Microsoft® SQL Server 6

UNLEASHED

David Solomon
Daniel Woodbeck
Ray Rankins
Jeffrey R. Garbus
Bennett Wm. McEwan

SAMS
PUBLISHING

201 West 103rd Street
Indianapolis, IN 46290

I dedicate this work to my wife, Carola, who has endured more stress and hardship through my career than through her own. —David Solomon

This book is dedicated to Beth, whose support, insight, and gracious way of telling me I use too many words made this book more readable for all of you. I also would like to dedicate this book to Scott Rupple, whose patience, and willingness to tolerate the rantings and ravings of a promising, but slightly neurotic college student led me into a career using computers, client/server technology, and eventually, SQL Server. —Daniel Woodbeck

To the two shining beacons in my sea of life, Elizabeth and Jason, without whose love, understanding, and most of all, patience, I would be lost.—Ray Rankins

I dedicate this book to my wife, Penny, without whose help and support I would never have finished my chapters; and to my children, Brandon, Devon, Max, and Gillian, for the space they gave me to write. —Jeffrey Garbus

"To the love of work, where the line between leisure and toil is no line at all." —Bennett Wm. McEwan

Copyright © 1996 by Sams Publishing

Trademarks

Publisher	Richard K. Swadley
Acquisitions Manager	Greg Wiegand
Development Manager	Dean Miller
Managing Editor	Cindy Morrow
Marketing Manager	Gregg Bushyeager

Acquisitions Editor
Rosemarie Graham

Development Editor
Leslie Koorhan

Software Development Specialist
Steve Flatt

Production Editor
Kimberly K. Hannel

Copy Editors
Nancy Albright, David Bradford, Susan Christophersen, Ryan Rader, Bart Reed

Technical Reviewer
Robert L. Bogue

Editorial Coordinator
Bill Whitmer

Technical Edit Coordinator
Lynette Quinn

Formatter
Frank Sinclair

Editorial Assistants
Carol Ackerman, Andi Richter, Rhonda Tinch-Mize

Cover Designer
Tim Amrhein

Book Designer
Gary Adair

Copy Writer
Peter Fuller

Production Team Supervisor
Brad Chinn

Production
Stephen Adams, Carol Bowers, Michael Brumitt, Mike Dietsch, Jason Hand, Sonja Hart, Louisa Klucznic, Ayanna Lacey, Clint Lahnen, Kevin Laseau, Casey Price, Bobbi Satterfield, Laura Smith, SA Springer, Josie Starks, Andy Stone, Susan Van Ness, Colleen Williams

Indexer
Ginny Bess

Overview

Part IV System Administration

Part V Introduction to Open Client Programming

Appendix

Contents

Part III   Performance and Tuning

Part IV System Administration

Part V Introduction to Open Client Programming

Appendix

Acknowledgments

I want to acknowledge the hard work of my co-authors on this book, particularly Dan Woodbeck, who made certain this book reflects the spirit of SQL Server 6.0 as much as its technical content, and Ben McEwan, who had the most to learn during its creation. I also want to thank Rosemarie Graham at SAMS Publishing, who shepherded this book through with her customary determination and patience, and has helped me through some difficult transitions. -*David Solomon*

I'd like to thank my wife Beth, for her patience, understanding, and for tolerating the annoying squeak of a hardwood floor at 3:00 am while I paced about the hall racing to meet yet another deadline. I couldn't have done any of this without your help. In addition, I'd like to thank my friends on Microsoft's SQL Server development team who answered more technical questions than I'm willing to admit to. You folks write some of the best code I've seen Microsoft produce. -*Daniel Woodbeck*

I wish to acknowledge my wife, Elizabeth, and son, Jason for their understanding and patience during the long, late hours put in to make this book a reality. I would also like to acknowledge Brian Tretter for providing some of the ideas and material used as the basis for some of the chapters in this book. And finally, I would also like to acknowledge and thank those special teachers I have had in my lifetime who instilled in me a joy of learning and the importance of good writing and communication skills. -*Ray Rankins*

I'd like to thank the people from Microsoft who gave us early access to the SQL Server 6.0; SAMS Publishing staff for helping us get these books finished; our clients for giving us the "War Stories" we're sharing with you herein; my co-authors and other employees at Northern Lights for their support and very hard work; and last but not least my family, for understanding. -*Jeffrey Garbus*

Some of the material in this book has appeared in articles written by Daniel Woodbeck that appeared in *Microsoft SQL Server Professional* magazine. The material was used with permission from *Microsoft SQL Server Professional* magazine© All rights reserved. Pinnacle Publishing Inc., P.O. Box 888, Kent, WA 98035-1088. 206-251-1900; 800-788-1900; fax: 206-251-5057.

About the Authors

David Solomon, president of Metis Technologies in Troy, NY, writes, speaks, teaches, and consults on SQL Server design, application, and implementation. With more than five years of experience in SQL Server, he is an expert on query analysis and troubleshooting, logical database design, and application design and implementation. He specializes in advanced SQL techniques and physical database design.

Daniel Woodbeck is an instructor and consultant for ARIS Corporation in Bellevue, WA. Dan started working with SQL Server in 1991, developing client/server applications for Baxter International using Microsoft SQL Server for OS/2 1.0 and PowerBuilder 1.0. Dan has the unique perspective of having worked for both Sybase and Microsoft, doing consulting and training for Sybase as part of Sybase Professional Services and teaching internal education classes for Microsoft's database and development tool technologies to consultants and developers in the Microsoft Consulting Services division. Dan is a Sybase Certified Professional as well as a Microsoft Certified Product Specialist on both SQL Server and Visual Basic. He currently teaches the Sybase curriculum as well as the Microsoft curriculum for Windows NT, SQL Server, Visual Basic, and Microsoft Access.

Ray Rankins is currently a managing consultant for Northern Lights Consulting and a Certified Sybase Professional Database Administrator. Prior to joining Northern Lights, he worked for Sybase Professional Services as a consultant and instructor and was involved in the development of the Sybase Performance and Tuning class. Ray has been working with Sybase and Microsoft SQL Server since 1987 as a DBA, application developer, database designer, project manager, consultant, and instructor and has worked in a variety of industries including financial, manufacturing, health care, retail, insurance, communications, and state and federal government. His expertise is in SQL Server performance and tuning, SQL Server application design and development, client/server architecture, and Very Large Database design and implementation.

Jeffrey R. Garbus is president of Northern Lights Software, Ltd. Since 1989, Jeff has taught thousands of programmers, systems administrators, and database designers about SQL Server administration and tuning, based on his experience as a consultant to some of the most complex SQL Server installations in the world. His current interests are in design, tuning, and maintenance of Very Large Databases (VLDBs).

Ben McEwan is the Manager of Software Development for Northern Lights Software. He has been responsible for the programming and development of the Aurora Utilities suite since February 1995. Ben teaches classes on SQL Server, Open Client, and Visual Basic/SQL Server integration. His specialty is the practical use of emerging technologies.

Introduction

Welcome to Microsoft SQL Server 6.0

Congratulations! You have bought the premier Windows-based database management product on the market today. Microsoft SQL Server 6.0 introduces many features and capabilities that are characteristic of far more advanced (and expensive!) database managers.

SQL Server 6.0 is a relational database management system (RDMS or RDBMS, depending on where you grew up!) that is capable of handling large amounts of data and many concurrent users while preserving data integrity and providing many advanced administration and data-distribution capabilities.

Here are a few of the capabilities of SQL Server 6.0:

- Complete data integrity protection, from complex transaction support and advanced security to objects that support your business rules as an implicit part of your database.
- Integration with Windows NT, allowing complete multi-threading, symmetric multi-processing on SMP systems, and integration into distributed administration environments.
- Outstanding performance on a low-cost platform.
- First-class administration tools (see the following).

Is This Book For Me?

This *Unleashed* book is meant for anyone who is responsible for designing, building, administering and tuning SQL Server 6.0. Among other things, this book contains performance information you may not find anywhere else, including SQL Server internals, tuning methods, and advanced SQL techniques that are undocumented or not well described.

- *System Administrators* will learn how to install and administer SQL Server. You will also learn about important standards and protocols to ensure that SQL Server applications can be maintained and supported for the long haul, and you will understand how SQL Server integrates into Windows NT to help you understand how to tune server-wide performance and configuration.

- *Database Administrators* will learn to make the best use of SQL Server 6.0 objects and datatypes, and will learn to write effective stored procedures and triggers. The "Performance and Tuning" section of the book will help you understand what's going on under the hood of SQL Server, including a detailed analysis of the query optimizer and the physical storage mechanisms used by SQL Server. You can start to understand what performance you can reasonably expect with SQL Server so that you can focus on problems that you can really fix and on practical solutions.

- *Programmers* will learn how to write code that runs well on SQL Server, and will acquire a complete understanding of how SQL Server interprets SQL statements when running. We also provide a solid foundation for your work in C and Visual Basic with DB-Library and ODBC in Part V, "Introduction to Open Client Programming."

What Will I Learn from This Book?

If you have installed Microsoft SQL Server 6.0, you probably have seen the program group pictured in Figure I.1.

FIGURE I.1.

SQL Server places a set of administration utilities in a single program group in Program Manager during server installation. These utilities are a good starting place for exploring the capabilities of SQL Server.

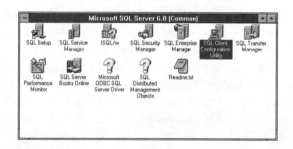

Understanding SQL Server starts with understanding—both functionally and conceptually—the tasks these utilities represent. In general, this book is *task-oriented*, not tool-oriented. If you need specific instructions on what a particular tool does, or how to use a particular button, the online help is a good starting place. This book explains the important tasks, describes when they need to occur, and then shows you how to perform them with the appropriate tools.

For your convenience, here is a quick list of the utilities provided with SQL Server, their general uses, and how we refer to each utility in the course of this book:

- SQL Setup is the installation and configuration management tool. After SQL Server is installed, you only use the setup utility to upgrade a server release, change network, language, or security settings, or to remove SQL Server. You can also use this utility to rebuild your master database in a crisis. This utility is examined most closely in Chapter 24, "SQL Server Installation and Connectivity."

■ SQL Service Manager (the stoplight icon) allows you to start and stop SQL Server and related services, including the SQL Executive. Usually, SQL Server will start whenever your NT operating system does. You can control this in the Control Panel, under Services. In production situations, you will rarely need to bring SQL Server itself down or restart it. We discuss how to use SQL Service Manager in Chapter 24 as well.

■ ISQL/W is one of the two utilities you will use on a daily basis. This tool enables you to open a session or several sessions with one or several servers. Then you can submit *ad hoc* Transact-SQL queries and get results. You can also analyze query behavior with this tool. It is typical for programmers to use ISQL/W to test queries without the complications introduced by an application program to make certain that the SQL code is efficient and performing as expected. System and Database Administrators use the tool to perform routine and emergency maintenance tasks. We provide sample Transact-SQL code examples for ISQL/W throughout this book and you may find yourself always keeping a session or two open to test a query or look at the contents of a table.

■ SQL Security Manager provides a graphical method of mapping NT security entities (users and groups) to those in SQL Server for integrated or mixed security. If your organization is using standard security, you set up login IDs using SQL Enterprise Manager or Transact-SQL statements. We look at the different security options in Chapter 27, "Security and User Administration."

■ SQL Enterprise Manager is the other utility you will use on a daily basis. The Enterprise Manager is new to SQL Server 6.0, and its capabilities are very broad, though in places a little thin. Throughout this book, we will discuss tasks as diverse as creating users, setting up tables, and setting up replication, all of which can be performed using SQL Enterprise Manager. Almost all of the tasks can also be performed by writing Transact-SQL statements as well. In cases where there is a Transact-SQL method, we will show you that first, and then discuss how to perform the task in the SQL Enterprise Manager.

■ SQL Client Configuration Utility, as its name would imply, enables you to manage the configuration of SQL Server client software. In particular, it helps you examine and maintain different versions of the connectivity software on client systems. We look at client configuration management as part of installation in Chapter 24.

■ SQL Transfer Manager allows you to copy data into and out of SQL Server. (Experienced SQL Server users will understand better when I say that Transfer Manager is a souped-up, graphical bulk-copy program.) We talk about data transfer issues in Chapter 24 as well.

■ SQL Performance Monitor is a special invocation of the Windows NT Performance Monitor that provides only SQL Server information instead of the broad range of system information regularly available. We talk about use of the NT Performance Monitor in Chapter 32, "Measuring SQL Server Performance."

What's in This Book?

This book consists of five sections:

- Part I, "The SQL Server Architecture," discusses client/server architecture in general and looks closely at how Microsoft SQL Server implements a client/server database system.

- Part II, "Transact-SQL Programming," discusses the language constructs of Transact-SQL and discusses how objects are created and maintained. You will learn about the different datatypes in SQL Server and how their use can affect performance, data maintenance, and capacity. We look closely at programming issues in writing procedures and triggers, examine cursor programming, and explain the ins and outs of transaction programming.

- Part III, "Performance and Tuning," describes in detail how SQL Server stores data, how it decides on optimization strategies, and how locking and multi-user issues impact overall performance. Perhaps the most important point here is that you can start to understand the kinds of expectations you should have for the system: when the query performance is as good as you can expect, and when it can get a lot better. Chapter 22, "Common Performance and Tuning Problems," describes some performance pitfalls that are easy for newcomers to SQL Server to miss, but also easy to avoid once you know they are there.

- Part IV, "System Administration," describes the tasks needed to get SQL Server up the first time and to keep it running all the time. (The Performance and Tuning section worries about making SQL Server fast; the System Administration section worries about making it reliable.) You will learn to make backups, how to restore them, and how to develop a backup and maintenance regimen that ensures your data is safe. Chapter 37 looks at some of the issues associated with building very large databases (VLDBs).

- Part V, "Introduction to Open Client Programming," provides a first look at the programming issues with SQL Server. Of course, this is a topic for a whole other book, but you learn in these chapters the basics of DB-Library and ODBC programming for both Visual Basic and C++.

What's Next?

If SQL Server 6.0 is not yet installed, you might want to start with Chapter 24 to get SQL Server up and running, and then continue on to the other sections of this book.

If You Are New to SQL Server...

Start at the beginning and read about how this stuff is built. (You will never make the time later and you really need to understand this stuff to make good use of SQL Server.)

As a System Administrator, you should read Chapter 3 because you will need to know some SQL. Then you can jump right to Chapter 23 and work through the administration section.

As a Database Administrator, you will need to understand Transact-SQL programming, so work through the book in order from Chapter 3 to about Chapter 14. Before you design a system ready to go into production, you should finish the performance section and try some stuff using a hands-on approach. Then you need to understand thoroughly Chapters 28 (on database logging) and 31 (on server configuration and performance). Read Chapter 22, "Common Performance and Tuning Problems," before you take a production system on-line. If you are working with large databases, be sure to read Chapter 37.

As a programmer, you should probably read the chapters in order through Chapter 10, then make the time to look at Chapters 12 through 16 to make sure you understand the kinds of performance issues and problems you might run into. If you will be writing in Visual Basic or C++, read the section on Open Client Programming. (It may help you choose the best architecture for your application.) Finally, make the time to read 19, "Application Design for Performance," and Chapter 20, "Advanced SQL Techniques."

Conventions Used in This Book

We've tried to be consistent in our use of conventions here. Names of commands and stored procedures are presented in a special monospaced, computer typeface. In the text itself, we have tried to present all SQL keywords in the text in uppercase, but because SQL Server does not make a distinction between upper- and lowercase for SQL keywords in actual SQL code, many code examples show SQL keywords in lowercase.

We have purposely not capitalized the names of objects, databases, or logins/users where that would be incorrect. That may have left sentences starting like this, "sysdatabases includes..." with an initial lowercase character.

Code and output examples are presented separately from regular paragraphs and also are in a monospaced, computer typeface. Here is an example:

```
select id, name, audflags
from sysobjects
where type != "S"

id           name                           audflags
---------- ------------------------------ ----------
144003544  marketing_table                130
```

When we provide *syntax* for a command, we've attempted to follow the following conventions:

Key	Definition
command	Command names, options, and other keywords
variable	Indicates values you provide
{}	Indicates you must choose at least on of the enclosed options
[]	Means the value/keyword is optional
()	Parentheses are part of the command
¦	Indicates you can select only one of the options shown
,	Means you can select as many of the options shown, separated by commas
...	Indicates the previous option can be repeated

Consider the following example:

```
grant {all ¦ permission_list} on object [(column_list)]
     to {public ¦ user_or_group_name [, …]}
```

In this case, the `object` value is required, but the `column_list` is optional. Note also that items shown in plain computer type, such as `grant`, `public`, or `all`, should be entered literally as shown. Placeholders are presented in italics, such as `permission_list` and `user_or_group_name`; a placeholder is a generic term for which you must supply a specific value or values. The ellipses in the square brackets following `user_or_group_name` indicates that multiple user or group names can be specified separated by commas. You can specify either the keyword `public` or one or more user or group names, but not both.

Our editors were enormously helpful in finding inconsistencies in how we used these conventions. We apologize for any that remain; they are entirely the fault of the authors.

Good Luck!

You are in good shape now. You have chosen a fine platform for building database applications, one that can provide outstanding performance and rock-solid reliability at a reasonable cost. And you now have the information you need to make the best of it.

We wish you all the best with SQL Server.

The SQL Server Architecture

PART

I

Overview of
Client/Server

1

4

Welcome to the first chapter of this book. To give you some background before tackling the rest, this chapter covers the following topics:

- Comparative architectures
- Definition of client/server
- Roles of clients and servers

Roots of Client/Server Computing

Strictly speaking, *client/server* is a style of computing where a client process requests services from a server process. Client/server computing is a broad area within *cooperative processing,* a field that looks at interactive computing between systems. What most distinguishes client/server computing is how processing is distributed between independent applications.

That's all well and good, but in the real world of business computing, the term *client/server* has come to describe the interaction between *fourth-generation language* (4GL), front-end applications, and *relational database-management systems* (RDBMSs). That is certainly how the term will be used in this book.

Client/server computing represents the marriage of two older processing models: mainframe or host-based computing and PC/LAN (local area network)-based computing. Let's look more closely at these two models to understand the purpose of client/server.

For this discussion, let's break down a typical business data-processing application into four components:

- *User interface* elements control keyboard and screen features, including the implementation of function keys, the field-to-field behavior of the cursor, and the display of data.
- *Application program* elements manage screen-to-screen behavior of the system and menuing as well as mapping field information to a logical data model.
- *Logical data processing* is the application of *business rules* to application data. This includes data validation and referential integrity. *Data validation* involves ensuring that a provided value is in a valid format or within a valid range of values (Is price greater than $0.00? Is social_security_number in the format ###-##-####?). Referential integrity involves verifying that the data "referenced" in one table exists in a "related" table (Does the pub_id value in the titles table exist in the publishers table? Is item_number found in the items table?). It also includes rules particular to a specific organization or application (for example, promised ship dates are always seven days from the date of order; only managers may fill in an override column; and so forth).
- *Physical data processing* maps logical data to a physical storage structure. It handles locking, data caching, and indexing, as well as the actual reads and writes from media.

Host-Based Computing

In the *host-based* environment, almost all processing occurs on the central host. What little local processing does occur (for instance, with an advanced terminal) is restricted to cursor handling from field to field and handling of individual keystrokes. After a screen of data is transmitted, the host resumes control.

In this environment, applications and data are centralized and exist solely on the host computer. Communications are almost never a bottleneck, even when the host and the terminal are separated by hundreds of miles and only share a relatively slow asynchronous connection. Application development and maintenance are also centralized, providing an important measure of control and security. Administration of the system (backup, data maintenance) is handled centrally as well.

Host-based computing has been the platform for most business database applications for the past 20 years: Mainframes and traditional minicomputers have provided solid, reliable performance, but at a tremendous cost. Purchase prices are stratospheric compared to PCs, but the intolerable burden of mainframes has been the cost of maintenance. The combined effect of high purchase prices and exorbitant maintenance fees was that processing cycles centralized on the host became far more expensive than the processing cycles on a PC.

PC/LAN-Based Computing

When those central mainframe costs were billed to a department manager's budget, the manager turned to a PC to solve departmental problems. The low cost and high availability of PC computing was extremely attractive to people who were forced to wait in line to pay high prices for mainframe processing.

Of course, the real nightmare of host processing has always been the tremendous backlog of applications waiting to be developed and maintained. PC users found they could build their own applications (they were admittedly amateur, but often more usable than the enterprise applications) faster than they could fill out the forms requesting apps from the central MIS group.

NOTE

> Years ago, a colleague of mine switched to a PC to do all his data analysis and number crunching, even though his data sets were typically large and fairly complex. He explained, "It takes my PC seven minutes to do what the mainframe can do in one-half second, but I have to wait a week to run my job on the mainframe."

Small, private, PC-based databases grew into multiuser, LAN-based databases because it made sense—users found ways to share data and be more efficient. Although fileserver-based LANs are well qualified to handle most office-automation (OA) tasks (word-processing document storage, shared printing devices, and central OA application maintenance), performance is problematic when managing databases with large amounts of data and/or increasing numbers of concurrent users. Moreover, much of the data entered in those PC-based databases was redundant with information stored in other systems. The reentry or data conversions required to populate the data often resulted in corrupt, duplicate, or inaccurate data.

The performance problem relates to the breakdown of application processing on the LAN. User-interface processing is performed entirely on the local PC, as is application processing. Logical data processing also occurs on the PC, which can create a data integrity problem (discussed later in this chapter). Physical data processing is split between the local PC and the central fileserver.

A fileserver is a lot like a hard drive attached to your computer by a very long cable (the network), and that cable is usually shared by many users. When your application needs to find a particular record in a database, it retrieves a set of physical blocks from the fileserver file. It is up to the application to find the required record in the data stream that is transmitted.

The efficiency of each request (defined as the ratio of data required to data returned) depends significantly on the capabilities of the application programmer. Using clever indexing strategies, a skilled programmer can write applications in the fileserver environment that support hundreds of thousands (even millions) of records.

On the other hand, ad hoc query performance can be disastrous. Users without a sophisticated understanding of how to manipulate indexes to improve performance can initiate queries that—while accurate—require that the system return all records for review by the local PC. Not only is this time-consuming, but it also can lock up system resources for the hours it takes to retrieve the results.

The problem is that the fileserver doesn't know anything about the data itself. All it understands is the physical storage of information on the hard drive. The result is that a simple query could take hours, filling the network with useless traffic and slowing down every other operation at the same time.

NOTE

Here is a useful analogy to help you understand LAN-DBMS computing.

If you call information to get a telephone number for John Murphy on Cedar Street, the conversation might go like this:

OPERATOR: "Information. What city, please?"

YOU: "Murphysville, please. I would like a number for John Murphy on Cedar Street."

OPERATOR: "Please hold for the number."

[Pause]

RECORDING:
"Abbott, James, 555-1234."
"Abbott, Martin, 555-1299."
"Abby, Philip, 555-9999."

…(Two hours later—are you still waiting?)
…

"Murphy, James, 555-8888."
"Murphy, John, 555-6666."

Of course, by this time, John Murphy has probably moved to another city.

You didn't call to have someone play a recorded telephone book—you called to get a specific number. With LAN-based databases, the server sends your application the telephone book, and it's up to the application program to find the number you need.

The other problem with the PC/LAN-based approach to database applications is as much cultural as technical. There are plenty of outstanding PC programmers and sophisticated power users, but every shop seems to have its share of dBASE programmers whose background in computer systems left them with no understanding of the craft of software development.

This latter group tends to be very productive in the early stages of development, but software maintenance is another issue. Because data-integrity checks are housed in the application software, and application software is distributed, version control and related data-integrity control can often fall victim to deadlines and software enhancements.

The fact of life is that application development, report development, and data analysis are gravitating toward individuals with less experience and less training in the information disciplines. This means that the "system" (to be better defined later) needs to become more intelligent, more protective of data integrity, and more efficient.

The host-versus-LAN dichotomy is summarized in the following table:

Host	LAN
High speed	Low cost
Central administration	Local processing
Geographical distribution	High-speed communication
Maturity	Opportunity

The issue of maturity versus opportunity is where a lot of people are stuck right now. Mainframes represent a stable, predictable environment, with dependable utilities, well-developed infrastructures, and large budgets. PCs represent a dynamic, uncontrolled world, short on administrative utilities, long on risk, and with very low cost expectations from management.

Client/Server to the Rescue!

Client/server computing seeks to merge the best of both worlds: the sheer power and central control of mainframes with the lower cost and better processing balance of PCs. How is this achieved?

First, what is client/server computing? For many, *client/server* is another way of saying *cooperative processing.* By that definition, any time two computers are communicating, you are in a client/server world. Broadly speaking, client/server is a subset of cooperative processing, which is a peer-to-peer architecture.

In the real world (that is, when you see the words in the classified ads), client/server refers to the interaction between user workstations and central database servers. The workstations run application programs that query and update data stored centrally on the database server.

The following are the key points about this client/server model:

- The client process and server process may be (but are not required to be) connected by a LAN or a wide area network (WAN). They both could be running on the same computer.

- The basic language used to communicate between the client and a database server is Structured Query Language (SQL).

> **NOTE**
>
> SQL is a highly abstract language in which the programmer or user describes his requirements (add a row of data to a particular table, display rows having the following characteristics, and so forth) without needing to understand or define the physical approach to answering the question. The database server is fully responsible for interpreting an abstract request, finding the fastest method to retrieve the data, and managing the locking and data integrity.
>
> Because SQL is so abstract, the implementation of client and server software tools and client/server applications does not require the close coordination ordinarily required for cooperative processing. In client/server, both sides write to a common API with some confidence that the final result will provide sufficient functionality and good performance.

Client/server provides a new approach to the central/local distribution of work and responsibility. Like a host-based system, client/server is capable of exerting stringent central control over data integrity, administration, and security. Because data is stored centrally, client/server enables the administrator to back up work centrally and to perform periodic maintenance against data stored in a central and secure location.

Because application programs run entirely on the client systems and only database requests are handled centrally, intricate and processor-intensive user interfaces (for example, Windows applications and highly graphical data presentations) are performed using local processors and local memory.

> **NOTE**
>
> The other resource that can become a bottleneck is the network, especially in a multiuser environment with graphical applications. Anyone who has tried to execute intricate X Window applications with multiple X terminals on a busy network will tell you that executing graphical-application processing on a host can cause serious performance degradation on a LAN. (With lots of users, CPU and memory resources on the server can quickly run dry.)
>
> Local application and interface processing (using local CPUs and local memory) make the client/server model work.

Client/server is particularly efficient (when properly implemented) at responding to ad hoc queries. A LAN-DBMS often responds to simple requests by delivering huge amounts of useless data, but client/server systems return an answer. This answer, called a *result set,* is only the rows and columns of data you requested from the server in a SQL statement.

As mentioned before, SQL should not dictate a specific method of answering a query; it defines only the data required. How does the server know how to answer the question?

SQL Server includes a *query optimizer,* the responsibility of which is to analyze the SQL query, consider the data it is to act on, and decide on an *optimization plan.* The SQL Server optimizer is very powerful and a major factor in the success of the product. (The optimizer is also a fascinating part of the system, and understanding how it works can have a major impact on system performance. For more on the optimizer, take a look at Chapter 12, "Understanding the Query Optimizer.")

The other implication of client/server computing (particularly under the SQL Server model) is that application programming can be distributed without creating havoc in the database. SQL Server (and now other competitive products) provides several data-integrity structures to perform server-side validation and processing within the database.

Because the server is able to manage data integrity, this burden can be lifted (in part or in whole) from the application development at the client. Consider each item in this list. Where was this processing taking place before? Data integrity was managed within the application, not the database. Application programmers were fully responsible for data integrity. An error in implementing data integrity in an application would likely result in having "bad" data in the database. The detection, identification, and clean-up of this data could require hundreds (or thousands!) of hours. Database administrators (DBAs) could do no more than provide guidelines, review code, and hope for the best.

The DBA is able to become more active now. The database has extensive capabilities and the DBA can use the data integrity objects to enforce guidelines on the server side. In many cases, this enables the elimination of thousands of lines of redundant code within applications. Applications become simpler, they are faster to develop, and it is less likely to be a disaster when they contain an error.

The Critical Factor: Cost

Of course, the driving force behind the move to client/server is cost. Mainframe hardware and software are expensive to buy and expensive to keep. Annual maintenance costs alone make MIS managers see red (instead of black), and the rightsizing trend is intended to bring systems cost to an acceptable level. For some organizations, this can mean the elimination of a mainframe or not having to perform an expensive mainframe upgrade to handle new application requirements.

> **NOTE**
>
> There is some discussion of using mainframes as giant database servers, and some organizations are already doing this. Because NT systems are now able to provide more storage options in hundreds of gigabytes, they will be more attractive as superservers. As of this writing, mainframe DASD storage costs approximately 30 times what NT drives cost for the same capacity (and that gap is actually widening).
>
> Mainframes as database servers represent an enormous integration problem as well: There is a very limited choice of RDBMS software, and sophisticated connectivity on the mainframe is substantially more difficult than on Windows NT. The proprietary architecture of mainframes imposes a substantial burden on an integrator because of the problems in transferring knowledge and tools from one environment to the other.

Cost issues extend beyond the purchase and maintenance costs of computing equipment. LANs are not cheap and they can become enormously complex. On the other hand, most organizations are building LANs and WANs for other uses, including office automation, telephony, and videoconferencing. Client/server architecture creates substantially less traffic on the network than some of these other systems.

Many businesses have bought into client/server to gain access to advanced development tools, such as PowerBuilder, Visual Basic, Visual C++, and many useful query and analysis products as well. The opportunity to develop products in less time does more than reduce development costs; it also enables an organization to move more rapidly into new markets, to improve customer service, and to be more competitive.

> **WARNING**
>
> It is crucial that you understand the business case for client/server in your organization in order to gauge management's expectations of your new systems. Many MIS shops have succeeded in implementing newer technologies, but have failed in the eyes of management because of a marked difference between what was implemented and what management expected.

This book looks at SQL Server from several perspectives. In this first part you learn about the fundamental architecture of SQL Server. In Part II you learn the basic structures that SQL Server supports and how to address those structures. In Part III you will begin to understand how SQL Server implements those structures in order to implement the system to get the best performance. Part IV looks at SQL Server from an administrative standpoint. This is so you can understand the strengths and weaknesses of the product, along with the background you need to develop an aggressive approach to maintaining and tuning the server. In Part V you will look at some programming interfaces for writing client applications.

Summary

You and your organization have traded in the maturity and stability you were used to with mainframe systems for the dynamism and opportunity of the client/server environment. Maybe you decided to step up from a LAN DBMS to a database capable of supporting hundreds and thousands of users and hundreds of gigabytes of information.

This book provides you with the information you need to bolster the system and to provide the reliable service your organization expects from its data resources.

The Microsoft Client/ Server Architecture

2

From the time that client/server became an overused, misinterpreted computer buzzword, different vendors have been attempting to refine their implementations of the concepts discussed in Chapter 1, "Overview of Client/Server." This section compares different database engine architectures—the heart of any client/server database-management system (DBMS). From that comparison, the history of the Sybase/Microsoft client/server architecture, starting in 1986 with the first release of SQL Server 1.0, will be more understandable. The chapter culminates with a discussion of how Microsoft, through increased investments in time, developers, and support personnel, has created a version of SQL Server that is very much its own, but still has recognizable Sybase roots.

Comparative Database Architectures 101

In the current client/server world, there are two dominant architectures for writing database engines. Understanding both aids in understanding how yours will work, so let's take a look at both.

The first type is the multiprocess engine, which is characterized by multiple executables running simultaneously. Typically, these engines will consume significantly higher system resources than the other type, but they appear (with limited testing) to scale to dramatically larger platforms more easily than their counterparts.

The second type is the single-process, multithreaded architecture, which is used by SQL Server. Instead of running distinct executables or applications for each task, this architecture relies on multithreading work within a single application. The benefit is substantially lower hardware requirements for a given performance level.

Multiprocess Database Engines

Some database engines rely on multiple executable applications to perform user query work. In this architecture, each time a user logs in, he or she is actually starting a separate instance of the database engine itself. Each user, therefore, is running his or her own instance of the database application. In order to coordinate many users accessing the same sets of data, these executables work with other global coordinator tasks to schedule operations among these various users. Applications in a database of this type communicate using a proprietary *interprocess communication* (IPC) facility. Although not necessarily efficient, dynamic data exchange under Microsoft Windows is one IPC.

Multiprocess database engines are typically used on mainframe databases and are popular on the MVS operating system because MVS provides IPC facilities for applications.

The most popular example of a multiprocess database engine isn't typically run on mainframes. Oracle Corporation's Oracle Server is a true multiprocess database engine. Sixteen different types of executables are loaded by the Oracle Server to perform different tasks. User connections start user-database executables, executables which manage multiuser access to data tables, executables that maintain transaction logging and versioning, and other features such as distributed transactions, data replication, and so on.

Each time users connect to an Oracle database, they load a distinct instance of the Oracle database executable. Queries are passed to that executable, which works in concert with the other executables on the server to return result sets, manage locking, and perform other necessary data-access functions. (See Figure 2.1.)

FIGURE 2.1.

With process-per-user architectures, a separate instance of the database engine starts for each user.

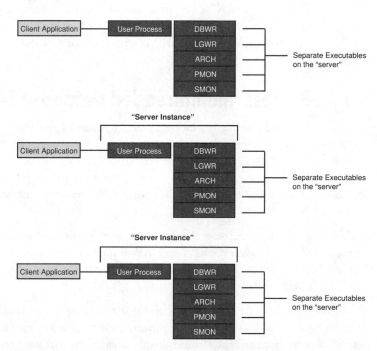

Pros and Cons of Multiprocess Database Engines

Most multiprocess database engines were developed before operating systems supported features such as threads and preemptive scheduling. As a result, "breaking down" a single operation meant writing a distinct executable to handle that operation. This enabled two important benefits for database processing: first, a database could support multiple simultaneous users, providing for data centralization on a network; second, it provided for scalability through the addition of more CPUs and the physical machine.

In a multitasking operating system (OS), the OS divides processing time among multiple applications (tasks) by giving each task a "slice" of the CPU's available work time. In this way, there is still only one task executing at a time. However, the tasks share the processor because the OS grants a particular percentage of the CPU's time to each task. As a result, multiple applications appear to be running simultaneously on a single CPU. The real advantage, however, comes when multiple CPUs can be used by the operating system.

Applications love operating systems that support multitasking as well as symmetric multiprocessing. The ability to schedule distinct tasks to distinct processors gives applications the true ability to run simultaneously. As a result, today's multiprocess, database-management systems scale to larger numbers of processors more readily than do their counterparts. Most industry polls and publications acknowledge that Oracle Server can scale to large numbers of processors and do so efficiently—that is, as new processors are added, Oracle takes advantage of that processor, so that there is a net gain in processing power for the database. As you'll see in the following discussion on multithreaded DBMSs, that may or may not be what your business really needs.

Single-Process, Multithreaded Database Engines

Multithreaded database engines tackle the thorny issue of multiuser access in a different way, but using similar principles. Instead of relying on a multitasking operating system to schedule applications on a CPU, a multithreaded database engine takes on this responsibility for itself. In theory, the database engine's ability to fend for itself gives it greater portability because the database will manage scheduling of individual task execution, memory, and disk access. (See Figure 2.2.)

Multithreaded systems are more efficient for a given hardware platform. Whereas a multiprocess database will use between 500KB and 1MB of memory for each user connection (remember, memory is protected and dedicated to an executable file), a multithreaded DBMS will use only 50KB to 100KB of RAM.

In addition, because the database executable itself manages these multiple threads, there is no need for a costly and inefficient interprocess communication mechanism. Instead, the database engine itself coordinates the multiple operations it must perform, and it sends these instructions to the operating system for final execution. In this way, the database time slices individual operations by taking individual threads, one at a time, and sending the user instructions on those threads to the operating system. Instead of the OS time slicing applications, the DBMS time slices threads.

In this way, the database uses a finite element of work (a thread) for a variety of operations (user instructions, locking data pages, disk I/O, cache I/O, and so on) instead of a multiprocess DBMS, which uses specialized applications for each.

This architecture forms the heart of all Sybase SQL Server versions through release 10.*x*, and without the multiprocessing features, also for SQL Server on OS/2. In fact, Sybase developers wrote the code that Microsoft distributed for its then-new operating system, OS/2. Microsoft has since assumed more and more responsibility for this code base, but the underlying architecture is identical to the one Sybase developed in its first release of SQL Server.

FIGURE 2.2.

A single-process, multithreaded database simulates operating-systems threads; as a result, the DBMS is responsible for scheduling user tasks and commands internally.

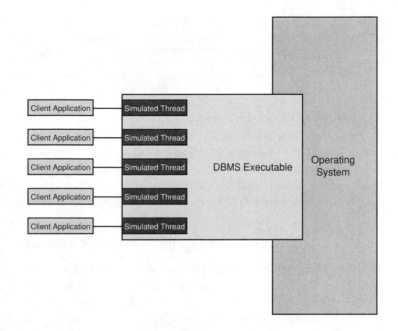

As you'll see in the discussion on how Microsoft has altered this idea with SQL Server for Windows NT, there are different means to implement thread services, memory management, and, most importantly, thread scheduling and SMP services.

Pros and Cons of Multithreading Database Engines

Sybase was quick to point out the performance it could achieve on relatively small hardware platforms when SQL Server first debuted. In fact, SQL Server was typically one of the fastest DBMSs (if not *the* fastest) for any given database size or hardware platform. That performance is derived in part from the efficiency of a multithreaded DBMS relative to other multiprocess competitors. A single executable running multiple internal threads consumes far fewer system resources, and it uses those it consumes much more effectively than in other architectures.

> **NOTE**
>
> As a developer using SQL Server 1.0 for OS/2 a few years ago, I was able to convince my management to buy what was, at the time, the hottest PC available—a 486/DX33 with 16MB of RAM, and 3 SCSI hard disks. With a 16Mbps Token Ring adapter, we were able to support 50 simultaneous users with almost instantaneous query response using databases as large as a full gigabyte (this was 1991). We thought this performance was amazing from a hardware platform that cost only $12,000 (again, this was 1991) but could run "real" applications.

> Today that $12,000 could buy a two-processor Intel machine with 64 MB of RAM, a
> Fast Ethernet (100Mbps) network card, a stack of 1.0 or 2.0G SCSI fixed disks, a
> 10GB database, and it could support literally dozens if not hundreds of users!

Of major benefit from this enhanced efficiency is the reduction in RAM requirements for the server, saving precious megabytes for data and procedure caching. Cache is a critical element for any serious database application, and maximizing both the quantity and usage of that cache is an important performance factor. Although the need for such efficiency has been somewhat mitigated by falling RAM prices, memory is still a precious commodity. As you'll see in the chapter on configuring SQL Server, there's no such thing as too much memory.

The most significant detractor of a multithreaded DBMS is more implementational than architectural, but it still reflects choices the database vendor can make.

Scalability with multithreaded DBMSs can be an issue, if only because the degree to which a multithreaded database is scalable is a function of the database vendor's ability to take a single operation and break it down so that multiple threads can work on that single operation. Up to now, the availability of symmetric multiprocessing hardware, particularly on Intel-based platforms, has been severely restricted—obviating the need for an SMP database. As these platforms continue to expand and become common items, a database's ability to take advantage of the additional processing power will be an important purchasing and implementational decision factor.

Single-process DBMSs are not inherently restricted from using SMP hardware. Quite to the contrary, their efficient use of threads makes them better candidates for such platforms because of their ability to squeeze the most from the least. However, SMP support competes with portability because different hardware vendors implement SMP support in different ways.

As a result, Sybase has been forced to implement an operating-system–neutral means of accessing operating system and hardware-level SMP support. This has contributed overhead to SQL Server, limiting its ability to scale to larger processor counts and hardware platforms. This is more a function of the parallelization of threads than anything else. SQL Server has implemented user connections as individual threads—but only as single-thread operations, not multithread operations. Therefore, when a user executes a query that scans a 4GB table, that user has only one thread of execution to do the scanning. Because threads are the most finite element of work in SQL Server, a single thread can be scheduled to only one CPU at any given time. Therefore, there is no parallelization of work for this user, because they are a single task, running on a single CPU at any given time. Any performance benefits resulting from SMP are the result of another processor being made available before the existing processor would be—which is a scheduling benefit, not a true processing benefit.

In fact, it is this very problem that Microsoft sought to address in SQL Server 4.2*x* for Windows NT and has succeeded in addressing in SQL Server 6.0 for Windows NT. The next section on Microsoft's Symmetric Server Architecture modifications to the base Sybase architecture defines how they've achieved this, and at what cost.

SQL Server for Windows NT and the Symmetric Server Architecture

With Windows NT, Microsoft was making the leap to building a true application server. Although many pundits would argue that they missed the mark with the first release, few would argue that Windows NT (in versions 3.5 and 3.51) is a true network-enabling, application-server platform. It is this very platform that forms the heart of Microsoft's effort to "go it alone."

> **NOTE**
>
> There is substantial confusion about what SQL Server 4.2 for Windows NT was or was not. If you talk to Sybase, it's a relic implementing an outdated feature set. If you talk to Microsoft, it's a complete reengineering of database technology. As usual, the truth is somewhere in between.

With Windows NT, Microsoft finally had a 32-bit operating system with preemptive scheduling, protected memory, and a kernel-based architecture that supported symmetric multiprocessing. It would be difficult for any application developer to pass up access to those kinds of resources—which has long been the Sybase approach. Instead of treating Windows NT like just another operating system, Microsoft decided to use it to best advantage.

Depending on who you talk to, anywhere from 70 to 85 percent of the core Sybase database kernel was tossed out and rewritten by Microsoft. The interesting part is that the behavior of the server that application developers saw didn't significantly change! With SQL Server for Windows NT, Microsoft created a database engine that looked like SQL Server, walked like SQL Server, and even quacked like SQL Server—but it was no ordinary SQL Server.

Microsoft rewrote SQL Server to use native operating system services for threads, memory management, disk I/O, symmetric multiprocessing support, and even Windows NT's networking services. This was a complete break with the past. Sybase was accustomed to writing all these facilities for itself—a necessity of its portability, in that Sybase can't count on features such as threads, protected memory, and network protocols in all the operating systems that Sybase wants to support.

Microsoft took a different approach, relying on the portability of Windows NT to achieve cross-platform compatibility. Because Windows NT can run on a variety of platforms, Microsoft can count on Windows NT services for connectivity and resource management. As a result, SQL Server from Microsoft runs only on Windows NT, but it runs on all platforms, including SMP platforms, that are supported by Windows NT. So what about this version number thing?

Microsoft wanted to ease customer concerns about migrating to a new database version and a new operating system; complete, guaranteed backward compatibility with existing SQL Server 4.2 for OS/2 databases was a must. So the decision to use the 4.2 version number was marketing driven. SQL Server, however, behaved exactly like the 4.2 for OS/2 release. Underneath, little was left untouched.

Thread Services for Microsoft SQL Server

The biggest change came in SQL Server's use of threads. Instead of simulating threads in the database kernel, as Sybase had done, SQL Server used native Win32 operating system threads— meaning those threads ran in protected memory spaces, preemptively scheduled by the Windows NT OS kernel. This, in marketing-ese, became the Symmetric Server Architecture shown in Figure 2.3.

FIGURE 2.3.

The Symmetric Server Architecture of SQL Server 6.0 for Windows NT features native operating system threads, a major departure from the threading internal to earlier versions of Microsoft and Sybase SQL Server.

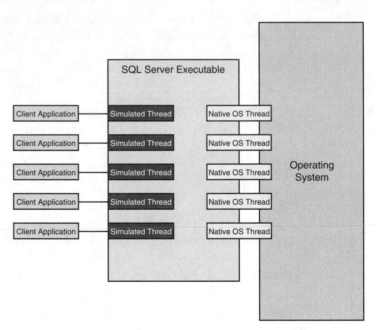

In the Sybase architecture, a user connection is given a distinct thread in the database kernel. This is true for Microsoft SQL Server as well, except that with MS SQL Server on Windows NT, that thread is a Win32 operating system thread. It is bound by the restrictions of Windows NT's memory protection, thread scheduling, and hardware-access rules, but it also has all the features of a Win32 thread—out-of-the-box support for multithreading, access to striped hardware devices, and memory protection for individual threads. With this architecture, a single corrupt thread no longer crashes the entire executable; instead, SQL Server can trap the offending thread and continue execution.

In MS SQL Server, there is a pool of 1024 "worker threads" capable of serving user connection requests. That thread pool is distinct from another of 255 threads, one for each disk device that SQL Server supports. (You'll learn more on this in Chapter 25, "Defining Physical and Mirror Devices.") Why a pool of threads? Important SQL Server configuration options indicate that SQL Server supports a maximum of 1024 worker threads. Because one connection gets one thread, the maximum number of user connections should be 1024—but instead, the numeric limit is 32,767. SQL Server will dynamically round-robin user connections to available threads, even if the number of user connections exceeds the threads available. If you're supporting more than 1,000 users on a single SQL Server, you obviously don't sleep much. But the capacity is present in SQL Server to expand beyond even its own resources.

In SQL Server 6.0, there are different pools of threads for different purposes, including parallel table scanning, backup striping, disk-device management, and user connections. Microsoft has already hinted that SQL Server 6.5 will expand thread usage for improved scalability on SMP hardware.

This architecture continues in SQL Server 6.0, and it has been enhanced to provide multiple threads of operation for single queries—a substantial advantage for using SMP hardware with SQL Server. You will learn more about this in Chapter 31, "Optimizing SQL Server Configuration Options."

Network Services for Windows NT

SQL Server always supported any network protocol you could want—so long as it was the native protocol of the operating system you used to host SQL Server. For Sybase and UNIX platforms, that meant TCP/IP. For OS/2, Named Pipes using NetBEUI (that lovely little nonroutable rascal), and for NetWare, IPX/SPX. This wasn't necessarily a limitation because most environments rarely mixed operating systems, and products such as SQL Bridge from Microsoft closed the gap between Named Pipes and TCP/IP.

With Windows NT, Microsoft changed network interoperability by offering an operating system that would work with anybody's protocol. Through the NWLink network subsystem, Microsoft ensured IPX/SPX interoperability with Novell NetWare clients and servers. Windows NT has always had built-in TCP/IP support, which SQL Server has used since being released on Windows NT. Through the two years that Windows NT has been available, Microsoft has added support for DECNet Sockets, Banyan VinesIP, and the Apple Datastream Protocol (ADSP, or AppleTalk).

Because SQL Server is written as a Win32 application, it too can take advantage of these networking services. As such, SQL Server supports all the protocols that Windows NT supports, allowing a Windows NT machine running SQL Server to support clients of almost any network—NetWare clients, UNIX workstations, Macintoshes, and even ordinary PCs.

With SQL Server 6.0, Microsoft has added an extra network library called the *Multiprotocol Network Library* (MPNL). MPNL takes two core Windows NT network services—network services and network-enabled operating system remote procedure calls—and integrates them. With MPNL, SQL Server can use Windows NT RPCs as its interprocess communication, and it can take advantage of Windows NT RPC features such as encryption. MPNL appears as just another option in Windows NT's setup routine. However, that network library enabled TCP/IP, IPX, and Named Pipes workstations to communicate with Version 6.0 SQL Servers using encrypted connections. These connections feature two-way encryption, meaning that both queries and result sets are encoded using RSA encryption (the encryption algorithm Microsoft used for RPCs).

> **WARNING**
>
> During the internal testing phases of SQL Server 6.0's development, I spoke with many people on the development team. Using MPNL in these interim beta releases resulted in a 10–15 percent performance decrease in network throughput, caused primarily by the overhead of using OS-level RPCs. In addition, selecting the "encryption" option caused another 10–15 percent performance degradation at the network level. My own informal testing of the released version of SQL Server 6.0 has shown that these levels hover right around 10 percent for each, but my testing methods were not formal or scientific. The features are unique and very useful for secured environments, but there is a modest cost to using them.

Windows NT and Disk Systems

Sybase SQL Server and Microsoft SQL Server for OS/2 (essentially the same product, with different distribution channels for most of their lives) supported fault tolerance through internal mirroring of physical disks and files. Sybase and Microsoft guaranteed fault tolerance, but there was no integration with the operating system or the underlying hardware platform. Microsoft changed yet another Sybase stand-by through its using of Windows NT.

From its first release, Windows NT has supported both RAID 0 (simple data striping across multiple physical disks) and RAID 5 (data striping with parity checks). Windows NT uses NTFS and stripe sets to spread data writes across multiple disks. Although SQL Server maintains full compatibility and support for its own mirroring, using the operating system is recommended unless hardware RAID devices are available.

SQL Server and caching disk controllers have never really been a good combination. SQL Server assumes that when it writes a data page to disk, the page is actually written on disk. However, caching controllers take that data page and write it to a hardware cache that SQL Server doesn't know about. Because of this, the page may or may not be actually written to disk. This situation hasn't changed much, although hardware vendors are now developing disk controllers with on-board caches that make themselves aware to the operating system—and on Windows NT—which means SQL Server knows about them as well. In most cases, SQL Server will "write through" the operating system so that neither Windows NT nor the hardware platform will cache data writes SQL Server thinks it has committed.

Microsoft has permanently changed the direction of its SQL Server by using an operating system that provides network connectivity, hardware scalability, and proper thread and memory protection. Sybase's efforts at portability focused on assuming a generic standard of nonexistence for most of these features, forcing them to be implemented in the database kernel. Microsoft, through its use of Windows NT's portability, has eliminated the duplication of this code and its incumbent overhead.

The Two APIs of Any Client/Server Database

Most computer professionals are familiar with some form of database technology. Business applications are worthless without some central data store. However, accessing that data is the job of programmers, who require two distinctly different languages. There is a host language, which for ages has been COBOL. However, COBOL isn't a database language—it's a generic programming language with file-access capabilities. To access a database, you need a language to get to that database.

Through most of the 1970s, database access came through embedded languages and precompilers. Statements that accessed the database were inserted using special codes or function calls that marked the source code as a flag for the precompiler. The source code was fed to the precompiler first, and the database-specific code was compiled into separate instructions. The host-language compiler took the standard COBOL code, turned it into a binary object, and linked it so the operating system could understand it as an executable.

Host Language APIs for SQL Server

That same process of using two different native languages to write an application goes into writing SQL Server applications, with an interesting twist—there is no precompiler. Instead, the database-specific calls reside in the source code of the application merely as strings—and they stay that way through the host-languages compilation process. In the resulting executable, all the database queries are still stored as strings. In fact, those queries won't see SQL Server until the source code is properly compiled and runs for the first time!

Most books and documentation written about SQL Server (or any client/server database, for that matter) don't address this issue. They discuss SQL syntax and they discuss client library API calls—but integrating the two is a topic most people just assume. It's a dangerous assumption. Improperly using DB Library or ODBC API calls, or similarly, Transact-SQL calls, can contribute to bad applications just as easily as bad design can.

This fundamental difference between interface types defines what a call-level interface is. Both DB Library and ODBC are call-level interfaces, in that the host application makes native language calls into a library of database functions. The data-manipulation statements are stored as strings, instead of being marked for precompilation like those in embedded languages.

For SQL Server, there are two different APIs that every application will use. The client host-language API that traditionally has been the SQL Server standard is DB Library. Sybase introduced DB Library with the original version of SQL Server, and Microsoft used DB Library for all versions of SQL Server. In fact, Chapter 38, "DB-Library Programming," discusses in detail Version 6.0–specific enhancements in this new release. Marking a change in SQL Server's focus, ODBC is actually now the strategic API for Microsoft—as evidenced by the substantial work being put into ODBC by Microsoft not only in terms of developing database drivers, but also by working with other companies such as Visigenic and InterSolv to move ODBC to non-Windows platforms such as UNIX and Macintosh.

Microsoft introduced support for embedded languages with the E-SQL Developer's Kit for OS/2 SQL Server. This toolkit gave PC-based COBOL and C developers access to an embedded language, if that was their preference. Most developers, however, have chosen DB Library as their API, and more are switching to ODBC.

SQL Is an API?

Transact-SQL is the second of the two APIs for SQL Server. Why define T-SQL as an API? Most importantly, it fits the definition! An API is an access point to the resources of an operating system or application that provides a specific set of services. Transact-SQL, through its enhancements to the SQL standard in the form of functions, datatypes, logical operators, and branching logic, is the access point to SQL Server's data-processing resources and services. It is the second of two APIs for SQL Server, because DB Library and ODBC are also access points to a different, but still necessary, set of resources and services.

SQL Server applications need both in order to function. A standard SELECT statement is useless unless it can be passed to SQL Server. A SQLLOGIN% C-language function is used to open a connection to SQL Server, but that connection is equally useless unless T-SQL statements can be passed over that connection, prompting SQL Server to pass results back to the client.

Sound like fun? It gets better. As already mentioned, Transact-SQL is a dialect of ANSI-standard SQL. ANSI has two primary standards—one codified in 1989, the other in 1992. SQL Server is ANSI 1989 compliant, but SQL Server 6.0 is not technically ANSI 1992 compliant.

How SQL Server Processes Queries

SQL Server doesn't process SQL statements until they are passed to the server over the network. There are some implicit assumptions here: first, that the client application is capable of formulating queries; second, that there is a network for transporting these query instructions to the server; and third, that the server is capable of using the network to return the results of the query.

These assumptions form the architecture that makes up the SQL Server client/server architecture. With any query you execute, whether interactively through ISQL/w or within an application, all of the following steps take place:

1. DB Library receives a SQL string from the client application.
2. DB Library associates that string with a particular user connection opened at the server.
3. DB Library passes the string along that connection to the network library.
4. SQL Server's Network Library "disassembles" the SQL string into a data packet for the network you are running. The data chunk of the packet conforms to SQL Server's formatting, which is called Tabular Data Stream.
5. The network delivers those packets to SQL Server.
6. SQL Server has a Network Library, too, which listens for queries to arrive.
7. The server-side Network Library reassembles the query into a string and passes that string to the SQL Server query processor.
8. SQL Server processes the query and, if it is a `select` statement, generates a result set.
9. SQL Server passes the result set to the server-side Network Library, which disassembles the result set into Tabular Data Stream packets.
10. The client-side Network Library receives the packets and reassembles them into a result set, which resides on the client in a connection-specific memory region.
11. DB Library API calls access the memory region, extracting the data held there and putting it into host-language variables (variables that are local to the client application) for display to the user.

Although this may seem like too many steps, the process has been broken down to a very low level. You'll take a look at this process in more detail in Chapter 38 and Chapter 39, "ODBC Programming."

What is most significant about this process is that regardless of the operating system, these steps are followed every time you send a query to SQL Server.

Summary

With SQL Server for Windows NT, Microsoft has taken a popular, high-performance architecture for client/server databases and made some critical modifications. While some may debate the "openness" of making SQL Server a Windows NT–only application, making the most of Windows NT's security, portability, and scalability means that SQL Server for Windows NT can run on a variety of platforms and scale to support very large applications.

Although all client/server databases make use of two APIs for developing applications, only SQL Server uses DB Library and Transact-SQL (or ODBC, if you're so inclined) to provide the two necessary means to access SQL Server's powerful features.

PART

II

Transact-SQL Programming

Introduction to Transact-SQL

3

IN THIS CHAPTER

What Is Transact-SQL?

To communicate with the SQL Server and to manipulate objects stored in SQL Server, client programs and stored procedures use a variety of *Structured Query Language* (SQL) called *Transact-SQL* or *T-SQL*. T-SQL provides most of the capabilities of *ANSI SQL 89 and 92*—the standard 1989 and 1992 versions of SQL as published by the American National Standards Institute, as well as several extensions to provide greater programmability and flexibility in the language.

Structured Query Language

SQL provides a language for accessing data objects using substantially less programming code than required by a third-generation language. A SQL query addresses data in sets rather than requiring you to construct a typical loop. For example, the following pseudocode resembles the code required to modify a set of rows in a table:

```
open file
while not(eof)
begin
   lock record
   read record
   if column-value = value
   write record
   unlock record
end
close file
```

Using SQL, you can accomplish the same task with a single statement like this:

```
update table-name
set column-name = new-value
where column-value = value
```

The individual SQL statement is far more likely to represent a work unit than is the atomic line of code in a third-generation language. This greater level of abstraction means better reliability, easier maintenance, and more readable, more meaningful code.

SQL provides some additional benefits:

- *No need for explicit locking statements*—the server manages all locking.
- *No reference to the physical location of the data*—the server translates a logical name into a linked set of physical locations.
- *No specification of indexing or search strategy*—the server identifies the most efficient method of finding the requested data.

Later chapters explore the mechanics of locking in SQL Server, the method the server uses to manage table storage, and query-optimization strategies. This chapter, however, discusses the basics of T-SQL.

T-SQL and ANSI-SQL

Standard SQL provides mechanisms to manipulate and manage data. Some components of SQL include

- *Data Definition Language* (DDL) to create and drop data structures and to manage object-level security
- *Data Modification Language* (DML) to add, modify, and remove data from tables

Standard SQL was originally conceived as a query-and-execution language, not as a full-fledged programming language. Transact-SQL extends SQL by adding program flow-control constructs (if and while, for example), local variables, and other capabilities that enable you to write more complex queries and to build code-based objects that reside on the server, including stored procedures and triggers.

Statements, Batches, and Elements of T-SQL

A Transact-SQL statement (almost) always includes at least one command: a verb indicating an action. For example, select asks the server to retrieve rows of data and update tells the server to change the contents of the specified rows. This chapter looks closely at four commands: select, insert, update, and delete.

> **NOTE**
>
> The one case where a command is not required is in the execution of a stored procedure. When the name of a stored procedure is the first element of a batch submitted to SQL Server, the execute command is optional.

Commands are one kind of *keyword* in SQL, reserved words that have special meaning to the server. Other keywords introduce new elements of a SQL statement. For example, the from keyword tells the server that a list of source tables follows. The where keyword introduces a list of logically connected conditions specifying the rows affected by a statement.

The application program or user submits T-SQL statements to the server in batches. A *batch* is a set of statements sent to the server at a single time. Every SQL Server application has a mechanism for telling the server to execute a batch of statements. For example, in the following isql session, the go directive tells isql to submit the three preceding lines as a batch to the server:

```
1> select au_lname, au_fname, phone
2> from authors
3> where state = "CA"
4> go
```

Server Processing Steps

When you submit a SQL batch to the server, the batch is parsed as a whole, optimized and compiled as a whole, and then executed statement by statement.

Let's look more closely at each of these steps. The server parses the batch to check the syntax of each command and keyword and to validate table and column names. During optimization, the server determines the most efficient method for resolving a query. (There is much more on optimization in Part III, "Performance and Tuning.") Compilation creates an executable version of the batch. Execution is the step-by-step performance of each statement in the batch.

If parsing or compilation fails for any reason (for example, a syntax error or a type mismatch occurs), the batch fails and no statements are executed. If the batch fails because of an error during execution, some subset of the entire batch might have been executed. You will need to look at the error messages returned by the server to determine what actually happened during execution.

Who Uses SQL and Transact-SQL?

Whether you are working from PowerBuilder, writing a C/C++ application in Windows NT or MS-DOS, or using Microsoft Access, Visual Basic, or Visual FoxPro, you will ultimately submit a SQL query to the server. Some tools do the dirty work for you by providing a visual interface to enable you to identify the components of the ultimate query and then submit the query behind the scenes. You might never see the SQL, but it is still there.

So, if you want to interact with SQL Server data, you need to submit a query in SQL. If you want to write a program to store as a SQL Server stored procedure, you need to write in Transact-SQL.

This chapter discusses the basic SQL data-retrieval and data-modification capabilities. Chapters 4 and 5, "Transact-SQL Datatypes" and "Creating and Altering Database Objects," explore SQL datatypes and the creation of tables and views. Chapter 6, "Transact-SQL Programming Constructs," shows you how to use the programming constructs with T-SQL; Chapter 7, "Transact-SQL Program Structures," reviews how to build objects based on SQL code.

> **NOTE**
>
> If you already know SQL, you might want to skim most of this chapter. Look at the notes, which highlight performance characteristics of SQL on SQL Server. Be sure to read about the use of worktables in ordering data and in performing aggregate functions.
>
> If you are just learning SQL, plow through this and try executing some of the queries presented to get a feel for the language.

This book is not intended to be a detailed text on SQL syntax; there are several other excellent books that can help you learn the intricate details of SQL programming. Here you'll get some SQL background and then forge into those areas where the Transact-SQL language differs from standard SQL.

How Do I Test SQL Queries?

If SQL Server is installed on your network, you need a SQL editor that enables you to write SQL statements and submit them to the server. There are three obvious choices:

- Use the Aurora Desktop product included on the CD-ROM in the back of this book. (We think it's a really cool and easy way to execute SQL, but we're biased because we wrote it.) Instructions for installing and using Aurora are included in a `readme` file on the CD.

- Use the Windows-based utility `isql/w`, which is included in the client utilities for SQL Server. After you run Setup to install the utilities on your workstation, start the application. Connect to a server; you are prompted for a login name and password. If you are the system administrator and nobody has ever used the server before, the login is sa and the password should be left blank. If this is not the case, get your login and password from your administrator.

- Use the MS-DOS-based utility `isql`, which is one of the utilities provided when you install the server. To run `isql`, you need to set some environmental variables (see Chapter 24, "SQL Server Installation and Connectivity," for more on this).

For now, let's assume that you can login to a server. For the following examples, use the pubs database.

NOTE

The pubs database is a sample database consisting of tables referenced in almost every example you will see in the system documentation and in every book or article you ever read about SQL Server. The database is automatically created and populated when you install SQL Server.

Later you'll learn what actually happens when you "use" a database. Type the following command:

```
use pubs
```

To execute this command, use the mouse to select a button that says "execute" or "go" or has a green arrow (depends on the program you are using) or, if you are using isql, type the word go on its own line. Now you are ready to execute the examples in this chapter.

Retrieving Data with *select*

When people think of SQL, they think first of the select statement. A select statement asks the server to prepare a result and return it to the client. In standard SQL, you use it to retrieve data from tables and views for review in a client application. In T-SQL, select also enables the user to retrieve information from the system and to set the values of local variables for further work on the server.

Tables, Rows, and Columns

Most SQL statements retrieve data from tables. Logically, a *table* is a two-dimensional structure consisting of rows (or *instances*) of data, each having one or many columns (or *attributes*; they used to be called *fields*). In Chapter 4, you learn to create tables. For now, you'll retrieve data from the tables in the pubs database.

The *pubs* database

The pubs database is a collection of tables containing sample data related to a fictitious book-distribution company. There are *publishers* who publish books, *authors* who write the books, *titles* (the books themselves), and *stores* that sell the books. There are also tables stating the relationship between the tables: the titleauthor table shows which author(s) wrote which title(s) and the sales table lists which store(s) purchased which and how many title(s).

> **NOTE**
>
> There are other tables with special characteristics to demonstrate additional features of the server, including the pub_info table to demonstrate *binary large objects* (BLOBs) consisting of text or images, and discount and royalty to show how to perform more offbeat joins and other kinds of queries.

If the pubs database is not installed on your server, you should install it or ask your administrator to do so. All of the examples in the Microsoft documentation, as well as many of the examples in this book, are based on this database.

Selecting Data from a Table

To retrieve data from a table, you submit a select statement. The (extremely) simplified syntax for the select statement is

```
select <column-list>
from <table-name>
```

The following example retrieves the last and first names of all rows in the authors table:

```
select au_lname, au_fname
from authors
```

The first and most important point about SQL is that it operates on *sets* of data, not individual rows. This statement returns all rows specified—in this case, all rows in the table. (Shortly, you'll explore how to limit affected rows with a where clause.)

SQL Result Sets

Take a look at the results returned from this query.

> **NOTE**
>
> If you get slightly different results, don't despair. In general, your pubs database configuration should be no different from mine, but I might have somewhat different indexes or some other variation.

Because you specified two columns in the select list, the result set contains two columns:

```
au_lname                                  au_fname
----------------------------------------- --------------------
White                                     Johnson
Green                                     Marjorie
Carson                                    Cheryl
O'Leary                                   Michael
Straight                                  Dean
Smith                                     Meander
Bennet                                    Abraham
Dull                                      Ann
Gringlesby                                Burt
Locksley                                  Charlene
Greene                                    Morningstar
Blotchet-Halls                            Reginald
Yokomoto                                  Akiko
del Castillo                              Innes
DeFrance                                  Michel
Stringer                                  Dirk
MacFeather                                Stearns
Karsen                                    Livia
Panteley                                  Sylvia
Hunter                                    Sheryl
McBadden                                  Heather
Ringer                                    Anne
Ringer                                    Albert
(23 rows affected)
```

> **NOTE**
>
> This is a complete result set, with each of the 23 rows displayed. Most of the result sets that follow are truncated, with ellipses (…) to stand for the missing rows. Complete results sets are only included where it is necessary to see all of the data to understand the example.

The results returned by most queries are actually similar to tables themselves, consisting of one or more columns with zero or more rows of data.

> **NOTE**
>
> You can redirect standard result sets into a new table using the into keyword. Some keywords yield a result set that is not a pure table. For instance, the compute keyword produces additional result rows that don't fit the column/row structure. You cannot direct a result set into a new table in combination with a compute clause.

Column-based Expressions

You can manipulate the contents of columns in the select list, as in the following example where the proposed increase in the price of books is 10 percent of the current price:

```
select title_id, type, price, price * .1
from titles
```

Here is the result set, containing four columns of data. The fourth column is an expression derived from price.

```
title_id type          price
-------- ----------- ------------------------ ----------------------
BU1032   business                     19.99                  1.99900
BU1111   business                     11.95                  1.19500
BU2075   business                      2.99                  0.29900
BU7832   business                     19.99                  1.99900
MC2222   mod_cook                     19.99                  1.99900
...
PS7777   psychology                    7.99                  0.79900
TC3218   trad_cook                    20.95                  2.09500
TC4203   trad_cook                    11.95                  1.19500
TC7777   trad_cook                    14.99                  1.49900

(18 rows affected)
```

In expressions, the basic arithmetic operators are available (+, -, *, /, %), as well as bitwise logical operators (AND &, OR |, XOR ^, NOT ~) and string concatenation (+).

Here is an example of string concatenation, combining the contents of two columns and a constant string expression:

```
select au_lname +", " + au_fname
from authors


------------------------------------------------------------
White, Johnson
Green, Marjorie
Carson, Cheryl
O'Leary, Michael
Straight, Dean
Smith, Meander
Bennet, Abraham
Dull, Ann
Gringlesby, Burt
Locksley, Charlene
Greene, Morningstar
Blotchet-Halls, Reginald
Yokomoto, Akiko
del Castillo, Innes
DeFrance, Michel
Stringer, Dirk
MacFeather, Stearns
Karsen, Livia
Panteley, Sylvia
Hunter, Sheryl
McBadden, Heather
Ringer, Anne
Ringer, Albert(23 rows affected)
```

Manipulating Column Names in the *select* List

Look closely at the column headings for each of the result sets provided in the previous section. Wherever a column appears unmodified in the select list, the column name is provided as the default column heading. Where any kind of expression or manipulation takes place, the column heading is blank.

To provide a column heading for a blank column, or to replace the default heading, you specify a *column alias*. Here are a couple of examples:

```
select title_id, type, price "original price", price * .1 discount
from titles
title_id type            original price          discount
-------- ------------    ----------------------  ----------------------
BU1032   business                19.99                   1.99900
BU1111   business                11.95                   1.19500
BU2075   business                 2.99                   0.29900
BU7832   business                19.99                   1.99900
MC2222   mod_cook                19.99                   1.99900
...
TC4203   trad_cook               11.95                   1.19500
TC7777   trad_cook               14.99                   1.49900
```

```
 (18 rows affected)
select "Full Author Name" = au_lname +", " + au_fname
from authors

Full Author Name
---------------------------------------------------------------
White, Johnson
Green, Marjorie
Carson, Cheryl
O'Leary, Michael
Straight, Dean
Smith, Meander
Bennet, Abraham
...
Karsen, Livia
Panteley, Sylvia
Hunter, Sheryl
McBadden, Heather
Ringer, Anne
Ringer, Albert

(23 rows affected)
```

The two examples do the same thing in different ways. The first, which is the ANSI-SQL standard method, states the alias after the column expression. Note that `"original price"` appears in quotes because the alias itself contains two words. The quotes do not appear in the result heading. In the second example, the alias precedes the column expression with an equal (=) sign. The two aliasing methods have the same effect.

TIP

Newcomers to SQL often forget commas in the `select` list, which is a difficult and subtle problem to catch unless you know it can happen. For example, look at this query and the result:

```
select city state from publishers
state
--------------------
Boston
Washington
Berkeley

(3 rows affected)
```

What happened to the state column? Without the comma between city and state, the word "state" was interpreted as a column heading for the city column. Unless you knew to look for this problem, you could spend hours trying to fix your server, your network, and your workstation without looking at the query.

A simple solution to troubleshooting SQL is to always ask an easy question first: How many columns did I request, and how many came back? If those numbers differ, look at the query and make certain you really asked for the right number of columns of data.

Using *distinct*

The distinct keyword removes duplicate rows from the result set. Without distinct, this query returns one result row per row in the source table:

```
select type
from titles
type
- - - - - - - - - - -
business
business
business
business
mod_cook
mod_cook
UNDECIDED
popular_comp
popular_comp
popular_comp
psychology
psychology
psychology
psychology
psychology
trad_cook
trad_cook
trad_cook

(18 rows affected)
```

Adding distinct instructs the server to remove duplicate rows from the result set:

```
select distinct type
from titles
type
- - - - - - - - - - -
UNDECIDED
business
mod_cook
popular_comp
psychology
trad_cook
```

The scope of the distinct keyword is over the entire select list, not over a single column. In the next query, containing two columns, the distinct keyword identifies unique *combinations* of city and state in the authors table. Here is the complete list of cities and states in the authors table:

```
select city, state
from authors
city                     state
- - - - - - - - - - - - - - - - - - - -    - - - - -
Menlo Park               CA
Oakland                  CA
Berkeley                 CA
San Jose                 CA
Oakland                  CA
```

```
Lawrence          KS
Berkeley          CA
Palo Alto         CA
Covelo            CA
San Francisco     CA
Nashville         TN
Corvallis         OR
Walnut Creek      CA
Ann Arbor         MI
Gary              IN
Oakland           CA
Oakland           CA
Oakland           CA
Rockville         MD
Palo Alto         CA
Vacaville         CA
Salt Lake City    UT
Salt Lake City    UT

(23 rows affected)
```

Here is the same result set, with `distinct`:

```
select distinct city, state
from authors

city                  state
--------------------  -----
Ann Arbor             MI
Berkeley              CA
Corvallis             OR
Covelo                CA
Gary                  IN
Lawrence              KS
Menlo Park            CA
Nashville             TN
Oakland               CA
Palo Alto             CA
Rockville             MD
Salt Lake City        UT
San Francisco         CA
San Jose              CA
Vacaville             CA
Walnut Creek          CA

(16 rows affected)
```

In the result set, note that many rows can contain the same value for a specific city or state; the distinct operator removes only duplicate combinations.

> **TIP**
>
> Don't use `distinct` if you don't need it. It forces the server to perform extra sorting and processing that will slow down your work when it is not necessary.

select *

You can include an asterisk (*) in the `select` list in place of a column or columns. The asterisk stands for all columns in a table.

```
select *
from publishers
```

As shown in the following example, this is a convenient shortcut for *ad hoc* queries because it displays all columns in logical order (the order in which they were declared when the table was created) and the user does not need to know the names of columns to display information.

```
pub_id pub_name                                   city                 state
------ ---------------------------------------    -------------------- -----
0736   New Age Books                              Boston               MA
0877   Binnet & Hardley                           Washington           DC
1389   Algodata Infosystems                       Berkeley             CA

(3 rows affected)
```

> **WARNING**
>
> Using `select *` is not recommended in programs of any type because it can lead to unexpected program behavior or to runtime application failures. The problem is that the server expands the * into a list of all columns in the table during the parsing stage. If a database administrator adds an additional column to a four-column table, queries that used to return four columns will then return five.
>
> The problem created by using `select *` becomes even more complex if the user is restricted from viewing the contents of the new column. Parsing of the * occurs prior to permissions being checked, so a user expecting a four-column result might be refused access to a result set he previously accessed because of permissions problems on a column he never knew existed.

Filtering Rows with *where*

SQL is a set-processing language, so data-modification and data-retrieval statements act on all rows in a table unless a `where` clause limits the scope of the query. The `where` clause must follow the `from` clause, as in this example:

```
select <column-list>
from <table-name>
where <condition>
```

In the following example, the `where` clause restricts the result set to authors from California:

```
select au_lname, au_fname
from authors
where state = "CA"
```

In this section you examine the methods available for limiting the number of rows affected by a query.

Equality and Inequality Operators

In the preceding example, the condition is in the form

```
<column name> = <constant expression>
```

The server evaluates each row to determine whether the search expression is true.

> **NOTE**
>
> The server does not always need to examine every row in a table to find rows that match a query. It can use indexes to speed searches if it decides that method is more efficient. The various search methods used by the server are described in detail in Chapter 12, "Understanding the Query Optimizer."

The search condition is more generally in the form

```
<expression> <operator> <expression>
```

where either expression is any valid combination of constant, variable, and column-based expressions, and where the operator is =, <> or != (equivalent symbols meaning not equals), >, <, >=, and <= (and !> not greater than and !< not less than).

For example, the following query compares price, year-to-date sales, and advance sales in the titles table:

```
select type, title_id, price
from titles
where price * ytd_sales < advance
```

Inequalities and Character Data

When you use inequalities to compare character strings, the server determines which string would appear first in the current server *sort order*. Using the default sort order, which is based on the ASCII character set cp-850, the server selects and orders character data based on the standard ASCII character set. For example, the condition

```
type < "mod_cook"
```

would find the value business, but would also find UNDECIDED because uppercase characters appear before lowercase characters in the ASCII character set.

Logical *or* and *and*

You can connect multiple search conditions with the or and and keywords. This example displays authors from California or from Salt Lake City:

```
select au_id, city, state
from authors
where state = "CA" or city = "Salt Lake City"
au_id       city                 state
----------- -------------------- -----
172-32-1176 Menlo Park           CA
213-46-8915 Oakland              CA
238-95-7766 Berkeley             CA
267-41-2394 San Jose             CA
274-80-9391 Oakland              CA
409-56-7008 Berkeley             CA
427-17-2319 Palo Alto            CA
472-27-2349 Covelo               CA
486-29-1786 San Francisco        CA
672-71-3249 Walnut Creek         CA
724-08-9931 Oakland              CA
724-80-9391 Oakland              CA
756-30-7391 Oakland              CA
846-92-7186 Palo Alto            CA
893-72-1158 Vacaville            CA
899-46-2035 Salt Lake City       UT
998-72-3567 Salt Lake City       UT

(17 rows affected)
```

between and Ranges of Data

You can search for data in a range using a condition in this form:

```
<expression> between <expression> and <expression>
```

In the following query, the search condition compares a column to a specific range. This is the most common use of the between operator.

```
select title_id, price
from titles
where price between $5 and $10
```

Note that between includes the endpoint values; thus between has the same effect as two conditions connected with and:

```
select title_id, price
from titles
where price >= $5 and price <= $10
```

Use not between to identify rows outside the range, as in this example:

```
select title_id, price
from titles
where price not between $5 and $10
```

Note that not between *excludes* endpoint values; not between has the same effect as two conditions connected with or:

```
select title_id, price
from titles
where price < $5 or price > $10
```

Lists of Possible Values with *in* (...)

Use in to provide a list of possible values for a column or expression:

```
select title_id, price
from titles
where type in ("mod_cook", "trad_cook", "business")
```

The server reviews the value of type in each row; if the value appears in the list, the condition is true for the row. Note that in has the same effect as multiple equality conditions (one per value in the list) connected with or:

```
select title_id, price
from titles
where type = "mod_cook"
    or type = "trad_cook"
    or type = "business"
```

Use not in to provide a list of ineligible values:

```
select title_id, price
from titles
where type not in ("mod_cook", "trad_cook", "business")
```

The value must not be found in the list for the condition to be true. Note that not in has the same effect as multiple inequality conditions (one per value in the list) connected with and:

```
select title_id, price
from titles
where type <> "mod_cook"
    and type <> "trad_cook"
    and type <> "business"
```

Wildcards with *like*

SQL also provides a pattern-matching method for string expressions using the like keyword and three wildcard mechanisms,: % (percent sign), _ (the underscore character), and [ ] (bracketed characters). (See Table 3.1.)

Table 3.1. Wildcard mechanisms with the `like` operator.

Wildcard	Meaning
%	Any number (0 to many) of any character(s)
_	Any single character
[]	Any single character listed in the brackets

You can freely combine wildcards in a single expression.

Let's look at some uses of the wildcard. In the first example, the `where` clause matches any row where the city starts with the word "Spring" (including Spring Hill, Springdale, Springfield, and even Spring itself):

```
select au_lname, au_fname, city, state
from authors
where city like "Spring%"
```

In the following example, the underscore matches only a single character in an expression, so the query finds only rows with a single character between the "B" and "1342" in the `title_id`.

```
select type, title_id, price
from titles
where title_id like "B_1342"
```

Possible matches for `title_id` include `"BA1342"` to `"BZ1342"`, but also include numerics (for example, `"B71342"`) and other non-alphanumeric characters (`"B*1342"` or even `"B%1342"`). Notice that `"B1342"` and `"BAB1342"` do not match the pattern because the underscore always stands for a single character.

The bracket notation enables you to define a set of valid values for a position in a string. For example, the next example more accurately specifies the value for `title_id` from the previous example (only the specific alphabetic characters U, A, or N should be permitted in that position):

```
select type, title_id, price
from titles
where title_id like "B[UAN]1342"
```

Note that you could also write this query as a set of equality statements, much like an `in` clause:

```
select type, title_id, price
from titles
```

```
where title_id = "BU1342"
    or title_id = "BA1342"
    or title_id = "BN1342"
```

As well as listing possible values, specify a range of values with a hyphen as in the following example, which permits any alphabetic character (upper- or lowercase) in the same position of the earlier titles query:

```
select type, title_id, price
from titles
where title_id like "B[A-Za-z]1342"
```

NOTE

This last example could conceivably be written with lots of equality conditions connected by or …

```
where title_id = "BA1342"
    or title_id = "BB1342"
    or ...
    or title_id = "Bz1342"
```

It would require 52 where clauses connected by or to replace the wildcard capabilities. The pattern-matching strengths of the [] become increasingly clear as the number of permutations and combinations increases:

```
where title_id like "[A-Z][A-Z][0-9][0-9][0-9][0-9]"
```

This example would require more than 6 million where clauses!

WARNING

Remember that the wildcard characters are only meaningful after the like keyword. In all other circumstances, the wildcard characters are treated as actual characters, usually with odd results. In this query, only rows with individuals whose names end in a percent sign (probably very few) would be returned:

```
select au_lname, au_fname
from authors
where au_lname = "G%"
```

Chapter 4 describes the column, variable, and expression datatypes available to the DBA and programmer. Look for information there on the interaction of specific datatypes with the comparison operators.

Ordering Result Sets with *order by*

In most cases, you cannot count on SQL Server data being sorted in any particular order. The rows returned in an unsorted result set are ordered according to the most efficient method for resolving the query. In order to force the output to be sorted by a particular value, you must specify an order by clause:

```
select au_lname, au_fname
from authors
order by au_lname
```

You can also sort based on two or more columns, separating the sort keys with commas, as follows:

```
select au_lname, au_fname
from authors
order by au_lname, au_fname
```

NOTE

Sorting result sets introduces a performance cost because the server adds an additional sorting step subsequent to preparing the set of rows to be returned. This additional step can be circumvented if the server can make use of an index on the sort columns.

You can specify the sort column by name or by position in the select list, as in the following example, where titles are sorted by year-to-date dollar sales, derived from price and ytd_sales (unit sales).

```
select title_id, price, ytd_sales, price*ytd_sales "ytd dollar sales"
from titles
order by 4
```

If you want to sort by an expression in the select list, you should make certain that the expression in the order by clause exactly matches the expression in the select list, as follows:

```
select title_id, price, ytd_sales, price*ytd_sales "ytd dollar sales"
from titles
order by price*ytd_sales
```

TIP

It's usually a good idea to name the full column or expression in the order by clause. Otherwise, when a programmer makes a change to the select statement (adding type after title_id, for example), he or she could inadvertently change the sort column.

Ascending and Descending Ordering

In the previous example, it might be more common to sort the data by sales in descending order, showing the best-performing items first. To reverse the sort order (highest items displayed first), use the desc keyword:

```
select title_id, price, ytd_sales, price*ytd_sales "ytd dollar sales"
from titles
order by price*ytd_sales desc
```

> **NOTE**
>
> By default, sort order is ascending. The asc keyword (for "ascending") is included as part of SQL for completeness, but is very seldom used.

asc and desc ordering only affects a single column. The following query displays best-selling books by type (ascending) and then by quantity sales (descending):

```
select title_id, type, ytd_sales
from titles
order by type, ytd_sales desc
```

Ordering by Columns not Appearing in the *select* List

Every example so far in this chapter has demonstrated sorting by a column or columns included in the select list. ANSI-SQL requires that sort columns be included in the select list, but SQL Server does not. Sometimes this leads to confusing results, as in the following query, where the data is sorted by the invisible city and state columns:

```
select au_lname, au_fname
from authors
order by city, state
au_lname                                 au_fname
---------------------------------------- --------------------
del Castillo                             Innes
Carson                                   Cheryl
Bennet                                   Abraham
Blotchet-Halls                           Reginald
Gringlesby                               Burt
DeFrance                                 Michel
Smith                                    Meander
White                                    Johnson
Greene                                   Morningstar
Karsen                                   Livia
Straight                                 Dick
Stringer                                 Dirk
Green                                    Marjorie
MacFeather                               Stearns
Dull                                     Ann
Hunter                                   Sheryl
```

```
Panteley          Sylvia
Ringer            Anne
Ringer            Albert
Locksley          Chastity
O'Leary           Michael
McBadden          Heather
Yokomoto          Akiko
```

```
(23 rows affected)
```

A user trying to determine the sort order of these results would be driven nuts trying to find the pattern.

Ordering by a column not in the `select` list can provide better performance. In the following example, the query displays a discount derived from price but sorts by the price column itself:

```
select title_id, discount = price * .15
from titles
where price between $10.50 and $15.00
order by price
```

The logical result of the query is the same as if you had ordered by the expression `price * .15`; however, because you only create indexes on columns (not on expressions), it is always better to sort by a column than by an expression derived from that column. If there were an index on the price column, this query would probably be generated without the intermediate worktable, providing substantially better performance.

NOTE

By now, you have noticed that the behavior of the server cannot always be predicted— that it will "probably" use an index or "in many cases" it will make use of an intermediate worktable. Even given a specific table structure and query, you cannot predict universally how the server will answer a question until you also understand the distribution of the data. It is the work of the optimizer to decide, on a query-by-query basis, what is the most effective method for resolving queries.

Experienced programmers often have a difficult time getting used to the idea that the server makes these decisions for them, but this is one of the primary benefits of the SQL Server implementation: Programmers can worry about how to logically define their requirements; database administrators worry about how to efficiently satisfy those requirements.

Retrieving Aggregate Data

SQL provides functions for describing data as a whole rather than as a set of rows. The *aggregate* functions (so named because they "aggregate" many rows of data into a single row) are listed in Table 3.2.

Table 3.2. The aggregate functions.

Function	Description
sum()	Totals numeric expressions
avg()	Averages numeric expressions
min()	Returns the lowest numeric expression, the lowest sorting string expression, or the earliest date
max()	Returns the highest numeric expression, the highest sorting string expression, or the latest date
count()	Returns the number of non-null expressions
count(*)	Returns the number of rows found

Take a look at the following query and result set. The avg() function returns a single average for all title rows in the table:

```
select avg(price)
from titles
```

```
--------------------
            14.77
```

```
(1 row affected)
```

Notice that the query examined all rows of the titles table but returned only a single row.

> **TIP**
>
> The result column for the aggregate has no default column heading. It is useful to assign headings such as "sum" and "avg" to SQL result sets, but you need to assign these headings in quotes because these words are reserved as names of functions:
> ```
> select avg(price) "avg" ...
> ```

Combine where clauses with aggregates to specify the rows to be included in the aggregate. In this example, the query asks for the average price of business books:

```
select avg(price) "avg"
from titles
where type = "business"
```

Include many aggregates in the same select list if they relate to the same rows within a table:

```
select avg(price) "avg", sum(price) "sum"
from titles
where type in ("business", "mod_cook")
```

```
avg                         sum
----------------------      ----------------------
          12.98                       77.90
```

(1 row affected)

Counting Rows with *count(*)*

An important aggregate function is count(*), which counts rows matching a set of conditions. The following query determines the number of authors in California:

```
select count(*)
from authors
where state = "CA"
-----------
         15
```

(1 row affected)

Aggregates and Null Values

Aggregate functions do not include null values. Consider a table, test_table, containing four rows, with the following values in the c2 column:

```
c2
-----
100
150
200
null
```

The following example provides the values for each of the aggregate functions; this displays the behavior of each of the aggregate functions on a table containing a null value.

```
select sum(c2) "sum", count(c2) "count", avg(c2) "avg",
      min(c2) "min", max(c2) "max", count(*) "count(*)"
from test_table
sum          count        avg          min          max          count(*)
-----------  -----------  -----------  -----------  -----------  -----------
        450            3          150          100          200            4
```

(1 row affected)

Null values do not imply any value (not even zero). Notice that the count(c2) is 3, meaning that three rows in the table contain non-null values in the column c2. The average disregards the null value and the minimum is 100, not zero or null, because nulls are disregarded.

Note, however, that the count(*) column includes all *rows*, regardless of nulls.

Sub-aggregates with *group by*

The count(*) query provides the overall average and sum of prices for business and modern cooking books, but how do you determine the average and sum of each of these individual types of books? The answer is to return subaverages and subtotals by type, using group by, like this:

```
select type, avg(price) "avg", sum(price) "sum"
from titles
where type in ("business", "mod_cook")
group by type
type            avg                     sum
-----------     ---------------------   ---------------------
business                      13.73                   54.92
mod_cook                      11.49                   22.98

(2 rows affected)
```

The result set includes one row per type value among the selected rows. Aggregates return a single row for each unique value in the column specified in the group by clause.

When two or more columns are included in the group by statement, aggregates are based on unique combinations of those columns. In the following example, the server returns the average and total price for business and modern cooking books for each combination of type and publisher id:

```
select type, pub_id, avg(price) "avg", sum(price) "sum"
from titles
where type in ("business", "mod_cook")
group by type, pub_id
type            pub_id avg                     sum
-----------     ------ ---------------------   ---------------------
business        0736                    2.99                    2.99
business        1389                   17.31                   51.93
mod_cook        0877                   11.49                   22.98

(3 rows affected)
```

Filtering Results with *having*

You can use the having keyword to select rows from the result set. If you wanted to display by type the average price of books costing more than $10, you would use a where clause:

```
select type, avg(price)
from titles
where price > $10
group by type
type
-----------     ---------------------
business                      17.31
mod_cook                      19.99
popular_comp                  21.48
psychology                    17.51
trad_cook                     15.96

(5 rows affected)
```

The where clause selects rows from the table before the averaging takes place.

A having clause enables you to select rows from the result set. This example displays only those types of books with an average price greater than $20:

```
select type, avg(price)
from titles
where price > $10
group by type
having avg(price) > $20
type
------------ ----------------------
popular_comp                   21.48

(1 row affected)
```

> **TIP**
>
> One useful application of the having keyword is to identify rows in a table that have duplicate keys. (Keys are unique identifiers. Duplicate keys are a terrible idea, but they often crop up during a data transfer from older systems.)
>
> To find all rows in the authors table that share the same key, use this query:
>
> ```
> select au_id, count(*)
> from authors
> group by au_id
> having count(*) > 1
> ```

Worktables and Aggregate Functions

In order to resolve a query containing a group by clause, the server uses an intermediate worktable. Figure 3.1 shows the role of the worktable in the resolution of a query. The server resolves where clauses and grouping while building the intermediate worktable. distinct, having, and order by are resolved after the worktable is generated while preparing the final result set.

FIGURE 3.1.

The worktable helps the server resolve complex queries involving grouping and ordering.

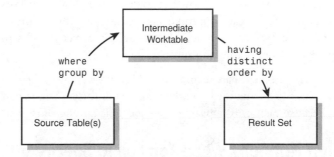

The server needs to use an intermediate result set to resolve this query:

```
select type, avg(price)
from titles
where pub_id = "1289"
group by type
having avg(price) > $15
order by avg(price) desc
```

First, rows matching the where clause are averaged into a worktable. Then the server filters and sorts the result set.

Joins

All of the queries considered so far have addressed only one table at a time, but most SQL queries need to address multiple tables at one time. For example, to display the titles of books and the names of publishers in a single query, you need to draw information from both the titles and publishers tables.

Let's look more closely at how you would write a query to join the titles and publishers tables.

When two tables are joined, they must share a *common key* or *join key*, which defines how rows in the tables correspond to each other. For example, in the case of titles and publishers, the tables share a common key, pub_id. In the publishers table, the pub_id uniquely identifies a row in that table. In the titles table, the pub_id uniquely identifies a row in the publishers table; it means that titles with this pub_id belong to publishers having the same pub_id.

When you join two or more tables in SQL Server, the server does not implicitly understand the relationship between the tables; you need to tell it about common keys. In the next example, the selection is drawn from two tables (see the from clause). The where clause of the query defines how those tables relate to each other.

```
sele ct title, pub_name
from titles, publishers
where titles.pub_id = publishers.pub_id
```

Notice that the from clause now names two tables. Also notice that the join condition specifies a table name before each column name (titles.pub_id). Column names must be *qualified* (that is, you must specify the exact table name) whenever there is possible ambiguity because of duplicate column names in multiple tables.

In this case, because pub_id appears in both the titles and publishers tables, the pub_id column needs to be qualified. On the other hand, the title and pub_name columns are not qualified because each only appears in a single table among those named in the from clause.

What Happens When You Fail to Specify a Common Key?

When you write a join without specifying a common key, the server returns all possible combinations of rows between the tables. Consider this example:

```
select title, pub_name
from titles, publishers
```

If the where clause were left out, the server would return a list containing each title many times, once for each publisher. This is a meaningless result because only a single publisher would have published each book.

A result set based on a query missing a proper join condition is called a *Cartesian product*. Cartesian products can take forever to resolve and—once resolved—are usually utterly useless.

Recipe for Writing Queries Containing Joins

Here is a simple recipe for writing joins if you have been assigned to write a specific query or report.

1. Build the select list, naming each column or expression.
2. Name the tables where the columns in the select list reside, as well as any tables required to connect those tables.
3. Provide the join conditions to connect the tables.

For example, imagine writing a query to determine the average price of all books purchased by a single publisher. In that case, the select list might look like this:

```
select pub_name, avg(price)
```

NOTE

This example uses an aggregate expression based on the price column. In spite of this added wrinkle, the join method is the same as elsewhere and the recipe described previously is valid.

The next step is to determine the tables where these columns are found, and any tables that must be identified between them, like this:

```
from titles t, publishers p
```

NOTE

Earlier, you saw how column aliases enable you to specify a substitute column name. The previous example included *table aliases,* which do not affect the final results but do enable you to simplify the SQL syntax. In a later section, you will see how self-joins require table aliases; however, in all other circumstances table aliases are completely optional. It is important to understand that, once you have specified an alias, any subsequent reference to a table *for this SQL statement* will require the table alias rather than the full name.

The final step is to name the where clauses and complete the SQL. Here is the complete query:

```
select pub_name, avg(price)
from titles t, publishers p
where t.pub_id = p.pub_id
group by pub_name
```

> **NOTE**
>
> You can combine joins with every other aspect of SQL including grouping, ordering, having, and other complex where conditions.

Dealing with More than Two Tables

You can join up to 16 tables at a time. This example joins the titles and authors tables to determine which author wrote each psychology title. Following the recipe for a join, here is the select list:

```
select au_lname, au_fname, title
```

In the from clause, you could simply name the tables authors and titles, but note that the tables do not share a common key. In order to connect them, you need to include the titleauthor table, which shares a common key with both tables:

```
from authors a, titles t, titleauthor ta
```

> **NOTE**
>
> Does the order in which the tables are named have an effect on the overall behavior of the server or on performance? In a very few cases, and only in cases where more than four tables are named, table order can have an impact on performance. See Chapter 12, Chapter 14, "Analyzing Query Plans," and Chapter 15, "Locking and Performance," for more on performance issues and how they relate to the actual syntax of a select statement.

Now it's time to name the join conditions. Because there are three joins, there are two required join conditions:

```
where ta.title_id = t.title_id
and a.au_id = ta.au_id
```

Now all that is required is to put the whole query together and add the condition to limit the result set to psychology books and you're done:

```
select au_lname, au_fname, title
from authors a, titles t, titleauthor ta
where ta.title_id = t.title_id
and a.au_id = ta.au_id
and type = "psychology"
```

The Meaning of * in a Multitable Query

In a multitable query, an unqualified asterisk (*) means "all columns from all tables." For example, in the following query, it means "every column from both the `titles` and `publishers` tables."

```
select *
from titles t, publishers p
where t.pub_id = p.pub_id
```

If you qualify the * as in the following example, you get only the columns from a single table.

```
select t.*, pub_name
from titles t, publishers p
where t.pub_id = p.pub_id
```

Subqueries

With SQL Server you can use a *subquery* in place of a constant expression to tell the server to derive a result before processing the remainder of the query. In the following example, you ask the server to show you all books published by a specific publisher. Note that a subquery might only return a single column of data:

```
select title
from titles
where pub_id =
    (select pub_id
     from publishers
     where pub_name = "Algodata Infosystems")
```

When a subquery appears as part of an equality condition (for example, pub_id = (...)), the server expects to resolve the subquery before it starts work on the main query, and *the subquery must return only a single row.*

> **TIP**
>
> To be certain to return only a single row, use a unique key or other unique identifier in the where clause of the subquery or use an aggregate.

Subqueries with *in*

Although a subquery only returns a single column of data, it can return multiple *rows* of data when used with in and not in. In the following example, the server displays all publishers of business books:

```
select pub_name
from publishers
where pub_id in
    (select pub_id
     from titles
     where type = "business")
```

The server returns a list of valid publisher IDs to the main query and then determines whether each publisher's pub_id is in that list. Here is the result set from the query:

```
pub_name
-----------------------------------------
New Moon Books
Algodata Infosystems(2 rows affected)
```

Subqueries versus Joins

The SQL Server treats the subquery in the same way as a join. Here is a query using a join condition to return a similar result:

```
select pub_name
from publishers p, titles t
where p.pub_id = t.pub_id
and type = "business"
```

Here is the result set:

```
pub_name-------------------------------------
New Age Books
Algodata Infosystems
Algodata Infosystems
Algodata Infosystems

(4 rows affected)
```

Subqueries with *exists*

Why does the server return duplicate rows in the result set? Because each query asks for *all matching rows.* There are two ways to solve this problem. The first method is to use the distinct keyword to force the server to find only unique results. The problem with distinct is that it requires an additional sorting step using a worktable, with an often severe performance penalty on large data sets.

The second method is to use the exists keyword to find only rows matching the condition, and to stop looking for results after the first match is found for a particular value. Here's the same query with an exists clause. Look at the example; then you'll step through it to understand how it is written and how it is resolved.

```
select pub_name
from publishers p
where exists
    (select *
     from titles t
     where p.pub_id = t.pub_id
     and type = "business")
```

There are a number of syntactic oddities to observe. First, note that exists takes neither an equals sign nor an in, and it does not apply to a relationship between columns but to a relationship between tables. Because of that, you do not specify a column name in the select list of the subquery; always write select * instead.

Finally, notice that the subquery refers to a table alias, p, in the where condition (p.pub_id), even though this table alias is not declared in the from clause of the subquery itself. The table alias p, of course, relates to the publishers table, which is declared in the outer portion of the query.

exists (and some other situations we won't look at right now) usually uses a *correlated subquery* in which the subquery will not run on its own. In order to resolve the correlated subquery, the server must execute the subquery once for each row in the outer query, testing for a match on pub_id.

Here is the result set of the query with exists:

```
pub_name
-----------------------------------------
New Age Books
Algodata Infosystems

(2 rows affected)
```

The duplicates are eliminated without an intermediate worktable.

not exists and not in

Certain results can be defined only with a subquery; for example, non-membership and non-existence can be expressed only in that way. For example, which publishers *do not* publish business books? This query cannot be expressed with a join, but it can be expressed using not exists or not in:

```
select pub_name
from publishers p
where not exists
    (select *
     from titles t
     where t.pub_id = p.pub_id
     and type = "business")
select pub_name
from publishers
where pub_id not in
    (select pub_id
     from titles
     where type = "business")
```

Subqueries with Aggregates in *where* Clauses

One specific case where a subquery is required appears when you want to use an aggregate function in a where clause. The next example returns the type and price of all books whose price is below the average price. This condition in a where clause would be illegal:

```
where price < avg(price)
```

The server requires that the average price be derived in a subquery, as follows:

```
select type, price
from titles
where price <
    (select avg(price)
     from titles)
```

> **NOTE**
>
> Don't confuse this use of a subquery with a having clause. Consider this example:
>
> ```
> select type, avg(price)
> from titles
> group by type
> ```

union

The SQL union keyword enables you to request a logical union of two or more result sets, listing rows where values are found in either result. This query requests the city and state of each author and each publisher in a single result set:

```
select city, state
from authors
union
select city, state
from publishers
```

The server resolves each element of the union, placing the results in an intermediate worktable. When all of the results are available, the server automatically removes duplicate rows from the final result.

> **TIP**
>
> To prevent the server from removing duplicates, use union all to force all result rows to be returned.

Each result set must have the same number of columns as the first result set, and each column must be of the same datatype as the one in the corresponding position in the first result set. The name of each column is drawn from the column names in the first result set.

> **NOTE**
>
> Column datatypes do not have to match exactly, but they do have to allow an implicit conversion. For example, the server automatically converts strings of different lengths, and it will convert numeric values of different types. It will not, however, automatically convert dates to numeric values, or numbers to strings. For more on implicit data conversions, see Chapter 4.

You can sort the result of a union operation. The order by clause appears after the final select statement, but it references the column names or expressions in the first select list. In the following sample query, authors' and publishers' cities and states are sorted by state, then city:

```
select city, state
from authors
union
select city, state
from publishers
order by state, city
```

This operation is most often used to connect active and archive data, or data that has been separated by year into a single result set. The following example draws data from the fictional salescurrent and saleshistory tables, where the two tables have the same structure:

```
select 95 "year", month, sum(dollar_sales)
from salescurrent
group by month
union
select 94, month, sum(dollar_sales)
from saleshistory
group by month
order by year, month
```

Notice that the union keyword enables you to create result sets using group by and where clauses, each of which is specific to its own select operation. Also note that the order by clause might optionally reference the column aliases defined in the first result clause instead of the column expressions.

Using *select* with *into*

You can direct the select statement to create a table consisting of the rows in the result set on the fly instead of returning the output to the user. This is a common mechanism for creating temporary tables that will be used for subsequent reporting. The structure of the table is defined by the select list itself. The columns are created in the order of the select list, with column names and datatypes drawn from the select list as well.

This example instructs the server to create a table with each of the book types included in the titles table:

```
select distinct type
into type_lookup
from titles
```

The resulting type_lookup table has one column named type whose datatype is the same as the datatype stored in the titles table.

When creating a table with select ... into, you can use any of the SQL syntax you have seen so far in this chapter. This query prepares a master list of all California cities for publishers, authors, and stores:

```
select city
into cal_cities
from publishers
where state = "CA"
union
select city
from authors
where state = "CA"
union
select city
from stores
where state = "CA"
```

NOTE

The into must be stated after the first select list when combined with a union statement.

It is often useful to create an empty copy of an existing table. This query creates an empty copy of salesdetail:

```
select *
into new_salesdetail
from salesdetail
where 1 = 2
```

Even though no rows are found, a table with no rows is created.

Adding Rows with *insert*

So far, you have explored SQL only for retrieving data. The next couple of sections look at queries that modify the data in tables using the keywords insert, update, and delete.

To add rows to a table, use the insert statement. You can either insert specific values that you state in the query or insert based on a selection from another table.

Inserting Specific Values

The following query inserts a row in the authors table, providing values for four of the nine columns in the table:

```
insert authors
    (au_id, au_lname, au_fname, phone, contract)
values
    ("123-45-6789", "Jones", "Mary", "415 555-1212", 1)
```

In the insert statement, the number of columns in the values list must match those in the column list. The datatype of the values must enable an implicit conversion to the datatype of each corresponding column. Columns that are not specified are set to their default value (see

Chapter 5 for information on default values) where one is defined; if there is no default value for a column not specified in the column list, a null value is inserted for the column.

> **NOTE**
>
> If a column does not allow null values, has no default value, is not an *identity* (automatically sequentially numbered) or *timestamp* (automatic version control) column, SQL Server will return an error if no value is provided in the insert statement. In those cases, in order to enter a row a value must be provided for the column.

The insert statement in which you provide specific values only inserts one row at a time. Each additional row requires that you specify the insert keyword again, providing again the name of the table and related columns.

Inserting Several Rows with *select*

In addition to inserting individual rows with a values list, you can also insert one row or many rows based on the result set from a select query embedded in the insert statement. In the following example, the query inserts rows in the fictitious authors_archive table based on rows in the authors table:

```
insert authors_archive
    (au_id, au_lname, au_fname, phone, city, state, zip)
select au_id, au_lname, au_fname, phone, city, state, zip
from authors
where state = "CA"
```

> **NOTE**
>
> A single insert statement can insert zero, one, or many rows. This is an important point to remember about inserting rows when writing insert triggers. For more on this, see Chapter 7.

Omitting the Column List

The column list in an insert statement is optional, but when it is left out, you must provide values for each column in the table *in the order in which the columns were defined*. If you fail to provide the correct number of columns, the server returns a syntax error and the insert fails. This query inserts a row in the publishers table, but does not specify any column names:

```
insert publishers
values
    ("1235", "New World Books and Prints", "Atlanta", "GA")
```

If you specify values in an incorrect order, the server traps invalid data types where appropriate. Otherwise, the wrong data simply appears in each column. For example, this insert to the `publishers` table has the city and state in the wrong order:

```
insert publishers
values
    ("1235", "New World Books and Prints", "GA", "Atlanta")
```

The server won't catch this error because all of the columns are character or variable-character datatypes, enabling implicit conversions and length adjustments. In this case, the value GA would be inserted as the city and the value At (truncated to two characters to match the state column definition) would be inserted for the state.

> **WARNING**
>
> Omitting column names from `insert` statements, particularly when the statements are embedded in application programs, stored procedures, and triggers, can result in ugly code-maintenance problems. What if someone added a column named zip to the `publishers` table? An `insert` statement including the column names to be inserted would succeed, although zip would be stored as a null value. But an insert without column names would fail because the statement now requires five values instead of four.
>
> Here is an important coding standard for your organization: all `insert` statements will name the columns to be inserted.

Modifying Rows with *update*

To modify values within tables, use the `update` statement. Update statements consist of three main components:

- The table to be updated
- The columns to be updated, with the new values
- The rows to be updated, in the form of a `where` clause

This statement changes the name of a publisher to "Joe's Press":

```
update publishers
set pub_name = "Joe's Press"
where pub_id = "1234"
```

An unqualified `update` statement (one without a `where` clause) modifies every row in the table:

```
update titles
set price = price * 2
```

TIP

By far the hardest element of SQL for experienced database programmers to grasp is the need for a where clause to define the set of rows to be updated. This is particularly true when writing an online update system where the row to be modified is visible onscreen.

When you pass the update statement, SQL Server has no idea which row or rows you might have onscreen; each statement is taken on its own, without a reference to other processing. Therefore, the statement

```
update publishers
set name = "Joe's Books and Prints"
```

instructs the server to change *every row in the table*.

You can only update one table at a time, but you can set values for many columns at a single time, as in the following statement that updates the entire address record for a contact:

```
update contacts
set address1 = "5 West Main St.",
    address2 = "Apartment 3D",
    city = "Hartford",
    state = "CT",
    zip = "03838"
where contact_id = 17938
```

TIP

It is always more efficient to set many columns in a single statement than to issue many update statements.

Removing Rows with *delete*

To remove rows from a table, issue the delete statement. delete statements include the name of the table and a where clause defining the rows to delete. This example removes all business books from the titles table:

```
delete titles
where type = "business"
```

An unqualified delete statement removes every row from the table:

```
delete titles
```

This is usually unintended (if not, see the next section on truncate table).

You can only delete rows from a single table at a time.

Clearing a Table with *truncate table*

There are times when you want to clear all rows from a table but leave the table definition as is. To clear a table, issue the `truncate table` command:

```
truncate table titles
```

`truncate table` simply deallocates all space allocations to a table and its indexes instead of removing each row from the table one by one. This is substantially faster than an unqualified `delete`, especially on large tables.

> **WARNING**
>
> You probably are not ready for this information, but you will be reminded of it later when you are reading about transaction logs and data backup.
>
> `truncate table` is fast because it does not log individual row deletions as it deallocates space. Your ability to recover your database in case of disaster is compromised after `truncate table` until you run a backup, and you will not be able to run an incremental backup (`dump transaction …`) until you have run a full backup (`dump database …`) first.

`truncate table` is most commonly used when moving large blocks of test data in and out of the server and when preparing the server for a rollout.

Summary

SQL provides a flexible, English-like method of retrieving and modifying data in tables. The query language is fairly simple yet powerful. It is the only way to access data in a SQL Server and is supported by every product that supports SQL Server itself.

The following chapters look at Transact-SQL, the extensions to the standard SQL language that enable SQL Server to store programmatic, SQL-based objects and to manage data integrity at the server.

Transact-SQL
Datatypes

4

IN THIS CHAPTER

Datatypes Supported by SQL Server

This chapter looks at the datatypes supported by SQL Server. *Datatypes* are predefined, named methods for storing, retrieving, and interpreting categories of data values. As in most programming environments, the system defines the datatypes available to you; you are not permitted to improvise your own.

> **NOTE**
>
> SQL Server supports user-defined datatypes, but these enable the user only to subclass an existing datatype, not to define a new type with new storage and retrieval characteristics. For more on user-defined datatypes, see Chapter 5, "Creating and Altering Database Objects."

You must choose a datatype whenever you create a column in a table or when you declare a local variable. In each case, the choice of a datatype determines the following:

- The kind of data that can be stored in the column (numbers, strings, binary strings, bit values, or dates)
- In the case of numeric and date datatypes, the range of values permitted in the column
- In the case of strings and binary data, the maximum length of data you can store in the column

> **WARNING**
>
> Column datatype selection is one of those incredibly important topics that has ramifications on space utilization, performance, reliability, and manageability of your system. Unfortunately, it is also something you need to do very early in the process of implementing SQL Server, long before you will really understand the ramifications of your choices.
>
> Whatever else you don't have the time to understand, be certain to understand this point:
>
> *After you have created a column and declared its datatype, you cannot change that datatype without dropping and re-creating the table. The more data in the table, the more time that process will take and the more disruption it will cause in system availability.*
>
> This chapter doesn't go into detail on physical storage structures (how rows and pages of data are stored, how indexes are physically managed, and so forth). Before you get deeply into production on systems that require optimal performance, you should finish this chapter and also carefully read Chapter 10, "Understanding SQL Server Storage

Structures." If you are planning to build very large tables or tables that need to perform extremely well, take the time now to read that chapter before you define your tables and columns.

Nullability and Datatypes

When you define a column, you must also decide whether to allow null values in that column. A column that allows nulls requires more space to store a value and might have other performance or storage implications. In this chapter, be sure to notice any special concerns related to nullability for each datatype.

NOTE

This chapter will probably be more helpful if you understand the context in which you define a datatype. Here is a brief example of a table-creation statement:

```
create table my_table
(id int not null,
value float not null,
description varchar(30) null)
```

This query creates a three-column table named `my_table`. Each column is assigned a datatype, and the variable-length column description is also assigned a maximum length of 30 characters.

For more about table definition, see Chapter 5.

Character and Binary Datatypes

Store strings using character datatypes. There are three valid datatypes for storing strings:

- `char`, for storing fixed-length strings
- `varchar`, for variable-length strings
- `text`, for strings of virtually unlimited size (up to 2GB of text per row)

Binary datatypes store *binary* strings, which are strings consisting of binary values instead of characters. The most common uses of binary data are for timestamp and image datatypes:

- `binary`, for fixed-length binary strings
- `varbinary`, for variable-length binary strings
- `image`, for storing large binary strings (up to 2GB of image data per row)

char and varchar

The most common string datatypes are fixed- (char) and variable-length (varchar) character types. Columns defined as char (or character) will store trailing blanks to fill out a fixed number of characters. Columns defined as varchar (or character varying) will truncate trailing blanks to save space.

Column Length

The maximum length of a character column is 255 columns. When you define a char or varchar column, you must also specify a column length to indicate the maximum number of characters the column will store. Here are some column definitions and likely datatypes:

```
name varchar(40)
state char(2)
title varchar(80)
comments varchar(255)
title_id char(6)
```

In the examples, name, title, and comments will vary in length. The server will not reserve space to handle trailing blanks, so a value of George in SQL Server will store only the first six characters in the name column. The columns title_id and state are fixed-length char types because the user is likely to (or *might* be restricted to) insert only strings of the stated length.

TIP

The decision to use char or varchar depends on how frequently the user will provide data of *exactly* the length specified in the column definition. Variable-length structures require additional overhead for their storage (1 extra byte per row to store the length of the variable-length data). In addition, SQL Server must store 1 extra byte per row if there is any variable-length data at all in the table definition. Finally, certain operations are more efficient with character data.

The extra cost in overhead of storing variable-length data is often worth the substantial space savings provided by not storing trailing blanks. If a column is defined as char(20) but averages only 8 bytes of data per row, SQL Server still stores (on average) 12 additional padding spaces per row. That might not seem like much, but over a million rows, that's at least 12MB of additional space.

Until you have a firmer understanding of how SQL Server stores data, you may not make the correct choice between char and varchar. As a rule of thumb, the more the data varies in length, the more important it is to use varchar. Note that there is no reason to define a varchar(1) column.

Chapter 10 discusses the details of physical data storage in more detail. (There, for example, you will find the specifics on variable-length column overhead.)

> **NOTE**
>
> Nullable character columns are stored as variable-length columns. For example, the `description` column in this table is stored exactly like a `varchar(50)` column:
>
> ```
> create table null_char_example
>     (id int not null,
>     description char(50) null)
> ```
>
> The `description` column is not stored with trailing blanks, and the server will use extra overhead in each row to keep track of the actual length of the data.

Character Insert Format

When inserting character data to the server or searching for a value in a `where` clause, pass the value in single or double (matched) quotations. The following `insert` statement provides four character values:

```
insert publishers
     (pub_id, pub_name, city, state)
values
     ("1234", "Stendahl Publishing", "Paris", "France")
```

> **NOTE**
>
> For some reason, when the original `pubs` database was defined, the `publisher`, `title`, `store`, and `author id` columns were all defined as character data. This is not usually as good a choice for a key as an integer or other numeric type, which can be stored far more efficiently. (See the section "Numeric Data Types" later in this chapter.)

Here is an example of an `update` statement with character data:

```
update publishers
     set pub_name = "Press of St. Martins-in-the-Field"
     where pub_id = "1234"
```

Truncation with Character Strings

SQL Server simply truncates character strings that are longer than the column definition, without reporting an error. Let's create a table with four rows to demonstrate the behavior of character strings under a variety of circumstances:

```
create table chars
(id int not null,
c1 char(6) not null)
```

74

Here are the `insert` statements:

```
insert chars values (1, "abc")
insert chars values (2, "abcdefg")
insert chars values (3, "    ef")
insert chars values (4, "ab ef")
```

Note that the second `insert` includes a character string that is longer than the defined length of the c1 column. The server truncates the string after six characters, but it returns no error message or warning.

Now retrieve the rows to see how the server stored them:

```
select id, c1, ">" + c1 + "<" c1_too
from chars

id          c1     c1too
----------- ------ -------
1           abc    >abc   <
2           abcdef >abcdef<
3               ef >    ef<
4           ab ef >ab ef<
```

As expected, the server has truncated the g from the end of the second entry. Also, notice how blanks are treated in a non-null `char()` column: The server stores the trailing blanks in the first row.

sysname Datatypes

Earlier in the chapter, it was mentioned that user-defined datatypes enable you to subclass an existing system datatype to provide a common structure for many columns sharing a single type and having consistent data-integrity requirements. When you install SQL Server, two user-defined datatypes are already available: `sysname` and `timestamp`. (For more on timestamp data, see the section "Timestamps" later in this chapter.)

> **NOTE**
>
> SQL Server uses `sysname` to identify `varchar(30)` columns bound by the naming restrictions for objects, columns, and databases, primarily regarding permitted and restricted characters.
>
> The `sysname` type is not typically assigned to columns in user tables. It is mentioned here so that you understand what it means if you happen across it in the `systypes` table.

binary and varbinary

SQL Server binary datatypes are similar to character datatypes. When you specify a column as `binary` or `varbinary` (or `binary varying`), you must also specify a maximum data length for the column. The server truncates binary values that are too long. As with character columns, variable-length columns have some overhead, but fixed-length ones pad shorter values with trailing hex zeros.

Treatment of binary columns is similar to character types in terms of null or non-null columns (see the section "Nullability and Datatypes" of character data earlier in this chapter). Null columns will require an additional byte of storage where a value exists, but will store less data if no value is available.

To specify a binary column, use the `binary` datatype, as in this example:

```
create table binary_example
    (id int not null,
    bin_column binary(4) not null)
```

Binary Data Insert Format

To insert binary data in a column, specify it without quotation marks, starting with `0x`, and provide two hexadecimal characters for each byte of data. This `insert` statement adds a row containing a 4-byte value into the sample table specified previously:

```
insert binary_example
    (id, bin_column)
values
    (19, 0xa134c2ff)
```

Timestamps

The most common use of binary columns is in the application of another preinstalled, user-defined datatype: the *timestamp*. Timestamp columns enable the user to uniquely identify *versions* of each row in the table.

> **NOTE**
>
> If you didn't understand that statement, you probably are not alone. Keep reading and it will probably make more sense.

There are three important steps involving timestamps:

- Creation of a table with a timestamp column
- Automatic updating of a timestamp column
- Optimistic locking using the timestamp value

To create a table with a `timestamp` column, use the timestamp datatype in the table-creation statement. Note that in this example, the column is named `ts`, but you may use any legal column name:

```
create table timestamp_example
     (id int not null,
     code char(3) not null,
     ts timestamp not null)
```

> **NOTE**
>
> A single table might have only one `timestamp` column.

To insert a row in a table and update the timestamp value, just insert the row. All updating of the timestamp is automatic, so you don't have to indicate a timestamp value. This `insert` statement is an example of a statement in which the server provides a unique timestamp value:

```
insert timestamp_example
     (id, code)
values
     (17, "AAA")
```

When you retrieve the rows from the table, you should see that the timestamp has been assigned a binary value. Look at the output that is received after inserting a row into the `timestamp_example` table:

```
select id, code, ts
     from timestamp_example

id          code ts
----------  ---- -------------------
        17  AAA  0x000000010000198a
```

> **NOTE**
>
> How does the server provide a unique timestamp for each row? Every modification to a row in a SQL Server table is written first to the transaction log. The server uses the unique row identifier in the transaction log as the timestamp value for that row.
>
> You can see the timestamp values steadily escalate if you execute the timestamp `insert` several times. When you retrieve the rows, you should see that the unique log identifier is incrementing by three or four per row. (The increment is not one because the log has additional work to record during an insert.) For more on log writes, see Chapter 12, "Understanding the Query Optimizer."

In fact, the server does not allow you to specify a timestamp value. This command will generate an error message:

```
insert timestamp_example
     (id, code, ts)
```

```
values
    (18, "BBB", 0x01)
```

The third step in the use of the timestamp column is with *optimistic locking.* Here's a brief description of how you implement optimistic locking, but see Chapter 15, "Locking and Performance," for a more in-depth discussion of this technique.

Optimistic locking uses a new system function, `tsequal()` (pronounced "tee-ess-equal," for *timestamp equal*). Most locking techniques warn concurrent users when they attempt to retrieve a record for modification. Optimistic locking warns users when they are performing conflicting modifications.

Consider two users, Mary and Al, each attempting to modify a row in the `timestamp_example` table used earlier. Each retrieves the row with a `select` statement, planning later to update the row:

```
select id, code, ts
from timestamp_example
where id = 17
```

Each user retrieves the current, unchanged value of the `timestamp` column. Mary then modifies the code value of the row with an `update` statement, using the `tsequal()` function to be certain that the row has not changed since she retrieved it:

```
update timestamp_example
set code = "BBB"
where id = 17
and tsequal(ts, 0x000000010000198a)
```

It's important to understand why this `where` clause is written as it is. In order to use the `tsequal()` function, the rest of the `where` clause must identify a unique row. The `id` column is a primary key for the table (and has a unique index, as it turns out), so the `where` clause specifies only one row. (If the value 17 were not found in the table, the `update` statement would complete and SQL Server would report that no rows were processed by the query.)

After the rest of the query identifies the row, SQL Server evaluates the `tsequal()` function for that row. It retrieves the value of the `timestamp` column (`ts` in this example) and compares it to the constant expression passed with the function (`0x000000010000198a` in this example). If those values are the same, the update is allowed.

If you retrieve a timestamp value from the server and then return that value to the server at the next step, why would the `tsequal()` function ever fail to match? Mary's update works because the timestamp failed, but during the update, the server automatically updates the timestamp value again. Now think about poor Al, about to update the same row in the table:

```
update timestamp_example
set code = "CCC"
where id = 17
and tsequal(ts, 0x000000010000198a)
```

Al's update fails in this example because the timestamp value he retrieved when he originally read the record is no longer the current value. When Mary updated the row, the timestamp value changed. Al gets error number 532:

```
The timestamp (changed to 0x000000010000387c) shows that the row has been updated
by another user.
```

> **TIP**
>
> If you are writing applications and are planning to use optimistic locking, you should definitely plan to trap this error and document how users can work around it.

Text and Image Data

The longest variable-length column is only 255 characters. The maximum row length in SQL Server is limited by the size of the data page, which is 2KB.

> **NOTE**
>
> The rows themselves are restricted to a maximum of 1962 bytes because of page and transaction log overhead. Chapter 10, "Understanding SQL Server Storage Structures," discusses row storage in detail and helps you understand the actual row-length limitations (there are many).

Many applications need to store much larger data than a 255-byte column or a 2KB page will allow. Long comments, detailed descriptions, telephone call-log notes, and graphical objects like digitized photos, screen shots, and online images all need much larger capacity than 2KB. SQL Server provides a mechanism for storing *binary large objects* (BLOBs) as large as 2GB per row using the text and image datatypes.

Defining Text and Image Columns

The sample table—texts—has three columns, including a text column—textstring:

```
create table texts
    (id int identity,
     item int not null,
     textstring text null)
```

Let's insert four rows in the table and then look at the characteristics of the text columns. You can insert a string into a text column exactly as you do a regular char or varchar column:

```
insert texts (item, textstring) values
    (1, null)
insert texts (item) values
    (2)
insert texts (item, textstring) values
    (3,"the rain in spain falls mainly on the plain")
insert texts (item, textstring) values
    (4,replicate("the rain in spain falls mainly on the plain", 7)
```

The first two text values inserted are null; the following two rows are not. The last row uses the replicate function to write a fairly long value. Notice that the insert statement will not insert a text value longer than about 1200 bytes.

TIP

Most of the string functions return only 255 characters because they are limited to the maximum length of a varchar. String concatenation of text data is also illegal.

---

writetext, readtext, and updatetext

SQL Server provides three statements to enable the manipulation of long string and binary data, to improve performance, and to simplify access to text and image columns. Text and image data is stored in a chain of separate 2KB pages, apart from the rest of the row data. In the row data itself, SQL Server stores a pointer to the page where the chain of text or image data begins. The three text/image statements—writetext, readtext, and updatetext—use that pointer to find the page chain and are able to write directly to that chain without modifying the underlying row. (In order to do this, you must already have a non-null page pointer stored in the row itself.)

To retrieve the page pointer for a row, use the textptr() function Here are the page pointers for the rows already inserted in the sample table—texts—along with the length of the text data (using the datalength() function):

```
select id, textptr(textstring) textptr,
    datalength(textstring) datalength
from texts

id          textptr                                  datalength
----------  ---------------------------------------  ----------
1           (null)                                   0
2           (null)                                   0
3           0x690100000000000010000009a080000 43
4           0x6a0100000000000010000000a1080000 225

(4 row(s) affected)
```

> **NOTE**
>
> The page pointers for the first two rows are null. Before you could use any of the three text/image statements, you would need to either update the column with data or a null value or insert data into the text or image column during the original `insert` statement.

Let's write a new `textstring` value to the third row using the `writetext` statement. Here is the syntax for `writetext`:

```
writetext table_name.column_name text_ptr
[with log] data
```

> **NOTE**
>
> The `writetext` and `updatetext` statements enable *nonlogged* modifications to text columns, which can substantially improve the performance of text operations (see Chapter 21, "Miscellaneous Performance Topics"). If the database option `select into`/`bulkcopy` has not been set, you must include `with log` to allow the modifications to be logged.

`writetext` completely replaces the existing text or image value with the new value. This `writetext` statement replaces the existing string with the replacement string. Notice that you must first retrieve the page pointer and then pass it to the `writetext` statement in a variable:

```
declare @pageptr varbinary(16)
select @pageptr = textptr(textstring)
      from texts
      where id = 3
writetext texts.textstring @pageptr
"Mary had a little lamp, its fleece was white as snow"
```

> **NOTE**
>
> All text and image operations, whether performed manually with `writetext` or automatically with `insert` or `update` statements, require two physical steps: SQL Server must first find a page pointer in the row itself, and then it must go to that page and perform the requested operation.

In the `writetext` example, there was an error in the text string; Mary should have had a little *lamb*. To change `lamp` to `lamb`, we can use the `updatetext` command. Here's the syntax:

```
updatetext table_name.dest_column_name dest_text_ptr
{NULL | insert_offset} {NULL | delete_length} [with log]
{inserted_data | table_name.src_column_name src_text_ptr}
```

Let's break this down and look at some examples of this statement. To replace existing text, specify where to start (`insert_offset`) and how many characters to replace (`delete_length`), and then provide the new data. To replace a single character with another single character, `delete_length` should be 1:

```
declare @pageptr varbinary(16)
select @pageptr = textptr(textstring)
    from texts
    where id = 3
updatetext texts.textstring @pageptr 21 1 "b"
```

A NULL value for `insert_offset` means that the data will be appended to the end of the existing data, so the rest of the rhyme is added to the existing text:

```
declare @pageptr varbinary(16)
select @pageptr = textptr(textstring)
    from texts
    where id = 3
updatetext texts.textstring @pageptr NULL 0
 ", and everywhere that Mary went that lamb was sure to go."
```

Instead of retrieving the data from a string constant, you can also use another text column as the source data. This example copies the contents of the third-row text data into the text column of the first row (first, though, you need to update the text column to create a text pointer). This example requires two page pointers for the source and destination pages:

```
update texts
    set textstring = ""
    where id = 1
declare @from_ptr varbinary(16), @to_ptr varbinary(16)
select @from_ptr = textptr(textstring)
    from texts
    where id = 3
select @to_ptr = textptr(textstring)
    from texts
    where id = 1
updatetext texts.textstring @to_ptr 0 NULL
texts.textstring @from_ptr
```

The NULL value for `delete_length` instructs SQL Server to delete all characters from the insert point to the end of the existing text data before inserting.

Although this example moves data between rows of the same table, you can also move data between text or image columns of different tables.

WARNING

Before you use text and image datatypes, see Chapter 21 for more information about the drawbacks of BLOBs and alternative implementation methods.

The last thing to do here is to use a `while` loop (see Chapter 6, "Transact-SQL Programming Constructs," for details) to append the same string repeatedly and build a very long value for one row in the `texts` table. This code will have comments delimited with `/* */` to help you understand what is going on:

```
/* declare three variables for from, to, and counter */
declare @from_ptr varbinary(16), @to_ptr varbinary(16), @ctr int
/* set up the pointers and initialize the counter at 1 */
select @from_ptr = textptr(textstring), @ctr = 1
      from texts
      where id = 3
select @to_ptr = textptr(textstring)
      from texts
      where id = 3
/* MAIN LOOP */
while @ctr < 10
begin
/* increment the counter */
      select @ctr = @ctr + 1
/* repeatedly double the size of the text by appending */
      updatetext texts.textstring @to_ptr NULL NULL
      texts.textstring @from_ptr
end
```

Let's see how long the text string is now:

```
select id, datalength(textstring) "col length"
from texts
where id = 3

id          col length
---------   ----------
3           55808
```

A `select` statement will only return the first 255 bytes of this value, but you can now use `readtext` to retrieve any sequence of characters in the column. This `readtext` statement retrieves the 50 bytes starting in position 40000 into the result set listed here:

```
declare @pageptr varbinary(16)
select @pageptr = textptr(textstring)
      from texts
      where id = 3
readtext texts.textstring @pageptr 40000 50

textstring
-------------------------------------------------
go.Mary had a little lamb, its fleece was white as
```

datetime Datatypes

SQL Server enables you to store date and time values. Columns using `datetime` or `smalldatetime` will store both a date and a time value for each row. This `create table` statement creates a two-column table, consisting of an `integer` and a `datetime` column:

```
create table date_example
    (id int not null,
    dateval datetime not null)
```

datetime versus *smalldatetime*

SQL Server supports two date-storage types, datetime and smalldatetime. Generally speaking, smalldatetime is less precise and covers a smaller range of dates, but it occupies less space. The details are outlined in Table 4.1.

Table 4.1. A comparison of `datetime` and `smalldatetime` columns.

	datetime	*smalldatetime*
minimum value	Jan 1, 1753	Jan 1, 1900
maximum value	Dec 31, 9999	Jun 6, 2079
precision	3 milliseconds	1 minute
storage size	8 bytes	4 bytes

> **NOTE**
>
> Here's a question to stump your friends with while watching *Jeopardy!*: Why does SQL Server track datetime values starting with Jan 1, 1753? The Gregorian and Julian calendars were 13 days apart until they were synchronized in September 1752. Date accuracy prior to 1753 is meaningless using our calendars.

datetime Inserts

datetime values are passed to the server in a character string. SQL Server is responsible for conversion and validation of datetime data. This statement inserts a date and time into the sample table created previously:

```
insert date_example
    (id, dateval)
values
    (19, "September 25, 1996 3:15PM")
```

SQL Server permits the entry of many date formats, and it will provide default values for the date and time if they are omitted. Table 4.2 summarizes the entry value and the return value for several date formats.

Table 4.2. SQL Server accepts many different date formats for entry.

insert format	datetime value	smalldatetime value
Sep 3, 1995 13:17:35.332	Sep 3 1995 1:17:35:333PM	Sep 3 1995 1:18PM
9/3/95 1pm	Sep 3 1995 1:00:00:000PM	Sep 3 1995 1:00PM
9.3.95 13:00	Sep 3 1995 1:00:00:000PM	Sep 3 1995 1:00PM
3 sep 95 13:00	Sep 3 1995 1:00:00:000PM	Sep 3 1995 1:00PM
13:25:19	Jan 1 1900 1:25:19:000PM	Jan 1 1900 1:25PM
3 september 95	Sep 3 1995 12:00:00:000AM	Sep 3 1995 12:00AM
4/15/46	Apr 15 2046 12:00:00:000AM	Apr 15 2046 12:00AM

Let's look at each of these examples. The first example in Table 4.2 demonstrates the complete date specification, including the month, day, and year, as well as time in hours, minutes, seconds, and milliseconds. Note that the datetime value is rounded to the nearest 3 milliseconds and the smalldatetime value is rounded to the nearest minute.

Lines 2 through 4 show alternative methods of entering dates, with slashes and periods, and with the name of the month specified as well. Dashes (–) are also a legitimate delimiter in this format.

Line 5 demonstrates how the server handles a time without a date value. When you specify a time without a date, the server provides the system date Jan 1, 1900.

TIP

In general, it makes no sense to enter a time without a date in SQL Server.

In line 6, the server uses the default value 12:00 midnight (a.m.) for the time when none is provided. You almost always need to use a range search method (between x and y) when searching for specific dates (see the section titled "Search Behavior with Dates" later in this chapter).

Line 7 shows how the server treats two-digit year values less than 50. As you can see, all two-digit years less than 50 are assumed to be in the twenty-first century ($20xx$), whereas two-digit years greater than or equal to 50 are treated as twentieth-century dates ($19xx$).

dateformat Options, Languages, and Date Formatting

By default, the server treats a date in the format *xx/yy/zz* as a month/day/year sequence. Microsoft calls this the *mdy* date format. SQL Server also supports several other date orderings. Using the set dateformat command, you can choose other date orders. Valid choices are *mdy, dmy, ymd, ydm, myd,* or *dym.*

This is a *session-level* option, which means that it must be set when the user logs in to the server. For example, to change your date ordering from the default to *yy/mm/dd* formatting, execute this statement:

```
set dateformat ymd
```

> **NOTE**
>
> When a user's language option is changed, it also changes his or her default date format. The server supports us_english (this is the default language) as well as french and german. A user's language option can be set at the server level for all users, as a characteristic of an individual's login account, or within a session by executing the set language statement.

Search Behavior with Dates

How do you find rows having a specific date or time value? Consider a table having the values listed in Table 4.2 (already shown) in a date column. The where clause of the select statement needs to specify a date range, not a single date value. The three select statements listed in the following example might be expected to bring back the same date, but the first will return rows only where the time is exactly midnight. The second and third select statements properly state a range of times within a single day:

```
/* this won't work ... only matches on time = midnight */
select *
from date_table
where date = "9/3/95"

/* this will work ... it states a range of times for the date */
select *
from date_table
where date between "9/3/95" and "9/3/95 23:59:59.999"

/* this will work ... and it might be easier to type */
select *
from date_table
where date >= "9/3/95" and date < "9/4/95"
```

In the last example, notice that the upper bound is *open* (less than) and the upper bound is *closed* (greater than or equal to). This is a general formula for returning a range of dates. Here are some other examples of search conditions returning a range of dates:

```
/* month */ where date >= "9/1/95" and date < "10/1/95"
/* year */ where date >= "1/1/95" and date < "1/1/96"
```

> **WARNING**
>
> As you work with SQL Server, you will discover other techniques for date manipulation. These include the date-parsing functions, `datename()` and `datepart()`, and the `convert()` function, which are all covered in the "Date Functions" section of Chapter 6. These functions can be used in search conditions to determine whether a date falls in a range. For example, you can use `datepart()` to determine the month and year of a date as in this `select` statement, which finds rows with a date in September 1995:
>
> ```
> select *
> from date_table
> where datepart(mm,date) = 9
> and datepart(yy,date) = 95
> ```
>
> The problem with using parsing functions in the search condition of a query is that the server cannot use an advanced performance strategy to speed the query. For example, if there were an index on the date column of this table, the range searches ("date between x and y" and "date >= x and date < y") listed in the example might provide a faster access path to the specific rows that match the search condition.
>
> When you ask the server to perform a function on a column in a search condition, the only way the server can resolve the query is to step through each row of the table, convert the date column in each row, and test its value. This method of query resolution is called a *table scan* and usually takes much longer than index access, particularly when tables are large.
>
> In general, to get better performance, avoid using parsing functions in your search conditions. For much more on this and related topics, see Chapter 20, "Advanced Transact-SQL Programming," Chapter 12, "Understanding the Query Optimizer," and Chapter 14, "Analyzing Query Plans."

Logical Datatype: Bit

SQL Server supports a logical datatype of *bit* for flag columns that store a value of 1 or 0. Bit columns are used for on/off or true/false columns. The following table includes a bit column:

```
create table bit_sample
    (id int not null,
    description varchar(30) null,
    active bit not null)
```

Bit columns have several unique characteristics:

- They do not permit null values.
- They cannot be indexed.
- Several bit columns can occupy a single byte (SQL Server collects up to eight bit columns into a single byte of physical storage).

> **NOTE**
>
> There are many uses for bit columns, including status flags, active account indicators, and item-availability columns. Advanced data-warehousing systems could use bit columns to stand for larger columns to substantially shorten data rows and improve performance.
>
> There are many instances in which a bit column is inappropriate. For example, inexperienced database administrators will create a bit column to indicate whether an account is active as well as a date column to store the activation date. The active bit column depends on the activation date in this example. This not only violates basic normalization rules, but it also requires additional overhead to keep the two columns in sync.

Numeric Datatypes

SQL Server provides many ways to store numeric values, which provide flexibility in precision, range of values, and data storage size. Numeric types fall into four basic categories:

- Integers, including `int`, `smallint`, and `tinyint`
- Floating-point datatypes, including `float` and `real`
- Exact numeric datatypes `numeric` and `decimal`
- Money datatypes `money` and `smallmoney`

Integer Datatypes

Integer columns store exact, scalar values. There are three integer datatypes, `int` (or `integer`), `smallint`, and `tinyint`, for storing varying ranges of values, as summarized in Table 4.3.

Table 4.3. Integers can store a larger range of values, but are larger than `smallint` and `tinyint`.

	int	*smallint*	*tinyint*
minimum value	-2^{31} (-2,147,483,647)	-2^{15} (-32,768)	0
maximum value	2^{31} (2,147,483,647)	2^{15-1} (32,767)	255
storage size	4 bytes	2 bytes	1 byte

Integers make useful keys because they can record a large number of exact values in very few bytes. Where possible, use integers for numeric columns because of the efficient storage mechanism. They are also handled natively and are thus much quicker on every platform. The following is a `create` statement including all three integer types:

```
create table auto_sales
    (id int identity,
    make varchar(25) not null,
    model varchar(25) not null,
    year smallint not null,
    age_at_purchase tinyint not null)
```

Consider how each of the integer type columns is used in this example. The `id` column should be an `int` column in order to allow up to two billion unique row keys in this table.

> **NOTE**
>
> The `identity` keyword tells the server to maintain an automatic counter using this column. The server will waste some counter values because of failed insertions, so even if you know exactly how many rows will be contained in a table, you need to make a provision for the counter to grow to a higher value. Using `smallint` for the key in this example could result in the server being unable to insert rows in the table once the next available value is higher than the maximum value for the datatype.
>
> For more on identity and other characteristics of tables, see Chapter 5, "Creating and Altering Database Objects."

In the example, the year of the car is a good use of `smallint` because the range of values is likely to be from about 1900 to 20xx.

> **NOTE**
>
> By the way, this is a terrible place to use a `smalldatetime` column. You are not recording the date of the car's manufacture (which would require date and time specificity), but the model year of the car. Aside from inefficient storage (`smallint` requires only two bytes, whereas `smalldatetime` requires four), `smalldatetime` does not permit date entry with only a year. For example, to find all orders in 1990, you would have to parse the order date:
>
> ```
> select order_id, ...
> from orders
> where datepart(yy, order_date) = 1990
> ```
>
> In the case of a model year, where the date specifics are not required, an integer value for the year is much easier to search for:
>
> ```
> select make, model
> from auto_sales
> where year = 1990
> ```

The age column in the `auto_sales` example is a good example of `tinyint` (until people start living for 256 years!).

WARNING

Remember that you cannot change the datatype of a column. If you discover late in the game that a decode table requires more than 256 unique keys, so a tinyint was a bad choice for a primary key, you will need to drop the table and re-create it with the proper datatype. You will also have to drop and re-create any table(s) that reference that key.

NOTE

An integer should be transmitted to the server as a number with no decimal place, as in this insert statement:

```
insert auto_sales
     (make, model, year, age_at_purchase)
values
     ("Ford", "Taurus", 1995, 42)
```

Pass integers in search conditions the same way:

```
select make, model
from auto_sales
where year >= 1993
and age_at_purchase between 18 and 25
```

Floating-Point Datatypes

SQL Server provides two approximate numeric datatypes, float (or double precision) and real, for handling numbers with a very large range of values requiring the same precision no matter how large or how small the number. In Table 4.4, you can see that float and real differ only in precision and storage size.

Table 4.4. float **columns take up more space per row than** real **columns, but they provide greater precision.**

	float	real
smallest value	±2.23E-308	±1.18E-38
largest value	±1.79E308	±3.40E38
precision	up to 15 digits	up to 7 digits
storage size	8 bytes	4 bytes

NOTE

`floats` and `reals` are often written in scientific notation. In Table 4.4, 1.79E308 means 1.79 times 10 raised to the 308th power.

Scientific notation makes it possible to talk about extremely large and extremely small numbers without needing to write out meaninglessly long numbers. To write 1.79E308 without scientific notation, I would have to write something like this:

179,000,000,000,000,000,000,000,000,000,000,000,...,000

(It would actually require 306 zeros. I only wrote 36 zeros and then I got lazy.) The part of the number where the numbers are meaningful (1.79) is called the *mantissa*. The part where the scale of the number is indicated (E308 or 10^{308}) is called the *exponent*.

`float` and `real` columns are useful for scientific and statistical data where absolute accuracy is not required and where the data in a single column might vary from extremely large to extremely small.

DATATYPE PRECISION

`float` columns use an internal algorithm to store numbers as a mantissa and exponent. The algorithm is not perfectly precise; what you put in is not always *exactly* what you get back. For example, a number with 15 significant digits entered in a `float` column might see some variance in the last digit.

That is why I was surprised to learn from a client at one of the New York City financial-trading companies that they had adopted a standard of using `float` for all stock and bond share prices. I had assumed that they would use `money` or `smallmoney` instead (see the following).

The problem with `money` and `smallmoney` is that they round to the fourth decimal place, which is inaccurate when dealing with shares trading at $^1/_{32}$ dollar ($0.03125) or $^1/_{64}$ dollar ($0.015125). Despite the fact that a `float` is an approximate money type, it was perfectly exact in this case, where the number of significant digits in the value does not approach the precision of the datatype.

What is important to keep in mind about `float` and `real` datatypes is this: What we commonly think of as precision is the number of decimal places that are accurately returned. In the case of approximate datatypes, precision is the number of significant digits in the value. The value of $^1/_{32}$—0.03125—requires five decimal places for storage, but a `real` or `float` datatype sees only four significant digits in the mantissa, 3.125, as well as an exponent, 10^{-2}. The value of $325^1/_{32}$—325.03125—also requires only five decimal places, but it requires eight-digit precision in a `real` or `float` datatype to record all the significant digits.

This means that the decimal precision of `float` and `real` data decreases as the number to store increases. A `real` column is sufficient to store $1/32$ exactly, but it will not store $325 1/32$ precisely.

Inserting *float* and *real* Data

To insert `float` or `real` data, simply supply the number (always include a decimal). If you need to specify both a mantissa and an exponent, use standard scientific notation in the form, $\pm m.mmmE\pm ee$, where *m.mmm* is the mantissa (up to 15 digits precision) and *ee* is the base-ten exponent, as in the following example:

```
insert float_example
    (id, float_col)
values
    (1, 1.395E3)
```

Precision of *float*

`float` permits the user to specify an optional precision, ranging from 1 to 15. `float` columns with a precision of 1 to 7 are stored as a `real` in 4 bytes; those with a precision of 8 to 15 bytes are stored like a `float` (without a specified precision) in 8 bytes.

Exact Numeric Datatypes

SQL Server supports two exact numeric datatypes, `decimal` (or `dec`) and `numeric`. The two are synonymous and interchangeable, but note that only `numeric` can be used in combination with `identity` columns. Use numeric data where the *precision* (number of significant digits) and *scale* (number of decimal positions) are known from the start. This is a useful datatype for handling monetary columns.

To create an exact numeric column, specify in the table-creation statement the datatype, along with the precision (maximum is 28) and scale (less than or equal to the precision) for the column, as in this example:

```
create table numeric_example
    (id int not null,
    num_col numeric(7,2))
```

The column, `num_col`, will store numbers up to ±99,999.99, with two digits following the decimal place.

The storage size for a numeric depends on the precision. A 28-digit numeric column will occupy 13 bytes per row.

Money Datatypes

The preceding sections show that `float` and `numeric` datatypes are useful options for monetary values. SQL Server also provides two datatypes specifically for this purpose: `money` and `smallmoney`. Both `money` and `smallmoney` are exact datatypes with four-digit decimal precision. (See Table 4.5.)

Table 4.5. `money` **columns require twice as much space per row as** `smallmoney`, **but they accommodate much higher numbers.**

	money	*smallmoney*
range	±922,337,203,685,477.5808	±214,748.3647
storage size	8 bytes	4 bytes

NOTE

You have probably noticed that the maximum `smallmoney` value is the same as the maximum integer value, but the decimal is shifted four positions to the left. Essentially, `money` and `smallmoney` are treated like integers for arithmetic operations; then the decimal shifts to the correct position for output.

NOTE

The correct format for entering money is with a dollar sign ($) and no commas:

```
insert dollar_table
     (id, dollars)
values
     (95, $12345.93)
```

IMPORTANT: Your language option does not affect the currency symbol or choice of decimal separator.

See Table 4.6 for a list of column datatypes.

Table 4.6. Column datatypes.

Datatype	Range of values	Size in bytes	Sample Input
Character datatypes			
char[(n)]	1<=n<=255	n (default is 1)	'Fred'
varchar[(n)]	1<=n<=255	data length (default is 1)	'14 Main St.'
text	BLOB up to 2, 147, 483, 647 chars	16+multiple of 2k	'Fred'
Binary datatypes			
binary(n)	1<=n<=255	n	0xa1b3
varbinary(n)	see binary,	n+1	0xf1
image	BLOB up to 2, 147, 483, 647 bytes	16+multiple of 2k	0xf1...
timestamp	Used for change management	16	N/A
Data datatypes			
datetime	Jan 1, 1900 to Dec 31, 9999 accuracy 3-millisecond interval	8	'jan 2, 1770 13:15:17.12'
smalldatetime	Jan 1, 1900 to Jun 6, 2079 accuracy minute	4	'jan 2, 1970 15:18'
Logical datatypes			
bit	0 or 1	1 (up to 8 bit columns/byte)	1
Numeric datatypes			
int	±2,147,483,647	4	1234567
smallint	±32767	2	2134
tinyint	0 to 255	1	32
float[(precision)]	machine dependent	4 (precision<16) 8 (precision>=16)	123.1397864
double precision	machine dependent	8	123.1397864
real	machine dependent	4	123.1324
numeric(p,s) decimal(p,s)	±10 to 38th power, p is precision (total digits, 1-38), s is scale (decimal digits, <=p)	2 to 17	12345.55
money	±$922,337,203,685,477.5807	8	$1596980.23
smallmoney	±$214,748.3647	4	$10000.25

System Tables and Datatypes

SQL Server datatypes are not keywords; instead, they are stored as *data values* in a database-level system table, systypes. The systypes table contains both system- and user-defined datatypes.

If you view all the names of the types, you will see all the entries described in this chapter. You will also see entries for nullable versions of many datatypes. For example, systypes includes both money and moneyn, one for non-null and one for nullable versions of the money datatype.

Summary

Datatype selection is one of the truly critical decisions the DBA must make when defining a database. Because a column datatype cannot be easily modified after a table is created, you need to anticipate the changing needs of your system and understand the ramifications of your datatype choices.

The next chapters in this part of the book show how to build SQL Server objects, referring to columns and variables belonging to these datatypes.

Creating and Altering Database Objects

5

In this chapter you learn two methods for maintaining SQL Server objects. One method requires writing Transact-SQL statements to develop and maintain objects; the other allows you to use a graphical interface. Why bother learning the syntactic approach when it is so easy to do the work using a graphical tool? Two reasons. First, as you become more accomplished with the language, you will find it easier to create a fast example for testing by writing code than by using the tool. Second, and more importantly, when you are finished designing your database using the SQL Enterprise Manager, you will need to make a backup version of that design, and you might even want to distribute that design (perhaps with minor modifications). The method of backing up and publishing a database *design* (as opposed to a database and its *data*) is to generate SQL scripts that can automatically reproduce the database structure.

Creating Database Objects

All objects created within SQL Server require a frame of reference, a logical way of putting your arms around all the related objects. This logical grouping of objects is referred to as a database. We assume you are working, now, in an existing database. Do *not* begin playing in the master or msdb databases; instead, create one of your own if you are experimenting or learning.

NOTE

If you don't have a test database and you are working on a server where it's acceptable to make some mistakes, here are some quick instructions on how to create a new test database. If it's not acceptable to make mistakes on your server, you should carefully read Chapter 28, "Database Logging and Recovering," before creating a test database. (You will need to be able to log in as sa to do this. If you can't log in as sa, ask your SQL Server administrator to create a database for you.)

To create a test database, use isql/w to execute this command:

```
sp_helpdb test
```

If you get an error message saying that the database "test" does not exist, that's good. (If not, try "test1" and "test2" and so forth until you find an unused name.)

Now execute this statement to create the database:

```
create database test on default = 2
```

This creates a two-megabyte database named test on a device that was set up for default use. If you get an error message saying that there is not enough space on the default disk, or if no default disk is found, there is more work to do and you need to go and read Chapter 28.

NOTE

This chapter demonstrates how to use the features of *SQL Enterprise Manager* (SQL-EM) regarding database object creation and management. It assumes that you are able to run the SQL Enterprise Manager application and that you have permissions, both over the network and on the SQL Server, to perform the operations discussed. If you do not have proper permissions to perform these functions, contact your SQL Server administrator.

In SQL Enterprise Manager, you can find the databases that are on your server by opening a connection to the server you are working with and opening the Databases folder. (See Figure 5.1.)

FIGURE 5.1.

SQL Enterprise Manager enables you to browse a variety of resources, including database names.

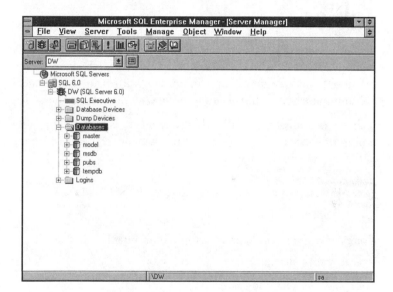

SQL Server supports a variety of database objects, which enable you to better utilize, access, and care for your data. In this chapter, you learn about the use and creation of the various SQL Server object types:

- Tables, to store SQL Server data.
- Temporary tables, to store temporary result sets.
- Views, to provide a logical depiction of data from one or more tables.
- Rules, to validate column data.
- Defaults, to provide a column value when none is provided by the client application.
- Constraints, to validate column data, and to maintain consistency between tables.

In this chapter, you also learn about other structures (not properly *objects*, but relevant to this discussion):

- User-defined datatypes, to maintain consistent rule and default enforcement among related columns.
- Indexes, to maintain uniqueness and improve performance.
- Keys, to document the structure of individual tables and relationships among tables.

SQL Server also supports two code-based object types, discussed in Chapter 7, "Transact-SQL Program Structures":

- Stored procedures
- Triggers

Tables

Tables are logical constructs used for storage and manipulation of data in the databases. Tables contain columns, which describe data, and rows, which are unique instances of data. Basic relational database design (in conjunction with your shop standards) determines table and column names, as well as distribution of columns within the tables.

Table creation is accomplished by using one of two tools: the SQL Enterprise Manager table editor, or Transact-SQL's `create table` statement. If you are typing a T-SQL statement, here is the fundamental syntax.

```
create table table_name
(column name datatype {identity ¦ null ¦ not null}
[, ...]
)
```

For example, you could create a four-column table called `demographics` using this statement:

```
create table demographics
(user_id numeric(10,0) identity,
last_name varchar(30) not null,
first_name varchar(30) not null,
comments varchar(255) null)
```

In SQL Enterprise Manager, you can graphically create tables using the Table Editor. To use Table Editor, you must open a database, and then open the Objects and Tables folders that are nested under Databases. If you right-click on the Tables folder, you are presented with the menu illustrated in Figure 5.2.

When you select the New Table item, you are presented with the Table Editor. This dialog box can also be activated by using the Manage|Tables... menu sequence, but this applies to the current database you have open.

FIGURE 5.2.

SQL Enterprise Manager uses a hierarchy of objects and collections to manage tables and other database objects.

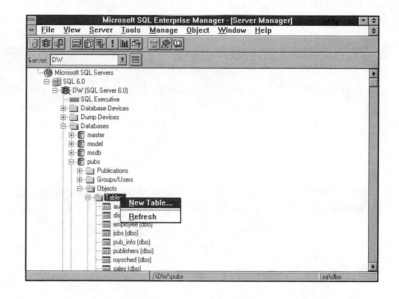

Figure 5.3 shows a table named `demographics`, which is comprised of four columns: `user_id`, `last_name`, `first_name`, and `comments`. This table at creation time is accessible only to the user who created it. This user may choose to grant permissions to other users (see Chapter 27, "Security and User Administration").

FIGURE 5.3.

SQL Enterprise Manager provides a graphical tool for creating and editing database tables.

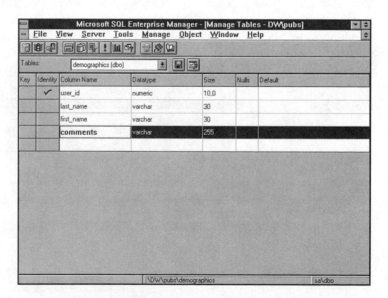

Table names are unique for a user within a database; this means that all users could potentially have their own tables entitled `demographics`. It also means that every user could have only one table called `demographics`.

To remove a table and its structure, use the drop command.

> **NOTE**
>
> The basic syntax to remove most database objects is drop *object_type object_name*.

```
drop table table_name

drop table demographics
```

> **WARNING**
>
> There is no UNDROP. Once it is gone, it is gone. The only way to get a dropped object back into the database is to have the systems administrator restore it from a dump. If that object did not exist in its entirety at the time of that dump, you are completely out of luck.

Dropping a table can be performed more easily in the Enterprise Manager application. Open the Tables folder for the database you are working with and select the table that you would like to drop. By right-clicking on the table name, you can display the menu illustrated in Figure 5.4. Select Drop from the menu, and the table, both its structure and data, will be destroyed, as if you had run drop `<tablename>`. Unlike the drop command, which requires no confirmation, Enterprise Manager prompts you first, just to make sure you are certain you want to drop the table. After you confirm your wishes, Enterprise Manager executes the drop command, and the table cannot be recovered.

FIGURE 5.4.

Administrators can use Enterprise Manager to edit, create, and destroy database tables.

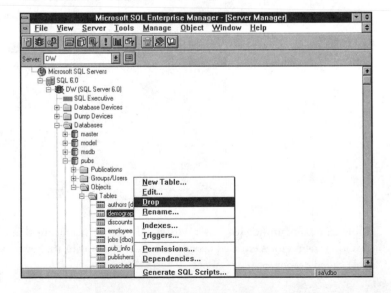

Enterprise Manager enables you to drop tables in groups, but by using the multi-select feature of its drag-and-drop interface. By holding the Ctrl key while you are selecting table names from the Tables folder, you can select multiple tables, all of which will be dropped. If you select a table name, hold the Shift key and select another table name in the list, Enterprise Manager highlights all the tables between these two points and includes them in the drop list. If you are familiar with other Windows applications that use multi-select, you can see that SQL Enterprise Manager behaves consistently with those other applications. In Figure 5.5, Enterprise Manager is prompting the administrator for confirmation of a multi-table delete.

FIGURE 5.5.

SQL Enterprise Manager supports the multi-select options customary to most Windows applications, enabling you to execute administrative tasks on multiple objects simultaneously.

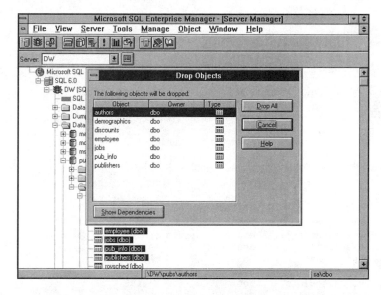

If you are running ISQL/w, you can get information on the table you have created by executing the `sp_help` system stored procedure.

> **NOTE**
>
> `sp_help` is the Swiss Army knife of SQL Server. Without any parameters, it provides a list of all objects and user-defined datatypes in a database. If you pass a table name, it will show you the structure of the table (see the next example). If you pass a procedure name, it will show you the parameters.

```
sp_help table name

sp_help demographics
Name          Owner     Type          When_created
------------  --------  ------------  -------------------
demographics  dbo       user table    Nov 13 1995  8:50PM
( 0 rows affected)
```

```
Data_located_on_segment
-------------------------------
default
( 0 rows affected)


Column_name      Type        Length Prec  Scale Nullable
---------------  ----------  ------ -----  ----- ------------------
user_id          numeric     6      10     0     no
last_name        varchar     30           no
first_name       varchar     30           no
comments         varchar     255          yes
( 0 rows affected)

Identity     Seed      Increment
-----------  --------  --------------------
user_id      1.0       1.0
( 0 rows affected)

Object does not have any indexes.

No constraints have been defined for this object.

No foreign keys reference this table.
```

Alternatively, sp_help without an object name gives you a list of all objects in the database:

```
sp_help
Name                 Owner    Object_type
-------------------  -------  ----------------------
demographics         dbo      user table
sysalternates        dbo      system table
sysarticles          dbo      system table
syscolumns           dbo      system table
syscomments          dbo      system table
sysconstraints       dbo      system table
sysdepends           dbo      system table
sysindexes           dbo      system table
syskeys              dbo      system table
syslogs              dbo      system table
sysobjects           dbo      system table
sysprocedures        dbo      system table
sysprotects          dbo      system table
syspublications      dbo      system table
sysreferences        dbo      system table
syssegments          dbo      system table
syssubscriptions     dbo      system table
systypes             dbo      system table
sysusers             dbo      system table
( 0 rows affected)

Sort Order:  Object_type Name
```

```
User_type      Storage_type    Length Prec Scale
          Nullable   Default_name   Rule_name
------------ ---------------- ------ ---- -----
             ---------- --------------- ----------
( 0 rows affected)
```

Sort Order: User_type

This information is particularly useful if you are trying to identify what objects are within a database or if you think you created a database object and don't remember what you called it, or if you are sure you created one and it does not appear to be there.

Although the traditional SQL Server methods inherited from Sybase SQL Server provide useful information, that information can be accessed more easily using SQL Enterprise Manager. In SQL-EM, you can view a table's columns, indexes, keys, and so forth in the Table Editor window described earlier. If you want to see the objects in a database, you can open that database's Objects folder for a list of object types, also presented as folders (see Figure 5.6). In each object type folder, the list of objects of that type is listed. By right-clicking on an object, you open SQL Enterprise Manager dialog boxes that enable you to create new objects of that type, as well as to modify or remove existing objects.

FIGURE 5.6.

SQL Enterprise Manager enhances traditional SQL Server functionality by presenting database object information in a more usable format.

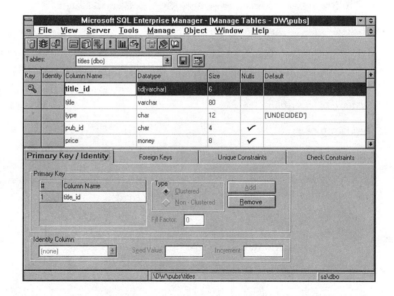

> **TIP**
>
> If you cannot find an object you created, run `sp_help` or look for it in the proper folder in SQL Enterprise Manager. Look for the table name and remember that *SQL Server object identifiers are case-sensitive.* Additionally, check to see whether the object owner changed. If you created an object as `user1` and are now the `dbo`, you have to qualify the name of the object (for example, `user1.demographics`).

Tables are comprised of up to 250 user-defined columns, each of which has three characteristics: a name, a datatype, and a property.

SQL Server Object Names

All SQL Server object names are up to 30 characters in length, and are case-sensitive. The 30-character limitation is imposed by the maximum length of the name columns in `sysobjects` and `syscolumns` system tables. Note that keywords, by definition, are case-insensitive.

The following is the full name of any SQL Server object:

```
database_name.owner_name.object_name
```

Note that the `database_name` defaults to the database you are in, and does not need to be explicitly named. `owner_name` defaults to the user name within the database of the person who signed in. If there is no object owned by the person who signed in, the server defaults to the database owner (`dbo`).

For example, this

```
pubs.dbo.authors
```

is a table named `authors`, owned by the `dbo`, in the `pubs` database (included with installation). The following

```
pubs.user1.authors
```

may coexist in that database and be owned by `user1`, and this

```
user1.authors.au_lname
```

is the name of a column in the table `authors` owned by `user1` in the current database; however, you know this only by looking at the names and making sense of them. If you look at this by convention only, it could as easily be a table called `au_lname` owned by `authors` in the database `user1`.

TIP

In a production database, all objects should be owned by the dbo to simplify owner-ship, avoid confusion, and ease a permission scheme. (See Chapter 27.)

SQL Enterprise Manager displays owner names as well. In the list of objects in a particular object folder, the owner name for an object always appears in parentheses immediately follow-ing the object name. Two objects with a similar name but different owners is sorted in ascend-ing order, using the object name first and then the owner name, as illustrated with the two demographics tables in Figure 5.7.

FIGURE 5.7.

*SQL Enterprise Manager tracks objects with common names by sorting on the Object Owner value (*dbo *and* dw, *respectively, for the* demographics *table).*

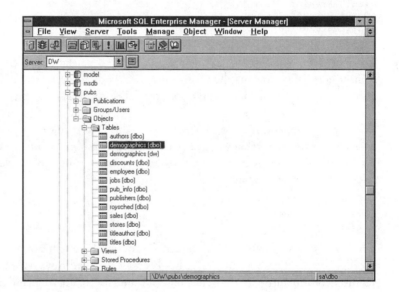

Column Properties

Columns can have the following properties:

- Null (a value does not need to be specified for a column)
- Not null (a value must be specified for the column)
- Identity (the server is to maintain a row counter on the table)

A value of null (in the column) means that the column has not been assigned a value. This is *not* equivalent to having a value of zero (for a numeric type) or spaces (for a character type). In fact, from a boolean standpoint, a null column value is not equal to a null column value, be-cause null is not a value at all; it is the absence of a value.

If a column has a property of not null, a value must be assigned at insert time or the row will not be inserted.

Identity columns are used for sequential, unique numbering of rows being inserted into the table.

```
create table table_name
(column_name {int ¦ smallint ¦ tinyint ¦ numeric(p,0)} identity [,...] )
```

Example

```
/* this table has first, last names and an automatic key */
create table names2
 (auto_key int identity,
 first varchar(30) not null,
 last varchar(30) not null
 )
```

You may have a maximum of one identity column per table, which will be (by default) not null. Identity columns may be of any integer or whole-number numeric datatype. In addition, you may set an initial value for the counter field, as well as to specify an incremental value for the counter to use. You could set the initial value to 1000 and count by 10, or set the initial value to 100 and count by 50. The syntax for this is to include, in parentheses, the seed value followed by the increment value. The defaults for these are 0 and 1, respectively, meaning that an identity field will start with value 0 and increment values in the field by 1 as new rows are added. The syntax is represented here:

```
create table foo
(field1 int identity (,10),
 field2 ...)
```

The right choice of datatype for an identity column is very important, because it is difficult to modify the datatype once the table has been created and rows have been added. In addition, identity columns are limited to the range of values for that particular datatype. In simpler terms, a column of type tinyint can store only 256 distinct values in the range of 0 through 255. By using an identity column, you have effectively limited your table to holding 256 rows!

If an upper or lower limit is reached for a datatype, inserts can no longer be processed on that table. SQL Server does not automatically reuse values that have been skipped or deleted, nor does the counter "cycle" back to the beginning to hunt for available values. In that way, your identity fields are limited by the datatype you select.

TIP

If your tables require an identity column and you anticipate them growing to be quite large, remember that any whole-number datatype will suffice. A numeric or decimal field allows you up to 38 decimal places for storing numbers. When specifying the datatype for such a column, use decimal (38,0) for the datatype. You'll have 38 decimal places, which should be plenty of row numbers (but if you don't use all those numbers, you may be wasting a lot of empty space).

To insert rows into a table with an identity column, do not specify the identity column in the insert statement. In the first example insert statement, the column names have been omitted and SQL Server expects values for all the columns in the table except the identity column. In the second example, the column names are specified; SQL Server expects values for only the named columns.

```
insert names values ("John", "Smith")
insert names (first, last) values ("Tom", "Jones")
select * from names
go

auto_key first            last
-------- ---------------- ------------------
1        John             Smith
2        Tom              Jones
```

The last value applied to an identity column for a session is available in the @@identity global variable. (See more on global variables in Chapter 6, " Transact-SQL Programming Constructs.") @@identity retains its value until the session inserts another row into a table with an identity column.

You can use the identitycol keyword in other SQL statements to refer to the identity column (or you can identify it by the column name):

```
select auto_key, first, last
    from names
/* OR */
select identitycol, first, last from names
/* update a row in names2 table */
update names2
    set first = "John"
    where identitycol = 2
```

Notes on Identity Columns

Updates to identity columns are never allowed. You have to delete the old row and insert the new row.

WARNING

Identity column values are not row numbers. SQL Server attempts to use sequential numbers for identity column values, but may not be able to based on seed value, increment value, and the failure of transactions to complete. Any of these three can contribute to gaps in the identity values SQL Server generates. SQL Server does not support internal row number operations, and identity columns are not a 100-percent-reliable method of implementing such processing!

The table owner, database owner, or sa can explicitly insert identity values if the following set option is enabled:

```
set identity_insert table_name on
set identity_insert names on
insert names (10, "Jane", "Doe")
set identity_insert names off
go
```

This option enables you to set a seed value for identity columns or to fill in gaps in identity sequences.

WARNING

It is possible, with this option on, to insert duplicate identity values into a table if there is no unique index or unique constraint defined on the identity column. Identity columns do not validate unique values—they merely generate numbers according to a sequence!

Views

Views are a logical way of looking at the physical data located in the tables. In fact, to a select statement, a view looks exactly like a table.

NOTE

A view does not represent any physical data, merely a window into the physical data. Dropping a view has no effect on the underlying table(s).

Creating a view is as simple as writing a select statement. Views (like other objects) require unique names *among all objects in the database.*

```
create view view_name [ (col_name, ...) ]
as select statement
[ with check option ]
```

If you omit the column names in a view, the view columns inherit the column names from the base table(s) at the time the view is created.

```
/* make view with two columns from authors table */
create view author_name as
    select last = au_lname, first = au_fname
    from authors
```

If you use column headings, as in this example, the column headings become the column names in the view.

NOTE

Make sure your column headings would also be valid column names.

In almost all ways, you may treat a view like a table:

```
/* retrieve all rows and columns from view */
select * from author_name
last                                first
--------------------------------    --------------------
White                               Johnson
Green                               Marjorie
Carson                              Cheryl
O'Leary                             Michael
Straight                            Dean
Smith                               Meander
Bennet                              Abraham
Dull                                Ann
Gringlesby                          Burt
Locksley                            Charlene
Greene                              Morningstar
Blotchet-Halls                      Reginald
Yokomoto                            Akiko
del Castillo                        Innes
DeFrance                            Michel
Stringer                            Dirk
MacFeather                          Stearns
Karsen                              Livia
Panteley                            Sylvia
Hunter                              Sheryl
McBadden                            Heather
Ringer                              Anne
Ringer                              Albert
( 23 rows affected)
```

To remove a view, use the drop view statement:

```
drop view view_name

/* drop the author_name view */
(d)drop view author_name
```

Examining Views in SQL Enterprise Manager

SQL Enterprise Manager also offers a Views folder similar to the Tables folder for a particular database. All views in the database are listed here. Double-clicking on a view displays a text-editor window where SQL-EM puts the original creation statement for the view. From here, you can edit the creation statement, resubmit it, and effectively re-create your view. (See Figure 5.8.)

FIGURE 5.8.

SQL Enterprise Manager provides a convenient interface for editing creation statements for views.

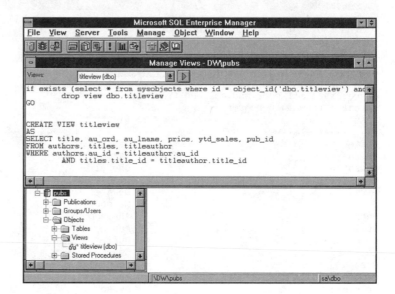

Views as Security—Vertical

You can use a view to limit access to selected *columns* in a base table. (See Figure 5.9.) This is a normal approach to restricting access to a user, while not requiring the user to write a lot of SQL. In this example, the view includes only three of the four columns in the `titleauthor` table.

```
/* create a view to show 3 of 4 titleauthor columns */
create view ta_limited as
    select au_id, title_id, au_ord
    from titleauthor
```

FIGURE 5.9.

The view displays only the named columns. Those columns not named are invisible to users accessing the table through the view.

au_id	title_id	au_ord	royaltyper
172-32-1176	PS3333	1	100
213-46-8915	BU1032	2	40
213-46-8915	BU2075	1	100
...	...	...	...
998-72-3567	PS2106	1	100

When you select from the view, you will only see the columns specified in the view. The royaltyper column in the titleauthor table is not displayed here and is unavailable from this view.

```
select * from ta_limited

au_id        title_id au_ord
-----------  -------- ------
172-32-1176  PS3333   1
213-46-8915  BU1032   2
213-46-8915  BU2075   1
238-95-7766  PC1035   1
267-41-2394  BU1111   2
...
899-46-2035  PS2091   2
998-72-3567  PS2091   1
998-72-3567  PS2106   1
( 25 rows affected)
```

When you use a view for security, grant the user permission to select from the view, but not from the base table.

This view can now be used to join titles and authors:

```
/* select title and author name using ta_limited view */
select au_lname, title
from authors a, titles t, ta_limited ta
where a.au_id = ta.au_id and t.title_id = ta.title_id

au_lname             title
-------------------  -------------------------------------------
Green                The Busy Executive's Database Guide
Bennet               The Busy Executive's Database Guide
O'Leary              Cooking with Computers: Surreptitious Balance Sheets
MacFeather           Cooking with Computers: Surreptitious Balance Sheets
Green                You Can Combat Computer Stress!
Straight             Straight Talk About Computers
del Castillo         Silicon Valley Gastronomic Treats
DeFrance             The Gourmet Microwave
Ringer               The Gourmet Microwave
Carson               But Is It User Friendly?
Dull                 Secrets of Silicon Valley
Hunter               Secrets of Silicon Valley
Locksley             Net Etiquette
MacFeather           Computer Phobic AND Non-Phobic Individuals:Behavior Variat
```

```
Karsen            Computer Phobic AND Non-Phobic Individuals: Behavior Varia
Ringer            Is Anger the Enemy?
Ringer            Is Anger the Enemy?
Ringer            Life Without Fear
White             Prolonged Data Deprivation: Four Case Studies
Locksley          Emotional Security: A New Algorithm
Panteley          Onions, Leeks, and Garlic: Cooking Secrets of the Mediterr
Blotchet-Halls    Fifty Years in Buckingham Palace Kitchens
O'Leary           Sushi, Anyone?
Gringlesby        Sushi, Anyone?
Yokomoto          Sushi, Anyone?
( 25 rows affected)
```

Views as Security—Horizontal

You can use a view to limit access to specific *rows* in a base table by writing a where clause in the view that restricts rows to those a user should see. In this example, the cal_publishers view contains only rows where the state has the value, CA.

```
/* create view with only California publishers */
create view cal_publishers as
    select *
    from publishers
    where state = "CA"
```

When you select from the view, only publishers from California are displayed:

```
/* retrieve all rows and columns from the view */
select * from cal_publishers

pub_id pub_name                  city                 state country
------ ------------------------- -------------------- ----- ---------------
1389   Algodata Infosystems      Berkeley             CA    USA
( 1 row affected)
```

Views to Ease SQL

Views can be used to simplify queries. It has been my direct and personal experience that the best programmers are the lazy ones; they find efficient ways of doing things and are therefore more productive. Views are useful for hiding complex joins or denormalized tables from end users and easing the SQL for programmers. In this example, the view joins three tables, allowing users to query a complex data structure as if the data were stored in a single flat table.

```
/* create a view to handle a three-way join */
create view titles_and_authors as
    select title, au_lname, au_fname, type
    from titles t, ta_limited ta, authors a
    where t.title_id = ta.title_id
    and a.au_id = ta.au_id

/* retrieve all rows and columns from the view */
select *
    from titles_and_authors
    where type = "business"
```

```
title                                       au_lname     au_fname   type
-------------------------------------       ----------   ---------- -------
The Busy Executive's Database Guide         Green        Marjorie   business
The Busy Executive's Database Guide         Bennet       Abraham    business
Cooking with Computers: Surreptitious Balanc O'Leary     Michael    business
Cooking with Computers: Surreptitious Balanc MacFeather  Stearns    business
You Can Combat Computer Stress!             Green        Marjorie   business
Straight Talk About Computers               Straight     Dean       business
( 6 rows affected)
```

NOTE

This view contains the `ta_limited` view that was created earlier. A view is permitted to refer to other views.

Views can contain the following:

- Aggregate functions and groupings
- Joins
- Other views (up to 16 levels of nesting)
- A `distinct` clause

Views cannot include the following:

- `select into`
- A `compute` clause
- A `union`
- An `order by` clause

You can use an `order by` statement when selecting from the view, however.

The inability to use a `union` has design implications when it comes time to segment data tables horizontally.

Data Modifications and Views

SQL Server allows you to insert into, update, and delete from views, with some restrictions.

`insert` adds rows to one base table. `update` and `delete` affect rows in one base table:

```
/* delete rows from a view ...
** corresponding rows in the table are deleted */
delete author_name
    where last = "Smith" and first = "Joseph"

/* change the name of a publisher */
update cal_publishers
 set pub_name = "Joe's Books and Magazines"
 where pub_id = "1389"
```

When a view includes columns from more than one table, you may not do the following:

■ Delete rows from the view (this would affect multiple base tables).

■ Update columns from more than one table in a single update statement:

```
/* this is NOT permitted */
update titles_and_authors
  set type = "mod_cook", au_fname = "Mary"
  where title = "The Gourmet Microwave"

/* INSTEAD, update each table in turn */
update titles_and_authors
  set type = "mod_cook"
  where title = "The Gourmet Microwave"
update titles_and_authors
  set au_fname = "Mary"
  where title = "The Gourmet Microwave"
```

Inserts are not allowed into views unless all underlying columns in the base table not included in the view either are defined to allow NULL values or have a default defined on the columns.

Inserts are allowed on views containing joins as long as all columns being inserted into the view belong to a single base table.

Finally, you cannot update, delete or insert into a view containing the distinct clause.

Views with check option

In previous releases of SQL Server, it was possible for users to insert or update a row, creating a row they could not retrieve with select:

```
insert into cal_publishers
     (pub_id, pub_name, city, state)
values
     ("1234", "Joe's Books", "Canton", "OH")

/* update creates an "invisible" row */
update cal_publishers
  set state = "OH"
/* would make ALL rows "Invisible" */
```

The with check option flag prevents insertion or updating of rows that will subsequently not meet the view criteria. Notice that with check option appears as the last element of the query.

```
create view view_name [ ( colname, ... ) ]
     as select_statements
     [with check option]
```

In this example,

```
/* create view with only California publishers */
create view cal_publishers_ck as
     select *
     from publishers
     where state = "CA"
with check option
```

```
update cal_publishers_ck
  set state = "OH"
```

The update fails because, after the update, the modified rows would fail to appear in the view. Here is the actual error message:

```
Msg 550, Level 16, State 2
The attempted insert or update failed because the target view either
specifies WITH CHECK OPTION or spans a view which specifies WITH CHECK
OPTION and one or more rows resulting from the operation did not qualify
under the CHECK OPTION constraint.
Command has been aborted.
```

Views created with encryption

Microsoft SQL Server enables you to encrypt creation statements. By including the keywords with encryption in the create view statement, you can prevent any user from viewing the original SQL source of a view (the create view statement that was originally executed). Many *Independent Software Vendors* (ISVs) use this feature to hide views and other objects that their applications create. Typically, views and stored procedures (discussed in Chapter 7) are encrypted according to standard internal security practices for your organization.

Getting View Information

sp_help lists all objects in a database, including views and tables. To get a list of just the views defined in a database, run the following select statement:

```
select name from sysobjects
    where type = "V"

name
----------------------------
titleview
author_name
ta_limited
cal_publishers
titles_and_authors
cal_publishers_ck
( 6 rows affected)
```

To see a list of columns in a view, use sp_help:

```
sp_help view_name
Name                      Owner         Type                When_created
------------------------- ------------- ------------------- --------------------------
cal_publishers_ck         dbo           view                Nov 14 1995  6:12PM
( 0 rows affected)


Data_located_on_segment
-----------------------
not applicable
( 0 rows affected)
```

```
Column_name                     Type                        Length Prec  Scale Nullable
----------------------------    ------------------------    ------ -----  ----- --------
----------------------
pub_id                          char                        4                    no
pub_name                        varchar                     40                   yes
city                            varchar                     20                   yes
state                           char                        2                    yes
country                         varchar                     30                   yes
( 0 rows affected)
...
 ( 0 rows affected)
```

Renaming Objects

You cannot change the owner of an object or its database, but you can change its name. To rename an object (for example, a table or a view), use sp_rename. In the example, the table name is changed from names2 to new_names2.

> **NOTE**
>
> Even though the name of the table has changed, objects like views and procedures that refer to the table by name are not affected by the change in the name. That's because SQL-based objects like views and procedures are stored both as text in the syscomments table (so you can output the original text with SQL-EM) and as a pre-parsed *query tree* identifying related objects by id instead of name. When a table name changes, a dependent view still works because the object id of the table (stored in sysobjects) does not change.

```
sp_rename old_name, new_name

/* change the table names2 to new_names2 */
sp_rename names2, new_names2
```

After a table has been created, columns cannot be removed, datatypes cannot be changed, and null status cannot be changed. However, columns can be renamed by using sp_rename:

```
sp_rename 'table_name.old_col_name', new_col_name

/* change the au_lname column to "last_name" */
sp_rename 'authors.au_lname', 'last_name'
```

> **NOTE**
>
> Quotation marks are optional when passing character data to stored procedures unless the character string includes punctuation or spaces (for example, authors.au_lname). Note that old needs a table name, but the new cannot have one.

Adding Columns to a Table

You can add columns to an existing table using the `alter table` command. Here is a simplified version of the `alter table` syntax that shows you how to add a column to a table:

```
alter table table_name add
    col_name datatype { null ¦ identity } [, ...]
```

In this example, the `alter table` command adds two new columns to the `names2` table:

```
/* add middle name and fax columns to names table */
alter table names2 add
middle_name varchar(20) null,
fax varchar(15) null
```

New columns may either be `identity` columns or they must allow null values; otherwise, rows existing in the database would become invalid. The keyword `null` is required in the command.

A table can only have one `identity` column. When you add an `identity` column with `alter table`, SQL Server generates identity values for all existing rows.

Adding Columns Using SQL Enterprise Manager

You also can add columns to tables by using the Table Editor in SQL Enterprise Manager. Double-clicking on a table brings up the Manage Tables window. By using the last empty line of the table editor, you can add a new column, specify its datatype, default value, and null status. By clicking the floppy-disk icon in the toolbar, you can save these changes. As with using T-SQL, Enterprise Manager commits the changes without requesting confirmation. Remember, once you add a column, you can't remove it!

Enterprise Manager also automatically flags an added column for NULL status, which is required when adding columns to existing tables.

Temporary Tables

Temporary tables are real tables created in the `tempdb` database, usually for the purpose of holding an intermediate result set. Temporary tables are identified by a number sign (#) before the table name. They exist only for the duration of a user session or the stored procedure in which they are created. If the server crashes unexpectedly, these tables are lost, with no recovery possible. All SQL Server users have permission to create temporary tables.

One way to create a temporary table is to use the `create table` statement:

```
/* create temp table in tempdb for use in this session */
create table #temp (a int, b int)
```

More typically, temporary tables are created with `select into`:

```
/* create titles and authors table in tempdb
** for use in this session */
select au_lname, au_fname, title, pub_id
    into #titles_and_authors
    from authors a, titleauthor ta, titles t
    where a.au_id = ta.au_id
    and t.title_id = ta.title_id
```

Now, a two-table join may be made between `publishers` and `#titles_and_authors` to find out what publishers use which authors.

Global and Permanent Temporary Tables

Ordinary temporary tables last only as long as your session, and are available only to your session. To create a *global* temporary table, that is, one available to all users, use two pound signs (##).

```
select *
into ##titles
from titles
```

The `##titles` table will be available to all users, but will be dropped when the session that created the table logs out.

You can create a *permanent* temporary table in `tempdb` by fully qualifying the table name with the name of the database:

```
select *
into tempdb..titles
from pubs2..titles
```

Permanent temporary tables exist until explicitly dropped or until the SQL Server is restarted (that is, after a shutdown or a crash). They are useful for nonpermanent data that needs to be shared between multiple users.

Rules

Rules provide a mechanism for enforcing domain constraints for columns or user-defined datatypes. The rules are applied before an `insert` or `update`, prior to the execution of the command.

Creating Rules

A rule is created in much the same way as any other database object:

```
create rule rule_name as
    @variable operator expression
    [{and¦or} ...]
```

Here are some examples of rules:

```
/* orders must fall into a range */
create rule order_quantity as
    @quantity between 100 and 150000

/* specify a list of valid colors */
create rule color_rule as
    @color in ('black', 'brown', 'red')

/* provide a rule for pub_id */
create rule pub_id_rule as
    @pubid like ('99[0-9][0-9]')
    or @pubid in ('0736', '0877', '1389')

/* date must be >= to current date */
create rule date_rule as
    @date >= getdate()
```

The variable (@date in the last example) is a placeholder and has no bearing on the column name. It must be no more than 30 characters in length, including the @.

Rules can use any of the comparison operators available in a where clause, so long as the comparison operator works for the underlying datatype of the field to which the rule will be bound. In other words, a like clause works only with strings, so creating a rule that uses like as a comparison operator wouldn't be much use on a column that stores integers. For further information on this, see Chapter 3, "Introduction to Transact-SQL," on using the where clause, datatypes, and datatype conversions.

Rules are a Transact-SQL method for implementing *domain integrity*, which is the capability of maintaining a valid list of values for a column. Domain integrity can also be implemented using ANSI-standard SQL syntax, which is discussed in the "Check Constraints" section later in this chapter. ANSI SQL syntax enables data object definitions to be portable to other ANSI-supported platforms, but using Transact-SQL statements means the data-definition language can be used only with SQL Server.

If a rule is not bound to any columns or user-defined datatypes, you can drop it with drop rule:

```
drop rule rule_name

/* remove rule from database */
drop rule key_rule
```

Rule Usage

A *rule* is a separate and distinct database object. In order for a rule to take effect, you must bind the rule to a column in a table or tables by using sp_bindrule:

```
sp_bindrule rule_name, 'table.column_name'
```

TIP

Remember that the quotation marks are necessary because of the separator, the period (.) in the parameter being passed to the sp_bindrule stored procedure.

This example binds the rule, key_rule, to the column user_id in demographics:

```
/* bind key_rule to user_id column in demographics table */
sp_bindrule key_rule, 'demographics.user_id'
```

You can instruct the server to stop applying a rule (*unbind* a rule) by using sp_unbindrule:

```
sp_unbindrule 'table.column_name'

/* unbind rule from user_id in demographics table */
sp_unbindrule 'demographics.user_id'
```

Rule Limitations

A rule can deal only with constants, SQL Server functions, and edit masks. It cannot perform a table lookup (use a trigger if this is necessary), nor can it compare a column against other columns in the table.

Only one rule may be bound per column. If you bind a rule to a column and there is an existing rule bound to the column, it is replaced by the new rule.

A rule will not be retroactively applied to existing data in a table, but it will be applied when an existing row is updated.

A rule may not be dropped if it is bound to a column or user-defined datatype; you must first unbind it from all columns and datatypes.

WARNING

Rules are not applied when you bulk copy data into the system.

TIP

Make sure the values in the rule are compatible with the datatype of the column to which it is bound.

Creating Rules Using SQL Enterprise Manager

SQL Enterprise Manager can do many things, but it can't create syntax for you. As a result, you should study the previous section carefully, because portions of the syntax described are necessary for creating rules using SQL Enterprise Manager. You'll see examples of this as we take a look at an alternate method for creating and managing rules.

SQL Enterprise Manager provides a Rules folder that holds a list of all rules contained in a particular database. By right-clicking on this folder, you can open the Manage Rules dialog box (see Figure 5.10). In this dialog box, you can define the rule name as well as the rule's description, which is how you define the restrictions the rule will implement.

FIGURE 5.10.

SQL Enterprise Manager provides a graphical interface for managing rules, but you still need to know some SQL syntax.

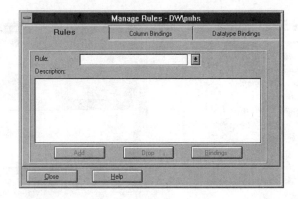

How do you define a description? You do it the same way that you define a rule, with a slight modification. The syntax that is included after the as clause of a rule is the same syntax you should use for the description. Therefore, if you write a rule creation statement as the following,

```
create rule title_id_rule as
@title_id like '[A-Z][A-Z][0-9][0-9][0-9][0-9]'
```

the description field should contain the

```
@title_id like '[A-Z][A-Z][0-9][0-9][0-9][0-9]'
```

text in it. Remember that the @title_id variable name is irrelevant. It could be @Fred or @Barney and have no effect on the application. (See Figure 5.11.)

After you create the rule, SQL Enterprise Manager enables you to define the bindings for the rule immediately by selecting the Column Bindings or the Datatype Bindings window tabs. (See Figure 5.12.)

FIGURE 5.11.
The syntax for creating rules in SQL Enterprise Manager is identical to that used by Transact-SQL.

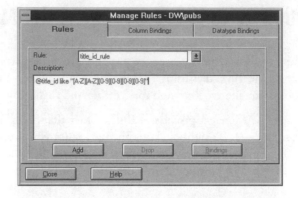

FIGURE 5.12.
SQL Enterprise Manager enables you to define rule and default bindings immediately during rule creation using both column-wise binding and datatype-wise binding.

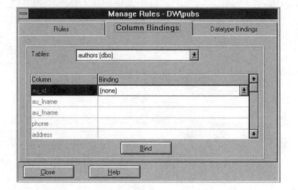

Remember that SQL Enterprise Manager relies on underlying T-SQL syntax to do its work. As such, when you work with establishing and removing bindings of rules and defaults, SQL Enterprise Manager, in the background, is running `sp_bindrule` and `sp_unbindrule` for you!

Defaults

Defaults provide a value for a column when one is not supplied at insert time. Like rules, they exist only as database objects and after creation, they must be subsequently bound to columns.

To create a default, use the `create default` statement:

```
create default default_name
    as constant_expression
```

Examples

```
/* default country value is "USA" */
create default country_default as
   'USA'
```

```
/* default age is 16 */
create default age_default as
   16

/* default time is the current system time */
create default time_default as
   getdate()
```

NOTE

There are *no quotation marks* around the 16. It is dangerously easy to make a mistake about the datatype of a default value. The server will not catch datatype mismatches until the first time the value is used in an `insert` statement.

To drop a default, use the `drop default` statement.

```
drop default default_name

/* remove default definition from database */
drop default age_default
```

Default Usage

You bind a default to columns in a table or tables by using `sp_bindefault`:

```
sp_bindefault default_name, 'table.column_name'

/* apply the default to country in demographics */
sp_bindefault country_default, 'demographics.country'
```

To unbind a default, use `sp_unbindefault`:

```
sp_unbindefault 'table.column_name'

/* remove default from country in demographics */
sp_unbindefault 'demographics.country'
```

NOTE

How many *d*s in `sp_unbindefault`? Only one. The standard naming system always removes duplicated letters when they occur between words in the names of system procedures. So, `bind` + `default` becomes `sp_bindefault` and `help` + `protect` becomes `sp_helprotect`. `add` + `dump` + `device` becomes `sp_addumpdevice`, however! (Only one d is removed.)

Declarative Defaults

SQL Server also permits the declaration of a default value for a column during table creation. Note that the `default` expression falls between the datatype and the nullability:

```
create table table_name
(col_name datatype
    [default expression]
    [{null ¦ not null ¦ identity}]
[, ... ]
)
```

Here the definition of the price column includes a default value of `$12.95`:

```
create table items
(item_id char(6)_not null,
price money default $12.95 not null)
```

Use the `alter table` statement to add or drop a default clause from a table:

```
/* To remove the default defined on price */
alter table items
    replace price default null
/* To define a default on ssn */
alter table items
    replace item_code default "N/A"
```

Defaults in SQL Enterprise Manager

SQL Enterprise Manager enables you to define two types of defaults for tables. If you use the Manage Tables dialog box illustrated earlier in this chapter, you can assign a default value either by using that dialog box at the time the table is created or by merely adding it in the interface. Using this method is equivalent to using the ANSI DEFAULT clause in a table creation statement, or using an ALTER TABLE command to add a DEFAULT constraint if the table already exists.

If you are going to create Transact-SQL based constraints, you must use the Defaults folder of the database with which you are working. By right-clicking on the Defaults folder, you can create a new default using the Manage Defaults dialog box.

If it looks strangely familiar, you're catching on. The interface is visually identical to the Manage Rules dialog box. However, instead of typing in the contents of a WHERE clause, as you did with rules, here you need only enter the default value itself. Remember that default values for CHAR and VARCHAR columns require paired quotes to mark the values as strings.

As with binding rules, the Column Bindings and Datatype Bindings window tabs for this dialog box enable you to define to which columns and/or datatypes this particular default will be bound.

Remember, if you are planning to use your data-definition language to create databases on a different ANSI SQL-compliant database, using Transact-SQL based defaults in this fashion will not work. You can only use ANSI-defined DEFAULT clauses as described previously. If you want your DDL to be portable, use the Manage Tables dialog box and create your defaults there.

Default Limitations

A column can have a default defined by a default clause or a default bound to the column, but not both.

A default can set only one constant or SQL Server function value; it cannot make a decision or perform a table lookup (use a trigger if this is necessary).

Only one default may be bound per column. If you attempt to bind a second default to a column, you get an error message from SQL Server—Error 15103 (Severity 16). You cannot bind a default to a column that was created with or altered to have a default value.)

Make sure the datatype of the value in the default is compatible with the datatype of the column to which it is bound. Like rules, a default is not retroactively applied to existing data in a table.

Make sure that defaults are consistent with any rule on the column; otherwise, rows with defaults will not be inserted (though this may be a way of forcing a nullable column to be made not null).

The default is applied before the rule is checked; this enables the rule to be applied to the default rather than to the null value.

Defaults are applied during bulk copy.

A default may not be dropped if it is bound to a column or user-defined datatype; you must first unbind the default from all columns or datatypes before dropping it.

When a Default Is Applied

Defaults are applied only when no value is specified for a column during insert. Consider this example:

```
/* define table with two columns */
create table table1
(id int not null,
price smallmoney null)

/* define a default price of $15 */
create default price_default as $15

/* bind the default */
sp_bindefault price_default, "table1.price"
```

In order to use the default value, the column must be assigned no value in the insert state-ment. An insert that does not specify columns must provide all values:

```
/* value is provided for price, default not applied */
insert table1
values (1, $30)
```

The following insert format uses the default:

```
/* default is applied */
insert table1 (id)
values (5)
```

Inserting an explicit null overrides the default:

```
/* Explicit null value provided for price, default not applied */
insert table1 (id, price)
values (1, null)
```

Examining Rules and Defaults

To list rules and defaults, along with all other objects in a database, use sp_help.

To list all rules or defaults in a database, use the following:

```
select name from sysobjects
    where type in ( "R", "D" )
```

To examine the rules and defaults bound to columns in a table, use this:

```
sp_help table_name
```

In the output of sp_help, the names of defaults and rules are displayed in the Default_name and Rule_name columns:

```
sp_help authors


Name                      Owner                   Type
------------------        -------------------     ----------------
authors                   dbo                            user table
Data_located_on_segment          When_created
------------------------          ------------------------
default                           Sep 27 1993  3:14PM

Column_name  Type      Length Nulls Default_name Rule_name
-----------  --------  ------ ----- ------------ ---------
  au_id      id           11    0 NULL            NULL
  au_lname   varchar      40    0 NULL            NULL
  au_fname   varchar      20    0 NULL            NULL
  phone      char         12    0 phonedflt       NULL
  address    varchar      40    1 NULL            NULL
  city       varchar      20    1 NULL            NULL
  state      char          2    1 NULL            NULL
  country    varchar      12    1 NULL            NULL
  postalcode char         10    1 NULL            NULL
```

You can get a wealth of information from the system tables if you know how. For example, to list all columns in a database bound to a rule, use this SQL:

```
/* list tables and columns for a rule */
select "table" = o.name, "column" = c.name,
    "user" = user_name(uid), "rule" = object_name(domain)
from syscolumns c, sysobjects o
    where o.id = c.id
    and object_name(domain) = "insert rule_name"
order by 1, 2
```

To list all columns in a database bound to a *default*, use the following:

```
/* list tables and columns for a default */
select "table" = o.name, "column" = c.name,
  "user" = user_name(uid), "default" = object_name(cdefault)
from syscolumns c, sysobjects o
where o.id = c.id
  and object_name(cdefault) = "insert default_name"
order by 1, 2
```

The text used to create a rule or default can be examined by using the `sp_helptext` stored procedure.

```
sp_helptext object_name
```

User-Defined Datatypes

A user-defined datatype is not really a new datatype; it is a way of describing an existing datatype. It provides a mechanism for enforcing data type consistency across and within a database or server. It also can simplify management of frequently used rules and defaults.

> **NOTE**
>
> A datatype is not a database object and therefore is not listed in `sysobjects`; it is listed in `systypes`, but follows object naming conventions.

Creating User-Defined Datatypes

Define and remove user-defined datatypes with `sp_addtype` and `sp_droptype`.

```
sp_addtype type_name,
    system_type,
    {null ¦ "not null" ¦ identity}


sp_droptype type_name
```

> **NOTE**
>
> System types that include *separators* (for example, parentheses in char or commas in numeric) must be enclosed in quotes.

Examples

```
/* add a social security number datatype */
sp_addtype ssn_type, 'char(9)', "not null"

/* add a price datatype */
sp_addtype price_type, money, null

/* drop the datatype */
sp_droptype price_type
```

User-Defined Datatype Notes

You may not drop a user-defined datatype if it is used in the definition of an existing column; you first have to drop all tables using the defined datatype.

You bind rules and defaults directly to the datatypes by using sp_bindrule and sp_bindefault:

```
/* bind price_rule to price datatype */
sp_bindrule price_rule, price_type

/* bind price_default to price datatype */
sp_bindefault price_default, price_type
```

Any column created with the price_type datatype automatically inherits the rule and default through the datatype, unless a rule or default has been explicitly bound to the column itself.

Defining and Using User-Defined Datatypes

The following is a typical sequence of events when using datatypes.

Create a user-defined datatype:

```
sp_addtype ssn_type, 'char(9)', 'not null'
```

Create a rule and default:

```
create rule ssn_rule as
   @ssn between '000001111' and '999999999'
   or @ssn = 'N / A'
create default ssn_default as
   'N / A'
```

Bind the rule and default to the datatype:

```
exec sp_bindrule ssn_rule, ssn_type
exec sp_bindefault ssn_default, ssn_type
```

Create the tables using the datatype:

```
create table test_table
(ssn ssn_type, name varchar(30) )
```

Typically, user-defined datatypes are defined in the model database and propagated to the user databases as the new databases are created.

Defining User-Defined Data Types in SQL Enterprise Manager

SQL Enterprise Manager can manage user-defined datatypes as well as rules and defaults. The User Defined Datatypes folder contains a list of all UDDTs defined for the database. From here, you can create, modify, and destroy any user-defined datatypes in a database. The interface is easy to work with. Because a UDDT requires a unique name and base datatype, those fields are mandatory in the dialog box shown in Figure 5.13. The Rule and Default fields are optional, but enable you to define the rule and default you want to use with this datatype.

FIGURE 5.13.

SQL Enterprise Manager makes managing user-defined datatypes easier by encapsulating the creation and binding of datatypes into a single interface dialog box.

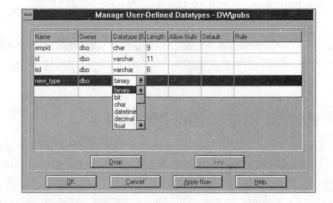

After you fill in the form, SQL-EM executes the proper CREATE statements and BIND procedures to create the UDDT you specified.

Binding Precedence with Rules and Defaults

Rules and defaults are maintained in a "stack of depth one":

```
/* bind a rule to a column */
sp_bindrule "rule_r", "table_t.col_c"
/* bind another rule to the column */
/* the first rule is replaced */
sp_bindrule "rule_s", "table_t.col_c"
/* unbind the rule - no rule is bound now*/
sp_unbindrule "table_t.col_c"
```

A rule or default bound explicitly to a column overrides a rule or default bound to a datatype. A subsequent bind to the datatype replaces the bind to the column as long as the column and datatype have the same rule or default prior to modification. If you unbind a rule or default from a column, future binds to the datatype apply to the column.

Indexes

The primary purpose of an index is to provide faster access to data pages than scanning every page. Secondarily, it is sometimes used as a mechanism for enforcing uniqueness.

Index Types

SQL Server provides two types of indexes, *clustered* and *nonclustered*. Both are B-tree indexes. For clustered indexes, data is maintained in clustered index order; as a result, only one clustered index per table may exist (because data can be physically sorted only one way!). Alternatively, you can have 249 nonclustered indexes per table, because nonclustered indexes maintain pointers to rows (not data pages).

An index can contain from 1 to 16 columns, but the total index entry width must be no greater than 255 bytes. Indexes are maintained and used internally by the server to improve performance or to enforce uniqueness. Under normal circumstances, the application programmer does not usually refer to indexes.

Clustered Index Mechanism

With a clustered index, there is one entry on the last intermediate index level page for each data page. This means that the data page is the *leaf*, or bottom, level of the index. (See Figure 5.14.)

In Figure 5.14, which diagrams a clustered index on last name, to find `"Fred Amundsen"` you look first in the root page. Because `"Amundsen"` is between `"Albert"` and `"Jones"`, you follow the `"Albert"` pointer to the appropriate Intermediate page. There, `"Amundsen"` is between `"Albert"` and `"Brown"`, so you again follow the `"Albert"` pointer to the data page. Note that the data page must be scanned (which is very quick) to find the actual data row.

FIGURE 5.14.

A clustered index stores pointers matching the physical sort of the data. At the lowest index level, rows in the index point to pages in the table itself.

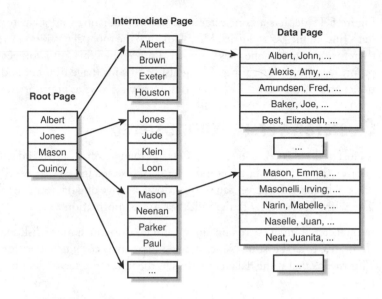

FIGURE 5.15.

The nonclustered index introduces an extra leaf level with one row of index for every row in the table.

Nonclustered Index Mechanism

The nonclustered index has an extra leaf index level for page/row pointers. (See Figure 5.15.)

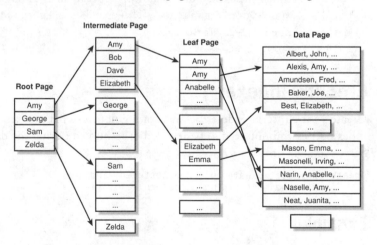

Figure 5.15 depicts a nonclustered index on first name (but a clustered index on last name). Let's find all the "Amy" entries. First, look into the root page. Amy is between "Amy" and "George"; therefore you follow the "Amy" pointer. Proceed like this until you get to the leaf page. At this point, read from the leaf page(s) the list of row ids (page number and row number combinations) and read each of the Amy entries, retrieving rows as appropriate.

Clustered versus Nonclustered

A clustered index *tends to be* one I/O faster than a nonclustered index for a single-row lookup, because there tend to be fewer index levels. Clustered indexes are excellent for retrieving ranges of data, because the server can narrow down a range of data, retrieve the first row, and scan the data without returning to the index for more information.

Nonclustered indexes are a bit slower and take up much more disk space, but are the next best alternative to a table scan. Nonclustered indexes may cover the query for maximal retrieval speed. This means that if the data required is in the index, the server does not need to return the data row.

> **WARNING**
>
> When creating a clustered index, you need *free space* in your database approximately equal to 120 percent of the table size. This enables space for the table to coexist in the database while it is being sorted.

Creating Indexes

Create your clustered indexes before creating nonclustered indexes, so that the nonclustered index entries will not need to be resorted or reshuffled during the data sort. (In reality, SQL Server actually drops and re-creates these indexes.)

```
create [unique] [clustered | nonclustered] index
    index_name on table_name (column [, ...])
```

Examples

```
create unique clustered index name_index
    on authors (au_lname, au_fname)

create index fname_index
    on authors (au_fname, au_lname)
```

By default (unless otherwise specified), an index is nonunique and nonclustered.

Notes on Indexes

Only one index can be defined on an ordered set of columns in a table (this is a new feature).

When an index is defined as unique, no two rows may have the same index value (null counts as one value!). The uniqueness check is performed at index creation, on insert, and on update.

Often, a clustered index is used for the primary key; this is not always the best performance selection. It is a good idea to have a clustered index on all tables; otherwise, space will not be reused from deleted rows. If there is no clustered index on the table, all new rows (and updated rows!) are placed at the end of the table.

As the number of indexes increases (past five or so) the overhead at update to maintain the indexes gets excessive; in an *executive information system* (EIS) where there is virtually no real-time update, the only constraint on the number indexes is disk space.

An OLTP system usually is configured with as few indexes as possible to speed update, insert, and delete activity.

Watch out for datatype mismatches in where clauses, especially char and varchar. They cannot be optimized effectively because the optimizer may be unable to use the data distribution statistics for the index. This is easy to do in unintentionally in stored procedures. Using user-defined datatypes can help avoid this problem.

Managing Indexes Using SQL Enterprise Manager

In addition to the syntax provided by Transact-SQL for managing indexes, SQL Enterprise Manager adds many important index management features into its interface. By selecting the Manage, Indexes menu sequence in SQL-EM, you are presented with the rather complex dialog box displayed in Figure 5.16.

In this dialog box, you can manage all aspects of table indexing, on a table-and-index basis. The left box displays the table structure, including datatypes and null status. The right combo box displays which index you are currently viewing. Selecting the combo box enables you to pick the index on the particular table you wish to view. The index attributes, such as whether the index is unique or clustered, are automatically displayed, and any options that were not used are available for selection should the index be rebuilt.

In addition, at the bottom of the screen, SQL Enterprise Manager calculates valuable index statistic information. By including the keys/page and levels information, you can plan how large an index will be, as well as how efficient that index will be for query resolution. Index usage is discussed further in Chapter 12, "Understanding the Query Optimizer," but the general principle is that an inverse relationship exists between the number of levels in an index and its efficiency for solving queries. Minimizing index levels (by minimizing key size) is a smart optimization technique.

FIGURE 5.16.

SQL Enterprise Manager extends the T-SQL index management syntax by providing useful index statistics and maintenance options.

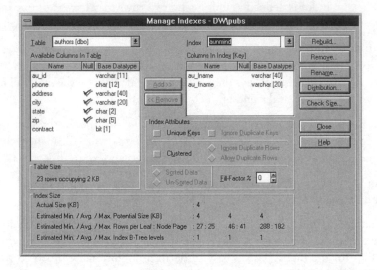

New indexes can be created by selecting the new index entry from the Index combobox. All the options are set to their defaults. You can pick the fields of the index, the index attributes, and so forth, and SQL Server will generate the proper creation statement and estimate the index size for you. You can add columns to the index by highlighting the column in the Available Columns in Table listbox and selecting the Add button. (See Figure 5.17.)

FIGURE 5.17.

Creating new indexes by using Enterprise Manager can be more efficient than using SQL syntax, because an administrator can view the size and relative efficiency of that index before it is created.

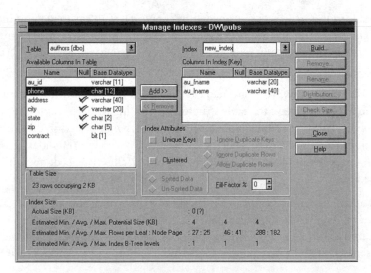

Adding new columns to, and removing existing columns from, a new index forces Enterprise Manager to recalculate the index size, keys/page ratio, and the number of levels. The initial values are approximated based on current data distribution information or statistics. For the most accurate information, you can update the statistics for an index or table.

The lower portion of this dialog box presents very useful, if advanced, information about indexes. The Index Size panel of the dialog box holds the computed sizes of both leaf and node pages of the index, as well as various other statistics. What are these statistics?

In a B-tree index, there are three classes of pages: a single *root* page, which is the entry point to the tree; typically multiple *node* pages, which are intermediate pages in the tree; and *leaf* pages, which are the lowest level of the index. Because root and node pages store different information than leaf pages do, they can, typically, store more information per page.

In the interface, the Actual Size value represents the total size, in kilobytes, of all index pages. To calculate the total number of pages in the index, divide this number by 2048 (2KB per page). The Estimated Min/Avg/Max Potential Size is the largest size this index could be given the current data distribution (more on that in a minute) and key size. The Estimated Min/Avg/Max Rows per Leaf:Node Page gives you information on the number of index keys a given leaf page can store, as well as the number of rows a given node page can store. Notice that for the aunmind index, the leaf page can store between 27 and 288 rows per leaf page, but the node page can store between 25 and 182 rows per node page. These values are calculated by using an algorithm discussed in Chapter 12, so refer to that chapter for more detail.

The Estimated Min/Avg/Max Index B-Tree Levels value shows you how high your tree is. This value is actually more critical in most cases than actual index size because it acts as a multiplier for page reads. A query that needs to navigate only from the root to the leaf has one level, that is, no node pages. In that way, the height value reported here represents the number of jumps a query must make from the root page to the leaf pages.

NOTE

Minimizing the number of index levels is an important part of optimizing queries. Although there are many methods to accomplish this (they are discussed in Chapters 12 through 15), the easiest method to implement is minimizing the index key size. The smaller your index keys, the more key values can fit on a given page, reducing both the total number of pages and the total number of index levels.

SQL Server depends on statistics it collects about table data to decide on index selection. The process of using these statistics is discussed in more detail in Chapter 12, but understanding what these statistics are and how important it is to maintain them is an appropriate discussion for this chapter.

SQL Enterprise Manager provides an easy way to browse and maintain table data statistics that are stored on the *distribution page*. The distribution page stores the distribution of data in the table as a histogram, that is, how many of value X does the table have, how many of value Y, and so forth. The statistics page is created at the time an index is created. However, the statistics page is never automatically updated unless the index is dropped and re-created. As a result, the statistics page may hold information that represents an inaccurate distribution of table data. By selecting the Distribution button in the Manage Indexes dialog box, you can view the current data distribution and update that information in the Index Distribution Statistics dialog box illustrated in Figure 5.18.

FIGURE 5.18.

SQL Enterprise Manager gives administrators a tool for examining and updating table data-distribution statistics, a first for any version of SQL Server.

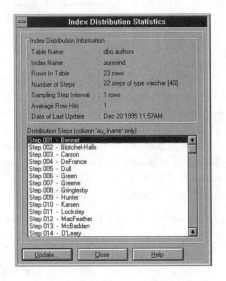

By clicking on the Update... button, you can update the statistics for this particular index or for all indexes on the table you have selected.

WARNING

Updating distribution page statistics can be a very time- and disk-intensive process. In order to build the statistics page, SQL Server must scan each row of the table and take a sample of the table data to construct the appropriate values. This causes a heavy drain on I/O and CPU resources and should be performed only during off-hours or normal maintenance cycles.

Constraints

Constraints provide an alternative method for defining data integrity requirements (to rules and defaults). SQL Server enforces three general types of constraints:

- Primary and unique key constraints
- Check constraints
- Referential integrity constraints

Primary-Key and Unique Constraints

SQL Server permits the declaration of a primary key or a unique constraint at table definition time. Unique constraints require that all non-null values be unique and allow a single null value for the column in the table. At definition, SQL Server automatically creates a unique index, nonclustered by default.

Primary key constraints require that all values in a table be unique, and the column(s) cannot allow null values. They also automatically create a unique index, though clustered by default.

All standard index creation options are available as part of the syntax for primary key and unique constraints. Here is the syntax for creating the constraints:

```
create table table_name
 ( col datatype [ {identity ¦ null ¦ not null} ]
     [ constraint constraint_name ]
         {unique ¦ primary key}
              [ {clustered ¦ nonclustered} ]
  [ , ... ]
 [ [, constraint constraint_name ]
     {unique ¦ primary key}
         [{clustered ¦ nonclustered}]
              (col [, ...] )
 [, ... ] ] )
```

Primary-key and unique constraints can be defined at the column level or the table level. A table level constraint can apply to a single column or multiple columns in the table. If you are defining a primary key or unique constraint on multiple columns (a composite key), the constraint must be defined at the table level:

```
/* create names table: primary key on ssn (table level) */
create table names
 (ssn varchar(9) not null,
 name varchar(20) not null,
 constraint names_pk primary key (ssn) )

/* create names2 table: primary key on ssn (column level),
   nonclustered, unique key on name, ssn, clustered (table level) */
create table names
 (ssn varchar(9) not null
     constraint ssn_pk primary key nonclustered,
 name varchar(20) not null,
 constraint name_key unique clustered (name, ssn))
```

Check Constraints

Check constraints specify a domain for columns (similar to rules) and may be slightly faster. They are defined for a table by using the `create table` or `alter table` command. Check constraints can be defined at the column level or the table level. Table-level constraints can perform multicolumn checks.

Multiple constraints can be associated with a single column. Check constraints cannot compare against values in other tables (use triggers), although they can look in the current row, and cannot contain aggregates.

```
create table table_name
 ( col datatype
     [ default constant_expression ]
     [ {identity ¦ null ¦ not null} ]
     [ [ constraint constraint_name ]
         check (search_condition) ]
   [ , ... ]
   [ [, constraint constraint_name ]
     [ [ constraint constraint_name ]
         check (search_condition) ]
     [ , ... ]
 )
```

Here are some examples of check constraints. The first example checks an `item_code` to make certain that inserted values consist of four characters, all numeric:

```
/* two column table with column level check
** constraint on key and default on price */
create table prices
 (item_code char(4) not null
    constraint item_code_constraint
    check (item_code like "[0-9][0-9][0-9][0-9]"),
  price smallmoney default $15 not null
 )
```

The inventory table created here consists of three columns. Note that the high and low columns each have a constraint requiring that the value be above zero, then a table-level constraint requires that the high and low volumes have a specific relationship to each other (high must be greater than low and they must be no more than 1000 apart).

```
/* inventory table with column level check
** constraints and table level constraint comparing
** two columns */
create table inventory
 (item_code char(4) not null
    constraint item_code_constraint
    check (item_code like "[0-9][0-9][0-9][0-9]"),
  high_volume int not null
    check (high_volume > 0),
  low_volume int not null
    check (low_volume > 0),
  constraint check hi_lo_check
    (high_volume >= low_volume
      and high_volume - low_volume < 1000)
 )
```

Referential Integrity Constraints

Referential integrity in a database is the property of all foreign keys having an associated primary key in the related tables. For example, if there is a `pub_id` in the `titles` table, there should be a corresponding publisher in the `publishers` table. You can also add constraints to enforce referential integrity at table creation time or later with an `alter table` statement. Referential integrity constraints prevent data modifications which would leave foreign keys pointing at non-existent primary keys. (For example, no title is permitted to have a `pub_id` that does not match an existing `pub_id` in the `publishers` table. See Figure 5.19.)

FIGURE 5.19.

Referential integrity defines the relationship between two tables. The referencing table contains a foreign key, pub_id, that references a primary key in the referenced table.

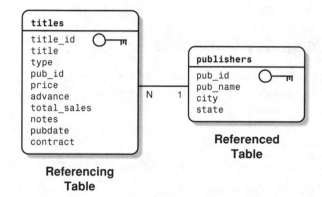

Constraints can enforce both primary and foreign key integrity checks without programming; this is called *declarative referential integrity*. Constraints can support both column level (single-part) keys and table level (multi-part) keys.

Single-part keys can also be defined as table-level constraints.

Declarative constraints roll back an update or insert when the RI constraint is violated. More advanced RI options currently require using triggers or SQL transactions.

Primary-Key Constraints

Primary key constraints require that all values in a table be unique, and require a value in each column identified in the primary key (no nulls) for every row. They automatically create a unique clustered index, and all standard index creation options are available.

```
create table table_name
 ( col datatype [ {identity ¦ null ¦ not null} ]
     [ constraint constraint_name ]
         primary key [ {clustered ¦ nonclustered} ]
   [ , ... ]
 [ [, constraint constraint_name ]
               primary key [{clustered ¦ nonclustered}]
            (col [, ...] )
 [, ... ] ] )
```

In each of these examples, ssn is defined as the primary key for the names table. A unique, clustered index will be created on that column automatically.

```
/* primary key on ssn (table level) */
create table names
 (ssn varchar(9) not null,
  name varchar(20) not null,
  constraint names_pk primary key (ssn) )

/* primary key on ssn (column level, nonclustered)*/
create table names
 (ssn varchar(9) not null
     constraint ssn_pk primary key nonclustered,
  name varchar(20) not null)
```

Foreign-Key Constraints

Foreign keys are declared by using the reference constraint in the create table or alter table statement. Reference constraints can be defined at the column level (single-part key) or at the table level (single- or multi-part keys).

```
create table table_name
 (column_name datatype
     [ [ constraint constraint_name ]
       references ref_table [(ref_col)] ]
 [, ... ]
 [, [ constraint constraint_name ]
     foreign key (column_name[, ...])
       references ref_table [(ref_col[, ...])] ]
 )
```

Here a salesdetail table is created that references two tables, titles and sales. Note that the titles reference is a column-level constraint on the title_id column, but the sales reference is a table-level constraint because the foreign key consists of two columns, stor_id and ord_num.

```
create table salesdetail
 (stor_id char(6),
  ord_num char(10),
  title_id tid
     constraint tid_fk_constraint
     references titles (title_id),
  qty int,
  discount real,
  constraint sales_fk_constraint
     foreign key (stor_id, ord_num)
     references sales (stor_id, ord_num)
 )
```

Constraint Notes

Reference constraints currently are restrictive only. Tables named in a references statement cannot have rows deleted if there are existing rows in the referencing table matching the primary key. Primary key columns cannot be updated if they are referenced by a reference constraint and there are matching foreign key entries in the referencing table.

Inserts or updates of foreign key values into a referencing table is not allowed if the value of the new foreign key entry does not exist in the primary key column of the referenced table. No reference checks are performed when primary keys are inserted.

Tables referenced in reference constraints must have a primary key constraint defined on the referenced columns or a unique index via a unique constraint or `create index` statement. If you do not provide the referenced column names in a reference constraint, there must be a primary key constraint on the appropriate columns in the referenced table.

The datatypes of the referencing table columns must exactly match the datatypes of the referenced table columns.

Constraint names must be unique within the current database. If the constraint name is not supplied, SQL Server generates a unique system-generated name.

To reference a table you do not own, you must have references permission on the table. (This is new!)

A table can include a reference constraint on itself. A referenced table cannot be dropped until the referencing table or reference constraint is dropped. Tables referenced in constraints must exist.

If tables are to cross-reference one another, use `alter table` to add a reference after the tables have been created or use the `create schema` command.

Modifying Constraints

You can add and drop primary and foreign key constraints by using `alter table`.

```
alter table table_name add        [constraint constraint_name ]
    { primary_key [ clustered ¦ nonclustered ]
        ( col_name [, ...] ) }
    ¦ foreign key (col [, ...])
        references ref_table [(ref_col [, ...])] }

alter table table_name
    drop constraint constraint_name
```

This example adds a primary key constraint to the `publishers` table and automatically creates a unique, clustered index on `pub_id`. Even though the primary key is a single column, this is considered a table-level constraint because it was added at the table level using an `alter table` statement.

```
alter table publishers
    add constraint pub_pk_constraint
        primary key (pub_id)
```

This `alter table` statement adds a foreign key constraint to the `titles` table, referencing the primary key established in the prior example. No rows can be added to `titles` if a corresponding `pub_id` cannot be found in the `publishers` table.

```
alter table titles
    add constraint pub_fk_constraint
        foreign key (pub_id)
        references publishers (pub_id)
```

The foreign key constraint on the `titles` table has been dropped and the restrictions on the table are lifted.

```
alter table titles
    drop constraint pub_fk_constraint
```

Adding Constraints

To add a constraint to an existing table, use the `alter table` statement. All new constraints are defined as table-level constraints; column-level constraints can be created only at table or column creation time.

```
alter table table_name add
    [constraint constraint_name ]
    { {unique ¦ primary_key }
        [ clustered ¦ nonclustered ]
        ( col_name [, ...] )
      ¦ check (search_condition) }
```

Here a check constraint is added to the `prices` table, requiring the `price` to be greater than zero.

```
/* add a table level check constraint: prices > 0
** note that constraint is table-level,
** but only checks a single column */
alter table prices add
    constraint price_chk
    check (price > $0)
```

As with any object, to modify a constraint, you must drop and re-create it.

Removing Constraints

To remove a constraint from a table, use the `alter table` command.

```
alter table table_name drop
    constraint constraint_name

/* remove the item_code constraint */
alter table prices
    drop constraint price_chk
```

Information on Constraints

For information on the constraints on a table, use `sp_helpconstraint`.

Example

```
sp_helpconstraint publishers
Object Name
-----------------------------------------------------------
----------------------------
publishers
( 0 rows affected)


constraint_type            constraint_name                constraint_keys
-----------------------    -----------------------------  ----------------
PRIMARY KEY (clustered)    UPKCL_pubind                   pub_id
CHECK on column pub_id      CK__publisher__pub_i__089551D8 (pub_id = '1756'
                           or (pub_id = '1622' or (pub_id = '0877'
                           or (pub_id = '0736' or (pub_id = '1389'))))
                           or (pub_id like '99[0-9][0-9]'))
DEFAULT on column country   DF__publisher__count__09897611 ('USA')

Table is referenced by
----------------------
pubs.dbo.titles: FK__titles__pub_id__0E4E2B2E
pubs.dbo.employee: FK__employee__pub_id__2FAF1EF9
pubs.dbo.pub_info: FK__pub_info__pub_id__3567F84F
```

Managing Constraints Using SQL Enterprise Manager

SQL Enterprise Manager, through the Manage Tables dialog box, enables you to define, manage, and remove constraint definitions graphically and to view constraint information. By selecting the Advanced Features button in the Manage Tables dialog box, you can extend the dialog box to show four different constraint types: primary keys, foreign keys, checks, and unique constraints. (See Figure 5.20.)

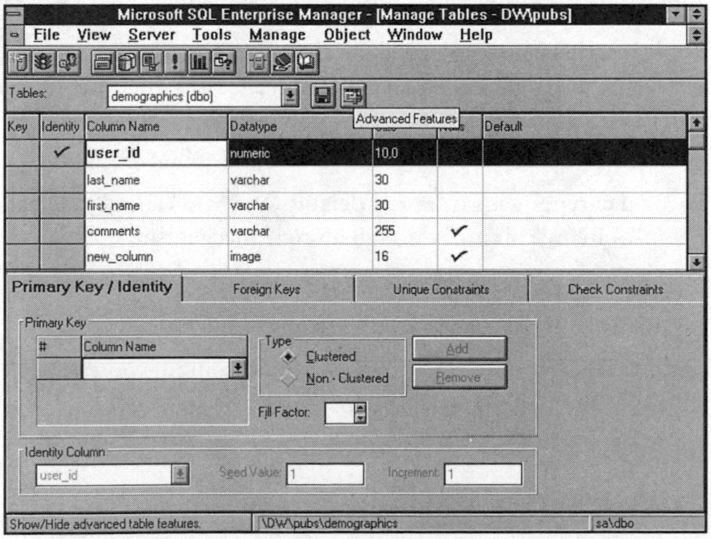

FIGURE 5.20.

SQL Enterprise Manager makes constraint management easier by graphically presenting the domain and reference constraints for a given table in the Manage Tables dialog box.

When you are defining primary-key constraints, remember that the primary key requires a unique index in order to work. Therefore, the primary key represents the unique row identifier for each row in a table. If you are defining primary keys that are to be referenced by other tables, make sure that you are defining foreign keys on those other tables.

When you define foreign-key constraints, remember that you are working from the current table, and that it holds *foreign key records that relate to a different primary-key table.* For example, the `titles` table in the `pubs` database serves as a primary-key table for a relationship with the `titleauthor` table. However, the `titles` table is also a foreign-key table in relation to the `publishers` table. As a result, to establish the proper key relationships, you have to create a primary key on the `publishers` table, then create a foreign key on the `titles` table. You also have to create a primary key on the `titles` table and then a foreign key on the `titleauthor` table that referenced `titles`. Understanding proper key creation order can prevent many headaches when dealing with large numbers of table relationships!

When defining unique and check constraints, you need worry only about the current table with which you are working. Because these two constraint types enforce domain integrity (the valid values possible for a column or set of columns), you don't need to worry about their creation order.

All the information about constraints, including their creation, modification, and configuration can be seen through this dialog box. Pieces of the information presented in the dialog box are retrieved by using the very same stored procedures described previously, so understanding both can give you a useful toolkit—preventing your dependence on an otherwise very graceful utility!

Guidelines on Constraints

Rules and check constraints both enforce domains.

Tables can have both rules and check constraints. The set of allowable values will be the intersection of the rules and check constraints. Constraints enable you to define data integrity requirements as part of a table creation statement. Table-level check constraints can access other columns in the table.

Using datatypes with rules and defaults, you can centrally manage the data integrity requirements of many columns through a single mechanism.

Constraint names must follow SQL Server object naming conventions, if named. If you do not name your constraint, it will be named for you:

- `tablename_colname_uniquenumber` for column constraint
- `tablename_uniquenumber` for table level constraint

For ease of maintenance, it is recommended that you explicitly name constraints.

Comparing Data Integrity Methods

Rules, defaults, and indexes are T-SQL extensions to the ANSI-89 SQL standard. Rules and defaults are reusable database objects and can be bound to many datatypes or columns. User-defined datatypes can simplify maintenance of rules and defaults for common columns and datatypes. Indexes can be created on columns other than primary key and unique columns to improve query performance.

Constraints

Constraints are ANSI-89 SQL-compliant. They are specific to the table in which they are defined. Check constraints can perform multi-column checks within a table. Because they are stored in the table definition, this documents data integrity checks within the table. Constraints also enable display of custom error messages when the constraint is violated.

Keys

SQL Server enables the definition of logical keys for a database design within the database. The key definitions are for documentation purposes only. The server does not use these for any purpose whatsoever. (As a result, the discussion here will be short.) Their only practical application is that some applications (for example, APT-Forms) use the key information to help define join candidates between tables within the application. These differ from constraints (which enforce referential integrity) and indexes (which enforce uniqueness—for example, of primary keys).

Do not confuse keys with indexes. Keys are logical entities, which have meaning to logical database designers. Indexes are physical database objects, whose purpose is performance:

Key Type	Description
Primary key	Unique row identifier
Foreign key	Primary key from another table, typically used for joins
Common key	Usually an alternate, shorter primary key, used for joins

Use these stored procedures to identify keys in your tables.

```
sp_primarykey table_name, col1 [, col2, ...]

sp_foreignkey table_name, pk_table_name,
    col1 [, col2, ...]

sp_commonkey table1_name, table2_name,
    col1a, col2a [, col1b, col2b , ...]

sp_helpkey table_name
```

Which One Should You Use?

Which one should you use? As with all things, the simple answer is "it depends." There are some important distinctions. First, constraints have proven to be consistently faster than T-SQL data validation objects such as rules and defaults. The reason for this is that constraint-based validation of data happens as a code path within the SQL Server executable, and data-validation object processes require fetches from disk to read the validation object. For example, if you establish a check constraint and a rule on a column, the check constraint is always faster.

Why? Because the constraint is part of the SQL Server executable, meaning its instructions are always in working memory. With a rule, the instructions for validating data are out in the disk subsystem, or, at best, reside in cache. Either way, instead of simply jumping to the code path, SQL Server must search for the resolved rule, execute the rule's instructions, and process the results. Because this involves reads to cache or disk, the process is inherently less efficient than using a check constraint. This principle also holds true for default constraints. As a general rule, constraints are always faster than the equivalent T-SQL data validation object.

In the case of referential integrity constraints, there are some other issues to consider. As of Version 6, SQL Server is only base-level ANSI 92-compliant. As a result, its referential integrity features support "restrict-only" operations. Therefore, if you have orders that you want deleted from the orders table whenever the corresponding customer is deleted, constraints do not work. Constraints work only where the goal is to *prevent* any multi-table operations. SQL Server will not *cascade* any multi-table operations.

In order to implement cascading multi-table operations, you must still write triggers using Transact-SQL coding. Creating triggers, particularly referential-integrity triggers, is discussed in Chapter 7 on SQL Server Programming Objects. Until SQL Server's ANSI 92 compliance is expanded to support declarative referential integrity with cascade options, triggers are your only choice for implementing cascading RI functions at the database level.

The issue of portability is important for some shops, as well. In areas where multiple relational databases are used, the capability of moving from one server platform to another quickly can be an issue. As a result, some shops insist on ANSI 92 SQL compatibility for data definition language. In such cases, your only choice is to use ANSI constraints, because SQL Server data validation objects are, by definition, proprietary enhancements to the ANSI 89 SQL standard. They do not work on any other server platform.

In the end, the issues boil down to functionality, performance, and portability. Based on the requirements of your applications, deciding on constraints versus T-SQL objects breaks down along these lines. If one doesn't work, the other probably will.

Summary

This chapter explores the creation and use of several database objects, all of which center on the manipulation and control of user data in tables. You could probably start designing a database design with what you know right now, but there is a great deal more to learn about how these tables and indexes are physically stored in the server, what kinds of database design choices you need to make to provide the best `select` versus `update` performance, how SQL Server really uses indexes, and so forth. Proper database design and implementation is a major factor in the long-term performance and usefulness of a system, and it turns out to be fairly difficult to change the design of a production system. So keep reading!

In Chapter 6, "Transact-SQL Programming Constructs," you learn about the extensions to the basic SQL language that make up Transact-SQL. These extensions are the building blocks for stored procedures and triggers, which you need to understand to begin designing effective databases for SQL Server.

Transact-SQL Programming Constructs

6

Many books discuss the relative merits of the ANSI-standard SQL language, not the least of which is the one published by ANSI. SQL Server supports 98 to 100 percent of the ANSI standard, but the ANSI standard does not really provide the capability of doing anything other than querying the database.

Because the SQL Server is much more robust and, as programmers, you demand more, SQL Server provides extensions to the standard for things such as extended functions and programming constructs. These extensions to the standard SQL are called *Transact-SQL* (T-SQL).

This section covers the following topics:

- SQL Server extensions to ANSI standard
- Functions: built-in, mathematical, string, and date manipulation
- Extensions to insert, update, and delete
- Programming constructs (if, while, and so forth)
- Cursors

SQL Server Functions

ANSI-89 SQL allows standard arithmetic operators (+, -, *, /, and ^) in both select and data-modification statements.

Examples

```
/* display 10% of each price */
select title, price, price / 10
    from titles
title                                               price
------------------------------------------------    ----------  ------
The Busy Executive's Database Guide                 19.99       2.00
Cooking with Computers: Surreptitious Balance Sheets 11.95      1.20
You Can Combat Computer Stress!                     2.99        0.30
Straight Talk About Computers                       19.99       2.00
Silicon Valley Gastronomic Treats                   19.99       2.00
The Gourmet Microwave                               2.99        0.30
The Psychology of Computer Cooking
But Is It User Friendly?                            22.95       2.30
Secrets of Silicon Valley                           20.00       2.00
Net Etiquette
```

```
Computer Phobic AND Non-Phobic Individuals: Behavior Variations 21.59        2.16
Is Anger the Enemy?                                              10.95        1.10
Life Without Fear                                                 7.00        0.70
Prolonged Data Deprivation: Four Case Studies                   19.99        2.00
Emotional Security: A New Algorithm                               7.99        0.80
Onions, Leeks, and Garlic: Cooking Secrets of the Mediterranean 20.95        2.10
Fifty Years in Buckingham Palace Kitchens                       11.95        1.20
Sushi, Anyone?                                                  14.99        1.50
( 18 rows affected)
/* use an operator in an update statement */
update titles
     set price = price * 1.1
     where type = "business"
/* perform concatenation with "+" */
select location = city + ', ' + state
     from publishers
location
-----------------------
Boston, MA
Washington, DC
Berkeley, CA
Chicago, IL
Dallas, TX
München,
New York, NY
Paris,
( 8 rows affected)
```

SQL Server data functions provide advanced data manipulation, including the following:

- String functions
- Math functions
- Date functions
- System functions

String Functions

Table 6.1 lists the SQL Server string functions, which can be used as part of any character expression. These functions enable manipulation, parsing, and conversion of character strings.

Table 6.1. SQL Server string functions.

Function	Definition
	Length and Parsing
datalength(char_expr)	Returns integer # of characters in char_expr, ignoring trailing spaces
substring (expression, start, length)	Returns part of string
right (char_expr, int_expr)	Returns int_expr characters from right of char_expr
	Basic String Manipulation
upper (char_expr)	Convert char_expr to uppercase
lower (char_expr)	Convert char_expr to lowercase
space (int_expr)	Generate string of int_expr spaces
replicate (char_expr, int_expr)	Repeats char_expr, int_expr times
stuff (char_expr1, start, length, char_expr2)	Replace length characters from expr1 at start with expr2
reverse (char_expr)	Reverses text in char_expr
ltrim (char_expr)	Remove leading spaces
rtrim (char_expr)	Remove trailing spaces
	Conversions
ascii (char_expr)	Ascii value of 1st character in char_expr
char (int_expr)	Converts ASCII code to character
str (float_expr [, length [, decimal]])	Numeric to character conversion
soundex (char_expr)	Returns soundex value of char_expr
difference (char_expr1, char_expr2)	Returns difference between soundex values of expressions
	In-string Searches
charindex (char_expr, expression)	Returns the starting position of the specified char_expr, else zero
patindex ("%pattern%", expression)	Returns the starting position of the specified pattern, else 0

Basic String Manipulation and Parsing

All of the string manipulation and parsing functions that you are used to in other languages are available in T-SQL. Of those listed, here are some tips:

- `data_length` is useful for determining the length of a variable string.
- `right` returns the rightmost *N* characters, but there is no "left" function; to retrieve the leftmost positions, use the `substring` function and start in position 1.
- `upper` and `lower` are case conversions, which are sometimes useful for text comparisons.

> **WARNING**
>
> Don't use these conversion functions in a WHERE clause without any other conditions. The SQL Server cannot use an index to resolve a function and so must scan the table. For more on this, see Chapter 19, "Application Design for Performance."

Conversions

The `soundex` function is useful in determining whether character strings are likely to sound similar. The function returns a value representing the first letter and each of the significant consonant sounds, as in this example:

```
select soundex('marsupial')

-----
M621
( 1 row affected)
```

In this example, the `soundex` value consists of the initial m followed by a number for each of the next three consonants (r, s, and p). Vowels, semivowels, and duplicated letters are ignored, and if the word has fewer than four useful sounds, the value is padded with zeros.

The idea is that if two strings have the same `soundex` value, they are likely to sound similar. For example, look at the results from this query:

```
select name, "soundex" = soundex(name)
from smith_table

name              soundex
---------------   -------
Smith             S530
Smyth             S530
Smithe            S530
Smythe            S530
Smithson          S532
Smithsonian       S532
Smithers          S536
Smothers          S536
```

Properly used, the soundex function provides the capability to search for certain values that sound similar but are spelled differently. The problem is that a WHERE clause based on a soundex function (and the related difference) will not be able to make use of an index:

```
select id, name
from smith_table
where soundex(name) = soundex("Smythe")
```

This query must scan the table, *even if there is an index on the* name *column*, because the query processor cannot optimize the query. You can actually store soundex values in a table and then index those values, if you need to search for them:

```
insert smith_table (name, sdx)
values ("Smythe", soundex("Smythe")

select id, name
from smith_table
where sdx = soundex("Smythe")
```

In this case, SQL Server can use an index on the sdx table, resolving the one constant soundex expression before starting the search.

There are substantial limitations with soundex and differences, mostly because of the oddness of English spelling. soundex will fail to match the names, "Klein" and "Cline" and will consider the word "Phone" an exact match with "Pen" but not "Fan." For these reasons, the soundex-based functions should be used cautiously in applications.

Wildcards

SQL Server provides *wildcards* to enable pattern matching in text searches. This is roughly like the matching you use in the Windows File Manager to look for a missing file. Table 6.2 lists the SQL Server wildcards, which are used with the like operator.

Table 6.2. SQL Server wildcards.

Wildcard	Meaning
%	Matches any quantity of characters, or no characters
_	(Underscore) Matches any single character (a placeholder)
[ ]	Specifies a range of valid characters, or an or condition (this is a SQL Server extension)

Within the brackets, there are a couple of operators available. The caret (^) in the first position means "NOT", so the pattern [YyNn] means "capital or lower case Y or N" where [^YyNn] means "any character EXCEPT capital or lower case Y or N."

The hyphen (-) means any character within a range, so the pattern [AC] means "capital A or C", but [A-C] means "any capital between A and C."

Examples

```
[ABG]           /* matches "A" or "B" or "G" */
[A-CF-G]        /* matches "A", "B", "C", "E", "F", "G" */
[^ABG]          /* matches any except "A", "B", "G" */
[^A-C]          /* matches any except "A", "B", "C" */
```

> **WARNING**
>
> It is *very* important to use wildcards with the `like` operator rather than `=`.
>
> ```
> /* this will work */
> select * from authors
>     where au_lname like "[Ss]mith%"
> /* this will not work as expected! */
> select * from authors
>     where au_lname = "[Ss]mith%"
> ```
>
> In the first example, the server returns rows with values such as "Smith", "smith",
> "Smithers", and "Smithsonian". In the last example, the server is being instructed to
> look for an author whose last name is "[Ss]mith%". You would not expect any rows to
> be returned.

The *escape* Clause

To include wildcard characters as literals in a search string, use an escape character.

SQL Server, by default, uses the square brackets (`[]`) to escape a wildcard, which means that
you want to use the wildcard as a literal character.

Example

```
/* find a string containing the value 20% */
select * from test_tab
    where description like "%20[%]%"
```

The ANSI-89 SQL Standard defines the escape clause to specify an escape character.

Syntax

```
like char_expression escape escape_character
```

Example

```
/* find a string containing the value 20% */
select * from test_tab
    where description like "%20#%%" escape "#"
```

An escape character retains its special meaning inside square brackets (unlike wildcard characters). It is valid only within its `like` predicate and does not affect other `like` predicates in the same statement. Finally, it affects only the single character following it.

String Function Examples

In this example, you build a name column from two columns, using the concatenation operator, +:

```
select au_lname + "," + au_fname
     from authors
```

```
 -------------------------------------------------------
White,Johnson
Green,Marjorie
Carson,Cheryl
O'Leary,Michael
Straight,Dean
Smith,Meander
Bennet,Abraham
Dull,Ann
Gringlesby,Burt
Locksley,Charlene
Greene,Morningstar
Blotchet-Halls,Reginald
Yokomoto,Akiko
del Castillo,Innes
DeFrance,Michel
Stringer,Dirk
MacFeather,Stearns
Karsen,Livia
Panteley,Sylvia
Hunter,Sheryl
McBadden,Heather
Ringer,Anne
Ringer,Albert
( 23 rows affected)
```

This example finds all rows where the last name has an identical `soundex` value to the name Green:

```
select au_id, au_lname, au_fname
   from authors
   where difference (au_lname, "Green") = 4
```

```
au_id    au_lname                           au_fname
-------- ---------------------------------- ----------------
213-46-8915 Green                           Marjorie
527-72-3246 Greene                          Morningstar
( 2 rows affected)
```

```
/* or */
```

```
select au_id, au_lname, au_fname
    from authors
    where soundex (au_lname) = soundex ("Green")

au_id      au_lname                        au_fname
--------- ------------------------------- -----------------
213-46-8915 Green                         Marjorie
527-72-3246 Greene                        Morningstar
( 2 rows affected)


/* replace characters within a string */
update authors
    set phone = stuff(phone, 4, 1, "-")
```

Functions can be embedded:

```
select rtrim(reverse(au_lname))
    from authors

-----------------------------------------
etihW
neerG
nosraC
yraeL'O
thgiartS
htimS
tenneB
lluD
ybselgnirG
yelskcoL
eneerG
sllaH-tehctolB
otomokoY
ollitsaC led
ecnarFeD
regnirtS
rehtaeFcaM
nesraK
yeletnaP
retnuH
neddaBcM
regniR
regniR
( 23 rows affected)
```

This example displays all titles containing the word `Computer`, using the `like` operator and wildcards to identify many rows:

```
select title
    from titles
    where title like "%Computer%"
title
--------------------------------------------------------------------
Computer Phobic AND Non-Phobic Individuals: Behavior Variations
Cooking with Computers: Surreptitious Balance Sheets
Straight Talk About Computers
The Psychology of Computer Cooking
```

```
You Can Combat Computer Stress!
( 5 rows affected)
```

Mathematical Functions

SQL Server performs standard arithmetic operations using normal precedence. Functions and parentheses are evaluated first, then multiplication and division, then addition and subtraction—all left to right. SQL Server also supports all standard trigonometric functions and a number of other useful ones. Table 6.3 lists the SQL Server mathematical functions.

Table 6.3. SQL Server mathematical functions.

Function	Description
abs (*numeric_expr*)	Absolute value of specified value.
ceiling (*numeric_expr*)	Smallest integer greater than or equal to the specified value.
exp (*float_expr*)	Exponential value of the specified value.
floor (*numeric_expr*)	Largest integer less than or equal to specified value.
pi ()	Returns the constant value of 3.1415926....
power (*numeric_expr,power*)	Returns the value of *numeric_expr* to the power of *power*.
rand ([*int_expr*])	Returns a random float number between 0 and 1, optionally using *int_expr* as a seed.
round (*numeric_expr, int_expr*)	Rounding off a numeric expression to the precision specified in *int_expr*.
sign (*int_expr*)	Returns the positive (+1), zero (0), or negative (-1).
sqrt (*float_expr*)	Square root of the specified value.

> **WARNING**
>
> The randomizer function needs a random seed in order to provide a random value.

Date Functions

SQL Server includes date functions for performing date parsing and date arithmetic. (See Table 6.4.) This is extremely useful for identifying, for example, the age of invoices.

Table 6.4. SQL Server date functions.

Function	Description
getdate ( )	Returns current system date and time.
datename(*datepart, date_expr*)	Returns specified part of *date_expr* value as a string, converted to a name (e.g. June) if appropriate.
datepart(*datepart, date_expr*)	Returns specified part of *date_expr* value as an integer.
datediff(*datepart, date_expr1, date_expr2*)	Returns *date_expr2 - date_expr1*, as measured by specified *datepart*.
dateadd(*datepart, number, date_expr*)	Returns the date produced by adding *number* of specified *datepart* to *date_expr*.

Date Parts

Date parts are used in conjunction with the date functions to specify an element of a date value for parsing or date arithmetic. (See Table 6.5.)

Table 6.5. SQL Server date parts.

Date Part	Abbreviation	Value Range (in datepart)
year	yy	1753-9999
quarter	qq	1-4
month	mm	1-12
dayofyear	dy	1-366
day	dd	1-31
week	wk	1-54
weekday	dw	1-7 (1=Sunday)
hour	hh	0-23
minute	mi	0-59
second	ss	0-59
millisecond	ms	0-999

Examples

```
/* what is the current date and time */
select getdate()
```

```
--------------------------
Nov 15 1995 10:39AM
( 1 row affected)
/* how old are unpaid invoices? */
select invoice_no,
    datediff (dd, date_shipped, getdate()) "invoice aging"
    from invoices
    where balance_due > 0
```

In the example, notice the sequence `date_shipped, get_date`, which avoids a negative number. Always put the earlier date first. Also, notice that we have requested the difference in number of days (`dd`) in the `invoice aging` column.

```
/* what month were these books published? */
select title, datename ( mm, pubdate )
    from titles
title
-------------------------------------------------------------------------------
------------------------------- -----------------------------
The Busy Executive's Database Guide                               June
Cooking with Computers: Surreptitious Balance Sheets             June
You Can Combat Computer Stress!                                  June
Straight Talk About Computers                                    June
Silicon Valley Gastronomic Treats                               June
The Gourmet Microwave                                           June
The Psychology of Computer Cooking                             November
But Is It User Friendly?                                          June
Secrets of Silicon Valley                                        June
Net Etiquette                                                  November
Computer Phobic AND Non-Phobic Individuals: Behavior Variations  October
Is Anger the Enemy?                                              June
Life Without Fear                                              October
Prolonged Data Deprivation: Four Case Studies                   June
Emotional Security: A New Algorithm                              June
Onions, Leeks, and Garlic: Cooking Secrets of the Mediterranean October
Fifty Years in Buckingham Palace Kitchens                        June
Sushi, Anyone?                                                   June
( 18 rows affected)
```

convert

The `convert` function is used to change data from one type to another when SQL Server cannot implicitly understand a conversion (for example, `float` to `real` to `integer` are all dynamically converted for comparison purposes).

Syntax

```
convert (datatype [(length)], expression)
```

Example

```
/* return one column of data ...the conversion is
** required to allow concatenation of literal
** string with a numeric */

select "Advance = "
     + convert (char(12), advance)
from titles
---------------------
Advance =      5000.00
Advance =      5000.00
Advance =     10125.00
Advance =      5000.00
Advance =         0.00
Advance =     15000.00
Advance =
Advance =      7000.00
Advance =      8000.00
Advance =
Advance =      7000.00
Advance =      2275.00
Advance =      6000.00
Advance =      2000.00
Advance =      4000.00
Advance =      7000.00
Advance =      4000.00
Advance =      8000.00
( 18 rows affected)
```

SQL Server makes any reasonable conversion; if you choose an unreasonable conversion, you get an error message.

Date Conversions

A special version of the `convert` function enables date datatypes to be converted to character types.

Syntax

```
convert (datatype [(length)], expression, format)
```

The `format` parameter tells SQL Server which date format to provide in the converted string. Table 6.6 lists the SQL Server date formats.

Table 6.6. SQL Server date formats available with the `convert` function.

Without Century	With Century	Format of Date in Converted String
	0 or 100	mon dd yyyy hh:miAM (or PM)
1	101	mm/dd/yy

continues

Table 6.6. continued

Without Century	With Century	Format of Date in Converted String
2	102	yy.mm.dd
3	103	dd/mm/yy
4	104	dd.mm.yy
5	105	dd-mm-yy
6	106	dd mon yy
7	107	mon dd, yy
8	108	hh:mi:ss
	9 or 109	mon dd, yyyy hh:mi:ss:mmmAM (or PM)
10	110	mm-dd-yy
11	111	yy/mm/dd
12	112	yymmdd

Notice that you can display dates in almost any kind of format without resorting to string manipulation.

Example

```
/* return pubdate in mon dd, yyyy format*/
select "Pubdate" = convert (char(12), pubdate, 107)
     from titles
Pubdate
------------
Jun 12, 1991
Jun 09, 1991
Jun 30, 1991
Jun 22, 1991
Jun 09, 1991
Jun 18, 1991
Nov 13, 1995
Jun 30, 1991
Jun 12, 1994
Nov 13, 1995
Oct 21, 1991
Jun 15, 1991
Oct 05, 1991
Jun 12, 1991
Jun 12, 1991
Oct 21, 1991
Jun 12, 1991
Jun 12, 1991
( 18 rows affected)
```

System Functions

System functions are used to display information about the SQL Server, database, or user. These tend to be used a lot by programmers and DBAs, but not very often by users.

Useful System Functions

System functions with optional parameters return values for the current user, database, and process if a parameter is not specified.

System functions enable quick conversion of system and object information without writing several join clauses. They are used heavily in system stored procedures. Table 6.7 lists the SQL Server system functions.

Table 6.7. SQL Server system functions.

Function	Definition
	Access and Security Information
host_id ( )	Current host process ID number of client process
host_name ( )	Current host computer name of client process
suser_id (["*login_name*"])	User's SQL Server ID number
suser_name ([*server_user_id*])	User's SQL Server login name
user_id (["*name_in_db*"])	User's ID number in database
user_name ([*user_id*])	User's name in database
user	User's name in database
show_role()	Current active roles for user
	Database and Object Information
db_id (["*db_name*"])	Database ID number
db_name ([*db_id*])	Database name
object_id ("*objname*")	Database object ID number
object_name (*obj_id*)	Database object name
col_name (*obj_id,col_id*)	Column name of object
col_length ("*objname*", "*colname*")	Length of column
index_col ("*objname*", *index_id*, *key #*)	Indexed column name
valid_name (*char_expr*)	Returns 0 if *char_expr* is not a valid identifier

continues

Table 6.7. continued

Function	Definition
	Data Functions
datalength (*expression*)	Returns length of *expression* in bytes
tsequal (*timestamp1*, *timestamp2*)	Compares timestamp values. Returns error if rows are found but timestamp values do not match

System Function Examples

```
/* return current user ID*/
select user_id ()
------
1
( 1 row affected)
/* return login name of the login whose ID is 10 */
select suser_name (1)
------------------------------
sa
( 1 row affected)
```

> **NOTE**
>
> The system user ID (suser_id) of the sa is always 1 because sa is the first login added to the syslogins table during installation.
>
> Likewise, the user ID (user_id) dbo is always user 1 (user_name "dbo") in every database because the dbo is the first user added to the sysusers table during database creation.

```
/* Return name of the object specified by the ID */
select object_name (112003430)

------------------------------
publishers
( 1 row affected)

/* Return list of all indexes for titles table */
select name from sysindexes
     where id = object_id("titles")
name
------------------------------
UPKCL_titleidind
titleind
( 2 rows affected)

/* compare timestamps for update */
```

```
update titles
    set price = $10.95
    where title_id = "BU1032"
    and tsequal(timestamp, 0x0010000000002ea8)
```

compute and compute by

The compute and compute by keywords enable you to prepare both detail and summary information in a single pass of the table.

compute

A compute clause reports overall aggregate values for a result set.

Example

```
/*list titles and prices, show overall max price*/
select title, price
    from titles
    compute max(price)
```

title	price
The Busy Executive's Database Guide	19.99
Cooking with Computers: Surreptitious Balance Sheets	11.95
You Can Combat Computer Stress!	2.99
Straight Talk About Computers	19.99
Silicon Valley Gastronomic Treats	19.99
The Gourmet Microwave	2.99
The Psychology of Computer Cooking	
But Is It User Friendly?	22.95
Secrets of Silicon Valley	20.00
Net Etiquette	
Computer Phobic AND Non-Phobic Individuals: Behavior Variations	21.59
Is Anger the Enemy?	10.95
Life Without Fear	7.00
Prolonged Data Deprivation: Four Case Studies	19.99
Emotional Security: A New Algorithm	7.99
Onions, Leeks, and Garlic: Cooking Secrets of the Mediterranean	20.95
Fifty Years in Buckingham Palace Kitchens	11.95
Sushi, Anyone?	14.99
	23

```
( 19 rows affected)
```

In this output, the most expensive book is listed as 23 (note the last line). The format of this output varies from one reporting tool to the next. Some tools (including isql) produce a header in the line before the output, but this is completely dependent on the application program. The server merely returns rows marked as compute columns, and it is up to the application to determine a format. Here is what the isql output might look like:

```
max

 =========================
                    22.95
```

> **NOTE**
>
> Many organizations do not use compute for a variety of reasons. First, because it is not ANSI-standard SQL, organizations avoid writing important queries that might need to be modified dramatically to be ported to other database environments. Second, any decent reporting tool will provide all of the totaling and subtotaling directly within the report definition, with much more flexibility about the actual handling of the computed values.
>
> If you plan to use compute, make sure you have spent the necessary time testing how your application reads and presents computed values.

compute by

A compute by clause displays subtotals within a result set, but not totals.

Example

```
/* display type, title and price,
** and show the maximum price for each type */
select type, title, price
    from titles
    order by type
    compute max(price) by type
type        title                                                     price
----------- --------------------------------------------------------- ----------
----------- --------------------------
UNDECIDED   The Psychology of Computer Cooking
                                                                      0
business    Straight Talk About Computers                             19.99
business    You Can Combat Computer Stress!                           2.99
business    The Busy Executive's Database Guide                       19.99
business    Cooking with Computers: Surreptitious Balance Sheets      11.95
                                                                      20
mod_cook    The Gourmet Microwave                                     2.99
mod_cook    Silicon Valley Gastronomic Treats                         19.99
                                                                      20
popular_comp Net Etiquette
popular_comp But Is It User Friendly?                                 22.95
popular_comp Secrets of Silicon Valley                                20.00
                                                                      23
psychology  Life Without Fear                                         7.00
psychology  Is Anger the Enemy?                                       10.95
psychology  Emotional Security: A New Algorithm                       7.99
psychology  Prolonged Data Deprivation: Four Case Studies             19.99
psychology  Computer Phobic AND Non-Phobic Individuals: Behavior Variations 21.59
                                                                      22
trad_cook   Sushi, Anyone?                                            14.99
trad_cook   Fifty Years in Buckingham Palace Kitchens                 11.95
```

```
trad_cook    Onions, Leeks, and Garlic: Cooking Secrets of the Mediterranean    20.95
                                                                                    21
( 24 rows affected)
```

If you look at the results, you should see a maximum price reported for each type.

To show subtotals and totals, combine compute by and compute in one select statement:

```
Example
/*display details with subtotals and grand totals*/
select pub_id, title_id, ytd_sales
      from titles
      order by pub_id
      compute sum(ytd_sales) by pub_id
      compute sum(ytd_sales)
```

pub_id	title_id	ytd_sales	sum(ytd_sales)	sum(ytd_sales)
0736	BU2075	18722		
0736	PS2091	2045		
0736	PS2106	111		
0736	PS3333	4072		
0736	PS7777	3336	28286	
0877	MC3026			
0877	MC2222	2032		
0877	MC3021	22246		
0877	PS1372	375		
0877	TC3218	375		
0877	TC4203	15096		
0877	TC7777	4095	44219	
1389	PC9999			
1389	BU1032	4095		
1389	BU1111	3876		
1389	BU7832	4095		
1389	PC1035	8780		
1389	PC8888	4095	4941	97446

compute and *compute by* Notes

Important point: compute by columns must match, *in order,* columns in the order by clause. You can specify only a subset of the order by columns. Consider a query containing this order by clause:

```
order by a, b, c
```

The only allowed compute by clauses are the following:

- compute by a, b, c
- compute by a, b
- compute by a

If you try to perform a compute by operation without a corresponding order by clause, the server returns this message:

```
A compute-by item was not found in the order-by list.
All expressions in the compute-by list must also be present in the order-by list
```

Expressions in a `compute` or `compute by` clause must match exactly the corresponding expression in the `select` list.

Example

```
select type, price, price*2
from titles
    where type = "business"
    compute sum(price), sum(price*2)

type          price
-----------   -------------------------   --------------------------
business      19.99                       39.98
business      11.95                       23.90
business      2.99                        5.98
business      19.99                       39.98
                                          110

( 5 rows affected)
```

isnull

Sometimes, when calculating aggregates or printing reports to end users, you want to have null values treated as if they are something else. To make them that "something else," you can use the `isnull` function, which substitutes a specified value for a null value in a column in a query or an aggregate.

The following examples refer to the `total_order` column in the invoices table. Here is a query with the contents of that column for all rows in the table:

```
select total_order
from invoices

total_order
----------
100
50
25
(null)
```

The `avg` function, like all aggregate functions, ignores nulls:

```
/* average of orders excluding nulls */
select avg ( total_order ) "avg"
    from invoices

avg
----------
58
```

Using the `isnull` function, you can force the aggregate function to treat a null value as if it had a specific value *for the current query*. The next two examples substitute the values 0 and 10 for any null values, respectively:

```
/* average of orders using 0 for orders
** that have a null  total */
select avg ( isnull ( total_order, 0 ) ) "avg using 0"
     from invoices

avg using 0
----------
43

/* average of orders using 10 for orders
** that have a null total */
select avg ( isnull ( total_order, 10 ) ) "avg using 10"
     from invoices

avg using 10
-----------
46
```

Use isnull, then, to force specific behavior for unknown or unavailable values, rather than ignoring the values entirely.

Programming Constructs

As previously mentioned, it is sometimes necessary to do more than is available in the ANSI standard—it is necessary to program. To that end, let's look at the following topics:

- Batches
- Comments
- Local and Global Variables
- Message handling
- Error handling
- while loops
- if...then loops
- begin...end loops

Batches

A *batch* is the entire packet that is passed from the client to the server, which can contain several SQL statements. Statements in a batch are parsed as a group, compiled as a group, and executed as a group. This means that none of the statements in the batch are executed if there are any syntax errors in the batch.

NOTE

If a stored procedure is not the first statement in a batch, it must be preceded by the exec keyword (which is otherwise optional).

Examples

```
/* this batch performs two selections */
select * from authors
select * from titles
go
/* this batch binds defaults to several columns at once */
sp_bindefault "my_default", "my_table.col_3"
exec sp_bindefault "my_default", "my_table.col_2"
go
/* this batch sets security on a table */
grant select, insert to mary on mytable
revoke select, insert from mary on mytable(col_3)
go
```

Note that because a batch represents everything shipped to the server, if you are going to separate your batches (which you often will—some tasks require their own batch), you need either to send twice or use some sort of separator that instructs the front end to ship separate batches. In many tools, this is the keyword go. go *is not* T-SQL. It is an instruction to the front end to ship to the server everything up to the go.

Comments

Comments can be included in batches, and it is a good practice to include descriptive comments in stored procedures.

Syntax

```
/* single or multi-line comment
[...]
*/
-- single-line comment
```

Two hyphens (--) precede a single-line comment that is terminated with an end-of-line (CR-LF) sequence.

Multi-line comments (with /*) must be explicitly terminated (*/).

Local Variables

Variables for use in a batch or stored procedure are defined with the declare statement.

WARNING
Local variables exist only for the life of the batch. When the batch is complete, all information stored in the local variables is lost forever.

Syntax

```
declare @variable_name datatype [, ...]
```

Example

```
/* declare two variables in a single statement */
declare @name varchar(30), @type int
```

Variable names must be preceded by a single @. Note that this limits variable names to 29 characters plus the @. Local variables are assigned values with a `select` statement, generally referred to as an *assignment* `select`.

Syntax

```
select @variable_name = expression
[, ...] [from ... [where ...]]
```

Examples

```
/* set a variable equal to a constant expression */
declare @int_var int
select @int_var = 12
go
/* multiple variables set in a select statement */
declare @single_auth varchar(40),
        @curdate datetime
select @single_auth = au_lname,
        @curdate = getdate()
    from authors
    where au_id = '123-45-6789'
```

Notes on Local Variables

A single `select` statement can be for data retrieval or variable setting, but not for both. It lasts for the duration of the batch or stored procedure in which it is declared and is not available to other processes.

From a compilation point of view, it is more efficient to declare multiple variables in a single `declare` statement and to set multiple variables in a single `select` statement.

If an assignment `select` that retrieves data returns multiple rows, the local variable is assigned the value for the last row returned. If an assignment `select` that retrieves data returns no rows, the local variable retains the value it had prior to the execution of the `select` statement. Note that this might not have been the expected result.

Global Variables

Global variables are used by the server to track server-wide and session-specific information. They cannot be explicitly set or declared. Global variables cannot be defined by users and are not used to pass information across processors by applicants (as defined in many third- and fourth-generation languages).

The server also provides some useful global variables. These are read-only variables that are available from any context. Although they are called "global" variables, they are not *server-wide* values. Instead, they provide information about your current session. Other users' values will almost certainly vary from your own at any given time. Here is a list of the more common global variables.

Function	Description
@@rowcount	Number of rows processed by preceding command
@@error	Error number reported for last SQL statement
@@trancount	Transaction nesting level
@@servername	Name of local SQL Server
@@version	SQL Server and O/S release level
@@spid	Current process id
@@identity	Last identity value used in an insert
@@nestlevel	Number of levels nested in a stored_procedure/trigger
@@sqlstatus	Status of previous fetch statement in a cursor

Although all of these variables are relevant at one time or another, there are some points about the most commonly used global variables that need to be made.

- @@rowcount changes after every statement except declare. If you need to use the value repeatedly or refer back to it after performing some intermediate processing, declare an int variable and then store the value of @@rowcount in that variable, like this:

```
declare @rows int
select @rows = @@rowcount
```

This is a particularly useful technique inside of a trigger, where you will often need access to @@rowcount to be certain that all the rows in the table are valid.

> **NOTE**
>
> When you write a trigger, you need to be especially aware of how @@rowcount is affected by every statement. Notice, however, that when you exit the trigger and continue processing, @@rowcount is restored to the value originally set by the statement that fired the trigger.

- @@error should be checked after every SQL statement, particularly in stored procedures and triggers. If you want to streamline your code a little more, you should always check @@error after data-retrieval and data-modification statements. If the value of @@error is not zero, an error was raised by the execution and you should take the next step.

  Client application programs rely on automatic mechanisms that alert the application or the user when server-originated errors occur. The way you trap those errors depends on your front end. You need to use @@error most frequently when you are writing server-based routines (stored procedures, triggers, and complex batches) where the decision to go ahead and work on the next SQL statement depends on the success of the prior statement.

- The value of @@trancount is greater than zero if a transaction is currently uncommitted within the session, and zero if there is no pending transaction. Refer to Chapter 8, "Transaction Management," for an in-depth discussion of @@trancount.

- @@version tells you the current release and operating system for the server. This is useful for technical support and sometimes helpful to identify an unnamed server in your network.

print

The print statement is used to pass a message to the client program's message handler. Messages can include up to 255 characters of text. You can only pass a literal character string or a single character-type variable to print. You cannot perform any concatenation or substitution in the print statement itself.

Syntax

```
print {character_string | @local_variable | @@global variable }
```

Examples

```
/* send a string to the message handler */
print "This is a message"
```

```
This is a message

/* send a variable to the message handler
** the variable needs to be of a character type */
declare @msg varchar(30)
select @msg = "Hello " + user_name()
print @msg

Hello dbo
```

Notice how the second example uses a variable to store the final string to be passed to the print statement. The concatenation performed in the select statement cannot be performed by the print statement. Instead, build your message in a variable using select and then print the variable.

Error Handling

SQL Server will handle most error reporting for you automatically, transmitting a message to the user and identifying the problem. The raiserror command is provided to enable you to initiate an error yourself. Returning and identifying an error condition to a calling procedure or batch is useful in stored procedures and complex batches. It is particularly useful when you encounter an error in a trigger and must issue a rollback command.

Error messages consist of four basic elements. The server and client applications use each of these elements to inform the user or administrator and to make programmatic decisions.

Error *number* is a unique integer value between 50,001 and 2,147,483,647 (2^{31} - 1). Client programs trap certain errors, but pass others straight through to the user. The server itself also monitors the errors being generated and can take action in response to an error.

- The error handler in a client program will identify errors it needs to trap to handle internally. Deadlocks are a common error handled by the programmer with no user intervention.

- Other general errors are often reported directly to the user. The attempt to enter a duplicate key in a table is often reported directly to the user.

- You can also set up alerts so that SQL Server can respond to specific error conditions by number. One common error to trap with an alert is a full database transaction log.

Severity describes the general type of error. Severity values include 0 and all of the integers from 10 to 25.

- Severity levels 0 and 10 are informational; both are returned to the client application as severity 0.

- Severity levels 11 through 16 are errors that the user can typically correct. They include syntax errors, security violations, data-validation violations, and other common database occurrences.

■ Severity levels 17 through 19 indicate a software or hardware problem. You can usually continue working, although the statement you executed to generate the error might not work. These errors should be reported to a system administrator immediately.

■ Severity levels 20 to 25 indicate system problems. They are fatal and, depending on the error, could result in the user losing his connection or might result in the whole server shutting down. In any case, something heavy is going down.

State describes the "invocation state" of the error. State is an integer value from 1 to 127. Because the state of the error depends on when it is called, you don't store the message state as part of the error.

NOTE

I'll be brutally honest here. I'm quoting the Microsoft SQL Server Books on Line. With over five years of experience in SQL Server, I still haven't heard a convincing explanation of how to use this information.

Message is the text of the error message to be reported to the user. It cannot exceed 255 characters.

To generate a SQL Server error programmatically, use the `raiserror` command, which places the error number you specify in the `@@error` global variable and transmits the error number, severity, state, and the text of the error message to the client application. It is also possible to transmit error messages to the SQL Server error log and the Windows NT event log.

Managing SQL Server Errors

SQL Server provides a number of internal error messages related to predefined events within the parsing, optimizing, and execution subsystems. These errors are stored in a system table, `master..sysmessages`. You can add your own messages to the `master..sysmessages` table and then refer to those messages in a `raiserror` statement. When you raise an error, you can send an *ad hoc* error message and number created directly in your SQL code, or you can refer to one of your predefined messages.

To provide better system documentation and greater consistency between development and support teams, you should store all error messages in `master..sysmessages`. SQL Server provides three stored procedures to help you maintain your error messages:

`sp_addmessage` adds messages to the table.

```
sp_addmessage msg_id, severity, "text of message"
  [, language[, {true¦false} [, REPLACE ]]]
sp_addmessage 52000, 16, "Invalid customer id in order", "us_english", true
```

SQL Server enables you to provide several different language versions of a single error message. When a program generates an error, the version of that error for the user's current language is returned to the user. The default language is us_english. The true|false element indicates whether the error should be recorded in the SQL Server error log when raised.

sp_altermessage changes the logging behavior of a message:

```
sp_altermessage msg_id, WITH_LOG, {true|false}
sp_altermessage 52000, WITH_LOG, "false"
```

The words WITH_LOG must be literally supplied; then you provide the true or false value to indicate whether the error should be logged when it occurs. Only the system administrator can run this command. Notice that you can even change the behavior of a system-supplied error message.

sp_dropmessage removes an error message from the table.

```
sp_dropmessage msg_id [, language | 'all']
```

```
sp_dropmessage 52000
```

You can drop all language versions of a message, or just a version of a message in a single language. If you don't provide a language value, the server drops the message in your current language.

It's much easier to manage error messages using SQL Enterprise Manager. Choose the Messages option in the Server menu. Then, to add a user-defined message, choose the New... button. Figure 6.1 shows you the New Message dialog box from SQL-EM.

FIGURE 6.1.

You can manage your error messages from SQL Enterprise Manager.

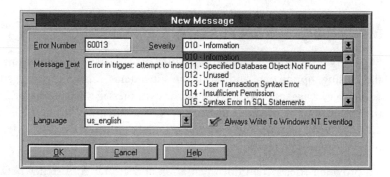

The *raiserror* Command

Although many error messages are generated automatically by the SQL Server, there will be times when a SQL batch or a SQL programming object (a trigger or stored procedure) will need to raise an error.

NOTE

Server-side errors are reported to the client application as part of the *Transaction Data Stream* (TDS). Most client applications implement an interrupt-based error handler using a callback function or event handler. How the client application deals with error events or how it displays errors to the user is entirely up to the application developer.

Here is the syntax for `raiserror`:

```
raiserror ({msg_id | msg_str}, severity, state
   [, argument1 [, ...]] )
   [WITH LOG]
```

NOTE

SQL Server supports an alternative syntax for `raiserror` with *ad hoc* messages:

```
raiserror msg_id msg_str
```

Before version 6.0, this was how errors were raised under all circumstances. Don't use this syntax in new applications unless they will also need to run in SQL Server 4.21.

Here are some examples of `raiserror`:

```
/* raise the error and send a message */
raiserror ( 52000, 16, 1 )
```

In this case, SQL Server requires that error message `52000` already exist in the `sysmessages` table. If you raise an error that does not exist, SQL Server returns this error:

```
Msg 2758, Level 16, State 1
RAISERROR could not locate entry for error 52000 in Sysmessages.
```

You need to add the message with `sp_addmessage`, then raise it.

To raise an *ad hoc* error message (one that is not already in `sysmessages`), provide the text of the message instead of the error message ID:

```
raiserror ("Invalid customer id in order", 16, 1)

Msg 50000, Level 16, State 1
Invalid customer id in order
```

Ad hoc error messages always use message ID `50000`.

`raiserror` enables you to provide *arguments* that are then substituted into the text of the message using syntax similar to the C-language `printf` command. This permits your error message to be more specific and useful. In this example, the actual customer ID that caused the error is passed as an argument to the `raiserror` statement:

```
raiserror ("Invalid customer id %s in order", 16, 1, "AB52436")

Msg 50000, Level 16, State 1
Invalid customer id AB52436 in order
```

The value AB52436 is substituted for %s in the message when it is returned. You can also pass arguments to messages stored in sysmessages. Here is the message added to sysmessages:

```
sp_addmessage 52000, 16, "Invalid customer id %s in order"
```

Now raise the error, referring to the specific message by its message ID and passing the argument:

```
raiserror (52000, 16, 1, "AB52436")
Msg 52000, Level 16, State 1
Invalid customer id AB52436 in order
```

You need to specify the datatype of the arguments you intend to pass in the message text. %s indicates a string and %d or %i is used for a signed integer. (There are other, more exotic types including octals and hexadecimals.)

When you consider raiserror in context, the benefits of predefined error messages and user-specified arguments are clearer. Here is a brief example of a stored procedure for deleting rows from a table. The database programmer is able to provide a detailed error message if the row cannot be deleted because it belongs to someone else:

```
create proc pr_del_cust
(@cust_id char(4))
as
declare @resp_user varchar(30)
select @resp_user = resp_user
    from cust_table
    where cust_id = @cust_id
if user_name() != @resp_user
begin
    raiserror (58000, 14, 1, @cust_id, @resp_user)
    return 1
end
delete cust_table
where cust_id = @cust_id
return 0
```

Here is error message 58000:

```
sp_addmessage 58000, 14, "Customer %s belongs to %s. You may not delete it."
```

If the user attempts to delete a row that does not belong to him, the server returns a descriptive and specific error:

```
pr_del_cust "AB12"

Msg 58000, Level 14, State 1
Customer AB12 belongs to david. You may not delete it.
```

Conditional Execution: *if...else*

Statements to be executed conditionally are identified with the `if...else` construct. This allows a statement or statement block to be executed when a condition is `true` or `false`.

Syntax

```
if boolean_expression
    {statement | statement_block}
[else
    {statement | statement_block}]
```

Example

```
/* check for average price of business books
** and return a message */
if (select avg(price) from titles
        where type = "business") > $19.95
    print "The average price of business books is greater than $19.95"
else
    print "The average price of business books is less than $19.95"

The average price of business books is less than $19.95
```

SQL Server also provides a `nullif` function. This function is true if the expressions in the parameters passed are equivalent:

```
declare @fred int
select @fred = 10
select @fred = nullif(5,5)
select @fred


- - - - - - - - - -

( 1 row affected)
```

In this example, the local variable `@fred` is defined and set to `10`. The third statement instructs the server to set the value of `@fred` to `null` if 5=5 (this might be column names, normally).

if exists

The `if exists` test is used to check for the existence of data, without regard to the number of matching rows. The existence test is superior to a `count(*) > 0` for an existence check, because the server stops processing the `select` as soon as the first matching row is found.

Syntax

```
if [not] exists (select_statement)
    {statement | statement_block}
[else
    {statement | statement_block}]
```

Example

```
/* check for authors named Smith */
declare @lname varchar(40), @msg varchar(255)
select @lname = "Smith"
if exists (select * from titles
        where au_lname = @lname)
    begin
    select @msg = "There are authors named " + @lname
    print @msg
    end
else
    begin
    select @msg = "There are no authors named " + @lname
    print @msg
    end
go
```

Note that using a print statement causes the information to be returned to the client's message handler (a pop-up dialog box, perhaps?) rather than as data.

Notes on *if...else*

If the boolean expression contains a select statement, the select statement must be enclosed in parentheses.

if statements can be nested up to 150 levels. (If you are nesting deeply, make sure your sa has configured your stack size adequately. Consider also whether you should be using a case statement.)

if exists is useful when performing referential integrity checks.

The if condition affects exactly one succeeding statement or statement block.

Statement Blocks: *begin...end*

To treat multiple SQL statements as a single block, use the begin...end construct.

Syntax

```
begin
    SQL Statements
end
```

Example

```
/* check for a smith and do two things */
if exists (select * from authors
        where au_lname = "Smith")
    begin
```

```
        print "Smith exists"
        exec found_proc
    end
else
    begin
        print "Smith not found"
        exec not_found_proc
    end
```

Although `begin...end` can be used almost anywhere, it is most commonly used in combination with `while` and `if...else`.

case

In situations where you might have a whole host of `if` statements, Microsoft SQL Server provides a `case` statement. This enables multiple possible conditions to be managed within a `select` statement.

Syntax

```
case expression
    when expression1 then expression2
    [...]
    [else expressionN]
    END
```

Expressions can be constants or booleans:

```
select substring (title, 1,30), 'This book is a' +
    case    type
        when 'popular_comp' then ' Computer book'
        when 'mod_cook'  then ' Cook book'
        when 'trad_cook'  then ' Cook book'
            else 'n Unimportant book'
    end,
'Sales are ' +
    case
        when ytd_sales < 5000 then "Poor"
        when ytd_sales between 5001 and 10000 then "Good"
        when ytd_sales > 10000 then "Awesome"
        else "Sales unknown"
    end
from titles
```

```
-----------------------------  -----------------------------------  ------------------
The Busy Executive's Database  This book is an Unimportant book Sales are Poor
Cooking with Computers: Surrep This book is an Unimportant book Sales are Poor
You Can Combat Computer Stress This book is an Unimportant book Sales are Awesome
Straight Talk About Computers  This book is an Unimportant book Sales are Poor
Silicon Valley Gastronomic Tre This book is a Cook book        Sales are Poor
The Gourmet Microwave          This book is a Cook book        Sales are Awesome
The Psychology of Computer Coo This book is an Unimportant book Sales are Sales
unknown
But Is It User Friendly?       This book is a Computer book    Sales are Good
```

```
Secrets of Silicon Valley       This book is a Computer book    Sales are Poor
Net Etiquette                   This book is a Computer book    Sales are Sales
unknown
Computer Phobic AND Non-Phobic  This book is an Unimportant book Sales are Poor
Is Anger the Enemy?             This book is an Unimportant book Sales are Poor
Life Without Fear               This book is an Unimportant book Sales are Poor
Prolonged Data Deprivation: Fo  This book is an Unimportant book Sales are Poor
Emotional Security: A New Algo  This book is an Unimportant book Sales are Poor
Onions, Leeks, and Garlic: Coo  This book is a Cook book         Sales are Poor
Fifty Years in Buckingham Pala  This book is a Cook book         Sales are Awesome
Sushi, Anyone?                  This book is a Cook book         Sales are Poor
( 18 rows affected)
```

You are reducing the amount of data returned and displayed from the title with a substring. Book types are identified by using a case type statement, which applies the when test to the value in the type and responds accordingly. The second case statement is a searched-case expression wherein the full boolean expression is part of the when.

coalesce

Closely related to the case statement is the coalesce statement.

Syntax

```
coalesce (expression1, expression2)
coalesce (expression1, expression2,...expressionN)
```

This function call returns the first non-null value in the sequential list and null if there is none.

Repeated Execution: *while*

To execute statements multiple times, use the while construct.

Syntax

```
while boolean_condition
     [{statement ¦ statement_block}]

[break]

[continue]
```

break unconditionally exits the while loop and continues processing with the first statement after the end statement. continue reevaluates the boolean condition and begins processing from the top of the loop if the condition is true.

Example

```
/* loop until average price equals or exceeds $25*/
while (select avg (price) from titles) < $25
```

```
begin
    update titles set price = price * 1.05
    /* if fewer than 10 books are less than
    ** $15, continue processing */
    if (select count(*) from titles
              where price < $15) < 10
        continue
    else
    /* If maximum price of single book exceeds
    ** $50, exit loop */
      if (select max(price) from titles) > $50
        break
end
```

If you want to understand what's going on, read the comments describing each step. Note that the condition governing the loop is evaluated before any processing begins.

NOTE

Of course, this is a horrible example of a `while` loop. Nobody in his right mind would keep running the same table scans over and over like this. So try to remember that the example is meant to help you understand how the looping structures (`while`, `break`, `continue`) are used and what they do.

Keep in mind that the traditional reason for looping syntax in a database application using a third-generation language would be to walk record-by-record through a file until you reach the *end of file* (EOF) mark. That makes no sense in SQL Server unless you are using a cursor. Instead, almost all of your interaction with tables using SQL is performed using *set processing*. For example, this query instructs the server to update all rows in the table sharing a certain characteristic:

```
update authors
set city = "Pittsburgh"
where city = "Pittsburg"
```

If you want to see better examples with `while`, check out the section titled "Cursors" later in the chapter.

Repeated Execution: *goto*

Here is goto—for the sake of completeness.

Syntax

```
goto label
...

label:
```

Example

```
declare @counter tinyint
select @counter = 0
top:
select @counter = @counter + 1
print "Structured programming scoffs at the goto"
if @counter <= 10
goto top
Structured programming scoffs at the goto
Structured programming scoffs at the goto
Structured programming scoffs at the goto
Structured programming scoffs at the goto
Structured programming scoffs at the goto
Structured programming scoffs at the goto
Structured programming scoffs at the goto
Structured programming scoffs at the goto
Structured programming scoffs at the goto
Structured programming scoffs at the goto
Structured programming scoffs at the goto
```

Example

```
goto label2
label1:
   insert into #mytemp values (1)
   return
label2:
   create table #mytemp  (a int)
   goto label1
error 208 invalid object name #mytemp
```

This example fails because the server cannot resolve the backward references.

Event Handling: *waitfor*

The `waitfor` statement is used to cause a query to pause for a period of time or until an event occurs. It is an event handler.

> **NOTE**
>
> SQL Server is an event handler.

Syntax

```
waitfor {delay "time" ¦ time "time" }
```

`delay` pauses for the specified amount of time. `time` waits until the specified time of day. The time specified for delay and time is in "hh:mi:ss" format—you cannot specify dates. `time` cannot exceed a 24-hour period, and you cannot specify a variable.

> **TIP**
>
> Although you cannot use a variable in the `waitfor time` or `waitfor delay` statement, you can use the `execute` statement to formulate a variable execution string like this one, which performs an action once per hour on the hour for a day (in this case, reports who is on line).
>
> ```
> declare @exec_string char(255),
>     @start datetime,
>     @ctr tinyint
> select @start = getdate(),
>     @ctr = datepart(hh, getdate())
> while datediff(hh, @start, getdate()) < 24
>     begin
>     select @exec_string = "waitfor time '"
>         + str(@ctr) + ":00:00'"
>     execute (@exec_string)
>     execute sp_who
>     end
> ```

Examples

```
/* Pauses until 10pm */
waitfor time "22:00:00"
/* display current logins every 30 seconds */
while 1 < 2
begin
    waitfor delay "00:00:30"
    exec sp_who
end
```

> **NOTE**
>
> Note that 1 will be less than 2 for a very, very long time!

return

To exit a batch unconditionally, use the `return` statement.

Syntax

```
return
```

Examples

```
select * from authors
print "finishing now"
```

```
return
/* return can be used with a conditional statement
** to terminate processing */
if not exists (select * from inventory
                where item_num = @item_num)
    begin
        raiserror 51345 "Not found"
        return
    end
print "No error found"
return
```

set Options

Options affect the way the server handles specific conditions. Options exist for the duration of
your connection, or for the duration of a stored procedure if used in a stored procedure.

Syntax

```
set condition {on | off | value}
```

Examples

```
/* instruct the server to return only the first 100 rows of data */
set rowcount 100
/* asks the server for the number of logical and physical page requests */
set statistics io on
/* requests execution time */
set statistics time on
/* tells the server to stop reporting the number of rows returned */
set nocount on
/* asks the server for the final optimization plan for the query */
set showplan on
/* parse and optimize, but don't execute the query (often used in conjunction
** with showplan for looking at a plan without running a query) */
set noexec on
/* checks the batch for syntax, and then stops. */
set parseonly on
```

Cursors

ANSI-SQL provides the capability of addressing a set of rows individually, one row at a time,
by a *cursor*. A cursor is a pointer that identifies a specific working row within a set. In this section, you explore the syntactic structures used to define and use cursors.

Before looking at how to use a cursor, you need to understand what cursors can do for your
application. Most SQL operations are set operations: a where clause defines the set of rows to
address, and the rest of the statement provides definitive instructions on what to do with
the rows.

Consider a typical reporting requirement in which the sales manager wants to evaluate the probable value of all sales opportunities for the next three months.

A typical table to track sales opportunities contains these columns:

```
create table leads
 (id int identity,
  cust int not null,
  est_sale int not null,
  close_date smalldatetime
      default dateadd(dd, 30, getdate()) not null,
  prob tinyint default 20 not null,
  sales_id char(3) not null,
  descr varchar(30) not null)
```

Here is some sample data that might occur in the leads table:

```
id  cust  est_sale  close_date         prob sales_id descr
--  ----  --------  ----------------   ---- -------- --------
 1   1    5000      Jan 17 1996 12:00AM 25   JJJ      software
 2   1    9000      Jan 28 1996 12:00AM 60   DDD      hardware
 3   1    9000      Jan 30 1995 12:00AM 70   RRR      hardware
 4   2    2000      Jan 31 1995 12:00AM 60   XXX      hardware
 5   3    8000      Jan 20 1995 12:00AM  5   MMM      misc
 6  12    2000      Jan 24 1995 12:00AM 95   PPP      software
 7   3    8000      Jan 19 1995 12:00AM 70   DDD      software
 8   1    2000      Jan 29 1995 12:00AM 50   JJJ      hardware
 9  23    4000       Feb 5 1995 12:00AM 55   DDD      hardware
10   1    2000      Jan 30 1995 12:00AM 55   SSS      hardware
11  43    4000      Jan 16 1995 12:00AM 25   RRR      software
12   2    6000       Feb 5 1995 12:00AM 50   AAA      misc
```

A simple sales projection method is to multiply the estimated sale (est_sale) by the probability of a sale occurring (prob), then total those discounted projections:

```
select est_total = sum(est_sale * prob)
from leads
```

Suppose that you want to write a sales projection that is far more scientific. Here are some facts you need to add to your sales projection:

- Some of the salespeople are way too optimistic, others too conservative. JJJ's probabilities are always 20 percent high, and DDD's are always 50 percent low.
- Customer number 2 is known for asking for bids he never buys. His projections should also be lowered by 80 percent (except JJJ's, which are already sufficiently discounted).

■ Anything projected for February should be discounted by an additional 20 percent.

■ Salespeople have been typically selling more hardware than they expect, so increase the sale amount in the projection by 15 percent.

Some Approaches

You could certainly write a program using a client-side application program, and many of these programs are written that way. What if there are 5 million lead rows, however? What impact will that have on your application?

You could use a set of temporary tables and build a standard query or set of queries to perform this step, but it might be easier to write a query that uses cursors, examining each row individually to see whether it fits any of the rules, and make any necessary adjustments.

> **NOTE**
>
> See earlier note. I really don't like cursors because they are *substantially* slower than the typical set processing mechanisms. In this chapter, I come not to praise cursors, but to bury them (that is, describe them).

Cursor Example and Some Syntax

Take a look at the following code. This is the actual cursor program to execute the sales projection, given the functional requirements stated previously.

```
declare leads_curs cursor for
select  cust_id, est_sale, close_date, prob, sales_id, descr
from leads
for read only

go

declare
  @cust_id int,
  @est_sale int,
  @close_date smalldatetime,
  @prob tinyint,
  @sales_id char(3),
  @descr varchar(30),
  @sum_sales int

select @sum_sales = 0

open leads_curs
fetch leads_curs into
  @cust_id, @est_sale, @close_date, @prob, @sales_id, @descr
```

```
while (@@fetch_status = 0)
begin
   if @sales_id - "DDD"            /* increase DDD's sales */
     select @prob = @prob * 1.5
   if @sales_id = "JJJ"            /* decrease JJJ's sales */
     select @prob = @prob * .8
   else
     if @cust_id = 2               /* decrease cust 2's sales */
       select @prob = @prob * .8
   if datepart(mm, @close_date) = 2 /* decrease feb sales */
     select @prob = @prob * .8
   if @descr = "hardware"          /* increase hardware sales */
     select @est_sale = @est_sale * 1.15

   select @sum_sales = @sum_sales + @est_sale * @prob / 100
   fetch leads_curs into
     @cust_id, @est_sale, @close_date, @prob, @sales_id, @descr
end

close leads_curs
select @sum_sales "Weighted projected sales"
deallocate leads_curs
go
```

Let's review in detail each element of the sample program.

Declaring Cursors

The sample program consists of two batches. The first batch creates the cursor; the second uses it.

```
declare leads_curs cursor for
select cust_id, est_sale, close_date, prob, sales_id, descr
from leads
for read only

go
```

The example declares a cursor that selects from a single table. The cursor will be used only to read values, not to update rows (for read only).

The cursor is optimized and compiled when it is declared. If the cursor contains a where clause and could use an index, it is a good idea to make it a SARG and support it with an index.

Cursor names are restricted by the same rules as object names—30 characters and no reserved characters. The select statement is a normal SELECT statement. (There are some restrictions, which are detailed later.)

Declaring Variables

When fetching rows (discussed in more detail later), you can do one of two things with cursor data:

- You can return the row to the user, in which case the data looks just like a one-row result set from a select statement.
- You can retrieve the data into variables.

```
declare
  @cust_id int,
  @est_sale int,
  @close_date smalldatetime,
  @prob tinyint,
  @sales_id char(3),
  @descr varchar(30),
  @sum_sales int

select @sum_sales = 0
```

In order to retrieve the data into variables, the variables need to be declared first. The variables should be of the same type and length as the columns specified in the select list of the select statement (no implicit conversion is allowed).

> **TIP**
>
> As a convention, you usually name the variables exactly the same as the column names in the select list. In the example, the columns are cust_id, est_sale, and so forth, and the variables are @cust_id, @est_sale, and so forth.

Opening Cursors

When you open a cursor, the server executes the select statement to fix the membership and ordering of the cursor set. When you open the cursor, the row pointer is above the first row in the cursor; you must fetch a row to move the pointer to the first row.

```
open leads_curs
```

You can repeatedly close and open a cursor. In that case, the cursor select is reexecuted to determine a revised ordering and membership for the set, and the row pointer is moved above the first row in the set again.

Fetching Rows

Once a cursor is open, you can fetch rows from the cursor set. In this case, the cursor is retrieving into variables. Note that one variable is required for every column in the select list.

```
fetch leads_curs into
  @cust_id, @est_sale, @close_date, @prob, @sales_id, @descr
```

The `fetch` keyword in this case is forward-going only. This means that each subsequent `fetch` statement moves you one row forward in the keyset. You will look at other ways to scroll through a cursor set with `fetch` in the "Scrolling Capabilities" section later in this chapter.

The Main Loop

This is the reason for writing a cursor, right? This is the main loop, where you retrieve all the rows one at a time, perform some conditional processing on each one, and then move on to the next.

```
while (@@fetch_status = 0)
begin
   if @sales_id = "DDD"            /* increase DDD's sales */
     select @prob = @prob * 1.5
   if @sales_id = "JJJ"            /* decrease JJJ's sales */
     select @prob = @prob * .8
   else
     if @cust_id = 2               /* decrease cust 2's sales */
        select @prob = @prob * .8
   if datepart(mm, @close_date) = 2 /* decrease feb sales */
     select @prob = @prob * .8
   if @descr = "hardware"          /* increase hardware sales */
     select @est_sale = @est_sale * 1.15

   select @sum_sales = @sum_sales + @est_sale * @prob / 100
   fetch leads_curs into
     @cust_id, @est_sale, @close_date, @prob, @sales_id, @descr
end
```

> **NOTE**
>
> This looks a lot like old-fashioned programming, something you might do in COBOL or PASCAL or BASIC. The problem is, SQL Server is rotten at old-fashioned programming.
>
> This program took about 8 seconds to run against 12 rows on my Pentium. (That's a long time for 12 rows!)
>
> The moral of the story is that old-fashioned programming is typically a bad choice in SQL Server. Write set-based programs whenever you can, even (most of the time) if it means making multiple passes of a single table or set of tables.

You should note the global variable, `@@FETCH_STATUS`, which has three states after you execute a `fetch` statement:

- `0` means that a row was successfully fetched.
- `-1` means that the fetch exceeded the results set (in this case, out of rows).

■ -2 means that the row returned is no longer in the table (it was deleted from the table after the cursor was opened but before the row was retrieved). In this case, the row retrieved will consist entirely of NULLs.

> **TIP**
>
> Some additional code is required in the main loop to handle the case when @@FETCH_STATUS is -2, and to do other appropriate error checking, before this result can go into production.

Closing the Cursor

When you finish working with a cursor, close it, then do your end-of-process programming. Some open cursors hold locks that block others' work, and an open cursor uses up other resources as well. You can reopen a closed cursor; the row pointer returns to the top of the set.

```
close leads_curs
select @sum_sales "Weighted projected sales"
```

Deallocating Cursors

When you finish working with a cursor, deallocate it. The cursor optimization plan takes up space in memory, so it should be freed up as soon as possible. Once a cursor is deallocated, you need to declare it again before issuing the open statement.

```
deallocate leads_curs
```

Updating with Cursors

The sales projection example demonstrates only how to read data by using a cursor. Cursors can also be used to modify (update or delete) rows in a table. In order to enable update and delete statements to deal with the current row in a cursor set, SQL Server includes the WHERE CURRENT OF cursor_name condition:

```
UPDATE table_name
SET column = expression [, column = expression[, ...]]
WHERE CURRENT OF cursor_name
DELETE table_name
WHERE CURRENT OF cursor_name
```

Here are a couple of examples:

```
update leads
set est_sale = est_sale * .8
where current of leads_curs
delete leads
where current of leads_curs
```

Cursor Declaration for Update

In order to update or delete using a cursor, you need to declare the cursor for update. Here is the complete syntax for the DECLARE statement:

```
DECLARE cursor_name [INSENSITIVE] [SCROLL] CURSOR
  FOR select_statement
  [FOR {READ ONLY ¦ UPDATE [OF column_list]}]
```

For now, let's look at the last line of the statement, where you set up the cursor as a read-only cursor or as an updatable cursor. (You look into INSENSITIVE and SCROLL in the next few pages.) If a cursor is declared as READ ONLY, you can only fetch rows, but you cannot use the WHERE CURRENT OF construction to modify the contents of the set.

In the example of the leads_curs, the updatable version looks like this:

```
declare leads_curs cursor for
select cust_id, est_sale, close_date, prob, sales_id, descr
from leads
```

You can declare a cursor FOR UPDATE or FOR UPDATE OF column_list. If you do not specify a list of columns, all columns in all tables are considered updatable. This means that you can update the contents of several tables during the processing of a cursor containing a join.

> **NOTE**
>
> Is it a good idea to update many tables using a single cursor? Possibly, but it seems as if it would be easy to get confused.

If you plan to update only one table in the cursor, but need to access information in another, the cursor should be declared FOR UPDATE. You can use the SHARED keyword to indicate which tables you will read from and which will be modified. In this example, you need to access the publishers table to increase prices on titles published in Massachusetts, but no modifications will be made to the publishers table:

```
declare tp cursor for
select title_id, type, price
from titles t, publishers p shared
where t.pub_id = p.pub_id
and state = "MA"
for update of price
```

In addition to limiting updates to the price column of the titles table, this cursor also maintains only shared locks on the publishers table, improving multi-user operations.

Scrolling Capabilities

If you use the keyword scroll in your cursor declaration statement, you can use fetch to move forward, backward, and to absolute row locations within the cursor set (the keyset).

For example, here is a scrollable version of the `leads_curs` declaration:

```
declare leads_curs scroll cursor for
select cust_id, est_sale, close_date, prob, sales_id, descr
from leads
for read only
```

Once you declare a cursor with the `scroll` keyword, the `fetch` statement is far more flexible. Here is the complete syntax for FETCH:

```
FETCH [[NEXT¦PRIOR¦FIRST¦LAST¦ABSOLUTE n¦RELATIVE n] FROM cursor_name
[INTO @variable_name1, @variable_name2, ...]
```

Let's look at some examples.

This is the standard `fetch` statement. The keyword `next` is optional. You do not need a scrollable cursor to use `next`:

```
fetch next from leads_curs
    into @cust_id, @est_sale, @close_date, @prob, @sales_id, @descr
```

Here, you retrieve the prior row:

```
fetch prior from leads_curs
    into @cust_id, @est_sale, @close_date, @prob, @sales_id, @descr
```

In this case, the cursor moves back one row. If the cursor is already on the first row of the set, the value of `@@fetch_status` is set to -1 to indicate that the `fetch` exceeded the cursor set.

This example retrieves the first row in the set:

```
fetch first from leads_curs
    into @cust_id, @est_sale, @close_date, @prob, @sales_id, @descr
```

Use `last` to fetch the last row in the set.

You also can retrieve a row in an absolute position in the set. For example, to retrieve the tenth row in the cursor, use this:

```
fetch absolute 10 from leads_curs
    into @cust_id, @est_sale, @close_date, @prob, @sales_id, @descr
```

Again, your program should check the value of `@@fetch_status` to be certain that the absolute position is valid.

NOTE

When you write a book, you have a tendency to ask unanswered questions, try things, and see what really works. It appears that the `absolute` option is really useful only if it can be used with a variable, as in this example:

```
/* Nice to have, but won't parse! */
fetch absolute @ctr from leads_curs ...
```

But variable expressions are not permitted in this position. The secret is to use the `execute` keyword to execute the `fetch` statement by first building it:

```
/* This works */
declare @ctr int, @fetchstmt varchar(50)
select @ctr = 5
select @fetchstmt =
  "fetch absolute " + str(@ctr) + " from tcurs "
execute (@fetchstmt)
```

I won't try to vouch for the performance you should expect with this approach. The combination of slow cursor performance and on-the-fly execution should give you something truly awful.

In general, avoid cursors. If you can't avoid cursors, avoid scrolling cursors. If you can't avoid scrolling cursors, avoid using the execute statement to do variable-driven, absolute addressing in the cursor.

The last `fetch` operator uses relative row scrolling:

```
fetch relative -5 from leads_curs
    into @cust_id, @est_sale, @close_date, @prob, @sales_id, @descr
```

Relative scrolling can be forward (positive values) or backward (negative values). This example scrolls back five rows in the set. Again, always check @@fetch_status after each relative scroll to make sure the new row position is still valid.

INSENSITIVE Cursors

If you declare a cursor with the INSENSITIVE keyword, the server makes a copy of the affected data into a temporary worktable. The contents of the worktable are what you actually see as you fetch rows in the cursor. The contents of an INSENSITIVE cursor do not change as the underlying data in the actual table changes, so you can use this mechanism to take a snapshot of data at a particular moment in time, then use a cursor to process and report on that data.

Obviously, an insensitive cursor is not updatable.

Avoiding Cursors

In general, you should try to avoid cursors. The sample cursor program took 8 seconds to process 12 rows. For the record, here is how you could use a CASE expression in a select statement to replace the cursor processing:

```
select "Sum of Sales" = sum(
    est_sale * prob * .01
    *
    CASE descr
    WHEN "hardware" THEN 1.15
    ELSE 1.
    END
    *
```

```
      CASE datepart(mm, close_date)
      WHEN 2 THEN .8
      ELSE 1.
      END
      *
      CASE sales_id
      WHEN "JJJ" THEN .8
      WHEN "DDD" THEN 1.5
      ELSE 1.
      END
      *
      CASE
      WHEN cust_id != 2 THEN 1.
      ELSE
          CASE sales_id
          WHEN "JJJ" THEN 1.
          ELSE .8
          END
      END
      )
from leads
```

This query took less than a second to run. On a large data set, a performance improvement of more than 80 percent is well worth a little hard work.

Summary

This chapter has considered the syntactic extensions and special features of the Transact-SQL. In the next chapters, you look at using these structures to manage transactions and write stored procedures and triggers.

Programming Structures

Table 6.8 summarizes the syntax presented in this chapter.

Table 6.8. Syntax summary.

Task	Syntax
Insert a comment	`/* multi-line comment`
	`[...]`
	`*/`
	`-- single-line comment`
Unconditional end of batch or procedure	`return`
Send a message	`print {character_string	@local_variable`
	`| @@global_variable } [ , arg_list ]`
Send an error message	`raiserror error_number`
	`{ character_string	@local_variable }`
	`[, arg_list]`
Register an error message	`sp_addmessage message_number, message_text`
Bind an error message to a constraint	`sp_bindmsg constraint_name, msg_number`
Declare a local variable	`declare @variable_name datatype`
	`[, ...]`
Set a local variable	`select @variable_name = expression`
	`[, ...] [from ... [where ...]]`
Evaluate a condition	`if boolean_expression`
	`{statement	statement_block}`
	`[else`
	`{statement	statement_block}]`

continues

Table 6.8. continued

Task	Syntax
Check for existence of rows	`if [not] exists (select_statement)`
	`{statement	statement_block}`
	`[else`
	`{statement	statement_block}]`
Create a statement block with `if` or `while`	`begin`
	`SQL_Statements`
	`end`
Execute repeatedly	`while boolean_condition`
	`{statement	statement_block}`
Declare a label execute from a labeled spot	`goto label`
	`...`
	`label:`
Wait for an event	`waitfor {delay "time"	time "time"	`
	`errorexit	processexit	mirrorexit}`
Modify the environment	`set condition {on	off	value}`

Transact-SQL
Program Structures

7

IN THIS CHAPTER

Now that you understand how to code batches, you need to find ways to make these batches permanent. This is done with triggers and stored procedures. *Triggers* are database objects that are bound directly to tables. *Stored procedures* exist independently from tables (although they typically reference tables).

Typical Trigger Uses

Why would you want to bind a collection of T-SQL statements directly to a table? There are a variety of good applications. The most common, probably, is enforcing special *referential integrity* (RI) requirements not supported by constraints. For example, by using a trigger, you can cascade updates and deletes of primary keys.

Triggers can enforce complex column rules. Check constraints can look in other columns in the same row, but cannot check other rows or other tables to verify data. A trigger can look practically anywhere to perform validation, and can even execute a remote procedure call to get information from another SQL Server or (through an extended stored procedure) a DLL in Windows NT that can access virtually any data source.

Another common trigger use is enforcing complex business rules. For example, if you want to make sure that salary increases do not exceed 25 percent, you could write a trigger to compare salary amounts before and after the calculation and, if necessary, undo (roll back) the changes, returning an error message to the client application.

Triggers are also used to maintain complex defaults. Chapter 5, "Creating and Altering Database Objects," shows how to implement declarative default values based on constant expressions (for example, the default value for country might be "USA") or a combination of constant expressions and system functions (default order date might use the getdate() function). Triggers enable you to define default values that depend on the values of other columns or even values from other tables. A common application for triggers is to provide accurate values for legislative districts or postal zones on the basis of address information entered by a user.

Finally, triggers can maintain duplicate data. For example, you could store mirror copies of data in other databases for performance reasons (although this is usually better handled by replication). It is very common to use triggers to maintain derived summary information. The ytd_sales column in the titles table is derived from the qty column in the sales table. The quantity of each entry in sales needs to be reflected in an increase in ytd_sales for that title.

When Is a Trigger Executed (Fired)?

A trigger is an integral part of the statement that fires it. This means that a statement is not complete until the trigger completes, and that any work done in the trigger will be part of the same transaction (unit of work) as the statement that caused the trigger to fire.

Without a trigger, a data-modification command works like this:

Command	Result
`delete publishers where`	Any existing RI constraints are checked.
	Row(s) are deleted if not referenced.

With a trigger, a data modification command works like this:

Command	Result
`delete publishers where`	Any existing RI constraints are checked.
	Row(s) deleted if not referenced.
	Execute commands in trigger and either roll back or allow deletion.

Triggers are executed only once for a single data-modification statement, regardless of the number of rows affected (zero, one or many). This means that if you delete, insert, or update multiple rows, your trigger code must take into account the possibility that multiple rows were affected.

Trigger Creation

A table can have up to three triggers—one each for `insert`, `update`, and `delete`—or a single trigger can be defined for any combination of the three.

Basic Syntax

To execute the `create trigger` statement, you need to provide a name for the trigger itself, along with the name of the table, and the action(s) that will fire it:

```
create trigger trigger_name
  on table_name
  for {insert ¦ update ¦ delete} [, ...]
as
SQL_Statements
[return]
```

Here is a simple example of a trigger:

```
create trigger titles_trigger
     on titles
     for insert
as
print "title inserted"
return
```

When the `insert` statement is executed for the `titles` table, the `"title inserted"` message is passed to the front end's message handler.

> **NOTE**
>
> This trigger is actually a problem. Remember that a trigger will fire one time, regardless of how many rows are affected by the statement. How many rows could be affected by an insert statement? That depends on the form of the insert statement that was executed. In this form, only one row could be inserted and the trigger is always correct:
>
> ```
> insert titles (column_list)
> values (value_list)
> ```
>
> But in the alternate form, where the insert statement uses a select statement to provide the inserted values, any number of rows could be inserted (zero, one, or many):
>
> ```
> insert titles (column_list)
> select column_list
> from table_name
> where conditions
> ```
>
> The trigger is a problem because it will report "title inserted" even when no rows were entered!
>
> The most important thing to take from this whole discussion of triggers is that triggers must handle the multi-row case.

To drop a trigger, use the drop trigger command.

> **TIP**
>
> Notice that when you drop a trigger you specify only the name of the trigger, not the name of the table. Be careful not to drop the wrong trigger inadvertently. To be certain that you are dropping the correct trigger, list the names of all the triggers for a table with this query:
>
> ```
> select name, object_name(instrig), object_name(deltrig), object_name(updtrig)
> from sysobjects
> where name = "table_name"
> and type = "U"
> ```

```
drop trigger trigger_name
```

You must be the table owner to modify an object's schema, which is what you are doing when you create a trigger on the table. Triggers do not take parameters and cannot be explicitly called or executed. This can make them difficult to debug. Be thorough.

Deleted and Inserted Tables

The inserted and deleted tables are special views of the transaction log that last for the duration of a trigger. They reflect the changes made in the table by the statement that caused the trigger to execute. The structure of the inserted and deleted tables exactly matches the structure of the table on which the trigger is created.

The inserted table contains the new rows that resulted from an insert or update. The deleted table contains the old rows that were removed as the result of a delete or update. Whenever there is an update trigger, SQL Server treats the update as a delete followed by an insert.

The inserted and deleted tables can be seen only inside a trigger and are unavailable once the trigger completes.

What Happens on Delete?

Figure 7.1 illustrates what happens when a delete trigger executes. After the T-SQL is issued, the trigger executes. The trigger sees the existing table as modified; this table has an exclusive lock on it that keeps other processes from reading the page until the lock is released. The trigger also sees the contents of the inserted and deleted tables, which are identical in structure to the publishers table. The deleted table has a row in it that corresponds to the row removed, and the inserted table is empty, due to the nature of the statement that caused it to fire.

FIGURE 7.1.

During execution of a delete *trigger, the inserted table is empty but a deleted table contains a copy of each of the deleted rows.*

publishers

pub_id	pub_name	city	state
0736	New Age Books	Boston	MA
0877	Binnet & Hardley	Washington	DC
1389	Algodata Infosystems	Berkeley	CA

1. Command executes:

```
delete publishers where pub_id = "0736"
```

2. The trigger sees:

publishers

pub_id	pub_name	city	state
0877	Binnet & Hardley	Washington	DC
1389	Algodata Infosystems	Berkeley	CA

deleted

pub_id	pub_name	city	state
0736	New Age Books	Boston	MA

inserted

pub_id	pub_name	city	state

Delete Trigger Example

Task: Write a `delete` *trigger for* `publishers` *that cascades deletions to the* `titles` *table.*

> **NOTE**
>
> What does *cascade* mean here? Cascading deletes means deleting rows in dependent tables. In an order-entry system, when you delete customers you also need to delete any orders by those customers.
>
> Some organizations do not allow cascaded deletions, whereas others require them. This is a case where your *business rules* can be reflected in the database structure.

Remember to check the number of rows affected (via `@@rowcount`) and return if `@@rowcount` is 0, because the `delete` statement causes the trigger to fire regardless of whether any rows were deleted.

Solution

```
create trigger cascade_del_trigger
     on publishers
     for delete
as

if @@rowcount = 0  -- no rows deleted
    return

/* cascade delete of pub_id(s) to related */
/* rows in titles table */
delete titles
    from titles t, deleted d
    where t.pub_id = d.pub_id

if @@error != 0
    begin
    print "Error occurred deleting related titles"     rollback tran
    end

return
```

Note some key features of the code. First, you check to see whether any rows were modified. Remember, the trigger fires whether data was modified or not; execution is dependent on execution of the T-SQL statement, not on whether the `delete` statement found any rows to delete.

> **NOTE**
>
> This is important. A `delete` statement could fail to find any rows but could require an exclusive, table-level lock just to look for rows. That lock would be retained right through the execution of the trigger, so it is critical *in all cases* to return from trigger execution as quickly as possible.

Next, because the list of modified rows is no longer available in the table, you look for the modified rows in the `deleted` table. In fact, you join the `titles` table (the table containing rows to be deleted from the trigger) to the `deleted` table so that you can remove the appropriate rows.

Finally—and this is very important—you check the return code of your T-SQL statement to trap any error conditions.

> **NOTE**
>
> This code *does not* check for any dependencies of the `titles` table. You have to write a trigger on the `titles` table to affect tables such as `sales` and `titleauthor`, which contain the `title_id`.

What Happens on Insert?

Figure 7.2 illustrates the `inserted` and `deleted` tables during an insert. At insert time, you see the modified `titles` table (although nobody else can) and the inserted row in the `inserted` table.

Handling Multi-Row Inserts and Updates

SQL Server enables multi-row inserts in a single `insert` statement via the `insert... select...` syntax. If inserting or updating multiple rows whose foreign key values need to be checked, the trigger should compare the count of all rows inserted or updated against a count of rows that contain valid keys. Here's how:

- Find out how many rows (with `count(*)`) are found when you join the `inserted` table to the primary key table.

- Compare that number to the value of `@@rowcount` at the beginning of the trigger. (Remember to store `@@rowcount` in a local variable before performing any operations affecting it within the trigger.)

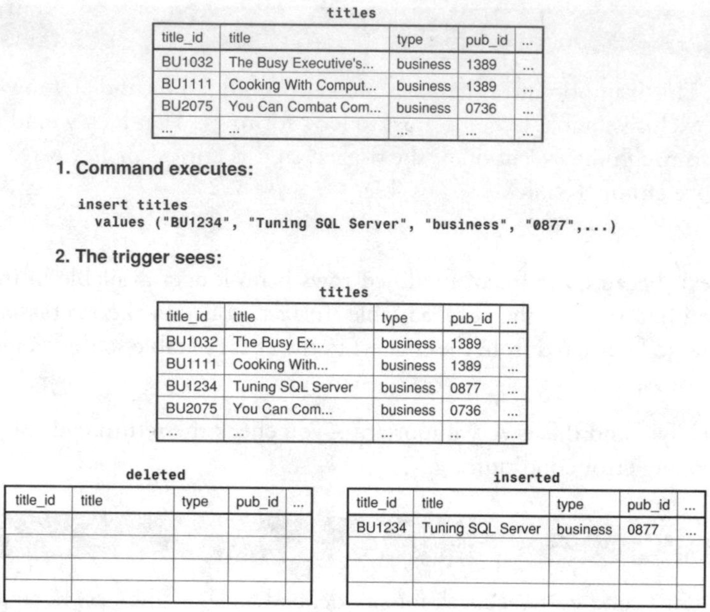

FIGURE 7.2.

When a trigger executes during an insert, the inserted *table contains the row or rows inserted by the operation. The* deleted *table is always empty.*

titles

title_id	title	type	pub_id	...
BU1032	The Busy Executive's...	business	1389	...
BU1111	Cooking With Comput...	business	1389	...
BU2075	You Can Combat Com...	business	0736	...
...	...	...	...	

1. Command executes:

```
insert titles
    values ("BU1234", "Tuning SQL Server", "business", "0877",...)
```

2. The trigger sees:

titles

title_id	title	type	pub_id	...
BU1032	The Busy Ex...	business	1389	...
BU1111	Cooking With...	business	1389	...
BU1234	Tuning SQL Server	business	0877	...
BU2075	You Can Com...	business	0736	...
...	...	...	...	

deleted

title_id	title	type	pub_id	...

inserted

title_id	title	type	pub_id	...
BU1234	Tuning SQL Server	business	0877	...

If the values are not equal, at least one of the rows is invalid.

```
create trigger tr1
on my_table
for insert, update
as
declare @rows int
select @rows = @@rowcount
if @rows = 0 return
if (select count(*) from inserted i, pkey_tab p
    where i.fkey = p.pkey) != @rows
/* At least one of the inserted/updated rows
   does not match a primary key */
/*  begin error processing */
begin
    raiserror (55555, 16, 1)
    rollback tran
    return
end
return
```

Because every SQL statement modifies @@rowcount, you must store its value (the number of rows modified by the statement that causes the trigger to fire) as soon as you enter the trigger. (declare is the only SQL statement that does not modify @@rowcount.)

In the example, you join the inserted table (that is, each row that is newly entering the table) to the list of *valid* foreign keys (that is, the primary keys in the parent table). If the number of rows in the result set of this join matches the number of rows inserted, referential integrity is preserved. If not, something is invalid and other error processing needs to take place.

NOTE

Do you actually manage referential integrity using triggers? Not unless you have special RI requirements. Constraints perform the same task more easily, more efficiently, and with less code to write and maintain.

What are some "special requirements" that would justify a trigger? What if you needed to allow specific users to violate RI, but only if they entered a special override code? A constraint could never handle that set of requirements, but it would be easy in a trigger. What if you needed to allow a user to enter a non-existent customer ID in an order, but if one were found, the system should enter the ID into the customer table automatically (this is sometimes called a *trickle*, the opposite of a *cascade*)? A trigger could find non-existent rows and enter them in another table.

Triggers exist to enforce the *special rules* that govern data integrity. Much day-to-day validation should be handled by constraints, rules, defaults, and other, lower-overhead structures. Only use a trigger when there is no other way around it.

TIP

When SQL Server executes `rollback transaction` in a trigger, the server cancels all work done so far within the trigger and the transaction that fired the trigger, completes work within the trigger, then *stops all processing on the batch*, returning control to the client application.

When you find a data consistency error in a trigger, it is almost always best simply to roll back the transaction rather than try to find the individual row update(s) that violate your business rules. Remember that triggers fire in the middle of a transaction, while locks are still held open. Long-running triggers, and particularly triggers that use cursors to validate individual rows in the inserted and deleted tables, cause online SQL Server systems to perform horribly.

Also, always raise an error when you roll back the transaction. If you roll back but do not raise an error, the user receives no information whatsoever from SQL Server that anything went wrong and will believe that his data modification was successful!

if update Test

The `if update` test provides a mechanism to find out whether a specific column has been modified during an insert or update operation. If a trigger checks the validity of a column, it should only do so if the value of the column has changed (or if dependent columns change). You can use the `if update()` test to improve the performance of your system by avoiding unnecessary work re-testing data that has previously been checked.

Syntax

```
if update (col_name)
    [ { and ¦ or } update (col_name) ...]
```

The test is true when either of the following conditions is true:

■ A non-null value has been inserted into the column.

■ The column was named in the set clause of an update statement (this does *not* necessarily mean the column's value changed).

Inserting Trigger Example

Task: Verify the referential integrity of the titles row(s) inserted into titles against the publishers table. Roll back the insert transaction if any rows violate RI.

Solution

```
create trigger tr_titles_i
on titles
for insert
as
declare @rows int   -- create variable to hold @@rowcount
select @rows = @@rowcount

if @rows = 0        -- no rows inserted, exit trigger
return

/* check if pub_id was inserted and if all pub_ids
   inserted are valid pub_ids in the publishers table */
if update(pub_id)  -- was an explicit pub_id inserted?
  and (select count(*)
      from inserted i, publishers p
      where p.pub_id = i.pub_id ) != @rows
  begin
    raiserror 33333 "Invalid pub_id inserted"
    rollback transaction
  end

return
```

In this example, you act only if rows were modified. You also act only if the column you care about (in this case, the foreign key) is affected by the SQL statement. This is true for either insert or update. As in the prior join example, you want the count of the join to match the count of the rows affected, thus demonstrating RI.

Conditional Inserting Trigger Example

Task: Verify the referential integrity of the titles row(s) inserted into titles against the publishers table. Remove any rows from titles that violate RI and allow the rest to remain in the table.

Solution

```
create trigger tr_titles_i
on titles
for insert
as
declare @rows int  -- create variable to hold @@rowcount
select @rows = @@rowcount

if @rows = 0        -- no rows inserted, exit trigger
return

/* check if pub_id was inserted and if all pub_ids
   inserted are valid pub_ids in the publishers table
   delete any invalid rows from titles */
if update(pub_id)  -- was an explicit pub_id inserted?
  and (select count(*)
       from inserted i, publishers p
       where p.pub_id = i.pub_id ) != @rows
  begin
  delete titles
     from titles t, inserted i
     where t.pub_id = i.pub_id
     and i.pub_id not in
         (select pub_id from publishers)
  raiserror 33334 "Some Invalid pub_id(s) not inserted"
  end

return
```

The only new code in this example identifies the rows in the deleted table that failed the test and should be deleted from the table. The query compares the rows returned by the subquery to the rows in the inserted table to determine which rows need to be removed from the titles table.

This is another example of a trigger that provides special RI capabilities to the database designer. If a constraint were used to enforce RI, it would refuse all the inserted rows if any individual row were invalid. Similarly, a trigger would ordinarily test all the rows in the set and simply roll back the whole insert if any individual row were invalid. This trigger allows only valid rows to be entered but permits partial transactions to be completed.

What Happens on Update?

Remember, the update is a delete followed by an insert. As a result, you get a row in both the inserted and deleted tables. (See Figure 7.3.) The nifty thing about this is the capability of comparing *before* and *after* images of the data.

FIGURE 7.3.

During an update *trigger, there will always be the same number of rows in the* deleted *table as in the* inserted *table. The* deleted *table contains the rows prior to the update, and the* inserted *table contains the modified rows.*

salesdetail

stor_id	ord_num	title_id	qty	discount
7896	234518	TC3218	75	40.0
7896	234518	TC7777	75	40.0
7131	Asoap432	TC3218	50	40.0
...	...	...	...	...

1. Command executes:

```
update salesdetail
  set qty = 100
  where stor_id = 7896
  and ord_num = 234518
  and title_id = TC3218
```

2. The trigger sees:

salesdetail

stor_id	ord_num	title_id	qty	discount
7896	234518	TC3218	100	40.0
7896	234518	TC7777	75	40.0
7131	Asoap432	TC3218	50	40.0
...	...	...	...	...

deleted

stor_id	ord_num	title_id	qty	discount
7896	234518	TC3218	75	40.0

inserted

stor_id	ord_num	title_id	qty	discount
7896	234518	TC3218	100	40.0

Updating Trigger Example

Task: When a salesdetail *row is inserted or updated, update the corresponding summary value,* total_sales, *in the* titles *table.*

Solution

```
create trigger tr_total_sales
on sales
for update, insert
as
declare @rows int   -- create variable to hold @@rowcount
select @rows = @@rowcount
if @rows = 0        -- no rows inserted, exit trigger
    return
/* update the ytd_sales in titles with qty
** in modified salesdetail rows */
if update(qty)
  begin
  update titles
    set ytd_sales = isnull(ytd_sales, 0)
/* use isnull function in case of no value */
/* use subqueries to get total inserts and deletions */
    + (select isnull(sum(i.qty), 0)
        from inserted i
        where i.title_id = titles.title_id)
```

```
          - (select isnull(sum(d.qty), 0)
              from deleted d
              where d.title_id = titles.title_id)
    end
return
```

This trigger uses two *correlated subqueries* to match modifications to the `sales` table to the corresponding rows in the `titles` table. SQL Server matches each title with relevant modifications, calculating the new value of `ytd_sales` based on the total of related values in `inserted` and `deleted`.

Trigger Limitations

The following SQL statements are not permitted in triggers:

- Any `create` command (this includes creation of temp tables; if you need to create a temporary table in a trigger, call a stored procedure that does that work)
- Any `drop` command
- `alter table/database`
- `grant`
- `revoke`
- `select into` (table creation)
- `truncate table`
- `update statistics`
- `reconfigure`
- `load database/transaction`
- `disk init/mirror/reinit/refit/remirror/unmirror`

Triggers During Transactions

A trigger is an integral part of the statement that fired it and of the transaction in which that statement occurs. `rollback transaction` inside a trigger rolls back all work to the outermost `begin transaction` statement, aborts processing in the trigger and the current batch:

```
/* trigger on the table called on insert */
create trigger tr_titles_i on titles for insert as
declare @rows int  -- create variable to hold @@rowcount
select @rows = @@rowcount
if @rows = 0 return
if update(pub_id) and (select count(*)
      from inserted i, publishers p
      where p.pub_id = i.pub_id ) != @rows
  begin
      rollback transaction
      raiserror 33333 "Invalid pub_id inserted"
  end
return
```

```
/* transaction inserts rows into a table */
begin tran add_titles
insert titles (title_id, pub_id, title)
    values ('BU1234', '0736', 'Tuning SQL Server')
insert titles (title_id, pub_id, title)
    values ('BU1235', 'abcd', 'Tuning SQL Server')
insert titles (title_id, pub_id, title)
    values ('BU1236', '0877', 'Tuning SQL Server')
commit tran
```

How many rows are inserted if `'abcd'` is an invalid `pub_id`? No rows are inserted because, unlike `rollback transaction` in a procedure, a `rollback transaction` statement in a trigger aborts the rest of the batch.

Statements subsequent to a `rollback transaction` within a trigger are executed. Remember to return following a `rollback transaction` in a trigger to prevent unwanted results. Do not issue `begin transaction` statements in a transaction. A transaction is already active at the time the trigger is executed.

You can set a savepoint in a trigger and roll back to the savepoint. Only the statements in the trigger subsequent to the savepoint are rolled back. The transaction will still be active until subsequently committed or rolled back; the batch will continue.

Do not roll back to a named transaction from within a trigger. This generates a run-time error, rolls back all work, and aborts the batch. For best results, include `save transaction` or `rollback transaction` statements in triggers.

Nested Triggers

If a trigger performs an `insert`, `update`, or `delete` on another table that has a trigger defined for that action, by default, that trigger will also fire. This is called a *nested trigger*. (See Figure 7.4.)

FIGURE 7.4.

A nested trigger on `table_b` *fires as part of the transaction on* `table_a`.

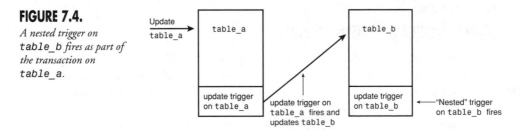

Triggers are limited to 16 levels of nesting. Check `@@nestlevel` to avoid exceeding limits. Nested triggers cannot see the contents of the `inserted` and `deleted` tables for other triggers. Nesting of triggers can be disabled at the server level by a system administrator with `sp_configure`.

Some Other Information about Triggers

Triggers are not *recursive*; that is, they do not fire if the trigger modifies its own table. Triggers do fire when a table is modified by a trigger on another table.

If you define a new trigger for a given action on a table, the most recently defined trigger takes precedence. If the old trigger is no longer defined for any action, the old trigger is automatically dropped. For example, after these two `create trigger` statements, the trigger ABC is dropped because XYZ is the current trigger for both `insert` and `update`.

```
create trigger ABC on A for insert, update as ...

create trigger XYZ on A for insert, update as ...
```

In the next example, ABC is not dropped because XYZ only handles the insert operation; ABC is still responsible for updates.

```
create trigger ABC on A for insert, update as ...

create trigger XYZ on A for insert as ...
```

A trigger does not have to be dropped before being re-created for the same single action (`insert`, `update`, or `delete`) on a table, but any new trigger must have a different name from any other existing object, including the trigger it is meant to replace.

Triggers do not override existing permissions; instead, they take advantage of the existing permission structure. If a user does not have permission to update a table directly, it cannot be updated via a trigger on another table on which the user has update permission unless both tables are owned by the same user. (Please refer to Chapter 27, "Security and User Administration," for more on the issue of security on dependent objects.)

Triggers cannot be defined on temporary tables or views. If modifying data through a view, triggers on the underlying tables are executed.

Triggers can execute stored procedures, including remote stored procedures. Work performed by local stored procedures (procedures executed on the local SQL Server) are treated as part of the fundamental transaction for the purposes of recovery and rollback. Work performed by remote procedure calls is not treated as part of a transaction (transactions cannot span SQL Servers as of Version 6.0), so that work cannot be recovered or rolled back.

Cursors can be used in triggers. Some uses for cursors in triggers include custom logging, maintaining duplicate data, and performing actions in individual rows in the `inserted`/`deleted` tables. Be extremely careful how you use cursors in triggers: the performance penalty introduced by cursors can cause major performance and concurrency problems.

214

Trigger overhead, like stored-procedure overhead, is relatively low. Nevertheless, it is useful to try to avoid doing work in triggers when an alternative method is available.

An `insert` trigger will not fire when you are bulk-loading data with the `bcp` program. A `delete` trigger will not fire when you issue the `truncate table` command.

Do not use `select` statements that return result sets to the end user within a trigger. An application issuing an `insert` command will most likely not be expecting (or be coded to process) result rows. Return information from triggers using `raiserror`.

Examining Triggers

You can use the SQL-EM Manage Triggers dialog box to retrieve and type the text of triggers. First, select a table for the trigger. Then use the Manage Triggers menu option. This will open a dialog box in which you can write new triggers, or retrieve and even modify existing triggers.

You can also perform a number of trigger-maintenance functions with SQL statements. List all tables and their triggers with this `select` statement:

```
/* display user tables and triggers */
select name, user_name(uid),
    "insert trigger" = object_name(instrig),
    "update trigger" = object_name(updtrig),
    "delete trigger" = object_name(deltrig)
  from sysobjects
  where type = "U"
  order by name
```

name		insert trigger	update trigger	delete trigger
authors	dbo			
discounts	dbo			
employee	dbo	employee_insupd	employee_insupd	
jobs	dbo			
pub_info	dbo			
publishers	dbo			
roysched	dbo			
sales	dbo	tr_total_sales	tr_total_sales	
stores	dbo			
titleauthor	dbo			
titles	dbo	tr_titles_i		

(11 rows affected)

Sort Order: name

Display trigger text with the following:

```
sp_helptext trigger_name
```

```
sp_helptext tr_total_sales
```

To list all objects referenced within a trigger, use this:

```
sp_depends trigger_name
```

```
sp_depends tr_total_sales

In the current database the specified object references the following:
name                                    type              updated selected
---------------------------------------- ---------------- ------- --------
dbo.jobs                                user table        no      no
dbo.employee                            user table        no      no
( 1 row affected)
```

To list all triggers and stored procedures that reference a table, use this:

```
sp_depends table_name

sp_depends employee

In the current database the specified object is referenced by the following:
name                                    type
---------------------------------------- ----------------
dbo.employee_insupd                     trigger
( 1 row affected)
```

Stored Procedures

A *stored procedure* is a database object that exists independently of a table. It can be called from a client, parameters can be passed and returned, and error codes can be checked. This section explores the following topics:

- Creating stored procedures
- Passing parameters in and out
- Handling return codes
- Effects on the optimizer

Stored Procedure Advantages

Store procedures provide many benefits over executing large and complex SQL batches from a client workstation:

- *Faster execution.* Stored procedures, after their first execution, become memory-resident and do not need to be reparsed, reoptimized, and recompiled.
- *Reduced network traffic.* Less SQL needs to cross busy network lines.
- *Modular programming.* You now have a way of breaking things into digestible pieces.
- *Restricted, function-based access to tables.* You can grant permissions in such a way as to allow a user access to tables *only* through the stored procedure.
- *Reduced operator error.* There is less information to pass.
- *Enforced consistency.* If users are accessing tables only through your stored procedures, ad-hoc modifications go away.
- *Automated complex or sensitive transactions.*

Running Stored Procedures

Stored procedures improve overall system performance by reducing network traffic and the optimization and compilation by the SQL Server:

First Execution	*Subsequent Executions*
Locate stored procedure on disk and load into cache.	Locate stored procedure in cache.
Substitute parameter values.	Substitute parameter values.
Develop optimization plan.	
Compile optimization plan.	
Execute from cache.	Execute from cache.

Note that the second time the stored procedure is run, it is in memory and is that much faster to locate. You do not need to parse, optimize, or create an executable, and that saves time as well.

> **NOTE**
>
> Later, you will see that skipping the optimize step is not always a good thing!

Creating Stored Procedures

To write a stored procedure, you need to provide the procedure with a unique name and then write the sequence of SQL statements to be included in the procedure. It is good programming practice to end the stored procedure with a return statement. Here is the simplified syntax for a stored procedure, and a quick example:

```
create proc procedure_name
as
SQL statements
[return [status_value]]

create proc pub_titles
as
select t.title, p.pub_name
  from publishers p, titles t
  where p.pub_id = t.pub_id
return
```

To execute a stored procedure, simply invoke it by name (just like you executed system stored procedures like sp_help). Use the execute keyword if the call to the stored procedure is not the first statement in the batch.

> **NOTE**
>
> Some of these rules seem awfully arbitrary unless you think about how the parser works. If the parser sees an unknown word appearing first in the batch, it tries to find a stored procedure with that name. In most other contexts, it will simply try to fit that unknown name into the syntax of the current statement being executed.
>
> For example, the parser might think that the stored procedure call in this next example was an alias for the titles table:
>
> ```
> select * from titles
> sp_help
> ```
>
> The server needs to know that this unknown word is really the name of a stored procedure. You indicate this with the execute keyword:
>
> ```
> select * from titles
> execute sp_help
> ```
>
> Whenever you are having a problem understanding the parsing and syntax rules, try to be a parser yourself and see if you can make sense out of the syntax you sent the SQL Server!

```
[exec[ute]] proc_name
```

```
pub_titles
```

```
exec pub_titles
```

```
title                                              pub_name
The Busy Executive's Database Guide                Algodata Infosystems
Cooking with Computers: Surreptitious Balance Sheets  Algodata Infosystems
You Can Combat Computer Stress!                    New Moon Books
Straight Talk About Computers                      Algodata Infosystems
Silicon Valley Gastronomic Treats                  Binnet & Hardley
The Gourmet Microwave                              Binnet & Hardley
The Psychology of Computer Cooking                 Binnet & Hardley
But Is It User Friendly?                           Algodata Infosystems
Secrets of Silicon Valley                          Algodata Infosystems
Net Etiquette                                      Algodata Infosystems
Computer Phobic AND Non-Phobic Individuals: Behavior Varia  Binnet & Hardley
Is Anger the Enemy?                                New Moon Books
Life Without Fear                                  New Moon Books
Prolonged Data Deprivation: Four Case Studies      New Moon Books
Emotional Security: A New Algorithm                New Moon Books
Onions, Leeks, and Garlic: Cooking Secrets of the Mediterr  Binnet & Hardley
Fifty Years in Buckingham Palace Kitchens          Binnet & Hardley
Sushi, Anyone?                                     Binnet & Hardley
```

To drop a stored procedure, use the drop proc statement:

```
drop proc proc_name
```

SQL Server and Temporary Stored Procedures

Microsoft SQL Server provides the capability to create temporary and global temporary stored procedures. By putting a # as the first character, a *temporary stored procedure* is unique to a user connection and is destroyed either when the user disconnects or when the server is shut down. *Global temporary procedures* begin with ## and are available to *any* user connection.

Display and Maintenance

Procedures can be renamed by using sp_rename. To modify a stored procedure, drop the procedure and re-create it; a stored procedure must be dropped before it can be re-created with the same name by the same user.

You cannot drop and re-create an object in the same batch. The following batch fails because SQL Server parses the whole batch before execution. When it reaches the create proc statement with the parser and checks to make sure that no such procedure exists before creating it, the procedure is still there so the whole batch fails:

```
/* this batch will fail to execute ... why?
Objects cannot be dropped and created in the same batch */
drop proc titles_for_a_pub
create proc titles_for_a_pub
as ...
```

The next example includes a go statement, which separates the two executions into separate batches. This example works fine:

```
/* this batch succeeds because drop and create are in separate batches */
drop proc titles_for_a_pub
go
create proc titles_for_a_pub
as ...
```

A better method is the following:

```
/* check if the procedure exists and drop it */
if exists (select * from sysobjects
    where name = "titles_for_a_pub"
    and type = "P" and uid = user_id())
  drop proc titles_for_a_pub
go
create proc titles_for_a_pub
as ...
```

Why even worry about this? It is a standard and very important practice to maintain copies of your stored procedures in scripts, both for documentation and for capability of modifying the procedures (there is no "modify procedure" or "alter procedure" statement).

To display text of a stored procedure in the database in which it was created, use the following:

```
sp_helptext procedure_name
```

```
sp_helptext titles_for_a_pub

text
----------------------------------------------------------
create proc titles_for_a_pub
    (@pub_name varchar(40))
as
select t.title from publishers p, titles t
    where p.pub_id = t.pub_id
    and pub_name like @pub_name
return

( 0 rows affected)
```

> **NOTE**
>
> SQL Enterprise Manager will reverse-engineer this information from the system table, `syscomments`, where the text of stored procedures (and triggers and views) is stored.

sp_help reports parameters' names and datatypes for a stored procedure.

```
sp_help procedure_name

sp_help titles_for_a_pub
```

Name	Owner	Type	When_created
titles_for_a_pub	dbo	stored procedure	Nov 16 1995 3:58PM

```
( 0 rows affected)
```

Data_located_on_segment
not applicable

```
( 0 rows affected)
```

Parameter_name	Type	Length	Prec	Scale	Param_order
@pub_name	varchar	40	40		1

```
( 0 rows affected)
```

Procedures and Parameters

Stored procedures can accept parameters to improve their usefulness and flexibility. The parameters are declared at the top of the procedure.

```
create proc procedure_name
    (parameter_name datatype [, ...])
as
SQL Statements
[return [status_value]]

[exec[ute]] procedure_name [expression] [, ... ]
```

Here is an example of a stored procedure with a single parameter, @pub_name. You need to declare a datatype for parameters, and you can use user-defined datatypes if they exist in the database where the procedure is created.

```
create proc titles_for_a_pub
    (@pub_name varchar(40))
as
select t.title from publishers p, titles t
    where p.pub_id = t.pub_id
    and pub_name like @pub_name
return
```

In this procedure, you are going to pass in a publisher name and perform a lookup based on that publisher name. Note that you use the `like` operator and therefore can do some pattern matching.

Example: Procedure Usage

Here is an example of how a procedure with a parameter might be used. Note that the quotes around the parameter value, Algo%, were required because the string included a special character, "%". Quotes are also required around character data that includes spaces, punctuation, or any reserved words.

```
titles_for_a_pub 'Algo%'

title
--------------------------------------------------------
The Busy Executive's Database Guide
Cooking with Computers: Surreptitious Balance Sheets
Straight Talk About Computers
But Is It User Friendly?
Secrets of Silicon Valley
Net Etiquette
( 6 rows affected)

exec titles_for_a_pub 'New Moon Books'

title
--------------------------------------------------------
You Can Combat Computer Stress!
Is Anger the Enemy?
Life Without Fear
Prolonged Data Deprivation: Four Case Studies
Emotional Security: A New Algorithm
( 5 rows affected)
```

Parameter names, like local variables, require an at sign (@), and can be up to 29 characters in length. You are still restricted by all the other SQL Server naming guidelines (no spaces or punctuation, case sensitivity, and so on). You can define up to 255 parameters per procedure.

If you use user-defined datatypes, be careful that they are defined in the database (and are not inadvertently deleted!). Rules, defaults, and column properties such as nullability and identity do not apply to parameters defined with user-defined datatypes. All parameters are nullable.

Microsoft SQL Server can use text and image datatypes as read-only stored procedure parameters.

Executing with Parameters

At execution time, parameters can be specified by position or by name. If passed by name, parameters can be passed in any order. Here is the basic syntax.

```
[exec[ute]] procedure_name
    [[@parm_name = ]expression] [, ... ]
```

Here is an example of a stored procedure that requires three parameters.

```
create proc myproc
    (@val1 int, @val2 int, @val3 int)
as
...
go
```

In this example, the parameters are passed by position. The execute statement does not provide any parameter names, so the values are assigned to the parameters in the order they were defined in the create statement (@val1, @val2, @val3).

```
/* parameters passed by position here */
exec myproc 10,20,15
```

In this example the parameters are passed by name. The execute statement provides specific parameter names for each value, so the values are assigned to the parameters explicitly according to the specifications of the execute statement.

```
/* parameter passed by name here */
exec myproc @val2 = 20, @val1 = 10, @val3 = 15
```

After you start passing parameters by name, all subsequent parameters must be passed by name.

Passing parameters by name is more flexible and self-documenting than passing parameters by position; however, passing by position is marginally faster.

Default Parameter Values

Stored procedure parameters can be assigned default values if no value is supplied during execution. You can improve your stored procedure code by defining defaults for all parameters.

```
create proc procedure_name
     (@parameter_name datatype = default_value
     [,...])
as
SQL Statements
[return [status_value]]
```

Example: Procedure Creation

```
/* check for a pub_name before executing query */
create proc titles_for_a_pub
     (@pub_name varchar(40) = null)
as
if @pub_name = null
  begin
  print "Pass in the pub_name as a parameter"
  return
  end
select t.title from publishers p, titles t
     where p.pub_id = t.pub_id
     and pub_name like @pub_name + "%"
return
```

Here, you pass in a parameter and verify that the parameter has actually being passed. If you had not specified a default, SQL Server would have sent a generic error message (and the procedure would not execute) if no procedure name were passed at execution time. If you specify a default value for a parameter, the stored procedure executes, giving you the chance to check the default and take action within the stored procedure.

If you execute without providing a parameter value, you get this error message:

```
/* without a parameter, you get the message */
titles_for_a_pub
go

Pass in the pub_name as a parameter
```

If you provide a parameter, you get the typical procedure execution:

```
/* with a parameter, you get the results */
titles_for_a_pub "Algo%"
go

title
------------------------------------------------
The Busy Executive's Database Guide
Cooking with Computers:Surreptitious Balance Sheets
Straight Talk About Computers
But is it User Friendly
Secrets of Silicon Valley
Net Etiquette
```

Passing Parameters In and Out

Stored procedure parameters can be passed both in and out. The output keyword identifies parameters that can be returned to the calling batch or procedure. Notice in the syntax the use of output in both the create proc and execute statements.

```
create proc procedure_name
  [ (@parm_name datatype = default_value [output]
  [, ... ] )]
as
SQL Statements
[return [status_value]]

[exec[ute]] procedure_name
     [[@parm_name = ] expression [output] [, ... ]
```

In this example, the procedure accepts two parameters, @title and @ytd_sales. The second parameter is keyed for output, meaning that its value at the end of the procedure will be available for return to the calling process. The procedure finds a row in the titles table for the @title value and then stores the value of the ytd_sales for that title in the parameter.

```
/* passing a parameter back to calling batch */
create proc ytd_sales
  (@title varchar(80) = null,
   @ytd_sales int output)
as
if @title = null
  begin
  print "Syntax: ytd_sales title, @variable [output]"
  return
  end
select @ytd_sales = ytd_sales
  from titles
  where title = @title
return
```

The execute statement needs to declare a variable to store the returned value (@sales_figure). The datatype of the variable should match the datatype of the output parameter. The execute statement itself needs to include the keyword output to complete the chain and permit the value of the parameter to be returned to the variable. The final select statement demonstrates the use of that returned value.

```
/* variable must be set up first to accept output value
** in this example, total sales are returned by position */
declare @sales_figure int
exec ytd_sales 'But Is It User Friendly?', @sales_figure output
select 'ytd sales of But Is It User Friendly?  = ', @sales_figure
go

---------------------------------------- ----------
ytd sales of But Is It User Friendly?  =  8780
( 1 row affected)
```

This example shows the same execution as directly above, except that the parameters are passed by name (@title = ...) instead of position.

```
/* in this example, total sales are returned by name */
declare @sales_figure int
exec total_sales @title= 'But Is It User Friendly?',
                 @ytd_sales = @sales_figure output
print "total sales of But Is It User Friendly?= %1!", @sales_figure
go
```

Returning Procedure Status

Every stored procedure automatically returns an integer status value: 0 is returned on success-ful completion, -1 through -99 are returned for SQL Server detected errors. Use a `return` state-ment to specify a return value greater than 0 or less than -99. The calling program can set up a local variable to receive and check the return status. Here's the syntax for the creation and the execution:

```
create proc procedure_name
 [ (@parm_name datatype = default_value [output]
   [, ... ] ) ]
as
SQL Statements
return [integer_status_value]

[execute] [@status_var = procedure_name
    [[@parm_name = ] expression [output] [, ... ]
```

When you create the procedure you need to define any error conditions and associate them with integral error codes. It's best if the error codes are well defined and consistent throughout your application (or, even better, throughout your organization). They must at least be docu-mented and well defined between a stored procedure and a calling batch. In this example, the value 15 means that the user failed to provide a necessary parameter, the value -101 means that no publisher with the specified name was found, and the value, and the value 0 means that the procedure ran without error. In a long stored procedure, it is useful to define error states in a comment in the procedure header.

```
/* procedure sets an error status on error */
create proc titles_for_a_pub
    (@pub_name varchar(40) = null ) as
if @pub_name = null
    return 15
if not exists (select * from publishers
        where pub_name = @pub_name)
    return -101
select t.title from publishers p, titles t
    where p.pub_id = t.pub_id
    and pub_name = @pub_name
return 0
```

During procedure execution, the `execute` keyword is followed by a local variable that can ac-cept a return status code. This allows the batch or application to take action if there was an error during procedure execution.

```
/* check for status and report errors */
declare @status int
exec @status = titles_for_a_pub 'New Age Books'
if @status = 15
    print "Invalid Syntax"
else if @status = -101
    print "No publisher by that name found"
```

SQL Server Status Codes

In addition to your own status codes, SQL Server provides error codes if a stored procedure terminates unexpectedly during execution. The following is a list of return status codes currently in use by SQL Server:

Status Code	Meaning
0	Successful return
-1	Missing object referenced
-2	Datatype mismatch error
-3	Process chosen as deadlock victim
-4	Permission error
-5	Syntax error
-6	Miscellaneous user error
-7	Resource error, such as out of space
-8	Nonfatal internal problem (bug)
-9	System limit reached
-10	Fatal internal inconsistency (bug)
-11	Fatal internal inconsistency (bug)
-12	Table or index corrupted
-13	Database corrupt
-14	Hardware error

Stored Procedures and Transactions

SQL Server notes the transaction nesting level before calling a stored procedure. If the transaction nesting level when the procedure returns is different from the level when executed, SQL Server displays the following message: Transaction count after EXECUTE indicates that a COMMIT or ROLLBACK TRAN is missing. This message indicates that transaction nesting is out of whack. Because a stored procedure does not abort the batch on a rollback transaction, a rollback transaction inside the procedure could result in a loss of data integrity if subsequent statements are executed and committed.

A `rollback transaction` statement rolls back all statements to the outermost transaction, including any work performed inside nested stored procedures that have not been fully committed (that is, `@@trancount > 0`). A `commit tran` within the stored procedure decrements the `@@trancount` by only one.

Develop a consistent error-handling strategy for failed transactions or other errors that occur within transactions. Implement this strategy consistently across procedures and applications. Implement transaction control in nested stored procedures. Check whether the procedure is being called from within a transaction before issuing a `begin tran`.

Because a `rollback transaction` from a procedure does not abort the batch calling the procedure, follow these guidelines:

- Procedures should make no net change to `@@trancount`.
- Issue a `rollback tran` only if the stored procedure issues the `begin tran` statement.

Here is a code template for a stored procedure that can provide transactional integrity whether it is run as a part of an ongoing transaction or if it is run as its own transaction:

```
/* proc to demonstrate no net change to @@trancount
** but rolls back changes within the proc
** VERY IMPORTANT: return an error code
** to tell the calling procedure rollback occurred */

create proc p1
as
declare @trncnt int

select @trncnt = @@trancount   -- save @@trancount value

if @trncnt = 0    -- transaction has not begun
  begin tran p1   -- begin tran increments nest level to 1

else              -- already in a transaction
  save tran p1    -- save tran doesn't increment nest level

/* do some processing */

if (@@transtate = 2) -- or other error condition
  begin
  rollback tran p1  -- rollback to savepoint, or begin tran
  return 25          -- return error code indicating rollback
  end

/* more processing if required */

if @trncnt = 0     -- this proc issued begin tran
  commit tran p1   -- commit tran, decrement @@trancount to 0
                   -- commit not required with save tran

return 0 /* successful return */
```

Here is a template for the calling batch that might execute the stored procedure listed here. The main problem you need to solve is to handle return codes properly and respond with the correct transaction handling.

```
/* Retrieve status code to determine if proc was successful */
...

declare @status_val int, @trncnt int

select @trncnt = @@trancount  -- save @@trancount value

if @trncnt = 0    -- transaction has not begun
  begin tran t1  -- begin tran increments nest level to 1
else              -- otherwise, already in a transaction
  save tran t1    -- save tran doesn't increment nest level

/* do some processing if required */

if (@@transtate = 2) -- or other error condition
  begin
  rollback tran t1   -- rollback to savepoint,or begin tran
  return             -- and exit batch/procedure
  end

execute @status_val = p1 --exec procedure, begin nesting

if @status_val = 25 -- if proc performed rollback
  begin           -- determine whether to rollback or continue
  rollback tran t1
  return
  end

/* more processing if required */

if @trncnt = 0     -- this proc/batch issued begin tran
  commit tran t1   -- commit tran, decrement @@trancount to 0
return             -- commit not required with save tran
```

Cursors in Stored Procedures

In stored procedures, the declare cursor statement does not have to be in a separate batch (these are called *server cursors*). As Figure 7.5 illustrates, if stored procedures are nested, they can access cursors declared in higher-level stored procedures in the call tree.

FIGURE 7.5.

If stored procedures are nested, they can access cursors declared in higher-level stored procedures in the call tree.

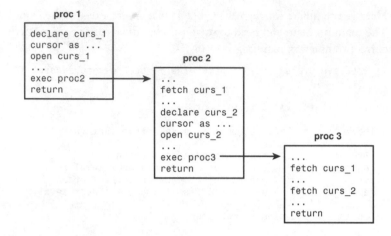

Example: Server Cursor

```
create proc title_price_update
as
declare @ytd_sales int, @price money
/*declare cursor*/
declare titles_curs cursor for
  select ytd_sales, price from titles
  for update of price
open titles_curs
fetch titles_curs into @ytd_sales, @price
if (@@fetch_status = 2)
  begin
    print "No books found"
    close titles_curs
    deallocate titles_curs
    return
  end
while (@@fetch_status = 0)
  begin
    if @ytd_sales = null
      begin
      update titles set price = @price * .75
        where current of titles_curs
      end
    else
        if @price > $15
            update titles set price = @price * .9
                where current of titles_curs
        else
            update titles set price = @price * 1.15
                where current of titles_curs
        fetch titles_curs into @ytd_sales, @price
  end
if (@@fetch_status = 1)
  raiserror 55555 "Fetch of titles_curs failed"
close titles_curs
deallocate titles_curs
return
```

Procedure Limitations and Notes

A stored procedure cannot create views, defaults, rules, triggers, or procedures, nor issue the use statement. (If you want a stored procedure to operate within the context of the database it is called from, create a system stored procedure.) You can create tables in stored procedures. Typically, you create temporary tables for storing intermediate results or as work tables. Temporary tables used within stored procedures are dropped at procedure termination. A table cannot be created, dropped, and re-created with the same name in a single procedure.

Stored procedures are parsed in a single pass and will not resolve forward or backward references. For example, when defining a stored procedure that references a temporary table, either the stored procedure must create the temporary table prior to referencing it, or the temporary table must exist at the time the stored procedure is created.

Procedures are reusable, but not reentrant. Stored procedures can be recursive.

Stored procedures can reference objects in other databases and call other procedures to a nesting level of 16 deep.

Objects Referenced in Procedures

To display a list of objects referenced by stored procedure, use `sp_depends`:

```
exec sp_depends procedure_name
```

To display a list of stored procedures that reference a specific table or view, use `sp_depends`:

```
exec sp_depends {table_name | view_name}
```

If you rename an object referenced by a stored procedure, the stored procedure still references the original object. If you drop the original object and create a new object with the original object's name, the stored procedure is recompiled to reference the new object. If you create a new object with the original object's name and the original object still exists, you need to drop and re-create the stored procedure to reference the new object.

If you drop any object referenced by the stored procedure and do not re-create it with the same name, you get a runtime error. If you drop an index used by the query plan of a stored procedure, SQL Server will generate a new query plan the next time it is executed.

Optimizing Stored Procedures

The SQL Server optimizer generates a query plan for a stored procedure based on the parameters passed in the first time it is executed. This query plan is then run from cache for subsequent executions. To force a new query plan to be generated, use the `with recompile` option either at creation time or execution time. `with recompile` specified at procedure-creation time causes the optimizer to generate a new query plan for every execution. If it is specified at procedure execution time, it causes the optimizer to generate a new query plan for that execution only and will be used for subsequent executions.

Examples

```
create proc advance_range
    (@low money, @high money)
    with recompile
    as
select * from titles
  where advance between @low and @high
return
go

/* if the procedure has not been created with the
** 'with recompile' option, execute as follows to
** recompile */
exec advance_range $1000,$2000 with recompile
```

Here are some cases when you might consider using with recompile:

- When a stored procedure can generate widely different query plans, depending on the parameters passed in, and there is no way of predicting the best query plan for all executions

- When statistics have been updated on a table and you want the stored procedure to generate a new query plan based on the updated statistics

- When an index has been added to a table that you want the optimizer to consider to generate a new query plan for the stored procedure

WARNING

If the procedure contains select * from *tablename* and alter table has been used to add a column to the table, with recompile will not force all the columns to be displayed. Instead, you have to drop and re-create the stored procedure to display the new column.

Remote Stored Procedures

Remote stored procedures are procedures residing on other servers. Fully qualify the stored procedure name with the server name to execute procedures on other servers.

```
[exec[ute]] server_name.db_name.owner.proc_name
```

Both servers must be configured for remote access. This is a cookbook procedure that your SQL Server administrator will understand, but there are many steps and the server needs to be cycled.

Transaction control statements do not affect work performed in remote procedure calls.

Stored Procedure Guidelines

Stored procedures should be solid, because they are server-resident and called frequently. Check parameters for validity and return an error if there is a problem. Ensure that the parameter datatypes match the column datatypes that they are compared with to avoid datatype mismatches. Check @@error after each SQL statement. Comment your code. Always use a return statement. Develop a method for maintaining versions of stored procedure source code.

Stored Procedure Debugging Techniques

Write a stored procedure as a batch first. To get the syntax right on a stored procedure, write small parts of it as a batch first, then store the procedure once the whole operation starts working.

Get showplan output with recompile. The output from showplan and DBCC are generated by the optimizer, which operates only when a procedure is recompiled. To see the effect of different parameters on optimization, create the procedure with recompile and then drop and re-create the procedure without recompile when you go into production.

Summary

When SQL Server was first introduced, stored procedures and triggers helped differentiate the product from competitive database products. Even now, the capability of writing effective stored procedures and triggers makes your system operate better, with better integrity and usually better performance.

Understand the capabilities and limitations of stored procedures and triggers before writing lots of code. A well-written application runs fast and clean; poorly written code makes the server run sluggishly and inefficiently.

Transaction Management

8

What Is a Transaction?

A *transaction* is a set of operations to be completed at one time, as though they were a single operation. A transaction must be fully completed or not performed at all. Standard examples of transactions include bank transfers (withdraw $500 from checking, add $500 to savings) and order-entry systems (write an order for five widgets, remove five widgets from inventory).

All SQL statements are inherently transactions, from `grant` and `create` statements to the data-modification statements `insert`, `update`, and `delete`. Consider the following `update` example:

```
update titles
set price = price * 1.02
```

This statement modifies all rows in the `titles` table. SQL Server guarantees that, regardless of the size of the `titles` table, all rows will be processed or no rows will be processed at all. What if half of the rows are modified and the server fails? When the server comes back up (but before the database is available for use) it rolls back the incomplete transaction, removing all evidence that it ever began, which is all part of the recovery process.

SQL Server also includes transaction-control syntax to group sets of SQL statements together into single logical work units:

- `begin transaction` starts a unit of work
- `commit transaction` completes a unit of work
- `rollback transaction` cancels a unit of work

The following example enters an order and depletes inventory in a single transaction:

```
begin transaction
   update inventory
      set in_stock = in_stock - 5
      where item_num = "14141"
   insert orders (cust_num, item_num, qty)
      values ("ABC151", "14141", 5)
commit transaction
```

SQL Server guarantees that the inventory will not change unless the order is also entered.

Look at the same example, but with the `rollback transaction` statement instead of `commit`:

```
begin transaction
   update inventory
      set in_stock = in_stock - 5
      where item_num = "14141"
   insert orders (cust_num, item_num, qty)
      values ("ABC151", "14141", 5)
rollback transaction
```

When the server encounters the `rollback` statement, it discards all changes in the transaction and returns the data to the state it was in before work began.

Transaction Programming

The programming issues associated with writing transactional SQL are fairly straightforward. After you issue a begin tran statement, the server performs all of the subsequent work without formally writing a final record of the work. At any time after issuing a begin transaction statement, you can roll back the entire transaction or commit it.

The SQL Server implicitly commits work executed outside of explicit transactional control. For example, this set of statements includes no explicit transactional syntax:

```
insert publishers (pub_id, pub_name, city, state)
    values ("1111", "Joe and Mary's Books", "Northern Plains", "IA")
update titles
    set pub_id = "1111"
    where pub_id = "1234"
delete authors
    where state = "CA"
```

Each of these statements will be treated as its own transaction. Thus, the server issues *implicit* instructions on transaction control for each individual SQL statement. The server would treat the preceding batch like this:

```
[implicit BEGIN TRANSACTION]
insert publishers (pub_id, pub_name, city, state)
    values ("1111", "Joe and Mary's Books", "Northern Plains", "IA")
[implicit COMMIT TRANSACTION]

[implicit BEGIN TRANSACTION]
update titles
    set pub_id = "1111"
    where pub_id = "1234"
[implicit COMMIT TRANSACTION]

[implicit BEGIN TRANSACTION]
delete authors
    where state = "CA"
[implicit COMMIT TRANSACTION]
```

Each statement would include implicit BEGIN and COMMIT instructions (indicated by italics).

What does that mean for the integrity of this batch? Each statement is guaranteed to be carried to completion or rolled back to the beginning. If the server were to go down unexpectedly after the titles update had started but before it was complete, the server would roll back any work already performed by the update statement. On the other hand, the work associated with the insert to publishers would have already been completed and committed (by the implicit COMMIT operation), so only part of the batch would be complete.

Transactions and Batches

In the previous example, you might have wanted the whole operation to complete or do nothing at all. The obvious solution is to wrap the entire operation in a single transaction, like this:

```
begin transaction
insert publishers (pub_id, pub_name, city, state)
    values ("1111", "Joe and Mary's Books", "Northern Plains", "IA")
update titles
    set pub_id = "1111"
    where pub_id = "1234"
delete authors
    where state = "CA"
commit transaction
```

Now the server treats all three operations performed in the batch as a single modification.

There is no inherent transactional quality to batches. As you have seen already, unless you provide the syntax to form a transaction out of several statements, each statement in a batch is its own transaction, and each statement will be carried to completion or fail individually.

Transactions can also span batches. For example, you could write an application that begins a transaction in one batch and then asks for user verification during a second batch. The SQL might look like this:

First Batch:

```
/* DON'T DO THIS ... EVER!!! */
begin transaction
insert publishers (pub_id, pub_name, city, state)
    values ("1111", "Joe and Mary's Books", "Northern Plains", "IA")
if @@error = 0
    print "publishers insert was successful. Please go on."
else
    print "publisher insert failed. Please roll back"
```

Second Batch:

```
update titles
    set pub_id = "1111"
    where pub_id = "1234"
delete authors
    where state = "CA"
commit transaction
```

In a few pages (in the "Transactions and Locking" section), you'll look at the locking issues associated with transactions. At that time, you will see that transactions force data modifications (insert, update, delete) to hold locks that persist until a commit transaction or rollback transaction statement is encountered.

Writing transactions that span multiple batches is usually a bad idea. The locking problems can get very complicated, with awful performance implications. (What if this waited for a user to say "OK" before going on, but the user went to Cancun and didn't come back for two weeks? Locks would be held until the user got back and said "OK.") In general, you want to enclose each transaction in a single batch, using conditional programming constructs to handle situations like the preceding example. Here is a better way to write that program:

```
/* DO THIS INSTEAD !! */
begin transaction
```

```
insert publishers (pub_id, pub_name, city, state)
    values ("1111", "Joe and Mary's Books", "Northern Plains", "IA")
if @@error = 0
begin
    print "publishers insert was successful. Continuing."
    update titles
        set pub_id = "1111"
        where pub_id = "1234"
    delete authors
        where state = "CA"
    commit transaction
end
else
begin
    print "publisher insert failed. rolling back transaction"
    rollback transaction
end
```

The important point in this example is that the transaction now takes place within a single batch.

Savepoints

SQL Server enables you to mark a *savepoint* in a transaction. Savepoints let you to do some work inside a transaction and then roll back just that work, based on other circumstances. In this example, the program sells several items and then tests inventory (which is automatically updated through a trigger) and rolls back a portion of the work if there is insufficient inventory.

```
begin tran

save tran item111     /* mark a savepoint before each insert */
insert order (ord_no, item_no, qty)
    values ("2345", "111", 15)
if (select in_stock from inventory where item_no = '111') < 0
begin
    rollback tran item111    /* roll back just this item if incorrect */
    print "Item 111 would be back-ordered, cancelling order"
end

save tran item999
insert order (ord_no, item_no, qty)
    values ("2345", "999", 5)
if (select in_stock from inventory where item_no = '999') < 0
begin
    rollback tran item999
    print "Item 999 would be back-ordered, cancelling order"
end

save tran item444
    insert order (ord_no, item_no, qty)
values ("2345", "444", 25)
if (select in_stock from inventory where item_no = '444') < 0
begin
    rollback tran item444
    print "Item 444 would be back-ordered, cancelling order"
```

```
end

commit tran
```

By wrapping the inserts in a transaction, the programmer gets two benefits. First, the overall effect of each insert can be observed before the work is committed, which makes it very easy to reverse the effects of problem updates. The second benefit is that all of the legitimate inserts included in the batch will go in, whereas the rest will be rejected. (In your business, it might not be appropriate to allow a partial transaction. The proper use of savepoints depends on a good understanding of transaction logic in your application.)

The scope of transaction savepoint names is local, so you don't have to worry about generating unique names for your savepoints. Savepoints and related rollback statements do not affect program flow. Rolling back to a savepoint enables processing to continue forward from that point.

Nested Transactions

It is important to note that SQL Server does not implicitly commit work when you log out. For example, what if you issue the following statement and then log out?

```
begin transaction
insert publishers (pub_id, pub_name, city, state)
    values ("1111", "Joe and Mary's Books", "Northern Plains", "IA")
```

Any uncommitted transactions will be rolled back automatically when you log out.

How does the server know you have uncommitted transactions? SQL Server retains a *transaction nesting level* for each user connection.

> **NOTE**
>
> SQL Server maintains a list of active connections in `master..sysprocesses`. The primary key of that table is `spid` (server process ID). You can retrieve the server process ID for your current connection using the global variable, `@@spid`:
>
> ```
> select @@spid0
> ```

The transaction nesting level can be retrieved for your connection with the global variable, `@@trancount`. You need to understand how each transactional statement affects the contents of `@@trancount` in order to write properly nested transactions and to manage transactions through triggers and stored procedures.

Table 8.1 summarizes the effect of transactional statements on `@@trancount`.

Table 8.1. How transaction control statements affect `@@trancount`.

Statement	*Effect on `@@trancount`*
`begin transaction`	`@@trancount = @@trancount + 1`
`commit transaction`	`@@trancount = @@trancount − 1`
`save transaction`	(no effect)
`rollback transaction`	`@@trancount = 0`
`rollback transaction` *save_name**	(no effect)

Here is a summary of how transactional control relates to `@@trancount`:

- When you log in to SQL Server, your session `@@trancount` is zero.
- Each time you execute `begin transaction`, SQL Server increments `@@trancount`.
- Each time you execute `commit transaction`, SQL Server decrements `@@trancount`.
- Actual work is committed only when `@@trancount` reaches zero again.
- When you execute `rollback transaction`, the transaction is canceled and `@@trancount` returns to 0. Notice that `rollback transaction` cuts straight through any number of nested transactions, canceling the overall main transaction. This means that you need to be careful how you write code that contains a `rollback` statement.
- Savepoints and rolling back to a savepoint do not affect `@@trancount` or transaction nesting in any way.
- If a user connection is lost for any reason when `@@trancount` is greater than zero, any pending work for that connection is automatically rolled back. The server requires that transactions be explicitly committed.

Take a look at how the server handles transaction nesting. In this example, transactions are nested two levels deep:

```
begin tran
   update titles
      set price = price * 1.1
      from titles
      where pub_id = "1234"
   begin tran
      update titles
         set advance = advance * 1.15
         where pub_id in
            (select pub_id from publishers
             where state = "MA")
   commit tran
   delete titles
      where type = "UNDECIDED"
commit tran
```

Let's track @@trancount through each statement. Assuming that @@trancount starts out at zero, Table 8.2 shows the effect of each statement on @@trancount.

Table 8.2. How statements in the example affect @@trancount.

Statement	Effect on @@trancount
begin tran	@@trancount = @@trancount + 1 = 1
update titles	@@trancount = 1
begin tran	@@trancount = @@trancount + 1 = 2
update titles	@@trancount = 2
commit tran	@@trancount = @@trancount - 1 = 1
delete titles	@@trancount = 1
commit tran	@@trancount = @@trancount - 1 = 0

Nested transactions are *syntactic only*. The only commit tran statement that has an impact on real data is the last one, the statement returning @@trancount to 0, which forces physical data to be written to disk.

Transactions and Locking

In order to ensure data integrity, SQL Server places exclusive locks on the pages involved in a transaction. In the previous example, pages in both the titles and publishers tables are involved. As SQL Server progresses through the query, locks are acquired on each table modified by a statement and are then held until SQL Server reaches a commit tran that sets @@trancount to 0 (or a rollback tran). A long-running transaction performing data modifications to many different tables can effectively block the work of all other users in the system (see the section titled "Long-Running Transactions" later in this chapter).

Because of this, you need to be aware of the performance and concurrency issues involved with writing transactions. When writing transactional code, here are some things you need to keep in mind:

- Keep transactions as short as your application allows.
- Avoid returning data with a select in the middle of a transaction.
- Try to write all transactions within stored procedures.
- Avoid transactions that span multiple batches.

Transactions and Triggers

Triggers are considered part of the transaction in which a data modification is executed. In this example, an `update` trigger on the `titles` table will fire as part of the transaction:

```
begin tran
    update titles
        set price = $99
        where title_id = "BU1234"
commit tran
```

@@trancount and Implicit Transactions

What is the value of `@@trancount` as SQL Server processes each of these statements? If `@@trancount` starts at 0, `begin tran` makes it 1, the `update` statement leaves it at 1, and it returns to 0 with the `commit tran` statement.

What is the value of `@@trancount` inside the `update` trigger? To determine that, you would need a trigger that prints out the contents of `@@trancount` during execution. Here is an example:

```
/* DON'T LEAVE THIS KIND OF TRIGGER LYING AROUND!! */
create trigger tr_stores_upd
on stores
for update
as
declare @tc varchar(80)
select @tc = "Trancount = " + convert(char(1), @@trancount)
print @tc
raiserror 99999 "this update statement will never commit ... test trigger in place
"
rollback tran
return
```

Here is what the `isql` session looks like when you update the `stores` table:

```
1> update stores
2> set city = "Pittsburgh"
3> go
Trancount = 1
Msg 99999, Level 16, State 1:
this update statement will never commit ... test trigger in place
```

Inside the trigger, `@@trancount` equals 1. As mentioned earlier, each individual SQL statement is a transaction in and of itself. From this example, you can see that SQL Server uses the same transaction-nesting methods with implicit and explicit transaction control. Also, you can see that any work completed in the trigger is part of the `update` statement itself. (See Figure 8.1.)

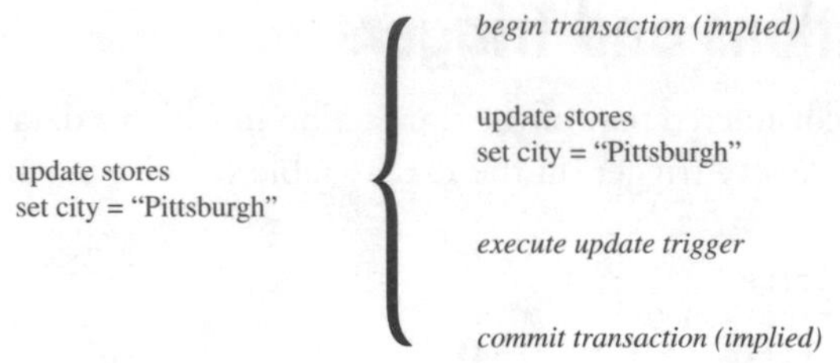

FIGURE 8.1.
A simple SQL data-modification statement.

update stores
set city = "Pittsburgh"

{
begin transaction (implied)

update stores
set city = "Pittsburgh"

execute update trigger

commit transaction (implied)
}

Watch what happens when the same trigger executes when the update runs as part of an explicit transaction:

```
1> begin tran
2> select "Before Update Trancount " , @@trancount
3> update stores
4> set city = "Pittsburgh"
5> select "After Update Trancount " , @@trancount
6> commit tran
7> go

 ------------------------ -----------
 Before Update Trancount           1

(1 row affected)
Trancount = 2
Msg 99999, Level 16, State 1:
this update statement will never commit ... test trigger in place
```

When the first begin tran executes, @@trancount is set to 1, as reported by the select statement. The update statement executes and the update trigger fires. The update trigger reports that @@trancount is 2 (again reflecting the effect on @@trancount of implicit transactions).

NOTE

Please don't allow this section to confuse you about transaction control and individual SQL statements. It is critical to understand that data-modification statements (insert, update, delete) have *no net effect* on @@trancount.

rollback transaction in a Trigger

In the previous example, you should note that the select statement after the update is not executed. Rollback-transaction statements, in addition to reversing the effect of the current data-modification statement, immediately return from the trigger and abort the batch, returning no automatic error message.

Consider this example, in which three `insert` statements are submitted as a batch to a table, `trigger_test`. The inserts are not stated as a transaction. Here is the `insert` trigger for the table, which ensures that the integer column, c1, is always less than c2:

```
create trigger tr_1
on trigger_test
for insert
as
if exists (select * from inserted
    where c1 > c2)
begin
    raiserror 99998 "c1 exceeds c2 — rolling back"
    rollback transaction
end
return
```

Here is the `insert` batch and the results:

```
1> insert trigger_test (c1, c2) values (1, 3)
2> insert trigger_test (c1, c2) values (3, 1)
3> insert trigger_test (c1, c2) values (1, 4)
4> go
(1 row affected)
Msg 99998, Level 16, State 1:
c1 exceeds c2 -- rolling back
1> select * from trigger_test
2> go
 c1          c2
 ----------- -----------
           1           3

(1 row affected)
```

As you can see, only the first `insert` statement is executed successfully. The trigger returns an error when the second statement fails the validation test. The error raised in the text of the trigger is returned, but notice that there is no error returned from the `rollback` statement itself. Finally, note that the final statement, which would pass the validation test if it were executed, is not executed.

Let's run the same `insert` (into an empty table) as a single transaction:

```
1> begin tran
2> insert trigger_test (c1, c2) values (1, 3)
3> insert trigger_test (c1, c2) values (3, 1)
4> insert trigger_test (c1, c2) values (1, 4)
5> commit tran
6> go
(1 row affected)
Msg 99998, Level 16, State 1:
c1 exceeds c2 — rolling back
1> select * from trigger_test
2> go
 c1          c2
 ----------- -----------

(0 rows affected)
```

Again, note that the trigger rollback canceled the batch, so the third `insert` was never executed. When the statement firing the trigger executes from within a transaction, the `rollback` in the trigger rolls back the whole transaction.

Please note that `rollback transaction` aborts a batch only from inside a trigger. *In all other cases, transactional syntax has no effect on program execution.*

Transactions and Stored Procedures

Writing all of your transactions in stored procedures can provide better performance by avoiding partial transactions, especially because the server provides error messages to help you manage the transaction nesting level within procedures. The biggest concern you have is how to handle `rollback transaction` statements within stored procedures. Mistakes in using `rollback` statements in procedures can result in data-integrity problems.

Consider this stored procedure, which inserts a row in a table, tests the table after the `insert`, and rolls back that `insert` if more than three rows exist with that value:

```
/* stored procedure example coded improperly (see below) */
create proc p2
(@parm int)
as
begin tran
insert tally_table (c1) values (@parm)
if (select count(*) from tally_table
    where c1 = @parm) > 3
begin
    raiserror 99997 "too many rows with that value - rolling back"
    rollback tran
    return 99997     /* error ... rolled back */
end
else
begin
    commit tran
    return 0         /* no error */
end
```

If you execute the stored procedure when the table contains only two rows with c1 = 1, the procedure runs properly and the `insert` is entered:

```
1> exec p2 1
2> go
1> select * from tally_table
2> go
 c1
 -----------
           1
           1
           1

(3 rows affected)
```

When you run the procedure again, the `rollback` statement will execute, and you will receive the following error message:

```
1> exec p2 1
2> go
Msg 99997, Level 16, State 1:
too many rows with that value - rolling back
1> select * from tally_table
2> go
 c1
 ----------
            1
            1
            1

(3 rows affected)
```

As expected, the procedure works properly and there are only three rows in the table after the insert fails.

The problem with this procedure arises only when it is executed from within a transaction. Consider this example:

```
begin tran
    exec p2 1
    exec p2 2
commit tran
```

What you intended by writing this as a transaction was that the inserts with value 2 would not occur unless you could make the related insert with value 1: both inserts should go in as a unit or no inserts should take place. Let's look at the output when the table contains three rows with value 1:

```
1> select * from tally_table
2> go
 c1
 ----------
            1
            1
            1

(3 rows affected)
1> begin tran
2>     exec p2 1
3>     exec p2 2
4> commit tran
5> go
Msg 99997, Level 16, State 1:
too many rows with that value - rolling back
Msg 266, Level 16, State 1:
Transaction count after EXECUTE indicates that a COMMIT or ROLLBACK
TRAN is missing. Previous count = 1, Current count = 0.
Msg 3902, Level 16, State 1:
The commit transaction request has no corresponding BEGIN TRANSACTION.
1> select * from tally_table
```

```
2> go
 c1
 ----------
          1
          1
          1
          2
```

(4 rows affected)

Before the batch, the table contains three rows; afterward, it contains four rows. The new row contains the value 2, so only half of the transaction was executed. The integrity of the transaction has been lost. Let's look at the output from the batch closely to understand what has occurred; then let's write the stored procedure and batch properly to make certain this does not occur.

```
Msg 99997, Level 16, State 1:
too many rows with that value - rolling back
```

This is our error message, generated because the first insert failed.

```
Msg 266, Level 16, State 1:
Transaction count after EXECUTE indicates that a COMMIT or ROLLBACK
TRAN is missing. Previous count = 1, Current count = 0.
```

This error occurs because the transaction nesting level (that is, the value of @@trancount) is different when the procedure starts from when it ends. Why? rollback transaction returns @@trancount to 0 regardless of the prior transaction nesting level. Clearly, this is a problem if the calling batch is unaware of the nesting level. Table 8.3 steps through the batch one statement at a time, understanding the impact of each statement on @@trancount (and on the transaction).

There are three specific events (noted in the table as a, b, and c) that you should look at to understand the problems in data integrity. Note (a) points out the problems caused by rollback transaction in a procedure. When you write the procedure, you need to make allowances so that a user can execute it whether or not a transaction is currently running. Note (b) shows that the second execution of the procedure, when it reaches the commit statement, forces @@trancount to zero, performing an actual commit of the data modifications since the prior begin tran statement. Finally, the commit statement at note (c) tries to decrement @@trancount, which is already zero. When this happens, the server returns the message seen earlier:

```
Msg 3902, Level 16, State 1:
The commit transaction request has no corresponding BEGIN TRANSACTION.
```

These two messages (3902 and 266) are your warnings that the transaction nesting is not properly managed in the stored procedure.

Table 8.3. Tracking `@@trancount` during procedure execution.

Calling Batch	Procedure	@@trancount
begin tran		1
exec p2 1		1
	begin tran	2
	insert tally table (c1) values (@parm)	2
	if (select count (*) from tally table	2
	where c1 = @parm) > 3	
	begin	0 (a)
	raiserror 99997 "too many rows with that value - rolling back"	
	rollback tran	
	return 99997 /* error . . . rolled back */	
	end	
exec p2 2		0
	begin tran	1
	insert tally table (c1) values (@parm)	1
	if (select count (*) from tally table	1
	where c1 = @parm) > 3	
	begin	0 (b)
	commit tran	
	return 0 /* no error */	
	end	
commit tran		0 (c)

There are several methods of coding stored procedures with transactions to ensure that the procedure works properly as a standalone transaction or as a part of a larger, nested transaction. Here is one example of how to write a stored procedure with transaction control:

```
/* proc to demonstrate no net change to @@trancount
** while still rolling back changes within the proc
** VERY IMPORTANT: return an error code
** to tell the calling procedure rollback occurred */

create proc p1
as
declare @trncnt int

select @trncnt = @@trancount   -- save @@trancount value

if @trncnt = 0    -- transaction has not begun
   begin tran p1  -- begin tran increments nest level to 1

else              -- already in a transaction
   save tran p1   -- save tran doesn't increment nest level
```

```
/* do some processing */

if (@@transtate = 2) -- or other error condition
  begin
  rollback tran p1  -- rollback to savepoint, or begin tran
  return 25         -- return error code indicating rollback
  end

/* more processing if required */

if @trncnt = 0     -- this proc issued begin tran
  commit tran p1   -- commit tran, decrement @@trancount to 0
                   -- commit not required with save tran

return 0 /* successful return */
```

As important as it is to write the stored procedure properly, it is equally important to write the batch calling the procedure to make proper use of the information provided by the stored proc return codes. Here is an example of how to manage nested procedures from the calling batch:

```
/* Retrieve status code to determine if proc was successful */
...

declare @status_val int, @trncnt int

select @trncnt = @@trancount  -- save @@trancount value

if @trncnt = 0     -- transaction has not begun
  begin tran t1    -- begin tran increments nest level to 1
else               -- otherwise, already in a transaction
  save tran t1     -- save tran doesn't increment nest level

/* do some processing if required */

if (@@transtate = 2) -- or other error condition
  begin
  rollback tran t1  -- rollback to savepoint,or begin tran
  return            -- and exit batch/procedure
  end

execute @status_val = p1 --exec procedure, begin nesting

if @status_val = 25 -- if proc performed rollback
  begin           -- determine whether to rollback or continue
  rollback tran t1
  return
  end

/* more processing if required */

if @trncnt = 0     -- this proc/batch issued begin tran
  commit tran t1   -- commit tran, decrement @@trancount to 0
return             -- commit not required with save tran
```

Whether or not you choose to adhere to these coding standards, the important point is that stored procedures and the batches that call those procedures need to be consistent with each other to provide you with proper data-integrity control. You must establish coding standards for both that enable transactional control to work whether the transaction commits success-fully or is rolled back.

Long-Running Transactions

There is no specific definition of a long-running transaction, but as transactions get longer, problems arise. Long-running transactions are not inherently different from shorter ones, but they do stress elements of the system that otherwise run quite well. In particular, you might encounter performance or concurrency problems because of issues related to the transaction log, the caching system, and locking.

Some of the symptoms of long-running transactions include the following:

- Your transaction log fills up. Some transactions can actually exceed the size of your transaction log. Unlike some other database systems, SQL Server does not enable you to define a temporary, emergency overflow log to handle this situation. Instead, you need to assign—permanently—a transaction log large enough to hold all of your largest transactions.

> **NOTE**
>
> Why not just clear half of the transaction and continue? The `dump tran` commands (and other transaction log-maintenance methods, such as `trunc. log on checkpoint`) do not allow the server to prune pending, uncommitted transactions.

- You are holding blocking locks that prevent all work from continuing by other users. You might be able to resolve this specific problem by looking at your lock escalation level (see Chapter 15, "Locking and Performance").
- Ordinarily, all transactional work is performed in memory. Only when a `commit` is executed are the changes to the transaction log flushed to disk; changes to tables and indexes wait until a system-initiated checkpoint. If a transaction gets too long, the caching system might run out of unused memory and initiate a checkpoint to release additional memory. This could slow down your transaction as well, and a `rollback` following a checkpoint is far more disk-intensive than one that is executed only in memory.

It is usually helpful to reduce the size of your transactions when you start to encounter perfor-mance or blocking problems. You can reduce transaction size by reducing the size of the logi-cal unit of work. For example, you could take a single-transaction task and execute it in two steps, each its own transaction. This might require that you write program code to handle the data integrity in cases where the first half of the transaction works, but the second half fails (you would need to write your own transaction handler to deal with the rollback processing).

Before changing the definition of a unit of work, you should look for technical fixes to your code to reduce the amount of log work required for each step. For example, if you can get the server to perform an update in place instead of a deferred update, you could substantially reduce the amount of information recorded in the transaction log to perform the same work. (See Chapter 12, "Understanding the Query Optimizer.") Reducing the number of indexes on a table also reduces the number of log writes required to handle complex modifications.

Summary

A transaction is a logical unit of work. SQL Server provides several automatic and programmatic mechanisms including Transact-SQL transaction control statements, the transaction log, and transaction isolation through locking to preserve data integrity while transactions are running. Transactions enable you to tie together logically related operations, allowing the server to maintain data integrity. Remember, when writing applications that include transaction control, you need to pay special attention to how you write and work with triggers and stored procedures.

PART

IN THIS PART

Performance and Tuning

How to Define Performance

9

What Can You Expect?

The first problem in tuning the performance of a SQL Server is to understand what level of performance you can reasonably expect from the server.

There are physical constraints on the server's performance, so some things are clearly improbable. For example, with today's technology SQL Server cannot scan a two-terabyte table from SCSI disks (the most common type of magnetic storage device used today) in under 1 second. In fact, the server can only scan at best about 2MB per second from a single disk. Later in this chapter you learn to measure the physical constraints of your server.

On the other hand, you clearly expect certain basic performance capabilities. For example, if you have a properly indexed table, you should be able to retrieve a single, specified row (random row retrieval) in under 1 second. (You should actually be able to retrieve hundreds to thousands of individual rows in under a second.)

Somewhere between what is improbable and what is easily expected, you need to understand what is—and what is not—possible on your server. You also need to be able to develop expectations as to what amount of elapsed time a specific query will cost (the *cost* of a query is defined here as the total elapsed time—the same measure your users probably use).

To help you develop proper performance expectations, this chapter discusses the following topics:

- Definition of performance
- Expectations
- Defining and tracking down bottlenecks
- A basic tuning approach

Definition of Performance

You might not define performance the same way as the DBA you meet at the local user's group does. There are three basic ways to define SQL Server performance; other definitions are simply combinations of them, as follows:

- *Response time for queries.* This means that what is important for you is to get answers back to your queries in a specific amount of elapsed time. At many shops, the standard is that response time must be subsecond. Of course, more complex queries take longer than a second, but measuring the response time for specific queries is an important measure of performance.

> **NOTE**
>
> As the story goes, ergonomic studies were done at IBM years ago (a cynic might suspect that these were performed by the hardware sales group) that demonstrated a

substantial drop-off of productivity if users had to wait more than a second for a response.

- *Throughput.* This is typically measured in *transactions per second*, or TPS. There are a variety of industry-standard benchmarks (TPC-A, -B, and -C, for example) that can help you compare the performance of database servers running on various platforms, but they will not help you define or predict the actual performance of the system because they do not reflect your own transactions.

  Carry out your performance benchmarking with your own queries and data to get meaningful throughput measures. You will need to make sure that your database and server are up to the challenge of managing the number of queries in the amount of time you need.

- *Concurrency.* This can reasonably be considered a subset of throughput. Here's the basic question: Can our system handle 5,000 users? Answering this question is usually a substantial task that requires you to profile predicted query and throughput traffic, and then to answer the response time and throughput questions under load. You need to configure for this (and test for this) differently than for throughput.

- *Combination of throughput and concurrency.* Capability to run *OLTP* (On-Line Transaction Processing), *DSS* (Decision Support Systems, also called Data Warehousing or *EIS* (Executive Information Systems), and *Batch* (Management and Off-Line Report Systems) simultaneously.

  This is the hardest thing to tune for, particularly on single-processor SQL Servers. More on this later.

Tradeoffs

You will find it reasonably simple to tune for a single performance need. Approaches that solve single performance include

- normalization (eliminating duplicate data)
- denormalization (storing duplicate data)
- creation or removal of indexes
- database segmenting to move specific objects onto specific physical devices
- partitioning tables across databases

You might even need to buy additional hardware or software.

Where solving a single problem is fairly straightforward, finding a way to solve multiple performance needs is usually a delicate balancing act. For example, you might choose to speed throughput by removing indexes used to improve query performance. Modifications to tables are much faster without the additional indexes, so transactions require less work and the system can handle more transactions per second. The tradeoff is that queries previously supported by an index now must perform a table scan. A query that used to take 3 minutes might now take several hours!

Common Tradeoffs

There are some common tradeoffs you need to consider when you are looking at performance issues. None of these tradeoffs is simple or has a standard response. As you evaluate your performance options, it is vital that you be able to state clearly what you are getting and what you are giving up.

Normalization versus Performance

Most *database administrators* (DBAs) develop database designs using a two-step approach that starts with a logical design and then moves to a physical design. (A *logical* database design is a representation of data intended to remove all duplication and to express clearly the relationship between data elements.)

The *physical* design is a plan for how to store the data represented by the logical design on a particular system. One of the first hurdles to overcome in physical design is understanding that it has a separate purpose from logical design. Logical design is for understanding the data; physical design is for performance.

> **NOTE**
>
> Making SQL Server run fast is not a popularity contest or a beauty pageant. Some DBAs are unhappy that they have to trade off their beautiful logical designs for less aesthetically pleasing physical designs to make the system fast. Al Davis says, "Just win, baby!" It's probably good advice.

The first tradeoff is normalization versus performance. A normalized database is easy to understand. It also requires more joins to resolve multi-entity queries, and joins are costly. If you denormalize, you reduce joins; thus many queries will run faster.

Storage versus Cost

This brings up the next tradeoff: storage versus cost. Denormalizing frequently demands more storage because it requires the storage of duplicate data, and that isn't free; however, it is often cheap compared to the cost of unresolved performance issues.

Retrieval versus Update

Duplication implies the next tradeoff: If you have redundant (denormalized) data, it is going to take more time and resources to update the redundant data.

Keep this in mind: Redundancy helps retrieval, but it costs extra time and I/O during updates.

Fast Execution versus Ad Hoc Access

Balancing OLTP and DSS is a specialized problem.

Before you can address your performance issues, you need to define your requirements and boundaries. You need to provide a physical design to enable the response times that you want to achieve. In the next three chapters you learn how to set and adjust these parameters.

Expectations

Let's take a look at some specific queries and try to identify what the expectations are. These queries are based on a table and index defined as follows (tables are partial, and just forget for a moment that you do not yet understand how SQL Server manages indexes).

```
create table orders( ...
        item_num int,
        warehouse int,
        ...)
create index ord_index on orders (item_num, warehouse)
```

Here are some potential queries you might run against the table with their response times.

A. (response time subsecond)

```
select sum(qty) from orders
where item_num = 1234 and warehouse = 432
```

B. (response time 600 seconds)

```
select sum(qty) from orders
where warehouse = 432
```

C. (response time 50 seconds)

```
select sum(qty) from orders
where item_num in (1234,2345) and warehouse = 432
```

Now let's pose the following questions: Which queries have acceptable response times? Which queries have expected response times? These are extremely important questions, and it is crucial to understand that they are *different* questions.

Look first at query A. Is the response time acceptable? Clearly, if you have subsecond response time, it is silly to waste time trying to decide if response time is acceptable. Move on to the next problem. Is the response time expected? If you have a reasonable amount of data for the test, again the answer is to look for real problems elsewhere.

Query B has response time that is unacceptable for most real-time operations, so we will define it as unacceptable. We must then ask ourselves, "Is the response time expected?" Should this query take 600 seconds?

This is a more difficult question to answer because it requires an understanding of the data, the physical design, and how the server uses the physical design. Let's handle this in reverse order of the questions just posed. First, how can the server handle the physical design? Can SQL Server use the index to resolve the query? Because the table is indexed on the item_num column, and item_num is not in the where clause, the server can not use the index. Therefore, the only way to resolve the query is with a *table scan*, which is the process of reading every page in the table. Next comes understanding the data: How many pages of data do we have to read to resolve the query? It also opens up a hardware question. How many pages of data can we read in a second? Platform dependent, we can read between 90 and 1,000 pages per second (typically) from a SCSI disk drive. This is a huge discrepancy, and makes another point clear:

You must understand the physical limitations of your system to be able to have reasonable expectations and from there to make physical design decisions.

Back to Query B. How many pages of data must we read? (SQL Server reads one page at a time). If the amount of data that needs to be read takes several hundred seconds, and you are willing to allow a few seconds for overhead, 600 seconds might be an expected result even though it is not an acceptable one. During your physical-design phase, you need to identify that you have a potential problem query, with expected results that are unacceptable, and you will need to figure out a way to improve performance (this can be an additional index, a summary table, or one of many other possible decisions).

Query C gets a bit trickier. It looks like a subset of Query A. (The In keyword should be treated as an or situation). Why does this take (at least) 50 times the elapsed time of Query A? Back to basics: Is the response time acceptable? Let's assume it isn't—that's why we're analyzing the query, after all.

One of the first things to do is break up the query. If both components of the query are resolved in less than a second, it's time to get on the horn with technical support and report a bug. You need to make an assumption—specifically, that the server is able to use an index to resolve this particular query. If one query takes less than a second (which we know from Query A) and the other takes 49 seconds, what is the problem? The most likely is that you suddenly have substantially more data for this item_num in the warehouse. Here it becomes necessary again to understand the bias of your data.

> **NOTE**
>
> There is a demo product in the back of this book that can help you understand what the server thinks is the bias of your data.

Defining and Tracking Down Bottlenecks

A *bottleneck* is the resource that is limiting the throughput of the rest of your processing because of inherent limitations. Therefore, eliminating a bottleneck has the net effect of shifting the bottleneck. With any luck, though, the new bottleneck will be wider.

A typical bottleneck is a physical disk drive. You might need to get data off of the disk drive a bit faster, and be limited by the speed of data retrieval off the drive. But is this the real problem? Is the problem the disk drive, the controller, or the operating system? Are you doing something inappropriate, like using operating system I/O?

It is essential to understand where bottlenecks can occur, and also where they tend to occur and under what circumstances. These potential bottlenecks are your *performance variables*—those things you adjust, tune, and balance to get the best possible results for your application.

Performance Variables

There are a variety of parameters which are going to drive performance. Some of them you can control; some you can not. Sometimes, decisions are thrust upon you.

> **NOTE**
>
> I can't tell you how many times I am given a hardware platform and then told to solve the problem. It is important to identify the problem and *then* pick a solution. Seems simple, doesn't it?

This section discusses variables that affect performance and defines which ones vary under your control.

Architecture

CPU/SMP Management
I/O
Network
Concurrency

Application

Query
Logical Design
Physical Design

> *Server*
>
> Configuration
> Optimizer
> Lock Management
>
> *Concurrency*
>
> Maintenance Activity
> Dump/Load
> Index Creation
> Batch Activity
> Concurrency Management

As you look over this list at categories and subcategories, you will find there are some variables that you can affect and some that are fixed and would require hardware upgrades to change.

The intent of this section is not to identify how to fix all of the problems associated with these variables (you'll be doing this throughout the book), but to identify potential problem areas about which you should start to think.

Architecture

Each subcategory has further subcategories. For example, under CPU/SMP management, how fast is your CPU? Can you make it faster? Probably not without an upgrade, but how about changing the number of CPU cycles needed by a transaction? This enables transactions to run with fewer CPU cycles, giving you a virtual CPU upgrade simply by writing better code.

Symmetric multiprocessing SMP is an open question requiring an understanding of the underlying software. For example, can you affect the number of CPU engines for a query? This is not a configurable option, and varies by server and version. MS 6.0 is the first level of server that enables multi-engine threading for queries (this is nifty). This enables idle processors to help a query that is so complex that response time is not adequate with a single CPU.

You cannot change the I/O rate for a physical device. You can, however, change the physical I/O requirements of a transaction by changing the physical design of the database or by reducing the amount of requested data. For example, limit the maximum number of rows to be retrieved from the database. Will a user really need all 4,000,000 rows? Usually not.

The network is a whole new world. You should always regard it as a bottleneck, and should make a point of reducing network traffic whenever and wherever possible. You can do this by reducing the number of packets transmitted or by increasing the TDS packet size. Finally, you can use a different network topology that better suits your requirements.

Concurrency issues are not tunable, but are sometimes containable. For example, if logging overhead is causing problems, you can try committing less frequently or putting the log on a higher-speed device. Additionally, if sequential reads are slower than you would expect, you might be able to redistribute the data on your disks. Overall server architecture also affects concurrency. For example, additional memory is going to be necessary. Along those lines, some dedicated hardware is normal for high-transaction-volume or high-concurrency systems.

Application

The most important issue from an application-tuning standpoint is to be sure your user asks the right query. I frequently suggest substantial user training, particularly where there are ad hoc queries involved, because horrid SQL is probably the number-one cause of bad performance. Bad queries can have a variety of flavors: unnecessary joins, insufficient joins, lack of search arguments (more on this later), or an inability to take advantage of server features (for example, the update in place).

Logical design issues might involve changing table normalization to reduce joins, or vertical segmentation to take infrequently referenced data out of the scanned table.

Physical design is what we tend to fix most often when we begin to tune performance. Correct index selection can often fix (read: improve the performance of) otherwise problematic queries, including adding and removing indexes. Adding indexes tends to help queries but hurt update performance. You can also provide summary data or redundant data. Finally, you can physically segment your data for the purpose of scanning multiple physical disks and spreading throughput across devices.

Cursors are a favorite way programmers can foul up performance, particularly concurrency. A poorly written cursor can lock huge amounts of data. Cursors are also a dramatically slower way to access data. Tell your programmers that cursors are a way of treating a set-processing language like a row-processing language and that it is usually the wrong approach.

Batch programming tends to be the Achilles' heel of applications. When the server engine decides it is time to swap out a process, it needs to perform overhead to be able to come back to the point where it left off. The more processing involved, the more overhead. As a result, as batch processes get longer and longer, the swapping takes up more and more CPU time. This means less time for OLTP processes.

Server

The database server is the most tunable component of your application. For example, you can configure and reconfigure memory, cache, locks, disk-resource dissemination, connections, and dozens of other things. There are also some components you cannot easily tune.

For example, you cannot rewrite the optimizer. The optimizer is going to pick its own path, join order, and/or other search tactic.

> **NOTE**
>
> You can, for a particular query or session, force a join order or index selection on the optimizer. (This is the topic of Chapter 16, "Managing the SQL Server Optimizer.") First you identify what the optimizer is doing, and then you identify ways of saying "I think that is a bad idea. Do it my way instead." Note that it is very unusual to pick a better join order than the optimizer picks.

Lock management is handled automatically by the server; the quantity of locks is configured by the system administrator. The SQL Server manages the use of the locks. You can favorably affect the server locking by keeping transactions short and by *not changing* transaction isolation levels. Also avoid situations where deadlocking becomes likely.

Server overhead can sometimes be handled with hardware, such as using a solid-state device for the log to increase transaction throughput where the log has been positively identified as a bottleneck. The audit queue, as a bottleneck, can sometimes be managed by throwing memory at the situation (that is, configuring the audit queue for more rows).

Concurrency

You will probably want to identify a batch window for performing, among other things, maintenance activity (such as dbcc and database dumps), index creations and re-creations (no, this is not something you normally need to do periodically), or other batch activity (reporting, mailing labels, long-running ad hoc queries). All of these activities are of the type that tends to hog an entire processor (or potentially a set of processors). It is also the type of activity that can lock tables or databases, which reduces OLTP concurrency.

Fitting all of your work into a batch window is sometimes a highly specialized art form, particularly in 24×7 shops (shops that require 24-hours-a-day, 7-days-a-week operation).

Tuning Approach

Before beginning to tune, gather as much information as possible about the circumstances surrounding the perceived performance problem. Remember that you can't tune for everything. You need to identify and prioritize problems before addressing them. For example, you have a problem query that runs for 40 hours. You can fix the problem by denormalizing and adding four indexes to the tables. The cost of this is six additional disk drives and three hours added to your batch (dump) window.

Ask yourself whether it is worth the cost. Are you fixing this query for the CEO of the company, who needs this report updated every two hours, or is this query being run every six months by an associate accountant who has completely fouled up your expense checks for the past four months? Sometimes the decisions are easy.

Spotlight obvious problems. Over the course of the next several chapters, you get a feel for what the problems are going to be, if you haven't had that type of experience already. If you are tuning, consider options that are transparent to users, such as indexes and segments.

Estimate your requirements prior to the final rollout. Find or build a tool that simulates user activity and act on the information you acquire. You can assume that whichever volumes of data your users swear they are going to use are lies, but at least you can turn back to them later and say, "I tuned for what you told me. Now that I can see what you need, I will act accordingly."

When you have specific problems, follow these steps:

1. Identify baseline time for your CPU and controllers so that you can identify *expected* results.

2. Identify whether the results are expected but unsavory or unexpected but unsavory.

3. Examine the problem query. Is it too complex? Does the query resolve the user's actual need (frequently, the answer is no. More than once, I've seen 25 pages of stored procedure doing what could have been 4 `select` statements).

4. Are the indexes appropriately selected in the physical design? Is the optimizer using the indexes you think it should? (This is covered in Chapter 16.)

5. Is the optimizer selecting the correct path/join plan/approach?

6. When in doubt, break down the query. Do individual components take too long?

Finally, prioritize the problem. Does the situation/user/application/and so on warrant physical-design changes or other work on your part?

Summary

Set your expectations appropriately based on a thorough understanding of your system's strengths and limitations. You will find that there are physical limitations to your system, which you must understand. Set your expectations and lay your plans accordingly.

Understanding SQL
Server Storage
Structures

IN THIS CHAPTER

To get the best performance out of a high-performance vehicle, you occasionally need to tune the engine. However, before you can begin tuning a high-performance vehicle, you need to have a good understanding of the internals of the engine and how it works. Likewise, in order to tune SQL Server effectively, you need to have a good understanding of the internal storage structures and how SQL Server stores and manages objects and data within the database.

This chapter explores the basic storage structures in SQL Server and how they are managed and maintained. This information will help you better understand performance issues raised in the subsequent chapters.

SQL Server Storage Structures

SQL Server doesn't see storage in exactly the same way a DBA or end-user does. A DBA sees initialized devices, device fragments allocated to databases, segments defined within databases, tables defined within segments, and rows stored in tables. SQL Server views storage at a lower level as device fragments allocated to databases, pages allocated to tables and indexes within the database, and information stored on pages.

There are two basic types of storage structures in a database: linked data pages and index trees. All information in SQL Server is stored at the page level. When a database is created, all space allocated to it is divided into a number of pages, each page 2KB in size. There are five types of pages within SQL Server:

- Data and log pages
- Index pages
- Text/image pages
- Allocation pages
- Distribution pages

All pages in SQL Server contain a *page header*. The page header is 32 bytes in size and contains the logical page number, the next and previous logical page numbers in the page linkage, the object_id of the object the page belongs to, the minimum row size, the next available row number within the page, and the byte location of the start of the free space on the page.

You can examine the contents of a page header by using the DBCC PAGE command. You must be logged in as sa to run the DBCC PAGE command. The syntax for the DBCC PAGE command is as follows:

```
DBCC PAGE (dbid ¦ db_name, page_no [, 0 ¦ 1 ¦ 2 ])
```

The display options (0, 1, 2) determine how the page contents will be displayed. 0 is the default and displays only the page header without the page contents. 1 displays the page header and a hex dump of the page contents individually by row. 2 displays the same information as 1, but displays the page contents as a single block of data.

> **NOTE**
>
> You need to run the DBCC TRACEON (3604) command prior to running DBCC PAGE, or DBCC PAGE will print its output to the errorlog rather than to the terminal.

Here is a sample page header:

```
DBCC TRACEON (3604)
go
DBCC PAGE (perftune, 424, 0)
go

PAGE HEADER:
Page header for page 0xac0000
pageno=424 nextpg=0 prevpg=0 objid=288004057 timestamp=0001 00000b46
nextrno=25 level=0 indid=0  freeoff=832 minlen=2
page status bits: 0x1
```

The following is an explanation of the fields visible in the page header:

- pageno is the current page number (logical page number assigned when page is allocated to database).
- nextpg is the pointer to the next page in the page linkage.
- prevpg is the pointer to the previous page in the page linkage.
- objid is the object ID of the object to which this page belongs.
- indid is the index ID of the index to which this page belongs.
- level is the level within the index in which this page is found.
- nextrno is the row number of the next row to be inserted on this page.
- freeoff is the location of the free space at the end of the page.
- minlen is the minimum allowable length of any row on the page.

If indid is 0, this is a data or nonindex page. If it is an index page (indid != 0), level indicates the level within the index in which this page is found. (Index levels and index structures are covered in more detail later in this chapter in the "Indexes and the B-Tree Structure" section.)

You might be wondering, with five different types of pages within a database, how SQL Server keeps track of what object a page belongs to, if any. The allocation of pages within SQL Server is managed through the use of *allocation units* and *allocation pages*.

Allocation Pages

Space is allocated to a SQL Server database by the CREATE DATABASE and ALTER DATABASE commands. The space allocated to a database is divided into a number of 2KB pages. Each page is assigned a logical page number starting at page 0 and increasing sequentially. The pages are then divided into allocation units of 256 contiguous 2KB pages, or 512KB (1/2 megabyte) each. The first page of each allocation unit is an allocation page that controls the allocation of all pages within the allocation unit (see Figure 10.1). The first allocation page is logical page number 0, and subsequent allocation pages are stored at each multiple of 256.

FIGURE 10.1.

Allocation units within a SQL Server database.

█	1	2	3	4	5	6	7
8	9	10	11	12	13	14	15
16	17	18	19	20	21	22	23
24	25	26	27	28	29	30	31
32	33	34	35	36	37	38	39
40	41	42	43	44	45	46	47
...							
...							
...							
248	249	250	251	252	253	254	255

█	257	258	259	260	261	262	263
264	265	266	267	268	269	270	271
272	273	274	275	276	277	278	279
280	281	282	283	284	285	286	287
288	289	290	291	292	293	294	295
296	297	298	299	300	301	302	303
...							
...							
...							
504	505	506	507	508	509	510	511

█	513	514	515	516	517	518	519
520	521	522	523	524	525	526	527
528	529	530	531	532	533	534	535
536	537	538	539	540	541	542	543
544	545	546	547	548	549	550	551
552	553	554	555	556	557	558	559
...							
...							
...							
760	761	762	763	764	765	766	767

...

█ = Allocation page

The allocation pages control the allocation of pages to tables and indexes within the database. Pages are allocated in contiguous blocks of eight pages called *extents*. The minimum unit of allocation within a database is an extent. When a table is created, it is initially assigned a single extent, or 16KB of space, even if the table contains no rows. There are 32 extents within an allocation unit. (See Figure 10.2.)

FIGURE 10.2.

Extent within an allocation unit.

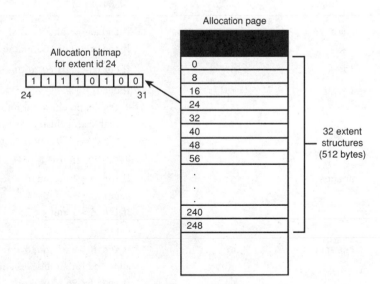

	257	258	259	260	261	262	263
264	265	266	267	268	269	270	271
272	273	274	275	276	277	278	279
280	281	282	283	284	285	286	287	← Extent
288	289	290	291	292	293	294	295
296	297	298	299	300	301	302	303
...							
...							
...							
504	505	506	507	508	509	510	511

An allocation page contains 32 extent structures for each extent within that allocation unit. Each extent structure is 16 bytes and contains the following information:

- Object ID of object to which extent is allocated
- Next extent ID in chain
- Previous extent ID in chain
- Allocation bitmap
- Deallocation bitmap
- Index ID (if any) to which the extent is allocated
- Status

The *allocation bitmap* for each extent structure indicates which pages within the allocated extent are in use by the table. (See Figure 10.3.)

FIGURE 10.3.

Diagram of the extent structures in allocation page 0 showing the allocation bitmap for extent ID 24.

Allocation bitmap
for extent id 24

1	1	1	1	0	1	0	0

24   31

Allocation page

0
8
16
24
32
40
48
56
.
.
.
240
248

32 extent structures (512 bytes)

If the allocation bit is on, the page is currently in use by the table or index. If the allocation bit is off, the page is reserved but not currently in use. The deallocation bitmap is used to identify pages that have become empty during a transaction that has not yet completed. The actual marking of the page as unused does not occur until the transaction is committed to prevent another transaction from allocating the page before the transaction is complete.

Pages not currently in use are reserved for use by that table or index and cannot be used by any other table or index within the database. This is the information you see reported by the sp_spaceused stored procedure. For example, consider the following output:

```
sp_spaceused titles
name           rows      reserved  data      index_size  unused
------------   --------  --------  --------  ----------  -----------
titles         18        48 KB     6 KB      8 KB        34 KB
```

reserved is the total number of kilobytes allocated to the table and its indexes (should be a factor of 8), data is the total number of kilobytes in use for data, index_size is the total number of kilobytes in use for all indexes on the table, and unused is allocated pages for the table and its indexes that are currently not being used. unused indicates the amount of space that can be used for the table or its indexes before additional extents need to be allocated. The titles table has 24 pages allocated to it—3 used for data, 4 used for its indexes, and 17 allocated pages that currently are not in use. This information is contained in the sysindexes table. (See Table 10.1.)

Table 10.1. The sysindexes table.

Column	Datatype	Description
name	varchar(30)	If indid >=1 and <= 250, name of index If indid = 0 or 255, name of table
id	int	ID of table related to this sysindexes row
indid	smallint	Index ID: 0 = table, no clustered index 1 = table and clustered index > 1 and <= 250 = nonclustered index 255 = text or image data
dpages	int	If indid = 0 or indid = 1, count of used data-only pages If indid > 1 and <= 250, count of leaf-level index pages
reserved	int	If indid = 0 or indid = 1, total number of pages allocated for all indexes and data If indid = 255, total number of pages allocated for text or image data

Column	Datatype	Description
		If indid > 1 and <= 250, total number of pages allocated to nonclustered index
used	int	If indid <= 1, total number of all used index and data pages for the table If indid = 255, total number of pages used for text or image data If indid >1 and <= 250, total number of pages for this index
rows	int	If indid <= 250, number of rows in the table If indid = 255, 0
first	int	If indid <= 1 or = 255, pointer to first data or text/image page If indid > 1 and <= 250, pointer to first leaf index page
root	int	If indid >= 1 and < 250, pointer to root page of index If indid = 0 or 255, pointer to last page in data or text/image chain
distribution	int	If indid >= 1 and < 255, pointer to distribution page for that index
OrigFillFactor	tinyint	The original fillfactor value used when the index was created
segment	smallint	Segment ID for segment from which this object is currently allocating space
status	smallint	Bitmap status for index: 1 - Abort command if attempt to insert duplicate key (IGNORE_DUP_KEY not specified) 2 - Unique index 4 - Abort command if attempt to insert duplicate row in nonunique clustered index (IGNORE_DUP_ROW not specified) 16 - Clustered index 64 - Clustered index allows duplicate rows (ALLOW_DUP_ROW set) 2048 - Index defined by PRIMARY KEY constraint 4096 - Index defined by UNIQUE constraint

continues

Table 10.1. continued

Column	Datatype	Description
rowpage	smallint	Maximum allowable number of rows per page
minlen	smallint	Minimum row width
maxlen	smallint	Maximum row width
maxirow	smallint	Maximum width of a nonleaf index row
keycnt	smallint	Number of columns in index
keys1	varbinary(255)	If indid >0 and <=250, description of index columns
keys2	varbinary(255)	If indid >0 and <=250, description of index columns
soid	tinyint	ID of sort order the index was created with (= 0 if no character data in the index)
csid	tinyint	ID of character set (= 0 if no character data in the index)

When a table or index requires more space, it checks the sysindexes table and compares the reserved column to the used column. If there are any reserved pages that are not used (reserved - used > 0), it allocates space to the table by using the following method:

```
if space is available on the current page then
    add record to the current page
else if there is a free page in the current extent
    add record to a free page in the current extent
    mark page as used
else if there is a free extent in the current allocation page
    allocate extent from current allocation page
    add record to first page in new extent
    mark page as used
else search all allocation pages for object following extent chain
        to locate a free extent
    allocate first free extent found
    add record to first page in new extent
    mark page as used
else
    allocate new extent from next allocation page in database with free extent
    add record to first page in new extent
    mark page as used
```

Data Pages

A *data page* is the basic unit of storage within SQL Server. All the other types of pages within a database are essentially variations of the data page. Figure 10.4 shows the basic structure of a data page.

FIGURE 10.4.

Structure of a SQL Server data page.

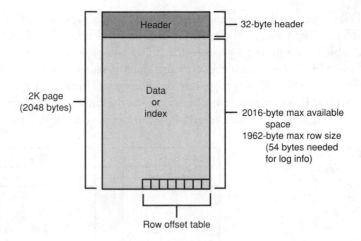

All data pages contain a 32-byte header, as described earlier. With a 2KB page (2048 bytes), this leaves 2016 bytes for storing data within the data page. In SQL Server, data rows cannot cross page boundaries; a data row must fit entirely within the data page. If there is not enough space at the end of a page to hold the entire row, it is stored on the next page in the page linkage. The maximum size of a single row within SQL Server is 1962 bytes, because pages in the transaction log are 2KB pages as well.

When a data row is logged, for example, during an insert, the entire row is written to a log page along with some logging information. This log information is 54 bytes per log record. Like data rows, log records cannot cross page boundaries. Because only 2016 bytes are available to store the log record, 2016 bytes minus 54 bytes of overhead leaves 1962 bytes for the data row. Therefore, 1962 bytes is the maximum data row size.

> **TIP**
>
> SQL Server enables you to create a table with data rows that could conceivably exceed 1962 bytes if it contains variable-length columns. SQL Server creates the table but gives you a warning message such as the following:
>
> ```
> The total row size, 2575, for table 't3' exceeds the maximum number of bytes
>  per row, 1962.
> ```
>
> If you attempt to insert a data row that actually exceeds 1962 bytes, or update the row so that its updated length exceeds 1962 bytes, you receive the following error message and the insert or update will fail:
>
> ```
> Msg 511, Level 16, State 2
> Updated or inserted row is bigger than maximum size (1962 bytes) allowed for
>  this table.
> ```

Data pages are linked to one another by using the *page pointers* (prevpg, nextpg) contained in the page header. (See Figure 10.5.) This page linkage enables SQL Server to locate all rows in a table by scanning all pages in the link. Data page *linkage* can be thought of as a two-way linked list, because each page contains the previous and next page pointer. This enables SQL Server to easily link new pages into or unlink pages from the page linkage by adjusting the page pointers. If nextpg equals 0, it indicates that the current page is the last page in the page chain. If prevpg equals 0, it indicates that the current page is the first page in the page chain.

FIGURE 10.5.

Linked data pages.

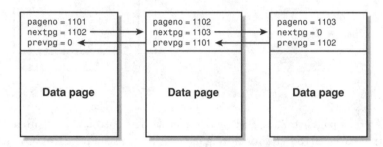

In addition to the page header, each data page also contains data rows and a *row offset table*. (Refer back to Figure 10.4.) The row offset table grows backward from the end of the page and contains the location of each row on the data page. Each entry in the row offset table is 2 bytes wide.

Data Rows

Data is stored on data pages in *data rows*. The size of each data row is a factor of the sum of the size of the columns plus the row overhead. Each record in a data page is assigned a row number. A single byte is used within each row to store the row number. Therefore, SQL Server has a maximum limit of 256 rows per page, because that is the largest value that can be stored in a single byte. Figure 10.6 displays the structure of a data row.

FIGURE 10.6.

Structure of a data row.

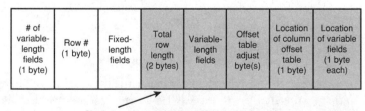

Shaded areas represent data present only when table
contains variable-length columns.

For a data row containing all fixed-length columns, there are four bytes of overhead per row:

- 1 byte to store the number of variable-length columns (in this case, 0)
- 1 byte to store the row number
- 2 bytes in the row offset table at the end of the page to store the location of the row on the page

If a data row contains variable-length columns, there is additional overhead per row. A data row is variable in size if any column is defined as varchar, varbinary, or allows null values. In addition to the 4 bytes of overhead described previously, the following bytes are required to store the actual row width and location of columns within the data row:

- 2 bytes to store the total row width
- 1 byte per variable-length column to store the starting location of the column within the row
- 1 byte for the column offset table
- 1 additional byte for each 256-byte boundary passed (adjust table)

Within each row containing variable-length columns, SQL Server builds a column offset table backward for the end of the row for each variable-length column in the table. Because only 1 byte is used for each column with a maximum offset of 255, an adjust byte must be created for each 256-byte boundary crossed as an additional offset. Variable-length columns are always stored after all fixed-length columns, regardless of the order of the columns in the table definition.

Figure 10.7 demonstrates what the row structure looks like for the following table with all fixed-length fields:

```
create table t1
        (cola char(10),
         colb char(25),
         colc int)
```

FIGURE 10.7.

Diagram of a row with all fixed-length fields.

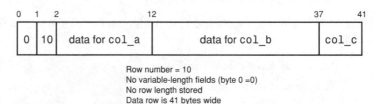

Row number = 10
No variable-length fields (byte 0 =0)
No row length stored
Data row is 41 bytes wide

Figure 10.8 demonstrates what the row structure looks like for the following table:

```
create table t2
        (col_a char(10),
         col_b varchar(25),
         col_c int,
         col_d varchar(10))
```

FIGURE 10.8.

Diagram of a row with variable-length fields.

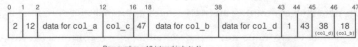

| 2 | 12 | data for col_a | col_c | 47 | data for col_b | data for col_d | 1 | 43 | 38 (col_d) | 18 (col_b) |

Row number = 12 (stored in byte 1)
2 variable-length fields (stored in byte 0)
Data row is 47 bytes wide (stored in bytes 16 and 17)
Adjust byte location at byte 43 (stored in byte 44)
Two bytes at end of record to store location of variable-length columns

Estimating Row and Table Sizes

Knowing the size of a data row and the corresponding overhead per row helps you determine the number of rows that can be stored per page. The number of rows per page is important when you explore performance issues in subsequent chapters. In a nutshell, a greater number of rows per page can help query performance by reducing the number of pages that need to be read to satisfy the query. Conversely, a fewer number of rows per page helps improve performance for concurrent transactions by reducing the chances of two or more users accessing rows on the same page that may be locked.

These topics are explored in greater detail in subsequent chapters, but for now, let's take a look at how you can estimate row and table sizes.

If you have only fixed-length fields in your table and none that allow null values, it is easy to estimate the row size:

Sum of column widths

+ 1 byte to store the row number

+ 1 byte to store the number of variable-length columns

+ 2 bytes per row in the row offset table

There is a minimum amount of overhead of 4 bytes for every data row. For example, consider table t1, described previously, which contains three fixed-length columns (char(10), char(25), and int). The total row size is the following:

(10 + 25 + 4) + 4 = 43 bytes per row

If the table contains any variable-length fields or nullable columns, the row width is determined as follows:

Sum of all fixed column widths

+ 1 byte to store the row number

+ 1 byte to store the number of variable-length columns

+ 2 bytes per row in the row offset table

+ sum of average size of variable-length columns

+ number of variable-length columns (1 byte per column)

+ 1 byte (for column offset table within row)

+ 2 bytes (for row length)

= subtotal

+ subtotal/256 rounded up to next integer

= average row size

Each row containing variable-length columns has a minimum 4 bytes of overhead, plus a minimum of 5 bytes of overhead if it contains at least one nullable or variable-length field. Let's examine table t2, which contains two fixed-length columns (char(10) and int) and two variable-length columns (varchar(25) and varchar(10)). Let's assume that the average data size for both col_b and col_d is half the column size—13 and 5 bytes, respectively. The calculation of the average row size is as follows:

(10 + 4) (for fixed fields)

+ 4 (for overhead)

+ (13 + 5) (for sum of average size of variable fields)

+ 2 (number of variable fields)

+ 1 (for columns offset table)

+ 2 (for row length)

= 41 (subtotal)

+ round(41/256) (adjust table bytes)

= 42 bytes (average row size)

NOTE

For a listing of SQL Server datatypes and their corresponding sizes, refer to Chapter 4, "Transact-SQL Datatypes."

When you know the average data row size, you can determine the number of rows per page by dividing the row size into the available space on the data page, 2016 bytes. For example, if your average row size is 42 bytes, the average number of rows per page is the following:

2016 / 42 = 48 rows per page

Remember to "round down" any fractions because you cannot have only a portion of a row on a data page. If the calculation works out to something like 24.8 rows per page, it actually requires two pages to store 25 rows because the 25th row will not fit entirely on the first data page. If you are using a fill factor other than the default (covered later in this chapter), you need to multiply the number of rows per page times the fill factor percentage as well. For this example, assume that the default fill factor of 0 is used, which indicates the data pages are 100 percent full.

When you know the average number of rows per page, you can calculate the number of pages required to store the data by dividing the total number of rows in the table by the number of rows per page. To follow the example, if you have 100,000 rows in the table, the number of pages required to store the data is the following:

100,000 / 48 = 2083.333...

In this case, you "round up" the value to get the actual number of pages (2084) required to store all the data rows. The size of the table in pages is also the cost in number of page I/Os to perform a table scan. A table scan involves reading the first page of the table and following the page pointers until all pages in the table have been read. The table scan, as you will explore in subsequent chapters, is the fallback technique employed by the SQL Server optimizer to satisfy a query when there is no less-expensive alternative, such as a clustered or nonclustered index, to find the matching data rows.

The Row Offset Table

The location of a row within a page is determined by using the row offset table at the end of the page. (See Figure 10.9.)

FIGURE 10.9.

Row offset table on data page.

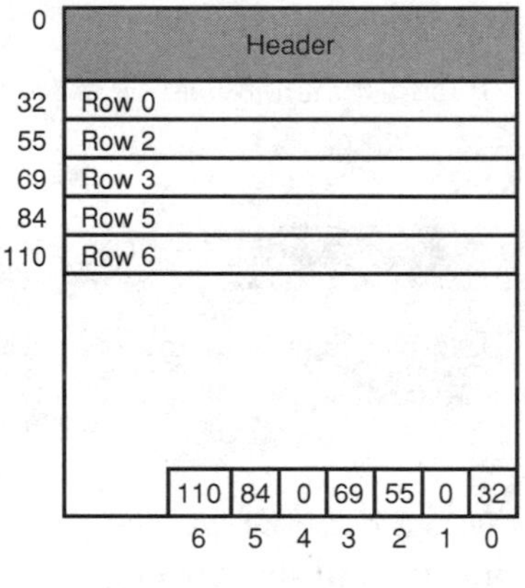

To find a specific row within the data page, SQL Server looks in the row offset table for the starting byte address within the data page for that row ID.

Note that SQL Server keeps all free space at the end of the data page, shifting rows up to fill in where a previous row was deleted and ensuring no space fragmentation within the page. However, the row ids for the remaining rows do not change. This helps reduce the amount of overhead involved to maintain row ID pointers in nonclustered indexes (covered later in this chapter in the "Indexes and the B-Tree Structure" section).

If the offset table contains a zero value for a row ID, that indicates that the row has been deleted. The next row to be inserted into the table reuses the first available row ID, and the row offset is set accordingly. Whether the new row is inserted at the end of the page or between existing rows depends on whether there is a clustered index created on the table that requires the rows to be in sorted order. Let's examine both scenarios, first looking at a table without a clustered index.

A table without a clustered index is stored as a heap structure. All new rows are added at the end of the table on the last data page. No sorting of the data rows is maintained. Assume that the page displayed in Figure 10.10 is the last page in the table.

FIGURE 10.10.

Deletion and insertion of a row without clustered index.

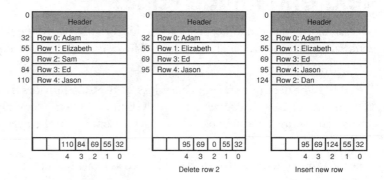

As row 2 is deleted, all remaining rows on the page are shifted upward, the offsets are adjusted, and the offset for row 2 in the row offset table is set to 0. As a new row is inserted back into the page, it is assigned row ID 2 but is inserted after the last existing row on the page. The offset for row 2 is set to the location of the new row on the page.

If the table has a clustered index defined on it, the rows must be kept in physically sorted order within the data page. Figure 10.11 demonstrates the sequence of events when deleting and inserting rows into a sorted table.

FIGURE 10.11.

Deletion and insertion of a row with clustered index.

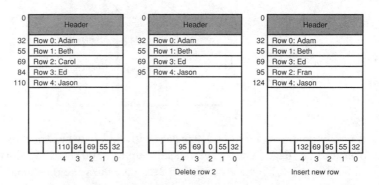

Again, you'll notice that all rows below row 2 are moved up on the page when row 2 is deleted, but the row ids don't change. The row offsets are adjusted to reflect the new row locations within the page, and the row offset for row 2 is set to 0. When a new row is inserted into the page, it is inserted in the proper sort order between rows 3 and 4, and row 4 is shifted down on the page. The new row, however, is reassigned row ID 2, and the offset table is adjusted accordingly for rows 2 and 4. Although the row IDs may not be in physical order, the actual data values are. Remember, the advantage of this approach is to minimize updates to row pointers in the nonclustered indexes. If the row ID for an existing row does not change, the index row pointing to that data row does not need to be updated.

Text and Image Pages

Occasionally, you need to store large text values or *binary large objects* (*BLOBs*) in a database—data values that could be millions of bytes. However, SQL Server is limited to a maximum row size of 1962 bytes.

To address the need to store large data values, SQL Server provides the text and image datatypes that enable you to store data values up to 2GB in size. This is accomplished by storing the text/image data across a number of linked pages separate from the page containing the data row itself.

The data row contains a 16-byte field, defined as a `varbinary(16)`, containing a pointer to the first page containing the text/image data for that column. The text/image data is then spread across many pages as necessary to store the data, up to 2GB. (See Figure 10.12.) Each text/image page contains an embedded pointer to the next linked text/image page for that column.

FIGURE 10.12.

SQL Server text/image pages.

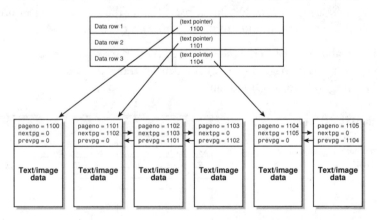

A *text/image page* is a standard data page with a 32-byte header, plus an additional 112 bytes of overhead per page. A text page can store up to 1800 bytes of information. Therefore, a data value that is 1801 bytes requires two 2KB pages to store the data.

If a row is inserted into a table containing a text/image column that allows null values and the column is initially null, the column is not initialized with a text page pointer saving 2KB of storage for that row. However, once the text value for that row is updated to something other than null, at least one text/image page is linked to that row even if the text/image column is subsequently set to NULL.

Text/image data is retrieved by reading the pointer in the data row, reading the data from the page pointed to by the text/image pointer, and following the embedded page pointers in the text/image pages until nextpg equals 0, signaling the end of the text data for that column.

For any table containing any text/image columns, an additional row is added to the sysindexes table with an indid of 255. The name of the index is system-generated by prepending a t to the table name. For example, the name in sysindexes for the titles table would be ttitles. This row is used for allocating and maintaining the text/image pages for that table. Text/image pages are allocated from a different set of extents than the data or index pages.

Indexes and the B-Tree Structure

To this point, you have examined only the table structure. A table with no clustered index is stored as a heap structure. All data is added at the end of the table. You can think of it as a single file where all new records are merely added to the bottom of the file.

This structure is the fastest way of adding data to the table. When there is no clustered index on the table, there is a row in sysindexes with an indid of 0. The root column of this row points to the last page in the table where inserts are to occur. (See Figure 10.13.) SQL Server adds records to this page until the page is full and then links in a new page to the table.

FIGURE 10.13.

SQL Server heap storage.

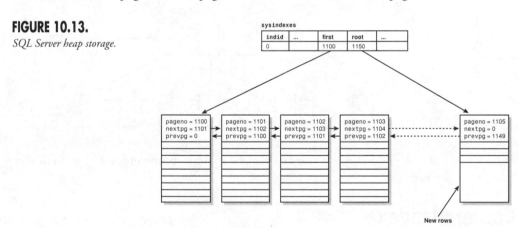

Needless to say, this is not a very efficient method for retrieving data. To find a specific record, you have to start at the top of the pile and read through each record until you find the requested record. This is referred to as a *table scan*. Because SQL Server doesn't know whether the first record found is the only record to be found, it continues reading all records until it reaches the end of the table. If a table is of sufficient size—for example, 100,000 pages—you probably don't want to have to scan all 100,000 pages to read or modify a single record.

You need to have a mechanism to identify specific records within a table quickly and easily. SQL Server provides this mechanism through two types of indexes: clustered and nonclustered.

Indexes are storage structures separate from the data pages in the table itself. The primary functions of indexes are to provide faster access to the data and provide a means for enforcing uniqueness of your data rows.

All SQL Server indexes are *B-Tree*, or *Balanced-Tree* structures. (See Figure 10.14.) There is a single root page at the top of the tree, branching out into *N* number of pages at each intermediate level until it reaches the bottom, or leaf level, of the index. The index tree is traversed by following pointers from the upper-level pages down through the lower-level pages. In addition, each index level is a separate page chain.

There may be many intermediate levels in an index. The number of levels is dependent on the index key width, the type of index, and the number of rows and/or pages in the table. The number of levels is important in relation to index performance, as you will see later in this chapter in the "Indexes and Performance" section.

FIGURE 10.14.

B-Tree structure.

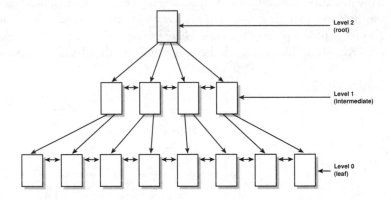

You need to have

SQL Server indexes are limited to a maximum of 16 columns in the index with a maximum total index key width of 255 bytes.

Clustered Indexes

When a clustered index is created on a table, the data in the table is physically sorted in clustered index key order. SQL Server allows only one clustered index per table because there is only one way to physically sort the data in the table. A *clustered index* can be thought of as a filing cabinet. The data pages are like the folders in a file drawer in alphabetical order, and the data rows are like the records in the file folder, also in sorted order.

The intermediate index levels can be thought of as the file drawers themselves, also in alphabetical order at a higher level up, assisting you in finding the appropriate file folder. Figure 10.15 shows an example of a clustered index.

FIGURE 10.15.

Clustered index structure.

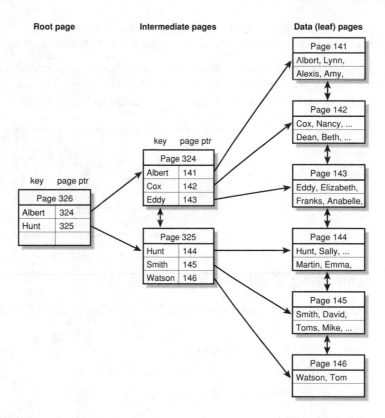

Notice how in Figure 10.15, the data is stored in clustered index order. This feature makes clustered indexes useful for range retrieval queries because the rows within the range are physically located in the same or adjacent data pages.

The data pages and clustered index are tightly coupled to each other. The clustered index contains a pointer to every data page in the table. In essence, the data page is the leaf level of the clustered index. To find all instances of a clustered index key value, you must eventually access the data page and scan the rows on that page.

SQL Server performs the following steps when searching for a data row by using the clustered index:

1. Queries sysindexes for the table where indid = 1 and get the address of the root page.
2. Compares the search value against the key values on the root page.
3. Finds the highest key value on the page where the key value is less than or equal to the search value.
4. Follows the page pointer to the next level down in the index.
5. Continues following page pointers as in steps 3 and 4 until the data page is reached.

6. Searches the rows on the data page to locate a match for the search value. If a matching row is not found on that data page, there are no matching rows in the table.

Because clustered indexes contain only page pointers, the size and number of levels in a clustered index is dependent on the width of the index key and the number of pages in the table. The structure of a clustered index row is detailed in Figure 10.16.

FIGURE 10.16.

Clustered index row structure.

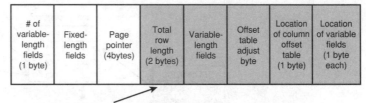

Shaded areas represent data present only when index contains variable-length columns.

Estimating Clustered Index Size

The formula for determining clustered index row width with all fixed-length fields is the following:

> Sum of fixed-length fields
>
> + 1 byte (number of variable columns)
>
> + 4 bytes (page pointer)

The formula for determining clustered index row width with variable-length fields is this:

> Sum of fixed-length fields
>
> + 1 byte (number of variable columns)
>
> + 4 bytes (page pointer)
>
> + 2 bytes (index row width)
>
> + sum of average width variable columns
>
> + 1 byte (adjust table)
>
> + 1 byte (location of offset table)
>
> + 1 byte per variable-length column

Assume you have a clustered index on a char(10) column that doesn't allow null values. Your index row size would be the following:

> 10 bytes
>
> + 4 bytes (page pointer)
>
> + 1 byte (number of variable columns = 0 in this case)
>
> = 15 bytes per index row

Because the clustered index contains a pointer to each data page in the table, the number of rows at the bottom level of the index is equal to the number of pages in the table.

If your data row size is 42 bytes, you can get 48 data rows per data page. If you have 100,000 rows in the table, it works out to 2084 pages in the table. Therefore, you have 2084 rows in the bottom level of the clustered index. Each index page, like a data page, has 2016 bytes available for storing index row entries. To determine the number of clustered index rows per page, divide the index row size into 2016 bytes and multiply by the fill factor. For this example, assume the default fill factor is being applied, which fills clustered index pages about 75 percent full:

2016 / 15 = 134.4 rounded down to 134 rows per page × .75 = 100 rows per page

At 100 rows per page, you need 2084 / 100 = 20.84, rounded up to 21 pages, to store all the rows at the bottom level of the index.

The top level of the index must be a single root page. You need to build levels on top of one another in the index until you reach a single root page. To determine the total number of levels in the index, use the following algorithm:

```
N = 0
divide number of data pages by number of index rows per page
while number of index pages at level N is > 1
begin
    divide number of pages at level N by number of rows per page
    N = N+1
end
```

When the number of pages at level N equals 1, you are at the root page, and N+1 equals the number of levels in the index. The total size of the clustered index in number of pages is the total sum of all pages at each level.

Applying this algorithm to the example gives the following results:

Level 0: 2084 / 100 = 21 pages
Level 1: 21 / 100 = 1 page

Thus, the index contains two levels, for a total size of 22 pages, or 44KB.

The I/O cost of retrieving a single row by using the index is the number of levels in the index plus a single data page. Contrast this with the cost of table scan for the example:

2 index levels + 1 data page = 3 page I/Os

Table scan = 2084 page I/Os

You can easily see the performance advantage during a `select` that having an index on the table can provide. An index is also helpful during data modifications to identify the rows quickly that are specified to be updated or deleted.

Nonclustered Indexes

A *nonclustered index* is a separate index structure independent of the physical sort order of the data in the table. (See Figure 10.17.) SQL Server allows up to 249 nonclustered indexes per table. Without a clustered index, the data is stored in the table as a heap structure, with no specific sort order applied.

FIGURE 10.17.

Nonclustered index structure.

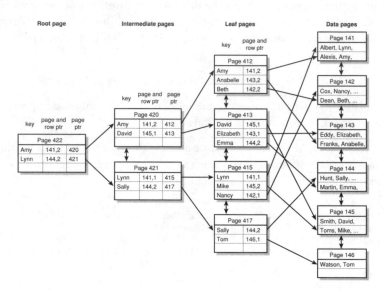

You can think of an nonclustered index like a index in the back of a road atlas. The towns are not located in any sort of structured order within a road atlas; rather, they seem to be spread randomly throughout the maps. To find a specific town, you look up the name of the town in the index that contains all towns in alphabetical order. For the town name you are looking for, you find a page number and the coordinates on that page where the town can be found.

A nonclustered index works in a similar fashion. The data rows may be randomly spread throughout the table. The nonclustered index tree contains the index keys in sorted order, with the leaf level of the index containing a pointer to the data page and the row number within the page where the index key value can be found. There is a row in the leaf level for every data row in the table.

The intermediate- and root-level pages contain the entire leaf level row information plus an additional page pointer to the page at the next level down containing the key value in the first row.

SQL Server performs the following steps when searching for a data row by using the nonclustered index:

1. Queries `sysindexes` for the table where `indid` > 1 and <= 250 and get the address of the root page for this index.

2. Compares the search value against the key values on the root page.

3. Finds the highest key value on the page where the key value is less than or equal to the search value.

4. Follows the page pointer to the next level down in the index.

5. Continues following page pointers as in steps 3 and 4 until the leaf page is reached.

6. Searches the rows on the leaf page to locate a match for the search value. If a matching row is not found on that leaf page, there are no matching rows in the table.

7. If a match is found on the leaf page, follows the pointer to the data page and row ID to retrieve the requested data row.

Because nonclustered indexes contain page and row pointers, the size and number of levels in a nonclustered index is dependent on the width of the index key and the number of rows in the table. The structure of an nonclustered index row is detailed in Figure 10.18.

FIGURE 10.18.

Nonclustered index leaf row structure.

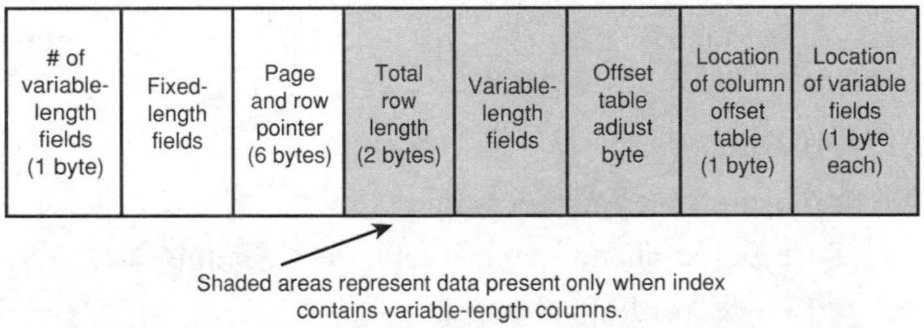

# of variable-length fields (1 byte)	Fixed-length fields	Page and row pointer (6 bytes)	Total row length (2 bytes)	Variable-length fields	Offset table adjust byte	Location of column offset table (1 byte)	Location of variable fields (1 byte each)

Shaded areas represent data present only when index contains variable-length columns.

The nonleaf rows of a nonclustered index contain the entire leaf row information—index key plus page and row pointer—and an additional page pointer to point to the pages at the next lower level. The nonleaf rows of a clustered index are constructed similarly to a clustered index. (See Figure 10.19.)

FIGURE 10.19.

Nonclustered index nonleaf row structure.

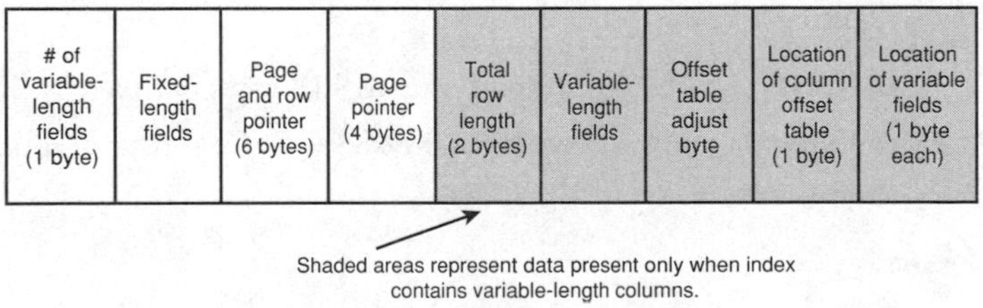

# of variable-length fields (1 byte)	Fixed-length fields	Page and row pointer (6 bytes)	Page pointer (4 bytes)	Total row length (2 bytes)	Variable-length fields	Offset table adjust byte	Location of column offset table (1 byte)	Location of variable fields (1 byte each)

Shaded areas represent data present only when index contains variable-length columns.

Estimating Nonclustered Index Size

The formula for determining nonclustered leaf index row width with all fixed-length fields is this:

> Sum of fixed-length fields
>
> + 1 byte (number of variable columns)
>
> + 6 bytes (page and row pointer)

Use this formula to determine nonclustered leaf index row width with variable-length fields:

> Sum of fixed-length fields
>
> + 1 byte (number of variable columns)
>
> + 6 bytes (page and row pointer)
>
> + 2 bytes (index row width)
>
> + Sum of average width variable columns
>
> + 1 byte (adjust table)
>
> + 1 byte (location of offset table)
>
> + 1 byte per variable-length column

Let's assume you have a nonclustered index on a char(10) column that doesn't allow null values. The leaf index row size is the following:

> 10 bytes
>
> + 6 bytes (page and row pointer)
>
> + 1 byte (number of variable columns = 0 in this case)
>
> = 17 bytes per leaf index row

Because the leaf level of a nonclustered index contains a pointer to each data row in the table, the number of rows at the leaf level of the index is equal to the number of rows in the table.

If you have 100,000 rows in the table, you'll have 100,000 rows in the nonclustered leaf level. Each nonclustered index page, like a data page, has 2016 bytes available for storing index row entries. To determine the number of nonclustered leaf index rows per page, divide the leaf index row size into 2016 bytes:

> 2016 / 17 = 118.6 rounded down to 118 rows per page × .75 = 88 rows per page

At 88 rows per page, you need 100,000 / 88 = 1136.4, rounded up to 1137 pages, to store all the rows at the leaf level of the index.

The nonleaf rows of a nonclustered index are like clustered index rows in that they contain pointers to all pages at the next level down in the index. Each nonleaf row contains the full index row from the leaf level plus an additional page pointer, 4 bytes in size. Therefore, the size of the nonleaf rows equals this:

> Size of leaf row
>
> + 4 bytes (page pointer)

For the example, the nonleaf rows are the following:

> 17 bytes (leaf index row size)
>
> + 4 bytes (page pointer)
>
> = 21 bytes per nonleaf index row

To determine the number of nonclustered nonleaf index rows per page, divide the nonleaf index row size into 2016 bytes and multiply by the fill factor. For this example, you use a fill factor of 75 percent:

> 2016 / 21 = 96 rows per page × .75 = 72 nonleaf rows per page

Like the clustered index, the top level of the index must be a single root page. You need to build levels on top of one another in the index until you reach a single root page. To determine the total number of levels in the nonclustered index, use the following algorithm:

```
N = 0
divide number of data rows by number of index rows per page
while number of index pages at level N is > 1
begin
    divide number of pages at level N by number of rows per page
    N = N+1
end
```

When the number of pages at level N equals 1, you are at the root page, and N+1 equals the number of levels in the index. The total size of the nonclustered index in number of pages is the total sum of all pages at each level.

If you apply this algorithm to the example, you get the following results:

> Level 0: 100,000 / 88 = 1137 pages
> Level 1: 1137 / 72 = 16 pages
> Level 2: 16 / 72 = 1 page

Thus, the nonclustered index contains three levels, for a total size of 1154 pages, or 2308KB.

The I/O cost of retrieving a single row by using the index is the number of levels in the index plus a single data page. Contrast this with the cost of table scan for the example:

> 3 index levels + 1 data page = 4 page I/Os
>
> Table scan = 2084 page I/Os

Although a nonclustered index defined on the same column as a clustered index typically consists of one additional level resulting in one additional I/O, it is still significantly faster than a table scan. You can easily see the performance advantage during a SELECT that having an index on the table can provide. An index is also helpful during data modifications to identify quickly the rows specified to be updated or deleted.

Indexes and Performance

You've seen how indexes, by their nature, can help speed up data retrieval by giving you a direct path to the desired data and avoiding a costly table scan. However, indexes have an adverse impact on update performance because the indexes need to be maintained on the fly by SQL Server in order to keep the proper sort order within the index and table.

The disadvantage of clustered indexes is that, during inserts, the rows must be inserted into the appropriate location to maintain the sort order. This is just like a filing system. If you don't put the files away in alphabetical order, your filing system becomes worthless. Similarly, SQL Server maintains the sort order of your data when you update, insert, and delete data rows.

If there is not a clustered index on the table, rows are added at the end of the table as a heap. Any nonclustered indexes have the new row added in the appropriate location within the index leaf page, depending on the index key value.

With or without a clustered index on a table, every time you insert, delete, or update a row and it causes the row to move within the table, all nonclustered indexes on the table need to be updated to reflect the new row location. With a large number of indexes on a table, the overhead during data modification may become excessive. For tables involved in *On-line Transaction Processing* (OLTP) types of applications, you should try to keep the number of indexes to less than five.

Let's now examine what occurs in SQL Server when you modify data with indexes on the table.

SQL Server Index Maintenance

SQL Server indexes are *self-maintaining* structures. That is, they allocate additional space as needed and deallocate space as rows are deleted, while maintaining the sort order of the index tree. There is typically no need to perform a "reorg" on SQL Server indexes to rebuild and re-sort the index tree, because SQL Server typically keeps the index tree balanced on the fly.

50-50 Page Splits

Normally, when inserting data into a table with a clustered index, the row is inserted into the appropriate position within the appropriate data and/or index page. If the data or index page is full, SQL Server performs a 50-50 page split. (See Figure 10.20.)

FIGURE 10.20.

50-50 page split.

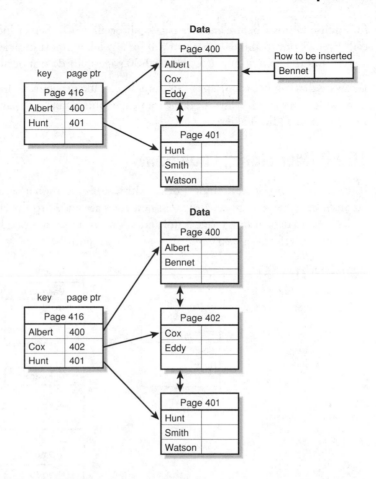

Whenever a page split occurs, the following steps also occur:

1. A new page is linked into the page chain.

2. Half of the rows on the affected page are moved to a new page.

3. The new row is inserted into the appropriate location.

4. The clustered index is updated to reflect the new data page; entries for new index pages are added to the next higher index level.

5. An entry for the new data row is added to all nonclustered indexes on the table.

6. All nonclustered indexes on the table are updated for each row that moved as a result of the page split.

A 50-50 page split obviously incurs index maintenance overhead and slows insert and update performance when it occurs. However, it helps to improve subsequent inserts and updates because the affected pages now are, on average, only about 50 percent full, leaving free space for additional rows before another page split occurs. SQL Server index and table pages typically average out to about 75 percent full for any table that is sufficiently active. This is desirable in an OLTP environment so that 50-50 page splits do not occur excessively.

Be aware that, on occasion, a page split might cascade up multiple levels within the index tree if the index pages are full as well. If the root page splits, a new root page is created and the index tree grows an additional level.

100-0 (Monotonic) Page Splits

If the table has no clustered index, or the clustered index is on a sequential key and data rows are inserted in sequential key order, all new rows are added to the end of the last page in the table. When a data or index page is full and a new row needs to be added to the end of the page, SQL Server performs a *monotonic page split*. (See Figure 10.21.)

FIGURE 10.21.

Monotonic (100-0) page split.

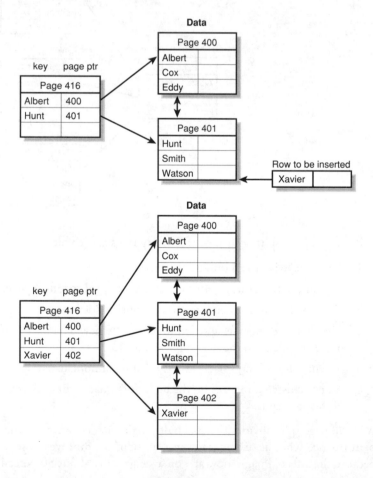

When a monotonic page split occurs, the following steps also occur:

1. A new page is linked into the page chain.
2. The new row is added to the new page.
3. An entry for the new data page is added to the clustered index; entries for new index pages are added to the next higher index level.
4. An entry is added for the new data row to all nonclustered indexes on the table.

As you can see, when you have a monotonic page split, there is less index maintenance and overhead involved. The downside to monotonic page splits or storage in a heap structure is that free space on previous pages is not reused because all new rows are added at the end of the page chain. The only way to recover this "lost" space is to rebuild the clustered index and reapply a new fill factor, which you will learn about shortly.

Overflow Pages

Let's examine what happens if you have a nonunique clustered index that allows duplicate rows and you need to add a duplicate value to the end of the page.

Look at Figure 10.22. At first, this insert looks similar to a monotonic page split, but it is slightly different in that the new page does not get recorded in the clustered index because it is in essence an "overflow" of a duplicate value from the previous page. An overflow page is generated only if the duplicate key value matches the last data row on the page and there is no more room to store additional rows on that page. The clustered index still points to the original data page, and the data page points to the overflow page.

Theoretically, this violates the normal B-Tree scheme but gives you a way of handling duplicate key values in a clustered index. If duplicate key values are split across normal data pages, you can miss the rows on a preceding data page if you use the normal method of traversing the index tree. For example, in Figure 10.22, if you had an index pointer to page 402 for the key value Eddy, you would traverse the index tree directly to page 402 and scan for all values of Eddy from that point forward, missing the entry for Eddy on page 400.

You may ask, with all the overhead involved in maintaining a sort order, why would I want to use clustered indexes? True, there is an overhead penalty paid when a page split occurs, but clustered indexes also provide a number of advantages:

- Because clustered indexes maintain a sort order and insert data into the appropriate location within the table, clustered indexes make use of free space in pages throughout the table, resulting in less wasted space.
- Clustered indexes can help improve performance for certain types of queries, such as range retrievals and queries with ORDER BY as you'll see in Chapter 11, "Designing Indexes for Performance."

- Clustered indexes take up much less space than nonclustered indexes defined on the same column(s).

- Clustered indexes typically provide a faster access path to the data than a similarly created nonclustered index, unless the nonclustered index can cover the query (which is also covered in Chapter 11).

- Clustered indexes are updated less often then nonclustered indexes. Review the previous examples. Every time you performed some form of operation on a data row, you had to update the nonclustered indexes. However, the clustered indexes needed to be updated only if you allocated or deallocated a data page.

FIGURE 10.22.

Overflow page.

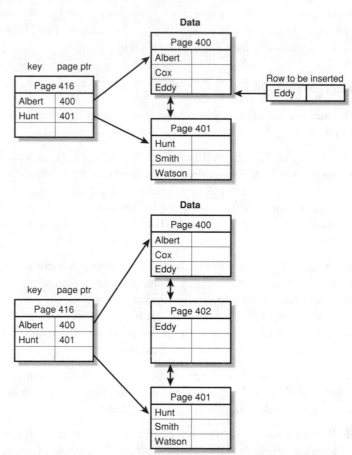

I once had a customer who had somehow become convinced that clustered indexes were a bad thing and got rid of all clustered indexes within his database. When I outlined the previous five points for him, he realized the error of his thinking and redefined his indexing scheme. In general, if you have one, and only one, index for a table, it is best to define it as a clustered index.

If you have multiple candidates for a clustered index and are not sure which column(s) to create the clustered index on, read Chapter 11, which covers index selection and provides guidelines on how to determine what indexes best support your queries and transactions.

Page Merges

As you delete data rows from pages, the remaining rows are shuffled upward on the page to keep all free space at the end of the page. However, if the clustered index key does not cause random inserts into these pages, the free space is not reused. This occurs if the clustered index is defined on a key value that tends to concentrate inserts to a specific portion of the table, such as at the end of the table if defined on a sequential key.

With no clustered index at all, the table is a heap structure and all inserts occur at the end of the page, with no preceding space being reused at all.

When all rows are deleted from a data page, the following occurs:

1. The page is removed from the page linkage.
2. The page is marked as unused in the extent structure bitmap on the allocation page for the allocation unit within which the page is located.

This page is still reserved for use by the table to which it is allocated. Unused pages are not deallocated from the table until all eight pages within the extent are marked as unused. At that point, the extent is deallocated and may be used by any object within the database that requires additional storage. Until the extent is deallocated, the table or index reuses the unused pages before a new extent is allocated to the table.

Pages within an index are managed similarly to data pages when rows are deleted—with one exception. When only one row is left on an index page, SQL Server merges the index row into an adjacent index page at the same level and removes the now-empty page from the index. This behavior helps to keep the index tree smaller and more efficient.

If the empty space within data and/or index pages is not reused, your table can become fragmented and might take up more space than anticipated. It also can cause your index tree to become unbalanced, with a crowding of data values at the end of the tree and the pages at the beginning of the tree being rather sparse.

This scenario is one of the few times you may have to perform a sort of "reorg" on your indexes to rebalance the index tree and defragment the data. Do this by dropping and re-creating your clustered index, reapplying a fill factor to the data to even out the distribution across the data pages.

The Fill Factor

The *fill factor* is a percentage specifying how full you want your index and/or data pages when the index is created. A lower fill factor has the effect of spreading data and index across more pages by leaving more free space in the pages. This reduces page splitting and dynamic reorganization, which can improve performance in environments where there are a lot of inserts and updates to the data. A higher fill factor has the effect of packing more data and indexes per page by leaving less free space in the pages. This is useful in environments where the data is relatively static, because it reduces the number of pages required for storing the data and its indexes and helps improve performance for queries by reducing the number of pages that need to be accessed.

The fill factor applies only at index creation time and is *not* maintained by the SQL Server. When you begin updating and inserting data, the fill factor eventually is lost. To reintroduce the fill factor, the index must be dropped and rebuilt. Providing a fill factor when creating a clustered index applies to the data pages for the table as well. A fill factor on a nonclustered index does not affect the data pages.

Setting the Fill Factor

The default fill factor is set at the server level, but it is typically provided at index creation. The typical default fill factor set at the server level is 0. A fill factor of 0 indicates that data and leaf pages are to be completely filled (100 percent) and the nonleaf pages filled to approximately 75 percent. This minimizes your data storage requirements, but it leaves some free space within the index tree to prevent excessive page splits within the nonleaf pages.

If you want to change the server-wide default for the fill factor, use the sp_configure command:

```
sp_configure 'fill factor',N
reconfigure
```

Typically, you specify the fill factor to be used for the index within the index creation statement:

```
create index idx_name on table (column)
with fillfactor=N
```

In both cases, N is the fill factor percentage to be applied. N can range from any valid integer between 0 and 100. 100 is typically used for static tables, and all data in index pages will be completely filled, except for the root page. For an OLTP environment, you may choose to use a fill factor value of 50, leaving your index and data pages only half full.

Because SQL Server indexes are self-maintaining and self-balancing, there is typically no need to reapply a fill factor to the index and/or data. With random activity and normal 50-50 page splits occurring, the data and indexes average out to about 75 percent full.

When might you need to reestablish the fill factor for your indexes or data? Some shops in intensive update situations drop and reload indexes periodically to spread the data and minimize page splits during heavy OLTP activity.

How might you determine whether you are experiencing excessive page splits? One way is to count the number of page splits recorded in your transaction log by running the following query:

```
select count(*) from syslogs where op = 16
```

By monitoring this value over time, you can determine when your page split count is increasing and also evaluate the effectiveness of various fill factor settings in reducing page splits.

If a table becomes very large and then very small, it is possible that rows may have become isolated within data pages. This space will not be recovered until the last row on the page is deleted and the page is marked as unused. To reclaim this space, you may choose to drop and re-create the clustered index.

Updates and Performance

All updates within SQL Server are essentially a DELETE followed by an INSERT, unless performed as a direct update in-place. With a clustered index on the table, the row is reinserted to the appropriate location on the appropriate data page relative to its physical sort order. Without a clustered index, the row is inserted into one of three locations:

- The same physical location on the same data page
- The same data page if there is room
- The last page in the heap

SQL Server performs two types of updates:

- Deferred updates
- Direct updates

Direct updates can occur as in-place or not-in-place updates.

Deferred Updates

A *deferred update* is a multistep process that occurs when the conditions are not met for a direct update to occur. Deferred updates are always required for the following:

- Updates that include a join
- Updates to columns used for referential integrity
- Updates in which the data modification statement can have a cascading effect

For example, consider a table with a unique index on an integer column and sequential data values stored in that column. The following update is executed:

```
update invoices set invoice_num = invoice_num + 1
```

If you start at the first row and update `invoice_num` from 1 to 2, and there is already a row with an `invoice_num` of 2, you violate the uniqueness of the index and the update will fail.

In order to perform this sort of update, SQL Server uses the deferred update method. With deferred updates, the following steps are executed:

1. All records to be modified are copied to the transaction log to reflect the old and new values for the column(s) to be modified.

2. SQL Server reads the transaction log, deletes the affected rows from the data pages, and deletes any affected index rows.

3. SQL Server rereads the transaction log, inserts the new rows from the log into the table, and inserts any affected index rows.

This method typically has the effect of generating more than the usual number of log records than a direct update. It also incurs the following additional overhead:

- Three data-page accesses for each data row
- Four log records generated for each updated row
- Two log records generated for each affected index row
- Two index traversals for each affected index
- Two scans of the log records

SQL Server may also apply the deferred method for inserts and deletes. Consider running the following `insert` on a table with no clustered index:

```
insert authors select * from authors
```

Because the table is a heap structure, all new rows are added at the end of the table. How does SQL Server know which rows are newly inserted rows and which are existing rows? SQL Server uses a deferred method of inserting the records by copying the data rows to be inserted into the transaction log. Then it reads the records in the transaction log, inserts them into the table, and inserts into any affected indexes as well.

Due to the additional processing overhead incurred when performing deferred updates, SQL Server attempts to perform direct updates whenever possible.

Direct Updates

Direct updates can be performed either in-place or not-in-place. A direct update not-in-place is still a DELETE followed by an INSERT, but the updates can be applied in a single pass. Direct updates not-in-place can take place if the following criteria are met:

- The number of rows affected can be determined at query compile time (that is, the WHERE clause has a search argument (SARG) that can be satisfied by a unique index).

■ The index chosen by the optimizer to satisfy the query is not being updated by the query.

■ No join clauses are used in the UPDATE statement.

For a direct update not-in-place, the row is deleted from the table, modified, and reinserted back into the table. Whether the updated row is inserted back into the table onto the same data page or a different data page depends on two things:

■ Whether there is still space available for the modified row on the current page

■ Whether the UPDATE caused a change to a clustered index key value forcing the row to be reinserted into a different data page

Figure 10.23 demonstrates a direct update not-in-place.

FIGURE 10.23.

Direct update not-in-place.

Update ... set lname = "Lynn" where lname = "Franks"

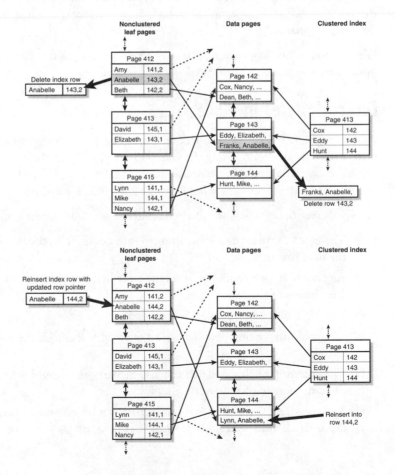

In this example, the UPDATE had to be performed not-in-place because the column being modified was the clustered index column, necessitating that the row be moved to a new page.

Even if the data row is reinserted in the same data page, it may be assigned a different row number than previously if there are any unused row numbers (row offset equals 0) less than the previous row ID for the affected row. This behavior necessitates that all index rows pointing to the data row be deleted and reinserted as well, in order to reflect the new page/row pointer information.

A direct update not-in-place produces the following overhead:

- A single data page access for each data row updated
- Two log records (DELETE, INSERT) generated for each updated data row
- Two log records (INSDELETE, INSINSERT) generated for each affected index row

If the column being modified is not part of an index and the row is deleted and reinserted in the same page with the same row ID, no index maintenance is required, because no index pointers need to be updated.

Direct updates not-in-place incur less overhead and are faster than deferred updates. Direct updates not-in-place are performed whenever possible.

Direct Updates In-Place

By default, SQL Server treats a direct update as a DELETE followed by an INSERT. An update in-place is a method for modifying the record directly, without the necessity for the DELETE. Because the row is modified in-place and doesn't move, updates in-place are faster than updates not-in-place—they incur fewer log writes and fewer index updates.

In SQL Server 6.0, the following criteria must be met for a direct update in-place to occur:

- The UPDATE cannot modify a clustered index column because this obviously requires the data row to move.
- An UPDATE trigger cannot exist on the table because the trigger requires the before and after image of the row.
- The table cannot be marked for replication.
- The column(s) being updated can be of variable length if the total row width doesn't change.
- The column(s) being updated can also be part of a nonunique nonclustered index if the index key is a fixed-width column.
- The column(s) being updated can be part of a unique nonclustered index if the index key is fixed-width and the WHERE clause criteria matches only one row.

SQL Server 6.0 also now enables direct updates in-place for multirow updates if the following criteria are met:

- The column being updated must be of fixed length.
- The column being updated cannot be part of a unique nonclustered index.
- The column being updated can be part of a nonunique, nonclustered index if the column is a fixed-width column.
- The index used to find the rows does not contain a column to be updated.
- The table does not contain a timestamp column.

A direct update in-place produces the following overhead:

- A single data page access for each data row updated
- A single log record (MODIFY) generated for each updated data row
- Two log records (INSDELETE, INSINSERT) generated for any affected index row (only if a column being updated is part of a nonclustered index)

Direct updates in-place incur the least amount of overhead of all the update methods. Direct updates in-place result in the fewest number of log records generated and the smallest opportunity for any index rows to need to be updated. SQL Server performs direct updates in-place whenever possible, rather than updates not-in-place.

Confirming Updates In-Place

One of the trickier tasks is determining whether a direct update occurs in-place or not-in-place. The SQL Server query optimizer reports only whether an update was direct or deferred, not whether it was in-place or not-in-place.

The only way to determine accurately whether a direct update occurs in-place or not-in-place is to examine the transaction log for the update in question.

The easy way to examine the transaction log records is to execute the UPDATE statement in question and to execute the following immediately:

```
select * from syslogs
```

As long as no one else has run a logged operation in that database between the time you execute your UPDATE statement and run the SELECT against the syslogs table, the last rows retrieved should be the rows related to the UPDATE in question.

If you are hoping for an update in-place, you want a row where op equals 9 sandwiched between a 0 and a 30. Table 10.2 lists some common op code values and the type of log record to which they relate.

Table 10.2. Transaction log op codes.

op	Description
0	BEGIN TRANSACTION
4	INSERT
5	DELETE
6	INSIND (indirect insert)
7	IINSERT (index insert)
8	IDELETE (index delete)
9	MODIFY (update in-place)
11	INOOP (deferred insert)
12	DNOOP (deferred delete)
13	ALLOC (page)
15	EXTENT (allocation)
16	PAGE SPLIT
17	CHECKPOINT
30	END TRANSACTION (commit or rollback)

If you have trouble remembering what the different op codes relate to, there is another way to examine the transaction log—use the DBCC LOG command. You have to log in as sa to run this command.

WARNING

Do not run DBCC LOG in a database if you have the 'trunc. log on chkpt.' option set to true for that database. There apparently is a rare situation where, if you are running DBCC LOG at the same time that the SQL Server is attempting to truncate the log, you could end up with a corrupted transaction log and your database will be marked as suspect.

If your log ever gets corrupted, you'd better hope you have a fairly recent backup of your database, because there is no way to fix a bad transaction log other than to restore your database to a point prior to the log's getting corrupted.

DBCC LOG displays a translated hex dump of the log contents. One nice thing it does for you is to translate the op codes into a textual representation of the type of operation.

To examine the transaction log, follow these steps:

1. Log in as sa.

2. Put the database in single-user mode to avoid having other users adding additional log records (not required, but recommended).

3. Run DBCC TRACEON (3604) to route DBCC output to your terminal.

5. Truncate the transaction log to make it as small as possible (again not required, but recommended because DBCC LOG can generate tons of output if the log hasn't been pruned recently).

6. Execute the UPDATE statement in question.

7. Execute DBCC LOG to print out the contents of the transaction log (this output can be quite large and you may want to redirect it to a file).

8. Examine the last few log records, which should correspond to your UPDATE command.

The BEGINXACT and ENDXACT records in the dbcc log output represent the beginning and end of the transaction. If an update in-place occurred, a MODIFY record should be between the BEGINXACT and ENDXACT records. You can match the transaction records to their corresponding BEGINXACT and ENDXACT records via the transaction ID (xactid). The following is sample output for a single row update in-place:

```
BEGINXACT(517 , 25)
attcnt=1 rno=25 op=0 padlen=3 xactid=(517 , 25) len=60 status=0x0000
masterid=(0 , 0) lastrec=(0 , 0)   xstat=XBEG_ENDXACT
spid=11 suid=1 uid=1 masterdbid=0 mastersite=0 endstat=3
name=upd   time=Nov 15 1995 12:37AM

MODIFY(517 , 26)
attcnt=1 rno=26 op=9 padlen=2 xactid=(517 , 25) len=52 status=0x0000
tabid=80003316 pageno=376 offset=296 status=0x0000
old ts=0x0001 0x000020b8   new ts=0x0001 0x000020ba

ENDXACT(517 , 27)
attcnt=1 rno=27 op=30 padlen=4 xactid=(517 , 25) len=40 status=0x0000
endstat=COMMIT time=Nov 15 1995 12:37AM
```

If the update is not in-place, there should be at least two records, a DELETE followed by an IN-SERT record.

The following output is an example of a single row update not-in-place:

```
BEGINXACT(517 , 21)
attcnt=1 rno=21 op=0 padlen=3 xactid=(517 , 21) len=60 status=0x0000
masterid=(0 , 0) lastrec=(0 , 0)   xstat=XBEG_ENDXACT
spid=11 suid=1 uid=1 masterdbid=0 mastersite=0 endstat=3
name=upd   time=Nov 15 1995 12:35AM

DELETE(517 , 22)
attcnt=1 rno=22 op=5 padlen=1 xactid=(517 , 21) len=72 status=0x0000
tabid=80003316 pageno=376 offset=275 status=0x0000
old ts=0x0001 0x000009d4   new ts=0x0001 0x000020b7
```

```
INSERT(517 , 23)
attcnt=1 rno=23 op=4 padlen=0 xactid=(517 , 21) len=76 status=0x0000
tabid=80003316 pageno=376 offset=275 status=0x0000
old ts=0x0001 0x000020b7    new ts=0x0001 0x000020b8

ENDXACT(517 , 24)
attcnt=1 rno=24 op=30 padlen=4 xactid=(517 , 21) len=40 status=0x0000
endstat=COMMIT time=Nov 15 1995 12:35AM
```

If you see any IINSERT and IDELETE records, these represent index row updates. The following output is an example of an update in-place on a nonclustered index column, resulting in the corresponding nonclustered index row update:

```
BEGINXACT(517 , 28)
attcnt=1 rno=28 op=0 padlen=3 xactid=(517 , 28) len=60 status=0x0000
masterid=(0 , 0) lastrec=(0 , 0)    xstat=XBEG_ENDXACT
spid=11 suid=1 uid=1 masterdbid=0 mastersite=0 endstat=3
name=upd   time=Nov 15 1995 12:41AM

IDELETE(517 , 29)
attcnt=1 rno=29 op=8 padlen=2 xactid=(517 , 28) len=56 status=0x0000
tabid=80003316 pageno=392 offset=222 status=0x0000
old ts=0x0001 0x00000cd4    new ts=0x0001 0x000020bc

MODIFY(517 , 30)
attcnt=1 rno=30 op=9 padlen=4 xactid=(517 , 28) len=56 status=0x0000
tabid=80003316 pageno=376 offset=280 status=0x0000
old ts=0x0001 0x000020ba    new ts=0x0001 0x000020bd

IINSERT(517 , 31)
attcnt=1 rno=31 op=7 padlen=2 xactid=(517 , 28) len=56 status=0x0000
tabid=80003316 pageno=392 offset=32 status=0x0000
old ts=0x0001 0x000020bc    new ts=0x0001 0x000020be

ENDXACT(516 , 0)
attcnt=1 rno=0 op=30 padlen=4 xactid=(517 , 28) len=40 status=0x0000
endstat=COMMIT time=Nov 15 1995 12:41AM
```

Summary

By now you should have a reasonable understanding of SQL Server storage structures and how they are maintained and manipulated. Having a reasonable understanding of this information will help you further understand the topics to be discussed in the subsequent performance and tuning chapters.

Now that you have a good understanding of the internals of your high-performance vehicle, SQL Server, it is time to starting tuning it to get the best possible performance for your applications.

Designing Indexes for Performance

IN THIS CHAPTER

There are a number of ways to improve SQL Server performance, but the greatest speed improvement will result from having indexes that the optimizer can use to avoid table scans and reduce the I/O costs of resolving queries. Proper index design is the most important issue in tuning SQL Server performance.

This chapter examines the SQL Server criteria for utilizing indexes and explores the issues and factors that influence index design.

Why Use Indexes?

There are two primary reasons for creating indexes in SQL Server:

- To maintain uniqueness of the indexed column(s)
- To provide fast access to the tables

If you have primary-key constraints, you need unique indexes to ensure the integrity of the primary key and avoid duplicates. However, you don't have to have indexes in order to access the data. SQL Server can always perform a table scan to retrieve data rows.

Table scans, however, are not an efficient mechanism to retrieve a single row from a million-row table. If the table could store 50 rows per page, it would require 200,000 page reads to access a single row. You need to have a more direct access path to the data.

Indexes can provide this direct access path. The tricky part is deciding which indexes to create, and also which type of index to create: clustered or nonclustered. In order to make the appropriate decisions, you need to know when SQL Server can use indexes and how they are used. You also need to understand the performance and size implications of indexes.

Index Usage Criteria

To effectively determine the indexes that should be created, you need to know whether they will be used by the SQL Server. If an index isn't being used, it's just wasting space and creating unnecessary overhead during updates.

The main criteria to remember is that SQL Server cannot use an index defined on a table unless the query contains a column in a valid *search argument* (SARG) or join clause that matches at least the first column of the index. You'll need to keep this in mind when choosing the column order for composite indexes. For example, if you had an index on an employee table as follows,

```
create index idx1 on employee (division, dept, empl_type)
```

each of the following queries could make use of the index:

```
select * from employee
where division = 'accounting'
and empl_type = 'exempt'
```

```
select * from employee
where division = 'accounting'
  and empl_type = 'exempt'

select * from employee
where division = 'accounting'
```

However, this query:

```
select * from employee
where empl_type = 'exempt'
```

would not be able to use the index because it doesn't specify the first column of the index. In order for the index idx1 to be used for the last query, you would have to reorder the columns so that empl_type was first, but then the index wouldn't be useful for any queries specifying only division and/or dept_num. To satisfy all queries in this case would require defining multiple indexes on the employee table.

You might think the easy solution is to index all columns on a table. This, although it takes up a significant amount of space, might work in a DSS environment. However, too many indexes can have an adverse impact on performance in an OLTP environment.

Indexes and Performance

Although providing a performance benefit for queries, indexes can be a hindrance to good performance for updates. This is due to the overhead incurred to keep indexes up to date when data is modified, inserted, or deleted. This is a common problem in databases that must support both OLTP and Decision Support-type applications.

In a *Decision Support System* (DSS), having too many indexes is not much of an issue because the data is relatively static. You'll typically load the data, create the indexes, and forget about it until the next data load. As long as you have the indexes to support the user queries and they are getting decent response time, the only penalty of having too many indexes is the space wasted for indexes that will not be used.

In an OLTP environment, too many indexes can lead to significant performance degradation, especially if the number of indexes on a table exceeds four or five. Think about it for a second. Every single row insert is one data-page write, and one or more index-page writes (depending on whether a page split occurs or not) for every index on the table. With eight nonclustered indexes, that would be at a minimum of nine writes to the database. For an update not-in-place of a single row, which is a delete followed by an insert, you'd be looking at potentially 17 writes to the database. Therefore, for an OLTP environment, you would want as few indexes as possible—typically only the indexes required to support the update transactions and enforce your uniqueness constraints.

Meeting the index needs of DSS and OLTP requirements is an obvious balancing act, with no easy solution. It often involves making hard decisions as to which queries will have to live with a table scan, and which updates will have to contend with additional overhead.

One solution is to have two separate databases, one for DSS applications and another for OLTP applications. Obviously, this would require some mechanism to keep the databases in sync. The mechanism chosen would depend on how up-to-date the DSS database would have to be. If you can afford some lag time, you could consider using a dump-and-load mechanism. If the DSS system required up-to-the-minute concurrency, you would probably want to consider using replication (see Chapter 35, "Introduction to Microsoft SQL Server 6.0 Replication").

I wouldn't recommend triggers as a method to keep two databases in sync. I once saw a system in which such a design had been implemented. The performance overhead of the trigger in the OLTP environment was much greater than any overhead caused by having the indexes on the tables. Believe me, replication is a much cleaner, behind-the-scenes approach.

Another possible alternative is to have only the required indexes in place during normal processing to support the OLTP requirements. At the end of the business day, create the indexes necessary to support the DSS queries, which can run as batch jobs after normal processing hours. When the DSS reports are complete, drop the additional indexes and you'll be prepared for the next day's processing.

Index Selection

Determining which indexes to define involves performing a detailed query analysis. This involves examining the search clauses to see what columns are referenced, knowing the bias of the data to determine the usefulness of the index, and ranking the queries in order of importance. You have to be careful not to examine individual queries and develop indexes to support one query without considering the other queries that are executed on the table as well.

Because it's usually not possible to index for everything, you'll want to index for the queries that are most critical to your applications or those that are run frequently by a large number of users. If you have a query that is run only once a month, is it worth it to create an index to support only that query and have to maintain it throughout the rest of the month? The sum of the additional processing time throughout the month could conceivably exceed the time it takes to perform a table scan to satisfy that one query.

If, due to processing requirements, you must have the index in place when the query is run, you might consider creating the index only when you run the query, and then drop the index for the remainder of the month.

Evaluating Index Usefulness

When the SARGs or join clauses in a query match the indexes on a table, SQL Server will evaluate all possible indexes and compare them to each other and to the cost of a table scan to determine the least expensive method to process the query in terms of page I/Os. SQL Server will use an index only if, depending on the type of query and the data in the table, the index will be more efficient than a table scan.

Also, SQL Server will typically use only one index per table to satisfy a query (the only exception to this rule is when a query contains an OR clause and SQL Server can apply the OR strategy. This topic is covered in Chapter 12, "Understanding the Query Optimizer"). If a query has multiple where clauses that can be satisfied by an index, SQL Server will evaluate all alternatives but choose to use only the index that will result in the most efficient query plan.

How does SQL Server determine the cheapest index to use, you might ask? For example, how does it know how many rows will be returned by the following query:

```
select * from table
    where key between 1000000 and 2000000
```

If the table contains 10,000,000 rows with values ranging between 0 and 20,000,000, how does the optimizer know whether to use an index or table scan? There could be 10 rows in the range, or 900,000. How does the SQL Server estimate how many rows there are between 1,000,000 and 2,000,000?

The Distribution Page

SQL Server keeps distribution information for each index on a separate page in the database called the distribution page. The location of this page is stored in the sysindexes table in the distribution column. The optimizer uses this information to estimate the number of rows that would match the search argument or a join clause for a query.

The optimizer stores two types of information in the distribution page:

- Sample data values for the first column of the index in a structure similar to (but not the same as) a histogram
- The density/selectivity of the index columns

The distribution page is built at index-creation time if the table contains data. If the table is empty, there is no distribution page created. In addition, the distribution page is not maintained by SQL Server as data is inserted/updated/deleted from the table. In order to update or, if necessary, create the distribution page, the DBA or table owner will need to run the update statistics command. The syntax is

```
update statistics table_name [index_name]
```

If only the table name is specified, update statistics will update statistics for all indexes on the table. If you want to update statistics for an individual index, specify the index name after the table name.

It is the general recommendation that if your data volume changes by more than 10 to 20 percent or if more than 10 to 20 percent of your indexed values have been modified, it is a good time to update statistics. If you want to confirm the last time index statistics were updated, use the stats_date system function. For example, to see the last time statistics were updated on the idx1 index on the pt_sample_lg table, execute

```
select stats_date(pt_sample_lg, idx1)
```

The distribution page is created by dividing the width of the first column in the index plus two bytes of overhead into the space available on the distribution page to determine the number of slots or "steps" it can store on the distribution page. (See Figure 11.1.) It then reads the leaf rows of the index and stores the appropriate values for the first column of the index into the steps on the distribution page.

FIGURE 11.1.

Distribution page.

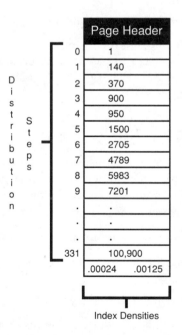

The space available on the distribution page is 2016 bytes (2048 minus a 32-byte header) minus additional space required for overhead and the index densities. The index densities are a float requiring 8 bytes each, and there are at least two densities stored on each distribution page (more on this in a bit) plus an additional 8 bytes. The total remaining space on the page is then 1992 bytes. With an integer key, the distribution step would be 6 bytes wide and the number of steps on the distribution page would be

1992 bytes / 6 bytes = 331 steps

With 10,000,000 rows in the table and 331 steps on the page, you can store a sample value for every

10,000,000 rows / 331 steps = 30,211 rows

The SQL Server walks the index, storing the key value on the distribution page for every 30,211 rows, starting with the first row in the table.

Look at the following query:

```
select * from table
where key between 1000000 and 2000000
```

The row estimates for a query will be a factor of the number of steps the search values are found on or between. In this example, SQL Server will compare the search values, 1,000,000 and 2,000,000, to the values stored on the distribution page. If it finds 1,000,000 at step 157 and 2,000,000 at step 182, the estimated number of rows would be:

182 - 157 = 25 steps
25 steps × 30,211 rows per step = 755,275 rows

If an index contains a number of duplicate values, the search value could be stored on multiple steps. For an equality search, if a search value matched a number of steps on the distribution page, the estimated number of matching rows would be equal to the number of matching steps × rows per step.

This is why a composite index with many duplicates on its first column isn't the optimum solution. If possible, it's often better to put the most unique column as the first column in a composite index. This will result in more selective statistics in the distribution page. However, it might make the index useless for certain queries where the first column is not specified, so you might have to make a trade-off here.

Distribution steps are used for equality search clauses (column = constant) only when a constant expression is compared against an indexed column whose value is known at query compile time. In SQL Server 6.0, this includes any constant values, arithmetic expressions, system functions, and string concatenation. SQL Server 6.0 evaluates the constant expression and uses the resulting value when compiling the query plan to compare against the distribution steps. Examples of expressions where distribution steps can be used include

- ```where col_a = getdate()```
- ```where cust_id = 12345```
- ```where monthly_sales < 10000 / 12```
- ```where l_name like "Smith" + "%"```

> **NOTE**
>
> In versions of SQL Server prior to 6.0, only if explicit constant values were specified in search arguments could the distribution steps be used.

Some constant expressions cannot be evaluated until query runtime. For these types of statements, you'll need some other way of estimating the number of matching rows. These include search arguments containing local variables or subqueries and also `join` clauses such as:

- `where price = @avg_price`
- `where total_sales > (select sum(qty) from sales)`
- `where titles.pub_id = publishers.pub_id`

Additionally, because distribution steps are kept only on the first column of the index, the optimizer must use a different method for determining the number or rows matching the specified portions of a multicolumn key. If there is an index on one of these other columns, it will examine the distribution page on that index to estimate the selectivity of the `search` clause on that column alone. Otherwise, the optimizer will use the index density values.

Index Densities

When the optimizer doesn't use distribution steps for equality searches (column = constant), it uses a value called the density. The *density* is the average proportion of duplicates for the index key(s). Essentially, this can be calculated as the inverse of the number of unique values in the table. For example, an index on a 10,000-row table with 2500 unique values would have a density of

$$1/2500 = .0004$$

The index density is applied against the number of rows in the table to estimate the average number of rows that would match any given value. Therefore, any single value compared against the index key on a 10,000-row table with an index density of .0004 would be expected to match

$$10,000 \times .0004 = 4 \text{ rows}$$

The lower the density value, the more selective the index is; the higher the density, the less selective the index. If an index consisted of all duplicates, the density would be 1 or 100 percent.

For multicolumn indexes, SQL Server now stores multiple densities for each sequential combination of columns. For example, if you had an index on columns A, B, and C, SQL Server would store densities for

A alone
A and B combined
A, B, and C combined

Typically, the density value should become smaller (that is, more selective) as we add more columns to the index. For example, if the densities were as follows:

A	.05
A, B	.004
A, B, C	.0001

and you had 10,000 rows in the table and a search value compared against A alone, you would estimate it to match:

.05 * 10,000 = 500 rows

If the query provided values for both A and B, you would expect it to match

.004 * 10,000 = 40 rows

If A, B, C are all specified, the query should match only

.0001 * 10,000 = 1 ro

NOTE

Prior to SQL Server 6.0, the distribution page contained only a single density value for all columns in the index.

All density values are stored at the end of the distribution page. (Refer back to Figure 11.1.) There are at least two densities stored, even for single-column indexes. One is used for determining join selectivity or for search arguments with unknown values and is referred to as the *alldensity value*. This density value is based upon all rows in the table, because the join or search value could match a value with a large number of duplicates.

The other density is used for search clauses when the value being searched for falls between two distribution steps. If there were a few values in the table with a large number of duplicates, the alldensity value could conceivably refer to a greater number of rows than would exist between the two steps. For example, consider a table with 10,000 rows with an index on a char(8) key:

8 bytes plus 2 = 10 bytes per step
1992 bytes / 10 bytes per step = 199 steps
10,000 rows / 199 steps = 50 rows per step

Let's assume there are 150 unique values in the table. The alldensity would be

1 / 150 = .0067

If a search value was found to be between two steps and the alldensity value was applied, it would estimate that

.0067 * 10,000 = 67

rows would match. However, there are only 50 rows per step, and if the search value falls between two steps, there cannot be more than 50 instances of the data value. For this reason, SQL Server stores a regular density value that excludes some values with a high number of duplicates—essentially those values that do not span multiple cells in the distribution. So, when there are a lot of duplicates, the join density is likely to be high and the search value density is likely to be low.

Viewing Distribution Page Values

Over time in an environment where the data is modified, your index statistics will become out of date. You'll need to run the update statistics command to generate new statistics based upon the current data values in the table.

If you want examine the current contents of the distribution page to determine if they accurately represent the data values stored in the table, you can use the dbcc page command. (See Chapter 10, "Understanding SQL Server Storage Structures.") The contents will be displayed in hexadecimal format, however, which is difficult to read and not very useful. Fortunately, SQL Server provides a command that will display the contents of the distribution page in a readable format:

```
dbcc show_statistics (table_name, index_name)
```

Following is a fraction of the output for the clustered index, tx_CIid, on the ID column for the pt_tx_CIid table:

```
Updated               Rows        Steps       Density
-------------------   ---------   ---------   -----------
Nov 19 1995  4:02AM   7282        330         0.000213248

(1 row(s) affected)

All density            Columns
--------------------   ----------------------------
0.000213248            id

(1 row(s) affected)

Steps
-----------
          1
         65
        214
        271
        369
        497
        604
        656
        745
        849
        961
```

```
    .
    .
    .
  316606
  316996
  317462
  317913
  318409
  318866
```

(330 row(s) affected)

Here you can see the values stored in the distribution steps as well as the stored index densities. Notice that there are two density values stored for a single column index, the regular density and the alldensity value. In this example, they are the same because the ID column is unique and there are no spikes in the data distribution where there would be a large number of duplicates.

If you prefer to see the index statistics in a graphical format, check out the demonstration copy of Aurora Distribution Viewer on the CD-ROM that accompanies this book. In addition to providing multiple ways of graphing the distribution page values, it also can keep a history of distribution page values for tracking the effectiveness of your update statistics strategy. The advantage of a graphical display is that it can help you track down spikes in your data distribution.

Index Design Guidelines

Now that you have an understanding of how the optimizer uses indexes and index statistics to optimize queries, let's examine some guidelines to consider when developing your index strategy.

Clustered Index Indications

One thing that I have found in my travels is that too often, the database designer (or as if more often the case, the database design tool) automatically assigns the clustered index to the primary key. This might be correct if the primary key is the primary access path for that table, but there are other good candidates for the clustered index to consider:

- Range searches
- Columns containing a number of duplicate values
- Columns frequently referenced in an ORDER BY
- Columns other than the primary key referenced in join clauses

In most applications, the primary-key column on a table is almost always retrieved in single-row lookups. For single-row lookups, a nonclustered index is usually only going to cost you one I/O more than a similar clustered index. Are you or the users going to notice a difference between three page reads and four page reads? Not at all. However, if you also have a retrieval such as a lookup on last name, will you notice a difference between scanning 10 percent of the table versus a full table scan? Most definitely.

Clustered indexes can improve performance for range retrievals because the clustered index can be used to set the bounds of a search, even if the query involves a large percentage of the rows in the table. Because the data is in sorted order, SQL Server can use the clustered index to find the start and end points within the range, and scan only the data pages within the range. Without a clustered index, the rows could be randomly spread throughout the table and SQL Server would have to perform a table scan to find all rows within the range.

Let's assume you have 2,000,000 titles in the table, with an estimated 1,000,000 books in the price range between $5 and $10, and you want to run the following query:

```
Select title from titles
where price between $5. and $10.
```

If you had a clustered index on the table, the rows would be grouped together by price; you could start your search at the first row where price is >= $5 and scan the rows in order until you find the last row within the range. (See Figure 11.2.)

FIGURE 11.2.

Clustered index range retrieval.

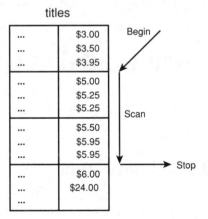

If there are 40 rows / page, with 1,000,000 rows within the range, it would cost you approximately:

> 1,000,000 / 40 = 25,000 data page reads

plus the number of index page reads required to find the first row in the range. This value should be equal to the number of levels in the index.

The same concept holds true for indexes on columns with a large number of duplicates. With a clustered index, the duplicate values will be grouped together, minimizing the number of pages that would need to be read to retrieve them.

Another good candidate for a clustered index is a column used frequently in queries for sorting the result set. Most sorts require that the table be copied into a work table in `tempdb` for sorting purposes. This incurs additional I/O overhead and also increases the potential for I/O and locking contention in `tempdb`. If you have a clustered index on the table and are ordering by the clustered index column(s) on the table, a work table can be avoided even if the query contains no search arguments. True, the optimizer will perform a table scan at this point, but since, by nature of the clustered index, it knows the rows are in sorted order, it can avoid the additional processing to sort the results.

NOTE

If you have a `search` clause on the table that will be satisfied by a nonclustered index but are ordering by the clustered index column(s), SQL Server will need to use a work table to sort the results. This is because the data in this case is being retrieved via nonclustered index order, not clustered index order. Therefore, rows are in random order when retrieved.

You also want to try to keep your clustered indexes on relatively static columns to minimize the re-sorting of data rows when an indexed column is updated. Any time a clustered index row moves, all nonclustered indexes pointing to that row will also need to be updated.

Clustered indexes can also be more efficient for joins than nonclustered indexes because they are usually much smaller in size, typically at least one level less (refer to Chapter 10 for a detailed discussion of index structures and sizes). A single page read might not seem like much for a single row retrieval, but add that one additional page to 100,000 join iterations and your looking at 100,000 additional page reads.

If you require only a single index on a table, it is typically advantageous to make it a clustered index; the resulting overhead of maintaining clustered indexes during updates, inserts, and deletes can be considerably less than the overhead incurred by nonclustered indexes.

Try to avoid creating clustered indexes on sequential key fields that are inserted monotonically, such as on an identity column. This can create a "hot spot" at the end of the table that results in locking contention on the last page of the table and the index. Additionally, the clustered index will not be reusing available space on preceding data pages because all new rows sort to the end of the table. This will result in wasted space and your table growing larger than anticipated. It is typically recommended that you try to cluster on a data value that is somewhat randomly distributed throughout your table. Some candidates for clustered index keys to randomize your data include the following:

- Date of birth
- Last name, first name
- ZIP Code
- A random hash key

Spreading your data throughout the table will help to minimize page contention as well as space utilization. If the sequential key is your primary key, you can still use a unique, nonclustered index to provide an access path via the index and maintain the uniqueness of the primary key.

Because there is only one way to physically sort the data in a table, you can only have one clustered index. Any other columns you want to index will have to be defined with nonclustered indexes.

Nonclustered Index Indications

Until tables become extremely large, the actual space taken up by a nonclustered index is a minor expense compared to the increased access performance. In an OLTP environment, however, you need to remember the impact on performance of each additional index defined on a table.

Also, when defining nonclustered indexes, you typically want to define indexes on columns with a low number of duplicates (that is, with low density values) so that they can be used by the optimizer effectively. A high number of duplicates on a nonclustered index can often make it more expensive in terms of I/O to process the query using the nonclustered index than a table scan. Let's look at an example:

```
Select title from titles
where price between $5. and $10.
```

Again, if you have 1,000,000 rows within the range, those 1,000,000 rows could be randomly scattered throughout the table. Although the index leaf level has all the index rows in sorted order, reading all data rows one at a time would require at least 1,000,000 page reads. (See Figure 11.3.)

FIGURE 11.3.

Nonclustered index range retrieval.

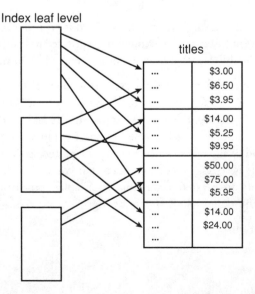

Thus, the I/O estimate for range retrievals using a clustered index is:

number of matching rows
+ number of index levels
+ number of index pages to be scanned to find rows

In the previous example, if you have 1,000,000 rows in the table, the page cost estimate would be

1,000,000 data pages + index pages

Contrast this with the cost of a table scan. At 40 rows per page, and 2,000,000 rows in the table, a full table scan would cost only 50,000 pages. Therefore, a clustered index (25,000 pages) would be most efficient, but if a clustered index is already defined on a better candidate column, then a table scan would actually be more efficient than a nonclustered index.

This same principle holds true for nonclustered indexes with a large number of duplicate values (index density is high). As a rule of thumb, nonclustered indexes will be more effective if < 10–20 percent of the data is to be accessed via the nonclustered index.

Nonclustered indexes can help also help improve performance for certain range retrievals by avoiding the need for a work table. This occurs when the column(s) in the order by clause match the column(s) in the nonclustered index and the index is chosen to satisfy the query. For example, if you had a nonclustered index on city, SQL Server could choose to use the nonclustered index to satisfy the following query:

```
select * from authors
   where city in "Boston", "San Francisco", "Chicago", "New York", "Indianapolis")
   order by city.
```

If the index is used, then the data rows will be retrieved in nonclustered index order, and the additional step of sorting the rows in a work table can be avoided.

In general, nonclustered indexes are useful for single-row lookups, joins, queries on columns that are highly selective, or for queries with small range retrievals. Although they might incur one additional page read per row lookup than a clustered index, they are typically preferable to table scans.

Also, when considering your nonclustered index design, don't overlook the benefits of index covering.

Index Covering

Index covering is a mechanism for using the leaf level of a nonclustered index the way the data page of a clustered index would work. Index covering occurs when all columns referenced in a query are contained in the index itself. Because the nonclustered index contains a leaf row corresponding to every data row in the table, SQL Server can satisfy the query from the leaf rows of the nonclustered index without having to read the data pages.

Because all leaf index pages point to the next page in the leaf page chain, the leaf level of the index can be scanned just like the data pages in a table. (See Figure 11.4.) Because the leaf index rows are typically much smaller than the data rows, a nonclustered index that covers a query will be faster than a clustered index on the same columns due to the fewer number of pages that would need to be read.

FIGURE 11.4.

Scanning the leaf pages of a nonclustered index to retrieve data values (index covering).

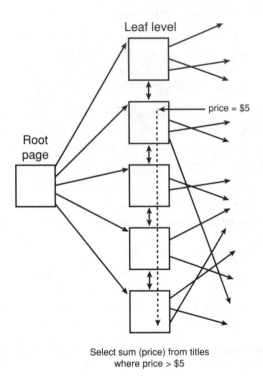

Nonclustered index on price

Leaf level

Root page

price = $5

Select sum (price) from titles
where price > $5

Adding columns to nonclustered indexes to get index covering to occur is a common method of reducing query time. Consider the following query:

```
Select royalty from titles
where price between $10 and $20
```

If you create an index on only the price column, SQL Server could find the rows in the index where price is between $10 and $20, but it would have to access the data rows to retrieve royalty. If there were 100 rows in the range, the page cost would be 100 data pages plus the number of index pages, which would have to be scanned. With an index on price, a money field that in this case is assumed to be not null, the index row width would be:

8 bytes + 7 bytes overhead = 15 bytes per row

With 15 bytes per row, SQL Server could store approximately 100 rows per page with a 75 percent fill factor, costing one additional index page to be scanned plus the number of nonleaf pages necessary to reach the leaf page.

> **NOTE**
>
> If you are not clear how these values are obtained, please read Chapter 10 for a detailed discussion about index structures and size estimation.

However, if you were to create the index on price *and* royalty, the query could be completely satisfied by the index. The number of pages required in this case would be a factor of the number of index leaf pages you would need to scan. An index on price and royalty, both money fields, would be 16 bytes wide.

$$16 + 7 \text{ bytes} = 23 \text{ bytes per row}$$

At 23 bytes per row, SQL Server could store approximately 65 bytes per row with a 75 percent fill factor. Because you can scan all 100 qualifying index rows in order in the leaf pages of the index, the I/O cost for this query would be only two leaf pages plus the number of nonleaf levels in the index.

Index covering also provides a number of performance benefits for queries containing aggregates. Typically, for SQL Server to use an index to satisfy a query, at least the first column of the index must be referenced in the where clause. However, with aggregates, SQL Server can recognize when an aggregate can be satisfied by a nonclustered index without any where clause at all. Consider the following queries:

```
select avg(price) from titles
select count(*) from titles where price > $7.95
select count(*) from titles
```

The first query can use a nonclustered index on price and scan all the index leaf rows to calculate the average price. The second query can again use the nonclustered index on price to find the first leaf row where price is > $7.95, and then just scan to the end of the index counting the number of leaf rows along the way.

The third query is even more interesting. You just want a count of all the rows in the table. You are providing any where clauses to cause it to use an index, so it will have to perform a table scan, right? Actually, SQL Server is somewhat clever with this one. Because it knows that any nonclustered index on the table will have as many rows as the table itself, it will use the nonclustered index with the smallest row size, and therefore the fewest number of pages, and simply count all the rows in the leaf level of that index.

> **WARNING**
>
> When considering padding your indexes to take advantage of index covering, beware making the index too wide. As index row width approaches data row width, the benefits of covering will be lost as the number of pages in the leaf level increases. As the number of pages approaches the number of pages in the table, the number of index levels increases, and index scan time will begin to approach table scan time.
>
> Also, if you add volatile columns to an index, remember that any changes to the columns in the data rows will cascade into indexes as well.

Composite Indexes versus Multiple Indexes

Remember, composite (compound) indexes will be selected by the SQL Server to satisfy a query only if at least the first column of the index is specified in a where clause. Also, because of the increased width of composite indexes, the index structure will consist of more levels and pages than a narrower index.

At times, it might be more beneficial to have many narrow indexes than one or more larger composite indexes. Having more indexes gives the optimizer more alternatives to look at and possibly derive a more optimal plan. Remember from earlier in this chapter that distribution steps are stored only for the first column in a composite index. If the first column has poor selectivity, SQL Server might not choose to use the composite index.

On the flip side of things, each additional index will negatively impact update performance.

So how do you determine the optimal index(es) for a table? Let's look at an example:

```
select pub_id, title, notes from titles
where type = 'Computer'
and price > $15.
```

The index candidates include:

- Clustered or nonclustered on type only
- Clustered or nonclustered on price only
- Clustered on type, nonclustered on price
- Nonclustered on type, clustered on price
- Clustered or nonclustered index on type, price
- Clustered or nonclustered index on price, type
- Clustered or nonclustered index on pub_id, title, notes, type, price

Which are the best options in which circumstances? The answer is entirely dependent on the data distribution and whether the indexes would be unique enough to be worthwhile.

For example, neither type nor price is a very unique value, so would a nonclustered index help in any case for either of them? Probably not, if this is a representative sample of the types of queries going against this table. If you had other queries that could take advantage of index covering (for example, select avg(price)), a nonclustered index might help.

What about a clustered index? That is the logical choice when a column contains a large number of duplicate values, or if a column is involved in range retrievals. Which column should you create the clustered index on, though? Price would probably be the better candidate, because there are more distinct prices than there are book types. Actually, there are so few book types—only six— that out of a thousand titles, would an index on type be helpful at all? How much I/O would an index on type save you in comparison to a table scan? Would the corresponding overhead be worth the minimal time savings?

What if you went the route of creating a composite index on type and price? That would help you if you were searching on type alone, and it would help further narrow the result set when you are searching on type and price. Unfortunately, that index won't help when you are searching on just price. Conversely, an index on price and type won't help when you search on type alone.

The question that needs to be asked at this point is which type of query is most critical? Which query must have good response time?

The last index suggested barely rates consideration. The attempt is to get index covering to take place. However, the index row is so wide that any I/O savings from index covering versus accessing the data in the table directly would be negligible.

As you can see from many of the questions raised in this exercise, you cannot examine just one query and devise the best indexing strategy. You need to examine all queries going against the database and design your indexes appropriately to support multiple queries.

Indexing for Multiple Queries

Indexing for multiple queries involves asking many of the questions raised in the previous section. It really requires that you sit down and perform a detailed query analysis and transaction analysis for all applications going against a database.

After the information has been gathered, you then need to begin ranking the queries/transactions in order of importance. The more critical queries should get a higher priority.

After you have ranked your indexes and decided which ones you are going to tune the system for, you need to examine the where clauses and see what types of indexes you'll need to support those queries. In order to evaluate the index usefulness, you'll also need to have a good understanding of the data and the data distribution. Determine which queries will actually make effective use of an index on a column. Don't assume that just because a column is referenced in a where clause, it needs an index. Consider also whether other, already-indexed columns are more selective or whether the index, based upon the selectivity, would even be used.

Start out by devising an indexing strategy for each query independently. Then begin comparing strategies, looking for overlap between them to find indexes that satisfy more than one query/ transaction. At this point, you might find that a composite index is more useful, or you might find that multiple smaller indexes would be better. Look for a crossover between queries on a significant sort column, or a common range retrieval between queries to identify a good candidate for the clustered index. Look for instances, such as aggregates, where you might be able to take advantage of index covering for a number of queries. Keep in mind the issues of overindexing if you have OLTP activity as well.

After you have devised your indexing strategy, go ahead and implement and test it, but be prepared to make changes. Few of us rarely, if ever, predict all query performance accurately the first time out. I have actually found trial and error to be an acceptable approach to aiding in index design, as well as an excellent learning process.

Let's look at a simple example and apply this strategy. Assume you have the following customer table:

```
create table customer
   (cust_id    char(6) not null,
    lname      varchar(15) not null,
    fname      varchar(15) not null,
    address    varchar(30) not null,
    city       varchar(30) not null,
    state      char(2) not null,
    zip        char(5) not null,
    zone       char(1) not null)
```

The customer table has 100,000 rows, six zones with distribution as follows:

> Zone A—70,000 rows
> Zone B—15,000 rows
> Zone C—10,000 rows
> Zone D—3,000 rows
> Zone E—1,5000 rows
> Zone F—500 rows

Cust_id is the unique, primary key, and states exist entirely within zones (for example, NY is in Zone A only). The following are samples of the critical queries run against the customer table:

```
select * from customer where zone = 'A'
select * from customer where zone = 'C' and state = 'NY'
select * from customer where cust_id = '345678'
select cust_id from customer where lname like "Smith%"
```

Let's select indexes for each query individually:

■ `select * from customer where zone = 'A'`

Because zone is not a very unique value for this query, you have the option of either a clustered index on zone or no index at all. For now, choose the clustered index on zone.

■ `select * from customer where zone = 'C' and state = 'NY'`

Again, zone is not a very unique value, and there is also state. Because states exist within a zone, you can always query state by limiting the result set to zone first. This is a good candidate for a composite index, and again, due to the poor selectivity, you can opt for a clustered index.

■ `select * from customer where cust_id = '345678'`

Cust_id is a unique primary key. Let's follow the normal trend and assume a clustered index on the primary key.

■ `select cust_id from customer where lname like "Smith%"`

Again, you have a range type retrieval with more than likely poor selectivity; you can assume a clustered index on lname.

Let's examine what we've got so far:

■ clustered on zone
■ clustered on zone, state
■ clustered on cust_id
■ clustered on lname

Obviously, there is some overlap here. Let's make the tradeoffs and decide which one should be the clustered index. Because cust_id is a unique key involved in a single row lookup, there is no appreciable benefit to having a clustered index on it when there are other candidates for clustered index.

Next, you have to decide between a clustered index on zone or lname. If you look closely at the lname query, it is only retrieving a list of cust_ids from customer for a list of last names. You could get away with a nonclustered index on lname, cust_id, which would actually be more efficient than a clustered index on lname.

Now you are left with a decision on the clustered index on zone. Because you have two queries that rely on zone, but one that needs to limit the result set to states within a zone, you can make the clustered index on zone and state. This way, one composite index can effectively satisfy two different queries.

To summarize, the indexes you create initially will be

■ clustered index on zone, state
■ nonclustered index on lname, cust_id
■ unique nonclustered index on cust_id

Remember, you cannot tune for everything and everyone. You won't be able to make everyone happy. At some point you will need to make a tradeoff of some sort:

■ OLTP performance needs versus DSS response time
■ Critical query versus noncritical query

- Frequently run query versus rarely run query
- Online queries versus batch queries

The art is balancing the tradeoffs effectively so that the system is deemed a success.

Summary

The most important aspect to improving SQL Server performance is proper index design. Choosing the appropriate indexes that will be used by SQL Server to process queries involves thoroughly understanding the queries and transactions being run against the database, understanding the bias of the data, understanding how SQL Server uses indexes, and staying aware of the performance implications of overindexing tables in an OLTP environment. In general, consider using clustered indexes to support range retrievals or when data needs to be sorted in clustered index order; use nonclustered indexes for single or discrete row retrievals or when you can take advantage of index covering.

It is also recommended that you have a good understanding of the SQL Server query optimizer to know how it uses indexes and index statistics to develop query plans. This might be a good time to read Chapter 12.

And always remember—keep your index statistics up to date!

Understanding the Query Optimizer

Query optimization is the process of analyzing the individual queries and determining the best way to process them. This involves understanding the underlying storage structures and the indexes defined on them to determine whether there is a way to process the query more efficiently. To achieve this end, SQL Server uses a cost-based optimizer. The query optimizer examines parsed SQL queries and, based on information about the objects involved, outputs a query plan. The query plan is the set of steps to be carried out to execute the query.

As a *cost-based* optimizer, the optimizer's purpose is to determine the query plan that will access the data with the least amount of processing time.

To allow the optimizer to do its job properly, you need to understand what types of queries can be optimized and learn techniques to help the optimizer choose the best query path. Having a good understanding of the optimizer will help you to write better queries, choose better indexes, and detect potential performance problems.

> **NOTE**
>
> To better understand the concepts presented in this chapter, you should have a reasonable understanding of how SQL Server manages data objects and indexes, and how indexes affect performance. If you haven't already read Chapters 10, "Understanding SQL Server Storage Structures," and 11, "Designing Indexes for Performance," it is recommended that you review them now.

Optimization Goals

The primary goal of the query optimizer is to find the cheapest access path to minimize the total time to process the query. To achieve this goal, the optimizer analyzes the query and searches for access paths and techniques primarily to do the following:

- Minimize logical page access
- Minimize physical page access

Disk I/O is the most significant factor in query processing costs. Therefore, the fewer number of physical and logical I/Os performed, the faster the query plan.

Query Optimization Steps

When SQL Server processes the query, it performs the following steps:

1. Parse and normalize the query validating syntax and object references.
2. Optimize the query and generate the query plan.

3. Compile the query plan.

4. Execute the query plan and return the results to the user.

The optimization step is broken down into multiple phases, as follows:

Phase 1: Query Analysis

1. Find search arguments (SARGs)

2. Find OR clauses

3. Find joins

Phase 2: Index Selection

4. Choose best index for SARG

5. Choose best method for ORs

6. Choose best indexes for any join clauses

7. Choose best index to use for each table

Phase 3: Join Order Selection

8. Evaluate join orders

9. Compute costs

10. Evaluate other server options for resolving joins (Reformatting Strategy)

Phase 4: Plan Selection

If a query is a single table query containing no join clauses, SQL Server skips Phase 3 (Join Order Selection) and jumps directly to Phase 4 (Plan Selection). The following sections explain these four phases of optimization.

Query Analysis

The first step in query optimization is to analyze each table in the query to identify all search arguments (SARGs), OR clauses, and join clauses. It is the SARGs, OR clauses, and join clauses that will be used in the next phase to select useful indexes to satisfy a query. For SQL Server to use an index to satisfy a query, at least the first column of the index must match a SARG, OR clause, or join column.

Identifying SARGs

SARGs exist to enable the optimizer to limit the rows searched to satisfy a query. The general goal is to match a SARG with an index to avoid a table scan. A search argument is defined as a WHERE clause comparing a column to a constant. The format of a SARG is as follows:

```
Column operator constant_expression [AND...] [MC1]
```

ANOT <.fIMC

Valid operators for a SARG are any one of =, >, <, >=, and <=. The inequality operator (!= or <>) is not a valid operator for a SARG. If you have an inequality operator, the optimizer will ignore that statement as a search argument because it cannot be used to match a value against an index, unless the query can be solved by index covering.

> **TIP**
>
> If you have a search clause containing an inequality operator, try to rewrite it as a SARG so that it can be recognized as a search argument by the query optimizer. For example, consider the following query:
>
> ```
> select title from titles where price != 0
> ```
>
> If there is a business rule enforced on the table to prevent any rows where price is less than zero, then the query could be rewritten as follows:
>
> ```
> select title from titles where price > 0
> ```
>
> and still return the same result set. The difference is that the second version contains a valid SARG that the optimizer will recognize and consider for matching with an index to satisfy the query. True, it may still result in a table scan, but at least it gives the optimizer the option to consider; it wouldn't have done so with the inequality operator.

Multiple SARGs can be combined with the AND clause. If an OR clause is specified, the SARG is treated differently, as you will see shortly. Following are examples of valid search arguments:

- `flag = 7`
- `salary > 100000`
- `city = 'Saratoga' and state = 'NY'`

As stated earlier, an inequality operator is not treated as a search argument. Additionally, if any operation is performed on the column, it is ignored as a search argument as well. Some examples of invalid SARGs follow:

- `gender != 'M'`
- `lname = fname` (comparison against a column, not a constant)
- `ytd/months > 1000` (operation performed on column)
- `ytd/12 = 1000` (operation performed on the column)

> **TIP**
>
> The last SARG, `ytd/12 = 1000`, can be rewritten to be treated as a SARG as `ytd = 12000`. When tuning performance of your system, keep an eye out for invalid SARGs. They are a common cause of poor performance because they prevent an index from being used. Many times, invalid SARGs can be rewritten as valid SARGs.

Improvising SARGs

Some SQL statements do not appear to follow the syntax for a valid SARG, but can be improvised as SARGs by the query optimizer. The following are clauses that can be improvised as SARGs:

- `BETWEEN` becomes `>=` AND `<=`

  `price between $10 and $20` becomes:

  `price > = $10 and price <= $20`

  `100 between lo_val and hi_val` becomes:

  `lo_val <= 100 and hi_val >= 100`

- `LIKE` becomes `>=` AND `<`

  `au_lname like "Sm%"` becomes:

  `au_lname >= "Sm" and au_lname < "Sn"`

The `LIKE` clause will be improvised as a SARG only if the first character in the string is a constant. The following statement would not be improvised into a SARG:

`au_lname like "%son"`

Also, watch out for the following `BETWEEN` clause in SQL Server 6.0:

`price BETWEEN $20 and $10`

This will be improvised into

`price >= $20 and <= $10`

which is an empty result set. SQL Server doesn't generate any error or warning message when this code is encountered.

> **TIP**
>
> In releases of SQL Server prior to 6.0, the optimizer would switch the upper and lower bounds of a BETWEEN if necessary so that the higher value was the upper bound. Unfortunately, this behavior is in violation of the ANSI standard and was changed in version 6.0 to comply with the ANSI standard.
>
> If you are porting an existing application from SQL Server Version 4.2 to 6.0, you may want to check any queries containing BETWEEN clauses to verify that the lesser value is always defined as the lower bound.

In some cases, the column in a SARG may be compared with a constant expression rather than a single constant value. The constant expression can be an arithmetic operation, built-in function, string concatenation, local variable, or subquery result. As long as the left side of the SARG contains a column alone, it's still a valid SARG.

Constant Expressions

The issue with a SARG containing a constant expression is whether the optimizer can evaluate the expression prior to query optimization and make use of the distribution steps, rather than have to use the density value to estimate rows. In SQL Server 6.0, the optimizer now evaluates the constant expression if the value can be determined prior to runtime, and uses the resulting value when evaluating any indexes on the column(s).

The following are examples of expressions that can be evaluated prior to optimization:

```
due_date > getdate()
ytd_sales < 100000/12
lname like "Smith" + "%"%
```

For SARGs containing subqueries or local variables, the value of the constant expression cannot be evaluated prior to optimization because the value can't be determined until query execution. Examples of constant expressions that cannot be evaluated prior to optimization include:

```
price < (select avg(price) from titles)
qty < @inventory
```

OR Clauses

The next statement for which the optimizer looks in the query are OR clauses. OR clauses are SARGs combined with an OR statement rather than an AND, and are treated differently than a standard SARG. The format of an OR clause is as follows:

```
SARG or SARG [OR ...]
```

with all columns involved in the OR belonging to the same table.

The IN statement:

```
column IN ( constant1, constant2, ...)
```

is also treated as an OR clause, becoming:

```
column = constant1 or column = constant2 OR ...
```

Examples of OR clauses include:

```
where au_lname = 'Smith'  or au_fname = 'Fred'
where (type = 'business' and price > $25) OR pub_id = "1234"
au_lname in ('Smith', 'Jones', 'N/A')
```

An OR clause is a disjunction; all rows matching either of the two criteria will appear in the result set. Any row matching both criteria should appear only once.

OR Strategy

An OR clause can be handled by either a table scan or by using the OR strategy. Using a table scan, SQL Server reads every row in the table and apply all search criteria to each row. Any row that matches one of the criteria is put into the result set.

If an index exists on both columns in the OR clause, however, SQL Server evaluates the possibility of applying the OR strategy.

The OR strategy involves essentially breaking the query into two or more parts, executing each part using the available index and retrieving the matching row IDs, performing a UNION on the row IDs to remove duplicates, and, finally, using the row IDs as a *dynamic index* to retrieve the final result set from the base table.

If any one of the parts requires a table scan to be processed, or if a table scan is cheaper than using the available index, SQL Server will simply use a table scan to resolve the whole query rather than apply the OR strategy.

The following shows how SQL Server would handle the following query if given an index that exists on both au_lname and state:

```
select * from authors
   where au_lname = "Smith"
      or state = "NY"
```

1. Estimate the cost of a table scan.

2. Break the query into multiple parts; for example:

    ```
    select * from authors where au_lname = "Smith"
    select * from authros where state = "NY"
    ```

3. Execute each piece and get the row IDs into a worktable in tempdb as a "dynamic index."

4. Union the row IDs to remove any duplicates.

5. Use the dynamic index to retrieve all qualifying rows from the worktable. (See Figure 12.1.)

FIGURE 12.1.

Using the dynamic index to resolve the OR *clause.*

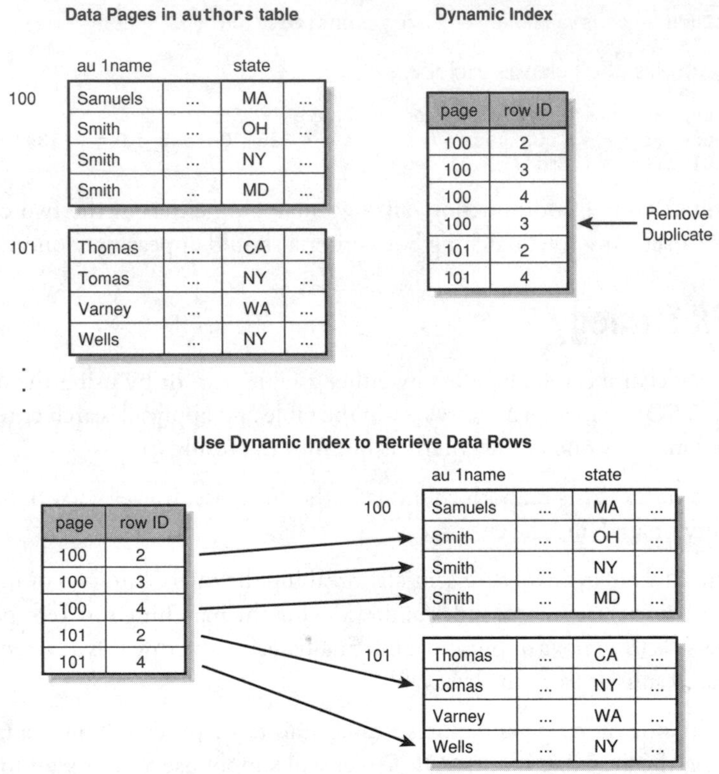

SQL Server will apply the OR strategy only if the sum of the total I/Os to use the OR strategy is less than the number of I/Os to process a table scan.

If the OR involves only a single column, for example,

```
au_lname = 'Smith' or au_lname = "Varney"
```

and a clustered index exists on the column, the optimizer will look at the alternative of solving it using a BETWEEN rather than using the OR strategy. Because the data is clustered, the optimizer knows that all values satisfying the OR clause are "between" the two values. Therefore, it could find the first matching row for the OR clause and simply scan the succeeding data pages until the last matching row was found. In some cases, this approach may result in fewer I/Os than using the dynamic index, as in the following:

```
select * from pt_tx_CIid
where id in (10000, 15000, 20000, 21000)
```

The OR clause would be translated into:

```
id = 10000 OR id = 15000 OR id = 20000 OR id = 21000
```

To process this using the OR strategy would involve using four separate lookups on the pt_tx_CIid table to get the matching rows into a worktable. Using the clustered index, this would have cost 2 pages per lookup, for a total of 8 page I/Os.

By treating it as follows

```
id BETWEEN 10000 and 21000
```

and simply scanning all rows in the range and applying the search criteria to each in a single pass to find all the result rows, it would have cost only five total page I/Os. Because the optimizer always seeks to use the method that results in the lowest I/O cost, SQL Server applied the BE-TWEEN strategy and avoided using the dynamic index for this query.

Join Clauses

The last type of statement that the query optimizer looks for during the query analysis phase is the *join clause*. A join clause is a WHERE clause in the following format:

```
Table1.Column Operator Table2.Column
```

A join clause always involves two tables except in the case of a self-join, but even in a self-join, you must specify the table twice in the query:

```
select name = e.name, manager = m.name
    from employee e, employee m
    where e.mgr_id = m.id
```

Flattening Queries

SQL Server will sometimes attempt to flatten a subquery into a join when possible to allow the optimizer to select the optimal join order, rather than be forced to process the query inside out.

IN, ANY, or EXISTS Subqueries

In SQL Server 6.0, any query containing a subquery introduced with an IN, ANY, or EXISTS predicate will be flattened into an existence join unless the outer query also contains an OR clause, or unless the subquery is correlated or contains one or more aggregates.

An existence join can be optimized the same way as a regular join, with one exception. With an existence join, as soon as a matching row is found in the inner table, the value TRUE is returned. At this point, SQL Server stops looking for further matches for that row in the outer table and moves on to the next row. For example, the following query would be converted to an existence join:

```
select pub_name from publishers
where pub_id in (select pub_id from titles where type = "business')
```

This behavior has been modified in SQL Server Version 6.0 from previous versions of SQL Server. Prior to 6.0, the preceding query would have been flattened into a normal join like the following:

```
select pub_name from publishers p, titles t
where p.pub_id = t.pub_id
and t.type = 'business'
```

The joins would essentially be processed the same way, but the result sets would be different.

If there were 4 rows in the titles table where type = 'business', you would get four rows in the result set using a regular join, but only two distinct publisher names. Using an existence join, you would get only the two rows for the publishers who have a match in titles.

Materialized Subqueries

If the outer query is comparing a column against the result of a subquery using any of the comparison operators (=, >, <, >=, <=, !=), then the results of the subquery must be resolved, that is, *materialized*, before comparison against the outer table column. For these types of queries, the optimizer must process them inside out.

An example of this type of query is as follows:

```
select title from titles
where total_sales = (select max(total_sales) from titles)
```

The subquery must be resolved first to find the value to compare against total_sales in the outer query.

Index Selection

When the query analysis phase of optimization is complete and all SARGs, OR clauses, and join clauses have been identified, the next step is to match them up with any available indexes and to estimate the I/O costs. The index I/O costs will be compared with each other and against the cost of a table scan to determine the least expensive access path.

If no useful indexes are found to match a SARG, OR clause, or join, a table scan will have to be performed on the table. A table scan is the fall-back tactic for the optimizer to use if there is no better way of resolving a query.

Evaluating Indexes for SARGs or OR clauses

To estimate the I/O costs of using an index for a SARG or an OR clause, the optimizer uses the index statistics stored on the distribution page for the index. If no distribution page is available or there is no index on the table, the following are the built-in row estimates that the query optimizer assumes for the different equality operators:

Operator	Row Estimate
=	10 percent
BETWEEN, > AND <	25 percent
>, <, >=, <=	33 percent

So, for example, consider a query containing the following search clause:

```
lname = "Smith"
```

With no index statistics, the optimizer will assume that 10 percent of the rows in the table will match the search value of "Smith". If index statistics are available and the value of the constant expression is known during query optimization, the optimizer will use the distribution step information to estimate the number of rows that match the constant expression. If the constant expression cannot be resolved until query execution, the optimizer will base its estimates on the index density.

> **NOTE**
>
> In previous releases of SQL Server, certain datatype mismatches would also prevent the optimizer from using distribution steps to estimate the number of matching rows in a query. The main culprit was the process of comparing a varchar against a char. This shortcoming seems to have been addressed in Version 6.0.
>
> For any datatype mismatch between a column and constant, if a legal implicit conversion can take place, SQL Server performs the datatype conversion to the column datatype and uses the distribution steps.

If a SARG contains the equality (=) operator and there is a unique index matching the SARG, then the optimizer estimates that one and only own row will match the SARG.

> **NOTE**
>
> For a more thorough discussion of index selection and index statistics, please refer to Chapter 11, "Designing Indexes for Performance."

Evaluating Indexes for Join Clauses

If the query contains a join clause, SQL Server will determine whether any usable indexes exist that match the column(s) in the join clause. Because the optimizer has no way of determining what value(s) will join between rows in the table at optimization time, it cannot use the distribution steps to estimate the number of matching rows. Instead, it will use the index density, which is an estimate of the number of matching rows in the table for any given value.

If index density is not available, then the estimate for the number of matching rows is determined as follows:

> 1 / number of rows in smaller table

For example, if you have an order table with 1 million rows joining with a customer table containing 5,000 rows, the join selectivity would be as follows:

> 1/5,000 or .0002

Therefore, for every row in the customers table, you would expect to find

> $1,000,000 \times .0002 = 200$

matching rows in the orders table (200 orders/per customer $\times$ 5,000 customers = 1,000,000 orders)

If you had a density value available on the join column(s), the density value would be used to estimate the number of rows per join between the two tables. *Density* is based upon the percentage of the number of unique values in a table. If you had 1,000 unique values in the orders table, the density would be as follows:

> 1/1,000 or .001

Using this density value, for each row in the customers table, you would expect

> $1,000,000 \times .001 = 1,000$

rows to match for any single customer.

A lower density value indicates a more selective index. As the density approaches 1, the index becomes less selective and approaches uselessness.

Ranking Indexes

Unless the OR strategy is applied, SQL Server can use only one index per table to satisfy a query. The index chosen will be the one that incurs the fewest number of I/Os to solve the query for that table.

Using the available or built-in statistics, the optimizer estimates the number of page reads necessary to retrieve the estimated number of rows using the candidate index. It then ranks the candidate indexes to determine the index that results in the least amount of I/O.

Keep in mind that there are instances (for example, large range retrievals on nonclustered index column) in which a table scan may be cheaper than a candidate index in terms of total I/O.

Estimating Page I/O

If there is no usable index, the optimizer performs a table scan. The estimate of the total I/O cost will be the number of pages in the table, which is stored in the sysindexes table.

If there is a clustered index, the I/O cost estimate will be the number of index levels in the clustered index plus the number of pages to scan. The number of pages to scan is based upon the estimated number of rows × the number of rows per page.

For a nonclustered index, I/O cost estimate will be

> The number of index levels
> + number of leaf pages
> + number of qualifying rows (number of data page reads)

The number of leaf pages is based upon the estimated number of rows × the number of leaf index rows per page. Because each leaf index row requires a separate data page lookup to retrieve the data row, the number of data page reads is equal to the number of matching rows in the leaf index level.

For a unique index and an equality join, the I/O cost estimate will be one data page plus the number of index levels traversed to access the data page.

Index Covering

When analyzing a query, the optimizer also considers any possibility to take advantage of index covering. Index covering is a mechanism for using the leaf level of a nonclustered index the way that the data page of a clustered index would work when all the data to satisfy the query (select columns and SARGs) can be found in the leaf level of the nonclustered index.

This can save a significant amount of I/O if the query does not have to access the data pate. In most cases, a nonclustered index will be faster than a similarly defined clustered index if the nonclustered index covers the query.

Index covering has particular benefits with aggregates. SQL Server will attempt to solve aggregates using index covering whenever possible, even when the query contains no SARGs. For example:

```
select avg (price) from titles
```

can be satisfied by scanning the leaf rows of a nonclustered index on price to determine the average.

If index covering can take place in a query, the optimizer will consider it and estimate the I/O cost of using the nonclustered index to cover the query. The estimated I/O cost of index covering is the number of index levels plus the number of leaf index pages to scan. The number of leaf pages to scan is based upon the estimated number of rows × the number of leaf index rows per page.

Join Order Processing

If the query contains any join clauses, the next phase in query optimization is to determine the best possible join order.

The optimizer will evaluate all possible join orders and, for each join order considered, will estimate the cost of the different index alternatives for each table in the join. If no useful indexes are available on one or more of the tables involved in the join, SQL Server will also consider applying the reformatting strategy to solve the query efficiently.

The optimal query plan for a join involves picking the best indexes for each table and the most efficient order to process the tables in the join.

Determining Join Order

Joins are performed as a set of nested loops, often referred to as *nested iterations*. Essentially, for each matching row in the outer table, you will perform a nested iteration on the inner table to find all matching rows to the outer row. This is repeated for each row in the outer table.

To process a nested iteration, you need to determine the order in which you will process the tables.

Consider the following query:

```
select au_lname, au_fname, title
   from authors a, titleauthor ta, titles t
   where a.au_id = ta.au_id
   and ta.title_id = t.title_id
```

Figure 12.2 shows the possible join orders that could be used to process this query.

FIGURE 12.2.

Possible join order for a query joining titles, titleauthor, *and* authors.

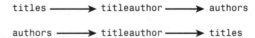

Because the SQL Server query optimizer is a cost-based optimizer, the order of the tables in the `from` clause does not dictate the order in which the tables will be joined. When processing a join, the optimizer will evaluate all reasonable join permutations and estimate the total I/O cost, in terms of I/O time. The plan resulting in the lowest estimate of I/O time will be the plan chosen.

As the number of tables increases, however, the number of permutations that the optimizer must evaluate increases as a factorial of the number of tables in the query, as shown in Table 12.1.

Table 12.1. Number of possible join permutations based upon number of tables in the query.

# of Tables	# of Join Permutations
2	2! = 2
3	3! = 6
4	4! = 24
5	5! = 120
6	6! = 720
7	7! = 5,040
8	8! = 40,320
9	9! = 362,880
10	10! = 3,628,800
11	11! = 39,916,800
12	12! = 479,001,600
13	13! = 6,227,020,800
14	14! = 87,178,291,200
15	15! = 1,307,674,368,000
16	16! = 20,922,789,888,000

Large, Multi-Table Queries

To minimize the number of permutations that need to be examined, the SQL Server will break up joins of more than four tables into all possible groups of four to evaluate the join permutations within each group of four. This is an iterative approach, repeated until the join order for all tables is determined. The purpose of this approach is to limit the number of permutations that the optimizer has to consider.

The algorithm used by SQL Server to process joins of more than four tables is as follows:

1. Group the tables into all possible groups of four.
2. For each group of four tables, estimate the join cost for each permutation possible.
3. Determine the group of four with the cheapest permutation. The first table of that permutation is marked as the outer table and taken out of the list of tables.
4. Repeat steps 1–3 for the remaining tables until only four tables remain and determine the best join order for those four as one final step.

The following is an example of this algorithm in practice.

Assume a query that joins six tables: T1, T2, T3, T4, T5, and T6.

Breaking the six tables into all possible groups of four, you would have the following:

> T1T2T3T4, T1T2T3T5, T1T2T3T6, T1T2T4T5, T1T2T4T6, T1T2T5T6,
> T1T3T4T5, T1T3T4T6, T1T3T5T6, T1T4T5T6, T2T3T4T5, T2T3T4T6,
> T2T3T5T6, T2T4T5T6, T3T4T5T6

For each group of four, SQL Server will find the lowest-cost permutation and make the outermost table for that permutation the outermost table for the entire query. Assume that the best permutation is T3T5T4T2. T3 will be set as the outermost table. The remaining tables will be regrouped into all possible groups of four, giving you the following:

> T1T2T4T5, T1T2T4T6, T1T2T5T6, T1T4T5T6, T2T4T5T6

Assume that the lowest-cost permutation out of each of these remaining groups of four tables is T4T2T5T6. Table T4 now becomes the second outermost table in the query.

SQL Server is now left with four tables, which the optimizer will evaluate as if it were a normal four-table join. Assuming that the best join order for the remaining four tables is T5T2T1T6, this join order will be appended to the two previously determined outer tables (T3 and T4). The result is that the final join order for the entire query will be as follows:

> T3,T4,T5,T2,T1,T6

This might seem like a lot of work, but the actual number of permutations examined can be substantially fewer, especially when the number of tables in the query exceeds eight or more tables.

The resulting number of combinations examined with this approach is the sum of N! / (N-4)! for each iteration. For this example, the number of permutations considered would be:

> 6!/(6-4)! = 720/2 = 360
> 5!/(5-4)! = 120/1 = 120
> 4! = 24

The total sum of all permutations considered is as follows:

> 360 + 120 + 24 = 504 permutations

This represents a savings of 30 percent. As the number of tables increases, the savings becomes even more significant, as shown in Table 12.2.

Table 12.2. Savings in number of join permutations examined using SQL Server optimizer approach.

# of Tables (N)	N!	Optimizer	Savings Method
6	720	540	30%
7	5040	1,344	73.3%
8	40320	3,024	92.5%
9	362880	6,048	98.3%
10	3628800	11,088	99.7%
16	20922789888000	148,512	99.999%

TIP

Even using the modified approach to identifying join permutations, large multitable queries are still rather costly to optimize. Sometimes, the time spent optimizing the query can be greater than the time spent processing the query.

In some earlier releases of SQL Server, the optimizer didn't do such a good job of handling queries with more than four tables. The order of the tables in the `from` clause would sometimes influence the query plan chosen. This sometimes forced developers to write queries in a specific manner, or sometimes break queries with more than four tables into smaller queries.

The current release of SQL Server, however, seems to handle multitable queries quite well. In testing that others as well as myself have done, the optimizer consistently tends to arrive at the most optimal plan regardless of the table order. It's typically not necessary to break up large queries anymore.

You may be concerned, however, with the time spent optimizing the query. To reduce the optimization time, you might consider putting the query into a stored procedure. With the query in a stored procedure, the query plan is determined only for the first execution, and then reused for subsequent executions, providing significant time savings if the query is repeatedly executed.

Another alternative is to override the join ordering phase of the query optimizer using the forceplan option. For details and warnings on using the forceplan option, please read Chapter 16, "Managing the SQL Server Optimizer."

Estimating Join Order Costs

For each join permutation considered, the optimizer needs to estimate the cost of that particular join order in terms of total I/O. For comparison purposes, the optimizer estimates the total logical I/Os per table and the total number of physical I/Os per table. It then sums the total logical and physical I/Os for the entire permutation, and translates that into a total elapsed time. The total elapsed time is used only for comparison purposes and does not reflect the actual time the query would take to run.

Currently, SQL Server rates a logical read as 2 ms and a physical read as 14 ms, a ratio between logical and physical of 1 to 7. These are fixed values regardless of the actual performance of the system you are running on.

The relative performance of a nested iteration is directly proportional to the number of times that the inner query will be done and the number of pages per lookup. The algorithm for determining the total number of I/Os for a nested iteration is as follows:

> \# pages accessed in outer table
> + (# matching rows in outer table
>   × # pages per lookup in inner table)

The total cost of the nested iteration is the total number of logical reads × 2 plus the total number of physical reads × 14.

When determining the total I/O cost, the SQL Server makes no assumptions about whether the table currently resides in cache or not. It will always assume that the first access of the table will be a physical page read, and any subsequent accesses or iterations on the table will be logical page reads. For every physical page read, there will also be a corresponding logical page read.

The only time that the data cache is considered is when there is insufficient cache to keep the inner table in memory. When this is the case, the optimizer assumes that, because the table cannot stay in cache, all accesses to the inner table will be physical I/Os.

Join Costing Example

Consider a few examples of possible join permutations that the optimizer would consider for the following query:

```
select * from titles t, titleauthor ta
 where t.title_id = ta.title_id and royaltyper < 50
```

For these examples, make the following assumptions:

> 15,000 `titles` (15 rows/page), 1,000 pages
> 25,000 `titleauthor` (50 row/page), 500 pages

Clustered index statistics on `royaltyper` in the `titleauthor` would indicate that 20 percent have `royaltyper < 50`.

There is sufficient data cache to keep both tables in memory.

titles to *titleauthor*, No Indexes

The first plan that the optimizer will consider is joining from the first table in the query to the second table in the query, using no indexes at all. In other words, it will consider doing a table scan on each table for each lookup.

For the outer table, `titles`, this would be single scan costing 1,000 pages. For each row in `titles`, you would have to look up the matching row(s) in `titleauthor`, using a table scan each time and checking to see whether `royaltyper` for the joined row is < 50. Because there are 15,000 rows in the `titles` table and no SARG to further limit it, you will perform 15,000 iterations on the `titleauthor` table. Each iterative table scan on `titleauthor` will cost 500 pages.

The total number of I/Os for this query would be estimated as:

1,000 pages in `titles`

+ (15,000 rows in `titles`×500 pgs/lookup in `titleauthor`)

= 7,501,000 I/Os

Next, you need to calculate the relative I/O cost for this permutation. Because you will perform one scan of `titles`, the first scan will incur 1,000 physical and logical reads. For the `titleauthor` table, because it can fit entirely in cache, only the first iteration will incur physical page reads. All subsequent iterations will be logical I/Os only. Therefore, there will be 500 physical and logical I/Os on the first iteration, and $14,999 \times 500$, or 14,500 logical I/Os, on the subsequent iterations. Factoring all this out into the relative I/O cost would result in the following:

1000 physical reads `titles`	14×1000	= 14,000
1000 logical reads `titles`	2×1000	= 2,000
500 physical reads `titleauthor`	14×500	= 7,000
7,500,000 logical reads `titleauthor`	$2 \times 7,500,000$	= 15,000,000
Total		= 15,023,000

The total cost (15,023,000) is the value that the optimizer will use to compare the query plan against the other alternatives.

Now you will examine some other hypothetical alternatives.

titles to titleauthor, clustered index on titleauthor.title_id

For this example, the I/O cost on the `titles` table remains the same. The difference will be on the `titleauthor` table. Rather than have to perform a table scan on `titleauthor` for each iteration, you can use the clustered index to find the matching rows. Let's assume that the index density indicates that for any join value, one row will match in the `titleauthor` table. If the clustered index consists of two levels, the I/O cost per lookup on the `titleauthor` table will be three pages (two index levels plus a data page lookup).

The total number of I/Os for this query would be estimated as follows:

> 1,000 pgs in `titles`
>
> + (15,000 rows in `titles` × 3 pages per lookup on `titleauthor`)
>
> = 46,000 I/Os

Because you still have no way of limiting the query any further at the beginning by `royaltyper`, you'll still have to join with every row in the `titleauthor` table during processing of the query to check the value of `royaltyper`. Therefore, at the end of query processing, you will still have examined every page in the `titleauthor` table, for a total of 500 physical page reads. Each iteration, however, will cost you only three pages, which will be assumed to be logical page reads.

The relative I/O cost would be as follows:

1,000 physical reads `titles`	14 × 1,000	= 14,000
1,000 logical reads `titles`	2 × 1,000	= 2,000
500 physical reads `titleauthor`	14 × 500	= 7,000
45,000 logical reads `titleauthor`	2 × 45,000	= 90,000
Total		= 113,000

As you can easily see, this plan (113,000) is much cheaper than the previous plan (15,023,000). There are still other plans to consider, however. What if you also had an nonclustered index on `title_id` in the `titleauthor` table?

titles to titleauthor, Nonclustered Index on titleauthor.title_id

Again, the I/O costs on titles remain the same. The only real difference between this query and the last one, which used the clustered index, is that the nonclustered index has one more level than the clustered index, and would cost you an extra I/O per lookup.

The total number of I/Os for this query would be estimated as follows:

> 1,000 pgs in `titles`
>
> + (15,000 rows in `titles` × 4 pages per lookup on `titleauthor`)
>
> = 61,000 I/Os

The relative I/O cost would be as follows:

1,000 physical reads `titles`	$14 \times 1,000$	= 14,000
1,000 logical reads `titles`	$2 \times 1,000$	= 2,000
500 physical reads `titleauthor`	14×500	= 7,000
60,000 logical reads `titleauthor`	$2 \times 60,000$	= 120,000
Total		= 143,000

This plan (143,000) is more expensive than the plan using the clustered index (113,000) but is still substantially cheaper than the table scan plan (15,023,000). If you only had a choice between a table scan and using the nonclustered index, the nonclustered index would still be much cheaper.

This pretty much exhausts the alternatives if you join from `titles` to `titleauthor`. Note that even having an index on titles wouldn't have aided either of these three plans because you have no SARG on `titles` to limit the rows that you want to join with `titleauthor`.

You do have a SARG on `titleauthor`, however. The following section examines some costing examples in which `titleauthor` is the outer table.

titleauthor to *titles*, No Indexes

Having no indexes means that, for the outer table, `titleauthor`, you'll need to perform a table scan to find the rows where `royaltyper` is < 50. This will be a single scan costing 500 pages. Because you have no index on `titles`, either, you will have to perform a table scan for each lookup on `titles`, costing 1,000 pages each lookup.

The question at this point is how many lookups will you need to perform on the `titles` table? Remember that if there are no statistics available to estimate the rows matching a search argument, the built-in statistics will be used. For your search argument:

```
royaltyper < 50
```

the built-in estimate is that 33 percent of the rows will match.

Therefore, a join will be performed only on the `titles` table for 33 percent, or 8,250 of the rows in the `titleauthor` table. If a row read during the table scan on `titleauthor` doesn't have a `royaltyper` < 50, then SQL Server will simply skip that row and compare against the next one. Therefore, the optimizer will estimate the you will perform 8,250 iterations on `titles`, rather than 25,000.

The total number of I/Os for this query would be estimated as follows:

> 500 pages in `titleauthor`
>
> + (8,250 rows in `titleauthor` $\times$ 1,000 pages/lookup in `titles`)
>
> = 8,250,500 I/Os

Because the titles table can fit entirely in cache, the relative I/O cost for this plan would be as follows:

500 physical reads `titleauthor`	14×500	= 7,000
500 logical reads `titleauthor`	2×500	= 1,000
1,000 physical reads `titles`	14×1000	= 14,000
8,250,000 logical reads `titles`	$2 \times 8,250,500$	= 16,500,000
Total		= 10,023,000

Next, look at a query plan for when you have a clustered index on `title_id` on the `titles` table.

titleauthor to *titles*, Unique Clustered Index on *titles.title_id*

Again, the I/O costs on `titleauthor` remain the same, but instead of using iterative table scans on `titles`, you'll use the clustered index. Because you have a unique clustered index on `title_id`, you know that one and only one row will match a single join value in the `titles` table. Each single row lookup via the clustered index on `titles` will cost you three pages (two index levels plus the data page). You will also use the built-in statistics of 33 percent to estimate the number of rows where `royaltyper` is < 50.

Therefore, the total number of I/Os for this query would be estimated as follows:

500 pgs in `titleauthor`

+ (8,250 rows in `titleauthor` $\times$ 3 pages per lookup on `titles`)

= 25,250 I/Os

Because you assume that only 33 percent, 8,250, of the rows in `titleauthor` match where `royaltyper` is < 50, and only one row in the `titles` table will join with a single value in the `titleauthor` table, you expect that you will access only 8,250 rows in the `titles` table. At 15 rows per page, that works out to

8,250 / 15 = 550

data pages that will be read during processing of this query. This translates into the total physical page estimate for the `titles` table. Based on this information, the relative I/O cost would be as follows:

500 physical reads `titleauthor`	14×500	= 7,000
500 logical reads `titleauthor`	2×500	= 1,000
550 physical reads `titles`	14×550	= 7,700
24,750 logical reads `titles`	$2 \times 24,750$	= 49,500
Total		= 65,200

This is the cheapest plan so far, but you're not done yet! Consider the plan cost if you also have a clustered index on `royaltyper`.

titleauthor to *titles*, Clustered Index on *titleauthor.royaltyper*, Unique Clustered Index on *titles.title_id*

Because you have a clustered index on `royaltyper`, you can use the index statistics to estimate the number of rows where `royaltyper` is < 50. In this example, the statistics indicate that 20 percent of the rows have `royaltyper` < 50. Therefore, you estimate that

$$25,000 \times .20 = 5,000$$

rows in `titleauthor` have a `royaltyper` < 50. Also, because you can use the clustered index to find the rows, you don't have to scan the entire table. You can start at the beginning of the table and scan the data pages until you find the first row where `royaltyper` >= 50. At 50 rows per page, that would be as follows:

5,000 rows / 50 rows per page = 100 pages.

Also, because you still have the unique clustered index on `titles`, one and only one row will match for every matching row in `titleauthor`, 3,000 rows. At 15 rows per page, you will have accessed

5000/15 = 334

data pages in titles while processing this query. Each single row lookup is still going to cost you three pages per lookup. Armed with this information, you can estimate the query cost to be as follows:

100 pgs in `titleauthor`

+ (5,000 rows in `titleauthor` $\times$ 3 pages per lookup on titles)

= 15,500 I/Os

100 physical reads `titleauthor`	14 × 100	= 1,400
100 logical `titleauthor`	2 × 100	= 200
334 physical reads `titles`	14 × 334	= 4,676
15,000 logical reads `titles`	2 × 15,000	= 30,000
Total		= 36,276

This would be the cheapest plan by far of all the ones considered if the table did actually have a clustered index on `royaltyper` in the `titleauthor` table and a unique clustered index on `title_id` in the `titles` table.

This example also underscores the reason that you need to understand how the query optimizer works. By knowing how the optimizer processes your queries examining search arguments, index statistics, and join orders, you can make better-informed decisions about your index design and write better queries.

For example, having a clustered index on `titleauthor.royaltyper` and a unique clustered index on `titles.title_id` was the cheapest plan (36,276), but wasn't that much cheaper than using no index on `titleauthor` (65,200) relative to the cheapest plan using no indexes at all (15,023,000). This could help you decide whether to index `royaltyper` on `titleauthor`, or create the clustered index on a different column where the cost savings would be more substantial for other critical queries.

Reformatting Strategy

As you saw in the previous set of examples, the worst-case cost scenario for joins is joining a table scan to a table scan. The resulting I/O cost is as follows:

> \# pages in the outer table
>
> \+ (rows in outer table × # of pages in the inner table)

This can be a significantly large I/O cost, even with tables where the page and row counts number only in the hundreds.

Occasionally, it may be cheaper to build a temporary clustered index on the inner table and use the index to process the query than to repeatedly scan the table. This is known as the *reformatting strategy*.

When reformatting occurs, SQL Server copies the contents of the inner table into a temporary worktable in `tempdb` and creates a clustered index on the join columns specified in the index. It then uses the clustered index when processing the join to retrieve the qualifying rows from the temporary worktable.

The cost of applying the reformatting strategy is the time and I/O required to create the temporary worktable and build the clustered index on it. The I/O cost of the reformatting strategy alone (that is, copying the table and building the clustered index) is determined as follows:

> $P2 + P2\log_2 \times P2$

where P2 = number of pages in inner table.

The reformatting strategy will not be used unless the estimated cost of processing the query using the reformatting strategy is less than the cost of joining using table scans. The total I/O cost for processing the query would be the reformatting cost plus the number of pages in the outer table (P1) plus the number of rows in the outer table (R1) × the number of scans on the outer table (for a normal nested iteration, there will only be a single scan of the outer table). The full equation to estimate total I/O for a query using the reformatting strategy would be the following:

> $(P2 + P2\log_2 \times P2) + P1 + R1$

If our outer table consists of 300 rows and 200 pages, and the inner table consists of 100 the cost of reformatting would be the following:

> $(100 + 100\log_2 \times 100) + 200 + 300 = 1300$ I/Os

The cost of processing this query using table scans would be the following:

$$200 + (300 \times 100) = 30200 \text{ I/Os}$$

In this example, the optimizer would choose to apply the reformatting strategy because is it substantially cheaper than joining with table scans.

> **TIP**
>
> It's nice that the optimizer has to capability to create a temporary clustered index on the fly to process queries on tables without supporting indexes. If you see the reformatting strategy being applied, however, it should set off a number of bells and whistles in your head, indicating that you probably don't have the appropriate indexes defined on your tables. True, reformatting is cheaper than joining a table scan to table scan, but it's still quite a bit more expensive than if the appropriate index were defined on the table(s) in the first place.

Outer Joins

If the query contains an asterisk (*) on either side of a join operator, that indicates that all rows from the table on the side of the asterisk are to be included in the result set whether or not it joins successfully with the inner table.

For example, to see all publishers whether or not you currently carry any of their `titles`, the following query could be written:

```
select pub_name, title from publishers p, titles t
    where p.pub_id *= t.pub_id
```

All `pub_names` will be retrieved from `publishers`. For any row that doesn't join successfully with `titles`, the `title` column will contain a `NULL` for that row in the output.

This syntax is referred to as an outer join. The table on the side of the asterisk is forced to be treated as the outer table, that is, it is to be the first table accessed in a nested iteration.

For this type of query, the optimizer will not evaluate the reverse join order.

GROUP BY/DISTINCT/ORDER BY

In addition to determining the best indexes and join orders, the optimizer will also determine whether worktables are required to further process a query. These are typically queries containing an ORDER BY, GROUP BY, or DISTINCT clause. Because worktables incur additional processing and I/O, the optimizer will make the determination whether a worktable is required or not.

GROUP BY

For a GROUP BY, a worktable must always be created to perform the grouping and hold any aggregate values being generated for each group.

DISTINCT

Because the DISTINCT clause applies across the entire row, a worktable is created to sort and remove duplicates. If a unique index exists on the table and all columns in the unique index are included in the result set, a worktable can be avoided because the unique index guarantees that each row is distinct.

ORDER BY

For an ORDER BY, the determination of whether a worktable is required is dependent upon the indexes on the table and the query containing the ORDER BY clause.

For a table with a clustered index, a worktable can be avoided for an order by if the following conditions are met:

- The ORDER BY clause specifies at least the first column in the clustered index as the first ORDER BY column
- Only columns that are part of the nonclustered index are listed in the ORDER BY clause
- The query is resolved using either the clustered index or a table scan

If these conditions are met, the worktable is not needed to sort the result set because the rows in the table are already sorted in clustered index order and will be returned in clustered index order.

For example, if the clustered index is defined on zone and state, a worktable is not needed for this:

```
select zone, state, customer, zip
from customers
order by zone, state
```

but a worktable would be required for this,

```
select zone, state, customer, zip
    from customers
order by zone, zip
```

because zip is not part of the clustered index. The data will be sorted by zone, but a worktable is needed to sort the data by zip within a zone.

If there is a nonclustered index on the table, a worktable can be avoided for sorting the results if

■ The query is resolved using index covering; and

■ The order by clause specifies at least the first column of the nonclustered index as the first ORDER BY column

For example, if a nonclustered index is defined on zone and state, a worktable is not needed for

```
select state
    from customers
order by zone
```

since the nonclustered index covers the query and the index rows are already sorted by zone. However, a worktable would be required for:

```
select zone, state
    from customers
order by state
```

because state is not the first column of the nonclustered index. The data will be sorted by zone and state within the index, but a worktable is needed to sort the data by state alone.

A worktable can also be avoided for sorting the results if

■ The ORDER BY clause specifies at least the first column of a nonclustered index as the first ORDER BY column

■ Only columns that are part of the nonclustered index are listed in the ORDER BY clause

■ The nonclustered index is used to satisfy the query by matching a SARG

If these conditions are met, no worktable will be needed to sort the result set because the rows will be retrieved from the table in nonclustered index order. For example if a nonclustered index is defined on zone and state, a worktable is not needed for

```
select zone, state, customer, zip
    from customers
    where zone = "A"
order by zone
```

as long as the nonclustered index is used to satisfy the query. Because the data is retrieved in nonclustered index order already due to the SARG on zone, no further sorting is necessary. However, a worktable would be required for

```
select zone, state, customer, zip
    from customers
    where zone = "A"
order by zone, zip
```

because zip is not part of the nonclustered index. The data will be retrieved by zone in zone order, but a worktable is needed to sort the data by zip within a zone.

> **NOTE**
>
> Prior to Microsoft SQL Server 6.0, any ORDER BY … DESC always required a worktable because SQL Server only scanned tables and indexes in ascending order. Since SQL Server 6.0 now supports reverse table and index scans, worktables are no longer required for an ORDER BY … DESC if the optimizer can perform a reverse table or index scan to retrieve the results and the other conditions discussed in this section are also met.
>
> If you mix ASC and DESC clauses in an ORDER BY, a worktable will always be needed to resolve the different sort orders.

Potential Optimizer Problems

So, you've written the query and read the plan, and the optimizer is not choosing the plan that you think is best. What's wrong with this query? Before you go into a detailed discussion about analyzing and debugging query plans (this is covered in detail in Chapter 14, "Analyzing Query Plans"), look at some of the more common problems that lead to the use of poor query plans.

Ensure That Statistics Are Up-to-Date

One of the more common problems encountered with performance in new production systems is the fact that no index statistics are available, or are woefully out of date. Before you start tearing queries apart, or your hair out, run update statistics on the tables in question and rerun your query.

Check to See That the SARGs Really Are SARGs

Look at your where clauses very closely. Are what appear to be SARGs actual SARGs in the eye of the optimizer? Watch out for inequality operators, operations on columns, and constant expressions that cannot be evaluated at query compile time.

See That the Index Actually Covers the Query

If you were expecting index covering to take place, double-check the query and index in question to make sure that all columns in the query are contained in the index. It's very easy for a nonindexed column to sneak its way into a query, forcing a data row retrieval.

Determine if the Stored Procedure Was Optimized Based on Different Parameters

Query plans for stored procedures are compiled once and placed into a procedure cache. The query plan created is based upon the parameters passed during the first execution. It's possible that the best plan for those parameters may not be the best plan for the current parameters. Chapter 13, "Stored Procedure Optimization," contains a complete discussion on how to deal with this problem.

Check if Reformatting Is Occurring

If reformatting is taking place, then there are no supporting indexes for the query, or the query contains invalid SARGs that cannot use any available indexes. At this point, you need to re-evaluate your indexing decisions, or rewrite the query to take advantage of an available index.

Summary

The SQL Server optimizer has continuously improved over the years, taking advantage of new techniques and algorithms to improve its capability to find the cheapest plan. Most of the time, the optimizer makes the correct decision. There are occasions when the optimizer makes the wrong decision, due either to inaccurate or incomplete information in the index statistics. When you suspect that the optimizer is making the wrong decision, SQL Server provides tools to analyze the query plans generated and determine the source of the problem. These tools are described in Chapter 14.

Stored Procedure Optimization

IN THIS CHAPTER

Stored procedures are one of the primary features of SQL Server. Almost every application developed on SQL Server makes use of stored procedures at some point. In fact, most administrative tasks in SQL Server are performed with stored procedures. For these reasons, it is important to understand how stored procedures are managed and processed by SQL Server in order to understand the performance benefits and issues when using stored procedures.

Stored Procedures and Performance Benefits

Stored procedures are parsed and compiled SQL code that reside in the database and can be executed from a client application by name. There are a number of advantages to using stored procedures in SQL Server:

- Reduced network traffic
- Faster execution
- Modular programming
- Restricted, function-based access to tables
- Reduced operator error
- Helps enforce consistency
- Can automate complex or sensitive transactions

Two of the main advantages of using stored procedures are reduced network traffic and faster execution of SQL.

In a client/server environment, the network must always be considered a potential bottleneck because all communication between clients and servers occurs over the network. Using stored procedures can help to reduce network traffic. A stored procedure can contain large, complex queries or SQL operations that are compiled and stored within a SQL Server database. They are then executed on the SQL Server when the client issues a request to execute the stored procedure. The SQL statements are executed locally within the SQL Server and typically only the final results are sent back to the client application. With the programming features (if...else, while, goto, local variables, and so on) built into Transact-SQL, the SQL Server itself can evaluate intermediate results and perform any necessary code branching without having to send intermediate results back to the client for processing.

Another performance gain that stored procedures provide over dynamic SQL is that all object references and SQL syntax are checked at the time the stored procedure is created. This parse tree is stored on disk in the sysprocedures table in the database where the stored procedure is created. When the stored procedure is executed, this parsing doesn't need to be performed. With dynamic SQL, the SQL statements must be parsed and all object references checked for each execution, even if the same SQL statements are executed repeatedly.

The main performance gain realized by using stored procedures, however, is SQL Server's capability to save the optimized query plan generated by the first execution of the stored procedure in procedure cache memory and reuse it for subsequent executions. Avoiding the optimization and compilation phase for subsequent executions can result in significant time savings on procedure execution, especially for complex queries or transactions. Refer to Table 13.1, which compares the differences between the first execution of a stored procedure and subsequent executions.

Table 13.1. Comparing the steps performed for first and subsequent stored procedure executions.

First Execution	*Subsequent Executions*
Locate stored procedure on disk and load into cache	Locate stored procedure in cache
Substitute Parameter Values	Substitute Parameter Values
Develop Optimization Plan	
Compile Optimization Plan	
Execute from Cache	Execute from Cache

How Stored Procedures are Optimized

The SQL Server query optimizer generates a query plan for a stored procedure based upon the parameters passed in the first time it is executed. The stored procedure parse tree is read in from disk, and SQL Server generates a query tree for the procedure in procedure cache. The parameters are then substituted and the optimizer generates a query plan in procedure cache. (See Figure 13.1.)

FIGURE 13.1.

Stored procedure query plans are read in from disk and a query plan is generated in cache for each concurrent user.

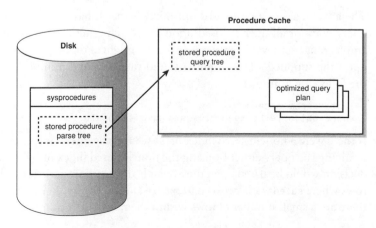

The stored procedure query plan remains in cache after execution for subsequent execution by the same or other SQL Server users, providing there is sufficient cache space available for the query plan to remain in cache.

> **NOTE**
>
> If procedure cache size is not configured large enough by the system administrator, there might not be enough free space in the procedure cache to load another query tree or to plan for all users needing them at the same time. Procedure cache space can be freed only if a query tree or plan is not currently in use. If there is insufficient space to load another query tree or plan, error 701, "There is insufficient system memory to run this query," occurs.
>
> Also be aware that there is a maximum number of procedures or other compiled objects allowed in procedure cache. The number of objects allowed in the procedure cache is a function of the procedure cache size and is displayed in the error log during SQL Server startup as the number of available *proc buffers*. If the number of procedures or objects in use exceeds the maximum, error 701 occurs.
>
> Refer to Chapter 30, "Configuring and Tuning SQL Server," for guidelines on estimating procedure cache space requirements.

It is important to note at this point that stored procedure query plans in SQL Server are reusable, but not re-entrant. What this means is that a query plan in cache can be in use by only one user at a time. If multiple users execute the same stored procedure concurrently, SQL Server generates newly optimized copies of the stored procedure query plan in cache for each concurrent user for whom a copy is not available.

The Stored Procedure Dilemma

The advantages of a cost-based optimizer is that it has the capability to generate the optimal query plan for all queries based upon the search criteria. For certain types of queries (for example, range retrievals) the query optimizer might at times generate different query plans based upon the supplied search arguments and the estimated number of matching rows. Consider the following example:

```
select * from orders
  where saledate between @lowdate and @highdate
```

If there were a nonclustered index on `saledate`, the query optimizer would have the option of resolving the query either by using the nonclustered index or by performing a table scan. This decision would be based upon the available distribution statistics and the estimated number of rows where `saledate` is between `@lowdate` and `@highdate`. For an execution of the query where there are a small number of rows within the range, the optimizer might choose to process the query using the nonclustered index. For a subsequent execution with a large number of values in the range, the optimizer might choose to process the query using a table scan.

However, the behavior of stored procedures for subsequent executions is to reuse the query plan residing in procedure cache that was generated for the first execution of the stored procedure. This provides a performance gain for queries that consistently use the same query plan, but can cause a performance loss if the wrong query plan is used for subsequent executions.

Consider the previous SQL example and put it into a stored procedure as follows:

```
create proc get_orders (@lowdate datetime, @highdate datetime)
as
select * from orders
  where saledate between @lowdate and @highdate
return
```

Suppose that the first time this procedure gets executed each day, it is passed parameter values to retrieve all order records for the previous day and is resolved via a table scan. This is the query plan that is placed in procedure cache for subsequent executions. Subsequent executions done on the same day, however, retrieve only order records since the last time the procedure was executed to provide for real-time monitoring of the orders being received throughout the day. Assuming the procedure is run every five minutes, the number of records to be retrieved is minimal, which could be sufficiently resolved using the nonclustered index. The query plan from the first execution of this stored procedure still exists in the procedure cache, however, so a new query plan is not generated. The procedure ends up performing a table scan for each execution, thus not providing the expected response-time performance for the query. There needs to be a way to get the SQL Server to recompile a new query plan for the subsequent executions.

Recompiling Stored Procedures

So how do you go about generating a new query plan when a stored procedure is using the wrong one for a particular execution? Fortunately, SQL Server gives you a couple of options. The first is to create the stored procedure with the `with recompile` option:

```
create proc get_orders (@lowdate datetime, @highdate datetime)
with recompile
as
select * from orders
  where saledate between @lowdate and @highdate
return
```

This option forces the SQL Server query optimizer to generate a new query plan for each execution. As you might suspect, this creates a lot of overhead with the optimizer, and you lose the performance gains typically realized with stored procedures by avoiding the query-plan compilation phase for subsequent executions. However, if you are looking at a few milliseconds extra for each execution versus the minutes or possibly hours a stored procedure might run if the wrong query plan is used, it's probably a worthwhile tradeoff because you can be virtually guaranteed that the proper query plan is being chosen based upon the parameters passed on each execution.

The second alternative is to create the procedure normally, but use the `with recompile` option on procedure execution like this:

```
exec get_orders @lowdate = "12/15/94", @highdate = "12/16/94" with recompile
```

Using `with recompile` on stored procedure execution causes the SQL Server optimizer to generate a new query plan based upon the supplied parameters only for the current execution. Other existing query plans in cache, except for the one it is replacing, remain unchanged. This method enables you to then explicitly specify when you want the optimizer to examine your parameters and generate a new query plan rather than create a new query plan for each execution as the `create proc … with recompile` option does. You typically use this method when you are running a specific instance of a stored procedure with atypical parameters.

> ### WARNING
>
> If there are multiple copies of a stored procedure query plan in procedure cache, the stored procedure currently being executed reuses the first available query plan the SQL Server finds in cache. There is no guarantee that a specific user will get the same query plan he generates with the `exec … with recompile` on subsequent executions. Likewise, another user might unexpectedly get the recompiled query plan, which may not be appropriate for the parameters he is passing in. The SQL Server still returns the appropriate results, but possibly not in the most efficient manner.
>
> Unfortunately, SQL Server provides no mechanism to explicitly flush query plans out of procedure cache. The only way to remove all query plans for a specific stored procedure from procedure cache is to drop and re-create the stored procedure.

Automatic Recompilation

What happens if you drop an index from a table referenced by a stored procedure, and the procedure query plan was using that index to resolve the query? In this instance, SQL Server detects that the index is no longer available and automatically recompiles a new query plan. In Microsoft SQL Server 6.0, the `CREATE INDEX` statement also causes automatic recompilation of stored procedures the next time they are executed. The `UPDATE STATISTICS` statement, on the other hand, does not cause recompilation of stored procedures.

Using *sp_recompile*

If you've updated statistics for a table, and want the query optimizer to reexamine the new statistics and generate new query plans for all stored procedures that reference that table, use the `sp_recompile` stored procedure as follows:

```
sp_recompile tablename
```

Using `sp_recompile` causes all query plans in cache that reference the specified table to be recompiled.

When to Use *with recompile*

Consider using the `with recompile` option when a stored procedure can generate widely different query plans depending on the parameters passed in and there is no way to predict the best query plan for all executions.

When to Use *sp_recompile*

The `sp_recompile` stored procedure should be applied when

- Statistics have been updated on a table and you want the stored procedure to generate a new query plan based on the updated statistics
- An index has been added to a table and you want the optimizer to consider the new index and generate a new query plan for the stored procedure

When Recompilation Doesn't Work

If a stored procedure contains a `select * from tablename…` statement, and `alter table` has been used to add a column to the table, the stored procedure does not pick up the new column(s), even when the stored procedure is executed using the `with recompile` option. This is because the column names and IDs for `select *` are resolved when the stored procedure is created and stored in the parse tree. To pick up the new columns, you need to create a new parse tree. The only way to do this is to drop and re-create the stored procedure.

This same situation applies when you rename tables referenced by a stored procedure. Because the stored procedure resolves object references by object ID rather than by name, the stored procedure can still reference the original table. For example, if you rename the `customer` table `old_customer`, your stored procedure continues to work, performing operations on what is now the `old_customer` table. If you subsequently create a new `customer` table, your stored procedures do not recompile to operate on the new `customer` table as long as the `old_customer` table exists. If you drop the `old_customer` table, the stored procedures that reference it are automatically recompiled and a new parse tree is generated to reference the new `customer` table. If you want to force the stored procedures to reference the new `customer` table without dropping `old_customer`, you need to drop and re-create all stored procedures that reference the `customer` table.

Alternatives to Using *with recompile*

Because of the performance issues already identified with using the with recompile option, you want to avoid using with recompile whenever possible.

Instead of creating a procedure with the with recompile option, consider the following solution:

```
create proc get_orders_smallrange (@lowdate datetime, @highdate datetime)
as
select * from orders
  where saledate between @lowdate and @highdate
return
go

create proc get_orders_bigrange (@lowdate datetime, @highdate datetime)
as
select * from orders
  where saledate between @lowdate and @highdate
return
go

create proc range_value (@lowdate datetime, @highdate datetime)
as
if datediff(hh, @highdate, @lowdate) >= 12
    exec get_orders_bigrange @lowdate, @highdate
else
    exec get_orders_smallrange @lowdate, @highdate
```

Using this approach, each subprocedure (get_orders_smallrange and get_orders_bigrange) is optimized on first execution with the appropriate query plan for the different range values specified in the parameters passed to it by the get_orders procedure. Thus, if a user executes get_orders with date values that are greater than 12 hours apart, get_orders executes the get_orders_bigrange procedure, which is optimized for processing large-range retrievals—possibly using a table scan. For a user executing get_orders with date values that are less than 12 hours apart, get_orders executes the get_orders_smallrange procedure, which is optimized for processing smaller range retrievals, possibly using an available nonclustered index. This approach should result in more consistent response times for queries by minimizing the possibility of a user executing a stored procedure with an inappropriate query plan for the parameters specified.

> **NOTE**
>
> Using this approach requires sufficient knowledge of the bias of your data to know when certain range values result in different query plans to design the stored procedure effectively.

Also be aware that this technique might increase your procedure cache memory requirements because users now have at least two procedure query plans (get_orders and either get_orders_smallrange or get_orders_bigrange) in cache. However, this approach is typically preferred over having your application check the range values and execute the appropriate stored procedure.

If the range check is hard-coded into your application source code and the bias of your data changes, you have to modify your application source code and recompile it. By performing the range check within the top-level stored procedure, you can easily drop, modify, and re-create the stored procedure to reflect changes in the bias of the data without having to change or recompile the application program.

One other programming consideration with stored procedures that relates to performance and optimal query-plan generation is when stored procedures perform different select statements based on condition branching. Examine the following stored procedure:

```
create proc get_order_data (@flag tinyint, @value int)
as
if @flag = 1
    select * from orders where price = @value
else
    select * from orders where qty = @value
```

At query compile time, the optimizer doesn't know which branch will be followed because the if...else construct isn't evaluated until runtime. On the first execution, the optimizer generates a query plan for all select statements in the stored procedure, regardless of the conditional branching. The query plan for each select statement is based upon the passed-in parameters.

Having distinctly different queries in the stored procedure could result in the wrong query plan being generated for one of the select statements, as its query plan might be based upon inappropriate values for that query.

Again, a better approach would be to break the different select statements into two separate stored procedures and execute the appropriate stored procedure for the type of query to be executed. For example:

```
create proc get_orders_by_price(@price int)
as
    select * from orders where price = @value
return
go
```

```
create proc get_orders_by_qty(@qty int)
as
    select * from orders where qty = @qty
return
go

create proc get_order_data (@flag tinyint, @value int)
as
if @flag = 1
    exec get_orders_by_price
else
    exec get_orders_by_qty
return
```

Summary

Stored procedures can provide a number of performance benefits within SQL Server. Having a good understanding of how stored procedures are optimized by SQL Server helps you to develop efficient stored procedures and achieve the maximum performance benefits they can provide.

Analyzing Query Plans

14

The SQL Server's cost-based query optimizer typically does a good job of determining the best query plan to process a query. There are times, however, when you might be a little bit skeptical about the plan that the optimizer is generating. At the least, you'll want to know the specifics about the query plan it is using to determine:

- Is the optimizer using the indexes that you have defined, or is it performing table scans?
- Are worktables being used to process the query?
- Is the reformatting strategy being applied?
- What join order is the optimizer using?
- On what actual statistics and cost estimates is the optimizer basing its decisions?
- How do the optimizer's estimates compare to actual I/O costs?

Fortunately, SQL Server provides some tools to answer just these questions.

Using and Understanding *showplan*

To determine the query plan that the optimizer has chosen to process a query, SQL Server provides the set showplan on option to display the query plan that will be executed. By examining the showplan output you can determine, among other things, which indexes (if any) are being used, what join order was selected, and whether any worktables are required to resolve the query. Interpreting and understanding this output will assist you in writing more efficient queries and choosing the appropriate indexing strategy for your tables.

The showplan option is a session-level setting. It will not affect other users and it is off by default when you first log in to SQL Server. To turn the showplan option on, execute the following statement in SQL Server:

```
set showplan on
```

If you are working in ISQL/W, you can set showplan on by typing the command in a query window and executing it, or by setting the Show Query Plan option on in the Query Options dialog box for that query window. (See Figure 14.1.)

Using either of these two ways to set showplan on causes the showplan output to be displayed in the query results window along with any data. A third way of setting the showplan output on is by checking it in the Options menu, as shown in Figure 14.2. This option causes the showplan output to be displayed in a graphical manner under the showplan tab (see Figure 14.3) and applies to all sessions open within ISQL/W.

FIGURE 14.1.

Setting the showplan option on for ISQL/W query window.

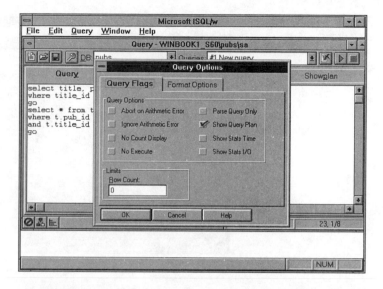

FIGURE 14.2.

Turning on the graphical showplan output for all query windows in ISQL/W.

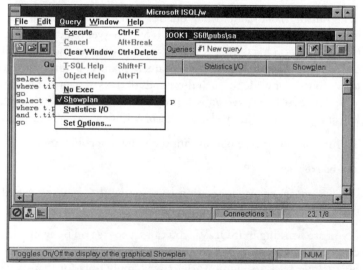

NOTE

I have found that ISQL/W's graphical showplan works well for simple queries but is difficult to interpret for larger, more complex sets of queries such as you would find in a stored procedure.

In addition, by learning to read and interpret the textual output for showplan, you will be able to use showplan in any development environment. For this reason, the showplan output that this chapter examines is that generated by the set showplan on option.

FIGURE 14.3.
ISQL/W's graphical
showplan *display.*

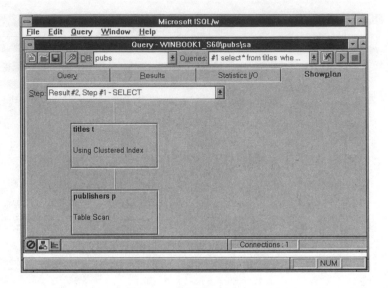

When using showplan to debug queries, you may also want to use it in conjunction with the noexec option. The noexec option tells SQL Server to generate a query plan but not submit it for execution. This option is useful when you are trying to rewrite a long-running query in order to get it to use a more efficient query plan. You don't want to have to wait hours for the query to run, or wade through thousands of rows of data just to see whether a query would use an index. Setting noexec on will prevent the query from actually executing, but SQL Server will still generate a query plan and display it if showplan is turned on.

To turn on the noexec option, run the following command:

```
set noexec on
```

Like showplan, noexec is a session-level setting that is off by default. It won't affect any other users or sessions that you might have open.

If you are working in ISQL/W, you can set noexec on by typing the command in a query window and executing it, or by setting the No Execute option on in the Query Options dialog box. (Refer back to Figure 14.1.) It will apply only for that query window because that is a separate session into SQL Server.

TIP

When the noexec option is turned on, the only command that SQL Server will execute is set noexec off. Always remember to set all your other session settings, trace flags, and so on before setting noexec on. Otherwise, you'll be pulling your hair out trying to figure out why you're not seeing the showplan output! Also, remember to turn it off when you want to actually execute the query or another command.

> **TIP**
>
> When the `showplan` option or the `statistics io/time` options are turned on and you run a system stored procedure, often the `showplan/statistics` output is rather voluminous, making it difficult to read the stored procedure output. Sometimes, depending on the query tool being used, the amount of output will exceed the tool's results buffer. Many of the system stored procedures are very large and complex stored procedures (run `sp_helptext` on a procedure such as `sp_help` sometime, and you'll see what I mean).
>
> To avoid generating all that output, you'd have to keep switching the `showplan/noexec/statistics` options off and on. If you're a lazy typist like me, this is not a viable option. I recommend opening a second session to the SQL Server for running system stored procedures such as `sp_help` and `sp_helpindex` where you don't have any of these options turned on. Use the other session for debugging your SQL code.

The following is an example of the information displayed by `showplan`:

```
/*QUERY for a simple join with SHOWPLAN ON*/
select sum(ytd_sales)from titles t, publishers p
where t.pub_id = p.pub_id
and p.pub_name = "New Moon Books"

STEP 1
The type of query is SELECT
Scalar Aggregate
FROM TABLE
publishers p
Nested iteration
Table Scan
FROM TABLE
titles t
Nested iteration
Table Scan
STEP 2
The type of query is SELECT

----------
28286

(1 row(s) affected)
```

The following sections break down the `showplan` output and examine the statements displayed.

STEP <stepnum>

Sometimes, SQL Server cannot process the entire query in a single step and must break it down into multiple pieces. The STEP <stepnum> statement displays which component of the query the optimizer is processing.

Typical queries that require multiple steps are queries with aggregates, GROUP BY or ORDER BY clauses, or queries that require a worktable to execute the query. The SQL Server must first retrieve the results from the base table(s) into a worktable in tempdb in the first step in order to calculate the aggregate or group, or to sort the result set. In the second step, it retrieves the result set from the worktable.

If you examine the sample query, you'll see that there is an aggregate in the query. In the first step, you perform the select from the tables. The value for sum(amount) is stored and calculated in a worktable in tempdb. In the second step, SQL Server retrieves the calculated sum from the worktable.

The type of query is <querytype>

This line simply states what type of command is being executed at each step. If the SQL statement is not the typical SELECT, INSERT, UPDATE, or DELETE, showplan will report the type of statement being executed. For example:

```
exec proc_1

STEP 1
The type of query is EXECUTE
```

The type of query is SELECT (into a worktable)

This statement indicates that SQL Server needs to select results into a worktable for processing—for example, when a GROUP BY clause is used:

```
select sum(ytd_sales), type from titles
group by type

STEP 1
The type of query is SELECT (into a worktable)
GROUP BY
Vector Aggregate
FROM TABLE
titles
Nested iteration
Table Scan
TO TABLE
Worktable 1
STEP 2
The type of query is SELECT
FROM TABLE
Worktable 1
Nested iteration
Table Scan
```

Notice that this query is a two-step query. The results are first retrieved from the titles table into a worktable to do the grouping and calculate the aggregate, and then the final result set is retrieved from the worktable in the second step.

GROUP BY

This indicates that the query contains a GROUP BY clause. Any query with a GROUP BY will always be a two-step query because a worktable must be used to calculate the vector or scalar aggregate.

Vector Aggregate | Scalar Aggregate

This indicates that the query contains one or more aggregate functions without a GROUP BY clause. A scalar aggregate contains a single value for the aggregate when the query does not contain a GROUP BY clause. A scalar aggregate is still a two-step query. The scalar aggregate is essentially a single-column, single-row worktable in tempdb used to keep a running total for each aggregate as the result rows are processed in the first step. In the second step, SQL Server retrieves the value stored in the scalar aggregate.

```
select sum(ytd_sales), avg(price)
from titles

The type of query is SELECT
Scalar Aggregate
FROM TABLE
titles
Nested iteration
Table Scan
STEP 2
The type of query is SELECT
```

A *vector aggregate* is created when the query contains one or more aggregates in conjunction with a GROUP BY clause. The vector aggregate is essentially a multicolumn table with one column for each column that you are grouping on and another column to hold the computed aggregate for each distinct group. There will be a row in the worktable for each distinct instance of the column(s) in the GROUP BY clause. (See Figure 14.4.)

FIGURE 14.4.

Worktable for vector aggregate.

type	avg (price)
UNDECIDED	NULL
business	13.73
mod_cook	11.49
popular_comp	21.48
psychology	13.50
trad_cook	15.96

NOTE

In many of the classes I teach, students have a tendency to misread the showplan output for queries with vector aggregates. They see the Table Scan output in the second step and assume that the optimizer performed a table scan on the base table, when actually it is the query against the worktable that is performing the table scan. SQL Server has to do a table scan on the worktable because it is not indexed.

Be careful not to make this same mistake. To determine the access path used by the optimizer, note the access path listed right after the FROM TABLE statement for the table in question.

FROM TABLE

The FROM TABLE line will typically be followed on the next line with the name of the table from which data is being selected. This can be a table in the FROM clause in the query, or a worktable. If aliases were used for tables in the query, the alias will follow the table name. The order of the FROM TABLE information in the showplan information indicates the join order used to process the query. In the following showplan example, the publishers table is the first, or outer, table in the join, and the titles table is the second, or inner, table.

```
STEP 1
The type of query is SELECT
Scalar Aggregate
FROM TABLE
publishers p
Nested iteration
Table Scan
FROM TABLE
titles t
Nested iteration
Table Scan
STEP 2
The type of query is SELECT
```

Nested iteration

As covered in Chapter 12, "Understanding the Query Optimizer," all joins are processed as a series of *nested iterations*, looping on the inner table for each row in the outer table. Essentially, all retrievals from a table are one or more sets of loops on the table to retrieve the matching data rows. When you see the Nested iteration statement in the showplan output, it indicates that one or more passes were made on the table.

Table Scan

This indicates that the access method used to retrieve data from the table listed above it was a table scan.

Using Clustered Index

This indicates that the data was retrieved from the table using the clustered index. The name of the index is not displayed because there can only be one clustered index on a table. This typically indicates that the query contains a search argument that can be satisfied using the clustered index.

Index: <index_name>

A nonclustered index was used to retrieve data from the table. The name of the index is displayed to indicate which nonclustered index was used. The nonclustered index can be used if there is a SARG that matches the index or if the query is covered by the nonclustered index.

Using Dynamic Index

If you see this statement in your showplan output, it indicates that the query contains an OR statement and the query optimizer applied the OR strategy to solve the query rather than a table scan. Refer back to Chapter 12 for a discussion of SQL Server's OR strategy.

Worktable Created for ORDER BY | DISTINCT

...
This step involves sorting

...
Using GETSORTED Table Scan

If the query contains an ORDER BY clause, a worktable needs to be created to sort the final result set if the data cannot be retrieved in index sorted order.

```
select * from titles
order by price

STEP 1
The type of query is INSERT
The update mode is direct
Worktable created for ORDER BY
FROM TABLE
titles
Nested iteration
Table Scan
TO TABLE
Worktable 1
STEP 2
The type of query is SELECT
This step involves sorting
FROM TABLE
Worktable 1
Using GETSORTED Table Scan
```

In this example, the rows are retrieved from the titles table into a worktable in `tempdb` in the first step. In the second step, the rows are retrieved from the worktable in sorted order using a table scan on the worktable.

If a query contains a DISTINCT clause, the result rows need to be copied into a worktable and sorted so that the duplicate rows can be removed.

```
select distinct type from titles

STEP 1
The type of query is INSERT
The update mode is direct
Worktable created for DISTINCT
FROM TABLE
titles
Nested iteration
Table Scan
TO TABLE
Worktable 1
STEP 2
The type of query is SELECT
This step involves sorting
FROM TABLE
Worktable 1
Using GETSORTED Table Scan
```

Worktable Created for REFORMATTING

The reformatting strategy is an alternative used by the query optimizer when no useful indexes are available on either of two tables involved in a join. Joining two tables without an index on either can be very costly. SQL Server compares the cost of joining the tables without an index to the cost of making a copy of one of the tables, creating a clustered index on it, and using the clustered index on the worktable to join it with the other table. Following is an example of the showplan output when the reformatting strategy is used:

```
select * from table1, table2
where table1.number = table2.number
(No indexes)

STEP 1
The type of query is INSERT
The update mode is direct
Worktable created for REFORMATTING
FROM TABLE
table2
Nested Iteration
Table Scan
TO TABLE
Worktable

STEP 2
The type of query is SELECT
FROM TABLE
table1
```

```
Nested Iteration
Table Scan
FROM TABLE
Worktable
Nested Iteration
Using Clustered Index
```

The following text walks you through the showplan output step by step to get an understanding of what is taking place.

In Step 1, the worktable is being created in tempdb, and the rows from table2 are copied into the worktable. A clustered index is then created on the worktable. In Step 2, table1 is joined on the worktable, using the clustered index on the worktable to find the matching rows for the join.

Worktable created for SELECT INTO

When you run a SELECT INTO statement, a new table is created in the specified database with the same structure as the table(s) being selected from. This statement in the showplan output is somewhat misleading in that it's not actually a worktable that gets created, but an actual table in the specified database. Unlike worktables created within other query plans, this table is not dropped when query execution completes.

The Update Mode is DEFERRED | DIRECT

When you perform an update operation (UPDATE, DELETE, INSERT, SELECT INTO), SQL Server can perform the update as a direct update or a deferred update. Refer back to Chapter 10, "Understanding SQL Server Storage Structures," for a full discussion of direct and deferred updates. This statement in the showplan output indicates which update method is being used on the specified table.

EXISTS TABLE: nested iteration

This is very similar to a standard nested iteration, except that the nested iteration is being performed on a table in a subquery that is part of an existence check in the query. An existence check on the subquery can take many forms, including, but not restricted to, EXISTS, IN, and = ANY. For example:

```
select pub_name from publishers
where pub_id in (select pub_id from titles
where type = "business")
STEP 1
The type of query is SELECT
FROM TABLE
publishers
Nested iteration
Table Scan
FROM TABLE
```

```
titles
EXISTS TABLE : nested iteration
Table Scan
```

In earlier releases of SQL Server, this query could have been flattened into a join but would have resulted in multiple rows for pub_name, one for each matching row in the titles table. The ANSI standard behavior for such a query is that it should only return distinct instances of pub_id. Therefore, the query is processed as an existence join check rather than a standard inner join.

WITH CHECK OPTION

This indicates that data is being inserted or updated in a view containing one or more subqueries that was defined with the WITH CHECK OPTION.

Using *DBCC* Trace Flags for Analyzing Query Plans

The showplan option is a very useful tool for determining the query plan that the optimizer has chosen to process the query, but it doesn't give you any indication why that plan was chosen. Unfortunately, sometimes it may not be clear why a particular plan is being used or it may appear that the wrong query plan was been chosen. So, how exactly do you determine whether the optimizer is choosing the appropriate plan?

Well, the hard way would be to force the optimizer to use different query plans and let it execute the various query plans to see which one actually results in the least amount of I/O and query processing time (see Chapter 16, "Managing the SQL Server Optimizer," for a discussion of how to force specific query plans). This would obviously be very time-consuming and would help you determine whether the optimizer was choosing the correct query plan, but still not necessarily why.

What you really want to know is whether the optimizer is recognizing your search arguments and join clauses, and what information it is using to come up with its row and page I/O estimates.

Fortunately, SQL Server provides us with some DBCC trace flags, which give you exactly that information. A list of the useful trace flags and the information they provide are listed in Table 14.1.

Table 14.1. Useful DBCC TRACEON commands for interpreting query plans.

Trace Flag	Information Displayed
-1	Sets trace flags for all connections rather than just the current connection when using DBCC TRACEON or DBCC TRACEOFF
302	Provides information on the index selection process for each table in the query
310	Provides information on the join order selection process
330	Displays cost estimates for each table in the showplan output
3604	Sends output to the client session
3605	Sends output to the SQL Server error log

You must be logged in as sa to have permissions to run the DBCC TRACEON command. You can cause some of the options to apply to all user connections by turning the trace flags on in SQL Server startup. If you start up SQL Server from a batch file or the command line, you can set trace flag options at SQL Server startup with the -T option:

```
sqlservr -d c:\sql60\data\master.dat -ec:\sql60\log\errorlog -T330
```

If you prefer to start up SQL Server using the SQL Service Manager, you'll need to set the SQL Server startup parameters in the SQL Server Setup program. Figure 14.5 shows how to set the 330 trace flag in the SQL Server Setup utility so that the trace flag will apply when starting SQL Server from the SQL Service Manager.

FIGURE 14.5.

Setting the 330 trace flag as a SQL Server startup parameter. Startup parameters set here will be used when SQL Server is started using the SQL Service Manager.

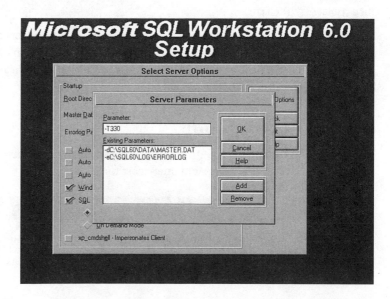

DBCC TRACEON (-1)

Most DBCC TRACEON commands, such as the 302 and 310 trace flags, display information only for the current user process in which they were executed. You also must be the sa to have the necessary permission to run the DBCC TRACEON commands.

If, as the sa, you want to turn a trace flag on globally for all user sessions, you can either specify it as a startup parameter, or you can use the DBCC TRACEON (-1) command. The DBCC TRACEON (-1) command will cause all DBCC TRACEON/TRACEOFF commands to globally apply to all currently open user sessions without having to shut down the SQL Server. In order for new connections to pick up the trace flags, you'll need to periodically run the DBCC TRACEON (-1) command.

One advantage of using the -1 trace flag over setting them as command-line options with the -T parameter is that you can turn them on and off without shutting down SQL Server. This is useful if you want to prevent generation of trace output during peak processing periods, or turn them on only during periods when particular problems occur.

The 3604, 3605 Trace Flags

By default, most DBCC TRACEON flags send their output to the SQL Server error log. To route the output to the client session, run the following command:

```
DBCC TRACEON (3604)
```

To turn off output to the client session, use the DBCC TRACEOFF command:

```
DBCC TRACEOFF (3604)
```

Unlike the other trace flags, all users have permission to issue the DBCC TRACEON (3604) command. Actually, for some of the DBCC trace flags that the sa can turn on for all users, the client application will still need to turn on the output to the client application with the 3604 trace flag in order to see the trace flag output.

DBCC TRACEON (330)

When the 330 trace flag is on, SQL Server reports additional information in the showplan output regarding the row estimates and query cost for each table.

> **NOTE**
>
> Note that the 330 trace flag is turned on automatically when you set the showplan option on in the ISQL/W Query menu. (See Figure 14.3.)

The following is the showplan output with the 330 trace flag turned on:

```
select title, pub_name
from publishers p, titles t
where t.pub_id = p.pub_id
order by type

STEP 1
The type of query is INSERT
The update mode is direct
Worktable created for ORDER BY
FROM TABLE
publishers p
Row estimate:  8
Cost estimate: 16
Nested iteration
Table Scan
FROM TABLE
titles t
JOINS WITH
publishers p
Row estimate:  18
Cost estimate: 60
Nested iteration
Table Scan
TO TABLE
Worktable 1
STEP 2
The type of query is SELECT
This step involves sorting
FROM TABLE
Worktable 1
Row estimate:  18
Cost estimate: 43
Using GETSORTED Table Scan
```

Note the two additional statements for each table, Row estimate and Cost estimate. The Row estimate is the estimate of the number of rows in the table that the optimizer estimates will satisfy the query. The Cost estimate is the I/O cost in milliseconds to retrieve the rows for each table. The total I/O cost for the entire query can be determined by summing the I/O cost displayed for each table. In this example, the total I/O cost for this query would be the following:

$$16 + 60 + 43 = 119 \text{ milliseconds}$$

Refer back to Chapter 12 for a discussion of how the optimizer determines the row and I/O cost estimates.

By displaying this information in the showplan output, you can more easily compare the effectiveness of different query plans with one another and see which one results in the lower total I/O cost. This would still require running different versions of a query, however, and forcing particular query plans by invalidating search arguments or using the techniques covered in Chapter 16. There must be an easier way to examine the different statistics, join orders, and cost estimates that the optimizer is looking at to find the cheapest query plan. Fortunately, there is.

DBCC TRACEON (302) and DBCC TRACEON (310)

The 302 and 310 trace flags give you a look into the cost analysis process that the query optimizer goes through when determining the best query plan. There are additional options available to view other aspects of the query optimization process, but these two trace flags provide the most useful information regarding optimizer query plan selection. These are the ones on which this chapter concentrates.

The 302 trace flag displays the index selection phase of the query optimizer. You'll be able to examine the search arguments and join clauses identified by the query optimizer and determine whether an index is found on the column(s) that matches the SARG or join clause, whether the statistics page is used, and what the row and page I/O estimates are for each candidate index.

The 310 trace flag is most often used in conjunction with the 302 trace flag, but it's not required. The 310 output displays the join selection phase of the query optimizer, which takes place after the index selection phase. Here, you'll be able to examine the possible join permutations and costs associated with each one that the optimizer is considering.

Like the other DBCC trace flags, you must be sa to turn on the 302 and 310 trace flags. These can be turned on for all users, however, by setting the trace flags on as startup parameters or by using the DBCC TRACEON (-1) command. The client application will still need to issue a DBCC TRACEON (3604) command to have the trace output displayed.

As the sa, run the following commands to turn on the 302 and 310 trace flags for your current session:

```
DBCC TRACEON (3604, 302,310)
```

If you want to turn the trace flag on for all user sessions, run the following command as sa:

```
DBCC TRACEON (-1, 302, 310)
```

The users will then need to run a DBCC TRACEON (3604) to have the 302 and 310 output returned to the client application.

Interpreting the DBCC TRACEON (302) Output

The 302 and 310 trace flags provide a textual representation of the query optimization process. This output, however, obviously was originally intended for the developers of SQL Server to debug the query optimizer code. Over the years, the output has become somewhat more readable but still can be a bit cryptic. In this section, you will examine the output from the DBCC (302) trace facility and decipher what each of the statements you may see actually represent.

Scoring Search Clauses

The first part of the 302 output is the search clause scoring phase. The process will be performed for each valid search argument identified in the query. If no search arguments are identified by the query optimizer for a table, there will be no search clause information displayed.

For each table on which the optimizer identifies one or more search clauses, you see its information displayed between two strings of asterisks.

```
*******************************
Entering q_score_index() for table 'pt_tx_CIid' (varno 1).
The table has 7282 rows and 118 pages.
Scoring the search clause:
AND (!:0xf14da4)  (andstat:0xa)
  GT (L:0xf14d84)  (rsltype:0x3c rsllen:8 rslprec:19 rslscale:4
  opstat:0x0)
    VAR (L:0xf14d1e)  (varname:amount right:f14d6a varno:1 colid:2
    coltype:0x3c colen:8 coloff:6 colprec:19 colscale:4 vartypeid:11
    varnext:f14c6a varusecnt:1 varstat:90 varlevel:0 varsubq:0)
    MONEY (R:0xf14d6a)  (len:8 maxlen:4 prec:6 scale:0 value:
    400000.00)

Cheapest index is index 0, costing 118 pages and generating 2403 rows
per scan.
Search argument selectivity is 0.330000.
*******************************
```

Pretty straightforward, easily readable output, huh? Now you'll break out the important pieces that you need to know to figure out what's going on.

Entering q_score_index() for table '<table_name>'

This indicates that you are in a scoring routine for the specified table to find the best index to use for a table, depending on the search arguments or join clauses.

varno <tablenum>

This indicates the location of the table in the FROM clause in the query. 0 is the first table, 1 is the second table, 2 is the third table, and so on.

The table has N rows and n pages.

This is the estimate of the overall table size. These values are taken from the sysindexes table. Essentially, this is the base cost of a table scan against which the cost of using any indexes will be compared to find the cheapest approach. Be sure to double-check these values, because there are instances in which they could be inaccurate or out of date, resulting in the wrong query plan being selected.

Scoring the search clause

This indicates that the optimizer is scoring a search clause on the specified table. This is where things get a bit tricky. Breaking out the different variables displayed should help things make a bit more sense.

The Type of Operator

```
AND (!:0xf14da4)  (andstat:0xa)
  GT (L:0xf14d84)  (rsltype:0x3c rsllen:8 rslprec:19 rslscale:4
```

SQL Server always reports one AND clause, even for queries with a single search argument. You can pretty much ignore the first one that you see. The next line below it indicates which type of operator is specified in the query:

- EQ:Equal to (=)
- LT:Less than (<)
- GT:Greater than (>)
- LE:Less than or equal to (<=)
- GE:Greater than or equal to (>=)

Remember, not equal (<>, !=) is not a treated as valid search argument by the optimizer and will not show up in the cost estimates.

NOTE

A BETWEEN clause is treated by SQL Server as

```
<= upper bound AND >= lower bound
```

as seen in the following example:

```
select count(*) from pt_tx_CIamountNCamount
where amount between 100000 and 120000


********************************
Entering q_score_index() for table 'pt_tx_CIamountNCamount' (varno
0).
The table has 7282 rows and 88 pages.
Scoring the search clause:
AND (!:0xf14e02)  (andstat:0xa)
  LE (L:0xf14dce)  (rsltype:0x3c rsllen:8 rslprec:19 rslscale:4
  opstat:0x0)
    VAR (L:0xf14e54)  (varname:amount left:f14d66 right:f14d80
    varno:0 colid:2 coltype:0x3c colen:8 coloff:6 colprec:19
    colscale:4 vartypeid:11 varusecnt:2 varstat:8c varlevel:0
    varsubq:0)
    MONEY (R:0xf14d80)  (len:8 maxlen:4 prec:6 scale:0 value:
    120000.00)
```

```
  AND (R:0xf14df6)  (andstat:0xa)
    GE (L:0xf14de2)  (rsltype:0x3c rsllen:8 rslprec:19 rslscale:4
    opstat:0x0)
      VAR (L:0xf14e54)  (varname:amount left:f14d66 right:f14d80
      varno:0 colid:2 coltype:0x3c colen:8 coloff:6 colprec:19
      colscale:4 vartypeid:11 varusecnt:2 varstat:8c varlevel:0
      varsubq:0)
      MONEY (R:0xf14d66)  (len:8 maxlen:4 prec:6 scale:0 value:
      100000.00)
```

Be careful dealing with BETWEEN clauses in SQL Server 6.0. In previous releases, it didn't matter whether you put the lower bound on the left or right of the search clause. SQL Server would swap the values to ensure that the lower bound was always the smaller value. With the release of SQL Server 6.0, the ANSI standard does not allow this treatment of a BETWEEN statement. If you state the query as follows,

```
BETWEEN upper_bound AND lower_bound
```

SQL Server will still process the query, but the row estimate will always be 0.

Also note that for any LIKE clause where the first character of the matching string is a not a wildcard character, it is treated as < upper bound AND >= lower bound.

Information on the Column

```
VAR (L:0xf14d1e)  (varname:amount right:f14d6a varno:1 colid:2
    coltype:0x3c colen:8 coloff:6 colprec:19 colscale:4 vartypeid:11
    varnext:f14c6a varusecnt:1 varstat:90 varlevel:0 varsubq:0)
```

- ■ varname indicates the name of the column involved in the search clause. In this example, the column name is amount.

- ■ varno is the table in the FROM clause to which this column belongs.

- ■ colid is the ID of the column in the table, as contained in syscolumns.

- ■ vartypeid is the datatype ID of the column. To find out the actual datatype name for this example:

```
select name from systypes where type = 11
```

The Datatype and Value of the SARG

```
MONEY (R:0xf14d6a)  (len:8 maxlen:4 prec:6 scale:0 value:
    400000.00)
```

This line indicates the datatype and value of the search argument supplied. In this example, the datatype is MONEY and the value is 400000.00. Note that SQL Server will convert a constant value to the column datatype.

Scoring the Indexes Matching the Search Clause

After identifying all the search clauses, the next step is to match the search clauses with any available indexes on the table. For any index that can satisfy the query, a cost estimate in terms of page I/Os will be generated for each index to determine the most efficient index to use. This cost estimate will be based either on distribution steps, index density, or built-in percentage estimates if the distribution steps and density information are either unavailable or cannot be used.

Unique type index found — return rows 1 pages N

If the search argument is an equality operation (=), SQL Server knows that only a single row can match a single value. The index *type* can be either clustered or nonclustered. The page cost is estimated to be a single data page read plus a number of index page reads equal to the number of levels in the index. Consider the following example:

```
select company from pt_sample_CIid
where id = 1000


********************************
Entering q_score_index() for table 'pt_sample_CIid' (varno 0).
The table has 5772 rows and 243 pages.
Scoring the search clause:
AND (!:0xf14c6e)  (andstat:0xa)
  EQ (L:0xf14c5a)  (rsltype:0x38 rsllen:4 rslprec:10 rslscale:0
  opstat:0x0)
    VAR (L:0xf14c10)  (varname:id right:f14c40 varno:0 colid:1
    coltype:0x38 colen:4 coloff:2 colprec:10 colscale:0 vartypeid:7
    varnext:f14b4a varusecnt:1 varstat:84 varlevel:0 varsubq:0)
    INT4 (R:0xf14c40)  (len:4 maxlen:4 prec:4 scale:0 value:1000)

Unique clustered index found--return rows 1 pages 2
Cheapest index is index 1, costing 2 pages and generating 1 rows per
scan.
Search argument selectivity is 0.000173.
********************************
```

A unique index was found on the id (varname = id) column for the table pt_sample_CIid, and the search argument is an equality operator. The cost of finding a single row for this table is two pages: one index page read to find the data page plus one data page read.

If the index is not a unique index, then the optimizer must estimate the number of matching rows using the index statistics.

Scoring clause for index <index_id>

This line indicates which index, by index id, matches the search clause and therefore is being evaluated as a potential access path. If index id equals 1, it's the clustered index. If the index id is between 2 and 250, it is scoring the corresponding nonclustered index.

```
Scoring clause for index 1
Relop bits are: 0x10
Qualifying stat page; pgno: 913 steps: 197
Search value: MONEY value:300000.00
No steps for search value--qualpage for LT search value finds
value between steps 18 and 19--use betweenSC
Estimate: indid 1, selectivity 9.060227e-001, rows 6597 pages 72
```

Scoring SARG interval, upper | lower bound

If the query contains an interval search (that is, BETWEEN, LIKE, or a pair of greater-than and less-than predicates), SQL Server will score both the upper and lower bound for the interval. It will determine the location of the upper bound on the statistics page, determine the location of the lower bound on the statistics page, and estimate the matching number of rows between the upper and lower bound.

```
Scoring clause for index 1
Relop bits are: 0x8,0x4
Scoring SARG interval, upper bound.
Qualifying stat page; pgno: 913 steps: 197
Search value: MONEY value:120000.00
No steps for search value--qualpage for LT search value finds
value between steps 173 and 174--use betweenSC
Scoring SARG interval, lower bound.
Qualifying stat page; pgno: 913 steps: 197
Search value: MONEY value:100000.00
No steps for search value--qualpage for LT search value finds
value between steps 168 and 169--use betweenSC
Net selectivity of interval: 2.551812e-002
Estimate: indid 1, selectivity 2.551812e-002, rows 185 pages 3
```

Relop bits are: ...

You can ignore this line. It simply is reiterating the integer bitmap value of the conditional operator.

Index Statistics

The next few lines of output give information on which index statistics are used (distribution steps, density, or built-in percentages) to estimate row count (refer to Chapter 12 for discussion of index statistics and the distribution page). The following sections examine the different alternatives and what the output looks like.

Qualifying stat page; pgno: <pagenum> steps: <numsteps>

A valid statistics page was found for this index at logical page address *<pagenum>*. The statistics page has *<numsteps>* steps on it. The information on this statistics page is what the optimizer will be basing its decisions on when evaluating that index.

TIP

One of the more common errors made by newcomers to SQL Server is to create a table and all indexes on it before loading the data. If update statistics is not run subsequent to the data load, there will be no statistics page for any of the indexes. SQL Server will not create a statistics page for an index created on any empty table because there is nothing with which to populate the statistics page.

Also, remember to keep your statistics up-to-date so that the optimizer can make more valid assumptions about your data distribution when it is estimating the number of matching rows. The rough rule of thumb is to update statistics when more than 10–20 percent of your data has been modified/inserted/deleted.

If you want examine the contents of the distribution page, you can use the DBCC PAGE command (see Chapter 10), but the contents will be displayed in hexadecimal format and are not very useful. Fortunately, SQL Server provides a DBCC command that will display the contents of the distribution page in a readable format. The command is as follows:

dbcc show_statistics (*table_name*, *index_name*)

Following is a fraction of the output for the clustered index, tx_CIid, on the id column for the pt_tx_CIid table:

```
Updated              Rows        Steps       Density
-------------------- ----------  ----------  ------------------------
Nov 19 1995  4:02AM  7282        330         0.000213248

(1 row(s) affected)

All density             Columns
----------------------- -----------------------------
0.000213248             id

(1 row(s) affected)

Steps
----------
         1
        65
       214
       271
       369
       497
       604
       656
       745
       849
       961
.
.
.
```

```
316606
316996
317462
317913
318409
318866
```

(330 row(s) affected)

Here you can see the values stored in the distribution steps as well as the stored index densities.

If you prefer to see the index statistics in a graphical format, check out the demonstration copy of Aurora Distribution Viewer on the CD-ROM included with this book. In addition to providing multiple ways of graphing the distribution page values, it also can keep a history of distribution page values for tracking the effectiveness of your update statistics strategy.

Search Value: <DATATYPE> value: <NNNNNNNN>

This repeats the datatype and value information from the search clause. This is the value that will be used for comparison against the index statistics.

Match found on statistics page

An exact match of the search value was found on the distribution page. This will be followed by one of the following four messages to indicate where the match was found within the distribution page and the number of steps it matched:

- `equal to a single row (1st or last) -- use endsingleSC`

  Search value matched the first or last step on the distribution page

- `equal to several rows including 1st or last -- use endseveralSC`

  Search value matched multiple steps near the beginning or end of the distribution page

- `equal to single row in middle of page -- use midsingleSC`

  Search value matched a single row in the middle of the distribution page

- `equal to several rows in middle of page -- use midseveralSC`

  Search value matched multiple rows in the middle of the distribution page

If no exact match is found on the distribution page, SQL Server looks to see which steps the search value would fall between.

No steps for search value—qualpage for LT search value finds

This indicates that no exact match for the search value was found on the distribution page. Based upon where within the distribution steps the search value falls, SQL Server will display one of the following three messages:

- `value between step K and K + 1 -- use betweenSC`

  The search value falls between the two steps listed.

- `value < first step -- use outsideSC`

  The search value is less than the first distribution step value.

- `value > last step -- use outsideSC`

  The search value is greater than the last distribution step value.

If the search value falls less than the first step or greater than the last step, this could indicate that statistics are out-of-date, especially if the index is created on a sequential key value.

This could be a potential problem if there is a large number of rows outside the distribution steps, but the optimizer estimates that there are only a few rows. If the estimate of where the search value falls within seems inconsistent with your knowledge of the actual data, it is probably time to update statistics for that table or index.

Because SQL Server knows the number of rows between steps, it can make an estimate of the number of rows that match the search value depending on which of the preceding matches is applied.

The *xxxxxx*SC statement indicates the algorithm that will be applied to estimate the number of matching rows. The row estimate is determined as a factor of the number of distribution steps matched and the index density. For example, if a search value falls between two step values, SQL Server cannot determine exactly how many duplicates there may be for the search value between the two steps. The estimate will be either the smaller of the index density times the number of rows in the table, or the number rows between the steps.

Consider a table with 100,000 rows, 333 steps on the distribution page, and an index density of .00025. The search clause is an equality search (column = constant). If a search value is found between two steps, the number of candidate rows is either:

> 100,000 rows /333 steps - 2 = 298 rows between 2 steps
>
> or
>
> 100,000 rows × .00025 = 25 rows based on index density

In this case, SQL Server would use the density estimate that 25 rows would match the search argument rather than 298. This is the typical case for an equality search when the search value falls between two steps.

For search arguments other than equality searches (column = constant) where the search value falls between two steps, the row estimates are determined as follows:

- column < constant   selectivity = ((stepnum + .5 / numsteps) - (density /2)
- column <= constant selectivity = ((stepnum + .5 / numsteps) + (density /2)
- column > constant   selectivity = 1 - ((stepnum + .5 / numsteps) - (density /2)
- column >= constant selectivity = 1 + ((stepnum + .5 / numsteps) - (density /2)

Net selectivity of interval: #.###

This information is displayed if a range search is specified in the query that matches an available index. A BETWEEN clause will display this information twice, once each for the lower and upper bound. The net selectivity is based upon the number of steps in the range.

When Distribution Steps Cannot Be Used

A common problem for the optimizer is search arguments that are valid but don't have known values until runtime. This occurs when the constant expression in the search argument contains a local variable or is compared against a subquery. For example:

```
select count(*) from pt_tx_CIamountNCamount
where amount > (select avg(amount) from pt_tx_CIamountNCamount)
```

or

```
declare @max_amt money
select @max_amt = max(amount) from pt_tx_CIamountNCamount
select count(*) from pt_tx_CIamountNCamount
where amount = @max_amt
```

There is no way for the optimizer to know what value the subquery or local variable will have at runtime, because the value cannot be determined until the query is executed, and the query cannot be executed until a query plan is generated.

Sounds like a bit of a Catch-22, doesn't it? Actually, the only limitation on the optimizer in these cases is that it cannot use the distribution steps to estimate row counts for equality operations; rather, it will have to use the index density. Index density is the percentage of unique values in the table. For any other type of operator (for example, >, <), it will have to use built-in, or "magic" percentages. The magic percentages used are dependent on the type of operator:

- equality (=)   10 percent
- closed interval (>= AND <, BETWEEN)   25 percent
- open interval (>, <, <=, >=)   33 percent

In releases before SQL Server 6.0, the query optimizer would also be unable to resolve the value for search arguments where the constant expression contained a function, mathematical operation, or string concatenation. This restriction appears to have been lifted in version 6.0.

SQL Server will now resolve the function, mathematical operation, or string concatenation before invoking the query optimizer. The resulting value can then be compared against the distribution steps, if available, instead of using the index density or "magic" percentages.

When the distribution steps cannot be used, the 302 output will contain the following:

```
SARG is a subbed VAR or expr result or local variable (constat=number)-- use
magicSC or densitySC
```

In most cases, it is preferable for the optimizer to compare values against the distribution steps instead of using the index density, and especially preferable over using the "magic" percentages. Consider the following example:

- 100,000 rows
- .00025 index density (4000 unique values)
- 20,000 rows where id = 100
  ```
  declare @id int
  select @id = 100
  select count(*) from table_1 where id = @id
  ```

If the distribution steps were used, SQL Server would estimate that approximately 20,000 rows would match the search argument where id = 100. Because you are using a local variable, however, SQL Server will use the index density instead to estimate the number of rows, and, in this case, that would be 100,000 × .00025, or 25 rows. Quite a significant difference in row estimates between the two approaches, possibly resulting in a less than efficient query plan being chosen.

Another situation where the optimizer is forced to use the "magic" percentages is when the distribution page is unavailable, or no index exists on the column specified in the search argument. With no index on the column, SQL Server will just automatically use the "magic" percentages—no information on index selection is displayed:

```
select count(*) from pt_sample
where id = 1000
******************************
Entering q_score_index() for table 'pt_sample' (varno 0).
The table has 5772 rows and 244 pages.
Scoring the search clause:
AND (!:0xf14d74)  (andstat:0xa)
```

```
  EQ (L:0xf14d60)  (rsltype:0x38 rsllen:4 rslprec:10 rslscale:0
  opstat:0x0)
    VAR (L:0xf14db6)  (varname:id right:f14d46 varno:0 colid:1
    coltype:0x38 colen:4 coloff:2 colprec:10 colscale:0 vartypeid:7
    varusecnt:1 varstat:84 varlevel:0 varsubq:0)
    INT4 (R:0xf14d46)  (len:4 maxlen:4 prec:4 scale:0 value:1000)

Cheapest index is index 0, costing 244 pages and generating 577 rows
per scan.
Search argument selectivity is 0.100000.
********************************
```

Notice that this query contains an equality operator. The last line states that the selectivity of the search argument is 0.100000, or 10 percent, the "magic" percentage for an equality operator.

If an index exists but no distribution page has been created, the following text is displayed:

```
No statistics page — use magicSC
```

Determining Final Cost Estimates and Selectivity of Indexes

After the row estimates have been determined using one of the preceding methods, the next step is to determine the I/O cost estimates and overall selectivity of the indexes. Examine the 302 output for the query:

```
select count(id) from pt_tx_CIamountNCamount
where amount > 300000
********************************
Entering q_score_index() for table 'pt_tx_CIamountNCamount' (varno
0).
The table has 7282 rows and 88 pages.
Scoring the search clause:
AND (!:0xf14dac)  (andstat:0xa)
  GT (L:0xf14d98)  (rsltype:0x3c rsllen:8 rslprec:19 rslscale:4
  opstat:0x0)
    VAR (L:0xf14e26)  (varname:amount right:f14d7e varno:0 colid:2
    coltype:0x3c colen:8 coloff:6 colprec:19 colscale:4 vartypeid:11
    varnext:f14df6 varusecnt:1 varstat:90 varlevel:0 varsubq:0)
    MONEY (R:0xf14d7e)  (len:8 maxlen:4 prec:6 scale:0 value:
    300000.00)

Scoring clause for index 1
Relop bits are: 0x10
Qualifying stat page; pgno: 913 steps: 197
Search value: MONEY value:300000.00
No steps for search value--qualpage for LT search value finds
value between steps 0 and 1--use betweenSC
Estimate: indid 1, selectivity 9.973933e-001, rows 7263 pages 80
Scoring clause for index 2
Relop bits are: 0x1000,0x800,0x10
Qualifying stat page; pgno: 945 steps: 197
Search value: MONEY value:300000.00
```

```
No steps for search value--qualpage for LT search value finds
value between steps 0 and 1--use betweenSC
Estimate: indid 2, selectivity 9.973933e-001, rows 7263 pages 7320
Cheapest index is index 1, costing 80 pages and generating 7263 rows
per scan.
Search argument selectivity is 0.997393.
*********************************
```

Estimate: indid I, selectivity #.###, rows R pages P

This information is displayed for each index considered, showing the estimated number of matching rows, the page I/O estimate to retrieve the rows, and the overall selectivity of the index expressed as a floating point value of the percentage of matching rows.

In the preceding example, you see this information twice for the one search argument because you have two indexes on the amount column that can be considered.

For the clustered index, indid 1, you see the estimate of the number of matching rows to be 7253 rows, costing 80 pages to retrieve them. The selectivity is .997393, or approximately 99.7 percent of the rows in the table.

For the nonclustered index, indid 2, the number of matching rows is the same and selectivity is the same, but the I/O cost is 7320 pages.

Both of these alternatives will be compared against the cost of a table scan, which is equal to the total number of pages in the table. The access path resulting in the fewest number of page I/Os is selected as the cheapest approach and is the next bit of information displayed by the optimizer.

Cheapest index is index I, costing P pages and generating R rows per scan.

This line merely reiterates the cost estimates for the index determined to be the cheapest access path. Note that if the index id = 0, a table scan is the cheapest access path.

In the preceding example, the cheapest index is the clustered index (indid 1), resulting in 80 page I/Os. Note that this is only slightly less than a table scan (88 pages), because of the high number of matching rows. If there were no clustered index on the table, a table scan would have been cheaper than the nonclustered index (7320 pages).

Search argument selectivity is N.

This displays the selectivity of the chosen index for a search argument as a decimal value.

Scoring Join Clauses

After scoring all search arguments for the query, the next step is to score any join clauses. With joins, a specific value cannot be looked up on the distribution page because the value to be compared is entirely dependent on the row to be joined at runtime.

Therefore, similar to how you deal with search arguments with unknown values, the optimizer uses the index density to estimate the number of rows which match any single row in a join clause. If index density is not available, the join selectivity is determined as follows:

> 1/# of rows in smaller table

The following is an example of a query with join clauses and the resulting DBCC TRACEON (302) output:

```
select company, amount from pt_sample_CIid s, pt_tx_CIid t
where t.id = s.id


********************************
Entering q_score_join() for table 'pt_sample_CIid' (varno 0).
The table has 5772 rows and 243 pages.
Scoring the join clause:
AND (!:0xf14d84)  (andstat:0x2)
  EQ (L:0xf14d70)  (rsltype:0x38 rsllen:4 rslprec:10 rslscale:0
  opstat:0x0)
    VAR (L:0xf14d28)  (varname:id right:f14cda varno:0 colid:1
    coltype:0x38 colen:4 coloff:2 colprec:10 colscale:0 vartypeid:7
    varnext:f14b4a varusecnt:1 varstat:84 varlevel:0 varsubq:0)
    VAR (R:0xf14cda)  (varname:id varno:1 colid:1 coltype:0x38
    colen:4 coloff:2 colprec:10 colscale:0 vartypeid:7 varnext:f14bb6
    varusecnt:1 varlevel:0 varsubq:0)

Unique clustered index found--return rows 1 pages 2
Cheapest index is index 1, costing 2 pages and generating 1 rows per
scan.
Join selectivity is 5772.
********************************


********************************
Entering q_score_join() for table 'pt_tx_CIid' (varno 1).
The table has 7282 rows and 118 pages.
Scoring the join clause:
AND (!:0xf14d84)  (andstat:0x2)
  EQ (L:0xf14d70)  (rsltype:0x38 rsllen:4 rslprec:10 rslscale:0
  opstat:0x0)
    VAR (L:0xf14cda)  (varname:id right:f14d28 varno:1 colid:1
    coltype:0x38 colen:4 coloff:2 colprec:10 colscale:0 vartypeid:7
    varnext:f14bb6 varusecnt:1 varstat:84 varlevel:0 varsubq:0)
    VAR (R:0xf14d28)  (varname:id right:f14cda varno:0 colid:1
    coltype:0x38 colen:4 coloff:2 colprec:10 colscale:0 vartypeid:7
    varnext:f14b4a varusecnt:1 varstat:884 varlevel:0 varsubq:0)

Scoring clause for index 1
Relop bits are: 0x80,0x4
Estimate: indid 1, selectivity 2.132651e-004, rows 1 pages 2
```

```
Cheapest index is index 1, costing 2 pages and generating 1 rows per
scan.
Join selectivity is 4689.
********************************
```

Scoring the JOIN CLAUSE:

This indicates that the optimizer is now scoring a join clause rather than a search clause for this query. Notice that the output is pretty much identical to the search clause output, except for the fact that you won't see it using distribution steps to estimate the query cost.

Join selectivity is #####.

SQL Server displays the join selectivity as an integer representation of the denominator of the index density. In the example, the clustered index on `pt_sample_CIid` is a unique index. Because the index density is determined as 1/# of unique values in the table, for `pt_sample_CIid`, this would be 1/5772. Therefore, the join selectivity is the denominator of the index density, or 5772.

For the `pt_tx_CIid` table, the index is not unique, so the density information is used to determine the number of distinct values in the table. In this case, the index density is .0002132651. Multiply that times the number of rows in the table to get the estimate of the number of rows that match any single unknown value:

$$7282 \times .0002132651 = 1.55 \text{ rows}$$

which the server rounds down to approximately 1 matching row per lookup. Therefore, the join selectivity is as follows:

$$1/.0002132651 = 4689 \text{ unique values in pt\_tx\_CIid}$$

After you have examined the search clause and join clause index selection process, the next step is to examine the join order processing phase.

Cost join selectivity is ####. Best join selectivity is ####.

If a table involved in the join also contains a search argument, SQL Server will estimate the best join selectivity as the selectivity of the join clause or the search clause, whichever is lower. Look at the previous example with an added search argument:

```
select company, amount from pt_sample_CIid s, pt_tx_CIid t
where t.id = s.id
and t.amount > 400000


********************************
Entering q_score_index() for table 'pt_tx_CIid' (varno 1).
The table has 7282 rows and 118 pages.
Scoring the search clause:
```

```
AND (!:0xf14e14)  (andstat:0xa)
  GT (L:0xf14df4)  (rsltype:0x3c rsllen:8 rslprec:19 rslscale:4
  opstat:0x0)
    VAR (L:0xf14bb6)  (varname:amount right:f14dda varno:1 colid:2
    coltype:0x3c colen:8 coloff:6 colprec:19 colscale:4 vartypeid:11
    varusecnt:2 varstat:91 varlevel:0 varsubq:0)
    MONEY (R:0xf14dda)  (len:8 maxlen:4 prec:6 scale:0 value:
    400000.00)

Cheapest index is index 0, costing 118 pages and generating 2403 rows
per scan.
Search argument selectivity is 0.330000.
******************************

******************************
Entering q_score_join() for table 'pt_sample_CIid' (varno 0).
The table has 5772 rows and 243 pages.
Scoring the join clause:
AND (!:0xf14e08)  (andstat:0x2)
  EQ (L:0xf14d70)  (rsltype:0x38 rsllen:4 rslprec:10 rslscale:0
  opstat:0x0)
    VAR (L:0xf14d28)  (varname:id right:f14cda varno:0 colid:1
    coltype:0x38 colen:4 coloff:2 colprec:10 colscale:0 vartypeid:7
    varnext:f14b4a varusecnt:1 varstat:84 varlevel:0 varsubq:0)
    VAR (R:0xf14cda)  (varname:id varno:1 colid:1 coltype:0x38
    colen:4 coloff:2 colprec:10 colscale:0 vartypeid:7 varnext:f14bb6
    varusecnt:1 varlevel:0 varsubq:0)

Unique clustered index found--return rows 1 pages 2
Cheapest index is index 1, costing 2 pages and generating 1 rows per
scan.
Join selectivity is 5772.
******************************

******************************
Entering q_score_join() for table 'pt_tx_CIid' (varno 1).
The table has 7282 rows and 118 pages.
Scoring the join clause:
AND (!:0xf14e08)  (andstat:0x2)
  EQ (L:0xf14d70)  (rsltype:0x38 rsllen:4 rslprec:10 rslscale:0
  opstat:0x0)
    VAR (L:0xf14cda)  (varname:id right:f14d28 varno:1 colid:1
    coltype:0x38 colen:4 coloff:2 colprec:10 colscale:0 vartypeid:7
    varnext:f14bb6 varusecnt:1 varstat:84 varlevel:0 varsubq:0)
    VAR (R:0xf14d28)  (varname:id right:f14cda varno:0 colid:1
    coltype:0x38 colen:4 coloff:2 colprec:10 colscale:0 vartypeid:7
    varnext:f14b4a varusecnt:1 varstat:884 varlevel:0 varsubq:0)

Scoring clause for index 1
Relop bits are: 0x80,0x4
Estimate: indid 1, selectivity 2.132651e-004, rows 1 pages 2
Cheapest index is index 1, costing 2 pages and generating 1 rows per
scan.
Cost join selectivity is 4689.
Best join selectivity is 2403.
******************************
```

The cost join selectivity on the pt_tx_CIid table in this example is the same as the normal join selectivity estimated in the previous, 4689. You also have a search clause on pt_tx_CIid, however, which is even more limiting than the join clause. By using the search argument, you can narrow down the number of rows to be joined even further. Therefore, in this case, the best join selectivity is the number of rows matching the search clause.

Interpreting the *DBCC TRACEON (310)* Output

The DBCC TRACEON (310) trace flag displays the cost analysis of the possible join permutations for the query. Here's an example of the 310 output for a simple two-table join:

```
select company, amount from pt_tx_CIid t, pt_sample_CIid s
where t.id = s.id


QUERY IS CONNECTED

J_OPTIMIZE: Remaining vars=[0,1]

permutation: 0 - 1

NEW PLAN (total cost = 3544342):
JPLAN (0x23afa48) varno=0 indexid=0 totcost=1888 pathtype=sclause
class=? optype=? method=NESTED ITERATION outerrows=1 rows=7282
joinsel=1 lp=118 pp=118 cpages=118 ctotpages=118 corder=1 crows=7282
cjoinsel=1

JPLAN (0x23afa90) varno=1 indexid=0 totcost=3542454 pathtype=sclause
class=? optype=? method=NESTED ITERATION outerrows=7282 rows=7282
joinsel=4689 lp=1769526 pp=243 cpages=243 ctotpages=243 corder=1
crows=5772 cjoinsel=1 joinmap=[0]


NEW PLAN (total cost = 34418):
JPLAN (0x23afa48) varno=0 indexid=0 totcost=1888 pathtype=sclause
class=? optype=? method=NESTED ITERATION outerrows=1 rows=7282
joinsel=1 lp=118 pp=118 cpages=118 ctotpages=118 corder=1 crows=7282
cjoinsel=1

JPLAN (0x23afa90) varno=1 indexid=1 totcost=32530 pathtype=join
class=? optype=? method=NESTED ITERATION outerrows=7282 rows=7282
joinsel=4689 lp=14564 pp=243 cpages=2 ctotpages=243 corder=1 crows=1
cjoinsel=5772 joinmap=[0] jnvar=0 refindid=0 refcost=0 refpages=0
reftotpages=0 ordercol[0]=1  ordercol[1]=1


permutation: 1 - 0
WORK PLAN (total cost = 1367732)
```

```
NEW PLAN (total cost = 28628):
JPLAN (0x23afa48) varno=1 indexid=0 totcost=3888 pathtype=sclause
class=? optype=? method=NESTED ITERATION outerrows=1 rows=5772
joinsel=1 lp=243 pp=243 cpages=243 ctotpages=243 corder=1 crows=5772
cjoinsel=1

JPLAN (0x23afa90) varno=0 indexid=1 totcost=24740 pathtype=join
class=? optype=? method=NESTED ITERATION outerrows=5772 rows=7282
joinsel=4689 lp=11544 pp=118 cpages=2 ctotpages=118 corder=1 crows=1
cjoinsel=4689 joinmap=[1] jnvar=1 refindid=0 refcost=0 refpages=0
reftotpages=0 ordercol[0]=1  ordercol[1]=1



TOTAL # PERMUTATIONS: 2
TOTAL # PLANS CONSIDERED: 4

FINAL PLAN (total cost = 28628):
JPLAN (0x23af128) varno=1 indexid=0 totcost=3888 pathtype=sclause
class=join optype=SUBSTITUTE method=NESTED ITERATION outerrows=1
rows=5772 joinsel=1 lp=243 pp=243 cpages=243 ctotpages=243 corder=1
crows=5772 cjoinsel=1

JPLAN (0x23af170) varno=0 indexid=1 totcost=24740 pathtype=join
class=join optype=SUBSTITUTE method=NESTED ITERATION outerrows=5772
rows=7282 joinsel=4689 lp=11544 pp=118 cpages=2 ctotpages=118
corder=1 crows=1 cjoinsel=4689 joinmap=[1] jnvar=1 refindid=0
refcost=0 refpages=0 reftotpages=0 ordercol[0]=1  ordercol[1]=1
```

Again, this information at first glance appears a bit cryptic, but I'll give you the keys that you need to wade through this information to fully comprehend what is going in the join processing phase of your query.

QUERY IS [NOT] CONNECTED

This statement indicates whether the proper number of join clauses have been specified to avoid a Cartesian product. You typically hope to see that the query is connected, because Cartesian products can be very expensive in terms of I/O, even on moderately sized tables.

J_OPTIMIZE: Remaining vars = [...]

This indicates the beginning of the join order processing for the tables in the query. The numbers specified in the brackets correspond to the tables in the order listed in the from clause. These numbers are the same numbers assigned during the search clause processing phase (that is, varno).

Permutation: 0 - 1 - ...

If this is a multitable query containing a join, this statement indicates the join order begin costed out. This information is repeated for each valid join order that the optimizer considers (for example, 0 - 1 - 2, 2 - 0 - 1, and so on). The numbers correspond to the tables as listed in the query's FROM clause:

> 0 = first table in from clause (varno = 0)
>
> 1 = second table in from clause (varno = 1) and so on

NEW PLAN (total cost = ######):

One of these will be printed for each join permutation considered. The total cost indicates the total I/O cost calculated for this plan in milliseconds.

Following the NEW PLAN line will be the JPLAN information, which is repeated for each table in the query. The order each in which they appear in the output is the order they are being joined for this permutation. The first JPLAN listed under NEW PLAN is being considered as the outermost table, the second NEW PLAN is the first inner table, the third JPLAN would be the second inner table, and so on. The output looks similar to the following example:

```
JPLAN (0x23afa48) varno=0 indexid=0 totcost=1888 pathtype=sclause
class=? optype=? method=NESTED ITERATION outerrows=1 rows=7282
joinsel=1 lp=118 pp=118 cpages=118 ctotpages=118 corder=1 crows=7282
cjoinsel=1
```

This information is somewhat cryptic, but when you learn to decipher it, you'll see that it contains a bunch of useful information. Table 14.2 shows what some of the useful variables represent.

Table 14.2. Description of variables displayed by DBCC TRACEON (310).

Variable	Description
varno	Table number as listed in the from clause (0,1,...). Matches the varno listed in the 302 output.
indexid	ID of the index being used on this table for this permutation. 0 = base table 1 = clustered >1 and <= 250 = nonclustered
totcost	Total I/O cost in milliseconds for this table for this permutation. This is the information displayed for the chosen plan as the cost estimate in the showplan output when the DBCC TRACEON (330) flag is turned on.

Variable	Description
pathtype	The access path being used for this table for this permutation: sclause - Search Clause (using index or table scan to find matching rows) join - Join clause orstruct - OR strategy (using dynamic index)
method	The search method used to process this table: NESTED ITERATION - Standard method for reading from table making one or more passes (iterations) REFORMATTING - Using reformatting strategy: building temporary clustered index on the fly OR OPTIMIZATION - Using OR strategy: dynamic index
outerrows	Number of iterations to be performed on this table; corresponds to number of rows in outer table. For the outermost table, outerrows will be 1.
rows	Estimated number of matching rows in this table. This information comes from the search clause processing phase and is based upon the index statistics or built-in statistics. The value here corresponds with the value reported in the 302 output for this table using the specified index.
joinsel	This is the best cost join selectivity as reported by the 302 output for this table using the specified index.
lp	The estimated number of logical page reads. This value is equal to the number of pages per lookup (cpages) times the number of iterations (outerrows).
pp	The estimated total number of physical page reads. For the outer table, this will equal the total number of pages scanned for the single pass of the table. For an inner table, this will equal the total number of pages physically read after all iterations.
cpages	Estimated number of page I/Os per lookup (index + data pages).
ctotpages	Total number of individual pages to be accessed for this table. If the inner table size is less than the size of the data cache, the total number of physical page reads will be the same as the total number of pages to be accessed (ctotpages) for this table. If the table is larger than the data cache size, the total number of physical page reads will be equal to the number of pages per lookup (cpages) times the

continues

Table 14.2. continued

Variable	Description
	number of iterations (`outerrows`), or the same as the number of logical page reads.
`crows`	Estimated number of data rows scanned per lookup.
`corder`	The ID of the most significant sort column for this table for this query (corresponds to `colid` in `syscolumns` for this table).
`cjoinsel`	This is the join selectivity for this index for this table, as reported by the `302` output.
The following values are displayed when the reformatting strategy is considered:	
`refindid`	This is the id of the temporary clustered index created by the reformatting strategy to be used to satisfy the query.
`refcost`	This is the estimated I/O cost in terms of milliseconds to apply the reformatting strategy (refer to Chapter 12 to see how this value is determined).
`refpages`	This is the number of pages per lookup using the temporary clustered index.
`reftotpages`	The total number of pages to be accessed for this table when the reformatting strategy is applied.

The I/O cost for each table (`totcost`) is determined as follows:

(total logical page reads (`lp`) for each table × 2ms)

+ (total physical page reads (`pp`) × 14ms)

The total plan cost is the sum of the total I/O cost (`totcost`) for each table in the query.

IGNORING THIS PERMUTATION

At times, the optimizer will determine that some permutations are so unlikely to cost less than any plans examined thus far that it will ignore those permutations altogether. This saves processing time for the optimizer, but it may at times make the wrong assumption and ignore a plan that might be cheaper.

If you want to verify that the optimizer isn't ignoring a plan that may be cheaper, reverse the order of the tables in the FROM clause. This will cause the optimizer to process the table permutations in the reverse order and estimate the I/O cost for the previously ignored permutation. For example, consider the following query:

```
select company, amount from pt_tx t,  pt_sample_lg s
where t.id = s.id
```

A portion of the 310 output for this query would be as follows:

```
QUERY IS CONNECTED

J_OPTIMIZE: Remaining vars=[0,1]

permutation: 0 - 1

NEW PLAN (total cost = 253881056):
JPLAN (0x25afa48) varno=0 indexid=0 totcost=1408 pathtype=sclause
class=? optype=? method=NESTED ITERATION outerrows=1 rows=7282
joinsel=1 lp=88 pp=88 cpages=88 ctotpages=88 corder=0 crows=7282
cjoinsel=1

JPLAN (0x25afa90) varno=1 indexid=0 totcost=253879648
pathtype=sclause class=? optype=? method=NESTED ITERATION
outerrows=7282 rows=51948 joinsel=7282 lp=15867478 pp=15867478
cpages=2179 ctotpages=2179 corder=0 crows=51948 cjoinsel=1 joinmap=[0
]

NEW PLAN (total cost = 384636):
JPLAN (0x25afa48) varno=0 indexid=0 totcost=1408 pathtype=sclause
class=? optype=? method=NESTED ITERATION outerrows=1 rows=7282
joinsel=1 lp=88 pp=88 cpages=88 ctotpages=88 corder=0 crows=7282
cjoinsel=1

JPLAN (0x25afa90) varno=1 indexid=1 totcost=383228 pathtype=join
class=? optype=? method=REFORMATTING outerrows=7282 rows=51948
joinsel=7282 lp=14564 pp=1368 cpages=2 ctotpages=1368 corder=1
joinmap=[0] jnvar=0 refindid=1 refcost=334948 refpages=2
reftotpages=1368 ordercol[0]=1  ordercol[1]=1


permutation: 1 - 0
IGNORING THIS PERMUTATION
```

I'll first break out the individual components of this output.

The first join order examined is from pt_tx to pt_sample_lg (0 - 1). The first plan considered for this join order (NEW PLAN (total cost = 253881056) is a table scan on the outer table, pt_tx (varno=0, indexid=0), and a table scan on the inner table, pt_sample_lg (varno=1, indexid=0). The total cost of the first plan considered is 253,881,056 milliseconds.

The processing method used on both tables in the first plan considered is the normal query processing (NESTED ITERATION). Because the outer table, pt_tx, is scanned only once (outerrows=1), the number of logical page reads (lp=88) is the same as the physical reads (pp=88, cpages=88 × outerrows=1). The total I/O cost (totcost=1408) for the pt_tx table is as follows:

> 88 logical page reads × 2ms = 176ms
> + 88 physical page reads × 14ms = 1232ms
> = 1408 ms

Next, the optimizer determines the total I/O cost for the pt_sample_lg table (varno=1).

The total number of pages per iteration on the pt_sample_lg is also 2,179 pages (cpages=2,179) because a table scan would be performed for each iteration. The total number of iterations performed is 7,282 (outerrows=7282). This value equals the total number of rows in the outer table, pt_tx (varno=0, rows=7282). Therefore, the total number of logical page reads (and in this example, physical page reads as well) is as follows:

> 7282 iterations
> × 2179 pages per iteration
> = 15,867,478 total page reads

Notice that in this example the physical page (pp=15867478) and logical page (lp=15867478) counts are the same for the pt_sample_lg table. This is because the system on which this query was run didn't have sufficient data cache available to fit the entire pt_sample_lg in memory. Therefore, for every iteration, SQL Server will have to perform all physical reads rather than logical reads. If the table could have fit in cache, the total number of physical page reads would have equaled the total number of pages accessed, 2179 (ctotpages=2179).

This is the total number of pages in the table, which is also the cost of a table scan. Because a table scan is performed for each iteration, the total number of pages per iteration is 2,179 (cpages=2179) scanning 51,948 rows per lookup (crows=51948). The total I/O cost for the inner table, pt_sample_lg, is 253,879,648 milliseconds (varno=1, totcost=253879648). This value is determined as follows:

> 15867478 logical page reads × 2 ms = 31,734,956ms
> 15867478 physical page reads × 14 ms = 222,144,692ms
> = 253,879,648 ms

The total I/O cost for the first plan is estimated to be 253,881,056 milliseconds, or nearly three days!

Because neither of these tables has a usable index for this query, the optimizer considered applying the reformatting strategy on the pt_sample_lg table (varno=1, method=REFORMATTING). This is the second plan considered (NEW PLAN (total cost = 384636)). The costs for the outer table, pt_tx (varno=0) are the same for this plan, but the cost for pt_sample_lg are the costs associated with applying the reformatting strategy on pt_sample_lg.

The reformatting strategy itself has an I/O cost of 334,948 milliseconds (refcost=334948). The number of pages per lookup using the temporary clustered index (refindid=1, indexid=1) is 2 (refpages=2, cpages=2), and the total number of pages accessed is 1,368 (reftotpages=1368, ctotpages=1368). Because you now have a clustered index on the table and do not have to read the entire table into cache, the number of physical page reads is the same as the number of pages accessed, 1,368 (pp=1368). The total number of logical I/Os is as follows:

> 2 pages (cpages=2)
> × 7282 iterations (outerrows=7282)
> = 14,564 logical page reads

The total I/O cost for the `pt_sample_lg`, including the cost of reformatting, is as follows:

$$14564 \times 2\text{ms} =$$
$$+\ 1368 \times 14\text{ms} =$$
$$+\ 334{,}949\text{ ms (cost of reformatting)}$$
$$=\ 383{,}228\text{ ms (totcost=383228)}$$

This is a more reasonable 6.4 minutes. Quite obviously, the cost of using the reformatting strategy is considerably less than the cost of joining via a table scan on the inner table. At this point, however, the optimizer makes the assumption that the reformatting plan is the lowest plan to be found and ignores the alternative permutation of `pt_sample_lg` as the outer table and `pt_tx` as the inner table. Just for fun, and because I am always somewhat skeptical myself, I'll force the optimizer to evaluate this alternative first by switching the order of the tables in the FROM clause:

```
select company, amount from pt_sample_lg s, pt_tx t
where t.id = s.id
```

The `310` output for this example is as follows:

```
QUERY IS CONNECTED

J_OPTIMIZE: Remaining vars=[0,1]

permutation: 0 - 1

NEW PLAN (total cost = 9178944):
JPLAN (0x25afa48) varno=0 indexid=0 totcost=34864 pathtype=sclause
class=? optype=? method=NESTED ITERATION outerrows=1 rows=51948
joinsel=1 lp=2179 pp=2179 cpages=2179 ctotpages=2179 corder=0
crows=51948 cjoinsel=1

JPLAN (0x25afa90) varno=1 indexid=0 totcost=9144080 pathtype=sclause
class=? optype=? method=NESTED ITERATION outerrows=51948 rows=51948
joinsel=7282 lp=4571424 pp=88 cpages=88 ctotpages=88 corder=0
crows=7282 cjoinsel=1 joinmap=[0]


NEW PLAN (total cost = 291796):
JPLAN (0x25afa48) varno=0 indexid=0 totcost=34864 pathtype=sclause
class=? optype=? method=NESTED ITERATION outerrows=1 rows=51948
joinsel=1 lp=2179 pp=2179 cpages=2179 ctotpages=2179 corder=0
crows=51948 cjoinsel=1

JPLAN (0x25afa90) varno=1 indexid=1 totcost=256932 pathtype=join
class=? optype=? method=REFORMATTING outerrows=51948 rows=51948
joinsel=7282 lp=103896 pp=44 cpages=2 ctotpages=44 corder=1 joinmap=[
0] jnvar=0 refindid=1 refcost=48524 refpages=2 reftotpages=44
ordercol[0]=1  ordercol[1]=1


permutation: 1 - 0
IGNORING THIS PERMUTATION
```

```
TOTAL # PERMUTATIONS: 2
TOTAL # PLANS CONSIDERED: 2

FINAL PLAN (total cost = 291796):
JPLAN (0x25af128) varno=0 indexid=0 totcost=34864 pathtype=sclause
class=join optype=SUBSTITUTE method=NESTED ITERATION outerrows=1
rows=51948 joinsel=1 lp=2179 pp=2179 cpages=2179 ctotpages=2179
corder=0 crows=51948 cjoinsel=1

JPLAN (0x25af170) varno=2 indexid=1 totcost=256932 pathtype=join
class=join optype=SUBSTITUTE method=REFORMATTING outerrows=51948
rows=51948 joinsel=7282 lp=103896 pp=44 cpages=2 ctotpages=44
corder=1 joinmap=[0] jnvar=0 refindid=1 refcost=48524 refpages=2
reftotpages=44 ordercol[0]=1  ordercol[1]=1
```

Note that, in this example, the total plan I/O cost of applying the reformatting strategy on the pt_tx table with pt_sample_lg as the outer table is 291,796 milliseconds, or approximately 4.9 minutes. This plan is about 1.5 minutes cheaper than the cheapest plan estimate in the previous example with pt_sample_lg as the outer table.

This is one of the rare instances when the order of the tables in the FROM clause does make a difference in the plan chosen. It's not a significant difference, but it's a good example to show how to use the DBCC trace flags to validate the optimizer's decision.

OR Strategy Example

Just for fun, take a look at the DBCC TRACEON (302,310) output for a query with an OR clause.

```
select * from pt_sample_CIid
where id = 1000
or id = 100000
```

I'll break out the 302, 310 output into parts and help you understand what's being evaluated/estimated at each point.

```
********************************
Entering q_score_index() for table 'pt_sample_CIid' (varno 0).
The table has 5772 rows and 243 pages.
Scoring the search clause:

TREE IS NULL

q_new_orsarg built new SARGs:
AND (!:0xf34b6c)  (andstat:0x0)
  LE (L:0xf34b58)  (rsltype:0x0 rsllen:0 opstat:0x20)
    VAR (L:0xf114f6)  (varname:id left:f11426 right:f11486 varno:0
    colid:1 coltype:0x38 colen:4 coloff:2 colprec:10 colscale:0
    vartypeid:7 varusecnt:5 varstat:4d varlevel:0 varsubq:0)
    INT4 (R:0xf11486)  (len:4 maxlen:4 prec:6 scale:0 value:100000)
  AND (R:0xf34b4c)  (andstat:0x0)
    GE (L:0xf34b38)  (rsltype:0x0 rsllen:0 opstat:0x20)
      VAR (L:0xf114f6)  (varname:id left:f11426 right:f11486 varno:0
      colid:1 coltype:0x38 colen:4 coloff:2 colprec:10 colscale:0
      vartypeid:7 varusecnt:5 varstat:4d varlevel:0 varsubq:0)
      INT4 (R:0xf11426)  (len:4 maxlen:4 prec:4 scale:0 value:1000)
```

```
Scoring clause for index 1
Relop bits are: 0x40,0x8,0x4,0x1
Scoring SARG interval, upper bound.
Qualifying stat page; pgno: 3529 steps: 321
Search value: INT4 value:100000
No steps for search value--qualpage for LT search value finds
value between steps 272 and 273--use betweenSC
Scoring SARG interval, lower bound.
Qualifying stat page; pgno: 3529 steps: 321
Search value: INT4 value:1000
No steps for search value--qualpage for LT search value finds
value between steps 11 and 12--use betweenSC
Net selectivity of interval: 8.132573e-001
Estimate: indid 1, selectivity 8.132573e-001, rows 4694 pages 28
Unique clustered index found--return rows 2 pages 28
Cheapest index is index 1, costing 28 pages and generating 2 rows per
scan.
Search argument selectivity is 0.000347.
*******************************
```

Because the OR clause is on the same column, the optimizer evaluates the cost of using the clustered index on id in a single pass to find all rows where id = 1000 or 100,000. Essentially, this is the same as doing a search where id is between 1000 and 100,000. The cost of this approach would be 28 pages to yield 2 rows.

The next step will be to evaluate the cost of performing two separate lookups on pt_sample_CIid using the unique clustered index on id.

```
*******************************
Entering q_score_index() for table 'pt_sample_CIid' (varno 0).
The table has 5772 rows and 243 pages.
Scoring the search clause:
AND (!:0xf34880)  (andstat:0x8)
  EQ (L:0xf11440)  (rsltype:0x38 rsllen:4 rslprec:10 rslscale:0
  opstat:0x0)
    VAR (L:0xf114f6)  (varname:id right:f11426 varno:0 colid:1
    coltype:0x38 colen:4 coloff:2 colprec:10 colscale:0 vartypeid:7
    varusecnt:5 varstat:10c5 varlevel:0 varsubq:0)
    INT4 (R:0xf11426)  (len:4 maxlen:4 prec:4 scale:0 value:1000)

Unique clustered index found--return rows 1 pages 2
Cheapest index is index 1, costing 2 pages and generating 1 rows per
scan.
Search argument selectivity is 0.000173.
*******************************

*******************************
Entering q_score_index() for table 'pt_sample_CIid' (varno 0).
The table has 5772 rows and 243 pages.
Scoring the search clause:
AND (!:0xf3488c)  (andstat:0x8)
  EQ (L:0xf114a0)  (rsltype:0x38 rsllen:4 rslprec:10 rslscale:0
  opstat:0x0)
    VAR (L:0xf114f6)  (varname:id right:f11486 varno:0 colid:1
    coltype:0x38 colen:4 coloff:2 colprec:10 colscale:0 vartypeid:7
    varusecnt:5 varstat:10c5 varlevel:0 varsubq:0)
    INT4 (R:0xf11486)  (len:4 maxlen:4 prec:6 scale:0 value:100000)
```

```
Unique clustered index found--return rows 1 pages 2
Cheapest index is index 1, costing 2 pages and generating 1 rows per
scan.
Search argument selectivity is 0.000173.
********************************
```

By using the unique clustered index in two separate lookups, it would cost 2 pages per lookup to find both qualifying rows for a total of 4 pages.

This is the end of the search clause processing phase. Even though you have no join in the query, there is still a join processing phase to estimate the total I/O cost using the cheapest access method determined during the search clause processing. The 310 output for this query is as follows:

```
QUERY IS CONNECTED

J_OPTIMIZE: Remaining vars=[0]

permutation: 0

NEW PLAN (total cost = 64):
JPLAN (0x25afa48) varno=0 indexid=0 totcost=64 pathtype=orstruct
class=? optype=? method=OR OPTIMIZATION outerrows=1 rows=2 joinsel=1
lp=4 pp=4 cpages=4 ctotpages=0 corder=0 crows=2 cjoinsel=0


TOTAL # PERMUTATIONS: 1
TOTAL # PLANS CONSIDERED: 1

FINAL PLAN (total cost = 64):
JPLAN (0x25af128) varno=0 indexid=0 totcost=64 pathtype=orstruct
class=join optype=SUBSTITUTE method=OR OPTIMIZATION outerrows=1
rows=2 joinsel=1 lp=4 pp=4 cpages=4 ctotpages=0 corder=0 crows=2
cjoinsel=0
```

This shows that the optimizer is using the OR strategy (method=OR OPTIMIZATION) rather than a table scan or normal single-scan index retrieval. Notice that the total physical page reads are 4 (pp=4) and the logical page reads are 4 (lp=4). This is the sum of the I/O cost for the two separate lookups using the clustered index. Four pages is significantly less than 28 pages, which would have been the I/O cost if a normal single-pass index scan were performed.

TOTAL # PERMUTATIONS: N

This represents the total number of possible join orders to be considered. Refer back to Chapter 12 for a discussion of how SQL Server evaluates all possible join permutations. For 2 tables, the number of permutations is 2. For 4 tables, the number of permutations is 24.

TOTAL # PLANS CONSIDERED: N

This value represents the total number of all possible query plans that the optimizer actually evaluated to determine the lowest query cost. This will be the sum of all query plans evaluated for each permutation considered. Any permutations that were ignored will not be figured into this value.

FINAL PLAN (total cost = N):

This section of the output simply reiterates the costing information for the permutation with the lowest estimated I/O cost. This is the "final" plan, which will be used to process the query. This is the information that is interpreted and displayed by the showplan output.

Using *statistics io* and *statistics time*

To this point, you've seen how the optimizer evaluates your queries, estimates the number of I/Os and the I/O processing time, and picks what it determines to be the cheapest query plan. The decisions that the optimizer makes are based upon index statistics and row estimates.

You may next want to compare the optimizer estimates against the actual number of I/Os and actual query processing time to verify the estimates being generated by the optimizer.

statistics io

SQL Server supplies a set option that causes the actual logical and physical page reads incurred by the query to be displayed. This option is the statistics io option and is turned on by executing the following command:

```
set statistics io on
```

If you are working in ISQL/W, you can set statistics io on by typing the command in a query window and executing it, or by setting the Show Stats I/O option on in the query options dialog for that query window. (See Figure 14.6.)

Setting statistics io on either of these two ways will cause the statistics io output to be displayed in the query results window, along with any data. A third way of setting the statistics io output on is by checking it in the Options menu, as shown in Figure 14.7. This option causes the showplan output to be displayed in a graphical manner under the Statistics I/O tab (see Figure 14.8) and applies to all sessions open within ISQL/W.

FIGURE 14.6.

Setting the statistics io *option on for an ISQL/W query window.*

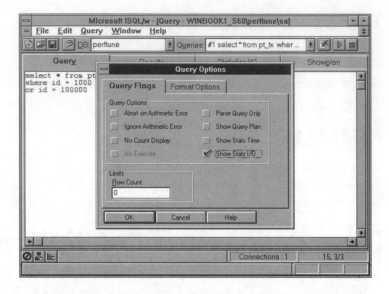

FIGURE 14.7.

Turning on the graphical statistics io *output for all query windows in ISQL/W.*

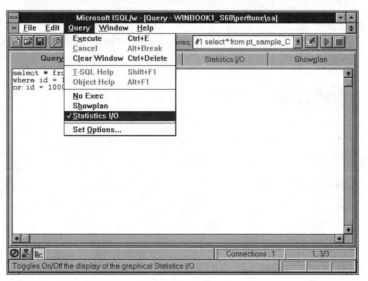

The graphical display makes nice, pretty pictures and gives you a quick glance of what the I/O counts look like, but it's difficult to determine the specific I/O counts from the display. The following examples use setting the showplan option on manually and reviewing the textual output.

FIGURE 14.8.

ISQL/W's graphical display of statistics io.

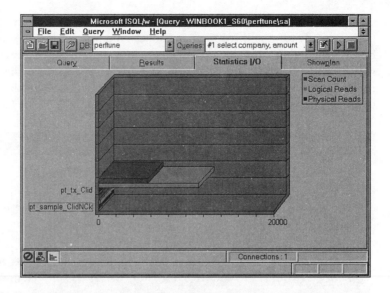

The statistics io option displays the total logical page reads per table, the total physical page reads per table, and the scan count (that is, number of iterations) for each table. Following is a query and a sample of the statistics io output generated for it:

```
select sum(amount) from pt_sample_CIidNCk s, pt_tx_CIid t
where s.id = t.id

---------------------------
501,590,426.50

Table: pt_sample_CIidNCk  scan count 1,  logical reads: 243,  physical reads: 15
Table: pt_tx_CIid  scan count 5772,  logical reads: 11667,  physical reads: 118
```

In this example, pt_sample_CIidNCk is the outer table and is scanned once (scan count 1). pt_tx_CIid is the inner table and is scanned 5,772 times. SQL Server performed 243 logical reads and 15 physical reads on pt_sample_CIidNCk, and 118 physical reads and 11,667 logical reads on pt_tx_CIid. Because every physical page read requires a logical page read for SQL Server to process the page, the count of physical page reads will never exceed the number of logical page reads. You could experience a high number of logical page reads, however, and few or zero physical page reads. If physical reads are 0, then the table was entirely in cache when the query was executed.

One good use of the statistics io output is to evaluate the effectiveness of the size of your data cache. By turning this option on, you can monitor the logical versus physical reads to see how much of your table(s) are staying in cache over time. If the physical page counts are consistently as high as the logical page reads, then the table is not staying in cache and you may need to modify the SQL Server configuration to increase data cache size (see Chapters 30, "Configuring and Tuning SQL Server," and 31, "Optimizing SQL Server Configuration Options.").

NOTE

In the example, the physical read count on pt_sample_ClidNCk is a result of SQL Server 6.0's capability to pre-fetch extents when doing sequential page reads. Because you are performing a table scan and all pages are sequential, SQL Server is able to recognize this and make use of the pre-fetch mechanism to minimize individual physical page reads.

For the example, the RA pre-fetch configuration variable was set to the default value of 3. For every initial physical page read, SQL Server was pre-fetching three extents into cache as a background process, so subsequent page read requests were satisfied by pages already in cache. In effect, you were getting approximately 2 extent reads, or 16 pages, per physical I/O request. If you divide the total number of pages read, 243, by the number of pages per read request, 16, you end up with approximately 15 physical page reads.

Therefore, one additional use for statistics io is to evaluate the effectiveness of your RA pre-fetch settings.

The other common use of statistics io is to evaluate the page estimates generated by the query optimizer for a query plan. If the actual numbers differ significantly from the optimizer's estimates for number of pages estimated by the optimizer, it would indicate that the optimizer is making an inaccurate estimate. This could be because of a bug or weakness in the optimizer's costing algorithm, or statistics that are woefully out of date. You should probably try updating statistics first and rerunning the command with statistics io on before you call Tech Support with a complaint about the query optimizer.

NOTE

In my experience, the SQL Server optimizer typically does a pretty good job of estimating page I/O. Obviously, they are estimates based upon index statistics, so they are not typically going to exactly match the actual page I/Os. I wouldn't suspect an optimizer problem unless the estimates were substantially different from the actuals, probably any difference greater than 1,000 pages or more than a 10 percent margin of error.

Also, you only want to compare the logical I/O counts against the SQL Server estimates. When the optimizer is making its I/O estimates, it makes no assumptions about any data that may already be in cache. Rather, it takes the more pessimistic view that all initial page reads on a table will be physical page reads.

Take a look at the final plan displayed by the DBCC TRACEON (310) command for the previous query, and compare the page estimates against the actual I/O statistics generated:

```
FINAL PLAN (total cost = 28628):
JPLAN (0x21af150) varno=0 indexid=0 totcost=3888 pathtype=sclause
class=join optype=SUBSTITUTE method=NESTED ITERATION outerrows=1
rows=5772 joinsel=1 lp=243 pp=243 cpages=243 ctotpages=243 corder=1
crows=5772 cjoinsel=1

JPLAN (0x21af198) varno=1 indexid=1 totcost=24740 pathtype=join
class=join optype=SUBSTITUTE method=NESTED ITERATION outerrows=5772
rows=7282 joinsel=4689 lp=11544 pp=118 cpages=2 ctotpages=118
corder=1 crows=1 cjoinsel=4689 joinmap=[0] jnvar=0 refindid=0
refcost=0 refpages=0 reftotpages=0 ordercol[0]=1  ordercol[1]=1
```

The optimizer estimated that there would be 243 total logical page reads on the outer table pt_sample_CIidNCk (varno=0, lp=243). This matches exactly with the actual I/O count generated by statistics io. For pt_tx_CIid (varno=1), it estimated 11,544 logical page reads and 5,772 iterations. It did perform 5,772 iterations on the pt_tx_CIid table, but actually performed 11,667 logical page reads, a difference of 123 pages with an error margin of only 1 percent. At 2 milliseconds per page, this is only about .25 seconds, not a significant amount of time.

And speaking of time, how closely do the time estimates generated by the optimizer correspond to the actual execution times.

statistics time

To display the total CPU and elapsed time to execute a query and the time to parse and compile the query, turn on the statistics time option. This option can be turned on with the following command:

```
set statistics time on
```

If you are working in ISQL/W, you can set statistics time on by typing the command in a query window and executing it, or by setting the Show Stats Time option on in the Query Options dialog for that query window (see Figure 14.9).

Setting statistics time on using either of these two ways will cause the statistics time output to be displayed in the query results window, along with any data.

FIGURE 14.9.

Setting the statistics
time *option on for an
ISQL/W query window.*

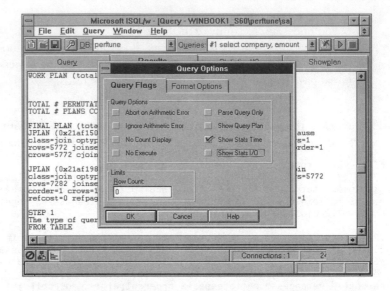

TIP

Again, make sure that you turn noexec off before running a query with statistics
time on or the query will not be executed and no time statistics for execution of the
query will be generated. The query will still be parsed and compiled, however, so time
statistics for those will be generated.

Compare the actual execution time with the estimated I/O times generated by the optimizer
for the following query:

```
select count(*) from pt_sample_CIidNCk s, pt_tx_CIid t
where s.id = t.id

SQL Server Parse and Compile Time:
   cpu time = 10 ms.


...........................
501,590,426.50

Table: pt_sample_CIidNCk  scan count 1,  logical reads: 243,  physical reads: 15
Table: pt_tx_CIid  scan count 5772,  logical reads: 11667,  physical reads: 118

SQL Server Execution Times:
   cpu time = 0 ms.  elapsed time = 4436 ms.
```

The times estimated by the SQL Server optimizer can be viewed with the DBCC TRACEON (310)
trace flag:

```
FINAL PLAN (total cost = 28628):
JPLAN (0x21af150) varno=0 indexid=0 totcost=3888 pathtype=sclause
```

```
class=join optype=SUBSTITUTE method=NESTED ITERATION outerrows=1
rows=5772 joinsel=1 lp=243 pp=243 cpages=243 ctotpages=243 corder=1
crows=5772 cjoinsel=1

JPLAN (0x21af198) varno=1 indexid=1 totcost=24740 pathtype=join
class=join optype=SUBSTITUTE method=NESTED ITERATION outerrows=5772
rows=7282 joinsel=4689 lp=11544 pp=118 cpages=2 ctotpages=118
corder=1 crows=1 cjoinsel=4689 joinmap=[0] jnvar=0 refindid=0
refcost=0 refpages=0 reftotpages=0 ordercol[0]=1  ordercol[1]=1
```

In this example, the SQL Server time estimate (28,628ms) is significantly higher than the actual execution time. But in this case, the SQL Server estimated a greater number of physical reads than actually occurred. Apply the I/O time estimates against the actual logical and physical page counts:

$$(118 + 15) \text{ physical reads} \times 14\text{ms} = 1862 \text{ ms}$$
$$+ (11667 + 243) \text{ logical reads} \times 2\text{ms} = 23820 \text{ ms}$$
$$= 25682 \text{ ms}$$

This value is still considerably higher than the actual execution time. In addition, the query optimizer's time estimate does not factor in network I/O times. If you have a moderately large result set, the time to send the results across the network can exceed the actual query processing time. The elapsed time reported by `statistics time` is the total time from when the query execution was initiated to when the final DONE packet is sent to the client application. It includes all time spent by the query to send results to the client, any time spent waiting for CPU cycles, and any time spent waiting for a lock request to be granted.

In other words, don't expect the estimated time displayed by the `DBCC TRACEON (310)` trace flag to match with the actual execution elapsed time. The optimizer time estimates are primarily for comparison purposes by the optimizer. The time estimates for logical and physical page access times, 2ms and 14ms respectively, are hard-coded values and don't necessarily represent actual I/O rates for the platform on which you are running.

The real useful purpose for the `statistics time` option is to record the actual CPU and elapsed time values for queries and transactions to benchmark and compare execution times for queries. You can also use the output to identify queries with high parse and compile times. Some queries may even have higher parse and compile times than execution times. These would be good candidates to place in stored procedures to reap the benefits of reusable query plans residing in procedure cache, and avoiding the expensive parse and compile steps for each execution.

Before I finish discussing `statistics time`, it is worthwhile to point out a slight difference in how the CPU time is calculated versus how the elapsed time is calculated. This can sometimes result in odd-looking values, such as cases in which CPU time is greater than elapsed time, or when CPU time is 0 and there is substantially more elapsed time.

The elapsed time is based upon the system time. It is determined by subtracting the system time when the query initially started execution from the system time when SQL Server sends the final DONE packet to the client application.

The CPU time is factored as the number of CPU ticks tallied for the query converted to milliseconds. A CPU tick is the time interval between clock interrupts on a system. The number of milliseconds per CPU tick is determined by dividing the clockrate by 1,000.

Look at the first scenario in which CPU time exceeds elapsed time. (See Figure 14.10.)

FIGURE 14.10.

Example of how CPU time can exceed elapsed time.

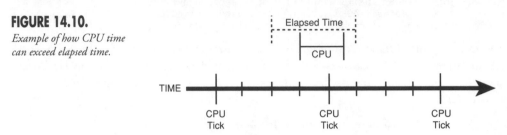

Scale: CPU Tick = 100 ms

Notice how the process starts just before a clock tick and completes just after. Because it was processing at the time of a clock interrupt, a CPU tick was tallied for that process. If you assume that a CPU tick translates to 100 ms, then the CPU time for this process would be 100ms. The actual elapsed time from start to finish appears to only be about 75ms, however. Thus you have a case in which the reported CPU time is more than the elapsed time.

Now look at a second scenario in which you have CPU time of 0 with substantially more elapsed time. (See Figure 14.11.) In this case, the process starts CPU processing just after a CPU tick and completes before the next CPU tick. Total elapsed time from start to finish in this instance appears to be around 175ms. Here you have a case in which CPU time is 0, even though the process did incur CPU processing time.

FIGURE 14.11.

Example of how zero CPU time can be accounted.

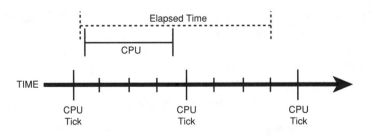

Scale: CPU Tick = 100 ms

Summary

SQL Server provides a number of tools to view and evaluate the query plans being generated by the query optimizer. You can use the showplan option to view the query plan being chosen by the optimizer, and the DBCC TRACEON (302, 310) trace flags to determine how the optimizer chose that query plan. The statistics io and statistics time options can be used to evaluate the actual performance of queries and validate the cost estimates of the query optimizer.

Through the use of these tools, you may sometimes discover that the optimizer is choosing the wrong plan, or at other times, you may simply want to force the optimizer to process a query differently than it chooses to. In Chapter 16, we'll examine some methods for forcing particular query plans and the conditions for when you might want to do this.

Locking and Performance

15

SQL Server Locks Defined

In any multiuser database, there must be a consistent set of rules for making changes to data. The rules might be "there are no rules," but that is still a rule. For a true transaction-processing database, the database-management system is responsible for resolving potential conflicts between two different processes that are attempting to change the same piece of information at the same time. Such a situation cannot occur because the atomicity of a transaction cannot be guaranteed. For example, if two users were to change the same data at approximately the same time, whose change would be propagated? Theoretically, the results would be unpredictable because the answer is dependent on whose transaction completed *last*. Because most application try to avoid "unpredictability" with data wherever possible (imagine your payroll systems returning "unpredictable" results, and you'll get the idea), there must be some way to guarantee the sequential, and atomic, nature of data changes.

The responsibility for ensuring conflict resolution between users falls on the SQL Server locking manager. Locks are used to guarantee that the current user of a resource (data page, table, index, and so on) has a consistent view of that resource from beginning to completion of a particular operation. In other words, what you start with has to be what you work with throughout your operation. Nobody can change what you are working on in mid-state, in effect, intercepting your transaction.

Without locking, transaction processing is impossible. Transactions, being defined as complete units of work, rely on a constant state of data, almost a "snapshot in time" of what they are modifying, in order to guarantee their completion. Transactions and locking, therefore, are part of the same whole—ensuring the completion of data modifications.

SQL Server Lock Granularities

Historically, all SQL Server locking management has been internal to SQL Server; there was no application level of locking granularity or control. Although there is now such control for lock type (see Chapter 16, "Managing the SQL Server Optimizer"), the granularity for SQL Server locks is still fixed.

The smallest unit of work for any SQL Server operation, including locking, happens at the 2K data-page level. In other words, SQL Server will lock all of the rows on a particular page when that page is read or changed. For efficiency purposes, SQL Server can also use extent locks, but it uses these only to allocate new space for data tables. For queries that affect large percentages of available rows, SQL Server might choose to upgrade a collection of page locks to a table lock. In effect, SQL Server trades in a collection of locks of a smaller granularity for one of larger granularity. Any lock, regardless of granularity, consumes the same quantity of resource overhead. Therefore, a single table lock is more efficient than 5,000 individual page locks, even though this does introduce a concurrency issue.

SQL Server Lock Types

SQL Server relies on a variety of lock types and lock granularities in its work. The three basic lock types are as follows:

- *Shared locks (SLocks)*—Used by processes that are *reading* pages, N shared locks can be on any page; a single shared lock will prevent *any* exclusive locks from being acquired. SLocks are held only for the duration of the read on a particular page.

- *Update Locks (ULocks)*—Used by processes that will update data but have not yet done so, ULocks are read-compatible with SLocks during the pre-modification phase. ULocks are automatically updated to XLocks when the data change occurs.

- *Exclusive Locks (XLocks)*—Used by processes that are currently changing data pages, XLocks prevent both ULocks and SLocks from being acquired. XLocks are held on all affected pages until an explicit transaction has completed, or until the command has completed in an implicit transaction (a transaction that has no explicit `begin tran`/ `commit tran` pair in its statements).

Table 15.1 summarizes the lock types and levels for SQL statements.

Table 15.1 Lock types and levels for SQL Server commands.

Statement	Index Used		Index Not Used	
	Table Level	Page Level	Table Level	Page Level
`select`	shared intent	shared	shared intent	shared
`select… holdlock`	shared intent	shared	shared	
`update`	exclusive intent	update then exclusive	exclusive	
`insert`	exclusive intent	exclusive	exclusive intent	exclusive
`delete`	exclusive intent	update then exclusive	exclusive	

Shared Locks

Shared locks are used by SQL Server for all read operations as well as "desire to update" operations. A read lock is by definition not exclusive, meaning that a theoretically unlimited number of shared locks can be on any page at any given time. In addition, shared locks are unique in that the particular page being locked is locked by a process only for the duration of the read on that page. For example, a query such as `select * from authors` would lock all of the pages in the authors table when the query starts. After the first page is read, the lock on that page is released, but the remaining locks are held. After the second page is read, its lock is released but the others remain. In this fashion, a select query returns a snapshot of data from the table—and that table data cannot be modified during such a read operation.

Shared locks are *compatible*, to use SQL Server terminology, with other shared locks as well as with update locks. In this way, a shared lock does not prevent the acquisition of shared locks and update locks on a given page. Those user connections requesting SLocks or ULocks are not prevented from doing so if an SLock already exists on a page. However, SLocks do prevent the acquisition of exclusive locks.

For all releases of SQL Server prior to Version 6.0, SQL Server mandated the prevention of dirty reads. *Dirty reads* are the capability to change data that is currently being read. The read is considered dirty because the actual data value being returned by the read query could be the value before the change, or it could be the value after the change. The result itself is dependent on the timing of the operations involved. Because this is, by definition, an unpredictable result, SQL Server has always prevented such things from occurring using SLocks to prevent any XLocks from being acquired.

> **NOTE**
>
> SQL Server actually disables the locking manager, and any locking capabilities, for databases that have the READ ONLY option turned on using sp_dboption. If your database is read only, using this option will yield the easiest database maintenance *and* the best performance improvement available.

Update Locks

Update locks are used to mark pages as those that a user connection would like to modify. An update lock is compatible with shared locks, in that both can be acquired on a single data page. Update locks are partially exclusive in that only one update lock can be acquired on any page. In effect, an update lock signifies that a user wants to change a page, keeping out other connections that also want to change that page. As a result, ULocks are useful in avoiding deadlock—a situation discussed in detail later in this chapter. When there are existing SLocks on a page and a user connection acquires an update lock, the ULock waits for all of the shared locks to be released. At that point, SQL Server automatically promotes the ULock to an XLock, allowing the data change to proceed.

If the user connection sending the data-change request has done so through an explicit transaction (by including begin tran/commit tran statements in the submitted batch), the XLock is held for the duration of the transaction—that is, until either a commit tran (endtran) is encountered, a rollback tran is encountered (endtran), or the server is stopped and restarted (in the case of an aborted transaction).

If the user connection sending the data-change request has not defined an explicit transaction, the newly acquired XLock will be released after that particular statement has completed (endcmd).

Exclusive Locks

Exclusive locks are reserved for those operations that are changing data. Exclusive locks are prevented when a data page is being read, and all data reads are prevented during data modifications. In this way, XLocks prevent dirty reads from occurring. The next chapter discusses methods of modifying this default behavior for SQL Server.

Exclusive locks are incompatible with any other lock type. If a page has read locks on it, the exclusive lock request is forced to wait in a queue for the page to become available. If an exclusive lock is on a page, any read requests are similarly queued until the XLock is released.

XLocks are held for the duration of an explicit transaction, or for the duration of a statement in a simple batch.

Transact-SQL Statements and Associated Locks

Different Transact-SQL operations affect locking in different ways, and the combinations of SQL statements can also have an impact.

SELECT queries will always acquire shared locks. As described earlier, those shared locks will be released in sequential order as pages are read. The only exception to this is to use the HOLDLOCK keyword, which is discussed in detail in the next chapter.

INSERT, UPDATE, and DELETE queries always acquire some type of exclusive lock to perform data modifications. If the page to be modified currently has read locks on it, the INS, DEL, or UPD statements first acquire an update lock, which are subsequently upgraded to an XLock after the read processes have finished. If a data page has no current SLocks, SQL Server automatically acquires an XLock for the statement or transaction.

Locking with Cursors

All this seems very simple; one area, however, that directly affects locking and data changes centers on the use of cursors. Because cursors perform row-at-a-time operations on tables, a single row can be associated with many rows on a single page. Hence, attempts to update different rows in different cursors can cause concurrency problems as different user connections fight for the same data page. Understanding how cursors implement locking can prevent application developers from writing queries that improperly use SQL Server's updateable cursors.

For cursors that are declared FOR READ ONLY, SQL Server uses a shared lock on the current page that is being read by the cursor. In other words, a fetch from a cursor result set causes SQL Server to put a shared lock on the page containing the row that was fetched. The shared lock is held for the duration of the fetch operation. All of the other pages that the cursor is browsing are unlocked during the execution of the cursor, with the exception that shared locks are applied to pages individually as rows are fetched.

For cursors that are declared FOR UPDATE, SQL Server uses an update lock on the page containing the current row being fetched. That update lock is held for the duration of the fetch operation. If the data row being fetched is modified, the ULock is upgraded to an XLock and held as an XLock for the duration of the transaction. If the update statement that changed the data page is not part of a multistatement transaction or an explicitly-defined transaction, the XLock reverts to an update lock after the change has completed. The ULock is then released when fetch operations move to another page. If the update statement involved is part of an explicitly defined or multistatement transaction, the XLock is held for the duration of the transaction and then released.

Cursors that are declared FOR UPDATE can use SLocks instead of ULocks if they are declared with the SHARED keyword. Using FOR UPDATE SHARED (see the cursor syntax section in Chapter 6, "Transact-SQL Programming Constructs," for syntax examples) allows SQL Server to use SLocks instead of ULocks for updateable cursors. The implication of this is that, because a cursor is *not* using a shared lock, it is possible for a different operation to acquire an update lock. Remember, only one update lock is allowed for any given page. Using SHARED allows multiple connections running multiple cursors to fetch rows that will be updated simultaneously, enhancing concurrency. The shared locks used when the SHARED keyword is specified are automatically upgraded to XLocks when a cursor row is updated. This process is identical to the upgrade/downgrade process for ULocks and updateable cursors.

This option is particularly useful for multitable cursors. If you are updating only one of the tables, using the SHARED keyword enables you to avoid putting ULocks on all the tables involved in the cursor set because you can modify only one of the tables at any given time.

Lock Escalation for Large Data Sets

SQL Server attempts to conserve locking resources by upgrading page-level locks to table locks when certain thresholds have been reached. Historically, that threshold has been to upgrade page locks to table locks when 200 page locks have been acquired on any given table. At that point, SQL Server releases the individual page locks and allocates a single table lock for the user connection. Chapter 16 shows you how to bypass this escalation by defining your own query-level locking scheme, and Chapter 32, "Measuring SQL Server Performance," shows you how to set server-wide configuration values to configure the various thresholds that SQL Server uses. Both of these chapters address features that are specific to SQL Server 6.0, so 4.2*x*-level users will find many reasons to upgrade their servers in these two chapters!

Index Locking

SQL Server locks indexes differently than tables. As you'll learn in the next two chapters, SQL Server's locking, by default, is internally managed. There are ways to manually override this control, but only for user-defined queries on user tables. Index locking issues are entirely internal, and actually use a substantially different mechanism.

Because SQL Server uses B-tree indexes, all SQL Server indexes have a single root page. As queries use indexes to retrieve rows, that root page receives more than its fair share of attention. As a result, locking this page during index scans and index-based reads creates high levels of contention for the index. Instead of locking all index pages for an index-based read, SQL Server locks and unlocks index pages as they are read through the index tree. In this way, a lock is held on an index page only so long as necessary to scan the key values for that page.

With B-tree indexes, there is always the possibility for page-splitting to accommodate index and table growth. (Refer to Chapter 11, "Designing Indexes for Performance," for more information about B-trees in general and SQL Server's use of them in particular.) When page splits occur, both index pages receive exclusive resource locks, which are held for the duration of the transaction. After the data modification has completed, the exclusive locks are released and the index is rebalanced, if necessary.

Using Transaction Isolation Levels in SQL Server 6.0

SQL Server is directly responsible for managing individual locking tasks. As you will find in the next chapter, there are provisions for manually overriding SQL Server for this. However, there is another aspect to locking and lock management that is directly tied to transactions; SQL Server also provides for the management of *transaction isolation levels*. Transaction isolation levels are categories of locking behavior within transactions that are defined by ANSI. ANSI has described four different classes of transaction isolation level, and each implements a different behavior regarding concurrency versus consistency.

Transaction Isolation Level (TIL) 1, which is descriptively referred to as READ COMMITTED, is the default SQL Server behavior, and it has been so historically through all versions of Microsoft and Sybase SQL Server. With READ COMMITTED as the TIL, read operations can read pages only where transactions have already been committed (that is, no dirty reads).

TIL 0, which is named READ UNCOMMITTED, allows SQL Server to read pages that are currently being modified— in effect, support for dirty reads.

TIL 2 allows a single page to be read many times within the same transaction. The designator REPEATABLE READ means that transactions can read a page as needed, regardless of the number of times necessary.

TIL 3 is designed to prevent a transaction from reading a row that has been changed, and then unchanged. Dirty reads could potentially occur on pages that have been modified. If those transactions have been rolled back, a phantom value would appear in the query's result set. The SERIALIZABLE option prevents this from happening.

All of these options are configured using the SET TRANSACTION ISOLATION LEVEL command. By default, SQL Server uses READ COMMITTED for all behavior. READ UNCOMMITTED is available as an option for allowing dirty reads and setting TIL 1. Levels 2 and 3 are synonymous under SQL Server; setting *either* REPEATABLE READ or SERIALIZABLE with this command will enable *both* of these options. They cannot be set independently because both implement reads on committed transactions.

> **NOTE**
>
> Remember, using the SET command to change how SQL Server processes queries remains valid for the *duration of the user connection*. If a user logs out, and reconnects, the new connection will revert to SQL Server's standard behavior, which is READ COMMITTED.

You can determine the current isolation level of a user connection by using the DBCC USEROPTIONS command (it does not accept any arguments) to determine current configuration option values enabled by SET commands.

Simulating Row-Level Locking

Because SQL Server performs all locking at the page level, the issue of concurrency is complicated when attempting to address row-level access. Certain applications might require row-level access to support highly transactional systems, and workarounds are required to make those systems work in SQL Server. There are two common ways to address the issue of row-level locking. The least efficient is row padding, and the most complex to implement involves optimistic locking.

Row padding is based on a simple concept: If SQL Server locks at the page level, make rows big enough so that only one row fits on a page. Presto! Magnifico! Row-level locking, right? The answer, of course, is a bit more complex. Yes, you will have only one row locked at any given time if that data page is locked. However, the storage requirements to support this are substantial; each row, even though it needs to be only 963 bytes (half of the space available on a page—1,962 bytes/2 = 962 bytes—plus one extra byte), the rows will effectively be 2,048 bytes in size. The reason? Only one row can fit on each page. That makes for a very, very big row. In addition, remember that SQL Server optimizes and costs queries based on the number of pages involved. That number has just increased substantially because the number of pages will match the number of rows. Depending on the application and the business needs at hand, row padding could very well be a viable alternative to page-level locking. However, carefully consider database size, growth, and application needs before implementing this solution!

The other option is colloquially referred to as optimistic locking because locks are not used to manage updates. In order to implement optimistic locking, some table structure prerequisites must be met. First, the table must be capable of supporting direct updates—meaning the operation is logged as a change, not a logical `delete`/`insert` pair. Second, it must have a primary key so that rows can be uniquely identified in a where clause. Finally, the table must have a timestamp column.

Instead of simply updating a row directly, an application must first read the row from the database. The value of the timestamp column must be kept at the client application. Having read the row, the application submits a new query to change the row. However, the `update` statement must include a WHERE clause that compares the timestamp value held in the client application with the timestamp value on disk. If the timestamp values match (the value that was read is *still* the value on disk), then no changes to that row have occurred since it was read. As such, the change attempted by the application will proceed. If the timestamp value in the client application *does not* match the value in the data table, then that particular row has been changed since the read operation occurred. As a result, the row the application is attempting to modify is not the row that currently exists. As a result, the change cannot occur because of the phantom-values problem.

Optimistic locking is achieved by putting a timestamp column on a table. Any applications must then use a READ-then-UPDATE process, driven from the client application, in order to do this. Finally, the `update` statement itself must make use of the TSEQUAL function. TSEQUAL compares two timestamp values to see if they are unique. TSEQUAL is used to compare the timestamp value returned by the read (and held in a buffer on the client application) with the timestamp value in the data table. If they match, the update will proceed. If not, the update will fail because the `where` clause cannot be satisfied.

The following sample illustrates how this works:

1. The client reads a row:

   ```
   select * from data_table where primary_key_field = <value>
   ```

2. The client prepares an `update` statement with new data values for this row.

3. The client submits the following `update` statement:

   ```
   update data_table set data_field_1 = foo where primary_key_field = <value>
   ➥and tsequal (timestamp, 0x13590813570159017)
   ```

In this step, the UPDATE statement is using the same WHERE clause as the `select` statement, identifying the same row using the same primary key value. This is required to make sure you get the same row, and it explains why a primary key is necessary for this to occur. However, in addition to specifying the primary key, the WHERE clause also uses the TSEQUAL function. TSEQUAL takes two distinct timestamp values and compares them for equality. In this case, the UPDATE statement is comparing the timestamp field of `data_table` with an explicit value,

0x13590813570159017. So how does the application get this value? By reading the row before the UPDATE statement and fetching it from the result set.

If TSEQUAL evaluates to TRUE, the row has been found and will be modified because both conditions of the WHERE clause have been met. If the TSEQUAL function is FALSE<, no rows will be affected because none of them would match both WHERE clause conditions.

Although optimistic locking is more efficient in terms of disk resources than row padding, sending multiple query statements back and forth across a busy network simply moves the additional overhead off of the disk subsystem and into the network and processor subsystems. As a result, there is no way to implement row-level locking without incurring additional overhead somewhere in the application. This last point is an important one to remember, because it defines SQL Server's page-level locking as the most efficient for the greatest variety of applications. Row-level locking needs should be carefully examined for deciding on their necessity; the overhead cost might outweigh the benefits, and only the architect of the application and the application's business needs can define those parameters.

Examining Current Lock Activity

SQL Server locking activity can be monitored using three different utilities. The sp_lock stored procedure supplied by SQL Server returns a snapshot-in-time of all currently allocated locks being managed by SQL Server. This stored procedure is useful only for the particular instance that it runs in because locks are allocated and deallocated dynamically by SQL Server.

```
sp_lock
go

spid    locktype             table_id    page    dbname
----    --------             ---------   ------   ----------
1       Sh_intent   123123456    0                master
1       Ex_table    321312312    0                Pubs2
2       Sh_intent   456456456    0                Pubs2
2       Sh_page     456456456    132123           Pubs2
```

Combining this procedure with sp_who will let you find out who is locking whom. If page 0 is locked, for example, that is a table lock.

The locktype column encodes the following information:

- *The type of the lock.* Shared locks are assigned a prefix of Sh_, whereas exclusive locks receive Ex_. Update locks are assigned a type of Update.

- *The unit of work the lock is assigned to.* Units of work can be either table, page, or extent. (Remember, extent locks are used only for space allocations, not normal querying operations.)

- *Whether the lock is intentional.* For example, does this lock want to acquire a shared or exclusive lock on a page?

- *If the locktype value has a suffix of _blk, it is blocking another process.* A user connection cannot access the unit of work held by this lock.

You can also tell if a particular lock is holding a table because the page value will be 0 for all table locks.

Another option for viewing the current quantity of locks allocated by SQL Server is to use Performance Monitor. Using Performance Monitor is discussed in Chapter 30, "Configuring and Tuning the SQL Server," but in this case, PerfMon is capable of keeping track of the total number of locks allocated by SQL Server, as well as locks allocated on a per-unit basis (that is, total number of shared locks, total number of table locks, and even total number of shared table locks). You'll learn to find the specific counters in Chapter 32, so the critical point here is to understand that SQL Server enables you to chart its locking activity for use in debugging particular concurrency problems.

Finally, an alternative to sp_configure lives in the SQL Enterprise Manager application. By clicking on the Current Activity button in the SQL-EM toolbar (its icon is a bar graph), you can view all of the current system logins and their activities. By clicking the Object Locks notebook tab, you can get a prettier version of sp_lock output that is also categorized by database table and login ID. (See Figure 15.1.) Optionally, you can select the Detail Activity tab and see individual login IDs. (See Figure 15.2.) Scrolling to the right reveals the Lock Type and Locked Object fields of the grid; these show which objects a given user connection has locked and the lock type currently allocated.

FIGURE 15.1.

SQL Server Enterprise Manager provides a facility for viewing current locking activity by object within the SQL Server.

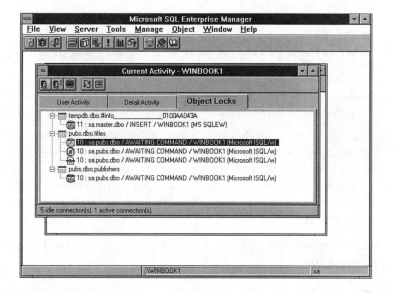

FIGURE 15.2.

Viewing current locking activity by user within the SQL Server (note that for display purposes, we have truncated the column headings to get the information to fit on one screen).

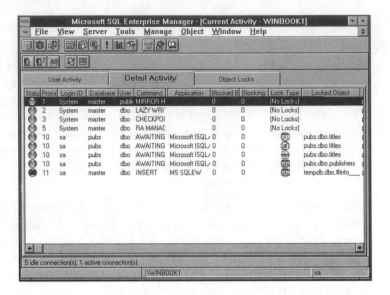

These three options are typically ignored if SQL Server is performing both reliably and quickly. If neither of these is true, they become very useful utilities in debugging concurrent access issues that can hamper SQL Server's performance.

Configuring SQL Server Locking

SQL Server offers a single configuration for locking—the locks parameter. This controls the total number of locks SQL Server can allocate at any given time. A lock of any type consumes a fixed quantity of overhead, so the lock type is unimportant from this perspective.

As a general rule, you should start out configuring SQL Server with a ratio of approximately 20 locks per user connection. If applications running against SQL Server do large numbers of scanning operations or affect large percentages of tables with individual queries, you will want to monitor lock activity closely. Increasing numbers of users, increasing numbers of rows affected by queries, or both, are indicators that the number of locks available to SQL Server might be insufficient.

Using the sp_configure stored procedure to configure the Locks parameter is discussed in Chapter 30.

Deadlock

Deadlock is the interesting circumstance of having two different user connections fighting for the same resources. The situation is similar to what happens at major corporations every morning. One person brings in coffee, the other brings in doughnuts. The person with the doughnuts wants the coffee, but *before* having to give up the doughnuts. The person with the coffee wants the doughnuts, but *before* having to give up the coffee. In effect, you have two people trying to keep what they have and grab what the other has at the same time. Welcome to deadlock.

In the case of SQL Server, deadlock uses the same metaphor, with a slightly more technical implementation. One user connection acquires a lock on a particular page. The next step is to acquire a lock on the next page affected by a transaction. However, a different user connection is already locking that page, and requesting a lock on the page the first user connection has locked. In this situation, neither user connection can continue until the other has finished, and neither can finish until the other has continued.

The traditional Sybase architecture for detecting and resolving this problem was replaced in Microsoft SQL Server 4.2 for Windows NT. It has been enhanced for SQL Server 6.0 to improve both detection and resolution. The details are considered Microsoft proprietary information, but the general process relies on a separate "monitor" that runs internally within SQL Server. This process continually checks for deadlocks, and it automatically aborts one of the conflicting user processes.

The user process that is aborted has its transaction aborted, but not its batch. The user process that has its transaction aborted is sent error number 1205, indicating that the user process "has been chosen as the victim of a deadlock process." Victim is the right word, since the transaction is aborted and rolled back without any intervention from the user.

All SQL Server applications that use transactions should check for error number 1205, or for return code -3. Both of these error values indicate an aborted transaction as the result of deadlock. If it is detected, typically an application should respond by simply resubmitting the transaction. Because the other user connection involved has been allowed to continue, it will probably have released its locks by the time the transaction is resubmitted.

Unfortunately, the nature of multiuser databases ensures that occurrences of deadlock can only be reduced, not eliminated entirely. As a result, *all* applications should check for error 1205, all stored procedures should check for return code -3 when calling other stored procedures, and application developers should write transactions such that deadlock can be minimized.

So How Do I Minimize the Chance for Deadlock?

The steps involved in avoiding deadlock are easy in principle, but they might be more difficult to implement depending on the needs of your application.

The easiest way to avoid deadlock is to put all transaction-based SQL code into stored procedures. The performance advantages of stored procedures becomes most apparent here because stored procedures allow a transaction to be completed in a dramatically shorter time frame than would be possible submitting "naked" SQL statements. As a result, the duration that locks are held within transactions is similarly reduced, which reduces the potential for deadlock.

WARNING

For application developers using client application development environments that use their own database API, you should always allow the development tool to create stored procedures for SQL Server databases wherever possible for this reason. Tools such as PowerBuilder, Visual Basic, Enterprise Developer, and others all implement their own abstraction layer APIs that shield developers from calling database-specific SQL calls directly. As a result, these tools are much more portable, but at a cost. Behind the scenes, each is submitting "dynamic" or "naked" SQL statements to SQL Server. As a result, application-development tools that do not provide a means to access SQL Server-specific features typically encounter problems with highly-transactional systems. If you are using, for example, PowerScript, Visual Basic's Data Access Objects, or the ODBC API directly, you should use existing options that provide access to stored procedures. This is not necessarily a consideration for decision-support systems, but for transaction-based systems on SQL Server, it can make a substantial performance and concurrency difference.

Another method of speeding transactions is to avoid putting queries that return data in a transaction. The data read allocates additional read locks that extend the time window update locks are held, increasing the probability of deadlock. Instead, explicitly defined transactions should be limited to what they were intended for—changing data. If read operations are part of a batch, put them outside the begin tran/commit tran pair. They only add locking overhead and extend lock duration needlessly.

Whether using stored procedures or submitting dynamic SQL, using the minimum locking level needed to complete the transaction is always ideal. Although HOLDLOCK is a useful option for maintaining shared locks and for implementing repeatable reads, excessive use of these features is a common cause of deadlock. If you have queries that are reading data as a "snapshot in time," consider writing these queries to use the NOLOCK option discussed in Chapter 16, "Managing the SQL Server Optimizer."

Finally, the simple matter of referencing tables in the same order (alphabetical by name, by table ID, or some other common sorting order) is a good way to redefine the access method for tables. As a result, if tables are accessed in similar order, the very issue of two connections requesting two different resources is obviated. Locks will be acquired and deallocated in (from user connection to user connection) a relatively sequential order, preventing deadlock by avoiding contention for resources.

Examining Deadlock

Because a user transaction is aborted (remember, it's the transaction, not the batch!), any locking information that could be returned by sp_lock is no longer available. The user connection with the aborted transaction had all of its locks deallocated by SQL Server when the transaction was aborted. However, there is still a way to debug the situation and find out what went wrong.

Using the DBCC TRACEON command, you can specify the 3605 and 1204 trace flags to display deadlock output messages in the SQL Server errorlog file. (Refer to Chapter 26, "Defining, Altering, and Maintaining Databases and Logs," for more information on proper use and maintenance of the errorlog file.) Only the sa login can turn on these trace flags, so debugging deadlock situations will involve testing multiple applications and having a system administrator available to turn on the trace flags and monitor output of deadlock information to the errorlog file.

Having turned on these options, the people responsible for debugging the problem (which typically means you, at 4 a.m.) can run the user processes that generate a deadlock. When the deadlock is generated, SQL Server automatically detects the deadlock and kills one of the user transactions. In the errorlog file, SQL Server contains information similar to what is listed here, highlighting the conflicting processes, the pages they are fighting over, and who was chosen as the victim.

```
95/11/21 23:15:13.39 spid10   *** DEADLOCK DETECTED with spid 11 ***
spid 10 requesting SH_INT (waittype 0x8004), blocked by:
  EX_TAB: spid 11, dbid 5, table 'authors' (0xf43010)
  (blocking at 0x246f9a0)
pcurcmd SELECT(0xc1), pstat 0, input buffer: select * from authors where
au_id = "409-56-7008"
and au_lname = "Bennet"

spid 11 waiting for SH_PAGE (waittype 0x8006), blocked by:
  UP_PAGE: spid 10, dbid 5, page 0x190, table 'titles' (0xb71be83), indid 0
  EX_PAGE: spid 10, dbid 5, page 0x190, table 'titles' (0xb71be83), indid 0
  (blocking at 0x246f9b8)
pcurcmd SELECT(0xc1), pstat 0, input buffer: select * from titles where title_id
 = "BU1032"

VICTIM: spid 10, pstat 0x0000 , cputime 40
```

In this example, User process 11 is marked as being involved with a deadlock. SPID 10 is requesting a shared lock on the authors table but is being blocked by an exclusive table lock from SPID 11. Further down the output, you can see that SPID 11 is waiting for a shared page lock on the titles table but is being blocked by SPID 10. As a result, the VICTIM is SPID 10. Hence, SQL Server will abort SPID 10's current transaction (similar to SPID 10 submitting the ROLLBACK TRAN statement but with SQL Server's "encouragement"), and all the work of that transaction will be undone, as well as the locks for that transaction being deallocated.

Summary

Up to SQL Server 6.0, all locking of all resources was controlled solely by SQL Server. With Version 6.0, some locking can be managed at the query level (discussed in the next chapter), or by using specific configuration options (discussed in Chapter 31, "Optimizing SQL Server Configuration Options"). SQL Server's smallest lock unit of work is the 2KB page, meaning that SQL Server does no row-level locking. Although row-level locking can be simulated, it comes at the cost of potentially substantial overhead.

Most important, remember that deadlock can be only minimized, never eliminated; understanding how to minimize deadlock will be an important skill to make the applications you develop on SQL Server both more reliable and faster. Use stored procedures, use the least-restrictive lock type possible (you'll see how to do this next), and make your transactions run as quickly as possible. A well-designed application on insufficient hardware is almost always faster and more reliable than a poorly designed application on a killer box!

Managing the SQL Server Optimizer

16

Before You Start Shooting Off Toes...

SQL Server uses a cost-based optimizer. As a result, the costs that it works with are computed values— computations developed by people. Because people are sometimes fallible, it stands to reason that the computations these people create also might be fallible. This creates the need for discussion of how to tell SQL Server what to do, but only in those instances where it can't figure out the best way to complete a query on its own.

This last point is the real issue: how often does SQL Server require manual intervention to optimally execute a query? Considering the overwhelming number of query types and circumstances in which those queries are run, SQL Server does a surprisingly effective job of query optimization.

For all but the most grueling, complex query operations, my own testing has shown that SQL Server's optimizer is quite clever and is very, very good at wringing the best performance out of any hardware platform. For that reason, you should treat this chapter as a collection of exception handles— these should be used only where other methods have already failed. SQL Server 6.0 provides you with the heretofore unprecedented ability to shoot yourself in the foot. It even lets you choose whether to pop your toes off one at a time or wipe out both feet with one simple blast.

Before wantonly applying the topics discussed in this chapter, remember one very important point: Used indiscriminately, these features can effectively hide serious fundamental design flaws in your database or application. And in fact, if you are tempted to use these features (with a few more moderate exceptions), it should serve as an indicator that problems might lie elsewhere in your application.

Having determined that no such flaws exist and that SQL Server really is choosing the wrong plan to optimize your query, this chapter can show you how to override the two most important decisions the optimizer makes: choosing the index, if any, to solve the query, and choosing the lock type and level to manage multiuser access to tables.

> **WARNING**
>
> If you haven't already read the previous four chapters, I strongly encourage you to do so now. If you are new to SQL Server, I suggest you go back through them again and make sure you have a solid grasp of the topics they cover. Understanding how SQL Server behaves normally is paramount to making it behave for a particular exception!
>
> SQL Server's optimizer is quite good. SQL Server has a reputation for rather blinding performance, and that reputation is owed in no small measure to the query processor. Remembering this as you peruse these chapters will help you keep a perspective on how selective you should be in applying these concepts.

Throughout this chapter, one point must remain clear in your mind: these options are considered exception cases and are meant to cope with particular problems in particular queries in particular applications. As such, there are no global rules or rules of thumb to speak of, because the application of these features by definition means that normal SQL Server behavior doesn't work.

The practical result of this idea is that you should test every option in *your* environment, with *your* data and *your* queries, and use the techniques discussed in the previous four chapters to optimize your queries. The fastest-performing query wins, so don't be afraid to experiment with different options—but don't think that these statements and features are globally applicable or fit general categories of problems, either! There are, in fact, only three rules: *test*, *test*, and *test*!

SQL Server uses indexes to improve query performance, and it locks to guarantee consistency. We'll look at forcing, or, in Microsoft's terms, *hinting* index selection first, including a common but unofficial method of doing what is now possible. Associated with index selection is the capability to force a particular join order for multitable queries, which is topic number two for this chapter. In the discussion on locking, we'll discuss new Microsoft-specific T-SQL keywords that enable you to define a query-level locking scheme that overrides the one SQL Server might have chosen for you.

Forcing Index Selection

In prior versions of SQL Server, there was an officially undocumented but commonly known method to force index selection on the optimizer. By including the index ID number after the table name in a query, SQL Server would use that index. With SQL Server 6.0, there is now a documented and commonly known method, using index hinting, that allows you to define, at the table level, the index SQL Server should use.

This select statement displays the names of tables and the index names and IDs for those tables. Here is an example of the kind of output you can expect:

```
select "table"=o.name, "index"=i.name, indid
from sysindexes i, sysobjects o
where i.id = o.id
and o.type = "U"    /* user tables only (no system tables */
order by 1, 2, 3

table                      index            indid
------------------------   --------------   -----
pt_sample                  pt_sample           0
pt_tx                      pt_tx               0
pt_sample_CIkey2           CIkey2              1
pt_sample_CIcompany        CIcompany           1
pt_sample_CIidNCk          CIid                1
pt_sample_CIidNCk          NCk                 2
pt_tx_CIamountNCamount     CIamount            1
pt_tx_CIamountNCamount     NCamount            1
pt_tx_NCamount             pt_tx_Ncamount      0
```

```
pt_tx_NCamount        NCamount2         2
pt_tx_CIid            tx_CIid           1
```

After you have the index names and IDs, you can use them to specify the index to be used by the query. Remember, an index of 0 reflects a scan of the base table, an index of 1 is for the clustered index, 2–250 are the nonclustered indexes, and 251–255 are reserved. Remember also that there will be a 0 or a 1 but not both listed here.

We'll use showplan to observe the index the server uses to resolve several queries. In this query, the server has three meaningful options for identifying the correct result rows: a table scan, a clustered index search, or a nonclustered index search.

```
set showplan on
go

select *
from pt_sample_CIidNCk
where id between 1 and 500 and
key2 between 30000 and 40000
go
```

Left to its own devices, the optimizer selects the clustered index:

```
STEP 1
The type of query is SELECT
FROM TABLE
pt_sample_CIidNCk
Nested iteration
Using Clustered Index
```

In order to force selection of a specific index, specify the index name for the index you would like SQL Server to use in parentheses after the name of the table in the from clause. This example forces the use of NCk index (see the preceding list of tables and indexes):

```
select *
from pt_sample_CIidNCk (index = NCk)
where id between 1 and 500
and key2 between 30000 and 40000
go
```

As instructed, the optimizer uses the nonclustered index to find rows matching the query:

```
STEP 1
The type of query is SELECT
FROM TABLE
pt_sample_CIidNCk
Nested iteration
Index : NCk
```

> **NOTE**
>
> In versions prior to SQL Server 6.0, the server enabled you to specify only the index ID, and not the name. The problem with index IDs is that they might change when an index is dropped and re-created. Because you specify the name of the index when you create the index, you are safer specifying an index name.

Using the same method, you can force the optimizer to use the clustered index by selecting an ID of 1:

```
select *
from pt_sample_CIidNCk (index = 1)
where id between 1 and 500
and key2 between 30000 and 40000
go

STEP 1
The type of query is SELECT.
FROM TABLE
pt_sample_CIidNCk
Nested iteration
Using Clustered Index
```

In this example, you've forced the clustered index. Using an index ID of 0, you can even force a table scan:

```
select * from pt_sample_CIidNCk (0)
where id between 1 and 500
and key2 between 30000 and 40000
go

STEP 1
The type of query is SELECT
FROM TABLE
pt_sample_CIidNCk
Nested iteration
Table Scan
```

Let's look at the performance of this query given each of these choices. `set statistics io` can be used to determine the number of logical I/Os to execute the query. (See Table 16.1.) (Physical I/Os are problematic because everything is resident in cache by the time you run the query a second time.)

Table 16.1. Summary of logical I/Os to resolve the query by optimization plan.

Index	Logical I/Os
Clustered: CIid (1)	7
Nonclustered: NCk (2)	632
Table Scan (0)	243

Clearly, the server found the most efficient path in this query!

A Case Study

Let's look at a case study where a user might decide that he can outguess the optimizer.

Table 16.2 shows the table structure for a simple transaction table, pt_tx.

Table 16.2. Partial output from `sp_help pt_tx`.

column	datatype	len
id	int	4
amount	money	8
date	datetime	8

There is a nonunique, nonclustered index on the date column.

Consider this query, which looks for the total amount for all Sunday entries:

```
select sum(amount)
from pt_tx
where datename(dw, date) = "Sunday"
```

The output from showplan shows that SQL Server has chosen a table scan strategy for this query, at a cost of 88 logical reads:

```
STEP 1
The type of query is SELECT
Scalar Aggregate
FROM TABLE
pt_tx
Nested iteration
Table Scan
STEP 2
The type of query is SELECT
```

Here is the data distribution by the day of the week:

```
select datename(dw, date) "day of week", count(*) "num rows"
from pt_tx
group by datepart(dw, date), datename(dw, date)

day of week      num rows
---------------  --------
Sunday           25
Monday           1236
Tuesday          1185
Wednesday        1220
Thursday         1248
Friday           1289
Saturday         1079
```

If you run a covered query (see Chapter 14, "Analyzing Query Plans") against this table using the nonclustered index on date, you will find that a nonclustered index scan will cost 55 logical I/Os.

The question is, *did the optimizer fail to find the best path?* If the server were able to scan the nonclustered index (at a cost of 55 I/Os) and if it were able to convert the date value in the index before deciding whether to read a data page, it would need to read a page from the table itself only 25 times (once for each row where the day of week is Sunday). The total cost of the query would be:

index scan cost	55
data read cost	+25
	----
total cost	80

This is less than the cost of the table scan by 9 percent (80 versus 88).

Based on this reasoning, let's force the use of the nonclustered index and look at the cost:

```
select sum(amount)
from pt_tx (index = date_ix)
where datename(dw, date) = "Sunday"
```

The cost of this query is 7,337 I/Os, or almost 100 times the cost of a simple table scan. SQL Server did not evaluate the value of the function before deciding whether to read a page from the table. Instead, for each value in the nonclustered index, SQL Server retrieved the corresponding page from the table, *and then determined whether the row matched the search condition.*

Moral of the Story

There are not a lot of really cool techniques available to SQL Server but unknown to the optimizer. If you find one, it more than likely will be fixed or added in a subsequent release.

From time to time, SQL Server will choose poorly, particularly when deciding between nonclustered indexes. For this reason, forcing an index should always be treated as a last resort. Instead of forcing an index, you should usually focus your time on why an incorrect index is being picked. A likely culprit is out-of-date statistics or a SARG that is not a SARG.

Forcing Join Order

Forcing join order is another technique to get presumably better performance from SQL Server. You have seen that the order of the joins is as important to performance as index selection. It is tempting to ask, "If I change the join order from the one the server selected, can I pick better?"

> **NOTE**
>
> I have to admit that I haven't been able to outguess the server very effectively, but I've certainly been able to pump up the volume of I/O requests.

You force join order with the forceplan option:

```
set forceplan {on | off}
```

After `forceplan` is on, the optimizer will not evaluate various join orders; instead, the table join order is the order of tables in the from clause. In this query, the optimizer found the most efficient plan by reversing the order of the tables from the order in which they are named:

```
set showplan on
set statistics io on
go

select * from titles, publishers
where titles.pub_id = publishers.pub_id
go

STEP 1
The type of query is SELECT.
FROM TABLE
publishers
Nested iteration
Table Scan
FROM TABLE
titles
Nested iteration
Table Scan
Total writes for this command: 0
Table: titles scan count 3, logical reads: 9, physical reads: 0
Table: publishers scan count 1, logical reads: 1, physical reads: 0
Total writes for this command: 0
```

We can see that the join order is `publishers` outside, `titles` inside. Current versions of the `showplan` option list tables outer to inner.

> **TIP**
>
> You can also verify the order by looking at the statistics io output, scan count. In the preceding example, a scan count of 1 says that the table incurred 1 iteration (the outer table), and the scan count of 3 was the inner table (passed through 3 times). Therefore, `publishers` was the outer table.

Force a join order with the `forceplan` option. (As a matter of tidiness, make sure you set it off when you are done with it.)

```
set forceplan on
go

select * from titles, publishers
where titles.pub_id = publishers.pub_id
go

set forceplan off
go

STEP 1
The type of query is SELECT.
FROM TABLE
titles
```

```
Nested iteration
Table Scan
FROM TABLE
publishers
Nested iteration
Table Scan
Table: titles scan count 1, logical reads: 3, physical reads: 0
Table: publishers scan count 18, logical reads: 18, physical reads: 0
Total writes for this command: 0
```

The `forceplan` option instructs the server to execute the query using the join order listed in the `from` clause, and to skip trying to pick a better join order. In this example, `titles` is being forced to be the outer table in the query, and `publishers` the inner table. You can see that you are more than doubling the amount of required reads to resolve the query. In large joins, performance can degrade by several orders of magnitude.

One of the things I do when I am tuning a database for a client who has a performance problem is to go in and add additional indexes, which allows the server to pick different join orders more effectively (allows a join order to use an index instead of a table scan). It is not unusual to have a change in join order change a query from 30 minutes to 30 seconds. In the case I just described, all I had to do was take a table that was indexed on (a,b) and index it additionally on (b,a).

> **NOTE**
>
> SQL Server 6.0 introduces *reverse index traversal* (discussed earlier), allowing a middle table in a join to use the index in both directions.

Although forcing a join order can be educational, it can cause problems as the data distribution changes. The optimizer notices when index statistics are updated, but you have to remember to go and change all of the code that is forced to a particular plan.

Temporary Tables

When you are joining many tables, join order is not your only problem. You can also run into built-in limitations regarding the number of joins or restrictions about inner/outer tables in outer joins. There are many cases where no optimizer could resolve the query in a single pass (although SQL Server will try).

In these cases, you might want to use a temporary table to build one or many intermediate results, then join those intermediate results together to get a final result. With large, complex queries, queries with many search clauses, and those requiring an intermediate work set that is substantially smaller than the source table(s), consider creating temporary tables. This is by far the most common way to bypass the optimizer.

Query-Level Locking Selection

As a second category of "optimizer hint," SQL Server includes a collection of keywords for defining the particular lock type and lock granularity a query can use for a specific table. Note that this occurs at the query level, and not at the table level. SQL Server 6.0 doesn't enable you to specify a particular lock for all queries of a type on a table. The locking level for those queries must be either chosen by the optimizer (the default behavior) or supplied in the form of an optimizer hint using the keywords discussed later in this chapter.

There are nine distinct optimizer hints. The first is index selection, which has already been covered. The remaining eight are dedicated to locking selection:

- ■ NOLOCK. select statements do not apply read locks on pages, and dirty reads are allowed.

- ■ HOLDLOCK. This is the traditional HOLDLOCK that has been part of SQL Server for many versions. It holds page or table locks until a statement or transaction has completed and does support repeatable reads.

- ■ UPDLOCK. New to SQL Server 6.0, this option uses update locks instead of exclusive locks for data page modification. Refer to the section on update locks in Chapter 15, "Locking and Performance," for more details on update locks.

- ■ PAGLOCK. New to SQL Server 6.0, PAGLOCK forces SQL Server to use individual shared page locks and prevents escalation from page locks to a single shared table lock.

- ■ PAGLOCKX. New to SQL Server 6.0, PAGLOCKX works like PAGLOCK except that it applies an exclusive page lock where an exclusive table lock would normally be used.

- ■ TABLOCK. Forces SQL Server to put a single shared lock on the table, rather than attempt to use individual page locks for the table.

- ■ TABLOCKX. Forces SQL Server to put a single exclusive lock on the table, rather than attempt to use individual page locks for the table.

- ■ FASTFIRSTROW. Because of SQL Server's new Parallel Data Scanning features, SQL Server can execute a table scan-and-sort operation faster than using a nonclustered index, because the combined operation spread over multiple threads results in faster execution over a single thread and a nonclustered index. However, rows cannot be returned to the workstation until the sort has completed, potentially delaying initial delivery of the result set. FASTFIRSTROW tells the optimizer to use the nonclustered index instead of the scan-and-sort operation to speed the response time of the first row. Overall query performance might suffer, but the initial results will be returned more quickly.

With each of these options, issues of consistency and concurrency arise, as they did in the previous chapter. These issues are magnified, however, by the application developer's control of these features replacing SQL Server's control of these features. So, how can you efficiently and effectively make use of these features?

First and foremost, these keywords enable you to overcome performance and locking problems that are created by SQL Server itself. They should be used only to solve a specific, identifiable problem.

For example, many transaction-processing databases must be online 24 × 7 × 365. As a result, the question of how to implement reporting has resulted in some curious inventions. Many shops simply do hourly or half-hourly transaction log dumps to disk. The backups are restored to DSS or reporting-only databases on the same server, or even on a different server. From that reporting server, reports can be run on almost-live data.

The critical issues with doing reporting on live transaction data are many. First, reports must run select statements, which require shared locks. However, updates, inserts, and deletes require exclusive locks. As a result, the read operations for reporting interfere with exclusive lock requests, creating concurrency issues— forcing the use of a separate reporting-only database or server.

The NOLOCK keyword fixes this by allowing reports to view live transaction data without interfering by using shared locks. This removes one of the restrictions to using live data for reporting, but the issues of CPU usage and I/O on the data pages involved remain. It isn't a perfect solution, but it's a step in the right direction.

For large numbers of users, queries can create contention because of SQL Server's effort to minimize locking overhead by escalating a collection of page locks (now configurable, as discussed in the previous chapter). You can eliminate this contention for table locks entirely by specifying all queries to use page-level locking, using PAGLOCK and PAGLOCKX. Although this does create overhead on the server, informal testing has shown that the locking manager's overhead is not a significant factor in query performance. The locks for which the locking manager is responsible make a far larger contribution to query performance for large numbers of users than does the manager itself.

As such, using PAGLOCK and PAGLOCKX can increase the concurrency of your queries by allowing queries to lock only those pages that it needs to reference, rather than locking all table pages for large operations. This is particularly true for PAGLOCKX, which allows other connections to read and write pages that are not affected by its query's operations.

The new FINDFIRSTROW option highlights the need for testing in *your* environment in order to make these new options work properly. With Parallel Data Scanning features enhancing table- and index-scanning operations, it is actually faster to perform a table scan, and then sort the data rows, than it is to use a nonclustered index that has the keys for the order condition. As a result, the data rows are not returned as quickly as they would be if a nonclustered index is used. So, using FINDFIRSTROW enables you to force SQL Server to use the available nonclustered index instead of the scan-and-sort operation, to return rows more quickly to the client. As a result, the query appears to run faster on the client because results start returning sooner, but in fact it takes longer to prepare the entire result set for the client.

> **NOTE**
>
> The idea for returning the first row of a result set immediately to create the impression of fast query performance is not new. In fact, Microsoft's own JET database engine (the core engine of both Microsoft Access and Microsoft Visual Basic) uses this technique to make users think they are getting data back sooner than they are. JET returns rows to the client as they are generated, so that the client gets at least some data right away. The tradeoff is that this increases network performance and client application overhead, because multiple fetches are required to get the entire result set back. As usual, applications have a set of six-of-one-half-dozen-of-the-other compromises that you, the application developer, get to choose from. Testing is the only way to ensure that you are maximizing SQL Server's performance potential.

With all of the hinting keywords, it is possible to specify multiple keywords for the same table, if they are separated by spaces. The most restrictive option is the only one that will be used in that query, so the others become redundant and are ignored by the query processor.

Summary

SQL Server provides many facilities for forcing optimizer behavior. Indiscriminate use of forcing indexes and forcing join orders often causes more harm than good, but it can be a useful tool for overcoming query-optimization problems. Where necessary, use temporary tables to reduce the cost of large joins.

If you are encountering locking problems, such as substantial quantities of blocked processes or highly contentious queries and tables, the locking hints in this chapter provide an effective means of managing locking granularity for queries.

With this chapter, there is a mandatory testing step that must precede any use of these keywords. If you don't know what's really going wrong with a query, using these options will make life much more painful, not less so. However, with thorough testing, these hints can alleviate locking contention and let client applications work more effectively. Testing! Always think TESTING!

Database Design and Performance

17

The purpose of a logical database design is to understand and describe your data.

Logical database designers are very good at drawing diagrams explaining the relationship of the data within an organization and even explaining the diagrams in front of a group. Usually, they can even take the logical design to the next few steps, most notably assigning attributes to their entities (that is, identifying which columns go into which tables).

Many shops swear by this design, and require this logical design to be the physical design, simply because it is easy to understand.

This is not a good approach. A logical design does not have the same purpose as a physical design. *The primary purpose of a physical design is performance.*

Designing databases for performance, however, requires an understanding of the underlying DBMS. You have learned much from the preceding chapters in this book. This chapter explores physical database design techniques for improving SQL Server performance.

Database Design Issues

There are three primary design issues to consider when developing a physical database design:

- Data integrity
- Ease of use
- Performance

When developing a physical database design, you want the design to support your data consistency and *referential integrity* (RI) requirements easily. If a data element is represented exactly once within a database, it is easier to track and maintain than if it is represented multiple times. Referential integrity must also be maintained and, if possible, enforced at the server level.

> **TIP**
>
> One of the more frequently asked questions is whether to handle integrity checking (of all sorts) at the client level or at the server level. The ideal answer is to check in both places. Check at the client level because it is cheaper and faster; check at the server level to guarantee database integrity across all applications uniformly, including those that might not perform integrity checks.

A DBA also should consider ease of comprehension in a physical database design. Tables should be browsable so that end users can easily find the data they need and know what data a table contains.

Finally, the DBA typically wants to make database access and modification fast. Speed of data retrieval and update is usually the yardstick used to measure the success of a physical database design. Often, designing a database for access speed or to improve update performance requires modifying the physical design of the database—for example, duplicating or partitioning frequently used data from infrequently used data.

Unfortunately, it is often impossible to design for all three criteria (data integrity, ease of use, and performance) because they tend to be mutually exclusive. For example, breaking up a table to improve access speed makes it harder to browse and pull data together for the end users. During physical database design, decisions need to be made regarding balancing these objectives.

What Is Logical Design?

Logical database design is the process of defining end users' data needs and grouping elements into logical units (for example, tables in an RDBMS). This design should be independent of the final physical implementation. The actual physical layout of the tables, access paths, and indexes is provided at physical design time. Database design tradeoffs have ramifications in physical design and performance because an RDBMS cannot detect a poorly designed database and compensate accordingly.

Logical design is intended to reduce (eliminate) redundant data and thereby minimize row size. This has the effect of increasing the number of joins required to pull related data elements together. The ultimate goal of logical design is to make it easy for a user to grasp a gestalt of his data and for the DBA to design the physical database.

Normalization Conditions

In order to understand how to change the database in the physical design to suit your performance needs, you first need to understand relational database *normalization*, which is the end result of logical database design. Here's a review of the basic terminology and conditions of normalization:

- An *entity* (table) consists of *attributes* (columns) that define *properties* about each *instance* (row) of the entity.
- Each instance of data refers to a single event.
- There is a way of uniquely identifying each row, which we call a *primary key*. The primary key enables you to decide which row you want to reference.
- The primary key can be a single column or multiple columns (a *compound* or *composite key*).
- Primary keys cannot be null (if there is no way of uniquely identifying a row, it does not belong in a relational database).

Normal Forms

There are up to five levels of normalization, or five *normal forms*, in the logical design process. The idea behind normalization is to provide data and keys to find the data and to ensure that the data exists in only one place. In this book, third normal form is considered a normalized database because it is pretty much the level the industry considers a normalized database.

First Normal Form

In order for a database to be in *first normal form*, all repeating groups have to have been moved into separate tables; one column contains exactly one value.

This example is not in first normal form because it has a repeating group of titles; there are many titles for the single `Publisher` row:

Publisher	Title1	Title2	Title3
Smith Publishing	The Tale of...	Cooking with...	Computer and ...

The following example is in first normal form. There are now several rows for `Publisher`, one for each `Title`:

Publisher	Title
Smith Publishing	The Tale of...
Smith Publishing	Cooking with...
Smith Publishing	Computer and...

Second Normal Form

When *second normal form* is met, nonkey fields must depend on the entire primary key. A database without compound primary keys is automatically in second normal form (if first normal form is met).

This example is not in second normal form because the key is `Publisher` and `Title`, but `Publisher Address` relates only to one part of the key field (`Publisher`) but not to `Title`:

Publisher	Title	Publisher Address
Smith Publishing	The Tale of...	New York, NY
Smith Publishing	Cooking with...	New York, NY
Smith Publishing	Computer and...	New York, NY

To correct the example, break the table into two parts. Publisher-specific information belongs in the `Publisher` table:

Publisher	Publisher Address
Smith Publishing	New York, NY

Title-specific information belongs in the `Title` table:

```
Publisher          Title

Smith Publishing   The Tale of...
Smith Publishing   Cooking with...
Smith Publishing   Computer and...
```

Third Normal Form

Third normal form dictates that nonkey fields must not depend on other nonkey fields.

This example table is not in third normal form because the `Location` column depends on the department, not the employee, even though `Employee` is the key field:

```
Employee           Dept            Location

Smith              10              Bldg C
Jones              10              Bldg C
Thomas             10              Bldg C
Alders             8               Bldg D
```

To bring the table into third normal form, break it into two parts, one for `Employee` that indicates the department:

```
Employee           Dept

Smith              10
Jones              10
Thomas             10
Alders             8
```

and the other for `Dept`, indicating the location:

```
Dept               Location

10                 Bldg C
8                  Bldg D
```

Benefits of Normalization

A normalized database reduces redundancy and, therefore, storage requirements in the database. Data integrity also is easier to maintain in an environment where you have to look in only one place for the data, where each entity is represented only once.

In addition, when the database is normalized, the rows tend to get narrower. This enables more rows per data page within SQL Server, which can speed up table scanning and queries that return more than one row, improving query performance for single tables.

Drawbacks of Normalization

There are some drawbacks to a normalized database design, however, mostly related to performance. Typically, in a normalized database, more joins are required to pull information together from multiple tables (for example, to get employees along with their current location requires a join between the `Employee` table and the `Dept` table).

Joins require additional I/O to process, and are therefore more expensive from a performance standpoint than single-table lookups.

Additionally, a normalized database often incurs additional CPU processing. CPU resources are required to perform join logic and to maintain data and referential integrity. A normalized database contains no summary data, because summary data violates normalization in two ways: it is redundant information and it has no independent business meaning. To calculate summary values requires aggregating multiple rows of data, which incurs both greater CPU processing and more I/O.

Normalization and the Database Design Picture

Normalization provides a good place to start a physical database design because data is logically grouped and consistent. (I once had a student request to put those first seven words in writing and sign my name. Apparently, his shop didn't understand the difference between the purposes of the two designs.) Third normal form should always be applied to all database design, at least initially. Denormalization is something that is done intentionally—and with malice and forethought—for the purpose of performance.

Remember, however, *normalization can cause substantially more I/O than a denormalized database.* Redundancy can reduce physical I/O, which might be judged to be more expensive than storage costs. Redundancy, however, incurs additional cost at update time.

Denormalizing the Database

Denormalizing is the process of taking a normalized logical design and intentionally disobeying the rules for the purpose of increasing performance. To denormalize effectively, you must understand the bias of the data that is to be loaded into the database and how the data will be accessed.

Advantages of Denormalization

Denormalization can help minimize joins and foreign keys and help resolve aggregates. Because these are resolved within the database design, you might be able to reduce the number of indexes and even tables to process them.

Guidelines

Here are some basic guidelines to enable you to determine whether it is time to denormalize your database design:

- Balance the frequency of use of the data items in question, the cost of additional storage to duplicate the data, and the acquisition time of the join.

- Understand how much data is involved in the typical query; this affects the amount of redundancy and additional storage requirements.

- Remember that redundant data is a performance benefit at query time, but is a performance liability at update time because each copy of the data needs to be kept up to date. You typically write triggers to maintain the integrity of the duplicated data.

Basic Denormalization Techniques

Be aware that denormalization is a technique for tuning a database for a specific application, and as such tends to be a last resort when tuning performance. Adding indexes to a table is a tuning method that is transparent to your end users and applications; modifying the database schema is not. If you change the database design, your application code that accesses that database needs to be modified as well.

A variety of denormalization methods can be used to modify the physical database design in an effort to improve performance:

- Adding redundant data by duplicating columns or defining summary data
- Changing your column definitions by combining columns or shortening existing columns
- Redefining your tables by combining tables, duplicating entire tables or portions of a table, and partitioning tables into multiple tables

Redundant Data

Redundant data helps performance by reducing joins, or computations, which in turn reduces I/O and CPU processing, respectively. It tends to be either an exact copy of the data or summary data.

Duplicate data should be of exactly the same name, type, and domain, and have the same integrity checking as the original data. Triggers should be used to maintain integrity between the original and the duplicate data. Note that the more volatile the data, the more often you will incur overhead to maintain the duplicate data. You need to balance frequency of use and the cost of the acquisition join against the frequency of modification and the cost of the extra update.

It is occasionally a good idea to duplicate static data to avoid joins. In Figure 17.1, moving the title to the `salesdetail` table saves you from having to perform a lookup when you need that data for, perhaps, a report on sales by title. Is this a good candidate for duplication? The advantage is that it will improve performance, and the title is a *nonvolatile* data attribute (that is, it won't change much). The disadvantage is it might make the `salesdetail` table a lot larger.

FIGURE 17.1.

Duplicating the title
column from the titles
table in the
salesdetail *table.*

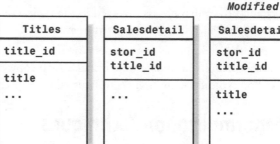

Why is this denormalized? Because there is redundant data and `title` does not depend on the entire key (`stor_id`, `title_id`) of the `salesdetail` table.

Foreign Key Duplication

Another candidate column for duplication is a foreign key to reduce the number of joins required to retrieve related information.

Figure 17.2 shows a normalized version of a database, requiring a three-table join to retrieve the name of the primary author for a title. If you want to be able to know the primary author for a book 80 percent of the time you retrieve the title, how can you reduce the joins? The easiest way is to add the author ID or author name for the primary author to the `titles` table. (See Figure 17.3.) Author name or author ID is a good candidate for duplication because it is unlikely to change very often.

FIGURE 17.2.

*In a normalized version of
this database, a three-table
join is required to retrieve
the name of the primary
author.*

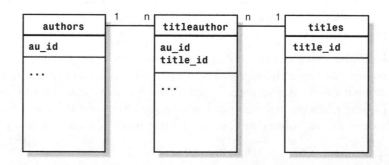

FIGURE 17.3.

Duplicating the primary au_id value in the titles table reduces that to a two-table join for better performance.

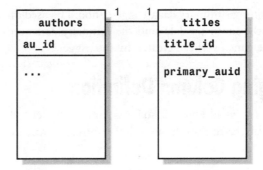

Derived or Summary Columns

Derived columns contain data that is duplicated for the purpose of avoiding repeated calculations. This is called *summary data.*

In any environment, application designers have recognized that certain summary values need to be maintained and available constantly in order to speed their retrieval. If you store frequently accessed sums, averages, and running tallies, reports and queries can run substantially faster, but data modification is slowed somewhat.

Figure 17.4 shows the titles table with a derived column, total_sales, which contains a sum of the qty column from the salesdetail table for the rows related to that title. The total_sales is updated automatically every time a qty is inserted or modified in the salesdetail table. This speeds data retrieval but adds overhead to modifications on salesdetail.

FIGURE 17.4.

Storing a derived value in the titles table, total_sales, which is the sum of qty for the corresponding rows in the salesdetail table.

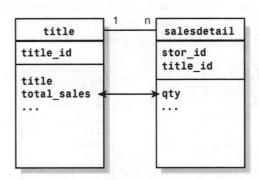

In this example, it is less expensive to maintain a running total_sales column than it is to calculate the total sales every time it is needed. This decision is based on comparing the frequency of the request for the quantity information with the additional cost of the update on salesdetail.

When defining summary data, triggers should be used on the detail tables to maintain the integrity of the summary data, and the summary data needs to be used often enough to justify the update-time overhead created by the triggers.

Changing Column Definition

You've seen that adding redundant columns and derived columns can enhance performance. You can also see an improvement in performance when you shorten critical columns by using two strategies:

- Contrived columns
- Shortening long columns

When the columns get narrower, a narrower index enables more keys to be searched with fewer I/O operations. The corresponding data rows can also wind up being smaller, enabling more rows per data page, which minimizes the number of I/Os required to scan the data.

Contrived Columns

A *contrived* column is typically a substitute for a long key; it has no business use of its own.

In Figure 17.5, is there enough information in the customer table to make rows unique? Is Name unique enough? City? State? Zip? Address? Maybe not. George Foreman presumably lives with each of his five sons, all named George, making six George Foremans (Foremen?) at one residence. How about Social Security Number? Some people haven't got one. Some people lie. Sometimes the Social Security Administration makes a mistake and issues a duplicate number. What do you do? What makes sense for a foreign key in the order table? Unfortunately, not necessarily any of the existing columns do.

FIGURE 17.5.

The customer table has no easily identifiable primary key for the order table to reference. A contrived key can be used as both primary key in customer and foreign key in order.

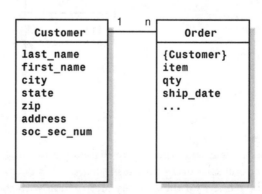

To use a contrived column, add the contrived key to the table and treat it as the primary key for all purposes. Use it as a foreign key in all related tables. This is most helpful in long or multicolumn key situations. You will save storage in the short *and* long run. Using a contrived column will result in a much shorter key than trying to decide how many columns guarantee uniqueness and using all those columns as the foreign keys.

Access performance also improves because index columns are narrower, speeding up individual lookups and joins. In addition, a contrived key is a column that generally doesn't change, so you don't have to worry as much about maintaining the foreign key values. If the customer name is part of the key and is used as a foreign key, any name change has to be cascaded to all foreign key entries as well, increasing the overhead on updates to customer. With a contrived key, you can update customer information without affecting the primary and foreign keys.

Redefining Tables

Creating duplicate tables tends not to be the only solution, and it is frequently not the best solution. It is, however, a viable method of reducing I/O and search speed for specific types of queries.

There are two basic methods of duplicating tables: subsets and partitioning.

Subsets are duplicates of the original data—by row, column, or both. (Note that the replication server can do this across SQL Servers automatically!)

Data Partitioning

Data *partitioning* takes on two basic varieties:

- Vertically, by separating infrequently used columns
- Horizontally, by separating infrequently used rows

Not all data are good candidates for duplication or partitioning.

If the data is fairly stable, it might be useful to consider duplicating or partitioning a table; volatile data is less likely to work well. The more volatile the data, the more you have to double your work. Triggers are necessary for maintaining data consistency and integrity of duplicate data, which incurs additional overhead on data modifications. In addition, if both tables of a partition must be checked to satisfy a query, additional code must be written (either a union or a join) to bring the results together into a single result set.

Duplicate data also means that you will incur an additional storage expense. On the other hand, you might need to scan less data to derive the same results. In addition, your joins will be faster (because the tables are smaller), and you might gain a benefit by archiving some of your historical, infrequently accessed data.

Although the potential benefits of duplication and partitioning might be large, the amount of extra maintenance might be correspondingly large.

Vertical Partitioning

Vertical partitioning is a denormalization technique by which you split a table, by columns, into two or more tables. This technique is typically used to minimize the size of the primary table, or to move infrequently accessed columns to a separate table. Consider the following situation:

> "Our invoicing job will not fit in the overnight batch window. We need to reduce join time between orders and items."

In Figure 17.6, a table with several descriptive columns can be partitioned vertically. The information needed for the active processing is all in the Item_Active table; less-used information is stored in the Item_Inactive table. The Item_Active table is considerably smaller and has a higher row density (rows per page). Given this implementation, order-entry operators can still look at descriptions, take orders, and so forth by performing a simple join between Item_Active and Item_Inactive. Because these are point queries, retrieving one row at a time, the additional cost of the join is negligible. However, the nightly batch process that needs to scan a large number of item numbers and prices at a time speeds up significantly.

FIGURE 17.6.

Vertically partitioning a table creates an active set of data with substantially higher row density.

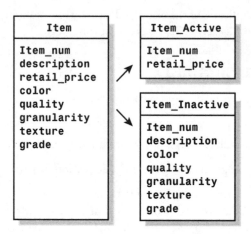

The advantage, if you choose to partition columns, is that the number of locks held on tables might be reduced, and table scans might be faster. However, if excessive joining takes place between vertically partitioned tables, and it adversely impacts performance, you might need to reevaluate your decision.

Horizontal Partitioning

Table scan time grows proportionally with table size. When activity is limited to a subset of the entire table, it makes sense to isolate that subset. This is useful not only for production, but for test tables. Horizontal partitioning is a method of splitting a table at the row level into two or more tables.

The method used to partition the rows horizontally varies depending on how the data is used. The most common method used is by date, partitioning the most current, active data from the historical, inactive data. Other partitioning options include partitioning by activity, department, business unit, geographical location, or a random hash value.

Consider the following situations:

> "98 percent of the time we are using 5 percent of the rows; the rest of the rows are getting in our way."

or

> "The most recent 15 percent of the data is being used 85 percent of the time. Why perform statistics updates on the whole 200,000,000 rows when only a part of the table is volatile?"

Figure 17.7 illustrates an `orders` table partitioned horizontally, with active rows in one table and inactive rows in another.

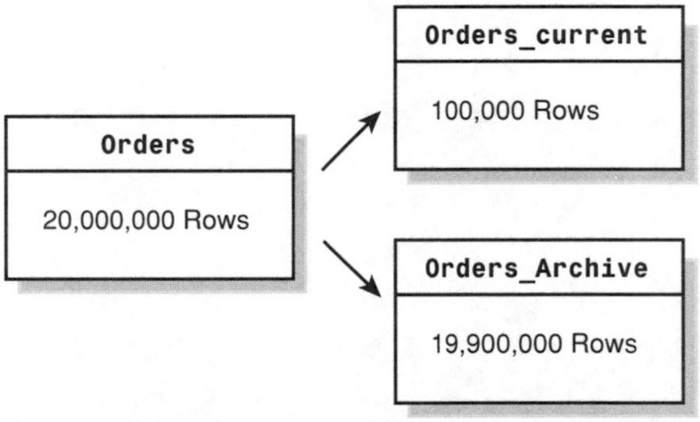

FIGURE 17.7.

You can reduce scan time, index size, and index levels by partitioning a table horizontally.

One of the main drawbacks to consider when horizontally partitioning tables is that retrieving data from more than one table as a single result set requires the use of the `UNION` statement. If you use a random hashing scheme to partition the data, it also is harder for end users to determine where the data resides, making the database less browsable.

Views as a Partitioning Tool

One advantage of vertical partitioning over horizontal partitioning is that the vertical partitioning can be hidden from the end user or application developer through the use of views. If you split a table by columns, a view can be created that joins the two table partitions. Users can then select from the view as if it were a single table.

Views cannot be used to hide horizontal partitioning from end users or applications, because in the current releases of SQL Server, the `UNION` statement is not permitted in views.

Summary

A fully normalized database, although easier to maintain, does not necessarily lend itself to optimal performance. To determine whether the database design needs to be modified to improve query performance, identify the problem queries and look at the base tables on which the queries rely. Identify any potential join problems due to column widths and types or due to the large quantity of rows that need to be accessed. Then consider modifying columns or creating derived, summary, or contrived columns where they might be helpful. Additionally, identify any potential scanning problems in the base tables and consider partitioning tables if there are no alternatives. Due to the impact on end users and application developers, the first choice for query optimization tends to be adding additional indexes, rather than modifying the physical database design.

Database Object Placement and Performance

18

You've seen, in the earlier sections on administration, that there are many databases on a server. You've also seen that a database can reside on many devices. (See Figure 18.1.) And finally, you've seen that a device can contain many databases.

FIGURE 18.1.

A single database can span several logical devices. The `create database` *statement here allocates 100MB on each device for use by the database* `perftune`*.*

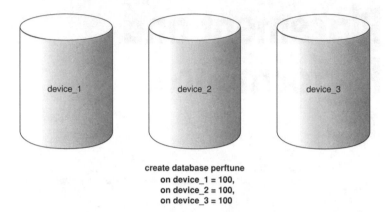

```
create database perftune
   on device_1 = 100,
   on device_2 = 100,
   on device_3 = 100
```

Here, then, is the 64-dollar question: When you create and/or load a table, where does it go? This chapter discusses the location of physical data, how to manage its location, and the performance ramifications of choosing from different database and object-storage and object-placement options.

The historical choice is implemented by SQL Server, and it focuses on using named segments to manually place objects onto particular disk devices and database fragments. SQL Server provided this feature because it was the best way to maximize the use of multiple fixed disks and disk controllers on a hardware platform that was incapable of presenting those hard disks as a single, logical volume.

The recommended option for SQL Server 6.0 is to use some variation of *RAID*, or *Redundant Array of Inexpensive Disks*. In this chapter you take a look at the implementation of segments and how to use them, and examine their implementational issues. After doing so, you learn a way to not only avoid the substantial administrative overhead associated with using named segments, but to actually get better performance in the bargain using RAID technology. For those of you who always read the last 10 pages of a mystery novel before ever looking at Chapter 1, you might want to skip to the last section of this chapter for the discussion on RAID.

In Figure 18.1 you see a database that is being associated with three devices, perhaps with the following statement:

```
create database perftune on device_1 = 100, on device_2 = 100, on device_3 = 100
```

Now you create a table:

```
create table perf_table (a int, b varchar(255) null)
```

Where will the table reside? Let's break this into two questions:

1. Where will the table structure reside?
2. Where will the table data reside?

The official answer is that it will be completely random. (In practice, you'll see that it is slightly less than random.) Based on the structures already created, you cannot control on which devices your data will reside. (See Figure 18.2.)

FIGURE 18.2.

When you don't use segments, allocation of space to a table among several devices is unpredictable.

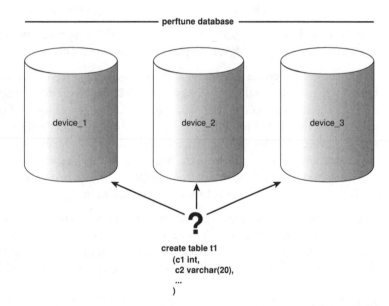

The key phrase is "Based on the structures already created." That's because you *can* control the device where your objects reside—by creating named segments.

A *segment* is a pointer to a device. Remember that definition, because it is quite different from a *fragment*, which is a section of a database on a particular device. Segments and fragments are interrelated in that a segment points to a fragment, meaning it points to a specific device. When creating a segment, you define the name of the segment (how you will refer to it when using it for object creation) and the device to which the segment points. A single segment can point to only one device at any one time. Segments can be moved or *extended*; segment foo, for example, can start out pointing to device DATA_DEV_1 and then be extended to point to DATA_DEV_2.

The create table statement causes a number of changes to a database, including the creation of the table itself. The pointer to the table will go into the sysobjects system table. Another pointer to the table will go in the sysindexes system table. One row per column in the table will go into the syscolumns system table. Note that the common denominator here is "system table." All system tables, with the exception of syslogs, reside on the system segment, which is defined by SQL Server when the database is created. The system segment, when initialized, points to the first device listed in the create database statement. System tables in the master database—whether server-level or database-level—also reside on the system segment in the master database.

The object itself (your table) is created on the segment named default. The default segment is a segment created by SQL Server when the database is created. By default, all objects are created on the default segment. Neat nomenclature, eh? The default segment also points to the first device in use by the database, similar to the system segment.

The third SQL Server–generated segment is called logsegment, and it holds only one table—syslogs. The syslogs table can be placed and managed only on the log segment.

If you (unwisely) create a database without specifying a separate log device, all three sets of tables (system tables on the system segment, user tables on the default segment, and the syslogs table on the logsegment segment) will compete for the same blocks of space. They will do so in a rather interesting fashion. All of the system tables are initialized first, and therefore grow on the first device. Tables that are created on the default segment start out on the first available device and continue to grow from the beginning of the database space allocation. The syslogs table, however, is actually allocated from the back of the space allocation. In other words, syslogs starts from the end and moves forward to the beginning.

In Figure 18.3, you can see that the tables you create will start at the beginning of the database's space allocation and continue to grow toward the end of the space allocation. The syslogs table, however, will be allocated from back to front. As a result, if a transaction log is not on its own device, they will both compete for the same space and eventually will collide.

FIGURE 18.3.

Unless the log is on its own device, it can grow large enough to fill the entire database.

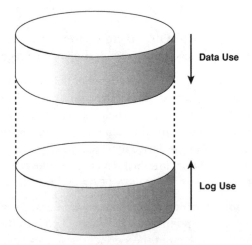

Data Use

Log Use

When the `logsegment` and `default` segments have met, you run out of database space. In this manner, log growth and size cannot be controlled because the transaction log is competing with other database objects for the *entire database space allocation*. So how do you control log table growth? By putting the transaction log on its own device.

When you execute the `create database` statement, you have the option of putting the transaction log on its own device. Doing so is highly recommended because the log will then use only the space allocated to it on that device. It will not be able to use any of the other devices allocated for the database.

Why Segments?

Why do you want to define and use segments? The first reason is performance. The most typical bottleneck in all of data processing is the limitation of speed imposed by the disk drives and their corresponding controllers. If you split your I/O across disk drives, you should be able to increase your performance by increasing the bandwidth of the bottleneck. This includes throughput for queries, as well as the capability to spread reads across devices and for update-intensive objects. Some objects—specifically logs and indexes—are hit so heavily that you might want to put them on their own devices.

The second reason you might want to use segments is control. An object can not grow beyond its segment. As a result, you can limit the growth of potentially explosive tables by placing them on a segment that includes only that space you wish to allocate to the table. Typical uses are the database log (the `syslogs` table, which resides on the `logsegment` segment, and which typically goes on its own device), and volatile tables such as live data feeds. Examples of these include stock-ticker information and physical monitoring equipment, such as shop-floor and pollution-control equipment. You want data accumulated, but if you suddenly get a huge number of data points into the database on orders of magnitude higher than typical and/or expected, you might consider losing some data points in exchange for the entire database not filling up unexpectedly.

> **WARNING**
>
> Segments are not for everybody. At a guess, about one in 10 shops I've seen actually uses segments. About one in three of those shops actually needs it. This is bad, because there is additional administrative overhead required for maintaining segments, which is discussed shortly.

> **TIP**
>
> Before going to the extra trouble of using segments, first identify positively that there is an I/O bottleneck. You might be able to do this with operating-system tools that your operating-system administrator can provide to you (and help you run). If you have not identified I/O (or cannot) to a specific table as a bottleneck, I strongly advise you look elsewhere for your performance gain.

Segment Definition

Now that you know not to do it without cause, here's how to do it. You begin with a `create database` statement like this example:

```
create database perfdb on vdev1 = 100, vdev2 = 100, vdev3 = 100
```

To create named segments, you first must use the database. Segments are *database-specific*: they have meaning only in the database in which they were created.

```
use perfdb
go

exec sp_addsegment seg1, virtual_device_1
exec sp_addsegment seg2, virtual_device_2
exec sp_addsegment seg3, virtual_device_2
exec sp_extendsegment seg3, virtual_device_3
go
```

Figure 18.4 displays the database and segment allocation at this point. (There will also be segments defined for `default`, `system`, and `logsegment`.)

FIGURE 18.4.

perfdb segment definitions after segments are defined. Notice how a single device can be designated as a part of several segments.

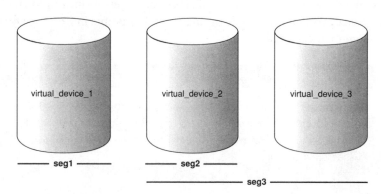

As you can see by looking at the code and the figures, seg1 refers to all of the space allocated to `perfdb` on `virtual_device_1`, seg2 refers to all of the space allocated to `perfdb` on `virtual_device_2`, and seg3 refers to all of the space allocated to both `virtual_device_2` *and*

virtual_device_3. Let's dispel some common misconceptions. First, the total space allocated to the database is 300MB. The total space allocated to seg1 is 100MB; to seg2, 100MB; and to seg3, 200MB. Note that you cannot add up the space allocated to the segments and get the database size. This causes some confusion when users receive an error message from the server along the lines of Unable to allocate space for object *object_name* on segment *segment_name*. If you were not using segments, this means that you ran out of space in the database or that syslogs has filled up. For named segments, it does not mean that the database is full; it simply means that there are no free extents on the virtual device(s) assigned to the segment. The object can not grow.

Let's go back to the original questions: If you place an object on seg1, where does it go? virtual_device_1. On seg2? virtual_device_3. On seg3? virtual_device_2 or virtual_device_3. In the seg3 case, it is still unclear whether the object will be allocated an extent on virtual_device_2 or virtual_device_3, but you know for certain that it will not be on virtual_device_1.

Next problem: what if there is more space available on vdev1? For example, assume virtual_device_1 is all the space on a two-gigabyte SCSI device. You are using only a small portion of the disk. You are also using only a small portion of the virtual disk you have defined on it. If you exceed the 100MB, will the object try to grab more space on the device? Again, the answer is no. The segment and space on the segment are limited to space allocated to the database by create database or alter database statements. (More on alter database shortly.) What if space on virtual_device_1 is allocated to another database? Again, still no difference. The many-to-many relationship of devices to databases does not affect segments, because segments are database-specific.

Placing Objects on Segments

You have at this point provided a mechanism to isolate individual devices defined for databases. Now you need to assign objects to these areas. The common way to place an object on a segment is to specify the segment in the table's creation statement. By using the on *<segment_name>* keyword, you can specify a distinct segment to initialize the table. The sp_placeobject stored procedure enables you to move an existing table from one segment onto another segment. The third option uses a unique feature of clustered indexes. By creating a clustered index for a table on a different segment, SQL Server puts both the index and the table data on the new segment.

```
create table volatile_table (a int, b varchar(255) null) on seg1
create index index1 on volatile_table (a) on seg2
create table spread_table table on seg3
```

Note a few things in this sample code. First, volatile_table will reside on seg1. This isolates the table from the other physical disks and might improve performance of tables on these devices if volatile_table was being requested heavily. Next, index1 is a nonclustered index. Clustered indexes are treated as being part of the same structure as the underlying table, so if you place a clustered index on a segment, it affects the underlying data as well. The `spread_table` table might acquire space on either `virtual_device_2` or `virtual_device_3`. Finally, both `index1` and `spread_table` table will compete for space on `virtual_device_2`. (See Figure 18.5.)

FIGURE 18.5.

Objects are assigned to segments and acquire space according to the definition of those segments.

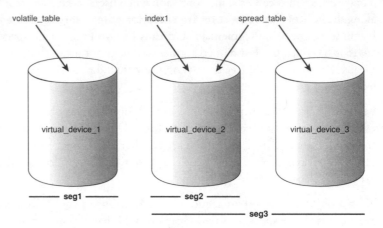

For performance reasons, you will often want to disseminate resources across devices.

When you place an object on a segment that spans devices, you are not guaranteed that the object will span those devices. When the server wants to allocate space, it looks in the `sysusages` table for the first available device fragment that has an available extent. The practical implications are that for the `spread_table` table, space will be allocated on `virtual_device_2` until there is no more space available before it allocates space on `virtual_device_3`. This might not be the most efficient for query performance, but it will be the most efficient for space allocation.

The upshot of this is that if you load a table and want it spread evenly across the devices at load time, you will have to spread it across the devices specifically.

How to Split a Table Across Devices to Increase Throughput

When you want to spread out the contents of a table between many devices, you need to define a segment for each device. Later on, to spread ongoing growth fairly evenly among all those devices, you need to define a segment consisting of all relevant devices. (See Figure 18.6.)

FIGURE 18.6.

Spreading out the contents of a table between many devices.

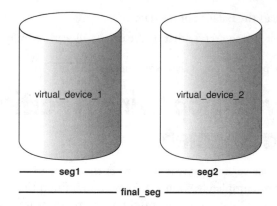

To accomplish this, you need to use `sp_placeobject` as described in Chapter 26, "Defining, Altering, and Maintaining Databases and Logs." In a nutshell, `sp_placeobject` controls FUTURE allocation of space for an object. To do this, follow these steps:

1. Create segments as appropriate on your database. The setup in Figure 18.6 could have been created as follows:

```
use perfdb
go

exec sp_addsegment seg1, virtual_device_1
exec sp_addsegment seg2, virtual_device_2
exec sp_addsegment final_seg, virtual_device_1
exec sp_extendsegment final_seg, virtual_device_2
```

2. Create your table and clustered index on the segment where you want to load the first portion of the data, as shown here:

```
create table spread_table (a int, b varchar(255)) on seg1
create clustered index index1 on spread_table (a) on seg1
```

WARNING

If you create your clustered index after placing the table onto a new segment, you will move all of your data to the new segment!

3. Use BCP (or another load facility) to load in half of the data.

4. Instruct the server to allocate all new pages from the other segment:

```
sp_placeobject seg2, spread_table
```

5. Load the balance of the data.

6. Instruct the server that future extent allocations may come from either device:

```
sp_placeobject final_seg, spread_table
```

How to Stop Using a Particular Device for a Segment

You can use `sp_dropsegment` to instruct the server to stop using a particular device for a segment or to completely remove a segment definition (if there is not already an object for that device). For instance, you might want to instruct the server that you do not want `virtual_device_1` to be used for default or system segments any longer.

```
exec sp_addsegment index_segment, virtual_device_1
exec sp_dropsegment "default", virtual_device_1
exec sp_dropsegment "system", virtual_device_1
```

Introduction to RAID Technology

RAID, or Redundant Arrays of Inexpensive Disks, is a relatively new technology, having debuted near the end of the 1980s. The concepts behind RAID are not new; RAID simply provides a structured framework in which to discuss those concepts. The most basic concept is simple: instead of using a single, fixed disk to store data, use multiple disks simultaneously and in parallel. When you do this, I/O operations are much faster because the read and write operations happen in parallel across multiple read-write heads on multiple fixed disks, rather than across a single read-write head on a single disk. Simple parallelization of I/O in this way has demonstrated immediate, and drastic, performance improvements. SQL Server has traditionally used segments to achieve this, by breaking up a table across multiple disks.

There are currently six common RAID levels defined:

- RAID Level 0
- RAID Level 1
- RAID Level 2
- RAID Level 3
- RAID Level 4
- RAID Level 5

RAID Level 0

A RAID Level 0 device provides data striping across multiple disks without providing any mechanism for data redundancy. (See Figure 18.7.) The data is divided into the appropriate number of chunks and striped across all disks in the array. All data reads and writes are handled asynchronously.

The advantages of RAID 0 is the high I/O rate due to small block size and the capability to read from and write to multiple disks at once. The transfer time for a data request to a RAID 0 device is proportional to the number of devices participating in the array.

FIGURE 18.7.

RAID Level 0 diagram.

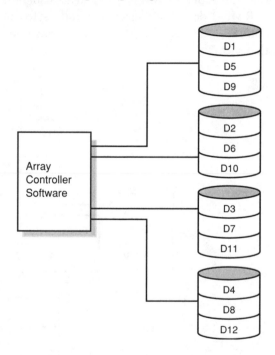

RAID Level 1

RAID Level 1 is your traditional, hardware-level disk mirroring. (See Figure 18.8.) Each disk in the array has one or more exact copies of the disk. There is no data striping. RAID 1 devices provide the highest level of reliability of all the RAID devices while providing a high I/O rate due to small block sizes. RAID 1 devices support small reads and writes with performance nearly equivalent to that of a single disk, especially if the array performs mirrored writes concurrently. Data access time can also be improved if the controller software allows simultaneous read requests to be spread over both disks.

RAID 1 devices often provide a faster and more efficient mirroring mechanism than SQL Server software-level mirroring.

One disadvantage to RAID 1 is that there is no built-in mechanism for data striping—it is up to the database designer/DBA to spread tables and indexes across devices to evenly spread the I/O. RAID Level 1 also requires the greatest number of disks of any the RAID technologies (each disk requires an equivalently sized duplicate to provide data redundancy).

As far as performance, large writes to a RAID 1 device will generally execute at a speed slower than a single spindle due to the overhead of maintaining a duplicate copy of the data. RAID 1 offers no performance improvement over a single disk when writing data and will definitely be slower if a separate controller is not used for the mirror drive. Read performance, however, will be the same or better than reads from a single spindle. This is because requested data can be read from either side of the mirrored pair and does not normally need to read from both disks. With some RAID 1 devices, intelligent controller software can improve read performance by reading from the device closest to the requested data or by splitting concurrent read requests across both devices.

FIGURE 18.8.

RAID Level 1 diagram.

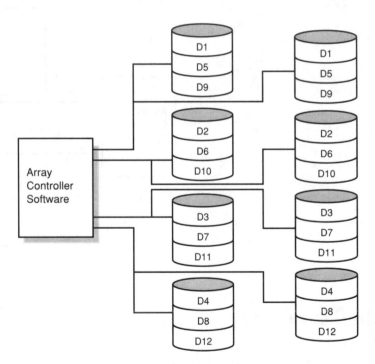

RAID Level 2

A RAID Level 2 device is a parallel-access array. All disks are accessed and written concurrently for every access to a RAID device. RAID 2 uses a bit-level interleaving scheme to spread a data chunk across all data disks in the array. (See Figure 18.9.) Data redundancy is implemented by spreading the corresponding check bits across check disks.

The advantages of using a RAID 2 array are that the array handles error detection and correction rather than individual disks, and the cost of redundancy in terms of drives is less. Redundancy is maintained using check bits of the data rather than an exact copy. The disadvantage of RAID 2 is that failure of one disk shuts down the entire array.

FIGURE 18.9.
RAID Level 2 diagram.

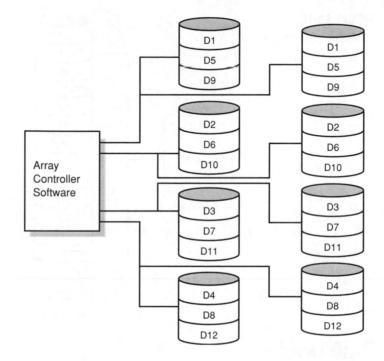

RAID Level 3

RAID 3 also implements a parallel access array. It differs from RAID 2 in that data blocks are spread across devices. A single disk contains parity information (XOR) in order to rebuild a failed device in the array. (See Figure 18.10.)

The advantages of using RAID 3 are that the synchronized parallel access supports fast large data transfers, and there is a lower cost of maintaining redundancy in terms of the number of devices required compared to RAID 1. RAID 3 also allows hot swapping of a failed data drive (that is, the array does not have to be shut down in order to replace a failed device). The failed device can be swapped out on the fly and the contents will be re-created on the replacement from the contents of the parity disk.

The primary disadvantages of using a RAID 3 device are that the single parity disk is a bottle-neck for the entire array, and failure of parity disk disables the entire array. Also, because of the parallel access architecture, RAID 3 is not efficient for small block reads.

FIGURE 18.10.
Raid Level 3 diagram.

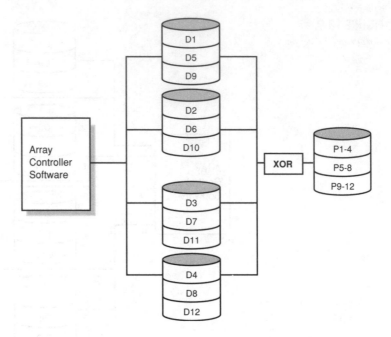

RAID Level 4

A RAID Level 4 device is an independent array. Unlike the parallel-access arrays, a single I/O request does not require concurrent access to all disks in array. Data blocks in a RAID 4 device are striped across all data devices in the array. A single disk contains the parity information (XOR) necessary to rebuild a failed device. (See Figure 18.11.)

The primary advantage of RAID 4 over RAID 2 and 3 is that because it is an independent array, it can process multiple data requests simultaneously. The disadvantage of RAID 4 is that write performance is compromised by the overhead of maintaining the disk parity.

To maintain the parity information, the controller software must read parity information to internal buffers, compute the new parity information, and then write the updated parity information as well the data to the appropriate devices. This is commonly referred to as the *read/modify/write sequence.* In addition, the single parity disk creates an I/O bottleneck in the array as well as creates a single point of failure.

FIGURE 18.11.
RAID Level 4 diagram.

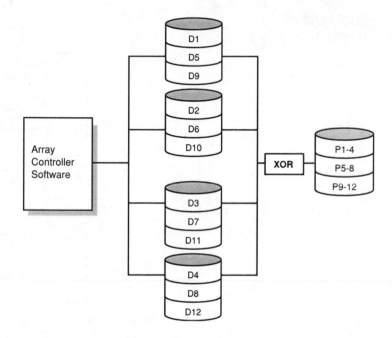

RAID Level 5

RAID 5 is similar to RAID Level 4 except that it doesn't maintain a single parity disk. Instead, parity information for the data contained on one disk is spread across the other disks in the array. (See Figure 18.12.)

The additional advantage to this approach is that it eliminates the bottleneck and single-point-of-failure problems of having a single parity disk. The disadvantage of RAID 5 is the slower write performance due to the read/modify/write sequence.

FIGURE 18.12.

RAID Level 5 diagram.

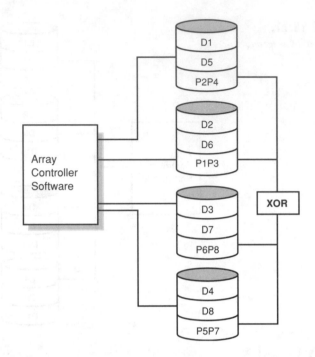

SQL Server and Storage Device Performance

SQL Server typically performs small block reads and writes, reading data in 2KB chunks at a time. This often leads to the expected performance gain often not realized when using storage devices that use larger block sizes to achieve performance gains or caching controllers that buffer large block reads.

> **NOTE**
>
> You might be able to take better advantage of the performance of devices that perform large block reads if you configure the read-ahead capabilities of SQL Server as described in Chapter 30, "Configuring and Tuning SQL Server."

DSS and Data Warehouse type applications may benefit from large block devices if they are performing large sequential reads of adjacent data pages. OLTP applications generally perform operations on small blocks of data randomly spread across devices; therefore, they benefit more from devices that perform small block I/O efficiently.

Which RAID Device to Use?

There are three tradeoffs involved in choosing a RAID device:

- Cost
- Performance
- Reliability

All three factors tend to be mutually exclusive:

- High performance equals higher cost and lower reliability.
- High reliability equals higher cost and lower performance.

If you're looking into a RAID solution, you need to choose the subsystem that best maps to the desired goal of performance, reliability, and cost, making the tradeoffs where necessary.

DSS and Data Warehouse implementations require good read performance and high availability. In an OLTP environment, the goal is both high device reliability and maximum write performance. A `tempdb` device requires high read and write performance, but high reliability is typically not required.

> **NOTE**
>
> With the capability to set up Stripe Sets in Windows NT (see the following section) to support RAID levels 0, 1, and 5, the cost issue of RAID is somewhat mitigated. However, you still need to weigh performance against reliability to determine which RAID implementation to use for different SQL Server environments.

RAID Levels Commonly Used with SQL Server

The three RAID levels most commonly implemented in a SQL Server environment are Levels 0, 1, and 5. RAID Level 0 typically provides the best read/write performance of the RAID devices for the lowest cost, but with the tradeoff of the lowest reliability. A RAID 0 device might be a good device to use for a large `tempdb` to help minimize `tempdb` I/O contention.

RAID Level 1 provides the highest reliability of RAID devices and high performance for small block I/O operations. Typically, RAID 1 provides the best tradeoff between reliability and performance and is a good candidate for log devices and critical OLTP databases.

RAID 5 provides high reliability and excellent performance for reads, but lower performance for writes. It also requires fewer devices than RAID 1 to maintain redundancy. RAID 5 is typically a good candidate for DSS and Data Warehouse databases where OLTP activity is at a minimum and most of the activity is read-oriented.

SQL Server and RAID—Additional Notes

When setting up the log and data devices for a SQL Server database, you want to try to get the log and data on separate I/O devices, and preferably on completely separate I/O channels so there is no contention between log writes and data reads and writes. This will give you the best I/O performance for your database. Because of the striping nature of RAID 0 and RAID 5 devices, if you mix SQL Server data and log on these devices, both log and data will be striped across same set of disks. Although striping reduces the chances of a log write going to the same disk at the same time as a data read or write, there is no guarantee that log and data I/O will always be going to separate physical disks. To eliminate any I/O contention between data and log and get the best performance when using RAID, it is recommended that you use separate RAID devices each for data and log.

For a transaction log, you might also want to consider using a mix of RAID 0 and 1, essentially a striped set of mirrored disks. This gives you the best of both worlds—the highest level of reliability (RAID 1) with the highest write performance for concurrent writes (RAID 0).

RAID devices provide flexible alternatives for storage devices requiring large volumes, high performance, or high reliability. Choosing the appropriate RAID device requires balancing cost versus performance versus reliability in order to find the proper fit.

Hardware-Based RAID Subsystems

With Microsoft SQL Server, there are two sets of options for using RAID technology: you can use Windows NT to create stripe sets, or you can use a hardware-based RAID disk subsystem.

Hardware-based RAID, although more expensive than using Windows NT, can also be more reliable. For mission-critical, transaction-processing applications, you should be using hardware-based RAID. With H/W based RAID systems, everything should be duplicated and hot-swappable. Disk drives should be hot-swappable, and most manufacturers of high-quality RAID subsystems have additional disks already plugged into the cabinet, waiting to be turned on in the event of a disk failure. The disks themselves should be hot-swappable, meaning the physical disk can be removed and replaced without turning off the server or disk subsystem.

Power supplies should also be hot-swappable, and a redundant power supply should already be in the cabinet. Should either of the power supplies fail, the remaining power supply should immediately take over, preventing service interruptions. Most hardware-based RAID systems also use dual controllers—one for managing the disk interface to the computer, the other for managing the striping of data. If possible, both of these controller types should also be duplicated, to prevent controller failure from becoming a single point of failure. Swappable controllers are obviously a more complicated effort, so understand that massive controller failure is still going to keep you up late trying to repair it.

As with all RAID implementations, remember that approximately 25 to 30 percent of the rated disk capacity will be consumed by the parity bit information that is part of RAID 5. You need to remember this when you are capacity planning for databases. Putting a 5GB database on a 5GB RAID array will lead to disappointing results; for 5GB, count on a 7GB or 8GB array being necessary!

Windows NT Stripe Sets

For ultimate disk-level, fault-tolerant protection, hardware-based RAID is the preferred choice. There are situations, however, when cost and fault-tolerant expectations need to be lowered, and can be. In these cases, Windows NT can supply both performance improvements and data-integrity enhancements through the use of Windows NT Stripe Sets. Stripe sets allow the operating system to collect space from various drives, and treat them as a RAID array. Windows NT does support RAID 5, and it will write parity bits according to that specification. The advantage here is one of dollar cost. Using existing hard disks in an existing server, I can create a stripe set that provides a majority of the performance offered by hardware RAID, with some of the fault tolerance as well. Windows NT will write parity bits, but drives and power supplies are not necessarily hot-swappable.

Stripe sets, including step-by-step instructions for their creation and management with the Windows NT disk administrator, are discussed in the Sams title *Windows NT Server Survival Guide*, and are also included in the Administering Windows NT multimedia education course available from Microsoft.

RAID versus Segments

Segments provide functionality outside of parallel I/O and fault tolerance. The ability to control growth of objects by limiting that growth to a particular device isn't something Windows NT or a hardware-based RAID system can control. If your database requires this feature, segments are your only option.

If, however, you are using segments purely as a performance enhancement, then you will be pleased and surprised to learn that not only is RAID faster, it's more reliable *and* cheaper to administer. A RAID volume presents itself as a single logical disk—drive E:, or drive F:, or whatever you care to label it. By creating a disk device and database on that drive, you have immediately paralleled I/O and fault tolerance.

> **NOTE**
>
> During the development of SQL Server 4.2 for Windows NT, the Program Manager for performance and tuning issues on the SQL Server development team at Microsoft tested the use of segments versus using Windows NT-based RAID. Despite days of configuration, his best manually configured scenario using named segments was still 10 percent *slower* than using Windows NT stripe sets. Not only do stripe sets eliminate the overhead of administrators manually configuring segments, but you also get a faster database.

Summary

SQL Server can use a variety of underlying disk-related technology for improving database performance and reliability. SQL Server for Windows NT has kept features introduced in SQL Server 4.2 (named segments), primarily for the purpose of backward compatibility. Advanced in hardware technology have largely rendered these features obsolete.

For small departmental applications, implementing stripe sets with three or four physical disks is a viable option for providing both guaranteed fault tolerance and a performance enhancement. Both of these advantages come without the administrative overhead associated with named segments. Even on smaller servers, buying extra hard disks and using stripe sets is cheaper than having an administrator manage segments manually.

For truly mission-critical, high-transaction-volume applications, hardware-based RAID is the best choice for both performance and data fault tolerance. The fault tolerance, hot-swappability of components, and extra performance that hardware-based RAID provides cannot be matched by Windows NT's built-in features, but bring your checkbook. The prices are high, but the cost of losing your data through failure or downtime may be even higher.

Application Design for Performance

19

Sometimes it seems as though there are a thousand ways to make your application run slowly. This chapter reviews some elements of system design and implementation that affect performance and then focuses on application-design characteristics that also have an impact on system performance.

At the most general level, system performance is determined by several components:

- Server resources, including fast CPU, sufficient memory, and fast disks
- Network configuration, including sufficient bandwidth for the traffic
- Client configuration, including fast CPU and sufficient memory

More specifically, a bad database or application design can render a good hardware configuration useless. For example, a database design requiring repeated scans of a very large table can bring a powerful server to its knees.

> **NOTE**
>
> There is a pessimistic theory of systems stating that all systems will ultimately fail. Systems that fail to gain acceptance obviously fail, but those that gain acceptance always grow in usage and demand until they can no longer handle the load and fail.
>
> No matter how powerful your hardware and software configuration, then, it makes sense to build a system optimally to delay the time when your configuration is no longer able to handle the demands on the system.

The obvious areas to focus in on building efficient SQL Server systems include the following:

- Logical database design, to keep data as concise as possible and improve update performance
- Physical database design, to improve query performance
- SQL query syntax, to take advantage of server capabilities
- Proper balance of client and server workload

This last item is the focus of this chapter.

Considerations in Balancing Performance

What you are looking for as you build client/server applications is the perfect mix of client processing and server processing. In order to predict how operations should be distributed, you need to understand the special strengths and weaknesses of servers and clients.

Servers

When properly optimized and configured, a SQL Server is most efficient at finding a needle in a haystack—that is, at finding a handful of rows in a huge table or performing hundreds of concurrent modifications on a large table. It is efficient at performing fairly complex data modifications, and its deadlock detection and resolution scheme is acceptable if deadlocks are not too frequent. The server is acceptably efficient at scanning a medium-sized table and evaluating complex search criteria. The SQL Server can efficiently enforce fairly complex business rules within a database. Overall, the server is best suited to handling set-based data retrieval and modification operations in your system.

A SQL Server is extremely *inefficient* at executing thousands of operations in a loop (as with a cursor) and at scanning an enormous table (though no more inefficient than other relational database systems). Large data loads on tables having dozens of indexes will run slowly.

Clients

A properly configured client workstation is most efficient at displaying complex user interfaces, handling data formatting and column- or row-specific data validation. The client can process and display small- and moderate-sized result sets, and it is efficient at handling row-wise operations on those sets.

Implications of Server and Client Capabilities

Once you understand the fundamental strengths of the components, there are several decisions you need to make regarding application design. Some of those decisions are very straightforward and indisputable; others are harder and involve trade-offs.

The Network as Bottleneck

You should not disregard the importance of the network in client/server systems. In general, you should always treat the network as a primary bottleneck. Even if your system has sufficient *potential* bandwidth to handle a specific operation efficiently, network availability is by far the most unpredictable performance factor. Moreover, under load, operations that run well for a single user might be unacceptably slow when multiple users are running them.

Let's look at ways to reduce network load and make applications more efficient.

Reducing Query Size

SQL (the language) allows complex set operations to be defined in a single statement. Consider the difference between the code required to modify a set of rows having a certain characteristic in a typical third-generation language and SQL. Here is pseudocode representing the work of a 3GL to search a set of rows and modify certain ones:

```
open file for update to filehandle
set up rowset
while not (eof)
begin
   lock next row
   read next row into rowbuffer
   if column1 = value
   begin
      update column2 = newvalue
      write rowbuffer
   end
   unlock this row
end
close file
```

Here is a sample SQL statement to perform the same work:

```
update tablename
set column2 = newvalue
where column1 = value
```

In and of itself, then, the SQL language provides a mechanism for reducing query size; however, complex batches can include dozens or hundreds of SQL queries. For example, the sp_help stored procedure is about 48KB of code. If every time a user needed to know table and column definitions he had to submit a 48KB query, the strain on the network could be substantial.

One useful way to reduce network traffic, then, is to use stored procedures instead of submitting large SQL queries. A stored procedure with several parameters seldom requires more than a small network packet (512 bytes) to transmit. If your system will have hundreds or thousands of users attached to a single server, using procedures instead of sending large SQL batches will improve network performance.

Reducing Result Sets

The other major drag on the network is large result sets. This is a genuine problem in decision-support systems, which by their nature deal with very large amounts of data and often need to return large sets of rows.

On the other hand, I have seen many client systems where programmers fail to take real advantage of the server, instead returning large numbers of rows to the client and then processing the rows on the client system to find the actual rows desired. For example, consider this query:

```
select last_name, first_name, m_init
from names
where upper(last_name) = "GREEN"
```

The query will probably run horribly (the upper function invalidates a SARG and requires a table scan) unless the table is quite small. An experienced SQL programmer will think of several reasonable solutions, including this one:

```
select last_name, first_name, m_init
from names
where upper(last_name) = "GREEN"
and last_name like "G%" or last_name like "g%"
```

The revised query may be able to use an index to identify the rows starting with a capital or lower case "G." This should speed up the query substantially, allowing use of an index, but a lot depends on exactly what the data looks like.

On the other hand, an inexperienced SQL programmer's reaction to the poor performance of the original query might be to return all rows to his application and then identify those rows matching his criteria locally, figuring that his local use of an upper() function will be faster than that on the SQL Server.

In this case, the inexperienced programmer is wrong, and this approach hurts both his individual query and every other activity on the network while he monopolizes bandwidth to transmit data.

Certain applications, particularly decision-support applications, legitimately need to bring back enormous quantities of data to the user. It might still be possible to keep that data off the network by submitting the query from a connection established locally on the server. (Use isql/w or the command-based isql program to do this.) That connection can create a file containing the large result set, which can be transferred to another physical computer far more efficiently than a large set could be transferred with the Transaction Data Stream (TDS).

Remember that it is almost always more efficient for the server to prepare aggregate results (with group by) than for the raw data to be passed to a workstation and processed there. In addition to the benefit of keeping the result set small, SQL Server also has access to indexes and caching mechanisms that make totalling easier and faster on that device than on a client workstation.

Row Processing

A major application question is how to perform row-by-row processing. SQL Server 6.0 introduces cursor processing for the first time, but the performance of cursor applications is a serious problem. There are several application problems (most often, batch update processes, complex reports, and logical integrity checks) that seem to call for row-wise processing. It is worth some time looking for alternative approaches because of the enormous performance penalty introduced by cursor processing. See Chapter 20, "Advanced SQL Techniques," for a discussion of the problems and solutions to row-wise, cursor-based processing (and for some alternatives).

Data Validation Methods

An ongoing debate in SQL Server applications is where and how to perform data validation. It was fairly simple in earlier software generations to decide how and where to do data validation. The application was required to enforce all business rules, from individual column values to interdependencies between columns in a row to complex interdependencies among several tables (including referential integrity).

One of the great benefits of SQL Server is the ability to implement rules, defaults, constraints, and triggers that define the data integrity and consistency requirements for a table or set of tables. At this time, the application designer has several methods of enforcing consistency:

- *Application-based integrity.* This is the traditional place to enforce business rules in a 3GL application, where the database has little or no capability to manage the content or consistency of data. There are correct ways to implement this approach to be certain that you have the desired effect and that locking and transactional problems don't completely lock up the system.

- *Procedure-based integrity.* All data modifications can be performed through stored procedures, allowing all validation to be implemented in those procedures. This is a fairly common choice because it allows a single set of code to manage all data. It's easy to maintain, and it can provide better performance if properly implemented. In this approach, transactions do not typically span procedures (and therefore batches), so fewer locks are held for a long time.

- *Server-based integrity.* This is integrity based on rules, constraints, defaults and triggers. This is the only approach that allows users to update freely using standard SQL statements, even if they know nothing about the structure or data-integrity requirements of the database. This approach is modular and efficient, but it can sometimes be difficult to debug because of the interaction of code in different objects.

- *Mixed-model integrity.* This is integrity enforced at several levels. This is a very common approach, often allowing the best combination of performance, flexibility, and user interface.

Data Validation and Performance

There are performance, code-maintenance, and interface issues associated with the method used to enforce business rules on the database. Code running at the client level will reduce the load on the server, but the client does not have access to other rows in the table or in other tables. Enforcement objects at the server level will increase the load on the server and can create persistent blocking locks that can damage performance. Server-based enforcement objects will apply to all applications and can keep application development simpler and more reliable; server-based objects also permit changes to the rules applied to data shared among several applications with a single modification. Only application-based validation can provide useful, column-level assistance during input and modification steps.

Let's look at each of these approaches and understand its long-term implications. Here are some examples of business rules that might need to be validated before a data modification could be permitted:

> **NOTE**
>
> You should understand that there is no right way to do this, although there are several wrong ways. Your choice of how to implement data validation will depend on your hardware and software configuration, application design and implementation philosophy, and usage and performance requirements.

Rule 1: Items can be deleted only if the in-stock value is 0

Rule 1 could be implemented in a couple of ways. It would be incorrect to read the row and verify that the in-stock value is 0 locally and then delete the row with confidence:

```
select instock
from item
where item_no = 1343
go

/* check instock in a local program */
delete item
where item_no = 1343
go
```

Clearly, the problem is that someone else could jump in and modify the value of instock on the item between the time you retrieve the row and when you delete the row. You could solve this with a persistent lock using holdlock in a transaction:

```
begin transaction
select instock
from item
where item_no = 1343
holdlock
go

/* check instock in a local program */
delete item
where item_no = 1343
commit transaction
go
```

This solves the potential hole in data integrity, but it leaves a persistent page-level lock on the page while you do application-side processing (transactions held open across batches). This can result in livelocks and deadlocks, which are both damaging to performance.

> **NOTE**
>
> You could delete the row by simply including the application condition in your SQL code like this:
>
> ```
> delete item
> where item_no = 1343
> and instock = 0
> ```
>
> What if the delete fails to find any rows? Does that mean there is no item or the item has a nonzero instock value? The failure to find a row based on either condition will cause the delete to fail.

There is a mechanism that provides sufficient data integrity without creating the locking problem introduced by transactions that cross batches. SQL Server provides an optimistic locking mechanism using timestamp values to guarantee that the version of the row being modified or deleted is the same one that was read.

```
select instock, timestamp
from item
where item_no = 1343
go

/* check instock in a local program */
delete item
where item_no = 1343
and tsequal(timestamp, 0x123456671312)
go
```

In this example, the programmer retrieved the binary timestamp value along with the instock value in the first step and then used that timestamp value in the tsequal() function to guarantee that the version of the row deleted is the same as the version retrieved. The important point about this function is how different error cases are treated: the server finds the row based on other conditions and then validates the version with the timestamp value. If the row is not found, the server returns 0 rows processed, as you would expect. If the row is found but the timestamp value fails to match, the server returns a specific error message (Error 532). (For a more thorough discussion of the use of timestamp columns, see Chapter 4, "Transact-SQL Datatypes.")

The approaches described so far would all work as well or better if performed during a stored procedure. All the locking windows would be narrower, substantially improving performance and reducing the potential impact on other users. Validation of the deletion could also be easily implemented in a trigger:

```
create trigger tr_item_del
on items for delete as
if @@rowcount = 0 return
if exists
    (select * from deleted
    where instock != 0)
```

```
begin
     raiserror 55555 "Error: attemp to delete non-zero instock value"
     rollback tran
end
return
```

The trigger simplifies the problem of an application programmer by handling the error case completely. The data is safe from errors made by individual application programmers who forget to apply the rule or do so improperly. The trigger does require some additional overhead during the deletion, and locks are held during trigger execution. But the overall performance impact of enforcing Rule 1 using a trigger is probably less than that of the other approaches.

Rule 2: Customer status can only be ACTIVE, INACTIVE, or PENDING

Rule 2 establishes a list of valid values for an individual column. It is simple enough to enforce this rule in an application program, although there is a chance that a programmer will make an error and allow invalid entries in one program. In addition, users accessing the database using a simple SQL interface like isql/w can put any value in the column using a simple insert statement. Nevertheless, validation in the application has two specific benefits. First, the application can prompt the user immediately if an entry is invalid. (This immediate feedback is critical to good user interface.) A server-based validation technique would prompt the user only when the entire row was submitted to the server. Second, performing column-level validation at the workstation avoids unnecessary network traffic and unnecessary work by the server.

To get efficient use of shared resources (the network and server) and good user interface (field-level prompting) as well as protection against application errors and interactive SQL users, it is common to implement a combination of both client-based and server-based validation techniques. In the case of Rule 2, using both application-level tools and a rule or constraint to validate customer status provides the best of both worlds, although it does require additional maintenance if the values change frequently.

Can you perform column-level validation in a stored procedure? Of course, and if all data modifications have been channeled through procedures, it might be appropriate. The benefit of using procedures instead of rules is that all database-consistency requirements are defined in a single unit of code.

Can column-level validation take place in a trigger? It can, but it shouldn't. Remember that triggers execute *after* the modifications are performed on the table. There might be a tremendous amount of disk activity (mostly reads, as modifications are made in memory until they are committed to disk) to support a data modification. Whenever you can, prevalidate work instead of waiting until the trigger fires, as long as that prevalidation does not require additional work (see Rule 1).

Rule 3: Orders can only be entered for valid customer IDs

This is classic referential integrity, in which the referencing table's foreign key (`order.cust_id`) must match a primary key in the referenced table (`customer.cust_id`). You can certainly write code to ensure that the customer exists, either in an application program or in a stored procedure. This will require the same kind of transactional and locking work seen in Rule 1.

SQL Server provides two mechanisms for handling referential integrity more efficiently: constraints and triggers. In general, constraints will be more efficient because they are implemented in C code as an implicit part of the SQL Server application rather than in SQL (see Chapter 20 for more on the difference in performance between native C and SQL code performance), so whenever possible we use constraints rather than triggers. (Remember not to rely on constraints when an application must run version 4.21 as well as version 6.0.)

Rule 3a: Orders can only be entered for customers having a status of "ACTIVE"

Here is an example where referential integrity requirements are more complex than a constraint would completely handle. Here, a constraint could catch the first level of data-integrity problems (only valid customers), but a trigger would be required to check the status of the customer.

```
create trigger tr_order_ins_upd
on orders for insert, update as
if @@rowcount = 0 return
if exists
     (select * from inserted i, customers c
      where i.cust_id = c.cust_id
      and c.status != "ACTIVE")
begin
     raiserror 55556 "Order entered for inactive customer"
     rollback tran
end
return
```

The trigger code is simplified because the constraint has already handled referential integrity. (Note that additional code would be required to allow updates to orders already in the table if the customer status is now "INACTIVE".)

A mixed approach taking advantage of the capabilities of many elements of the system usually provides the best results, but it might entail more sophisticated documentation and maintenance than you want to deal with. On the other hand, most single-mode approaches require a compromise on performance or functionality, and sometimes both.

Complex Transactions

Some applications require *complex transactions* to take place in real time (or as close to real time as possible). Complex transactions could be multirow updates requiring concurrency, or they could involve a dozen tables in a chain of nested triggers. What complex transactions have in common is the following:

■ A substantial number of pages must be locked, possibly in many tables

■ A large number of log entries are generated

What is substantial? What is a large number? There are no firm numeric guidelines, but if running the transactions is causing serious locking or performance problems, your transactions are complex enough to be worth addressing.

Consider an example of an update to a table that requires a dozen updates to related tables. The best case would be to include those updates as part of a single transaction, but currently the response time is unacceptable to users of the system. What is the best way to perform these complex applications?

The first step is to be absolutely certain that the application is properly coded and that the database design is fully optimized. (You certainly should know by now that too many indexes can slow update performance.) Problems with concurrency or performance can often be sufficiently resolved using basic optimization techniques, allowing transactions to happen in real time.

The resources that are stressed during execution of a long-running transaction are the locking system, the transaction log, and memory. Locking large numbers of pages will certainly result in blocking—"live" locks as well as some number of deadlocks. If concurrency problems arise, you might be able to reduce them by decreasing the fillfactor on small, heavily used tables. Changing the clustered index on a table can sometimes resolve locking problems as well. Using a cursor can reduce locking contention, but at a terrible price in performance.

Transaction log problems are most common with very large transactions—large enough to fill the transaction log between a BEGIN TRAN and a COMMIT. But a smaller transaction can cause this kind of problem if sufficient numbers of users are running it at one time. Log capacity isn't the only issue, however. A single transaction could take a long time to commit. If the log is a serious bottleneck, consider moving it onto a nonvolatile RAM drive such as a *solid state drive* (SSD).

Memory can also cause problems with long-running transactions, and you should allow sufficient space in memory for several users to run a complex transaction concurrently.

If long-running transactions continue to present a performance problem, the next step is to consider ways to perform the transaction in a batch mode during off hours. (Make certain that the operation fits in with the rest of your maintenance schedule.) If you cannot wait for a nightly batch, or if you are running a 7 × 24 shop, you will need to run a periodic sweep of worktables to perform these operations in the background.

> **WARNING**
>
> Be careful how you implement background housekeeping operations. If you want to run multiple instances of the operation, you need to build in the code to guarantee data consistency. Remember that background operations will introduce additional overhead, but they will speed up the perceived performance of the system by users waiting for a response from the system after an update.

Multiple Server Transactions

There are a handful of ways to implement transactions that span multiple servers. In general, you should avoid two-phase commit applications in favor of using the built-in replication that comes with SQL Server. The most significant problem with two-phase commits occurs when one of the servers is unavailable: at that point, no transactions involving that server can proceed.

In a replication approach, transactions involving a server that is unavailable are recorded and subsequently delivered to that server after it becomes available. Avoid designs that require complete concurrency between servers for the looser coupling offered with replication.

Some General Advice

In order, the things most likely to ruin application performance are

- bad database design
- bad application design
- bad SQL
- bad server configuration

It might not be a coincidence, but that is also a list of things most difficult to fix in an application. So you need to tend to your database and application design first.

Summary

SQL Server applications perform well when they achieve the right balance of client and server work, and when each of the individual components of the system perform well. Sometimes your design options will be constrained by the functional requirements of the application, especially when it comes to transaction implementation and data validation.

A final point: Never forget that *perceived* performance is as important as actual performance. Users are usually far more sensitive to operations that are slow to *start* doing work or hang up their systems for a long time than they are to operations that take a long time but are unobtrusive.

Advanced SQL Techniques

20

This chapter addresses advanced SQL techniques, particularly for improving individual query performance by understanding the impact of specific syntactic structures on optimization and execution of a query. Specifically, this chapter

- Identifies problematic statements and queries in application designs before they are created on the server

- Finds problematic or performance-hindering statements in queries and stored procedures, and tests different methods for fixing these statements and queries

Who Can Use This Chapter?

It is likely that this chapter will be useful for almost anyone responsible for writing efficient SQL. It would be best, however, for you to know some SQL before starting work on this chapter. The following are the general groups of users and developers who will benefit from this chapter:

- Application developers who write queries as part of their applications

- SQL Server developers writing queries and stored procedures for client application developers

- System administrators and DBAs responsible for writing stored procedures for client application developers

Where Else Can You Find Help?

System administrators and DBAs who want to optimize SQL Server configuration options and physical database design should look at the appropriate chapters in this part of the book on performance and tuning techniques.

Aggregate Query Resolution

This section covers how SQL Server uses worktables to resolve queries with GROUP BY and aggregate functions. In general, aggregate functions automatically require the use of a worktable, which introduces some overhead. Although this overhead cannot be avoided, the worktable also has functional implications for certain types of queries. You will look at the use of HAVING with GROUP BY, compare HAVING and WHERE clauses, and consider some advanced issues related to the use of GROUP BY.

HAVING Clauses with *GROUP BY*

When used with GROUP BY, HAVING restricts the *groups* that are returned by the query after the computation has been completed. When used without GROUP BY, HAVING restricts the *rows* that are returned by the query after the computation has been completed (see the following section, "WHERE versus HAVING").

HAVING does *not* affect the rows that go into a computation; it affects only the rows or groups that come out of a computation. In this example, the server will filter the final results to remove rows containing an average price less than $10:

```
select type, avg(price)
from titles
group by type
having avg(price) >= $10
```

Compare that query to the following, in which the server filters out rows having a price less than $10 before performing the averaging:

```
select type, avg(price)
from titles
where price >= $10
group by type
```

HAVING will always be evaluated *after* the computation has completed in the query, but before rows are returned.

WHERE versus *HAVING*

If both WHERE and HAVING clauses restrict rows, why not use HAVING all the time? If a query has no aggregate functions and no GROUP BY clause, SQL Server will implicitly interpret the HAVING as a WHERE. If a query has aggregate functions or a GROUP BY clause, HAVING is interpreted literally as HAVING, which forces SQL Server to use a worktable to resolve the query.

Query Tracking: *HAVING*

This query uses a HAVING clause to retrieve only selected rows from an aggregate result. Look closely at how the server resolves the query in two steps, using a worktable.

> **NOTE**
>
> The following information is accessed using the SHOWPLAN option, in which SQL Server displays its intended access method for resolving a query. It also includes output from the statistics io option, which provides details about SQL Server physical and logical data access during actual execution. Later in this section, you also examine output from DBCC TRACE flags. If you are unfamiliar with these methods of examining query performance, please refer to Chapter 12, "Understanding the Query Optimizer," for detailed assistance in retrieving and interpreting this information.

```
select id, avg(amount)
from pt_tx
where id < 200
group by id
having avg(amount) > $20000
```

In the following showplan output, the server plans to execute the query in two steps. In the first step, SQL Server will build the grouped (*vector*) aggregate; in the second step, it will return only rows in the worktable matching the HAVING criteria.

```
STEP 1
The type of query is SELECT (into a worktable).
GROUP BY
Vector Aggregate
FROM TABLE
pt_tx
Nested iteration
Index : pttx_1
TO TABLE
Worktable
STEP 2
The type of query is SELECT.
FROM TABLE
Worktable
Nested iteration
Table Scan
```

The output from statistics io shows that the worktable is scanned several times as the aggregate is prepared.

```
Table: pt_tx  scan count 1,  logical reads: 1,  physical reads: 0
Table: Worktable  scan count 1,  logical reads: 89,  physical reads: 0
Total writes for this command: 0
```

Grouping and Worktables

This section looks at advanced issues with GROUP BY and worktables, examining the following:

- The role of the worktable
- The impact of ORDER BY and HAVING on worktables
- HAVING with and without GROUP BY

Role of the Worktable

The worktable stores temporary results that cannot be evaluated, processed, or returned to the user until after the server has completed the current step. Worktables are used to prepare many kinds of results, including the ones covered in the following sections.

Vector Aggregate

```
select type, count(*)
from titles
group by type
```

Ordered Result Set (No Useful Index)

```
select type, title
from titles
order by type, title
```

How Does SQL Server Process Queries Involving a Worktable?

Figure 20.1 illustrates how the server uses a worktable in resolving a query. WHERE and GROUP BY are resolved as the processor moves rows from the base table(s) to the worktable. HAVING and ORDER BY are resolved as the processor builds a final result set based on the worktable.

FIGURE 20.1.

WHERE clauses and GROUP BY take place between the source table(s) and the worktable; HAVING *and* ORDER BY *operate on the worktable in producing a final result set.*

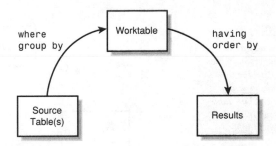

If the server can determine that the column value is dependent on the grouping value, it will perform the grouping properly (and will probably derive the function on-the-fly when displaying results). Here's an example where the GROUP BY clause refers to the actual column, while the select list contains only a function based on that column:

```
select user_name(uid), count(*)
from sysobjects
group by uid
```

Special Topics in Join Processing

This section covers the following special topics in multi-table optimization:

- Joins with or
- Overriding the optimizer
- Breaking up large queries

> **NOTE**
>
> Please review Chapter 12 in detail before reading this. I assume that you understand the fundamentals of single- and multi-table optimization in this section, and I use this information to lay out areas where you can improve query performance.

Joins with *or*

A curious problem arises when you join three tables with two conditions, where a row is included in the result set if either join condition is true. Consider the set of tables shown in Figure 20.2.

FIGURE 20.2.

In this three-way join, results include rows in the title table matching rows in the sales table, as well as rows in the titles *table matching rows in the* titleauthor *table.*

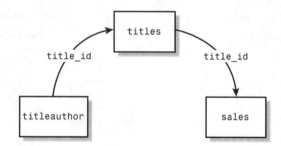

Here's an example of a query that joins three tables based on an or condition:

```
select title
from titles t, titleauthor ta, sales sa
where t.title_id = ta.title_id
or t.title_id = sa.title_id
```

On its surface, this query seems to request a list of all titles that either have an author specified or have been sold. I observed a strange behavior with this type of query, however. When either of the optional join tables is empty, the server returns no rows. For example, consider this three-table join:

```
select count(*)
from A, B, C
where A.id = B.id or A.id = C.id
```

Table 20.1 shows the contents of the three tables.

Table 20.1. Contents of Tables A, B, and C.

Table A

id	CA
1	1
2	2

Table B

id	CB
1	1
2	2

Table C (empty table)

id	CC
none	none

Based on the contents of the tables, you would expect that the count would find two rows where table A matched table B. The query appears to work when all the tables contain at least one row, but it fails when any table is empty.

Actually, the query is incorrectly written and fails under all circumstances. The following adds a couple of rows to table C and then tries the query again.

```
1> insert C values (1, 21)
2> insert C values (2, 22)
3> go
(1 row affected)
(1 row affected)
1> select count(*) from A, B, C
2> where A.id = B.id
3> or A.id = C.id
4> go

    -----------
         6

(1 row affected)
```

With only two rows in A, how did the server find six rows in the join? To understand better, look at the output of the join:

```
select A.id A, B.id B, C.id C
from A, B, C
where A.id = B.id or A.id = C.id
A           B           C
----------- ----------- -----------
          1           1           1
          1           1           2
          1           2           1
          2           1           2
          2           2           1
          2           2           2
```

When SQL Server does not understand your join condition or can find no path to optimize the join, it builds a Cartesian product (the set of all possible combinations) and then tests the validity of each row against the search conditions provided. In this case, you have many duplicate rows, including rows where A is matched to an incorrect B or an incorrect C.

You need to restate the question: Show how many rows in A have a match in B or a match in C. Here is the proper way to write the query:

```
select count(*)
from A
where id in
    (select id from B)
or id in
    (select id from C)
```

This query becomes more problematic if you need to retrieve information from table B or C to be included in the final result set. Your method of resolving that kind of query will depend on your specific requirements, but you will probably need to use a temporary table and prioritize B or C.

In any case, avoid using or to connect join clauses because it does create duplicate and invalid data.

Overriding the Optimizer

Here's a question. When might the optimizer be wrong?

You have looked at how to override the optimizer. Now I'll discuss some of the circumstances when it might be an effective approach.

In general, you should override the optimizer if you are absolutely certain that you know something it does not. Here are some examples:

- Indexes did not exist at optimization time
- Statistics are out of date
- Device performance is different from assumption

The following sections provide a brief look at each of these topics.

Indexes Did Not Exist at Optimization Time

When you create a temporary table inside a stored procedure, there are times when it is appropriate to index that temporary table so that you can access that index properly during a subsequent join, as in this example:

```
create proc p_temptable as

/* create a temporary table */
select title_id, au_id, title,
     au_fname, au_lname, au_ord, advance / royaltyper, price
into #temp_ta
from titles t, authors a, titleauthor ta
where t.title_id = ta.title_id
and a.au_id = ta.au_id

/* index the table for subsequent joins or other operations */
create unique clustered index on #temp_ta (title_id, au_id)
create nonclustered index on #temp_ta (title)

/* now execute queries ...
** will the procedure use the indexes or identify the best join order? */
select au_id, sum(qty)
from sales s, #temp_ta t
where s.title_id = t.title_id
group by au_id
order by 2 desc

... (other queries)

return
```

Stored procedure optimization occurs only once, so at procedure execution time, the temporary table indexes (as well as any index statistics, of course) are unavailable to queries such as the aggregate query in the example. You may want to force a join order or identify a useful index on the temporary table to run the query.

Statistics Are Out of Date

In most cases, the best cure for badly out-of-date index distribution statistics is to update your statistics. But updating statistics takes time and locks tables. Remember that an index is extremely valuable, even if its statistics are incorrect. Statistics are used only to choose a path, not to execute it. Force the correct index choice and you may get good performance.

Remember, though, that hard-coding a program to use a particular index path might cause trouble later on, when indexes are up to date. Forcing an index is best used with an ad hoc query when you know something about the specific here-and-now situation rather than about a global condition that will change over time. The optimizer is far better at adjusting to changing conditions than your programs are likely to be.

Device Performance Is Different from Assumption

The optimizer assumes that the ratio of logical to physical read performance is 14 to 2. What is the effect of this assumption on a typical join? Consider the example in Table 20.2.

Table 20.2. Effects of the ratio on a typical join.

Table	Table A	Table B
Size	10MB (5000 pgs)	2MB (1000 pgs)
Rows	1MB	250KB
NCI levels/size	4 levels, 500 pgs	3 levels, 100 pgs

Here is the query you are trying to optimize:

```
select count(*)
from A, B
where A.id = B.id
```

When the server estimates the work required to perform the join, it makes assumptions based on what will fit in cache. If an object will fit entirely in cache, the server assumes that one scan of a table or index will include a physical and a logical cost—number of pages to read $\times$ (14 ms + 2 ms), where any subsequent scan of the same object will require only a logical cost (pages to read $\times$ 2 ms).

> **NOTE**
>
> Some of the calculations here are a little more crude than what the server is able to do in its algorithm. The server takes into account issues such as percentage of cache to use, and considers index covering and reformatting strategies. I am considering only alternative join orders in performing a join.

You will now work out the estimated cost of performing the join without assuming any specific values for logical and physical reads. Instead, you will carry two variables, LC (logical cost) and PC (physical cost), and then look at how the ratio of those values affects actual performance.

First, assume that A is the outer table and B the inner (A->B join order), and use a nonclustered index (NCI) on B to correlate tables. Also, assume that table B and the nonclustered index fit in cache.

```
COST(A->B) = 5,000 pgs * PC
             + 1,100 pgs * PC
             + 1,000,000 rows * 4 levels * LC
    = 6,100 * PC + 4,000,000 * LC
```

In layman's terms, the cost equals:

- The number of pages to read all of table A times the physical cost of each read, *plus*
- The number of pages in the nonclustered index times the physical cost to read them, *plus*

■ The number of rows in table A times the number of index levels to traverse to find matching rows in B times the logical cost to read them once for each row in A.

Now assume a B->A join order, using a nonclustered index on A to correlate rows. Assume that the nonclustered index of table A (but not the data pages) will fit in cache.

```
COST(B->A) = 1000 pgs * PC
           + 500 pgs * PC
           + 250,000 rows * (4 levels * LC + 4 pages * PC)
         = 1,001,500 * PC + 1,000,000 * LC
```

If you substitute varying values for the ratio of performance between logical and physical reads, you get the graph in Figure 20.3. Some plans are more sensitive to device speed than others. In this example, as the physical device gets faster with respect to memory, the cost of treating B as the outer table in a join is reduced dramatically. SQL Server assumes that the performance ratio of physical to logical reads is 14:2.

FIGURE 20.3.

Expected query performance based on device speed and access path.

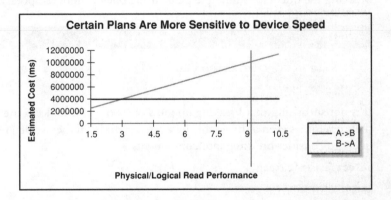

Clearly, how memory and disk speed relate will impact actual performance. Ordinarily, the ratio is more like 20 to 1 between memory and traditional disk storage, and much higher for nontraditional storage such as WORM and CD-ROM drives, especially without aggressive caching strategies. It is reasonable for the optimizer to discount this benefit because of the effects of multiuser processing consuming available cache, requiring a fall-back to physical memory when memory is insufficient.

Are there times when the actual physical drive performance will be better than 7 to 1? If you set up tempdb in RAM, or if you are using a Solid State Device (a nonvolatile, RAM-based hard drive), you may see numbers substantially better than that. Also, new RAID devices include smart read-ahead strategies that could provide substantially better performance than you have experienced in the past. Finally, if you have limited cache space on your server, or if the cache periodically is running over into the NT page file (a really, really bad idea, by the way), memory performance could be fairly bad.

The type of device is as important as the access path in some instances; therefore, you may find that drive performance is one area in which you can look to outguess the optimizer and force a specific order.

Breaking Up Large Queries

The following sections examine how to break up large queries.

Defining Large Queries

A *large multi-table query* is a query consisting of many tables with sufficient rows in the table to make a join expensive. The critical issue in multi-table queries is *join order*. The server may not be able to find an efficient join order with all of the tables in the query. The query may require breaking the query into multiple parts, using one or more temporary tables.

> **NOTE**
>
> This is a strategy that the optimizer will not try.

It is not surprising that breaking up joins of six or eight tables is useful. What is surprising is that sometimes even a three-table join can benefit from the use of a temporary table. Here is a query to consider breaking into components:

```
select sum(t1.amount)
from A, B, C
where A.id = B.id
and C.id = A.id
and B.id = C.id
and C.key2 between 1000 and 15000
```

The SHOWPLAN shows that the server chose the join order B -> A -> C:

```
STEP 1
The type of query is SELECT
Scalar Aggregate
FROM TABLE
B
Nested iteration
Table Scan
FROM TABLE
A
Nested iteration
Using Clustered Index
FROM TABLE
C
Nested iteration
Using Clustered Index
STEP 2
The type of query is SELECT
```

The problem is that table C, the innermost table, has two separate, fairly selective indexes that might be useful for this query: a clustered index to use with a SARG and a nonclustered index that could support the join. Because of the join selectivity estimates, the server has determined (correctly) that using the clustered index at the innermost level is the most efficient approach to this three-table join.

Here are the statistics for each table, retrieved using SET statistics io ON:

```
Table: A  scan count 7282,  logical reads: 14755,  physical reads: 0
Table: B  scan count 1,  logical reads: 88,  physical reads: 0
Table: C  scan count 11308,  logical reads: 34404,  physical reads: 0
```

How to Break Up a Query

You want to break up queries to allow SQL Server to get the best effect out of all candidate indexes. In the case considered here, only one of the two useful indexes on table C is being used, while table B is being scanned. Here is what you do to make this work:

- Separate the query into components that each have an effective strategy.
- Try several approaches to see which gives the lowest total STATS IO values.
- Use one or many temporary tables to store and re-join values, especially when you have a highly selective index.

It is most likely that breaking up a query will be useful when a SARG in the query is fairly selective (it will significantly reduce the number of relevant rows in a single table), but it is not used in the optimization plan. The best SARGs will use a clustered index.

At the first step in breaking up a query, you want to take advantage of that selective index to reduce the overall number of rows in play, partly to reduce the complexity of subsequent steps but also to reduce the size of your temporary table.

> **NOTE**
>
> This approach to large queries is likely to be less effective if the entire temporary table will not fit in cache.

```
select C.id, B.amount
into #temp
from B, C
where C.id = B.id
and C.key2 between 1000 and 15000
```

Here is the SHOWPLAN output for the first step in the plan. The clustered index on the inner table C is used to dramatically reduce the cost of each scan on that table:

```
STEP 1
The type of query is TABCREATE
```

```
STEP 2
The type of query is INSERT
The update mode is direct
Worktable created for SELECT INTO
FROM TABLE
B
Nested iteration
Table Scan
FROM TABLE
C
Nested iteration
Using Clustered Index
TO TABLE
#temp
```

In the second step, you join the remaining table(s) with the temporary table to get a result:

```
select sum(t.amount)
from A, #temp t
where t.id = A.id

drop table #temp
```

The server will choose to use the permanent table A as the inner table if the index on id is sufficiently selective and if indexes fit in cache. Otherwise, the temporary table, if small enough, will be the inner table. You may want to test this out, examining statistics outputs and optimization plans to make certain that the server finds the most effective plan. You might want to force a join order or use an index if the server is not making the best choice.

The optimization plan for the second part of the query shows that the server is scanning the new temporary table as the outer table and then using the index on A to build the final result:

```
STEP 1
The type of query is SELECT
Scalar Aggregate
FROM TABLE
#temp t
Nested iteration
Table Scan
FROM TABLE
A
Nested iteration
Using Clustered Index
STEP 2
The type of query is SELECT

STEP 1
The type of query is TABDESTROY
```

Figure 20.4 shows the original and revised join orders. You can see that the join order presented when the query was broken up allowed the server to make the most efficient use of the indexes available. The more tables involved in the query, the more likely you are to find a better optimization strategy by breaking up the join into more than one step.

FIGURE 20.4.

Breaking up a query into many parts allows more flexibility in identifying an efficient join order.

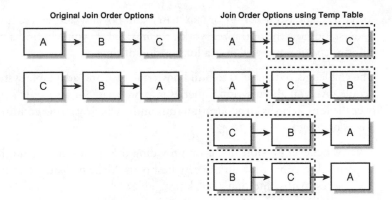

Here is the `statistics io` output from the query. The cost of the original query was about 48,000 logical reads. This query required less than half that many reads to complete:

```
Table: B  scan count 1,  logical reads: 88,  physical reads: 0
Table: C  scan count 7282,  logical reads: 22152,  physical reads: 0
Table: #temp_____000024884F  scan count 0,  logical reads: 554,
         physical reads: 0

Table: A  scan count 550,  logical reads: 1109,  physical reads: 0
Table: #temp_____000024884F  scan count 1,  logical reads: 5,
         physical reads: 0
```

Recommendations

The following are some recommendations for how to break up query tables:

- Understand outer/inner processing with multi-table joins.
- Look for situations in which the optimizer does not use all available indexing resources.
- Look for situations in which nested scans of large tables are occurring.
- Break up queries by building temporary result sets.
- Try to encourage the optimizer to make use of many indexes.
- Use the first step to reduce the number of rows being processed.

Summary

This chapter looks at some ways to manipulate SQL statements to get the best performance out of the SQL Server optimizer. In general, it's important to remember that the optimizer is not perfect and that it must make assumptions about the state of the data or its accessibility that are not necessarily true. It also has specific methods of resolving certain syntactic structures (such as GROUP BY or ORDER BY) and possibly adding complexity. So, the more you understand how the optimizer works, the more likely you will find a way to write queries that will run consistently well over a long period of time.

The challenge, of course, is to build powerful, fast, and adaptable systems. Some of the advice people give you about writing queries is appropriate for a specific situation, but problematic over the long term as an application runs under widely varying conditions. So here are two last pieces of advice:

- Whenever possible, focus on providing the optimizer with all the information it might need to come up with the very best plan. Make no assumptions, force no indexes or access paths, and don't break up queries.

- When it's not possible, make concessions and force a specific optimization by forcing an index or join order or even breaking up a query. If you do, document those choices and include a regular review of the code in your standard application maintenance schedule to ensure that the choices you made months or years ago are still appropriate today.

Miscellaneous Performance Topics

IN THIS CHAPTER

There are a number of performance-related issues in SQL Server about which both the programmer and the DBA/system administrator need to be aware. Many of these topics do not fit neatly into previous chapters on understanding and tuning the performance of SQL Server. This chapter presents a selection of these topics and discusses the various performance implications of each, providing tips and guidelines to alleviate or avoid some of the performance problems.

BCP and Performance

Two Microsoft SQL Server utilities can be used to transfer data. SQL Transfer Manager provides an easy, graphical way to transfer both objects *and* data from one SQL Server database to another. The *bulk copy program* (BCP) is a command-line utility that copies SQL Server data into or from an operating system file. The operating system file is defined in a user-specified format.

The BCP program is a very useful utility for transferring data from non–SQL Server data sources into SQL Server (for example, loading a DB2 data extract into a SQL Server database). BCP is the fastest way to insert data into a SQL Server table. This is because during load, BCP does not enforce rules, triggers, or constraints as a normal `insert` statement does. In addition, if the appropriate conditions are met, BCP can also avoid logging of the rows being inserted, greatly reducing the overhead involved and resulting in much faster load times.

When there are no indexes on a table, BCP performs a "fast" BCP load. The actual data rows being inserted into the table are not logged as they would be by a normal `insert` statement. Instead, only the new page allocations to that table are logged.

> **NOTE**
>
> In addition to having no indexes on the table, the database must also be configured for `select into/bulkcopy` operations, or else BCP reverts to the slow form of BCP load.
>
> Also, if a table you are inserting into is marked for replication, the individual rows will need to be logged for the replication process in order for them to be replicated. This also results in a slow, logged BCP to be performed.

> **WARNING**
>
> Selecting the `select into/bulkcopy` option disables transaction log dumps for that database. After completion of a nonlogged activity (`select into`, fast BCP load), a full database dump should be performed.

Minimizing Data Load Time

In addition to performing fast versus slow BCP loads, there are a number of other methods of tweaking the BCP load performance.

Network Packet Size

Network packet size determines the number of bytes (per network packet) sent to and from the SQL Server. Your SQL Server configuration determines the minimum packet size allowed. However, this option can be overridden on an individual basis with the -a option to BCP.

Increasing packet size can enhance performance on bulk copy operations. The default network packet size used by BCP when copying data into a Microsoft SQL Server is 4096 bytes; 512 bytes is the smallest network packet size. If a larger packet is requested but cannot be granted, BCP will default to 512 (the performance statistics generated at the end of a BCP run will show the actual packet size used). Testing has found that packet sizes between 4096 and 8192 bytes provide the fastest performance for BCP operations.

BCP Loading and Indexes

Generally, there are two reasonable sequences of events for initial loading of data into SQL Server. Here is the first sequence:

1. Create the clustered index.
2. Load the data.
3. Create any nonclustered indexes.
4. Update your statistics on the clustered index.

Here is the second sequence:

1. Load the data.
2. Create the clustered index and any nonclustered indexes.

Typically, the second sequence is the most efficient method. Although the cost is high to build all indexes after the data is loaded, the total elapsed time will be substantially less than the time it would take to perform a slow BCP into a table with the indexes in place.

Remember, however, that if the data in the source file is not in clustered index sort order, you'll need 120 percent of the size of the table as free space *within that database* for SQL Server to be able to sort the data and build the clustered index. Due to database size constraints, you might need to use the first sequence and load the data with the clustered index in place.

> **TIP**
>
> If the source data file is in clustered index order, you can load the data into the table without the clustered index. After the data is loaded, create the clustered index with the `sorted_data` option. This option simply creates the clustered index without resorting the data; it doesn't reorganize the table.
>
> If, however, this option detects a row out of order during the creation of the clustered index, the index `create` will fail. You will then be forced to run a standard clustered index `create` and have the necessary free space available.
>
> Also, if you must load the data with the clustered index in place, the load will proceed more quickly with sorted data than with unsorted data.

It is always faster to drop nonclustered indexes, load the data, and re-create the nonclustered indexes than it is to load the data with the indexes in place. This is due to the significant amount of overhead that is incurred to maintain those indexes during the data load. However, it will entirely depend on whether you are performing a complete refresh of the data or are performing an incremental data load in order to determine whether it is feasible to drop all indexes prior to running BCP.

Another advantage to creating indexes after the data load is that the index statistics will be up to date because the indexes are created with data in the table. It will not be necessary to run the `update statistics` command.

Incremental Loads versus Full Loads

If you are replacing all data for a table, it is faster to drop all nonclustered indexes and truncate the table prior to the data load. When the data is loaded, you then re-create the nonclustered indexes. Be aware, however, that if data volumes are high, index creation time can be substantial. In some cases, if the index rebuilds take an excessive amount of time (several hours), it may pay to absorb the overhead of leaving the nonclustered indexes in place during the data load. This typically applies when performing incremental data loads.

If you are making substantive increases in the amount of data being added to the table (approximately 20 percent or more as a rule of thumb), it will generally be faster to drop the nonclustered indexes, load the data, and then rebuild the indexes.

> **WARNING**
>
> Because rules, triggers, and constraints are not applied during BCP load, integrity controls are bypassed. You will need to ensure that the data is completely valid to avoid violating any data or referential integrity conditions (more on this later). For this reason, BCP is often not used for incremental data loads.

If you are not significantly increasing the amount of the data in the table, there are a variety of methods for performing an incremental BCP load.

One alternative is to run the BCP load with all indexes on the table. Although this BCP load is the slowest, you won't have to re-create the indexes; however, you will need to update statistics on the table subsequent to the load.

A second alternative for incremental loads is to drop all nonclustered indexes and load with just the clustered index in place. This approach will speed up the BCP load, but the table will still be essentially unusable by applications that depend on the nonclustered indexes for access performance until the indexes are re-created. Depending on the size of the table, index creation could take hours or even days.

The third option is to run the incremental BCP load with no indexes on the table. This allows the fastest load process, but the slowest index creation time. The re-creation of the clustered index will acquire an exclusive table lock, which must be completed before the creation of nonclustered indexes can commence. It also prevents any user access to the table until the clustered index creation is complete. Unless you are adding over 25 percent of the data (that is, adding 500MB to a 2GB table), the time needed to re-create the clustered index and all nonclustered indexes will be prohibitive.

Multiple Concurrent BCPs

If you have to load multiple tables, and the tables are on different physical devices, you might want to consider running multiple BCP loads concurrently, one into each table. This should help to increase overall BCP throughput over running them in serial. Be aware that there will still be contention for the transaction log between the BCP load processes unless each table resides in a separate physical database with the transactions logs for each database on separate physical devices as well.

Slow BCP and Logging

When running a slow BCP load, the individual data rows are logged. Remember that for each row being inserted into the table, a corresponding row is being inserted into each existing nonclustered index on the table. This can result in a significant number of log records being generated. Large, logged BCP loads are notorious for filling up the transaction log. Because the BCP load is treated as a single batch transaction by default, the BCP records in the log cannot be truncated until the BCP process completes.

To avoid the log filling up, you can use the `-b` option to break the BCP load up into multiple batches. At the completion of a batch, SQL Server commits the inserted rows and checkpoints the database. The log records for those inserted rows can now be removed from the log. If you also turn on the `trunc. log on chkpt.` option for the database, the log will automatically be truncated. The size of the BCP batch depends on the size of your transaction log and the amount of other logged activity occurring at the same time.

> **NOTE**
>
> Using the -b option causes BCP to run slower due to the multiple checkpoints that occur during the load. Also, when the log gets truncated, all update/insert activity is suspended until the truncate completes. However, this alternative is much preferred over the log filling up.

One other advantage of using the -b option for large data loads is that should the BCP load process fail at some point, you can restart the BCP load from the first row of the batch being loaded at the time the BCP failed. All rows for the previous batches will have been committed and checkpointed. Check the load statistics reported at the end of the failed BCP to determine how many rows were copied. If 40,000 rows were copied into the table using a batch size of 10,000, you can restart the BCP load at row 40,001 using the -F option as follows:

```
BCP acctg..customers in customer.BCP -Usa -P -c -b10000 -F40001
```

BCP and Data Integrity

BCP does not invoke any data integrity checks during load, such as triggers, rules, or constraints, even in "slow" mode. Your data and referential integrity checks are completely bypassed. When bulk copying data into a table with triggers, rules, or constraints, you'll need to decide how you are going to resolve this issue.

To make sure that new data is valid, you'll need to run SQL code after the BCP load process completes in order to check the data validity and to decide how invalid rows are to be handled. For example, to check that the loaded data meets your referential integrity constraints, you could run the following code:

```
select cust_id, line_no
from purchase
where cust_id not in
    (select cust_id from customers)
```

This query lists all of the rows with invalid foreign key values in cust_id.

Because BCP does not invoke rules or check constraints, you'll need to write SQL queries to check that all values in a column match your rules or constraints. Here is an example:

```
select order_id, item_num
from orders
where price <= $0.0
```

This query returns all rows that do not meet the rule or constraint that price must be greater than zero. You can then make the determination whether to change the rule, remove the rows, or change the invalid data.

Sometimes triggers are also used to keep summary values in sync. For example, consider an item table that has a `total_sales` column that contains the sum of the `qty` column in the orders table for that item. In this case, your trigger code is structured to handle the incremental adding of data. The overall total value for `total_sales` could not be determined by the trigger code. You may have to fully recalculate all summary values for the detail rows in the orders table. Determine the SQL necessary to accomplish this task and execute the code, similar to the following example, which uses a correlated subquery:

```
update item
set total_sales =
    (select sum(qty)
    from orders
    where item.item_num = orders.item_num
    group by orders.item_num)
```

You might wonder how all this relates to performance. Well, any corresponding speed gains achieved by running a BCP load are going to be offset by the performance hit the system will take when you have to run these queries. If your tables are large, the processes to validate your data integrity could take hours. These processes will be very I/O and CPU intensive; they will cause other concurrent processes to run more slowly and might also lock tables from updates or retrievals until they are complete. Some of these processes could essentially bring the SQL Server to its knees.

You may at times find it more beneficial to use a standard insert process to add data to your table. This way all data integrity checks and trigger code are applied for each individual row inserted. True, this is more overhead on the insert process itself, but it will allow other processes to continue to run only slightly hindered.

Database Maintenance and Performance

The main issue to address regarding data maintenance and performance is that data maintenance tasks tend to be very resource intensive and, although you can run many of the SQL Server maintenance tasks online, there may be a significant impact on performance.

One of the main culprits is the dbcc command. The database consistency checker validates your tables' allocation pages and page linkages. In order to do this, dbcc performs a huge amount of physical I/O and locks tables from update activity while running. As a result, it can be very time-consuming as well as have a severe impact on online performance. Table 21.1 summarizes the performance impact of the dbcc commands.

Table 21.1. Summary of dbcc commands and performance implications.

Command Option	Locking and I/O	Performance
checktable and checkdb	Shared table lock(s); heavy I/O	Slow

continues

Table 21.1. continued

Command Option	Locking and I/O	Performance
checkalloc, tablealloc, and indexalloc	Shared table locks; heavy I/O	Slow
checkcatalog	Shared page locks on system tables	Fast

In an effort to minimize the total amount of time spent running the dbcc commands, you may want to consider running some of them in parallel. Database consistency checks, when broken down with checktable, tablealloc, and indexalloc, can be executed in parallel. For example, you can try running the dbcc checktable and dbcc tablealloc commands concurrently for a particular table. Also, performing consistency checks on different tables can be done in parallel, decreasing overall completion time. However, you'll need to determine what the break-even point is on your server for running dbcc processes in parallel before the combined contention between the multiple processes causes them to run slower than if they were run sequentially.

Other data-maintenance commands that affect performance adversely are index creation and update statistics. Both update statistics and nonclustered index creations acquire shared locks on the affected tables. This prevents updates for the duration of the command. Clustered index creation acquires an exclusive lock on the table until completion, preventing any access by other processes.

TIP

The update statistics command updates statistics for all indexes on a table unless you specify a specific index name:

```
update statistics table_name [index_name]
```

When run specifying just the table name, the index statistics are updated for each index on the table sequentially. By running it on individual indexes, you could run multiple update statistics processes concurrently, lowering the total time to update the statistics for a table and releasing the shared locks quicker.

Also, keep in mind that the index statistics are only used for non-unique searches. For unique indexes used only for single row retrieval (*not used for range searches*), the distribution page will not be used. Therefore, it would not be critical to update statistics on that index as frequently, if at all.

tempdb and Performance

All users within SQL Server share the same `tempdb` database for work tables and temporary tables, regardless of what database they are working in. This makes `tempdb` a potential bottleneck in any multiuser system. The primary bottleneck in `tempdb` is disk I/O, but there can also be locking contention between processes on the `tempdb` system tables.

There are four basic techniques for eliminating `tempdb` as a bottleneck:

1. Add memory to SQL Server
2. Put `tempdb` in RAM
3. Put `tempdb` on faster devices
4. Disseminate disk resources

Adding More Memory to SQL Server

Adding more memory to SQL Server can help improve `tempdb` performance by allowing more of the `tempdb` activity in `tempdb` to take place in SQL Server data cache. The main disadvantage to this approach is that it won't help much for `inserts` into temporary tables in `tempdb` because the modified data pages will still have to be written to disk upon `commit`. Therefore, there is still an I/O bottleneck on writes to `tempdb`. Also, there is no guarantee that additional cache will be used exclusively for `tempdb` because the data cache is shared by all databases in the system.

Putting *tempdb* in RAM

Microsoft SQL Server provides the option of creating `tempdb` in RAM. This allows the `tempdb` to be entirely memory-resident. Using `tempdb` in RAM is safe and will not harm database integrity or recoverability because `tempdb` is only used for intermediate operations and is re-initialized on each SQL Server restart.

Putting `tempdb` in RAM can provide significant performance improvement if it is very write intensive. However, if `tempdb` is not used effectively, the RAM allocated to `tempdb` is essentially wasted memory that could be used more appropriately as SQL Server data cache and could end up having an adverse impact on overall SQL Server performance.

The use of `tempdb` in RAM can accelerate `tempdb` operations but will deplete memory available for the SQL cache buffer, which reduces the amount of data pages that can fit in cache resulting in more physical I/O for regular table operations. Therefore, `tempdb` in RAM is only a viable solution if you have excess memory available in your system after meeting your data and procedure cache requirements.

Also, if you have a limited amount of RAM available on your system to be used for `tempdb`, this will constrain its maximum size unless you move it out of RAM. If unforeseen growth requirements for `tempdb` materialize, you will need to either add more memory to the system or move `tempdb` back to regular disk devices.

To determine whether placing `tempdb` in RAM might be beneficial for you, see if you meet the following conditions:

■ You have a significant amount of available system RAM (typically >= 128MB).

■ Your SQL Server cache hit ratio is poor, even with a lot of available buffer cache.

NOTE

You can determine your cache hit ratio by using SQL Performance Monitor. For information about using SQL Performance Monitor, see Chapter 32, "Measuring SQL Server Performance."

■ Your applications perform a lot of `tempdb` operations.

TIP

To determine the amount of `tempdb` activity, use `sp_lock` to monitor the locking activity in `tempdb` while queries are running.

Or you can monitor the number of objects being created in `tempdb` running a query against `sysindexes`. Here's an example:

```
SELECT SUM(id) FROM TEMPDB..SYSINDEXES
```

■ The `tempdb` operations are sized so that they will fit within the maximum size of `tempdb` made possible by your RAM configuration.

To determine the effectiveness of `tempdb` in RAM, perform the following steps:

1. Identify a set of sample queries that typify your most frequently performed `tempdb`-intensive operations.

2. Run these several times, noting the average execution time.

3. Reconfigure your system to put `tempdb` in RAM and run the identical queries. Note the difference in average execution time.

If the amount of improvement is not significant, it is probably better to take `tempdb` out of RAM and allocate the memory to SQL Server cache.

Faster Devices for *tempdb*

One other way to minimize I/O contention in tempdb is to place it on faster devices. These could be high-speed disk devices, disk devices with caching mechanisms, or, if supported by the operating system, *Solid State Disk* (SSD) devices. SSD devices are essentially nonvolatile RAM devices that appear to the operating system and SQL Server as standard storage devices. SSD devices contain a built-in backup mechanism to maintain its contents following a system or power failure. I/O rates to SSD devices are roughly equivalent to reads and writes from system memory.

> **NOTE**
>
> For tempdb, the backup mechanism of an SSD is not necessary because tempdb is re-initialized during SQL Server startup anyway. SSD devices are fairly expensive (approximately $70–100 per MB). With the ability to put tempdb in RAM, it would be more cost effective to add additional memory to the machine and assign it to tempdb. However, if you need a larger tempdb device than you have available RAM to allocate for tempdb in RAM, an SSD device could be used as an alternative solution.

By speeding up I/O operations in tempdb, you will not only minimize the I/O bottleneck; you will also be minimizing the potential for locking contention in tempdb. The shorter the amount of time it takes to create and insert data into a temporary table, the less time a lock will be held on the system tables.

A customer once reported that he was experiencing deadlocking problems in tempdb. Further research determined that the deadlocking was occurring on the system tables due to the number of users concurrently creating and dropping temporary tables. By placing tempdb in RAM, I/O operations were sped up considerably and the deadlocking problem went away. If you do not have sufficient RAM to configure tempdb in RAM, a Solid State Disk device is an alternative solution to this problem.

Disseminating Disk Resources

The goal of disseminating resources is to place the databases and logs within SQL Server across devices in such a way as to spread the I/O and minimize I/O contention. In an ideal world, we would have an unlimited supply of disk drives available so that we could place databases, logs, and objects on their own physical device when needed. However, very few of us, if any of us, live in such a world. We frequently have to make do with existing hardware.

The first 2MBs of tempdb exist by default on the master device. If tempdb activity is high, you might want to move this 2MB fragment off of master so tempdb I/O doesn't conflict with other activity on the master device. Unfortunately, SQL Server only allows you to expand `tempdb` onto another device, but not to move it off of the master device. So, how do you get rid of the 2MB slice of `tempdb`?

Well, if you are squeamish about directly modifying SQL Server system tables, you can simply drop the `default` and `logsegment` segments from the master device for `tempdb` after you have altered it to another device. This will prevent any temporary or worktables and the `tempdb` log from reading or writing the master device. However, the system segment will still be there, and system table reads and writes will still go to the master device. To move the system segment, you would need to define a user-defined segment `tempdb` on the master device first, because SQL Server requires that there be at least one segment defined on a database device.

With the previous solution, you can effectively get all of `tempdb` off the master device, but you will have a 2MB slice of the `master` database essentially unused. To move `tempdb` completely off the master device, you'll need to modify the system tables.

WARNING

Modifying the system tables requires that you have sufficient knowledge of the information contained in the system tables. Once you start playing around with system tables, you risk corrupting your system if you modify or delete the wrong information.

It is *strongly* recommended that you perform all system table modifications within a transaction. This way, you can verify your modifications before they are committed. If you really mess up your system tables, you can simply issue a `rollback` statement and you'll be back to square one to try again.

The general steps to move `tempdb` off of master are as follows:

1. Start SQL Server in single-user mode to prevent users from attempting to access `tempdb`. Booting in single-user mode also allows updates to the system tables.

2. Log in as `sa`.

3. Make a backup of the `master` database in case something goes horribly wrong and you need to restore `master`.

4. Create a dummy database on the desired device at the size you want `tempdb` to be. (You first need to create the device as well if the device does not already exist.)

5. Begin a transaction so you can roll back system table changes if an error is made.

6. Delete all references to the existing `tempdb` database from the `sysusages` and `sysdatabases` tables (that is, where `dbid = 2`).

7. Get the database ID for the `dummy` database and modify the `sysusages` and `sysdatabases` tables accordingly to change the `dummy` database references to `tempdb` (that is, change `dbid` in `sysusages` and `sysdatabases` to `2` and change the name in `sysdatabases` to `tempdb`).

8. Run `selects` against `sysusages` and `sysdatabases` to verify your changes to the system tables. If everything looks okay, commit the transaction; otherwise, roll back the transaction. Review the steps you performed to determine the cause of the problem and try again.

9. Shut down and restart SQL Server for the changes to take effect.

> **WARNING**
>
> This procedure should only be used on the `tempdb` database and not on any other database. Attempting this procedure on any database other than `tempdb` will corrupt that database. It only works on `tempdb` because `tempdb` is rebuilt each time the SQL Server is rebooted. Also be aware that incorrectly modifying the system tables can cause serious problems within the SQL Server.

The following code example displays a sample session. In this example, the new database which we are going to make `tempdb` will be called `newtemp`. The size of the new database will be 200 MB. We will create it on an existing device called `newdevice`. A dump device called `masterdump` has previously been defined as the dump device for the `master` database. The server has already been booted in single-user mode to allow updates to the system tables, and you are logged in as `sa`:

```
/* backup the master database */
dump database master to masterdump
go

/* create the database called newtemp on the device called newdevice */
/* This will eventually become the new tempdb */
create database newtemp on newdevice=200
go

/* remember to begin a transaction before modifying system tables!! */
begin tran
go

/* remove tempdb references for tempdb (dbid = 2)
   from sysusages and sysdatabases */
delete sysusages from sysusages u, sysdevices d
where vstart between low and high and dbid = 2
go

delete sysdatabases where dbid = 2
go

/* get the database id for the new database */
select name, dbid from sysdatabases
where name = 'newtemp'
```

```
go
name                               dbid
------------------------------ -------
newtemp                            10

/* modify the system table references to the dummy database
   to make it look like tempdb (set dbid = 2 and change name to tempdb) */
update sysusages set dbid=2 where dbid = 10
go

update sysdatabases set name='tempdb',dbid=2
where name =  'newtemp'
go

/* verify your modifications by checking sysdatabase and sysusages */

select name, dbid, suid, crdate from sysdatabases
where name = 'tempdb'
go
name                               dbid   suid   crdate
------------------------------ ------- ------ ----------------------
tempdb                               2      1   Dec  8 1994 10:36AM
select * from sysusages where dbid = 2
go
dbid    segmap      lstart      size         vstart
------ ----------- ----------- ----------- -----------
    2           7           0       51200    16793600
(1 row affected)

/* Everything looks okay, commit the changes */
commit tran
go

/* shutdown and restart SQL Server for changes to take effect */
shutdown with nowait
go
```

Other *tempdb* Performance Tips

When using `temp` tables for storing intermediate values, select only the columns actually required by the subsequent SQL statements into the temp table. This will help to reduce the size of the `temp` table and speed access of the data within the `temp` table because more rows will fit on a data page, reducing the number of data pages that will need to be accessed by the query. With a large number of users, this can help to minimize the amount of I/O and I/O contention within `tempdb`.

If a table in `tempdb` is going to be accessed frequently, consider creating indexes on `tempdb` tables where appropriate. The investment in time and space to create the index might be more than offset by the time and I/O savings that are realized if the table is frequently accessed or used in joins. Also, the index can be used to satisfy the queries rather than table scans.

TIP

SQL Server enables you to create temporary tables and indexes within a stored procedure and, subsequently, reference them within the same stored procedure. Unfortunately, at the time the queries are optimized, there is no data in the temp table for the query optimizer to estimate the index usefulness. By default, it assumes the table has 100 rows on 10 pages.

If you want SQL Server to optimize the query based upon actual data and index statistics, create the temporary table prior to executing the stored procedure that references it. You can do this easily by creating master procedures and subprocedures as follows:

```
create proc p1 as
select * into #tmp1 from customers
create index idx1 on #tmp1 (cust_id)
exec p2
return
go
create proc p2 as
select * from #tmp1 where id = 1001
return
go
```

The only thing to remember when implementing this solution is that the temporary table must exist at the time all stored procedures that reference it are created so that they can resolve the table's name. To do this, simply add a command in the stored procedure script file that creates the table. Only the table definition must exist, not any data in the table. You can use a where clause, which doesn't return any data rows, to create the temporary table template:

```
select * into #tmp1 from customers where 1 = 2
```

Cursors and Performance

SQL was originally designed as a set-oriented processing language. Queries, updates, and deletes operate on sets of data. The set can contain a single row or multiple rows. The where clause specified indicates which rows will be included in the set.

What if you want to examine the rows' contents and, based upon the values, perform an appropriate action? Within the original SQL language, this would require running multiple update processes, specifying different conditions in the where clause.

But what if you had the following situation?

- Increase the price of all items by 10 percent, where price is less than $50
- Decrease the price of all items by 15 percent, where price is greater than or equal to $50

If you tried to run these as two separate update statements, you could potentially update a row twice, no matter which order you run the queries. If an item was priced at $49.95, the first update would increase its price to $54.95 and it would then be updated again by the second update. Obviously, you have a dilemma.

Cursors were designed to give you the ability to handle these types of situations. Cursors give you a way of performing operations on a row-by-row basis.

However, this method of row-by-row access incurs significant processing overhead due to the looping constructs needed to step through the cursor result set one row at a time. The slower processing of cursors can result in increased locking contention between concurrent users.

You want to be careful to use cursors only when absolutely necessary. Often, cursor processing can be replaced by normal SQL set-oriented processing. Standard SQL set-oriented processing will typically run faster than a cursor performing equivalent operations even if it requires multiple table scans.

For example, consider the following cursor:

```
declare price_curs cursor for
select price from titles for update of price
go
declare @price money
open price_curs
fetch next from price_curs into @price
while (@@fetch_status <> -1)
begin
   if (@@fetch_status <> -2)
   begin
      if @price > $50
         update titles set price = price * $1.10
            where current of price_curs
      else if @price > $25
         update titles set price = price * $1.20
            where current of price_curs
      else
         update titles set price = price * $1.30
            where current of price_curs
   end
   fetch next from price_curs into @price
end

close price_curs
deallocate price_curs
```

The previous example does not need to be performed as a cursor because the result sets do not overlap. It could be replaced with the following code:

```
update titles set price = price * $1.10
   where price > $50
update titles set price = price * $1.20
   where price > $25
```

```
update titles set price = price * $1.30
  where price <= $25
```

In testing against a 5000-row table, the second example has been observed to run approximately 2.5 times faster than the same processing performed as a cursor.

> **NOTE**
>
> Although cursor processing is slower than set-oriented processing, there are times when row-by-row processing can improve the concurrent access to the data.
>
> Consider an update to price for all rows in the items table. With normal set-oriented processing, this would require a table-level lock, locking out all other access to the table until the update completes. With a cursor, locking is performed at the page level. This allows access to other pages in the table by other user processes. If each row is committed as a single transaction, the cursor will typically only lock a single page at a time.
>
> Be aware, however, that committing each row individually could generate significantly more log records.

Text and Image Columns and Performance

Inappropriate datatype selection is a common error for database designers new to Microsoft SQL Server. One of the more common mistakes made is the inappropriate use of the text or image datatype.

Remember from Chapter 4, "Transact-SQL Datatypes," that text and image columns are stored as a 16-byte pointer in the data row, pointing to a separate linked chain of pages to store the text/image data.

What will often happen is that the database designer will often decide, "I need a column for 4 to 5 lines of free-format comments. char doesn't get big enough, so I'll use text."

The problems with text and image columns should cause you to think twice before using them. These problems range from potentially enormous space consumption to a serious performance impact. Let's look closely at the drawbacks, and then consider some alternative implementations for storing large text and image data.

Text and image columns can demand a substantial amount of storage overhead in your database. Each row in the table storage itself includes a 16-byte pointer to the first page in a page chain. (If the data in the text or image column is null, the pointer is null as well.) To store the actual BLOB data, SQL Server allocates space for text data in each row in a linked chain of 2KB pages.

> **NOTE**
>
> This is an extremely important point. The server will not pack text data to use space efficiently. If the text column in a row contains the string, "Hello, World!," those 13 characters will occupy an entire 2KB data page. One million rows worth of text columns like that will take up 2GB, where they would only take up 13MB if stored in a conventional `varchar` column.

> **NOTE**
>
> See Chapter 10, "Understanding SQL Server Storage Structures," for the details of text and image storage.

When you update a row containing a text column, the amount of information logged could create a serious performance problem. Text columns can be updated without logging using the `writetext` command, but this has an impact on the recoverability of your database because the text data inserted is not logged.

> **NOTE**
>
> To allow nonlogged modifications such as a `writetext` requires that the `select into/ bulk copy` option be turned on for that database. This disables transaction log dumps.

In addition, any read of text/image data would require a minimum of two page I/Os (one read of the data page to get the text/image pointer and at least one page read for the text/image data).

There are some basic workarounds to avoid the problems of text and image datatypes:

- *Store it somewhere else.* This is not as dumb as it seems. Lots of applications store only the pathname to an operating-system file containing the text or image data. The path is returned to the application, which in turn executes an operating system file `open` command to read the data. (Lots of commercial applications are written this way. There are some intricacies in implementing security, but the database application may run more smoothly.)

- *Use* `varchar(255)` *or* `varbinary(255)`. Stringing together a set of `varchar` or `varbinary` columns from a sequential set of rows will take a little extra application work, but eliminating the overhead of the BLOBs may provide better performance. (For an example of this, look at how SQL Server stores the text of stored procedures, views, triggers, rules, and defaults in the `system` table and `syscomments`.) Another alternative is to break the text/image data across multiple varchar(255) or varbinary(255) columns within a single row. Again, your application program will need to break the data into the appropriate columns on insert and combine them on retrieval.

This approach can help to improve performance by reducing search time for Like strings, reducing storage overhead and I/O. The multi-column approach is not feasible, however, if your data rows exceed the SQL Server maximum allowable row size of 1962 bytes.

■ *Store the text or image information in a related table.* In the pubs database, the pub_info table stores BLOB data separate from the actual publishers table. This improves the performance of updates on the publishers table, and the pr_info (text) and logo (image) columns can be placed in a table on a separate database, allowing a nonlogged writetext.

Summary

There are a number of performance issues to be addressed when working with SQL Server besides server configuration and query tuning. We've looked at only a subset of those issues in this chapter, but they are most common issues within standard environments. Mostly, these are issues that you need to be aware of when working in a SQL Server environment so that you can prevent potential performance problems or address them accordingly if they should arise.

Common
Performance and
Tuning Problems

22

When tuning the performance of SQL Server, there are a number of esoteric features that can be tweaked and tuned to improve overall performance. However, when trying to diagnose existing performance problems, a number of items could be potential culprits. How do you know where to begin to look to track down the performance problem?

Having a good understanding of the preceding chapters will help you to understand how SQL Server processes queries so that you can identify the causes of performance problems and ways to improve them. However, it's one thing to understand the technology, and another to know how to apply it.

In my years as a SQL Server consultant, I've been called in on a number of occasions to track down performance problems. What I've learned is that the majority of performance problems have similar causes, typically the types of mistakes made by developers and DBAs who are new to SQL Server and don't have a full understanding of how SQL Server optimizes queries. Admittedly, I made many of those same mistakes in the past as well.

What I've learned over the years is that it helps to try to identify the common causes of performance problems before delving into areas such as spreading I/O across devices or denormalizing the database. This chapter takes a look at some of the more common causes of performance problems and presents ways to work around or prevent them.

Out-of-Date or Unavailable Statistics

A couple of years ago I was conducting a performance evaluation of an application at a customer site when the manager of another application-development group in the department asked if I could spend a few minutes with one of their developers to take a look at a performance problem they were experiencing. I had some free time later in the afternoon and decided to take a look at it.

The programmer's description of the problem was that initially the queries that populated the screen used to return values with subsecond response time, but over time the application was getting slower as they added data to the tables. This behavior set off a light bulb in my head and prompted me to ask the obvious question, a question so obvious I was almost embarrassed to ask it: "When was the last time you ran update statistics?" His answer was, "What is that?"

The moral of this story is, don't neglect to ask the obvious question. We ran update statistics on the entire database and, like magic, all queries went back to subsecond response time. The problem was solved in a total of about five minutes from diagnosis to solution.

What tipped me off was that the behavior the programmer described was textbook behavior of a database with out-of-date statistics, or no statistics at all (refer to Chapter 12, "Understanding the Query Optimizer," for a detailed discussion of index statistics and how they are used by the optimizer). This often occurs in development environments or newly created production databases. Remember, if indexes are created on empty tables, no index statistics are generated.

Without valid statistics to use, the query optimizer must use built-in statistics to estimate index usefulness, which often leads to invalid row and page estimates and might result in the wrong index or a table scan being used to process the query. A table scan might not present a noticeable performance problem when the table is only a few data pages in size, but as data is added and the table grows, performance begins to degrade more noticeably. When you see this behavior, it's a good indicator that index statistics need to be updated.

> **TIP**
>
> If you've updated the statistics on your tables and/or indexes, don't forget to run `sp_recompile` on those tables. Any existing stored procedures in procedure cache have a query plan associated with them based on the table statistics from the first time they were run. To force them to generate a new query plan based on the updated statistics, run the `sp_recompile` stored procedure on the tables. All stored procedures that reference those table(s) will compile a new query plan on the next execution.

Search Argument Problems

It's the curse of SQL that there are a number of ways to write a query and get the same result sets—some queries, however, might not be as efficient as others. A good understanding of the query optimizer will help you avoid writing *search arguments* (SARGs) that SQL Server cannot optimize effectively. This section highlights some of the common "gotchas" encountered in SQL Server SARGs that can lead to poor or unexpected performance.

No SARGs

Watch out for queries in which the SARG might have inadvertently been left out, like this:

```
select title_id from titles
```

A SQL query with no search argument (that is, no `where` clause) always performs a table scan unless a nonclustered index can be used to cover the query (refer to Chapter 14, "Analyzing Query Plans," for a discussion of index covering). If you don't want the query to affect the entire table, be sure to specify a valid SARG that matches an index on the table in order to avoid table scans.

Negative Logic

Any *negative logic* (for example, `!=`, `<>`, `not in`) always results in a table scan being performed, unless index covering can be applied (that is, all columns contained in the query can be found within the leaf level of a nonclustered index). An example of a SQL statement containing negative logic is as follows:

```
select * from orders
where price != $10.95
```

The not in or not equal (!= or <>) statement is not considered a SARG by the SQL Server optimizer and is not evaluated for index matching. This typically results in a table scan (unless an index covers the query) to resolve the query. When faced with a !=, consider any possible ways to rewrite the query. For example, if you know (based on your data integrity rules) that price cannot be less than 0, the following query

```
select * from orders
where price != 0
```

or

```
select * from orders
where price is not null
```

can be written, and might perform better if written like this:

```
select * from orders
where price > 0
```

This query might perform better than either of the previous two because it avoids the negative logic and is treated as a SARG. The supplied constant value enables SQL Server to examine the distribution page to estimate the number of rows to be returned in order to determine if an index can be used to satisfy the query rather than a table scan.

Operations on a Column in a *where* Clause

Any operation on the column side of a where clause causes it not to be treated as a SARG by SQL Server. Therefore, the optimizer cannot use an index to match the SARG with an index; a table scan must be performed to satisfy the query. Examples of this type of where statement are

```
select * from orders
where price * 2 < $50.00
```

and

```
select * from customers
where substring(last_name, 1, 1) = "P"
```

These two queries could be rewritten as

```
select * from orders
where price < $50.00/2
```

or

```
select * from customers
where last_name like "P%"
```

As rewritten, the queries return the same result set, but the where clauses are now treated as SARGs. The optimizer can now consider using an index to satisfy these queries rather than performing a table scan. The query against the customers table uses the distribution steps to estimate the number of rows where name begins with P. In SQL Server 6.0, the optimizer will evaluate the arithmetic expression prior to optimization and also use the the distribution steps to estimate the number of matching rows. This is much better than limiting the optimizer to a table scan because the optimizer cannot treat the expression as a optimizable SARG.

Unknown Constant Values in a *where* Clause

The previous discussion brings up an interesting point regarding how the optimizer treats constant expressions where the value *cannot* be known until runtime. These are expressions that contain subqueries or local variables. The SQL Server treats these expressions as SARGs but cannot use the distribution steps because it doesn't have a value to compare against the steps at query compile time. What it does in this situation is use the *index density* information. Index density is stored on the distribution page for the index along with the distribution steps and is a float value representing the average number of rows that would match against any given value for the index. The index density value is based on the uniqueness of the index. A less unique index will have a higher index density—that is, a greater percentage of rows may match any given value. (For an in-depth discussion of index density and distribution steps, please read Chapter 11, "Designing Indexes for Performance").

The optimizer will generally be able to better estimate the number of rows affected by a query when it can compare a known value against the distribution steps than when it has to use the index density to estimate the average number of rows that match an unknown value. This is especially true if the data in a table is not distributed evenly. When you can, you should try to avoid using constant expressions that cannot be evaluated until runtime so that the distribution steps can be used rather than the density value.

To avoid using constant expressions that cannot be evaluated until runtime in where clauses, consider putting the queries into stored procedures and passing in the constant expression as a parameter. Because the optimizer evaluates the value of a parameter prior to optimization, SQL Server will evaluate the expression prior to optimizing the stored procedure. For example, the following query contains a search clause with a local variable. The value of the local variable will not be known until runtime, so the index density would have to be used to estimate the number of affected rows:

```
declare @avg_price money
select @avg_price = avg(price) from orders
select * from orders
   where price < @avg_price
```

To avoid using the subquery or local variable in a where clause when comparing the price column in the orders table against the average price, create the following procedure:

```
create proc proc1 (@var1 money)
as
   select * from orders
      where price < @var1
```

Now use an assignment select statement to retrieve the average price into a local variable and pass it into the stored procedure as a parameter as follows:

```
declare @avg_price money
select @avg_price = avg(price) from orders
exec proc1 @var1
```

In this example, @var1 is evaluated and a query plan is generated for the stored procedure using a known value, so the distribution steps are used instead of the index density to estimate the number of rows that are less than the specified price contained in the parameter @var1. This results in a more accurate estimate of the number of affected rows. More accurate row estimates will typically result in more efficient query plans being chosen.

So for best results when writing queries inside stored procedures, use stored procedure parameters in your SARGs whenever possible rather than local variables. This allows the optimizer to optimize the query by using distribution steps, comparing the distribution steps against the parameter value. If you use local variables as SARGs in stored procedures, the optimizer is restricted to using index density, even if the local variable is assigned the value of a parameter.

If you ever need to perform an operation on a parameter inside the stored procedure, do it before using the parameter in a SARG and store the new value back into the parameter itself or, better yet, perform the operation on the parameter right within the SARG. For example, the following two procedures will return the same results, but will be optimized differently:

```
create proc proc1 (@var1 money)
as
    select @var1 = @var1 * 2
    select * from orders
      where price < @var1

create proc proc2 (@var1 money)
as
    select * from orders
      where price < @var1 *2
```

For the first procedure, proc1, the select against the orders table is optimized based upon the value passed into @var1 when the stored procedure is called, not the value @var1 contains during execution. If the value of 10 is passed in to @var1 when the procedure is first executed, the optimizer will use 10 as the value for @var1 to compare against the distribution steps for an index on price. At optimization time, the previous select statement that assigns a new value to @var1, select @var1 = @var1 * 2 has not yet been executed, so the original value of @var1 (10) is used to optimize the query. Even though this is not the value @var1 will contain when the query is actually executed, this method is still often preferable to using local variables because the distribution steps can still be used to optimize the query rather than index density or built in optimizer statistics.

The second procedure, proc2, however, *will* evaluate the expression in the SARG, @var1 * 2, and use the value of 20 to optimize the query the first time it is executed, comparing 20 against the distribution steps for an index on price. This is because SQL Server 6.0 evaluates the expression in the SARG before optimization. This should result in a more accurate row estimate using the distribution steps than would be obtained for proc1, and possibly a more efficient query plan to retrieve the same result set.

TIP

If you need to maintain the original value of a parameter for use later in the procedure, save it in a local variable and reassign it back to the parameter when needed, as in the following example:

```
create proc proc3 (@var1 money)
as
declare @initval money

select @initval = @var1

select @var1 = avg(price) * 2 from orders
select * from orders
     where price < @var1

select @var1 = @initval
select * from orders
     where price > @var1
```

When this procedure is optimized, the original value of @var1 will be used to optimize the final select statement in the procedure.

NOTE

For more information on stored procedure optimization, please read Chapter 13.

Datatype Mismatch

This used to be a problem in earlier releases of SQL Server but appears to have been eliminated in SQL Server 6.0. Previously, if the value being compared against the column was of a different datatype, the index statistics couldn't be used. This was especially easy to do in stored procedures when a char or varchar parameter was being compared in a SARG against a varchar or char column, respectively.

NOTE

Remember, SQL Server stores a char column that permits nulls as a varchar. Therefore, to match a parameter datatype to a column defined as char(10) null, you need to make sure you define the parameter as varchar(10) to ensure the datatypes match.

When examining the index-selection process in SQL Server 6.0 using the DBCC TRACEON (302) trace flags (as described in Chapter 14), observe that SQL Server 6.0 now converts the value to the datatype of the column prior to checking the index statistics, as long as an implicit conversion between the datatypes could be performed (for example, float converts to int and char converts to varchar, but char doesn't convert to int). To be on the safe side, however, it is still recommended that you try to match the datatype of the constant expression with the column datatypes.

or Logic in the *where* Clause

An or clause might cause a worktable to be created if the optimizer chooses to apply the *OR strategy* to create a dynamic index (refer to Chapter 12, "Understanding the Query Optimizer," for a discussion of the OR strategy). The dynamic index is created and used to process the query rather than a table scan if the I/O cost of creating and using the dynamic index is less than the I/O cost of a table scan.

> **NOTE**
>
> Remember, an in clause is treated like an or clause by SQL Server.
>
> For example:
>
> ```
> select * from titles
> where title_id in ("BU3075", "BU1025")
> ```
>
> is the same as
>
> ```
> select * from titles
> where title_id = "BU3075" OR title_id = "BU1025"
> ```

If any one of the search clauses must be resolved by a table scan, a single table scan is performed to resolve the query. Also, if the resulting cost of using the dynamic index is estimated to exceed the cost of a table scan, a table scan is performed.

If you are trying to avoid table scans when you have or clauses in your queries, make sure that all clauses involved in the or can be supported by an index and that the index is selective enough to avoid a table scan.

Other Query-Related Issues

The majority of performance-related problems are a result of the way a query is written. The SQL language allows a number of additional clauses and keywords to sort and group the data in different ways. Unfortunately, this incurs extra work and my cause queries to run more slowly. This section identifies some additional perfromance issues to be aware of when writing SQL queries and offers some tips to improve query performance.

The *distinct* Keyword

The distinct keyword causes a worktable to be created in tempdb for sorting and removing duplicate rows. This can seriously affect performance if the query returns a large result set because the entire result set is copied into a worktable in tempdb and sorted, and then the duplicates are removed before SQL Server sends the results to the client application. This can significantly add to the response time of the query and increase the amount of I/O performed on tempdb.

For single-table queries, if all columns of a unique index are included in the select list, the unique index guarantees that each row is unique and the worktable can be avoided. For multi-table queries, each table must also have a unique index on the join columns.

TIP

Watch out for overuse and misuse of the distinct keyword. I was once at a client site where they were complaining about query response time in their applications. It was several minutes before any rows were being returned to the client application, even for single-table queries. As it turned out, they were using the distinct keyword in every query being issued, even for join queries where no duplicate rows were being returned, because one of the tables had a unique index that was being retrieved. Dropping the distinct keyword from the queries resulted in data results being returned to the client application in seconds rather than minutes.

Be aware of instances when a unique index avoids duplicate rows in your result set, but the optimizer still insists on using a worktable to ensure that no duplicates are returned. Also, you should simply avoid using distinct unless absolutely necessary.

The *count()* Function

The count(*) function, without a where clause, results in a table scan unless there is a nonclustered index on the table that can be used to cover the query. For the following query, the smallest nonclustered index can be used to satisfy this query because SQL Server can determine how many rows are in the table by counting the number of rows in the smallest nonclustered index:

```
select count(*) from customers
```

However, if the query contains a where clause, a clustered or nonclustered index would need to exist on one of the SARGs to avoid a full table scan.

> **TIP**
>
> If you only want to determine the existence of a row in a table without needing to know the exact count, use the `if exists…` statement rather than `select count(*)…`. The `if exists…` statement discontinues processing as soon as a matching row is found, whereas `select count (*)…` continues processing to look for all matching rows.

> **NOTE**
>
> Remember also that the `count(colname)` function counts all non-NULL values for a column in a table. Unlike `count(*)`, a query with a `count(colname)` function will only be covered by an index if the column being counted is contained in a nonclustered index. If no nonclustered exists which contains the column, SQL Server will need to scan the entire table to count the non-NULL values, even if the column is defined as `NOT NULL`.

Whether an index can be used to satisfy a `count()` function or not, a single-column, single-row worktable will still automatically be created in `tempdb` for the purpose of calculating and storing the count. This will require a second step in the query plan to retrieve the count from the worktable.

Aggregate Clauses

Aggregates such as `avg`, `min`, `max` and `sum`, without a `where` clause, generally cause table scans unless the query can be satisfied by an index. Here is an example:

```
select sum(qty) from orders
    where order_num = "3124"
```

If an index exists on the `orders` table and contains the `order_num` column, the query can be satisfied by finding the data rows via the index and calculating the sum of `qty`. If an index exists on the `order_num` and `qty` columns, the query can be satisfied by scanning the index rows without having to access the actual data rows at all.

Also, the following query would be covered by the index and thus avoid a table scan if the index were created on the `qty` column:

```
select sum(qty) from salesdetail
```

If you are expecting an index to cover an aggregate query, but the query optimizer is performing a table scan, make sure that the query truly is covered by the index. All columns in the select list, as well as all columns in the where clause, must be included in the index definition.

Also, as with the count() function, a single column, single-row worktable will automatically be created in tempdb for each aggregate function in the query for the purpose of calculating and storing the aggregate value. Be aware of the increased I/O that occurs from writing to tempdb, as well as the performance considerations related to tempdb (refer to Chapter 21, "Miscellaneous Performance Topics," for a detailed discussion of tempdb performance issues).

TIP

If you want to retrieve the max and min values for a table on an indexed column, it is actually cheaper in terms of total I/O and processing time to run them as separate select statements rather than combine them in a single statement. This is because SQL Server cannot walk an index structure in two different directions. For example, to resolve the following query on customers with a nonclustered index on id,

```
select min(id), max(id) from customers
```

the query would be covered by the index, but would find the min(id) by reading the first row on the first page of the leaf level of the index. Then, to find the max(id), it would have to scan the entire leaf level of the index until it found the last row on the last page (see Figure 22.1). Based on the index in Figure 22.1, it would cost five page reads to find the min and max in a single query.

However, if you ran a query to retrieve just the min value, it would cost only one page. SQL Server would simply read the first row on the first page in the leaf level. (Remember from Chapter 10, "Understanding SQL Server Storage Structures," that the location of the leaf page is stored in the sysindexes table, so SQL Server does not need to traverse the index tree to find the leaf page).

To retrieve the max value, SQL Server would start at the root page and traverse the index tree, following the last row on the last page at each level until it got to the last row on the leaf level. Refer to Figure 22.1 again and note that this would cost two page reads (the root page plus the last leaf index page).

Therefore, the total number of pages read for two separate queries is only three pages versus five. This example only saves two pages, but in much larger tables and indexes, the I/O savings can be substantial.

FIGURE 22.1.

Finding the min *and* max *values in the leaf pages of a nonclustered or clustered index.*

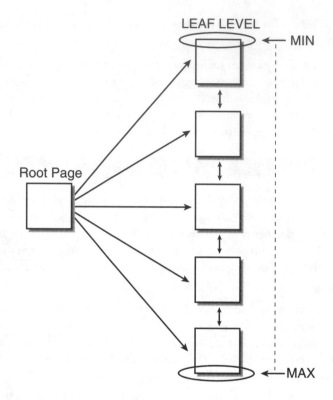

Order by and group by

The group by and order by clauses need to use tempdb as a work area for sorting and grouping the result set. When processing a small result set, the response should be subsecond. When a large result set is returned, response time can increase significantly due to the increased I/O in the tempdb database.

With the order by clause, you can avoid a worktable under two circumstances. The first is if there is a clustered index on the table and the result set is being ordered by the clustered index. Due to the nature of the clustered index, SQL Server knows the data is already sorted by the clustered index.

> **WARNING**
>
> If you are ordering by the clustered index but have a search argument on a column that has a nonclustered index that is used to resolve the query, a worktable will be generated to sort the result set because the result set is being retrieved in nonclustered index order rather than in clustered index order.

A worktable can also be avoided for an order by if the order by clause matches the SARG and the SARG can be satisfied by a nonclustered index, like the following:

```
select * from customer
    where id between 10 and 20
    order by id
```

Because the result set is being retrieved in nonclustered index order already, additional sorting is not required.

NOTE

In versions of Microsoft SQL Server prior to version 6.0, if you had an order by … DESC clause in your query, a worktable would have be generated in tempdb by the SQL Server to do the sorting because SQL Server was unable to retrieve the data in descending sort order.

SQL Server 6.0 can now perform reverse index scans. If an index is used to retrieve the data and the data is being sorted in descending index order by an order by … DESC clause, the index can now be scanned in reverse order and a worktable is not necessary to re-sort the final result set.

If you have any group by clauses in your queries, a worktable will always be generated by SQL Server to perform the grouping and the calculation of the aggregate(s) for each group.

Join Clauses

When running troublesome queries with the showplan option on, watch out for the following showplan message: Worktable created for REFORMATTING. This indicates that no useful indexes were available to satisfy the query, and the optimizer has therefore determined that it is more efficient to build a temporary clustered index on the inner table in tempdb on the fly rather than incur the I/O and processing cost of joining via iterative table scans.

WARNING

This can be a very costly solution in terms of additional I/O and tempdb usage. It is better to provide queries with the appropriate indexes rather than letting the optimizer generate one on the fly. If you see the reformatting message in the showplan output, you should perform a query analysis and reexamine your indexing strategy.

You also want to be careful to avoid and watch out for Cartesian products between tables in a join due to a missing join clause. Remember, as a general rule of thumb, if there are *n* tables in a query, there should be at least *n*-1 join clauses.

Provide All Join Options in Join Clauses

You can improve join performance in joins of three or more tables that share a key by providing all possible join clauses in the query.

The key to fast joins is selecting an efficient join order. When the server *joins*, it gets a value from one table and then looks for corresponding values in the next inner table. The order the tables are processed determines the amount of work required to answer the query.

The server uses the join clauses you provide in the query to define the universe of possible join orders. For example, if you write the following:

```
select *
   from titles t,salesdetail sd,titleauthor ta
   where t.title_id = sd.title_id
   and sd.title_id = ta.title_id
```

you have the following two possible join orders:

titles	→	salesdetail	→	titleauthor
titleauthor	→	salesdetail	→	titles

These two join orders are possible because of the two join clauses specified in the query.

Add the third leg of the triangle (t.title_id = ta.title_id) to the query to provide more possible join orders. (See Figure 22.2.)

FIGURE 22.2.

Adding the third join clause completes a triangle of join tables and gives the server complete freedom to choose the most efficient join order.

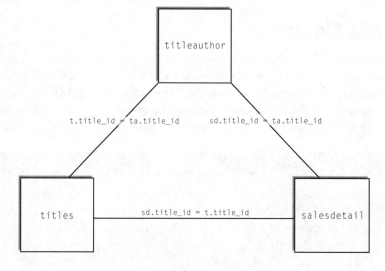

```
select *
from titles t,salesdetail sd,titleauthor ta
where t.title_id = sd.title_id
and sd.title_id = ta.title_id
and t.title_id = ta.title_id
```

Logically you haven't added anything (you will get the same result), but you have provided more possible join orders. There are three join conditions specified, so there are now six possible join conditions:

titles	→	salesdetail	→	titleauthor
titleauthor	→	salesdetail	→	titles
titles	→	titleauthor	→	salesdetail
titleauthor	→	titles	→	salesdetail
salesdetail	→	titleauthor	→	titles
salesdetail	→	titles	→	titleauthor

This means that with the additional join clause, you can actually triple your potential number of join orders. You won't necessarily always get a faster result, but you do improve your chances of getting that faster result.

SQL Server Configuration

SQL Server configuration has an impact on overall system performance. One of the most important configuration issues to examine when tracking down performance problems is SQL Server memory configuration.

> **NOTE**
>
> For a more detailed discussion about memory configuration and some of the more esoteric SQL Server configuration parameters and how they affect SQL Server performance, refer to Chapter 31, "Optimizing SQL Server Configuration Options."

Memory

Memory is probably the most important SQL Server configuration variable in relation to performance. The more data that can be accessed and worked on in data cache, the faster the system performs. You want to make sure that sufficient data cache has been configured for the databases and for the queries being run; don't assume that memory has been configured properly.

For example, I was at a customer site during a performance and tuning (P&T) engagement and asked them how much memory was on the machine. They reported to me that there was 48MB available. Mistakenly, I assumed that was how much they had configured for SQL Server.

One query in question was taking approximately 6 hours to run to retrieve 50,000 records. I tried running it with the showplan and noexec options on, and the query plan generated by `showplan` indicated the optimizer was using the expected index to process the query. I then turned off the `noexec` option and let the query run and noticed it was performing a significant amount of physical I/O.

At this point I decided to take a look at the SQL Server configuration and discovered that the SQL Server was only configured at 8MB of memory. No one had ever reconfigured it after installation!

Anyway, we increased the memory configuration to 32MB, which allowed all data pages required by the query to remain in memory. This also helped to significantly reduce the runtime of the query. Overall, we were able to cut the time required to run the query by about 6 hours—down to approximately 20 seconds!

Physical Database Design

The physical design of a database can have an impact on overall database performance. This section identifies some of the more common physical design issues to consider when tracking down performance issues or tuning the performance of a database.

Indexes

Watch out for missing indexes. You should verify that all indexes have been created as defined in design documentation. A common performance problem results from developers writing queries based on expected indexes that might have been created differently or not created at all. The queries, then, do not use the expected index, thus adversely affecting performance.

Over-Indexing

Avoid over-indexing your tables whenever possible in an *On-Line Transaction Processing* (OLTP) environment. Perform a thorough transaction-and-query analysis to carefully map out which indexes are really needed. You typically want to identify the most critical, highest-priority transactions that should be supported by indexes.

Index Selection

Poor index selection is another tuning item you should examine. Chapter 11, "Designing Indexes for Performance," contains a detailed discussion about index selection and usefulness. The following are a few things to keep in mind:

- For the SQL Server optimizer to consider using a composite index to process a query, at least the first ordered column in the index must be specified in the `where` clause.
- The first element in the index should be the most unique (if possible), and index column order in general should be from most to least unique in a compound key.

However, remember that selectivity doesn't help if you don't use the first ordered index column in your where clause, so choose the first ordered column that will also be used most in queries.

■ Understand that choosing the clustered index for the primary key is correct only some of the time. A more useful alternative is to choose the column(s) that will be accessed by ranges of data ("Give me all the consumers whose ages are between 25 and 45") or for grouping ("Give me sales by customer").

Clustered Indexes

Check to see if clustered indexes are being used effectively. Any table, if it has only one index, should typically have a clustered index before a nonclustered index because the overhead involved with maintaining clustered indexes is less than for nonclustered indexes. Also, the space required for a clustered index is significantly less than for a nonclustered index because the clustered index typically has one level less than a similar nonclustered index. This also helps improve query performance because it results in one less page-read-per-row lookup than does a nonclustered index on the same column.

Examine your clustered-indexing strategy closely. Too often, the clustered index is automatically assigned to the primary key. This is fine if it is the exclusive access path to that table and is used frequently in joins. However, there are other situations when it might be more efficient to create the clustered index on a different column(s) and create a nonclustered unique index to maintain and support the primary key.

Other possible candidates for a clustered index include the column or columns used most frequently to access data in the table, columns frequently specified in order by clauses, and columns frequently used for range retrievals.

> **TIP**
>
> Clustered indexes support range retrievals well because the data within the range is grouped together, minimizing the number of data pages that need to be accessed to retrieve the data rows. For further discussion on selecting clustered versus nonclustered indexes, refer to Chapter 14.

Avoid Hot Spots

Watch out for potential *hot spots* when inserting or updating data. Hot spots occur when the most recently inserted rows are clustered together. This typically occurs in tables without a clustered index because SQL Server inserts all new data rows at the end of the table. It can also occur with a clustered index if the clustered index exists on a sequential key and data is inserted in sequential-key order.

If the most recently inserted rows are also the most often accessed, there can be locking contention and potential deadlock problems on those data/index pages between multiple users. Consider implementing a clustered index that will spread the data throughout the table, thus avoiding hot spots. For example, if you have an orders table with a sequential key on order_id and data is inserted in sequential order, you might want to consider creating a nonclustered index on order_id and placing a clustered index on product_id so that new order entries are spread randomly throughout the table by product_id.

DSS versus OLTP

Try to avoid mixing *Decision Support System* (DSS) activities with high-load OLTP activity. DSS queries are often long-running and CPU-intensive, causing a slowdown of other transaction activity. In addition, DSS queries and reports typically require a large number of supporting indexes. The greater the number of indexes, the greater the overhead necessary to maintain all those indexes during update processing.

If possible, consider setting up a separate server on a separate machine with duplicate data for performing DSS tasks. This way, you can index the DSS system as heavily as needed and the DSS reports won't affect the OLTP activities.

> **NOTE**
>
> This topic is covered in more detail in Chapter 17, "Database Design Issues and Performance," and Chapter 37, "Administering Very Large SQL Server Databases."

Historical versus Active Data

You should check to see if a large amount of historical data that is rarely accessed is being kept online with recent, more active data. If so, consider moving the historical data off into a separate table or database to make the active table smaller. This reduces the amount of data and index pages that need to be searched and also reduces the overhead of index maintenance by making the index trees smaller. This topic is also covered in detail in Chapters 17 and 37.

Locking Issues

Watch out for obvious locking-contention problems, which can severely impact system performance. Some of the more likely culprits are disconnected client processes that have left a session in the SQL Server that is still holding locks, transactions that enable user input causing locks to be held for indeterminate periods of time, and nested transactions that don't fully commit properly (thus leaving locks held within a session).

> **TIP**
>
> For a complete discussion of locking issues and solutions, please refer to Chapter 15, "Locking and Performance."

Maintenance Activities

Watch out for maintenance activities, such as dump/load and DBCC, that could occur during normal processing periods. They are very I/O- and CPU-intensive and can have considerable impact on the performance of other online activities.

Summary

A number of potential causes and solutions to performance problems exist within SQL Server. Having a good understanding of the performance issues and SQL Server operations makes you effectively equipped to address and solve performance problems. You should now also have a good feel for the more likely culprits to examine to identify and solve performance problems quickly.

If you've considered and looked into the common problems addressed in this chapter and ruled them out as the cause of your performance problems, it might be time to dig a little deeper into the SQL Server. Just remember, when all else fails, feel free to give Tech Support a call. Who knows? You might have been one of the lucky(?) souls to uncover a bug or "undocumented feature" within SQL Server. Believe me, I've seen my share of those in the years that I have been working with SQL Server.

IN THIS PART

PART

IV

System Administration

Roles and Responsibilities of the System Administrator

23

This chapter looks at the roles and responsibilities of a SQL Server system administrator and how these roles differ from or overlap with those of a database or operating system administrator. You learn critical terminology and explore the following key concepts:

- System tables
- System stored procedures

Components of SQL Server

Recall from Chapter 2, "The Microsoft Client/Server Architecture," that the SQL Server environment consists of clients, servers, and a network that enables them to communicate. Let's review each of these components to understand the broad spectrum of administration required to keep SQL Server operational.

Client components include the following:

- Workstation hardware
- Network interface card (NIC)
- Operating system
- Network software
- Network library software
- Database library software (db-library/ODBC)
- Application software

These are the network components:

- Server and client NIC
- Network software
- Hubs, routers, and concentrators
- Cable

The following are server components:

- Server hardware
- NIC
- Windows NT Server
- Network software
- Network library software
- Server library software
- SQL Server software

As the SQL Server system administrator, you are probably only *officially* responsible for the SQL Server software and the various client libraries, but consider a different question: When the server becomes unavailable, which of these components could be the culprit? The answer is any of them. Client/server requires a mastery of several disciplines to maintain solid, reliable performance day in and day out.

As system administrator, you need to muster a team of experts—in client software, server software, and all the networking layers in between. As you work through this chapter, map the examples to your environment; this will enhance your capability for troubleshooting problems as they arise.

> **NOTE**
>
> People who are worried about job security in the client/server world should think about all the areas of expertise that are required to make a complex system such as SQL Server really work. Here's a very brief list of specializations:
>
> - Project manager
> - Analyst
> - Relational database designer
> - SQL Server administrator
> - Network/LAN (for example, Windows NT) administrator
> - Network administrator
> - Help-desk staff
> - Database administrator
> - Client OS (for example, Windows 95) specialist
> - Applications programmer

SQL Server Versions

SQL Server has been around for a number of years, and many releases and versions are in production in companies around the world. Microsoft first shipped SQL Server 1.0 for OS/2 in 1988, and it was actually Microsoft's first database product. At this early stage in the relationship, Sybase was responsible for actually porting the 32-bit UNIX version of SQL Server to 16-bit OS/2.

Microsoft followed version 1.0 with version 1.1, but both of these were quickly superseded by SQL Server 4.2 for OS/2. Version 4.2 introduced "feature set parity" with the major releases of Sybase SQL Server, which, depending on the platform, had version numbers between 4.0

and 4.2. Sybase continued to introduce new versions, such as 4.8 and 4.9x, and those enhancements weren't folded into the OS/2 version of SQL Server until an update, 4.2a (and then 4.2b), shipped concurrently with the first release of SQL Server for Windows NT.

SQL Server 4.2 for Windows NT was an interesting product. It represented Microsoft's coming-of-age in the development of this application because approximately 70 percent of the database kernel was completely rewritten and optimized for Windows NT. Microsoft's own marketing of the product caused some confusion about this point, however. Microsoft kept the 4.2 version number to ease people's concerns about compatibility—Release 4.8 from Sybase required extensive (and expensive) upgrade costs, and Microsoft put backward compatibility with the OS/2 server at the top of its feature list.

However, the database engine actually had features that would debut in Sybase 4.9.2, and even System 10. In fact, SQL Server 4.2 for Windows NT from Microsoft has the same query optimization enhancements that Sybase originally put in to the System 10 SQL Server.

Microsoft immediately differentiated SQL Server for Windows NT by re-architecting the database kernel—and writing it as a Win32 process so that it could only run on Windows NT. Hardware portability, provided by Sybase through various releases on various versions of UNIX, was accomplished through Windows NT's portability to both Intel-based and RISC-based platforms. Supported platforms for Windows NT now include MIPS, DEC Alpha AXP, and IBM/Apple/Motorola's PowerPC chip. In addition, symmetric-multi-processing support, which Sybase previously shipped in a different version of the software, is also directly supported through SQL Server's use of Windows NT.

Microsoft has gradually weaned its OS/2 customers off that platform and onto Windows NT—and for good reason. SQL Server for Windows NT is dramatically more stable, can address literally hundreds of megabytes of RAM (remember, OS/2 was still a 16-bit OS), and gigabytes of disk space. The combination of Windows NT and SQL Server is a far more stable, far better-performing server application platform than any supported on OS/2, and it now directly competes with a range of UNIX installations.

SQL Server 6.0 continues the trend of internal differentiation from the earlier version of the server co-developed by Microsoft and Sybase by adapting SQL Server to make use of more native Windows NT services, including the graphical user interface. Whereas SQL Server 4.2 for Windows NT introduced useful graphical tools for administering SQL Server, SQL Server 6.0 introduces a centralized administrative application for managing network-wide SQL Servers. In addition, SQL Server introduces new categories of features, such as parallelized query optimization and transaction-based data replication.

SQL Server clients can run on a variety of platforms, including DOS, Windows 3.*x*, Windows NT, Windows 95, Macintosh, and—by using ODBC—even UNIX. All of these platforms can take full advantage of SQL Server's services and features, allowing developers to write applications for whichever client platform their customers need.

System and Database Administration

In some organizations, no distinction is drawn between administration of SQL Server and its resident databases. A single individual or group is responsible for all these issues. Certainly, overall system responsiveness and integrity requires good coordination between the system and its databases, but there are distinctions between SQL Server and database administration. The systems administrator keeps the server available and focuses on the relationship between the server and its operating system. The database administrator focuses on database query performance, transaction throughput, and concurrency. Chapter 26, "Defining, Altering, and Maintaining Databases and Logs," examines database administration issues, but for the most part, this chapter concentrates on server administration issues.

The Systems Administrator (*sa*) Login

All administrative responsibilities need to be executed by an individual logged in—literally—as sa, for system administrator. Database-level tasks can be assigned to *database owners*, but administering server-level configuration and optimization parameters requires access to the special sa login.

Responsibilities of the System Administrator

The SQL Server system administrator is responsible for the overall performance and reliability of SQL Server. The following sections outline a list of some of the responsibilities of the system administrator. (This probably is a pretty good place to start defining the job description of an sa for your organization or workgroup.)

Server Installation and Upgrades

The system administrator installs the software on the server. (When performing an installation, obtaining assistance from a person skilled in the server operating system is always helpful.) A user that exists in the local Windows NT "Administrators" group must be added to the operating system to perform the SQL Server installation, if no such user exists. This user is also responsible for applying patches and bug fixes to SQL Server and for performing major version upgrades. When installation is complete, the system will contain a login for the sa. The step-by-step installation process is documented in Chapter 24, "SQL Server Installation and Connectivity."

Physical Device Configuration

SQL Server uses underlying system resources, including disk, memory, and network resources. The system administrator needs to identify physical storage areas and then define logical mappings to those areas.

Database Creation

After identifying logical devices, the sa creates databases on those devices and then often assigns ownership (and administrative responsibility) to another login.

System Configuration Settings

The system administrator manages system configuration settings, including the amount of server memory and how it is allocated, the number of concurrent user connections and open databases, and the number of locks and system devices. These settings affect system availability and performance.

Server Monitoring and Preventive Maintenance

SQL Server administration requires a well-defined regimen of preventive maintenance. Activities to include along with regular administrative activities are outlined in Chapter 26.

Backup and Maintenance of the System and User Databases

The `master` *database* is a crucial resource where system-wide information is recorded. All stored procedures are maintained in the master database. The `model` *database* is the template database for all subsequent database creations. As system administrator, you guarantee the availability and integrity of these databases.

Unless the sa designates specific owners of databases, the sa is also responsible for backup and restoration of user databases. The sa can transfer database ownership, creating database owners (DBOs) in the process, and these individual DBOs then assume such responsibilities.

Server Startup and Shutdown

Only the system administrator is permitted to start and stop the server process. You may require periodic shutdowns to change system parameters or to repair broken equipment.

In addition, the system administrator is the backup database administrator (DBO) for all databases.

System Security

SQL Server provides several levels of security: server login security, database security, and object security. The sa is responsible for server-level security.

System Tables

SQL Server stores almost all configuration, security, and object information in its own *system tables*. There are system tables within each individual database, colloquially referred to as the *database catalog*. There are system tables that are unique to the master database as well, and these are colloquially referred to as the *server catalog* or *system catalog*.

NOTE

The system tables that are unique to the master database are sometimes referred to as the *system catalog* or *data dictionary*. It's crucial to remember that system tables are stored within each individual database (including master). All databases, including master, model, tempdb, and so forth, have 18 system tables (such as sysobjects, sysusers, and sysindexes) that make up the database catalog. The master database is unique in that it holds 13 additional system tables that are global to the server (such as syslogins, sysdevices, and sysdatabases) and that also make up the server catalog.

Database Catalog System Tables

These databases are stored in every database, *including* master:

sysalternates	User aliases that allow a database user to be validated using a different server login name.
sysarticles	Stores the definition of a basic replication unit, including base table, publication to which it belongs, and article status. (See syspublications.)
syscolumns	Names and characteristics of every column in every table and view in the database.
syscomments	Contains the creation text of every view, rule, default, trigger, and procedure. This text is accessed through sp_helptext.
sysconstraints	Names and characteristics of table constraints.
sysdepends	Relationships between dependent objects (views to tables, stored procedures to tables, and so forth).
sysindexes	Index and space allocation information for every table.
syskeys	Documented keys for each table.
syslogs	Transaction log, a non-readable record of each logged modification performed within the database. (This is the only system table stored in the logsegment—see Chapter 26 for more on segments.)

sysobjects	Object definitions (tables, views, procedures, triggers, rules, defaults, constraints).
sysprocedures	Pre-parsed optimization trees for code-based objects (views, procedures, triggers, rules, defaults, constraints).
sysprotects	Permissions for users on objects (tables, views, procedures).
syspublications	Defines "folders" for individual replication articles, enabling other servers to subscribe to individual tables or groups of tables.
sysreferences	Names and characteristics of each referential integrity constraint declared on a table or column.
syssegments	Database partitions for storing different types or categories of objects and managing object growth below the level of the entire database.
syssubscriptions	Maps individual articles and publications to the servers that will use these objects. New rows are inserted as new subscribers request data from the source server and tables.
systypes	System- and user-defined datatypes available for columns when creating tables.
sysusers	Authorized logins who may access the database.

NOTE

Don't confuse the keys in syskeys with index columns or primary and foreign keys in constraints. Index columns determine the contents of an index, as well as the physical sort order of data (if clustered) and a unique identifier (if unique). Primary and foreign keys constraints define an enforced referential integrity relationship between tables.

Keys recorded in syskeys (established with sp_primarykey, sp_foreignkey, sp_commonkey) define the structure of tables *as system documentation only.* Their only real uses come when an application examines these values to suggest a join or to learn about the structure of the tables; however, the keys defined in syskeys are never enforced by SQL Server itself.

Server Catalog System Tables

The following databases are stored in master:

syslogins	Name, password, and configuration information about each serverlogin.
sysconfigures	System configuration values to be used at next system startup.

syscurconfigs	Current system configuration values.
sysdatabases	Database name, owner, status, and other information.
sysdevices	Physical storage resources available to SQL Server (both active database devices and backup devices).
sysusages	Data allocations and mappings of physical storage areas to individual databases.
sysprocesses	Process IDs, login information, and current status of each logged-in user.
syslocks	Current locks. (This is a memory table only—if the server goes down for any reason, all locks are released).
syslanguages	Installed language sets (in the United States, this is usually only us_english).
syscharsets	Installed character sets.
sysmessages	Server-wide error messages.
sysservers	All servers involved in remote procedure calls.
sysremotelogins	Mappings and login identifiers for users logging in from remote SQL Servers.

System Stored Procedures

SQL Server enables the database developer to store SQL routines within the database; these are *stored procedures*. Stored procedures provide faster performance, reduced network traffic, better control for sensitive updates, and modular programming.

Although stored procedures often support user table processing, SQL Server provides several stored procedures called *system stored procedures* that support system table processing. For example, the sp_helpdb stored procedure returns a complete listing of all system databases. Other system stored procedures (for example, sp_addlogin and sp_bindrule) modify system tables.

Special Characteristics

Names of system stored procedures start with sp_, are stored in the master database and are created by the instmstr script. If the creator of a stored procedure uses the sa login to connect, naming a stored procedure with sp_ and storing it in master gives administrators the capability to create new system stored procedures. You can also create your own system stored procedures.

> **NOTE**
>
> For shops that use both Sybase System 10 and Microsoft SQL Server 6, you'll notice that System 10 has moved the system stored procedures into a new system database called sybsystemprocs. Microsoft continues to store system stored procedures in master. It's one of what will continue to be a growing number of differences in these two products as the manufacturers update them independently.

When you execute a stored procedure whose name starts with sp_, the server first looks in your current database to find it. If the procedure is not found in your current database, the server looks for it in master.

Ordinary stored procedures are interpreted in terms of the current database when the procedure is created. For example, if you create a stored procedure in a user database, the stored procedure is immediately bound to the tables within the database. Note that in the following examples, any characters embedded inside a reversed pair of slashes and asterisks (/* and */) are interpreted as comments and are ignored by SQL Server:

```
/* create proc in user1db */
use user1db
go
create proc show_objects
as
select name, user_name(uid)
from sysobjects
go
```

You can execute this procedure from any database, but you will always see a listing of objects in user1db, the database in which the procedure was created. To invoke a procedure in one database from a different database, you must qualify the procedure name. The format is *database.owner.procedure*. If the database name is not provided, the object is assumed to be in the current database. If the owner is not provided, it will first look for an object owned by you; if you do not own an object of that name, it will then look for an object owned by the user dbo, the database owner. Assuming the previous procedure was created by dbo, you would execute the procedure in the following manner:

```
/* sample execution of procedure from database user9db */
use user9db
go
user1db..show_objects
go
```

System procedures are always interpreted in terms of the current database *when the procedure is executed.* Create a similar system procedure in master:

```
/* create this proc in master */
use master
go
create proc sp_show_objects
as
```

```
select name, user_name(uid)
from sysobjects
go
grant exec on sp_show_objects to public
go
```

When the procedure runs, the system returns the contents of sysobjects in the current database at execution time. Remember, you don't need to fully qualify the procedure name with its database and owner if you have prefixed it with sp_.

```
/* sample execution from user9db */
use user9db
go
sp_show_objects
go
```

You'll notice the last line of code in the preceding example includes a permissions statement. System stored procedures that are not created by the instmstr script have three requirements. First, they must be created by the sa login. Second, they must be created in the master database. Third, they must have their execution granted to the public group in the master database. Chapter 27, "Security and User Administration," discusses groups and users. For now, just remember to grant execution to the group public.

> **NOTE**
>
> With some practice, you will be creating these stored procedures yourself without giving it much thought. Do not forget, however, that a stored procedure must be prefaced by execute (or exec) if it is not the first command in a batch. The following is an example:
>
> ```
> /* From user9db, execute the */
> /* show_objects proc in user1db */
> /* AND the sp_show_objects proc */
> use user9db
> go
> user1db..show_objects
> exec sp_show_objects
> go
> ```

Useful System Procedures

The following are system procedures you will find useful:

sp_who	Current logins and operations (from sysprocesses in master database)
sp_lock	Current locks and table identifiers (from syslocks in master database)
sp_help	Objects in the database or detailed object information (from sysobjects, syscolumns, sysindexes, syskeys, and systypes)

`sp_helpdb`	Databases on the server (from `sysdatabases` in `master` database)
`sp_configure`	Current system configuration settings (from `syscurconfigs`, `sysconfigures` in `master` database)
`sp_helpdevice`	Physical storage and backup devices on the server (from `sysdevices` in `master` database)

TIP

If you plan to write your own system stored procedures, you probably want to identify your procs to avoid future versions of SQL Server from overwriting important, working procs with new standard system procedures. For example, if your company name is ABC Corp., you may want to prefix all your developed, stored procs with `sp_abc_`.

Summary

As an administrator of a SQL Server, you have several areas of responsibility. System tables record configuration and object information, and system stored procedures enable you to query and modify those system tables. (Although it is possible to update the system tables by hand, Microsoft strongly recommends against bypassing the system stored procedures to make changes directly to system tables unless instructed to do so by Microsoft Product Support Services.)

In the coming chapters, you examine the many responsibilities of the system administrator, explore the system tables involved in maintenance, and learn the proper usage of most system stored procedures.

SQL Server Installation and Connectivity

24

In this chapter, you take a look at installation and connectivity with SQL Server. You explore some broad guidelines and learn about the traps at this stage. This chapter gives detailed instructions about the process, but not about the specific selections because so many of the choices you need to make relate to your specific environment: your version of SQL Server, your platform, and your choice of client operating system.

SQL Server Hardware and Software Requirements

SQL Server for Windows NT is not shy about consuming hardware. What is amazing is not its appetite for anything related to hardware, including processors, disk space, disk controllers, RAM, and network access, but that it is able to use these resources so efficiently. Relative to other database servers, a very fast, scaleable SQL Server 6.0 platform can cost half to one-quarter of what a comparable UNIX platform would.

With SQL Server 6.0, Microsoft is acknowledging—in fact, promoting—SQL Server's capability to scale to even larger hardware platforms. Whereas SQL Server 4.2 could handle a 5GB (or even stretch to a 10GB) database, SQL Server 6.0 increases both of these numbers by an order of magnitude. Whereas SQL 4.2 could use four processors, SQL 6.0 can use eight. In fact, SQL Server's biggest problem is that only now are hardware vendors catching up to its appetite. Many Intel-based platform vendors, as well as Digital with its Alpha AXP-based systems, are just releasing machines that support a full gigabyte of RAM, multi-gigabyte disk subsystems, and eight or more CPUs. All of this is occurring at price points far below those of such well-known RISC platform vendors as HP, SUN, Data General, and so on.

So, what makes a good hardware platform for SQL Server?

Server Hardware Characteristics

SQL Server itself needs to be fast enough to handle the work of several users concurrently, and to manage all the overhead involved in running a complex product. The performance of the hardware platform focuses on the four critical areas of any system:

- CPU power to handle the computing load
- Adequate hard disk throughput for data access
- Sufficient RAM for SQL Server to effectively cache databases
- A network interface that doesn't strangle the other three

No one area is any more important than the others. As a SQL Server administrator, part of your job is to analyze the bottlenecks and performance inhibitors of your SQL Server platforms. Each of these components can be a potential problem, and keeping them performing in relatively equal fashion is an important job.

With Windows NT's built-in Symmetric Multi-Processing support, and SQL Server's use of that support through the Symmetric Server Architecture (discussed in Chapter 2, "The Microsoft Client/Server Architecture"), sufficient processing power shouldn't be a problem. If a single Intel Pentium 133MHz processor isn't sufficient, add another. If two aren't sufficient, add two more. If Intel-based systems don't work, any number of RISC vendors are available to make SQL Server run faster. To date, the fastest transaction test published for SQL Server is on a 2-processor DEC Alpha AXP machine, at a measured 308 transactions/second on the Transaction Processing Performance Council's TPC-B bench suite. TCP-B has since been replaced by TPC-C, but so far, few vendors have published results.

Physical memory capacity also is critical. After SQL Server has set aside the minimal memory that it needs for users, devices, and databases, the remaining server memory is used for cache. There is a simple rule about SQL Server and memory: more is better. The larger your tables, the more indexes you plan to create; the more users you expect, the greater the memory you should plan to install.

Here are some quick RAM guidelines:

- Development systems can run with only 16MB of actual RAM in the system, provided that replication is not involved.

- Production systems can have as much as you want to make available.

- If you are going to be using SQL 6.0's replication features, the "on the box" minimum memory requirement is 32MB. 64MB is the practical limit for such systems, though.

- SQL Server's RAM requirements and recommendations are consistent across all Windows NT's supported platforms, including the RISC platforms and PowerPC. 64MB of RAM on an Intel box is the same to SQL Server as 64MB of RAM on a PowerPC box.

Windows NT also takes advantage of multiple disk controllers and multiple hard disks, as does SQL Server. SQL Server 6.0 builds on this to improve parallelization of query operations as well, but that only means that it can take better advantage of the underlying hardware.

Networking seems to be the most-forgotten bottleneck for SQL Server systems. I have seen too many shops install SQL Server for Windows NT on multi-CPU Intel or MIPS boxes, with 128MB of RAM and dedicated RAID hardware subsystems. When query response times are dismal, nobody thinks to look at the 4Mbps Token Ring network on which they're running. Or the 2Mbps ArcNET network. These are necessarily deficient networks. In their day, they were sufficient for the needs of simple file and print sharing. But 16Mbps Token Ring or 10Mbps Ethernet is mandatory, and the new 100Mbps Fast Ethernet and 100Mbps *Asynchronous Transfer Mode* (ATM) networks will be the networks of choice for the next five years.

In the end, choosing hardware for SQL Server is a choice in compromises. Bypassing an extra CPU to make sure that the *network interface card* (NIC) is sufficient is a much better trade-off than vice versa. More RAM and more disk controllers are a better investment than a fifth processor, but a second processor may be better than the other two. Don't be afraid to test configurations, and don't be afraid to ask questions of other SQL Server users about their optimal hardware platform.

In Chapter 32, "Measuring SQL Server Performance," you learn how to use Windows NT's monitoring utilities to analyze bottlenecks and evaluate whether the cause is software-related, hardware-related, or both.

SQL Server Software Requirements

Windows NT's software requirements are easy. Windows NT Server is all you need. If you haven't upgraded to version 3.51, you should. It is not only faster than either 3.1 or 3.5, it is also the recommendation from Microsoft.

Also, Microsoft makes the interesting (and correct) recommendation that SQL Server *not* be installed on the Primary Domain Controller or Backup Domain Controller. Although the thin veneer of economics would suggest that running one hardware box for both of these is more economical than having dedicated PDC and SQL Server machines, the PDC requires substantial hardware in its own right to maintain domain security and accounts throughout the network. Backup Domain Controllers are also ill-suited to SQL Server work. Backup Domain Controllers are responsible for all logins to the domain, and on busy networks, that overhead can be substantial. For performance reasons, a dedicated server is best. If absolutely necessary, putting SQL Server on a BDC will work.

Upgrading to SQL Server for Windows NT 6.0

This next section makes the assumption that you already have SQL Server for Windows NT 4.2*x* installed. If you are not upgrading an existing server, you can skip ahead to step-by-step installation. These issues don't apply to you. If you are upgrading, however, consider this next section mandatory reading.

SQL Server 6.0 introduces a number of significant changes that affect how you choose to upgrade your server. The actual upgrade process can be very easy and quite painless. The good news is that backward compatibility, including support for existing 4.2*x*-based applications, has been a top priority. There are, however, some important planning issues to consider when adopting SQL Server 6.0.

For sites that want to run SQL 6.0 in parallel with existing 4.2*x*-level servers, there are a number of options. First, the SQL SETUP program can install SQL Server into a different drive and directory, and administrators can switch between SQL 4.2 and SQL 6.0 on the same machine. To accomplish this, two criteria must be met, as follows:

- ■ SQL Server 6.0 must be installed in its own subdirectory, not the existing subdirectory where SQL Server 4.2 is installed.

- ■ SQL Server 6.0 must use its own MASTER.DAT file. It cannot use the existing MASTER.DAT of the SQL Server 4.2 installation.

SQL SETUP installs SQL 6.0 registry keys into a different registry key folder than SQL Server 4.2, so no registry entry changes are required. Once installed, administrators can use DISK REINIT and DISK REFIT to restore the necessary sysdevices, sysusages, and sysdatabases table entries. Because the SQL Server 6.0-level services have been renamed, they will appear as different entries in the Control Panel's Service Control Manager. SQL Server 4.2 and SQL Monitor will appear as "SQLServer" and "SQLMonitor," whereas the new SQL Server 6.0 and SQL Executive services will appear as "MSSQLServer" and "SQLExecutive," thereby avoiding naming conflicts with the Service Control Manager.

The reason for avoiding naming conflicts? SQL Server 4.2*x* and SQL Server 6.0 can run side by side, simultaneously, on the same machine. Each must be configured to listen on a different default named pipe, but they can run side by side, making any migration path, fast or slow, more practical.

For those who want to install SQL 6.0 on a completely different machine, SQL Server 6.0 can read existing 4.2*x*-level backup files directly, and SQL Transfer Manager supports both platforms directly as well. This provides the capability to gradually move over to the new platform without compromising availability or backward-compatibility of the server or applications that access it. Although there is more effort involved in choosing this migration method, a single hardware failure won't destroy both servers.

For those who choose to upgrade directly from SQL 4.2*x* to SQL Server 6.0, the process is very simple. The SETUP program automatically detects the existence of the SQL Server 4.2 and steps through the upgrade process. In almost every case, this process can proceed uninterrupted, and clients will be using SQL Server 6.0 without realizing that the server underneath has changed. There is, however, one scenario in which this might not be true. That is the topic of the next section.

Upgrading SQL Server and Potential ANSI Keyword Violations

With the enhancements to Transact-SQL in SQL Server 6.0, there are many new keywords that were not part of SQL Server 4.2*x*. As such, existing object definitions in SQL 4.2*x* databases may cause conflicts with these new keyword definitions. To make the migration process as painless as possible, SQL Server 6.0 includes the CHKUPG.EXE utility. Located in the \BINN subdirectory of the SQL Server installation directory, CHKUPG connects to an existing 4.2*x*-level SQL Server and scans syscomments, looking for object definitions that may conflict with the keywords defined for Transact-SQL. This highlights the constraint with using CHKUPG:

it requires that the syscomments table hold all object definition statements so that CHKUPG can scan them in the table. Many third-party applications clear out the text column of syscomments for security purposes. In this case, CHKUPG will not work, and the object definitions will have to be manually scanned in the SQL Server system tables, both in master and in the other databases. In addition, the SETUP program also relies on syscomments for upgrade information—database and object definitions that are not present in syscomments will cause the upgrade to fail. SETUP will notify the administrator that an upgrade cannot be performed during the setup routine to prevent overwriting the existing server and databases.

CHKUPG uses the standard command-line syntax of all DOS-based SQL utilities and requires the specification of an output file for the report that it generates on keyword violations. A typical command line would be chkupg -Usa -Ppassword -oc:\chkupg.rpt. On my own 4.2*x* test server, I created a device named reference with a database named primary. In that database I created a table key, with column names such as constraint, check, and cursor. After the CHKUPG utility ran, it generated a report file the with results shown in Listing 24.1.

Listing 24.1. The CHKUPG utility generates a report of all ANSI keyword and reserved work violations in 4.2 databases that could cause upgrade problems.

```
=========================================================
Database: master
Status: 8
(No problem)
Missing objects in Syscomments
None
Keyword conflicts
User name: user
Login ID: user
Database: primary
=========================================================
Database: primary
Status: 0
(No problem)
Missing objects in Syscomments
None
Keyword conflicts
Column name: constraint
Column name: cursor
Object name: key
User name: user
=========================================================
Database: pubs
Status: 0
(No problem)
Missing objects in Syscomments
None
Keyword conflicts
None
```

You can see that the report shows which databases, objects, logins, and user definitions will cause the SQL 6.0 SETUP upgrade process to fail. With this information, administrators know where potential problems lie. They now have some choices to make about how these keyword issues can be resolved. The upcoming paragraphs discuss those options. Remember, this is *only* if CHKUPG doesn't give your server a clean bill of health. If CHKUPG doesn't say it's broken, you don't have to fix anything.

> **WARNING**
>
> Any server that will be upgraded from 4.2*x* to 6.0 should have CHKUPG run against it. If there are keyword violations, SQL Server SETUP will note them as part of the upgrade and *allow you to continue installing SQL Server*! This is problematic, because if the keyword violation is a database name, SQL Server is unable to validate or recover the database. In this case, SQL Server simply stops. You would be forced to re-install SQL Server and to use existing 4.2*x* backups to restore your server.
>
> Also, notice that SQL Server checks for missing objects in the syscomments table. Many ISVs who develop applications for SQL Server (PeopleSoft is most notable among many others) delete the text of their stored procedures from syscomments to prevent the code from being copied. If this is done, SQL Server cannot upgrade the server in place, because it cannot verify any ANSI keyword violations!

What to Do with ANSI Keyword Violations

There are two strategies for migrating servers currently using object identifiers that will generate new keyword violations. First, you can rename the offending objects, and change references to those objects in stored procedures and SQL statements within client applications that use those objects. This is not trivial, but it is the most thorough way to guarantee that applications can take advantage of SQL Server 6.0 without causing applications to cause otherwise preventable errors. This is the Microsoft-recommended method for migrating servers that will encounter this issue. If applications take advantage of stored procedure calls instead of passing "naked" Transact-SQL from the client, the work is much easier—simply change the references within the stored procedures, and the client applications will be "automagically" fixed. If changes to the object names are implemented, the identifier-change process must occur before SETUP is run to upgrade the server. SETUP cannot "upgrade in place" a 4.2*x*-level SQL Server that generates ANSI keyword violations under SQL Server 6.0. If you are not going to upgrade in place, but instead install SQL Server 6.0 on a different server and rely on BCP, you have another potential option.

With the new SET QUOTED_IDENTIFIER command, you have the option of installing SQL Server 6.0 on a separate machine, migrating the databases and objects to the new server using BCP, and using this command to keep the existing object names. Although not necessarily intended as a migration tool, SET QUOTED_IDENTIFIER changes how the query processor interprets double quotation marks. This command allows any T-SQL keyword to be used as an identifier, as long as the string value being used is enclosed in double quotation marks. Through the combination of modifying client applications to add double quotation marks surrounding object references and using SET QUOTED_IDENTIFIER, the object identifiers and definitions at the server can remain as they are. For example, the key table in the code example can be migrated to SQL Server 6.0 using ISQL and BCP. The fully qualified syntax references a database name of primary, an object owner ID of user within the database, the table name key, and the field name constraint. All four of these words are now T-SQL keywords because of SQL Server 6.0's ANSI language support. This statement can become valid if run in the following fashion:

```
SET QUOTED_IDENTIFIER ON
create table "key" ("constraint" int)
SET QUOTED_IDENTIFIER OFF
```

With this example, you can see that existing object definitions may not need to change. At the client application side, the source code for the application must be changed to add two things: double quotation marks to surround object references that would otherwise generate keyword-violation errors, as well as additional DB-LIB commands activating the appropriate SET option for each user connection. Remember, the SET command works at the *user connection* level, not the *global server* level. If your server generates ANSI keyword violations, the client applications must be modified in some form. The effort expended to achieve this is roughly equivalent, so putting the (marginally minimal) extra effort to rename the offending database objects will be time well spent.

The good news is that an extremely small portion of SQL Server installations have used database or object names that would violate ANSI keyword restrictions, so upgrading should be a simple matter of following the install process.

> **NOTE**
>
> Customers aren't the only ones to have been caught by their refusal to follow sound advice. Microsoft's own Systems Management Server, which uses an underlying SQL Server as its data storage area, used a column name of key for any primary-key fields. Because key is now an ANSI keyword (primary key and foreign key constraints, and so on), SMS 1.0 would not run on SQL Server 6.0. It would run only on SQL Server 4.2. Microsoft had to ship an update (Version 1.1) of SMS in order to use SQL Server 6.0.

Using Existing 4.2x Administration Tools

If you are installing SQL Server 6.0 over an existing SQL Server 4.2 installation, the existing SQL Server administration tools will also be automatically upgraded. New installation scripts (ADMIN60.SQL, OBJECT60.SQL, and so on) have been provided so that existing 4.2 tools can manage 6.0 servers. The tools themselves still see the 6.0-level server as a 4.2-level server, and are limited to the administrative functionality that they already contain. For example, I cannot use SQL Administrator to configure server-to-server replication. I need the SQL Enterprise Workbench for that, and other 6.0-specific features. With SQL Administrator, I can create devices and databases, and perform all the other operations that both servers have in common. The SQL Monitor application has been replaced with the SQL Executive (a topic of discussion in Chapter 34, "The Microsoft SQL Server Distributed Management Framework"), so any automated task scheduling is not possible in SQL Administrator. SQL Object Manager can perform any task against SQL Server 6.0 but is not equipped to configure database-level replication. Changes to SQL Server 6.0's support for tape drives have made the SQL Tape Utility unnecessary, so on "over-the-top" upgrades, it is removed from the machine.

Choosing a File System for Windows NT and SQL Server

With three to choose from, selecting a file system can seem a daunting task. Under OS/2, SQL Server actually performed better using FAT rather than HPFS. Under Windows NT, though, the issue is no longer performance. In fact, when SQL Server 4.2 for Windows NT first shipped, Microsoft made it clear that there were no direct performance differences between the file systems, and a series of tests bore out this claim.

So, how do you choose? The answer comes in the form of the features that you need to run SQL Server. The least likely choice will be FAT, because it is quite unusual to insist that a production SQL Server be dual-bootable to DOS and Windows NT. If your server does have this as a requirement, then FAT is your choice. HPFS and NTFS volumes cannot be read by DOS.

If you are dual- or triple-booting DOS, OS/2, and Windows NT (again, unlikely on a production SQL Server), then FAT is still your only option, as the lowest common denominator. If the machine is dual-booted between OS/2 and Windows NT, HPFS would be the better choice because OS/2 uses HPFS much more efficiently than it ever used poor old FAT.

If this is a production server, it's a good bet that Windows NT will be the only operating system. As such, NTFS becomes the choice because of its recoverability within the operating system, its capability to create stripe sets (multiple physical disks seen as a single drive letter), and its capability to implement RAID 5 fault tolerance on those stripe sets. (See Chapter 18, "Database Object Placement and Performance," on disk devices for more information on RAID and SQL Server.)

NOTE

NTFS actually uses a transaction-based metaphor for controlling file system recoverability—a concept that the Operating System group at Microsoft copied directly from database technology vendors.

There is a popular, but unverified, tale of a gentleman performing a file-copy operation between two disks in a computer using Windows NT and NTFS on both disks. He opened the case and disconnected the data cable from one of the disks. He sat by the machine for a few moments, and then reconnected the cable. Windows NT continued the file copy until it was complete.

To test his handiwork, this man did a file comparison of the two disks, and found that every byte of data had been copied properly. Ever try that with DOS?

In addition to recoverability features, NTFS also has improved file and disk security features, as well as enhanced protection against computer viruses. Because Windows NT's Executive (the OS kernel) doesn't allow direct access to hardware resources, viruses stored in NTFS partitions are unable to access such critical items as the boot sector or file system allocation tables. It's an extra layer of protection for what will be a storage place for critical information.

Step-by-Step Server Installation

SQL Server 6.0 uses a slightly modified version of the graphical SETUP utility shipped with SQL Server 4.2 for Windows NT. But the most important part of installation is knowing what you need to tell the SETUP utility. SETUP requires the following pieces of information:

- What is the destination drive and directory for the SQL Server system software?
- What is the destination and size for the MASTER.DAT device file?
- What code page and sort order are you going to use?
- What network protocols will you support?
- Do you want SQL Server and SQL Executive to start automatically?
- How is your SQL Server software licensed?

SQL Server Installation Path

Installation copies a number of files to the operating system file system, including the installation program, the server software itself, installation scripts, and utility files. You need to tell the server where this installation path is located in your directory structure.

The SQL Server administrator should have sufficient privileges to run the installation, which means write privileges to the disks on the server. (Later, you may choose to grant users access to the utility programs, the errorlog, or other parts of the server environment that they might find helpful.)

Master Device Location and Size

The next value required by the server is a location and size for the master device. The *master device* is always a file in the file system and is typically installed in the default location \sql60\data. The default size for the MASTER.DAT file (the physical name of the master device) must be at least 25MB. The discussion on database devices in the next chapter should help you properly size the master device, and also show you how to increase the size of the master device should you make it too small.

Mirror the master device (for more information, see Chapter 25, "Defining Physical and Mirror Devices"). It is an excellent fault-tolerance option for SQL Server, but does require a separate physical disk and controller to be properly implemented. Secure the directory well to prevent other users from stumbling on the master device. Name the file master.dev or something similar that makes its purpose unmistakable.

> **TIP**
>
> How large should the master device be? Under previous versions of SQL Server (this is still true under Sybase), devices could not be expanded after they were created. Take a look in Chapter 25 to see how to expand devices in SQL 6.0.

Code Page and Sort Order

SQL Server requires a unique *code page* combined with a unique *sort order* to define how data will be organized. SQL Server supports 10 distinct code pages. A code page corresponds to an alphabet in some ways. The code page defines the character appearance and unique number in the code set. For example, code page 437 (U.S. English) and code page 850 (Multilingual) contain the complete U.S. alphabet. Beyond the standard alphabet, however, the U.S. English code page contains additional graphics characters (blocks and lines in various positions), whereas the Multilingual code page contains accented letters from other alphabets, such as German umlauts and French accent ague and accent grave.

SQL Server can also order data in a variety of ways, within the definition of a single code page. SQL Server comes with 12 predefined sort orders, but other custom sort orders can be added using SETUP. A sort order defines how SQL Server will handle the organization of characters for both data storage and data retrieval operations. In effect, the sort order determines the results of ORDER BY and GROUP BY queries, because they rely on this underlying layer.

> **TIP**
>
> Microsoft has *informally* tested different sort orders and found that the combination of Code Page 850 with a *binary* sort order (meaning that the letters are sorted in ASCII numeric value) is about 20 percent faster than the next best combination.
>
> This may lead to unexpected results. Because the lowercase letters of the English alphabet are assigned larger numbers than uppercase letters, servers installed with this combination will return data in queries using ORDER BY, with lowercase letters sorted *after* uppercase letters. The reason? Binary sort order tells SQL Server that smaller-numbered letters are sorted before larger-numbered letters in the code page, and uppercase letters come first.
>
> Try to balance performance with flexibility: Although SQL Server does provide case-insensitive sort orders, these will affect system performance.

SQL Server Network Support

SQL Server for Windows NT 4.2 introduced a compelling feature: support for heterogeneous clients. NetWare, Named Pipes, TCP/IP, and Macintosh clients could all access a Windows NT–based SQL Server. Coming from the Sybase "any protocol as long as it's TCP/IP" world, this was a welcome relief for administrators wanting to put data in central locations, accessible by different types of clients.

SQL Server 6.0 builds on this to provide Integrated Login Security, a special feature of Microsoft SQL Server (see Chapter 27, "Security and User Administration"), over multiple network protocols. In addition, through the use of the new Multi-Protocol Network Library, SQL Server can encrypt connection attempts, queries, and data over network wires.

Selecting a protocol has never been easier. SQL Server supports a myriad, including the following:

- TCP/IP—Fastest in Microsoft's unofficial testing.
- IPX/SPX—Second fastest, according to informal tests.
- Named Pipes—Third fastest, and the only protocol permanently installed with SQL Server.
- DECNet Sockets.
- Banyan VinesIP—Including support for StreetTalk and the forthcoming ENS for Windows NT.
- ADSP—"AppleTalk" to the rest of us. This is supported using ODBC client software from Visigenic.

SQL Server installs Named Pipes support by default, but it can be removed at installation time.

Depending on your network protocol (TCP/IP, IPX/SPX, or Named Pipes), you need to decide on a listening port within the server. Processes that communicate with SQL Server send a message to the host operating system network address. The message is keyed with the internal address of the SQL Server process. The address that you establish will be used by every client and every server needing to communicate with this SQL Server.

In Named Pipes, the internal address of the process is a pipe name, with a default value of

```
\\SERVERNAME\PIPE\SQL\QUERY
```

where *SERVERNAME* is the published name of the host computer. The default pipe SQL Server uses can be changed using the SQL Client Configuration Utility on the client workstation.

In IPX/SPX, the server is assigned a standard port address within NetWare. There is a default value (normally 0x08bd) included with the server installation. If that value is already assigned, SQL Server provides several other values that you can try. (You are unlikely to encounter any other process with that identifier. Novell has assigned that number to SQL Server processes, and you will rarely find two SQL Servers running on a single Windows NT server.)

In TCP/IP, you identify a single integer port address within the server. For TCP/IP installations, contact an administrator for a value to use.

When you choose to install SQL Server 6.0 alongside an existing 4.2 installation, you can use different port numbers for the different servers. For IPX/SPX, you should use different IPX/SPX port numbers, selecting them from the provided list. For TCP/IP connections, selecting different IP port addresses for each server guarantees clients can connect to both servers.

> **TIP**
>
> If you are installing many SQL Servers at your organization, it is helpful to install SQL Server with the same port address everywhere, for the sake of consistency. If you choose not to standardize port addresses, publish port addresses to help those who do workstation setup and administration.
>
> You can use 5000, for example, unless that number is already used. If you are installing several SQL Servers on the same hardware, increment this number by 100 for each new server (check with the administrator to ensure that each value is available).

Although support for multiple protocols is important, with the introduction of integrated login security, SQL Server for Windows NT became part of the network security profile. The problem was that only Named Pipes clients could take advantage of this feature. In addition to the client and server network libraries listed previously, Windows 3.*x*–, Windows 95–, and Windows NT–based clients can also use the new Multi-Protocol Network Library to access SQL Server.

MPNL implements session-level connectivity using Windows NT Network *Remote Procedure Calls* (or RPCs). Using an underlying transport (NetBEUI, IPX, and TCP are supported currently), a client workstation can open a session-level connection with SQL Server using these RPCs instead of some other session-level IPC—such as sockets, SPX, and so on.

With MPNL, two new features are available. By selecting the appropriate check boxes in the SQL Server SETUP routine, administrators can take advantage of MPNL's encryption of TDS packets over the network wire. This enables encryption of packets sent and received across the network, providing a secure environment. The encryption relies on Windows NT encryption of network RPCs and uses RSA as its encryption method. Because both the server and client network libraries use these RPCs, two-way encryption is supported. Also with MPNL, any Windows-based client can take advantage of integrated login security over Named Pipes, TCP/IP sockets, or IPX/SPX, including Windows 3.*x*–based clients using Novell SPX over IPXODI.

Integrated security relies on the underlying domain security facility to provide authentication for SQL Server user connection. In SQL Server 4.2, this was achieved by querying the Named Pipes API to determine network validation and then allow access to the server through a trusted connection. SQL Server now relies on a prompt for domain connections to servers for which a Named Pipes or RPC domain structure does not exist. If, for example, a user needs to connect to a Novell network from a Windows NT workstation, and that user attempts to use MPNL to gain a trusted connection to SQL Server, the MPNL connection will prompt the user with a domain login and password dialog to validate the domain ID. That domain ID is valid for any server on the network that is both listening on the network with the MPNL and also has integrated security enabled. If any of the servers have mixed or standard security enabled, administrators will need to manage logins and permissions for each user on each server independently.

Automatically Starting SQL Server and SQL Executive

SQL Server and SQL Executive (the new version's replacement for SQL Monitor) run as *services* under Windows NT's Service Control Manager. As such, they can be configured to start automatically by the Service Control Manager. When the server is in production, this is the recommended method of installation, because SQL Server and SQL Executive can start whenever the server is started. During testing, you may want to leave this option off so that you can debug your Windows NT environment without having to worry about SQL Server. If you decide to change your mind about how SQL Server should start, you can set SQL Server's and SQL Executive's startup status using the Services applet in the Windows NT Control Panel. The service names are MSSQLServer and SQLExecutive.

Server Licensing

In Microsoft's campaign to disseminate disambiguation information (that is, their effort to stop confusing customers), SQL Server can be licensed in one of two modes. Before installing SQL

Server, make sure that you choose the proper licensing mode and the correct number of supported workstations. Microsoft has, unfortunately, so confused their customers that most are unsure if they are in compliance with their license agreement or not. Talk to your Microsoft representative to confirm the licensing plan for SQL Server, just to be safe.

Online Documentation

SQL Server has a new online documentation facility that uses Microsoft's MS Developer Network search engine. It is extremely useful, but it does take up more than 30MB of disk space. For test servers, I'd recommend installing it. The search engine is very easy to use, and the complete printed documentation is available online. For production servers, don't bother—you can always look things up on the testing server.

Having completed all of these steps, SQL Server's SETUP utility will now copy all of the files necessary to the source directory and path that you specified above, as well as build the master device and install the system databases. On an Intel DX4-100 machine with 32MB of RAM, this process took just over 35 minutes. Because SQL Server adds or changes entries in the Windows NT Registry, installation does require you to reboot the machine. SETUP will prompt you for this, and you're now ready to go!

Time to Log In!

You have installed SQL Server. The server is running. It's time to log in, look around, and see what's left to do. You'll use the ISQL/w (Interactive SQL for Windows) application on the server to log in as the sa.

> **NOTE**
>
> The only initial usable login on the server is sa, which has no password upon installation. (See the section titled "Changing Defaults—The Top Ten Items to Address upon Installation" later in this chapter.)

If you are successful, you should be able to transmit queries and receive results:

```
Congratulations, you have installed SQL Server!
```

If the Login Didn't Work

When ISQL/w running on the server fails to work, there are a few simple problems to check, based on the error message you receive.

The easiest message to resolve is `Login Incorrect` or `Login Failed`. Both of these messages mean that you found the server but your combination of name and password was entered incorrectly. If you just installed the server, you probably typed something wrong. If you installed the server a while ago, the `sa` password may have changed, or the `sa` login may have been disabled. If you really can't get in, make sure that the SQL Server process is running.

Another common message is `Unable to Connect: SQL Server is not available or does not exist`. SQL Server is probably not running. Use the SQL Server Manager applet (commonly known as the SQL Stoplight) to see the status of SQL Server. If necessary, restart the server and try again.

> **NOTE**
>
> This really is a more difficult message to interpret. Troubleshooting the `Unable to connect` message is discussed in detail later in the chapter, but most of the issues there relate to proper addressing and network connectivity. When you execute `ISQL/w` from the physical SQL Server and cannot find the server process, the usual problem is that the server process is not started yet.

If you are still stumped, see "Troubleshooting" later in this chapter. You might find a useful hint on how to resolve the problem.

Shutting Down with *shutdown*

To shut down the server, you execute the SQL statement `shutdown` after connecting to the server.

The `shutdown` command instructs the server to disable all logins except `sa`, waits for currently executing transactions and procedures to complete, checkpoints all databases, and then exits the server executable process. This is an orderly shutdown, which manages data integrity before downing the server.

The `shutdown with nowait` command shuts everything down immediately, without regard to process status. Transactions are not allowed to continue to completion and are rolled back upon restart. Databases are not checkpointed and need to do additional work to recover. This is not considered an orderly shutdown; data integrity is not damaged by a `shutdown with nowait`.

Although the `shutdown` command is available, SQL Server is typically stopped and started using either the SQL Service Manager ("Stoplight" application) or the stoplight icon in the SQL Enterprise Manager.

If you execute the `shutdown` statement and remain logged in while it proceeds, you lose your connection when the server shuts down and are notified of the dropped connection by your application program. Other users are not notified until the next time they try to use their connection. To avoid user panic and annoying calls, inform users before executing a shutdown.

Although SQL Server is considered a round-the-clock, 24×7 server, there are some common administrative tasks requiring a server shutdown:

■ *Changing configuration options.* There are a handful of *dynamic* configuration options that can change while the server is up. Most configuration options require modifications in the allocation of memory or resources that can be made only when the server is restarted.

■ *Removing aborted transactions from the log.* If a client disconnects, leaving a non-committed, non-rolled-back transaction in the log, that transaction might prevent a truncation of the database log. During the database recovery, aborted transactions are marked for rollback and the server is free to clean up the log.

■ *Setting server trace flags.* Server trace flags enable you to access DBCC and monitoring features. They must be set during server startup.

■ *Configuring mirroring of the master device.* The mirror parameter must be supplied to the dataserver executable before startup.

■ *Killing certain user connections.* The SQL Server kill statement can kill certain user processes, but other connections (for example, sleeping processes in earlier versions of SQL Server) simply cannot be killed without restarting the server.

Client Installation

Getting workstations ready for client/server is a big job, and the more workstations there are, the more logistic problems overshadow technical ones. If you have existing workstations that require work before they are ready for SQL Server, you have a more complicated problem in making changes to workstation configurations without impacting current capabilities.

In this section you look at the SQL Server client software installation to understand how SQL Server provides openness, portability, and modularity to application programmers.

db-Library Components

Two components, db-lib and net-lib, comprise SQL Server workstation software. db-lib is the set of functions directly accessible to the application, including calls to set up information in the login record (DBSETLUSER), to log in (dbopen), to store a query in the buffer (dbcmd), to execute the command (dbsqlexec or dbsend), and to process result rows (dbresults, dbnextrow).

db-lib is implemented differently on different platforms. DOS applications use an include file of db-lib function calls; Windows applications use resources in a dynamic link library (W3DBLIB.DLL for Windows version 3.*x*).

net-lib provides network transparency. (See Figure 24.1.) There are typically several net-libs available for each supported client operating platform. The net-lib receives the name of a SQL

Server from DB-Library and transforms that into a Named Pipe or full address and port identifier for network communication. Applications written for DB-Library name only the server; the rest of the network implementation is managed entirely through net-lib.

FIGURE 24.1.

Net-library provides network transparency to the application developer.

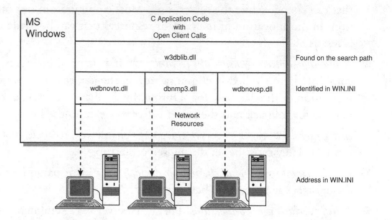

Each net-lib applies to a specific protocol and, if appropriate, a version of that protocol. For example, there is a specific net-lib for Windows for several different versions of TCP/IP (Novell, FTP, Microsoft, and so forth), as well as net-libs for Named Pipes and IPX.

Windows

Under Windows, you record the names of servers in a text file in the format of a Windows initialization file. With DB-Library, you store server names and addressing schemes in the WIN.INI file (in the Windows directory) under the heading [SQLSERVER]. If you have a DSQUERY value listed in the INI file, it is used by default if no server is named. Here is the [SQLSERVER] section from a sample WIN.INI file:

```
[SQLServer]
DSQUERY=DBNMP3
SERVER1=DBMSRPC3
```

Troubleshooting

Client/server works great—when you get it working. Then it works until someone changes something.

Troubleshooting client/server is no different from troubleshooting any other kind of system, except that the vendors are unbelievably nonuseful. Why? Because there are simply too many products (and too many combinations of products) for them to be smart about all of them.

You need to be single-minded about *isolating the problem.* Here are some questions to consider:

- Is the problem on the server, the client, or the network?
- Is the problem in the workstation application or the operating system?
- Is the problem in the connectivity software or the equipment?

Here's the stated problem: "I can't log in." Or, "I can log in, but I can't send a query." Or, "I can log in, but periodically, my connection hangs." This section presents some of the steps that you can take to isolate this problem.

Step 1: Does SQL Server work?

Start simple. Run the SQL Server Manager (`stoplight`) application. Select the MSSQLSERVER service from the combo box. If the server isn't started, the light is red. If the server was started but isn't showing up, no lights will be lit, and the message `Server status is indeterminate` will appear in the status bar at the bottom of the window. Your first step is to look at the errorlog and the Windows NT Event Log's Application subsystem to check for SQL Server error messages.

Step 2: Can You Access SQL Server from ISQL/w?

The server is working, so now you should find out whether anyone can log in. Remove the network and all the client issues and try to log in from the server. Log in to the hardware where SQL Server resides and invoke `ISQL/w`. If you can't log in, you may be out of maximum connections (the message for this is quite specific).

You also may have a problem in your addressing on the server itself. Remember the port you assigned to the server when you ran the installation? That's also how your client needs to address the server. Look in the Windows NT Registry on the server to make sure that the network and port address listed there is correct. You also may have to set server environmental variables to make this work. In addition, check the client software installation to ensure that the correct port number is specified on the client as well.

At any rate, don't bother trying to get a client process to talk to the server over the network until an `ISQL/w` session can communicate with the server locally.

Step 3: Can You Talk to the Physical Server at All Over the Network?

If a client is having a problem initiating a SQL Server session, first try to initiate a non–SQL Server connection. Try to access a shared drive on the server. If you are running Windows and Named Pipes, see whether an NT server shows up in your workgroup under File Manager's Disk Connect Network Drive option.

If you can't find or ping the server at the operating-system level, you have a network problem. The problem could be a loose or bad cable connection, a bad Ethernet card, out-of-date or incompatible network software, incorrect Ethernet frame types, bad packet sizes… well, you get the idea. This is the part where you call your networking friend and say, "Fix it. It's broken."

Again, don't bother continuing to try to log into SQL Server until this problem is solved.

Step 4: It Worked Yesterday...What Changed?

This is one of the most perplexing problems you will face. It is especially problematic in Windows.

A Windows workstation worked yesterday, does not work today, but the user swears that nothing changed:

"What did you do?"

"Nothing."

"Are you sure??"

"Well, I did install Excel…."

"Aha!"

Microsoft (and a lot of other vendors) ships DB-Library with many of its products. (Some vendors ship really old, horrible versions.) If the installation program also changes the workstation search *path* (which, unfortunately, is common), the new DB-Library jumps to the front of the path and sabotages any attempt to find SQL Server.

Step 5: Can You Log into SQL Server?

If you can't log in, first check the capitalization and spelling of your name and password. SQL Server logins and passwords are case-sensitive and also prevent the use of special characters. As a result, capitalization problems can prevent logins. If the capitalization is correct and your password still doesn't work, your sa should be able to give you a new password if that appears to be the problem. If you are the sa, you have bigger problems.

Step 6: Does It Happen Only When the Number of Users Increases?

One of the simplest solutions to occasional server lockups or problems with logins is duplicate client TCP/IP addresses. These conflicts cause the server to go complete berserk, so manage those addresses carefully. You can avoid this problem altogether on Windows NT networks that use TCP/IP by using *DHCP*, or *Dynamic Host Configuration Protocol*. DHCP dynamically "leases" TCP/IP addresses to workstations when they sign on to the network, preventing this problem. There are other implementation issues surrounding the use of DHCP, but it is a viable alternative to hard-coding TCP/IP addresses.

Changing Defaults—The Top Ten Items to Address upon Installation

There are some things that you should do as soon as you can log in. SQL Server is a great product, but sometimes you have to wonder. Some default settings are just senseless and you need to change them just as soon as you log in as sa.

Securing *sa* Access

The sa has no password and complete control over the server. You need to fix that—*pronto*. (For more on security, see Chapter 27.)

Turning Off the Master Device Default Status

If you don't change this value, you can mistakenly install user databases on the master device. Ultimately, this could mean a painful database recovery if you have to reinitialize the master device, and you may have to free up the space later to make additional room for the master database.

To turn this value off, use the following:

```
sp_diskdefault master, defaultoff
```

For more on default disks, see Chapter 25.

When you back up to diskdump, the backup is amazingly fast and equally fruitless. Nothing is backed up because there is no physical device attached. To avoid tragic mistakes, remove the diskdump device:

```
sp_dropdevice diskdump
```

Increasing the Size of *tempdb*

You probably don't know how large tempdb will need to be yet, but 2MB certainly won't be enough. Use disk init to set up a logical device for tempdb (see Chapter 24) and alter the database to extend tempdb onto the new device (see Chapter 25). For now, 20MB might be a good place to start.

Setting Obvious Configuration Settings

In Chapter 30, "Configuring and Tuning SQL Server," you review the configuration and tuning settings in detail, but here are three values that are always wrong:

- Open databases
- Memory
- User connections

Databases don't consume much server memory, so set this value near the maximum number of databases that you expect to create on the server, with additional room for master, model, tempdb, and msdb:

```
sp_configure "open databases", 20
go
reconfigure
go
```

The memory setting probably needs to be changed. The correct value depends on your server. Don't forget that memory is specified in 2KB pages (10240 = 20MB).

Connections should be set as low as reasonable because connections do consume memory (about 50KB each):

```
sp_configure "user connections", 25
```

Setting Up the Model Database Objects, Users, and Datatypes

You might want to set up the model database with all the objects (rules, defaults), users (guest, others), and user-defined datatypes that you will want in every database on this server. This is optional.

If this is your first server in your organization, it is really unlikely that you have made any of these decisions yet. If you have other servers, you may already have a set of standards. Make certain that you create everything in model before you create your first user database. Otherwise, you need to copy everything manually into both model and the user database(s) later on.

Installing the *pubs* Database

The pubs database is provided with every server, and you should install it on most servers. pubs contains sample tables, views, and data that you can query to observe how the SQL works or how to implement special objects or concepts. This also is optional. All of the examples in the SQL Server documentation—and in most articles you read—use pubs objects.

Summary

If you have already decided on SQL Server, you still need to find all the pieces to make it work. Think of client/server as a scavenger hunt. One medium-sized client eventually bought more than 100 products from more than 40 vendors to build a client/server system.

Your client/server installation will depend on your ability to find high-quality components and knit them together into a seamless system. It's not a one-day job; it's a continuous process of building a reliable, functional, simple system.

Use the following checklist to make sure that you have addressed all of the major points covered in this chapter.

Checklist: Deciding on Your SQL Server Environment

- Server hardware vendor and configuration (IBM, MIPS, NEC, HP, Compaq, DEC, and so on)
- Network type (Ethernet, Token Ring)
- Network protocol (TCP/IP, IPX, Named Pipes)
- Client workstation operating system (DOS, Windows, Macintosh)
- Client workstation configuration (CPU, Speed, RAM, and so on)
- Client development and reporting products (PowerBuilder, Visual Basic, C++, Forest & Trees, ReportSmith, Clear Access, and so on)
- Server administration tools (Aurora)
- Network administration tools

Defining Physical and Mirror Devices

25

The server is installed. Now what? For the server to be useful, you need to be able to create and load user databases. With SQL Server, you must first define the physical area that is to be used for the databases; this is done with SQL Enterprise Manager, or using the `disk init` statement. (See Figure 25.1.)

FIGURE 25.1.

You must set up devices before setting up databases.

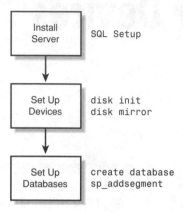

In this chapter you explore device mirroring at the software level. When you *mirror* devices, SQL Server keeps an exact copy of each used page from one device on another that you specify. You set up mirroring with the `disk mirror` statement. You also compare advantages and disadvantages of hardware-level disk mirroring, software-level device mirroring, and RAID (Redundant Array of Inexpensive Devices) striping.

Disk Initialization with *disk init*

Chapter 26, "Defining, Altering, and Maintaining Databases and Logs," discusses database creation and configuration. Before you can set up databases, SQL Server needs to map logical device names to physical disk resources. The logical names that you assign here ("devices") are used again at database creation (and segment placement) time.

> **NOTE**
>
> Upon server installation, you will have three devices initialized to house the `master`, `model`, `tempdb`, and `msdb` databases. The `master`, `model`, and `tempdb` databases are held on the device with a logical name of `master`. You define the physical location of the master device file with the SQL Server `Setup` utility. The `msdb` database is placed on two disk devices, called `MSDBData` and `MSDBLog`. Although you can create user databases on these devices, you should use these devices only for the databases previously mentioned, particularly for production servers.

Several databases can reside on a single physical device, and storage for a single database can span many devices. (Also, a single physical disk can contain several devices.) Figure 25.2 illustrates the many-to-many relationship between devices and databases (discussed at length later in this chapter).

FIGURE 25.2.

A physical device is defined to SQL Server as a logical device, on which can reside 0, 1, or many databases. A database can span several physical devices.

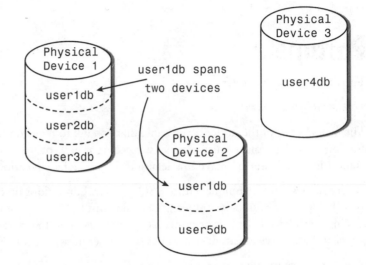

The `disk init` statement provides the server with a method of mapping databases to physical drives. You will use databases to contain (provide a context for) data objects such as tables, indexes, and stored procedures.

> **NOTE**
>
> Because `disk init` is used only when defining physical resources to the server, it is easy to forget the syntax. If you are unsure, look it up rather than guess at it.
>
> When working with the parameters, remember that the tricky parts are getting the physical name right, making sure that the vdevno is unique on the server, and stating the size parameter in *pages* (not megabytes).

The `disk init` statement requires four mandatory parameters. Every device has both a logical name (a reference for SQL Server) and a physical name (a reference for the operating system file). In addition, the size of a device is defined at creation time.

```
DISK INIT
NAME = 'logical_name',
PHYSNAME = 'physical_name',
VDEVNO = virtual_device_number,
SIZE = number_of_2K_blocks
[, VSTART = virtual_address]
```

(f)

Parameters

The first parameter for `disk init` is the logical name:

`NAME = 'logical_name'`

The *logical name* of the device is the name that you use to refer to the device when creating or altering a database on it, mirroring it (succeeding topic), or using the `sp_diskdefault` command (discussed later) to make it a default disk for database creation.

Device names must be unique within a SQL Server. Limitations on device names are the same as with any other SQL Server object: the name must be unique among devices and 30 characters in length with no spaces or punctuation (`data_device`, `log_device`, `index_device`). Don't forget that the server treats device names (like other meaningful identifiers) as case-sensitive.

The second parameter is the physical name:

`PHYSNAME = 'physical_name'`

The *physical name* of the device is its actual location within the operating system. The address is a file system name.

NOTE

Until recently, Microsoft SQL Server used only disk devices. With SQL Server 6.0, Microsoft has introduced support for removable-media databases and devices. However, since standard writeable devices have become so cheap (SCSI disk are less than $300 per gigabyte for internal drives), the usability of removable media is questionable.

The third parameter of `disk init` is the virtual device number:

`VDEVNO = virtual_device_number`

The virtual device number is a unique identifier used by SQL Server to identify unique page numbers (it is the high-order byte of an address, hence the 255-device limitation on the servers). These addresses are used to help map the many-to-many relationship between the system tables, `sysdevices`, `sysusages`, and `sysdatabases`.

Device numbering begins with 0, and device 0 is set at installation time to be the master device. The first available device number is 3, because MSDBData uses VDEVNO = 1 and MSDBLog uses VDEVNO = 2.

NOTE

In previous versions of SQL Server, devices consumed memory for their allocation. As a result, SQL Server needed to be configured to minimize memory allocations for devices without starving the server of database space. With SQL Server 6.0, that is largely not a problem because of its access to plentiful quantities of RAM. People familiar with running SQL Server for OS/2 or Sybase SQL Server will notice a missing configuration option for defining the maximum number of devices the server allocated when started.

The fourth parameter is the size, which is the size of the device in pages:

```
SIZE = number_of_2K_blocks
```

It also has been rumored that the page size will be variable in the future.

TIP

SQL Server generally is excellent at performance, throughput, and a host of other things, but leaves much to be desired in consistency with administration commands. Sometimes turning flags on means setting them to 1, sometimes it means setting them to true, sometimes setting them to defaulton, and so forth.

In this case, note that size is in pages. When you create a database, the sizes will be in megabytes, but the confirmation message that database creation returns specifies the number of *pages* allocated. Egad!

Moral: If you are unsure about the units of work for a particular command, then read the manual. Also, the SQL Enterprise Manager application (discussed shortly) has defaulted all space allocation parameters in dialog boxes to *megabytes*; this is noted in the dialog boxes themselves.

The sixth line of disk init specifies these parameters:

```
[, VSTART = virtual_address]
```

It is unusual to have to specify this parameter. It defaults to zero; leave it alone unless directed by Microsoft Product Support Services (PSS).

The following example of disk init creates a new device in the default SQL Server installation directory:

```
disk init
name = 'data_device_1',
physname = 'c:\sql60\data\d_dev_1.dat',
vdevno=3,
size = 512000
```

In this example, the disk init statement creates a device whose logical name is 'data_device_1'. The device is mapped to a physical location 'c:\sql60\data\d_dev_1.dat'. The virtual device number is 3, and its size is 1GB (= 512,000 × 2KB).

How long does disk init take? That varies with your version of SQL Server. At one point in its evolution, disk init would zero out every page and could take hours. With the Windows NT releases of the server, a disk init of 2GB takes only a couple of minutes.

> **NOTE**
>
> In the case of many SQL Server commands (disk init is one of these), no news turns out to be good news. If there is an error with a disk init statement, you will hear about it. If the command appears to take a few seconds and there is no error, it probably worked. Just run sp_helpdevice to make sure (see an example later in this chapter).
>
> After a while, you will get used to it, but for now, just make a note: If you don't get an error message, it probably worked.

Physical file creation for disk devices must meet two criteria:

- The file must not already exist (it will be created by the disk init process).
- The file must be writeable by the process that is running SQL Server. This means that if you configured the server to start under the Administrator account, the Administrator user would have to have write permission in the directory and file permission on the file after creation. For this reason, staring SQL Server using the LocalSystem account is recommended because LocalSystem has access to necessary permissions and privileges.

In the next example, a disk device of 40MB (20,480 pages) is created. A file of 40MB is created during initialization and an entry is made in the sysdevices system table:

```
disk init
name = 'data_device_2',
physname = 'c:\sql60\data\data_dev1.dat',
vdevno=4,
size = 20480
```

NOTE

Errors from `disk init` statements are normally not very descriptive. For example:

```
Error 5123: DISK INIT encountered an error while attempting to open/create the
physical file. Please consult the SQL Server for more details.
```

When you do consult the errorlog file, you usually find one of three errors:

- The directory or filename is invalid
- The file already exists
- There is not enough space to create the file

Here are some sample errorlog entries after a `disk init` error:

```
94/10/29 13:26:30.25 kernel   udcreate: Operating system error 112
(There is not enough space on the disk.) encountered
94/10/29 13:26:38.61 kernel   udcreate: Operating system error 80
(The file exists.) encountered
```

Normally, you can delete a physical file that was created during a failed `disk init`. If you can't delete it, SQL Server failed to release the locks on the file. To delete the file and reclaim the space, you may need to shut down and restart the server and try again. Before doing that, make absolutely certain that the `disk init` didn't actually work. You might be trying to delete a valid device!

Using SQL Server Enterprise Manager

The SQL-EM application allows you to define devices, mirror existing devices, and drop devices, all with a point-and-click interface.

To define devices, you must connect to a registered server. As with most SQL-EM operations, you can choose the option from the toolbar, from the menu structure, or by right-clicking the particular component of SQL Server that you want to work with in the Server Manager window. Selecting the devices icon in the toolbar, the Manage|Devices menu selection, or right-clicking on the Database Devices folder in the Server Manager window pops up the Manage Database Devices — <*servername*> window, as illustrated in Figure 25.3.

Double-clicking on one of the device names in the chart brings up a detail window on that particular device, showing the physical location, logical name, and size for that particular device and the specific databases (and their size allocations) on that device, as shown in Figure 25.4.

FIGURE 25.3.

The SQL Enterprise Manager displays information about database devices.

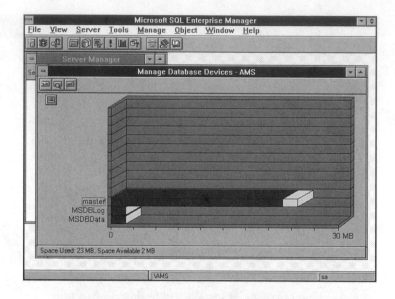

FIGURE 25.4.

You can see the allocation of device space by database in the detail window.

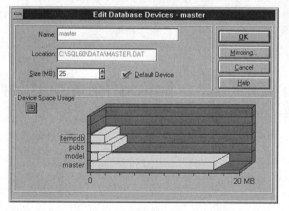

Returning to the Manage Database Devices window and clicking the first button on the toolbar brings up the New Device dialog box, where you can define new disk devices for storing databases. (See Figure 25.5.) Notice how the units of measure for these devices are all expressed in megabytes—a welcome change for anyone accustomed to the teeth-gnashing that is associated with keeping track of SQL Server's inconsistent measurements!

FIGURE 25.5.

Define the name, location, and size of a database device using the New Database Device window.

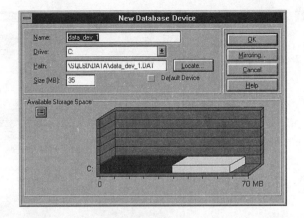

In Figure 25.5, the administrator is defining a device called data_dev_1. That device is 35MB in size (how many pages is that?), and you can see in the darker segment on the C drive that disk device will consume almost 50 percent of the space available on the disk. The D drive has almost no free space on it. Notice that there is no place to define the vdevno for this device. SQL-EM will automatically determine the largest-used device number, increment it by 1, and use the new value for the vdevno. Notice also that you can immediately specify mirroring properties for the device, as well as whether or not it is a default device, directly from this dialog box.

As with all operations in SQL Enterprise Manager, the application is merely executing Transact-SQL commands "behind the curtains" so that, instead of constantly digging up the command reference for disk init, you can point-and-click your way around a server to define devices. In this example, SQL Server is supplying a disk init statement to itself with a logical name of data_dev_1, a physical name of c:\sql60\data\data_dev_1.dat, and a size parameter value of 17,920 2KB pages (35MB).

SQL Server will process this statement in the same way as though you had typed it in yourself.

Effects of *disk init*

The disk init command can be performed only by the sa. After the disk initialization is complete, the space described by the physical address is available to SQL Server for storage and a row is added to the sysdevices table in the master database.

Figure 25.6 shows the contents of a small sysdevices table (use select * from sysdevices).

FIGURE 25.6.

The contents of the sysdevices *table in an Aurora Desktop window.*

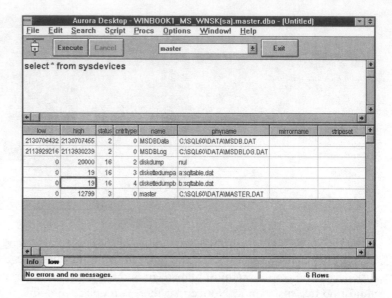

The sysdevices table contains one row for each device that the server can access. (Devices include disks for storage of data, and tape and file devices for backups.) Relevant columns in sysdevices include the name of the device (and its mirror, if it has one—you learn about that later), device status, and page range. Can you find the virtual device number? It is actually the high-order byte of the "low" column.

The status is a bitmap describing what the device is used for and what options have been set (if any). The layout of the status byte is provided in Table 25.1.

Table 25.1. Bitmap values for the status column of sysdevices.

Decimal	Hex	Description
1	0x01	Default disk
2	0x02	Physical disk
4	0x04	Logical disk
8	0x08	Skip header
16	0x10	Dump device
32	0x20	Serial writes
64	0x40	Device mirrored
128	0x80	Reads mirrored
256	0x100	Secondary mirror side only
512	0x200	Mirror enabled

For instance, the status of the master device is 3 (= binary 00000011), which corresponds to "database device" and "default disk" (1 + 2 = 3).

By far, the easiest way of decoding the status bit and virtual device number is to use the system stored procedure sp_helpdevice.

Here is the syntax of sp_helpdevice:

```
sp_helpdevice [<logical_device_name>]
```

sp_helpdevice can be used without parameters to get a list of defined devices. Figure 25.7 shows all defined devices within a SQL Server.

FIGURE 25.7.

A list of all defined devices in an Aurora Desktop window.

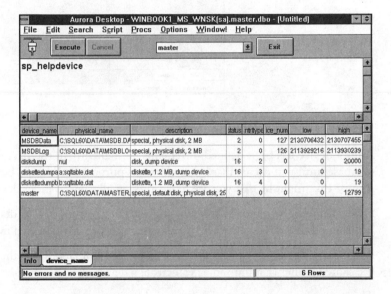

Pass sp_helpdevice the name of the disk device to get information on a specific disk. The information retrieved is shown in Figure 25.8.

The master device status is 3 (disk device + default device); its controller type is 0 (a device for storage, not backup); its virtual device number (device) is 0; and its low and high values represent the logical page numbers that define the space to be used on the device (12,800 pages = 25MB).

FIGURE 25.8.

Specific disk information in an Aurora Desktop window.

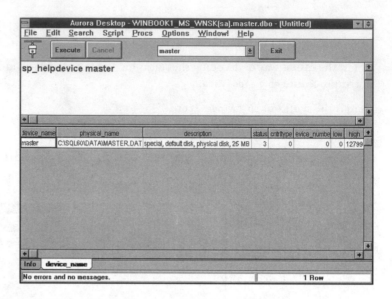

Removing Devices with *sp_dropdevice*

After a device has been defined, it remains permanently in the data dictionary in the master database until you decide that it has served its purpose and should be removed. A typical reason for this might be that you are replacing a small, slower, older device with a newer one.

Devices cannot be removed if databases have been defined on the device; any databases must be dropped first. (The server will check sysusages for any allocated fragments for the device.)

A device may be dropped with the sp_dropdevice command. Only the sa can drop a device, in the same manner that only an sa can create a device.

The syntax for sp_dropdevice is illustrated here:

```
sp_dropdevice <logical_device_name>
sp_dropdevice data_device_1
```

If your device was created as an operating system file, you must execute the necessary commands to remove the file (dropping the device will not automatically delete the file). Also, to be able to use that space, you must shut down and restart the server to release its pointer to the device.

Default Disks

The point of defining disks with disk init is to store data on them. The data will be stored in databases that actually allocate space on disks for tables of data, their indexes and related objects, database transaction logs, and so forth. At database creation time, a database must have a disk on which to reside; if there are no devices available (no space left on any defined device), a database cannot be created.

When creating databases, you can (and should) specify the devices where the database will reside. In some cases, you may want the server to determine the devices where the database will reside; in those cases, the server may use only disks that you have indicated to be default disks. In other words, if a database is created and no device is specified, each default disk may be used as a database device.

The `sp_diskdefault` stored procedure requires a logical device name, and the default status of the disk device as mandatory parameters.

```
sp_diskdefault "device_name", {defaulton | defaultoff}
```

Here are some examples of `sp_diskdefault` usages.

```
exec sp_diskdefault data_device_1, defaulton
exec sp_diskdefault master, defaultoff
```

> **NOTE**
>
> You use execute or exec before any stored procedure that is not the first statement on the batch. This is a rule for the SQL Server parser.
>
> In the previous example in which you issue two procedure requests in a single batch, the first use of exec is optional, the second is required.

In the first example, you instruct the server that data_device_1 can be used as a default device.

In the second example, you tell the server that you do not want to use database space on the master device unintentionally. This does not mean that the master cannot be used; it does mean that the space cannot be used unless it is specifically allocated.

> **NOTE**
>
> The only device whose default status is automatically on is the master device. (Master is the *default* default device.) This means that if you issue a simple create database command and do not specify a device, the database might end up on the master device.
>
> You do not want the master device cluttered unintentionally. (It's a real problem if the master device becomes full—especially if you need to increase the size of the master database.) So, turn off the default bit of your master database right now!

Because the `sp_diskdefault` command affects server-wide resources, it is limited to systems administrators only.

The net effect of the `sp_diskdefault` command is that the 2^0 bit in the status bit of the sysdevices table for that device is set to 1 (if defaulton) or 0 (if defaultoff).

In most systems, a default is the single option chosen when no selection is made by the user. Because you can set the default bit on or off independently for each device, you can end up with several default disks (or none).

It probably seems a little strange to have several default devices. How does the server decide which default disk device to use? Space on default devices is assigned to databases alphabetically, exhausting all space on each default disk device, then proceeding to the next, until all requested space is allocated.

For example, consider the following `create database` command, which requests that 100MB be assigned to database `newdb` on a default disk device (or devices):

```
create database newdb on default = 100
```

Assume that you have the default disks and available space on each as outlined in Table 25.2. (OK, it doesn't follow the Greek alphabet correctly, but neither does SQL Server.)

Table 25.2. Default disks.

Disk Name	Available Space
alpha_device	10MB
beta_device	10MB
delta_device	10MB
gamma_device	1000MB

Where will the server place `newdb`? The obvious answer is, "There is room on the `gamma_device`, so it will go there." But this is not the way default disks are allocated. Remember that space on default disks is assigned to databases alphabetically.

Here's what happens:

- 10MB is allocated on `alpha_device`.
- 10MB is allocated on `beta_device`.
- 10MB is allocated on `delta_device`.
- The remaining 70MB is allocated on `gamma_device`.

The net effect is the same as if you had issued the `create database` command:

```
create database newdb
   on alpha_device = 10,
      beta_device = 10,
      delta_device = 10,
      gamma_device = 70
```

and the effect on the disks is the following:

Disk name	Available space
alpha_device	0MB
beta_device	0MB
delta_device	0MB
gamma_device	930MB

Note that this is not necessarily a performance problem. In fact, it is an advantage to spread active tables across disk controllers.

TIP

If you want to find out whether a specific device is a default device, you can check the device status bit in sysdevices (if the status is odd, the 2^0 bit is set and it is a default device). Alternatively, use the sp_helpdevice command. It specifies whether the device is a default device.

It's normally not a good idea to use default disks. Whatever work it saves you in remembering physical device names is nullified by the enormous pain you will endure to fix one bad command. Turn off all your default statuses and specify device names in your create database statements.

In fact, it is unusual to have default disks defined. Systems administrators tend to want to keep a very tight control on physical server resources.

Expanding Disk Devices

For those familiar with previous versions of SQL Server, this section title is sure to induce some head scratching. All previous versions of the Microsoft server, and all versions (including System 10) of the Sybase server, have maintained a fixed allocation for database devices. They could not be shrunk or enlarged, only dropped and re-created. Microsoft has added a new command, DISK RESIZE, to give administrators a way to increase the size allocation for their existing devices.

The syntax for DISK RESIZE is quite simple, as illustrated here:

```
DISK RESIZE
NAME = logical_device_name,
SIZE = final_size
```

The name parameter references a unique logical device name, and the size parameter is the *final size* for the device. As with DISK INIT, the size parameter must be specified in 2KB pages. This command is not generally used (if you're using it too much, you're not properly calculating your space needs in advance), but it is quite useful for expanding the master device so that the master database can grow. DISK RESIZE can be used on any valid SQL Server database device.

Disk Mirroring

Occasionally, devices fail.

You can ensure against problems caused by device failures by instructing the server to mirror two devices, keeping them in complete sync at all times. You can mirror devices at the hardware, operating system, or SQL Server level. In the last case, SQL Server handles all the disk mirroring work.

> **WARNING**
>
> Disk mirroring at the hardware level may work, and may reduce the load on the CPU, but it is necessary to stress-test the hardware mirroring before counting on it to work with SQL Server in a production environment. In Chapter 18, "Database Object Placement and Performance," you'll learn the pros and cons of using different disk storage systems and their affect on SQL Server

You should mirror, at a minimum, the master device and all your log devices. A failed master device without backup is agony; a failed master device with backup is merely a pain in the backside. (You learn more about this in the recovery section in Chapter 29, "SQL Server Database Backup and Restoration.") Failed log devices cook the database; if the log devices do not fail, data device failures can be mitigated at least through log recovery (again, more in Chapter 29).

If you mirror devices across controllers (see Figure 25.9) as well as across physical disks, you reduce potential single points of failure.

FIGURE 25.9.

Mirroring across devices still leaves you vulnerable to a controller failure. Mirroring across controllers protects against controller failures as well.

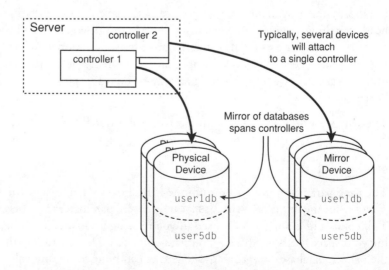

> **NOTE**
>
> SQL Server allows you to specify NOSERIAL for mirrored disk writes, but, in fact, it supports only SERIAL writes. SQL Server from Microsoft eliminated the NOSERIAL option for Version 6.0, but kept the syntax for compatibility with previous versions of SQL Server.

Although SQL Server currently has a limitation of 255 physical devices, mirroring does not take up any of these device connections. (Note the syntax.) Therefore, a mirror device is not a disk device; it does not require a distinct vdevno.

Finally, please note that the available space at the physical location of a mirror device must be at least as large as the device it is mirroring.

The disk mirror command syntax is illustrated here.

```
disk mirror
name = 'logical_device_name',
mirror = 'physical_device_name'
[ , writes = {serial ¦ noserial } ]
```

In the disk mirror syntax, *logical_device_name* is the name of the device that you initialized (on which you used the disk init command). The *physical_device_name* is the device that holds the contents of the mirror. Serial writes, the only option supported on Windows NT versions of SQL Server, ensures that, in case of a power failure, the write will go to at least one of the physical devices if the mirrors are on separate physical devices (they should be). The noserial option is kept only for compatibility with prior versions of SQL Server.

The syntax for the disk mirror command is presented here.

```
disk mirror
name = 'data_device_1',
mirror = 'r:\sql60\mirrors\d_dev_1.mir'
```

In the example, you mirror a device that you initialized and to which you assigned the logical device name data_device_1. A copy of all writes to the disk are also written to the physical device at 'r:\sql60\mirrors\d_dev_1.mir'. Drive R should be a separate physical disk, and, if possible, connected using a separate controller.

Sequence of Events

There are three steps in the disk mirror sequence of events:

1. The secondary device (mirror device) is initialized.
2. All used pages on the primary device are copied to the secondary device. Note that, as expected, this is not a fast process.
3. Bits are set in sysdevices—bit 2^6 (device mirrored) and 2^9 (mirror enabled).

> **WARNING**
>
> SQL Server mirrors at the device level, not the database level. If a database is spread across many devices, and any one database is not mirrored, the database is at risk of a physical failure. For a database to be fully protected, *every device associated with that database must be mirrored.*

Disk Mirroring Information

The easiest way to check on disk mirroring for a device is with the `sp_helpdevice` command.

Alternatively, you can identify all the disk devices (devices with `cntrltype` of 0—others are backup devices) using this SQL statement:

```
select * from sysdevices where cntrltype = 0
```

Deactivating Disk Mirroring:

1. You, as the sa, issue the `disk unmirror` command.
2. SQL Server, in an attempt to write to a primary or secondary device of a mirror pair, is unable to write to one of the devices.

The server maintains the bit flags within the device status in `sysdevices` to report on the status of the mirror. When mirrors fail or are disabled for any reason, the server updates the bit flags to indicate which mirror failed. Table 25.3 summarizes the bit flags as they relate to mirror devices. Note that other status flags (default or reads mirrored) could be set in addition to the flags described in the table.

Table 25.3. Status flags relating to mirror devices.

State of Mirror	Status Value	Decoded Status
Not mirrored	2 (2)	Physical disk
Mirrored	578 (2+64+512)	Mirrored, mirror enabled
Secondary failed	66 (2+64)	Mirrored
Primary failed	322 (2+64+256)	Mirrored, half mirrored

Unmirroring a device has the effect of modifying status bits and instructing the server to write to only one specific device of a mirrored pair.

If the mirroring is automatic, the server checkpoints the master database so that changes in the sysdevices table are permanently reflected on the disk.

The syntax for the disk unmirror command is illustrated here.

```
disk unmirror
name = 'logical_name'
[ , side = { 'primary' | 'secondary' } ]
[ , mode = { retain | remove } ]
```

The parameter *logical name* is the device that you initialized with the disk init command: the primary side is the device that you initialized; the secondary is the mirror that you specified. You can unmirror either the primary or the secondary device. Defaults are secondary and retain.

If you specify retain, the names of the unmirrored devices are kept in the sysdevices table indefinitely, and you can remirror (this is discussed shortly). Automatic unmirroring uses the retain option.

An example disk unmirror statement is shown here:

```
disk unmirror
name = 'data_device_1',
side = 'primary',
mode = remove
```

In the example, you are telling the server that you want to permanently remove the definition of the primary device from the data_device_1 device. The effect is that the mirror side becomes the primary (only) device.

```
disk unmirror name = 'data_device_1'
```

In this example, the server unmirrors the secondary device, and keeps the definition of the device in sysdevices. In this case, you can use the disk remirror command.

Disk Remirroring

After a device becomes unmirrored automatically, or manually with mode = retain, you, the sa, can instruct the server to restart the software mirroring. The disk remirror statement will fail unless the device was previously mirrored and the definition still remains in sysdevices.

An example of the syntax of the disk remirror command is presented here:

```
disk remirror name = 'logical_name'
```

Note that it is not necessary to specify anything else. The *logical name* in sysdevices already has the necessary information in the row or the command will fail (and you should have used the disk mirror command instead).

```
disk remirror name = 'data_device_1'
```

> **NOTE**
>
> Regardless of the elapsed time of the disk unmirroring process (one second unmirrored, with no updates occurring, for example), an unmirrored disk is considered to be out of synchronization with the primary, and the mirroring process begins anew. This means that the entire device is recopied onto the mirror (or primary, if that was the side unmirrored). Remember that this is not a fast process.

What happens when you have an older device that is being replaced because it is too old, small, or slow? What if you have several databases on the device (or parts of several databases on a device)? One technique is to execute the following steps:

1. Dump all the databases.
2. Drop all the databases. (You cannot drop a device if a database is on it.)
3. Drop the "old" device.
4. Cycle the server. (Remember, the device numbers are not reusable.)
5. Re-create the device.
6. Re-create the databases.
7. Reload the databases.

This is a lot of work. It also needs to be done when your users are not on the system (and you'd rather be home in bed). It is possible to use the disk mirroring commands to migrate data from one device to another. This may be extremely useful.

Here is the easy way (see Figure 25.10):

1. Mirror the current disk onto the new disk (or an appropriate slice of the new disk).
2. Unmirror the device, `side` = `primary`, `mode` = `remove`.

FIGURE 25.10.

It usually is more efficient to migrate data with mirroring than to back it up and restore it.

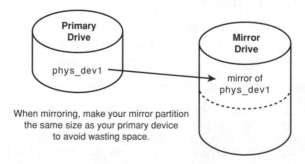

When mirroring, make your mirror partition the same size as your primary device to avoid wasting space.

You should mirror at least the master device and all log devices. With the low cost of disk space, there is little excuse not to mirror everything. Think about the cost of having the system down compared to the cost of a 2GB SCSI drive.

Mirroring the master device is *important.* If you lose master after a substantive change to your system configuration (but before a backup), you have to piece it back together. If you can't piece it back together, you may lose all contact with your user database(s).

Device SQL

It can be important to determine what devices are available, how much space is initialized on the devices, and how much space is actually utilized. This SQL returns that specific information in a neat report:

```
select 'Database device name' = name,
'In use by databases' = sum (size / 512),
'Space initialized' = (high-low+1)/512
from sysdevices, sysusages
where vstart between low and high
and cntrltype = 0
group by name, low, high
```

Controlling Device Mirroring with SQL Enterprise Manager

SQL-EM allows you to control all of these aspects of mirroring using the Manage Database Devices window that you saw earlier. When you click the Mirror button, SQL-EM displays the dialog displayed in Figure 25.11. With it, you can control all of the options defined previously using SQL syntax. As with the DISK INIT example described previously in the SQL-EM section, SQL-EM is executing the DISK MIRROR, DISK UNMIRROR, and DISK REMIRROR commands behind the scenes. The difference is, you now know what those commands are and how they should behave!

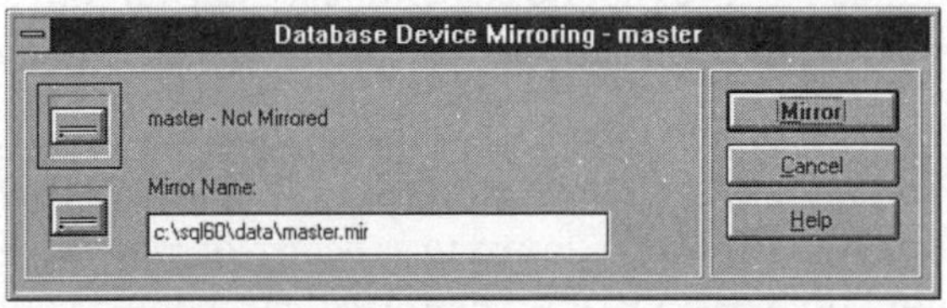

FIGURE 25.11.

Define mirroring in SQL-EM using the Database Device Mirroring dialog box.

Software Mirroring, Hardware Mirroring, and RAID

SQL Server mirrors data at the software level to ensure that mirroring is possible, regardless of hardware platform or configuration. There are alternatives, however, and most of them are recommended over SQL Server's own mirroring for reasons of cost, performance, or both. Many hardware vendors enable mirroring at the controller level. Alternatively, RAID provides an alternative to mirroring every device, along with a concurrent performance throughput benefit. What kinds of disk-level fault tolerance does SQL Server have available, and what are the trade-offs of using a particular method?

The next section covers three alternate methods of implementing disk fault tolerance for SQL Server, including Windows NT disk mirroring, Windows NT disk striping, and hardware-based RAID.

Software Mirroring

Software mirroring guarantees database stability against hardware failure. It is guaranteed by SQL Server, so if there is a problem, it is handled by MS-PSS. In addition, software mirroring enables you to mirror across controllers, minimizing single points of failure.

Software mirroring requires additional writes, however, which require more CPU cycles. Most users of this feature talk about a 10 percent performance hit from software mirroring.

Windows NT also provides operating-system level mirroring (technically considered RAID level 1) through the Disk Administrator application. Windows NT requires use of NTFS, or the native NT File System for mirrored drives. OS-level RAID 1, or *NTFS mirrored sets*, seems to demonstrate a slight performance increase on reads (the operating system simply accesses the drive available first), but writes do encounter a small penalty. Windows NT requires the equivalent of serial writes for all data modifications.

There is no error-checking or parity-bit allocation defined by the generic standard of RAID 1, and Windows NT does not do any error checking for mirrored sets. If the machine is capable of dual-booting to DOS, mirrored sets are unavailable (because they use NTFS, not FAT).

Windows NT also provides RAID support for levels 0 and 5. RAID 0 is simple data striping, where a single logical volume (expressed to Windows NT by a drive letter) actually consists of multiple physical devices (referred to as *platters* or *spindles*). This support is available only with NTFS, not HPFS or FAT. With RAID 0, there is only a performance improvement. Both read and write operations can be spread across multiple disks in parallel, improving throughput. RAID 0 does not provide any fault-tolerance options.

Instead, RAID 0 hands off fault-tolerance responsibilities to its big brother, RAID 5. Windows NT provides OS-level RAID 5 on NTFS partitions. RAID 5 not only stripes data across multiple disks, it also stripes a parity bit across the disks. RAID 5 guarantees the accuracy of data by ensuring that the data bits and associated parity bit are never written to the same physical disk.

RAID 5 is the most reliable of SQL Server's disk fault tolerance options, because RAID 5 provides for "hot fix" support. If a RAID 5 device fails, that device can be removed from the server while the database is processing. When a new device is inserted, the RAID management subsystem of Windows NT will automatically start rebuilding the previously defective disk until all of them are again synchronized. During this time, writes for both data and parity bits are routed to the remaining drives until the new disk is synchronized.

RAID 5 is a viable fault tolerance option, but still leaves a possible bottleneck. Although it can use multiple physical disks (it is recommended that you match this with multiple physical controllers), the power supply actually becomes a point of failure. That's where hardware-based disk mirroring and RAID 5 disk clusters come in.

Hardware Mirroring

Hardware mirroring reduces CPU work. (Hardware mirroring is handled by the controller, or, more important, duplexed controllers.)

Hardware mirroring is guaranteed by the hardware vendor, however. This means that if the mirroring does not work out, the hardware vendor will blame the software vendor, and the software vendor will blame the hardware vendor. This is not a pretty picture when all you want is your data back. (Database restoration is discussed in Chapter 29.)

> **TIP**
>
> If you are going to mirror at the hardware level, be sure to test the mirroring. When the server is under load, pull out one of the drives and see what happens. After mirroring is re-enabled, pull the other drive out and see what happens. (If you smell smoke or ozone, consider software mirroring.)
>
> One point about this: Network administrators have been pulling the plug on uninterruptible power supplies (UPSs) for years to make sure that the server can run even when the UPS has suffered a lapse in power from the power company. When you pull the power cord on the UPS, however, you can sometimes damage the UPS, and it stops working immediately.

Hardware RAID

With a hardware-based RAID subsystem, there are typically five devices. Four contain data and the fifth has redundant hash information. If any device fails, the RAID device notifies the operator and acts as if nothing happened as far as data transmission goes. The operator will replace the bad drive with a "hot" backup. The RAID device will automatically bring the new device up to speed.

Hardware-based RAID systems typically come with duplexed controllers, removing any one disk controller as a point of failure that could bring down the entire system. In addition, better RAID subsystems also provide duplicate power supplies, so that, should one fail, it can be hot-swapped while the other manages supplying five electricity-hungry disks with the power necessary to keep applications running. It has the added benefit of keeping the need to update your résumé to a minimum. The RAID architecture handles all mirroring automatically, and at the hardware level. It is a nifty technology.

RAID is expensive, however. No, that isn't true. It is breathtakingly expensive, and not just in purchase price. The parity bit that forms the core of RAID 5's fault tolerance consumes anywhere from 25 to 30 percent of the disk space available, so you'll have to count on needing at least 25 percent more disk than you would if you had bypassed on RAID. You might spend some time looking into advantages at the different RAID levels that you can set. You may decide that performance advantages are outweighed by an inconvenience factor.

Typically, you have to set RAID to level 5 to get the protection you want, and on many platforms, you might find that mirrored SCSI disks were faster after all, and don't cost what a good RAID subsystem would. The good news is that RAID subsystem prices are only coming down, and quickly.

Summary

You've learned how to implement storage devices using SQL Server, and looked at the use of internal and external mechanisms to provide fault tolerance and to ensure data reliability and availability. In the next chapter, you create databases using the space created on these devices.

Defining, Altering, and Maintaining Databases and Logs

26

IN THIS CHAPTER

This chapter addresses how to create and maintain databases and database logs. You learn several approaches to managing disk space on SQL Server, and also about SQL Server segments. If you are familiar with the term *segment* from a different database-management system, you need to disregard your preconceived definition when reading this chapter. It is likely that what is defined as a segment for some other database-management system is different from how SQL Server defines segments.

With SQL Server 6.0, part of an administrator's job regarding database creation and management is eased through the use of SQL Enterprise Manager. However, much of the fundamental logical and physical concepts that SQL Server is based upon are rooted in the original SQL syntax used to define and manage the components that are discussed in this chapter. Therefore, for the purposes of introducing topics and concepts, the initial references are to the traditional SQL syntax. Where appropriate, and after the discussion of concepts and SQL syntax, additional information and demonstrations follow concerning how to implement similar tasks using SQL Enterprise Manager. In order to be a competent administrator, you need to know what an application is doing behind the scenes to your server and databases. Teaching syntax first, and GUIs second, is a proven method for teaching skills, not just rote tasks.

What Is a Database?

The database concept is central to almost all implementation and administration tasks in SQL Server. During the database design phase of a project, you define the tables of interest to your organization. From a logical perspective, these related tables are collectively considered a single database. From a physical perspective, however, you can implement these tables in one or many SQL Server databases. The SQL Server database is important because it determines how data is stored physically—how data is mapped to physical devices. Physical space is assigned to a database during a database creation and additional space can be assigned to the database when the need arises.

Several key areas are based at the database level. All SQL Server objects must exist within the database—often referred to as "in the context of a database." Therefore, the limit on how large an object can grow is dependent on the amount of space allocated to the database. (At a detailed level, limits on object growth are truly dependent on the amount of space available to a segment in the database, which is described in the section titled "Segments and Object Placement," later in this chapter.) The database is also an important element in your security strategy because you must be a user of a database to be able to access objects within it. Some analysis tools, such as the Database Consistency Checker, act at the database level. Also, backups are typically conducted only at the database level, which means that a database is the standard unit of recovery available in SQL Server. (Table-level backups are supported, but only for very special disaster recovery situations. More on that in Chapter 29, "SQL Server Database Backup and Restoration.")

Databases and Space Management

Logical devices (see Chapter 25, "Defining Physical and Mirror Devices") make space usable to the SQL Server, and databases organize that space, making it available to SQL Server tables and their indexes as well as other objects. Databases cannot span physical SQL Servers, nor can tables and their indexes span databases. Therefore, the size of a database will limit the size of any tables and indexes it contains. However, if a table or index grows too large, you can increase the size of the database on the fly.

> **NOTE**
>
> Later in this chapter, you look at database segments and how they are used to manage table and index sizes within the database. Although people usually refer to the size of the database as determining the maximum size of a table or index, this is not fully accurate. Each object is created on a segment in a SQL Server database, and objects cannot span segments. Therefore, it is the amount of space available to the segment that determines the maximum size of an object.

Databases and Security

The owner of a database maps a system login to a database user. This is accomplished in one of four ways, described in detail in Chapter 27, "Security and User Administration." Permission to access objects is granted to a database user, either explicitly (to the user) or implicitly (to a user group). Therefore, if you do not allow a SQL Server login to be associated with a database user, you have eliminated that user's ability to access the objects within that database.

Databases and Backup

You will see later in this book in Chapter 29 that SQL Server utilities enable you to perform a *full backup* (a copy of the entire database) or an *incremental backup* (a copy of the transactions that have occurred since the last backup). Because transactions are logged in a table within a database, you need to be careful when creating related tables in different databases. For example, consider a table called customer in the customerdb database and a table called purchase in the purchase_db database. As part of a transaction, you add a new customer to the customer table and that customer's purchases to the purchase table. Each database logs the addition of rows in its own transaction log. If a disaster occurs and you lose the customer_db database, you might be forced to reload this database from backup (assume the purchase_db database is fine). It is possible that you would not be able to restore the customer_db database to the point at which the disaster occurred. Therefore, the purchase table would contain purchases for customers who are not in the customer table. When you decide how to distribute related tables in different databases, remember that you are possibly putting your data integrity at risk.

System Databases

A *system database* is a database created to support the operation of the server or a SQL Server facility. When SQL Server is installed, it creates at least three system databases—master, model, and tempdb. In a Version 6.0 installation, there is a fourth database created called msdb.

- The *master database* records all of the server-specific configuration information, including authorized users, devices, databases, system configuration settings, and remote servers.

- The *model database* is a template database. The contents of model are copied into each new database created after the system is installed.

- *tempdb* is the temporary database. This database is used as an interim storage area. It is used by the server (automatically) to resolve large or multistep queries or to sort data before returning results to the user (if a query contains an ORDER BY clause). It can also be used by programmers (syntactically) to provide a worktable to support application processing.

- *msdb* contains task scheduling, exception handling, and system operator information needed for SQL Executive. This database is discussed in detail in Chapter 34, "The Microsoft SQL Server Distributed Management Framework." The msdb database is a critical component of that framework.

> **NOTE**
>
> For shops that are running both Sybase and Microsoft SQL Server, one change made by Sybase but not copied by Microsoft is the movement of system stored procedures out of the master database and into a new Sybase-specific system database called sybsystemprocs. This database is specific to Sybase System 10. Any version of Sybase SQL Server prior to Release 10, and also all versions of Microsoft SQL Server, put the system stored procedures in the master database.

Database Creation

A primary task of the system administrator is to create databases. In this section, you learn the syntax of the CREATE DATABASE statement, as wells some of the implementation issues involved with database creation.

> **TIP**
>
> As you implement databases, remember that database creation can take a long time. Creation time depends mostly on your physical disk speed—the server initializes every page in a database—and can take between 20 and 60 minutes per gigabyte, depending on your platform. If you are implementing a very large database, this could affect your project schedule.

Syntax for *create database*

```
CREATE DATABASE database_name
[ON {DEFAULT | database_device} [= size]
    [, database_device [= size]]...]
[LOG ON database_device [= size]
    [, database_device [= size]]...]
[FOR LOAD]
```

When creating a database, you must provide a database name. Database names must be 30 characters or less, cannot include any punctuation or other special characters, and must be unique within the server.

> **NOTE**
>
> The naming conventions for database names vary widely between organizations. Some shops limit themselves to four or eight characters so that the database can easily map to DOS or MVS filenames. Others use long, descriptive names. Some shops standardize on encoded names, such as ACTV94TST01 (for "1994 activity test 1").
>
> Database names are case-sensitive; for example, you could create two databases, customer_db and CUSTOMER_DB. Many organizations standardize on uppercase for database names and object names to enable easier portability to other environments.
>
> I recommend that you keep database names short. After all, people will need to type them. And keep them meaningful and memorable. Names like AU149305 don't mean much to most mortals. Use names such as Accounting or acctg, which are easy to remember and easy to type, so your users and programmers won't be cursing you six times a day. For more on naming standards, see Chapter 36, "Defining Systems Administration and Naming Standards."

A database is created on one or more physical devices. Specifying the device is technically optional—but is highly recommended. (Remember, as the system administrator, your first responsibility is to maintain complete control of how SQL Server uses the physical resources of the platform hosting it!) When indicating the device, you use the logical name you specified as part of DISK INIT. (See Chapter 25 for more on setting up database devices.)

NOTE

If you do not specify the device on which to create the database, a default device will be used (see the "Default Disks" section in Chapter 25). Most DBAs like to know up front where a database is going to be placed. Therefore, always supply the device where you want the database to be created.

You also can specify the size of the database in megabytes. If a size is not indicated, the server will use the larger of the default size (a configurable value set to 2MB by SQL Server Setup) or the size of the model database (because the contents of model are copied into each new database created). It is a good standard practice to always provide SIZE to CREATE DATABASE.

NOTE

You specify disk size in pages, but you specify database size in megabytes. If you request more megabytes than are available on a device, the server will allocate all remaining space on the device, as long as there is enough room to make a complete copy of the model database.

This doesn't guarantee that you'll get all the space you asked for! In a wonderful bout of inconsistency, the confirmation message for the CREATE DATABASE statement displays the number of pages allocated on a particular device. Each time you run CREATE DATABASE, take the number of pages for each device and add them together. Divide that number by 512, and that number should equal the total space allocation you specified in megabytes in your original CREATE DATABASE statement.

You can also use the sp_helpdb stored procedure to verify that the created space and allocated space are the same.

Examples of *CREATE DATABASE*

The following are some sample CREATE DATABASE statements.

NOTE

Note how the SQL has been written to improve readability: Each individual device is listed on its own line. This does not affect how the command works, but it certainly makes it easier to read later on. And don't forget that you are saving all create statements in a script in case you need to execute them later.

The first example sets up a 12MB (8 + 4) database called marketing. In this database, 8MB is allocated for tables, indexes, system tables, and other objects (all of which are broadly classified as *data*), and 4MB is allocated for the transaction log.

> **NOTE**
>
> The transaction log is used by SQL Server to log certain activity within a database. Examples of logged activity include creating objects; adding or deleting database users; or adding, deleting, or modifying data in tables.

```
CREATE DATABASE marketing
ON data_device_1 = 8
LOG ON log_device_4 = 4
```

> **NOTE**
>
> In general, you should set up your log segment on a separate drive and, if possible, a separate controller. Performance will be much better. You will be able to perform incremental backups, and you will be better able to recover after a disaster. Please see Chapter 28, "Database Logging and Recovery," for more on transaction logs.

The next example sets up a 30MB (12 + 8 + 10) database called accounting. It provides 20MB for data and 10MB for the transaction log.

```
CREATE DATABASE accounting
ON data_device_1 = 12,
data_device_2 = 8
LOG ON log_device_1 = 10
```

This CREATE DATABASE statement includes several devices and sizes. If you include several devices, SQL Server acquires a fragment of the size you specify on each device. If there is not enough space on any single device listed, SQL Server will allocate as much space as it can on the device. A single database can have a maximum of 32 individual fragments.

The next example includes the keywords FOR LOAD. Create a database FOR LOAD if you are creating the structure for the sole purpose of restoring a database from a backup where the structure does not exist. For example, consider the situation in which you have encountered a database corruption and are forced to load from a backup copy. Normally, a corrupt database must be dropped—completely removed from the physical devices. However, you must load the backup copy into an existing database. Because the LOAD process is going to replace the existing structure with the data in the backup, there is no need to go through the time-consuming activity of initializing all the database pages. See Chapter 29 for more information on restoring databases.

```
CREATE DATABASE newdb
ON data_device_3 = 12,
data_device_4 = 8
LOG ON log_device_2 = 10
FOR LOAD
```

After a CREATE DATABASE … FOR LOAD, the only permitted operation on the database is LOAD DATABASE, the SQL Server method of restoring a database from backup.

What Happens When You Create a Database?

The server performs the following actions when you create a database:

1. Immediately allocates database space.

2. Inserts one row in sysdatabases (a system table in the master database) for the database. You will have a row in sysdatabases for every database in a server.

3. Inserts one row in sysusages (master database) for each device fragment.

4. Physically marks each extent. An extent is comprised of eight data pages. This activity is what takes the bulk of the elapsed time for a database creation.

5. Copies the model database into the new database.

If the database is created FOR LOAD, the server allocates the space from the specified devices but does not mark the extents or copy the contents of the model database into the structure. The actual marking of extents is an automatic part of the restore process (LOAD DATABASE). If you do not create the database FOR LOAD, you are performing the most time-consuming part of the create process needlessly.

> **NOTE**
>
> A hospital system using SQL Server experienced a database corruption. Minimizing downtime was critical. By using FOR LOAD, I was able to create the database structure in a few minutes—instead of performing a "normal" database create, which had originally taken over seven hours. This enabled the system to be up and running almost a full business day sooner than if I had not used FOR LOAD.

Here are the steps SQL Server performs when you specify FOR LOAD in a CREATE DATABASE statement:

1. Immediately allocate database space.

2. Insert one row in sysdatabases for the database.

3. Insert one row per device fragment in sysusages.

4. Set the database status bit 5 (value = 32), indicating that the database was created FOR LOAD.

Defining Databases Using SQL Enterprise Manager

SQL Enterprise Manager enables you to define, expand, and shrink databases the same way CREATE DATABASE enable you to do so syntactically. By clicking on the Databases icon in the toolbar, or by selecting Manage | Databases... from the menu, you can display the window shown in Figure 26.1.

FIGURE 26.1.

From SQL-EM, choose Manage Databases to display a graph of databases, their sizes, and the space available.

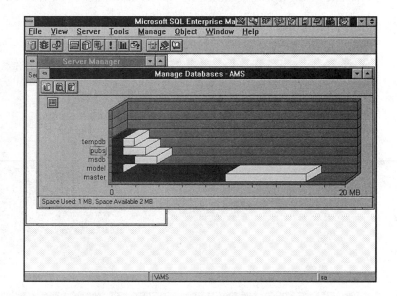

As with the Manage Database Devices dialog box (see Chapter 25), double-clicking on a particular database name in the window brings up detailed information on that database. (See Figure 26.2.) In addition, this is where you set database options (discussed later in this chapter) and assign permissions for users to database objects (discussed in Chapter 27).

FIGURE 26.2.

Details on a database are available from SQL-EM by double-clicking on a database name.

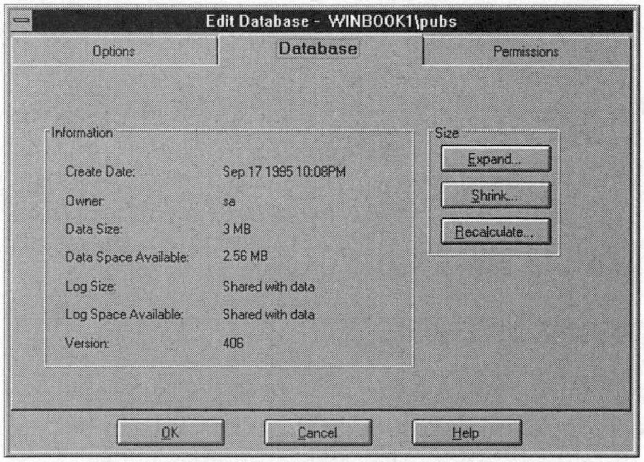

If you're creating a new database, clicking on the New Database icon in the toolbar (if you refer back to Figure 26.1, it's the first button on the left) brings up a dialog box where you can create databases, assign them to data and log devices, and see how creating a new database will affect your total available space on the server.

In Figure 26.3, the administrator is creating a 9MB database, using the `data_1` and `log_1` devices. The dialog legend at the left shows you how much space on each device the database will consume and how much, if any, is remaining. The Create for Load checkbox allows you to enable this option.

FIGURE 26.3.

Use the New Database dialog box to create a new database.

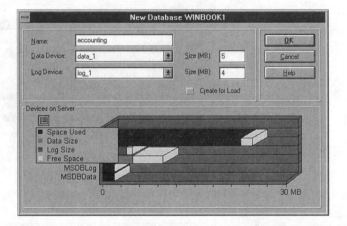

> **NOTE**
>
> With the SQL Enterprise Manager, you are limited to specifying just one data device and, optionally, one log device. If you want to spread the database across other devices, you must expand it using the dialog box shown in Figure 26.2, rather than the New Database dialog box displayed in Figure 26.3.

Sizing Databases

By definition, the size of the database is the size of all data fragments plus the size of all log fragments. The data area needs to be large enough to hold all of the system tables and your user tables, as well as any indexes. The log needs to be large enough for the transaction log.

Minimum Size

The minimum database size is the greater of the setting in `sp_configure` (2MB is the default value) or the size of the `model` database (also 2MB by default). If the `model` database will not fit into the allocated space, the database creation will fail.

Default Devices and Sizes

You don't need to specify a device name or a size. If you don't specify the size, the default size is the greater of the size of the model database and the value of database size in sysconfigures. For example, if database size is 2MB but the model database is 8MB, the default database size is 8MB.

> **NOTE**
>
> To change the minimum database size, you can either increase the size of the model database with ALTER DATABASE (see the section titled "Making Databases Larger," later in this chapter) or change the configured value (which is the recommended approach).
>
> To change the configuration setting to 8MB, use the sp_configure stored procedure:
>
> ```
> sp_configure "database size", 8
> reconfigure
> ```
>
> You need to restart your server before the new setting takes effect.

How Big Should the Database Be?

When you create a database, remember that the data area needs to be large enough to contain the system tables, user tables, and all indexes. You probably want to leave about 25 percent free space in your database as well. To estimate the eventual size requirements of tables, use the stored procedure sp_estspace.

> **NOTE**
>
> Use sp_estspace whenever you need to estimate how large a table and its indexes will grow. This stored procedure is available on the Microsoft CompuServe forum (go MSSQL). You can also find the script on the disk in this book; look for the file named estspace.sql.

It is important to remember that databases can easily get larger, but they can only get smaller with great difficulty. Shrinkable databases are a new feature for SQL Server 6.0 and are unique to that release. The general approach is to start the database small and let it grow as necessary.

How Big Should the Log Be?

The transaction log records all database modifications. If the log is full, no further modifications are permitted in the database. Under ordinary production circumstances, the only time SQL Server clears the transaction log is after an incremental backup.

The factors influencing log size are database activity level, the frequency of incremental backups, and the volume of simultaneous updates. Because these factors vary dramatically from one system to another, it is impossible to establish firm guidelines on sizing a database log. As a starting point, you might want to consider creating logs that are between 10 and 25 percent of the database size.

Long-running transactions also influence log size. If your system will be updating large amounts of data in a single transaction, the log must be large enough to hold the entire transaction. In that case, you might need the log to be 200 percent or more of the size of the data. If you want your logs to be smaller, you need to break up large updates into smaller transactions (which is usually a good idea anyway), and then dump the transaction log between the transactions to free up space in the log.

SETTING UP A SEPARATE AREA FOR THE TRANSACTION LOG

Most of the examples of database creation in this chapter include a separate allocation for the transaction log. This is accomplished by providing LOG ON information to CREATE DATABASE. Transaction logging and log management are discussed in great detail in Chapter 28, but it's important now to understand some of the characteristics of transaction logs.

A SQL Server transaction log is a record of all modifications made to a database. Every object creation, every security implementation, every row modification (INSERT, UPDATE, DELETE) is logged in a transaction log. (There are a handful of nonlogged activities, which are discussed later; but in a true production environment, all activities are fully logged.)

The transaction log is a *write-ahead log,* which means that logged activity is written to the transaction log before the modifications are made to the tables and indexes themselves. In most cases, the only information that is written to disk at the time of update is the logging information; the data will be brought up to date only at checkpoint time.

There are several crucial benefits to separating your log from your data in your CREATE DATABASE statement.

First, SQL Server incremental backups are actually just copies of the transaction log. If the data and log areas are not separated, the server cannot perform incremental backups; all backups for databases with integrated log and data areas will be full backups.

Second, you can get some performance benefits by separating log and data activity, especially if the devices are attached to separate physical disk drives in the server.

Third, without separate logs, recovery is more difficult. One implication of writing the log first is that the log is the unit of data integrity in SQL Server. If you lose your data but have your log, up-to-the-transaction recovery is possible (even likely). If you lose your log but still have your data, up-to-the-transaction recovery is not possible, and you can only recover up to the point of your last backup.

The best method of ensuring fault tolerance is to mirror all of the devices, or use RAID 5 technology, but sometimes that is not feasible. If you can mirror at least your log devices (which are always smaller than all database devices), you can ensure recoverability. If any log device fails, you still have an alternative device from which you can work. (See Chapter 25 for more information on mirroring.)

How Big Should You Make *tempdb*?

The `tempdb` database is a temporary work area used by the SQL Server to resolve large queries or queries requiring the creation of a worktable. (Queries that might need a worktable include those with `ORDER BY` or `DISTINCT` clauses. The `GROUP BY` clause always uses a worktable.) Users can also direct SQL Server to create temporary tables with `CREATE TABLE` or `SELECT ... INTO` statements.

Temporary tables are identified by the number sign (#) in the first character. For example, the following statement creates a temporary table, `#authors_and_titles`, in `tempdb`:

```
select au_lname, au_fname, title
into #authors_and_titles
from authors a, titleauthor ta, titles t
where a.au_id = ta.au_id
and ta.title_id = t.title_id
```

The size of the temporary table depends on the size of the tables referenced in the query (`authors`, `titleauthor`, and `titles`).

You cannot restrict users from creating temporary tables. The temporary tables will persist until the user explicitly drops the table (`DROP TABLE #titles_and_authors`) or until the user creating the temporary table logs out. Temporary tables created by stored procedures are dropped when the procedure ends.

Sizing `tempdb` depends on a number of factors: how often users create ad hoc temporary tables, whether application programs or stored procedures create temporary tables, how many concurrent users will need to create these tables at one time, and so forth.

TIP

The typical motivation for a programmer to use a temporary table is to avoid a second pass through a large table. By copying a small subset of the data to another location, the user can save many disk operations and improve performance. In general, you want to encourage programmers to think this way because it will improve overall system performance.

If you properly select indexes on the primary tables, it might not be necessary to create a worktable to resolve a query. For example, a programmer might want to retrieve data from a table in a particular order. If there was a clustered index created on the columns that the programmer wants to order the data by, the data could be retrieved directly from the primary tables. (The creation of a clustered index on the column or columns of a table will physically store the data in the table in the sort order specified.)

NOTE

If `tempdb` runs out of space, the transaction aborts and an error is reported in the error log and the Windows NT Event Log.

At first, make `tempdb` about 25 percent of the size of your largest database, unless you have reason to expect you will need substantially more.

Microsoft introduced a new `tempdb` option with Version 4.2 for Windows NT: `tempdb` in RAM. This configuring option enables SQL Server to allocate a block of memory for tempdb. In effect, all operations that require SQL Server to use `tempdb` are forced into RAM, instead of using a combination of physical disk and cache.

The performance improvement is dramatic, but there are some interesting details. First, SQL Server still caches `tempdb` in the data cache area. In effect, SQL Server can fetch data pages out of the database (which are in RAM) into data cache pages (which are also in RAM). Second, this requires a substantial amount of RAM, because SQL Server might be better able to allocate that RAM as database cache instead.

Microsoft's own recommendations call for `tempdb` to be loaded into RAM only if the server has more than 64MB of physical memory. Of course, doing so is also dependent on how heavily your queries make use of `tempdb`. Chapter 32, "Measuring SQL Server Performance," discusses using Windows NT's Performance Monitor utility, showing you how to use PerfMon to profile your database and queries to determine whether this option will help you.

Database Creation Authority and Database Ownership

Databases are created by the system administrator. The system administrator has the ability to grant CREATE DATABASE permissions, but this should be done only with great care.

Whoever creates a database owns it. However, ownership of a database can be transferred.

Allowing Others to Create Databases

Someone other than the system administrator can create a database if the system administrator grants that person the ability to execute the CREATE DATABASE command. (See Chapter 27 for more information.)

Ordinarily, you will not assign the database-creation ability to others, and you should not. Because database creation allocates system resources, you want to manage this task carefully and thoughtfully. Database creation should be a "system administrators only" task.

If you really need to allow others to create databases, do the following:

1. Use the master database:

   ```
   use master
   go
   ```

2. Add a database user in the master database for the particular login:

   ```
   sp_adduser john
   go
   ```

3. Grant the CREATE DATABASE privilege to the user:

   ```
   GRANT CREATE DATABASE TO john
   go
   ```

Transferring Database Ownership

Whoever creates a database is designated as its *owner*. It is very common to transfer ownership of a database to another user after the database is created. Database ownership is often transferred to distribute responsibility: A person other than the sa login is responsible for the normal operations of the database (adding users, granting permissions, and so on).

> **NOTE**
>
> The database is the only object that can change ownership. If you try to change the ownership of a table or other object, the system usually marks the entire database "suspect" and you will need to drop the database and restore from tape. I know, because I tried it.

Database ownership can be changed using the sp_changedbowner stored procedure. The sa login, or the database owner, can change the ownership as needed using this stored procedure.

Database ownership cannot be transferred using the SQL Enterprise Manager. You must run the sp_changedbowner stored procedure if you want to change database ownership.

Making Databases Larger

Use the ALTER DATABASE command to make databases larger. You can enlarge a database while the system is online and the database is in use.

Syntax for *ALTER DATABASE*

The ALTER DATABASE command is similar to CREATE DATABASE.

```
ALTER DATABASE db_name
[ON device_name [= size], [...]]
[LOG ON device_name [= size]]
```

Specify the additional amount of space to be allocated, not the ultimate size of the database. The default increment is 1MB.

Consider the following example of using the CREATE DATABASE and the ALTER DATABASE command together.

```
CREATE DATABASE market_db
ON device1 = 50,
device_2 = 100
LOG ON logdev1 = 35
ALTER DATABASE market_db
ON device1 = 50
```

In this example, a 185MB database is created on three devices. The ALTER DATABASE command adds an additional 50MB, for a total of 235MB.

Altering a database using SQL Enterprise Manager uses dialog boxes similar to those used in database creation. Using SQL-EM, right-click on the database you want to alter; then select Edit from the popup menu that appears. This displays the Manage Databases dialog box. Clicking on the Expand button displays the dialog box shown in Figure 26.4.

Selecting a device for a specific database portion (data or log), you are instructing SQL Server to expand the space allocation for the current database on that device. In the previous example, no devices are selected. However, I can expand the log, or the data area, or both, by selecting devices for them. SQL Server can expand databases online with little performance impact for users, depending on the available hardware platform.

FIGURE 26.4.

SQL Enterprise Manager makes space allocation easier by presenting a visual image of current space usage and available space for expanding databases.

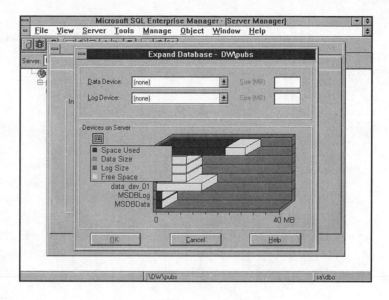

Adding Log Space

Adding log space to a database requires the LOG ON keywords (found in Version 6.0 only) in the ALTER DATABASE statement:

```
ALTER DATABASE market_db
LOG ON logdev2 = 35
```

This statement adds 35MB of space to the log of the market_db database.

Assigning Space to the Log

Typically, you assign log space with the LOG ON clause in the CREATE database or ALTER DATA-BASE statement. It is also possible to assign database space on a specific device to the log retro-actively (that is, after a CREATE or ALTER statement) with the sp_logdevice stored procedure, as in the following:

```
sp_logdevice databasename, devicename
```

Consider the following examples:

```
CREATE DATABASE test_db
ON device1 = 50,
device2 = 100
LOG ON logdev1 = 35
ALTER DATABASE test_db
ON newdevice = 50
```

After the ALTER statement, the database is 235MB, with 200MB of space for data and system tables (50MB on device1, 100MB on device2, and 50MB on newdevice) and 35MB of space for the transaction log (on logdevice1).

The space allocation on additional database devices is assumed to be used for data in SQL Server. In the preceding example, the allocation on newdevice is for data because there was no previous allocation of space for the database on the device. If you want to make newdevice a log device, use the sp_logdevice statement.

```
sp_logdevice test_db, newdevice
```

> **NOTE**
>
> In the previous example, the CREATE DATABASE statement sets aside 35MB on logdev1 for the transaction log. All subsequent allocations of space on that device will also be used for the log. The sp_logdevice procedure sets aside any space allocations on newdevice for the log as well.
>
> This is really the crucial point about space utilization: Space is assigned for data or log by device. This is a special case of the general use of database segments, which is examined in detail a little later in this chapter.

Exploring Databases

It's useful to get under the hood when it comes to databases, particularly if you ever need to do creative work with the system tables to enable a recovery. In the next sections, you're going to explore databases using standard stored procedures and then examine the system tables in more detail.

sp_helpdb

The system stored procedure, sp_helpdb, provides information about databases on the server. If you don't provide a parameter, the system provides a list of all databases on the server:

```
sp_helpdb
```

```
name             db_size   owner dbid created      status
---------------  -------   ----- ---- -----------  --------------------------
fred             4.0 MB    sa       9 Jan 18, 1995 no options set
master           3.0 MB    sa       1 Jan 01, 1900 no options set
model            2.0 MB    sa       3 Jan 01, 1900 no options set
perftune         5.5 MB    sa       6 Jan 06, 1995 select into/bulkcopy
pubs2            2.0 MB    sa       8 Nov 23, 1994 no options set
sybsecurity      8.0 MB    sa       7 Nov 10, 1994 trunc log on chkpt
sybsystemprocs   20.0 MB   sa       4 Nov 05, 1994 trunc log on chkpt
tempdb           2.0 MB    sa       2 Jan 05, 1995 select into/bulkcopy
testdb           4.0 MB    sa       5 Nov 07, 1994 no options set
```

If you provide a parameter, you get detailed information about a single database, as in the following example:

```
sp_helpdb pubs2

name             db_size owner dbid created      status
---------------- ------- ----- ---- ------------ ----------------------------
pubs2            2.0 MB sa        8 Nov 23, 1994 no options set

device_fragments size    usage               free kbytes
---------------- ------- ------------------- -----------
master           2.0 MB data and log                 480
```

The detailed information from sp_helpdb includes a list of database fragments, which are specific allocations of space on each device.

As you have already seen in this chapter, all of the information presented by these stored procedures is available in the Manage Database dialog box or one of its accessory dialog windows.

Database System Tables

When you create and modify databases, three system tables in the master database are involved: sysdatabases, sysusages, and sysdevices. (See Figure 26.5.)

FIGURE 26.5.

The sysusages table resolves the many-to-many relationship between sysdatabases and sysdevices.

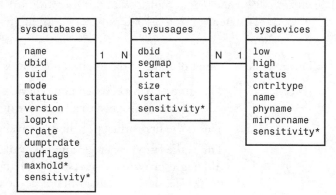

sysdatabases

The server adds a row to sysdatabases for each new database. The user specifies the name, but the server automatically selects the next available integer ID for dbid. There are several important columns in sysdatabases:

name	The name of the database, assigned by the database creator.
dbid	The system-assigned identifier for the database.
suid	The ID of the database owner; at database creation time, this is set to the ID of the login who issued the CREATE DATABASE statement. To change the database owner, use the sp_changedbowner stored procedure.

status	An integer consisting of several control bits with information about the database. See the section titled "The Database Status Flags" later in this chapter.
dumptrdate	The date of the last dump transaction. The server marks this date on the next transaction dump to ensure that all dumps are loaded in order during a restore from backup.

sysdevices

The CREATE DATABASE statements do not affect the sysdevices table, but each named device must exist in sysdevices. Information in sysdevices is used to build detailed rows in sysusages, so it is useful to look at sysdevices now. The important columns for this discussion are cntrltype, low, high, and name.

The maximum size of a device on SQL Server is 16 million pages (32GB). A unique range of 16 million pages is allocated to each device upon allocation; these are *virtual page numbers*.

NOTE

The virtual page range is determined by multiplying the virtual device number assigned in the disk init statement by 2^{24}, or approximately 16 million.

The following is a description of some of the important columns in sysdevices:

cntrltype	This differentiates between dump devices and database devices. A value of zero is assigned to all database devices.
low	This is the first virtual page number available on the device.
high	This is the last virtual page number available on the database device. Although the system reserves the entire range of 16 million pages to the device, the high value will reflect the device's actual capacity. To determine the number of pages on a device, use high - low + 1. To determine the number of megabytes, use (high - low + 1) / 512.
name	This is the logical name of the device.

The following is a sample listing from the sysdevices table for all physical database devices (cntrltype = 0).

```
select cntrltype, low, high, name
from sysdevices
where cntrltype = 0
order by low
```

```
cntrltype low          high         name
--------- ----------   ----------   -------------------------------
0         0            12799        master
0         16777216     16787455     sysprocsdev
0         33554432     33558527     sybsecurity
0         67108864     67112959     testdevice
0         100663296    100665343    test_dev
0         1342177728   134230015    introdev
0         150994944    151000063    instruct2_data
```

Values in the low column are even multiples of 16,777,216.

TIP

To determine the virtual device number, divide the low value by 16,777,216; the virtual device number for testdevice is 4.

The size of the testdevice is (67112959 – 67108864 + 1) = 4096 pages = 8MB.

sysusages

The CREATE DATABASE statement automatically adds one row in sysusages for each allocation of space on a device. For example, the CREATE DATABASE command,

```
CREATE DATABASE market_db
ON DATA_1 = 100, DATA_2 = 100
LOG ON LOG_1 = 50
```

allocates space on three devices, DATA_1, DATA_2, and LOG_1. Each of these allocations is recorded in a separate row in sysusages.

Take a closer look at the useful columns in sysusages:

dbid   The database identifier is used to relate information in sysusages with sysdatabases (dbid exists in sysdatabases as well).

segmap   This is used to map database fragments to segments (see the section "Segments and Object Placement," later in this chapter).

lstart   The first database (logical) page number is the logical page start within the database.

size   This is the number of contiguous pages.

vstart   The starting virtual page number enables you to map the database fragment to a specific virtual device. The fragment is located on the device if the vstart value falls between the low and high page numbers for the device in sysdevices.

Using SQL to Query the System Tables

The trick to joining sysdevices, sysdatabases, and sysusages is to understand how virtual device numbers in sysdevices are mapped to the vstart column in the sysusages table.

The following output displays the rows in sysusages for a single database. There are three fragments in the database, all on the same virtual device. sysusages includes one row per device fragment per database.

```
select *
from sysusages
where dbid = 9
order by lstart

dbid    segmap      lstart      size        vstart      pad     unreservedpgs
9       7           0           1024        67110912            664
9       7           1024        512         67111936            512
9       7           1536        512         67112448            512
```

The vstart value for each fragment falls between the low and high page numbers (67108864 and 67112959) for the testdevice, so each of these fragments is stored on the testdevice.

The actual SQL used to join sysusages to sysdevices uses a between test, as in the following fragment:

```
where sysusages.vstart between sysdevices.low and sysdevices.high
  and cntrltype = 0
```

NOTE

Some older SQL Server documentation tells you to join sysusages to sysdevices with the lstart column. This is wrong. Use vstart to make the join to sysdevices.

The following is the SQL used to list allocations of space on devices for each database:

```
select 'Database' = d.name, 'Device' = v.name, u.size
from sysdatabases d, sysusages u, sysdevices v
where d.dbid = u.dbid
  and u.vstart between v.low and v.high
  and cntrltype = 0
order by d.name
compute sum(u.size) by d.name
```

Database Space Usage

Use sp_spaceused to determine the amount of space used (and space available) in your database. If the database runs out of space for objects, you will not be able to add data to tables or indexes. You also might not be able to add new views or procedures, depending on where the space shortfall occurred.

The database runs out of space only when it tries to allocate a new extent to an object. For example, the server determines that a page split is required in an index, but the current extent is full. At that time, the server attempts to allocate a new extent (8 pages, which is usually 16KB) to the index. If all extents for the segment are reserved, the update fails and rolls back and the server reports an error (`out of space ON segment…`).

You usually want about 25 percent free space in your database at all times. This helps you avoid major work stoppages when you are hurrying to add additional space to the database.

The `sp_spaceused` procedure can report on the space allocated to a table if you pass the tablename as a parameter (`sp_spaceused tablename`). However, you should be more concerned with database space usage and availability at this time. No parameters are required to get database space usage for the current database, as in the following example:

```
sp_spaceused

database_name                    database_size
-----------------------------    --------------------
master                           8 MB
(0 rows affected)

reserved         data            index_size        unused
-------------    -------------   ---------------   -------------
5230 KB          4232 KB         208 KB            790KB
(0 rows affected)
```

> **WARNING**
>
> `sp_spaceused` can be off by as much as 2 extents per table.

The output from the procedure can be somewhat misleading, so review it closely. Database size is the total database size, including data and log allocations, but the reserved value is based only on data usage (not logs). If you have allocated data and log separately, you can subtract from the total database size the space allocated to the log to get the total data allocation.

To determine how much space is reserved for objects within the data allocation, take the reserved value in the previous example (5230) and subtract the pages reserved for the log (run `sp_spaceused syslogs`). That is the space reserved for objects.

To arrive at the space available for allocation to objects, subtract from the total allocation for data the amount reserved for objects.

In the case of the master database, where you cannot separate the data and log segments, you might have to add the space reserved by `syslogs` to the reserved value to get a total for the space being utilized. Then, subtract the total space utilized from the total size of the database to get the amount of space available for allocation.

Database Options

Use sp_dboption to enable or disable a database option for a database. Internally, this command sets a status flag for the database. The following list contains several options you can use to define standard processing or to support special requirements:

columns null by default	Permits the database owner to decide whether columns that do not specify nullability will permit nulls. For example, the following CREATE TABLE statement does not specify whether col_1 permits nulls or not. `CREATE TABLE table_1 (col_1 int)` Normally, col_1 would not permit nulls. If you set columns null by default to true before executing the CREATE TABLE statement, the column will permit nulls.
dbo use only	After setting a database to dbo use only, only the database owner (dbo) can issue the use statement for this database.
no chkpt ON recovery	Prevents a checkpoint record from being written to the log after the recovery process is complete.
offline	A removable-media database (mounted on CD-ROM, for example) is no longer accessible by SQL Server or its users.
published	This database is a source database for SQL Server 6.0 replication.
read only	Enables database users to select from the tables, but prevents all modifications. This option could provide a performance enhancement to decision-support systems.
select into/bulkcopy	Enables fast, nonlogged actions in a database, including SELECT … INTO, nonlogged WRITETEXT, and fast BCP.
single user	Limits database access to one user at a time.
subscribed	This database is a destination point for replication processing in SQL Server 6.0.
trunc log on chkpt	Automatically truncates the transaction log after every system-generated checkpoint.

> ### WARNING
>
> I have experienced a curious problem with `trunc log on chkpt` on certain systems. A checkpoint clears a portion of the cache to free space or update the data segments of the database. There are three kinds of checkpoints:
>
> - Checkpoints explicitly requested by the database owner
> - Checkpoints generated by the server to free space in the cache
> - Checkpoints issued by the server checkpoint process based on the server recovery interval
>
> On some SQL Server platforms, the `trunc log on chkpt` option truncates the log only after the third kind of checkpoint; a manual checkpoint did not truncate the log.
>
> For more about checkpoints, see Chapter 28. For now, try to understand the potential problem with truncation.
>
> Consider a long-running transaction such as an update of all rows in a large table:
>
> ```
> update titles
> set price = price * 1.02
> ```
>
> In this transaction, the titles table contains several million rows. The transaction is likely to be larger than the total capacity of the transaction log. You have two choices: You can increase the size of the log (ignore that choice), or you can try to run the transaction in smaller pieces, presumably clearing the log after each statement, as in the following:
>
> ```
> update titles
> set price = price * 1.02
> where title < "P"
> checkpoint
> update titles
> set price = price * 1.02
> where title >= "P"
> ```
>
> If the checkpoint results in a truncation, all is well. On some servers, the dbo-initiated checkpoint does not truncate the log and the log will fill up. What's worse, the explicit checkpoint reduced recovery time, further delaying the server-generated checkpoint that would otherwise have truncated the log.

Default Database Options

Upon server installation, the following items are true concerning database options:

- All database options are set to false in `model` and in all user databases.
- The `trunc log on chkpt` option for the master database is set to false.
- `select into/bulkcopy` is always true in `tempdb`.
- Any option enabled in the `model` database at the time a new database is created will also be enabled for this new database.

Setting Database Options

To set database options, use `sp_dboption`.

Syntax

```
sp_dboption databasename, option, {true ¦ false}
```

Example

```
sp_dboption market_db, "select", true
```

Notes

- You must be using the master database when you execute the `sp_dboption` stored procedure.

- You can abbreviate the name of the database option, as long as the server can distinguish the option from all others. Note that all keywords (such as SELECT) must be placed in quotation marks when they are passed as a parameter to a stored procedure.

- Options can be set `true` or `false`.

- `sp_dboption` without parameters will list all possible parameters.

- Only the `dbo` or `sa` can set database options. `dbo` aliases cannot set options.

Typically, changing an option involves the two steps shown in the following code:

```
use master  /* only set options in the master database */
go
sp_dboption market_db, "select into/bulkcopy", true
go
```

Setting Database Options Using SQL Enterprise Manager

SQL Enterprise Manager can also set database options, using the Options window tab of the Manage Databases dialog box, as shown in Figure 26.6. Instead of running `sp_dboption`, you can select the options you want activated or deactivated using the checkboxes provided in the interface.

SQL Enterprise Manager will automatically checkpoint the database, ensuring that changes take effect immediately upon an administrator clicking on OK to commit any database option changes.

FIGURE 26.6.

SQL Enterprise Manager can be used to configure specific database options.

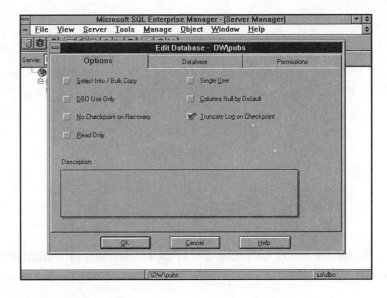

Examining Database Status

Use sp_helpdb to determine the value of status flags on a database. The status values are decoded to the far right in the output, and you might need to scroll to the end of the report to see the information.

The Database Status Flags

The status column in sysdatabases records information about a database in a bit field. Table 26.1 displays the bit representations of the status column.

Table 26.1. Status column bit representation.

Value	Status
2	Database is in transition
4	select into/bulkcopy
8	trunc log on chkpt
16	no chkpt on recovery
32	Crashed during load
64	Database not recovered yet
128	Database is in recovery

continues

Table 26.1. continued

Value	Status
256	Database suspect
1024	`read only`
2048	`dbo use only`
4096	`single user`
8192	Database being checkpointed
16384	`ANSI null default`
32768	Emergency mode

How to Turn Off the *SUSPECT* Flag on a Database

If you start the SQL Server before giving external storage devices a chance to warm up, or perhaps if a drive comes unplugged, the server will detect a failure of the device and mark all databases mapped to that device as SUSPECT (status column, bit value 28 = 256). Having that value in the status column will prevent the server from ever trying to recover that database. In order to regain access to the database, you need to turn off that bit and restart the SQL Server.

Soon you will learn how to manually update the sysdatabases table and remove the SUSPECT bit. But before you do anything unreasonable, you should check to make sure that you correctly understand the problem. If the server is up, run sp_helpdb on your database. Is the SUSPECT flag set? If it is not but you still can't access your database, you have a different problem.

If the database is marked SUSPECT, take a look at the error log. You want to see, fairly early in the server startup process, that it failed to start the device where the database is loaded. If you find this message, you are ready to roll. If not, keep reading and try to understand why the database was not recovered.

You need to log in as sa in order to manually update the sysdatabases table. The following example shows the necessary commands to enable you to directly update the status bit in the sysdatabases table:

```
use master
go
sp_configure "allow updates", 1
reconfigure with override
go
update sysdatabases
set status = status - 256
where dbname = "your database name here"
and status & 256 = 256
go
sp_configure "allow updates", 0
reconfigure
go
```

Now shut down and restart the server. If the drives are working, the system should come right up and the databases should be available.

The *model* Database

Whenever a database is created, the contents of the model database are copied to the new database. It is typical to place in the model database any objects that you intend to be located in all databases. Typically, model contains rules, defaults, user-defined datatypes, and any logins (for example, guest) who will be created in all databases.

> **TIP**
>
> User-defined datatypes are stored in systypes in each individual database. As new types are created in each database, each type is assigned a new integer identifier.
>
> For example, if ssn_type was the first user-defined type created in one database and age_type was first in another, each would be assigned the same identifier: 100. This would create a problem when you move information between databases, especially when you use the SELECT ... INTO command, where datatype identifier (the numeric value) is copied to the new table structure.
>
> The same problem is more severe in tempdb, where the lack of any matching type identifier typically causes sp_help to fail.
>
> I recommend that you define user-defined types first in the model database before creating any user databases. Then, when the user database is created, the user-defined types will be copied to this new database. I further recommend that as individual databases need to add further data types, you should create these data types in the model database first, and then re-create them in each user database.
>
> Bear in mind that tempdb is created every time the server restarts. When tempdb is created, it also gets a copy of the model database, which means that it gets a complete library of user-defined datatypes.

You should consider creating a system-stored procedure to handle centralized functions, rather than creating a procedure in model to be propagated to all databases. You should also consider placing lookup tables in a single central database, rather than propagating lookup tables into every database.

Dropping Databases

To drop a database, simply issue the DROP DATABASE command. Dropping a database removes all of the appropriate entries from the various system tables and removes the structure—making that space available to other databases. Only the dbo (or sa) can drop a database, and nobody can be using it at the time it is dropped.

```
DROP DATABASE database_name
```

When you drop a database you remove all objects, all data, and all logs associated with the database. The server removes all references to the database in sysdatabases and sysusages.

Sometimes, you won't be able to drop a database. To remove a corrupt or damaged database, use DBCC DBREPAIR, as in the following:

```
DBCC DBREPAIR (db_name, dropdb)
```

The following is an example of how to remove a corrupt database called corrupt_db:

```
DBCC DBREPAIR (corrupt_db, dropdb)
```

Segments and Object Placement

If you have a database with space allocated for data on two different physical devices, it is important to understand where the server will place tables, indexes, and other objects as they are created and expanded. For example, a database was created on devices DATA_1 and DATA_2 as follows:

```
CREATE DATABASE market_db
ON DATA_1 = 100, DATA_2 = 100
LOG ON LOG_1 = 50
```

When you create a table in the database, as in the following example, where does the server place the table—on DATA_1 or DATA_2?

```
create table Customer
(name char(30) not null,
 address char(30) not null)
```

The simple answer is that if you haven't set up any segments in your database, it doesn't matter. The server allocates space freely within the data area of the database until all of the allocations for data are full.

> **NOTE**
>
> By specifying in the CREATE DATABASE statement that the 50MB on LOG_1 was for log use only, you have already set up a *log segment*, a predefined segment that is for the exclusive use of the syslogs table. In this section, you will learn to create your own user-defined segments for storing tables that you want to isolate.

A segment is a label that identifies a set of storage allocations within a database. By using segments, you can control where the server places database objects, enabling those objects to expand only within specifically defined areas within the database. Segments can provide two broad benefits: improved performance, and greater control over object placement and growth within the database.

> **NOTE**
>
> Segments are not widely used in the SQL Server community. An estimate is that less than 5 percent of all SQL Server sites use any segments beyond those provided as part of SQL Server (see the section titled "Predefined Segments" later in this chapter).
>
> Consider the following discussion and look at the examples before deciding to implement segments. They provide some benefit but require substantial administrative attention, and they can complicate database restoration.

Segments for Performance

Typically, when segments are used to improve performance, the segments point to SQL Server devices that are mapped to different physical disk drives. The performance improvements typically seek to distribute database activity across disks (and controllers). Here are some examples of how activity can be distributed:

- Nonclustered indexes can be stored on one segment, while the table itself is stored on another. This can improve both read and write performance because index I/O can run parallel to table I/O.

  Note that clustered indexes always reside on the same segment as the table indexed. This requirement arises because the leaf level of the clustered index is the table itself.

- A large table can be divided among segments (and disks) to allow different parts of the table to be read at one time.

- Text and image data (Binary Large Objects, or BLOBs) can be placed on a segment, apart from the standard data pages. This can improve read performance when the table is heavily used.

Segments for Control

Segments also enable you to manage the size of objects within the database. Without segments, each object can grow to the full size of the data allocations in the database, contending for space with all other objects. In the previous example, the customer table and its indexes could grow to 200MB, unless other objects were also consuming space in the database.

When you use segments, objects can only grow to the size of the segment. In addition, by implementing segments, you will be able to place thresholds on each segment and define the necessary action when the objects in a segment come near to filling the segment.

Segment Definition

Use the `sp_addsegment` stored procedure to add a new segment to a database. Use `sp_extendsegment` to add other device allocations for the database to an existing segment.

Syntax

```
sp_addsegment segmentname, devicename
sp_extendsegment segmentname, devicename
```

Examples

```
use market_db
go
sp_addsegment Seg1, DATA_1
sp_extendsegment Seg1, DATA_2
```

Take careful note of the parameters of the `sp_addsegment` and `sp_extendsegment` stored procedures: segment name and device name. There are two characteristics you must understand about segments.

1. Segments are database-specific. When you create a segment, you establish a mapping to the usage of space on a specific device or set of devices for a database. Fragments of other databases on that device are not part of that segment.

2. Segments refer to all fragments on a device or set of devices for a database.

Take a look at two examples. In the first example, the accounting database is 240MB, with 200MB for data and 40MB for log. The first segment, `Seg1`, includes 50MB on `DATA_1` and 100MB on `DATA_3`. The second segment, `Seg2`, includes 50MB on `DATA_1` and 100MB on `DATA_3`.

```
use master
go
CREATE DATABASE acctg_db
ON DATA_1 = 50, DATA_2 = 50, DATA_3 = 100
LOG ON LOG_1 = 40
go
use acctg_db
go
exec sp_addsegment Seg1, DATA_1
exec sp_addsegment Seg2, DATA_2
exec sp_extendsegment Seg2, DATA_3
exec sp_extendsegment Seg1, DATA_3
go
```

Notes

Segment definitions are database-specific. So `Seg1` for `acctg_db` does not conflict with `Seg1` for `market_db` (see the preceding "Examples" section).

In the next example, add an additional 50MB to `acctg_db` on `DATA_3`. Now `Seg1` includes 50MB on `DATA_3` and 150MB on `DATA_3`.

```
ALTER DATABASE acctg_db
ON DATA_3 = 50
```

Segments refer to all fragments on a device or set of devices for a database. When you add 50 additional megabytes to the database on `DATA_3`, the additional space is automatically incorporated into every segment that refers to that device for the database. (See Figure 26.8.)

FIGURE 26.7.

A segment is database-specific. Two segments, each with the same name, are created for different databases. They uniquely identify usages on devices for that database.

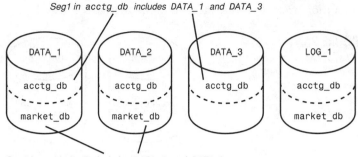

Seg1 in acctg_db includes DATA_1 and DATA_3

Seg1 in market_db includes DATA_1 and DATA_2

FIGURE 26.8.

Segments refer to all fragments on a device or set of devices for a database. Additional space allocated on a device already mapped to a segment becomes part of that segment.

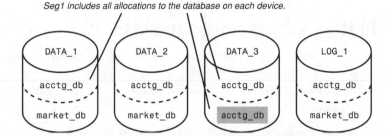

Seg1 includes all allocations to the database on each device.

> **NOTE**
>
> There is a many-to-many relationship between segments and devices. A single segment can include mappings to many devices. A single device can be part of many segments, even within a single database. The section "Segment System Tables," later in this chapter, discusses how this mapping is recorded in the sysusages table.

Predefined Segments

Whenever you create a new database, the server automatically creates three segments in the database:

- Default, for tables and indexes
- System, for system tables (including all object definitions)
- Logsegment, for storing `syslogs`

The default and system segments are mapped to all data allocations. The `logsegment` is mapped to any allocations for log. For example, in the first example you looked at, the allocations on DATA_1 and DATA_2 were mapped to the `default` and `system` segments:

```
CREATE DATABASE market_db
ON DATA_1 = 100, DATA_2 = 100
LOG ON LOG_1 = 50
```

Allocations for LOG_1 were mapped to the logsegment. (See Figure 26.9.)

FIGURE 26.9.

*When a database is created,
the* default, system,
and logsegment
*segments are defined
automatically.*

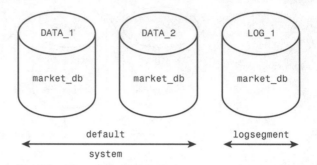

Placing Objects on Segments

Every object is placed on a segment when the object is created. System tables (except syslogs) are placed on the system segment and the transaction log (syslogs) is placed on logsegment segment. Everything else (specifically, tables and indexes) is placed on the default segment automatically.

To create an object on a specific segment, add

ON *segmentname*

to your create statement. This example places the Customer table (market_db database) on Seg1. As the table grows, it will use space on DATA_1 and DATA_2, the devices mapped to Seg1.

```
CREATE TABLE Customer
(name char(30) not null,
 address char(30) not null)
ON Seg1
```

The next example creates a nonclustered index on Customer on a different segment, Seg2. A table and its nonclustered indexes can be on separate segments.

```
CREATE INDEX Customer_nci1
ON Customer(name)
ON Seg2
```

The final example explicitly places a table on the default segment.

```
CREATE TABLE lookup
(code int not null,
 value varchar(20) not null)
ON "default"
```

> **NOTE**
>
> The word default must be enclosed in quotes, because default is a keyword referring to a type of system object.

Changing an Object's Segment

Use sp_placeobject to place all of an object's future growth on a specific segment.

> **NOTE**
>
> SQL Server allocates space to objects in eight-page (usually 16KB) extents. sp_placeobject instructs the server that all future extent allocations should come from devices mapped to the new segment. It does not prevent newly inserted rows from being added to pages that have already been mapped to the earlier segment.

Syntax

```
sp_placeobject segmentname, objectname
```

Example

```
sp_placeobject Seg3, Customer
sp_placeobject Seg3, "Customer.Index03"
```

After these statements are issued, all additional space allocations to the Customer table and to the Customer table Index03 index will come from Seg3.

> **NOTE**
>
> Place the clustered index on a different segment, as in the following:
>
> ```
> sp_placeobject Seg3, "Customer.ClusteredIndex"
> ```
>
> This has the same effect as placing the table on the new segment: All future space allocations to the table or clustered index will come from devices mapped to Seg3.

One way to use segments is to spread a large table across several devices. To distribute the table evenly, you need to create the table on one segment, load a segment of the data, and then run sp_placeobject to point to the next segment, as in the following example:

```
CREATE TABLE spread_table ( … ) ON Seg1
```

Now load 50 percent of the data:

```
sp_placeobject Seg2, spread_table
```

Now load the rest of the data. At this point, the data is evenly distributed between the two segments.

```
sp_placeobject Seg3, spread_table
```

All future allocations will come from `Seg3`.

> **NOTE**
>
> The interesting question is this: When should the clustered index be created? If you create the clustered index after the last `sp_placeobject`, the entire table will reside on the `Seg3` segment. So you need to create the clustered index early and enable it to grow across all three segments. To optimize the load, you will probably choose to create the clustered index after you load the first half of the data but before you place the table on `Seg2`.

Moving an Object to a New Segment

The method you use to move an object to a new segment, including all existing allocations, depends on the object. To move a table without a clustered index to a new segment, create a clustered index on the new segment and then drop the index.

```
CREATE CLUSTERED INDEX temp_index ON Table1(key) ON New_Seg
DROP INDEX Table1.temp_index
```

The first statement moves the table to `New_Seg` and builds a clustered index along the way. The second statement drops the index (if the sole use of creating the index was to enable you to move the table).

> **NOTE**
>
> Whether this is an efficient way to move a table to a new segment depends in part on the size of the table and the resources you have available to you. It might be faster to create a new table on the desired segment, insert rows from one table to the other, and then drop the old table and rename the new one. It also might be faster to use `bcp` to copy the data out and then in.
>
> Keep in mind that you cannot use the clustered index method to move a table that contains fully duplicate rows. Clustered index creation will fail if duplicate rows are discovered in the table.

To move a table that has a clustered index, drop the clustered index first, and then re-create it on the new segment.

```
DROP INDEX Table1.clustered_index
CREATE CLUSTERED INDEX clustered_index ON Table1(key) ON New_Seg
```

To move a nonclustered index to a new segment, drop the index and re-create it on the new segment.

```
DROP INDEX Table1.nc_index
CREATE INDEX nc_index ON Table1(nckey) ON New_Seg
```

TIP

Try to remember that sp_placeobject only affects the future growth of an object; it does not affect existing allocated space.

Removing a Device from a Segment

Use sp_dropsegment to remove a device from a segment definition or to remove a segment from a database. Remember, every object is created on a segment. If you remove a device from a segment definition, you control which objects can exist on a physical device.

There are some limitations to using sp_dropsegment:

- You cannot drop the last segment from a device.
- You cannot use sp_dropsegment on a segment if you have previously created or placed objects there.
- You cannot completely drop the predefined segments: default, system, and logsegment.

When you create a database, all data allocations are mapped to the default and system segments. When you create a new segment for a specific device, you probably want to remove the default and system segment mappings to that device to ensure that only objects explicitly placed there use the segment device.

For example, to create a segment to use with indexes in this database, you would create the index segment and then drop the default and system segments from the device, as in this example:

```
CREATE DATABASE market_db
ON DATA_1 = 50, DATA_2 = 50
LOG ON DATA_3 = 25

exec sp_addsegment index_segment, DATA_2
exec sp_dropsegment "default", DATA_2
exec sp_dropsegment "system", DATA_2
```

Figure 26.10 illustrates the segment mappings at the end of this process.

FIGURE 26.10.

You can drop the default and system segments from a data device after you have created a new segment on that device.

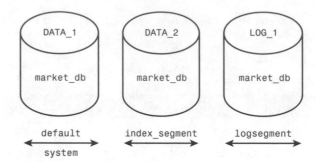

Information on Segments

Use sp_helpsegment to get information about segments in your current database. If you do not pass the segment name parameter, sp_helpsegment lists all segments in the database. If you pass the name of a segment as a parameter, you get detailed information about the segment, including a detailed list of fragments on devices and the fragment size, as well as a list of all objects stored on the segment.

> **TIP**
>
> Don't forget that "default" is a keyword. To find out about the default segment, pass the name in quotes.
>
> ```
> sp_helpsegment "default"
> ```

Segment System Tables

Segment changes have an impact on system tables in both the current database (syssegments and sysindexes) where the segments are being defined, and the master database (sysusages).

syssegments

When you create a segment, the server makes an entry in the syssegments table in the database. The entry consists of a *segment*, *name*, and *status*.

segment	A unique integer value assigned by the system. The maximum value is 31, and there can be no more than 32 segments in a database.
name	A unique name you assign with sp_addsegment.
status	A bit column indicating the default segment.

The following example shows the contents of `syssegments`. There is one row in `syssegments` per segment in the database; `syssegments` is a database-level system table.

```
segment name                          status
------- ----------------------------- ------
0       system                        0
1       default                       1
2       logsegment                    0
3       indexes                       0
```

sysusages

Creation of a segment also has an impact on `sysusages`. The `segmap` column in `sysusages` is a bitmap of segments mapped to that device fragment.

Segment Number	0	1	2	3	4
Bitmap Value	1 (2^0)	2 (2^1)	4 (2^2)	8 (2^3)	16 (2^4)
Segment Name	system	default	logsegment	Seg1	index_segment
Value	0	0	0	8	16

The value of `segmap` for the row in `sysusages` corresponding to DATA_2 is (0 + 0 + 0 + 8 + 16) = 24.

sysindexes

Object placement is recorded in the segment column of `sysindexes`. `sp_help` displays the segment in which an object is stored.

SQL to Query *syssegments*

To join `syssegments` to `sysusages`, you need to select on `dbid` and perform a *bit-wise and* (`&`) between the `segmap` column in `sysusages` and the segment values in the database. Your WHERE clause will look like the following:

```
WHERE segmap & power(2, segment) > 0
  AND db_id() = dbid
```

For example, to determine the number of fragments and the total megabytes allocated to each segment, execute the following command:

```
select s.name, count(*) "fragments", sum(size)/512 "allocation"
from master..sysusages u, syssegments s
where segmap & power(2, segment) > 0
  and db_id() = dbid
group by s.name
```

Segments are overlapping. In this database, there is a 3MB allocation to `default`, `logsegment`, and `system` on the same device, as shown in the following output:

```
name                            fragments   allocation
------------------------------- ----------- ----------
default                         1           3
logsegment                      1           3
system                          1           3
```

Summary

Databases are the main storage and allocation structure in SQL Server. Databases provide a way for you to logically and physically store data, they provide a way to perform backups and recovery with full transactional integrity, and they are a useful security mechanism, as you will see in the next chapter.

Segments improve database performance and control the growth of objects more carefully than a database alone can. Thresholds make segments far more useful because they enable the administrator to monitor the capacity and space availability of each storage unit.

Security and User Administration

27

Implementing a security and user administration plan in a SQL Server database is not a terribly difficult task when you understand SQL Server's security architecture and can develop an approach to implementing security. I'll recommend some approaches, but first I discuss the basics to help you implement an appropriate security regimen.

Overview

To access server data, a user needs to clear four security levels (see Figure 27.1):

- The workstation operating system
- SQL Server as an application on Windows NT
- The SQL Server database
- The SQL Server object

Think of each level as a door to a room: Either the door needs to be unlocked, or you need a key to open it. You can establish a virtually unlimited number of doors that can be set up to secure data within a database. Let's look at each level independently.

FIGURE 27.1.

SQL Server security consists of four access levels.

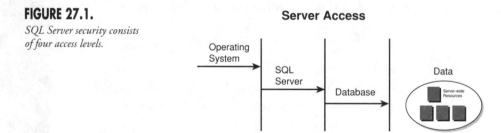

Operating-System Security Issues

A user might require some access to several operating systems to run a typical client/server application:

- A client workstation and its file, disk, and presentation resources
- A network operating system for the client/server application (as well as mail, file, and print services)
- The SQL Server host operating system where SQL Server is running

Normally, each of these processes—client, network, and SQL Server—runs on a distinct system; few applications use a locally hosted SQL Server database engine running on workstations.

A user does not require a login on the host machine where the SQL Server is running unless SQL Server is running locally. Windows NT requires a login to the operating system, so anyone administering SQL Server would need access to that workstation. SQL Server, however, can provide access to the server and its databases outside Windows NT's security, because it is directly network-port addressable. (See Chapter 24, "SQL Server Installation and Connectivity," for a detailed discussion of named pipe and network port addresses.)

Operating system security is the responsibility of the OS administrator or, more typically, of the network administrator. With the growing sophistication of client/server installations, these two distinct job descriptions are being handled by different employees, so coordination on changing the underlying OS when administering SQL Server security is even more important. As you'll see shortly, SQL Server's integration with network security makes this coordination even more critical.

NOTE

SQL Server provides two modes of defining access to the SQL Server itself. Standard security is the holdover from Sybase, where a user must supply a distinct login name and password in order to get access to the server. This login and password are distinct from any network logins, and also can be distinct from SQL Server to SQL Server.

With SQL Server for Windows NT 4.2, Microsoft introduced Integrated Login Security, which allowed SQL Server login names and passwords to be defined based on Windows NT network login names and passwords, allowing users to supply just one network login to get to SQL Server.

The next section starts out discussing the traditional standard security model and how to implement it. After that, you go through Integrated Login Security and discuss how to properly use it, and what the tradeoffs are between both access methods.

SQL Server Security: Logins

Access to a SQL Server is controlled through a server login and password. Logins can be standard SQL Server logins or integrated SQL Server logins. Whatever the type, the login ID grants access to the SQL Server process.

After a user has entered the server door (gained access to the server), a variety of database doors are available.

The door to the `master` database is always unlocked, and a person will end up in that room if you don't specify a different default when setting up the login or the user's `default` database is unavailable.

However, there are several other doors, including other system databases and any user databases that have been created.

SQL Server Database Security: Users

After you create a user login, you provide access to a SQL Server database in one of the following ways:

- Adding a user to a database (giving the user a key)
- Telling the database to treat a user as some other valid user (an alias—giving the user a copy of someone else's key)
- Creating a guest user (unlocking the door and propping it open)
- Making that login the owner of the database

When he is in a database, a user is able to see definitions for the objects contained in that database. This is because definitions are stored in the system tables, which any user of a database has select access to (except for certain sensitive columns). The user still needs permission to access each database object. (Database users are discussed in the "Database Access" section later in this chapter.)

Object-Level Security: Permissions

When you create an object (a table, procedure, or view), SQL Server automatically assigns ownership to you. Object ownership confers complete control over the object—its access, integrity, and administration. By default, only the object owner can select from a table until access is granted to others.

Object-level security is the last level of security. To provide access to an object, you must grant the user *permission* to use it. For example, a user can select from a table after the owner has granted the select permission. If that person does not have the necessary permission, access will be denied.

Although this is the last main level in your security scheme, object security can contain several sublevels. (The "Permission Approaches" section, later in this chapter, shows how the use of dependent objects can tighten the security in your system.)

For example, you can grant permission to a view but not to its underlying (base) tables. This enables an administrator to deny direct access to tables, but allow access to the data through the view. The same concept applies to stored procedures and triggers.

SQL Server offers a variety of ways to control access to data. SQL Server login and database user approaches affect the way in which a permissions strategy is implemented.

At the object level, most sites grant broad permissions and then limit or grant specific access as needed to minimize the administrative overhead in implementing a permissions plan. This usually involves granting to public or a user-defined group, and then revoking or granting specific permissions to a user-defined group or a specific user.

SQL Server Standard Logins

A SQL Server login provides access to the SQL Server. Logins are usually the first line of defense for the DBA in a security plan. (Remember that OS passwords are usually the responsibility of the OS administrator.) When you grant a login, the user can connect to the server and use the master database.

A SQL Server login usually requires a password, although there are exceptions. For example, upon initial installation, the sa login has no password. Passwords are not required for SQL Server logins, although it is recommended that you require passwords on all servers. Without passwords, it is difficult to implement any meaningful security on SQL Server.

Add logins with sp_addlogin:

```
sp_addlogin login_name, password [ , defdb [ , deflanguage ] ]
sp_addlogin rbrown, shake#crown
```

You receive this confirmation message:

```
New login created.
```

The next example shows the contents of syslogins after running sp_addlogin (adding a row to the syslogins table in the master database):

```
select suid, name from syslogins

suid    name
------  ----------------------------
1       sa
2       probe
3       mon_user
4       testuser1
5       jeff
6       rbrown
```

In SQL Server 6.0, only *login_name* is required. *login_name* must be unique for the server and must not be more than 30 characters long. Passwords also must not be more than 30 characters. In SQL Server 6.0, Microsoft has encrypted the password field of syslogins. In prior versions, SQL Server simply revoked permissions on the password column.

You can define a default database for each login. The default database does not grant any inherent privilege to use a database: It merely tells SQL Server to *attempt* to use the defined database at login time. If the login does not yet have access to the default database, the server issues an error message; the user is logged in and the current database is the master database. A login that does not have a default database specified will also default to the master database.

TIP

It's important to assign a default database and provide access to that database for each login in your system.

In a well-secured system, a user can't really do any damage to the master database. He can rattle around, select from the system tables, make a general nuisance of himself, maybe—but not do any real damage without the sa password.

To be safe, don't leave users in master. Set valid default databases for users so that they don't end up defaulting to master.

WHY CAN'T I USE THE DATABASE?

There are circumstances when you have done everything right, but users still end up pointed to the master database when they log in. Here are a few things to look for, starting with the obvious and moving toward the obscure.

Each of the specific error messages you receive is followed by this general error message:

```
Error 4001: Cannot open default database 'testdb'.
```

The following are common errors, their diagnoses, and the actions you should take.

Error received:

```
Message 916: Server user id 6 is not a valid user in database 'testdb'.
```

Diagnosis:

The login has not been added as a user to this database.

Action required:

Add the user to the database with sp_adduser, sp_addalias, or sp_changedbowner; or add the guest user to the database.

Error received:

```
Msg 927, Level 14, State 1:  Database 'test' cannot be opened - it is in
 the middle of a load.
```

Diagnosis:

The database cannot be used until a restore from backup is complete.

Action required:

Restore the database from backup. The user must wait until the restore is completed.

Error received:

```
Error 905: Unable to allocate a DBTABLE descriptor to open database 'testdb'.
Another database must be closed or dropped before opening this one.
```

> *Diagnosis:*
>
> Your system configuration settings need to enable more concurrently open databases.
>
> *Action required:*
>
> Increase the open databases setting with sp_configure. Meanwhile, a database needs to be closed before this database is available.

The default language option (deflanguage) is used at sites that have loaded other character sets besides us_english (the language that is always available to the server). If this parameter is provided, the user receives all system messages in the language selected.

Note that the optional parameters (defdb and deflanguage) can be updated later using the sp_defaultdb or sp_defaultlanguage stored procedures.

Of course, your users might ask whether they can change their own default database or password. A user can change his or her password using sp_password. Passwords should be changed frequently; about one every month should be appropriate. Also, users can change their default database with the sp_defaultdb command.

Special Logins

Two special logins are created as part of the installation of the SQL Server. These two logins are sa and probe.

sa

The sa login is a special login that is created as part of the installation process. The sa login owns the server. The sa login owns the system databases (master, model, tempdb, msdb, and any others installed by the sa). The sa login is the database owner (dbo) within those databases because it is the login that literally is mapped to the dbo user (more on dbo later in this chapter). (When an individual—a login—creates a database, the server records the suid column from the server's row in syslogins as the database owner in sysdatabases.) Regardless of actual database ownership, the sa is seen as the dbo of any user database.

probe

There also is a probe login that is provided as part of installation. This login is used between servers to manage *2-Phase Commit* (2PC) activities.

Generic Logins

Some sites add a general login, such as `templogin` or `sybguest`, to be used by temporary users of a server for in-house training or self-study. Often the logins have no password, or the password is the same as the login name. Of course, many administrators prefer an individual login for each user of a server; this provides better control and permits auditing of work by individuals when that is necessary.

How Logins Work

When a new login is created, a row is added to a system table in master called `syslogins`. Each login is assigned a unique system user ID (`suid`), which is an integer that identifies that user uniquely in the server. During login, the server matches the name passed in the login structure against the name column in the `syslogins` table. If a match is found and the password matches, the `suid` is stored in the memory allocated for the new connection.

The login name is not stored in any table except `syslogins`. The `suid` is the key used in all other tables that relate to a person's login, including those relating server access to database access.

> **TIP**
>
> To retrieve a list of `suid`s and login names, type the following line:
>
> ```
> select suid, name from syslogins
> ```
>
> Although you can select the password column if you are the `sa`, the values are encrypted in SQL Server 6 and above. Prior to SQL 6, the password column is plainly readable by the `sa`:
>
> ```
> select suid, name, password from syslogins
> ```

The system functions `suser_name()` and `suser_id()` convert login IDs to names and vice versa. For example,

```
select suser_name(2)
```

returns the value `probe` (because `probe` is always the second user inserted in the `syslogins` table). Conversely, the line

```
select suser_id("probe")
```

returns the value 2. When the functions are used without arguments, they return the login name or ID for the current user.

> **NOTE**
>
> These system functions are most useful in accessing data from system tables, where they enable you to decode a name or ID without needing to specify a join, as in the following example. These system functions are also frequently used in the SQL Server provided system stored procedures.
>
> ```
> use master
> go
> select spid, suid, suser_name(suid) "name"
> from sysprocesses
> order by suser_name(suid)
> go
>
>
> spid   suid   name
> ------ ------ ------------------------------
> 2      0
> 3      0
> 4      0
> 5      0
> 6      6      rbrown
> 1      1      sa
> ```
>
> You also should notice the rows in sysprocesses with an suid of 0 and no name. These processes are system processes in charge of mirror, network, and checkpoint handling.

Modifying Login Information

Again, don't worry if you don't have all the login information at the time that a login is added. It always can be changed using sp_defaultdb or sp_defaultlanguage:

```
sp_defaultdb login_name, databasename
```

Passwords

A password is used to verify the authenticity of a login. There is no minimum password length in Microsoft versions of SQL Server, but there is a maximum length of thirty characters. Passwords can include any printable characters, including A–Z, a–z, 0–9, or any symbols.

> **TIP**
>
> Add symbols or mix the case to make it difficult to guess a password.

Changing Passwords

Passwords can be changed by the user or by the sa. Change passwords with sp_password:

```
sp_password old_password, new_password [ , login_name ]
```

To change a password, a user passes the current password and the new password. If a user who is not the sa passes a login_name to sp_password, the system returns an error message.

An sa changing another user's password passes the sa password, the new user password, and the login name. If the sa omits the login name, the sa password will be changed!

SQL Server Integrated Logins

With SQL Server 4.2 for Windows NT, Microsoft introduced an interesting twist on the traditional Sybase security model: a feature that allowed logins to use their existing network IDs to access SQL Server. Microsoft called the feature Integrated Login Security (ILS), reflecting the integration of network and SQL Server security—two parts of an overall client/server security architecture that, up until this version, were completely exclusive.

There was, however, an important limitation: DOS- and Windows-based client workstations required using Named Pipes as their protocol for connecting to SQL Server. Native IPX/SPX or TCP/IP support wasn't available, but it was still possible to use Named Pipes over either of these protocols. The only problem for network administrators was the potential security gap caused by a resource that they couldn't control existing on their networks.

This restriction, although it appears esoteric, actually defines how ILS works. Windows NT servers have the capability to query the Named Pipes API to determine the network login and password information of each user on the network. SQL Server uses this Windows NT feature to validate network packets coming from workstations, bypassing any login or password information supplied for SQL Server. In effect, SQL Server "piggybacks" on Windows NT's network security.

There are actually two different submodes of integrated login security. Pure integrated security means that SQL Server will only accept ILS connections; therefore, all of the client workstations are connecting to SQL Server using Named Pipes. SQL Server will use only the network login and password for the workstation for validation. If an application attempts to use a different SQL Server login and password, SQL Server will ignore the explicit login and use the network login and password instead.

This is obviously very restrictive and requires running dual protocols in non-Windows NT network environments. Therefore, Microsoft also created *Mixed Login Security* (MLS), which allows connections on all of SQL Server's supported protocols. If a workstation is using Named Pipes, specifying a SQL Server login and password is optional. If the client does supply an explicit login and password, those explicit values are used for validation. If a Named Pipes client does not supply any SQL Server login or password information, an integrated connection is made. Clients other than Named Pipes are required to supply explicit login and password information. In mixed mode, non-Named Pipes connections are standard connections.

Using the new Multi-Protocol Network Library (MPNL) described in Chapter 24, "SQL Server Installation and Connectivity," true ILS connections can be used over Named Pipes, TCP/IP Sockets, and IPX/SPX connections.

Configuring Integrated Login Security

SQL Server setup for ILS involves a number of steps to configure. However, the most important step of all is how you plan your security architecture. Because Windows NT networking supports network security features that SQL Server does not, implementing Integrated Login Security requires careful planning and mapping of SQL Server's security regimen with that of Windows NT. It isn't necessarily rocket science, but it isn't trivial either.

Configuring SQL Server ILS involves four basic components:

- Run SETUP to configure SQL Server to start in Integrated security mode.
- Define Windows NT network users and passwords, and assign them to one of two groups: SQLUsers or SQLAdmins.
- Map the Windows NT network users to SQL Server logins.
- Test integrated connections using specific network logins.

Running *SETUP* to Configure SQL Server

To start SQL Server using ILS, you can use either the SQL Enterprise Manager application or the SQL Server Setup utility. When starting SQL Enterprise Manager, choose the Server | Configurations... menu sequence. Selecting the Security Options tab from the resulting window brings up the window shown in Figure 27.2.

FIGURE 27.2.

Set integrated security using the Server Configuration/ Options dialog box.

Your first task will be to decide which security mode you want. Standard forces everybody to use an explicit SQL Server login and password. Integrated forces everybody using either Named Pipes or the Multi-Protocol Network Library to use integrated connections. DECNet, VinesIP, and ADSP (AppleTalk) customers are out of luck. With Mixed mode, Named Pipes and MPNL connections can use either method, but DECNet, VinesIP, and ADSP workstations must use Standard security.

Within all DB-Library applications, the client process is able to identify itself to SQL Server using a *host name*, which is typically the application name or executable filename. With ILS, SQL Server overrides the value of this parameter and substitutes the network ID that the workstation is being validated with. Although it is not recommended or discouraged, it is effective at tying a particular login ID to a particular network ID or workstation.

SQL Server is able to audit both successful and failed ILS connections. Auditing these connections tells SQL Server to make entries in the Security subsystem of the Windows NT Event Log each time an event occurs.

Mappings are a crucial element to Integrated or Mixed security. Because Windows NT supports network logins that use special characters—such as spaces, dashes, and (most importantly) the backslash (\) character—to separate domain names from login names, SQL Server must somehow support them as well. However, SQL Server identifiers are restricted from using such symbols. Mappings allow you to substitute SQL Server approved characters for Windows NT approved characters. Typically, the default mappings will be sufficient, but make sure you discuss how network logins are defined with your LAN or Windows NT administrator for confirmation.

Exit the SETUP utility by clicking OK. SQL Server must now be restarted in order for these changes to take effect. You have just completed the first step to establishing integrated connections!

Creating Windows NT Users and Groups for SQL Server: Windows NT User Manager

All Windows NT User and Group creation is performed using the Windows NT User Manager. Because this is more of a network administration function than a database administration function, this section isn't going to focus on the ins and outs of defining network users and groups. Instead, you'll see why there should be two particular groups for SQL Server logins.

Windows NT's network security structure allows a single network login to be a participant in many different security groups on the network. Windows NT internally resolves the highest level of permission among these various, and potentially conflicting, groups and permission levels.

You need to supply a list of network IDs for people who should have access to SQL Server. Also, you should include specification of two distinct groups: SQLUsers and SQLAdmins. These new network users should be assigned to one of these groups. The network administrator is then responsible for creating the necessary IDs in User Manager.

> **NOTE**
>
> For clarification, I have chosen the names SQLAdmins and SQLUsers only because they are descriptive. They do not represent SQL Server keywords, and you could substitute names such as Fred and Ethel, which are equally as valid (if somewhat less descriptive) as group identifiers. As long as they are descriptively named, SQL Server doesn't really care.

SQL Server only supports a single user as part of a single group. Therefore, adding multiple existing network security groups from the Windows NT level could cause conflicts with SQL Server. Windows NT users who need access to SQL Server should be members of SQLUsers or SQLAdmins, but not both. This would cause the very conflict you are attempting to avoid!

Users assigned to the SQLAdmins group receive sa level authority, so be very careful about who you add to that group. Also, when SQL Server is first started in Integrated or Mixed security mode, SQL Server automatically grants sa privilege to any users in the Administrators group on Windows NT. Users added to the SQLUsers group have unique login and user IDs assigned at the SQL Server level, so that their permissions can be assigned individually, if need be.

Also, SQL Server creates database-level groups for each login group you create, so that the SQLUsers group as defined at the Windows NT level is also defined as the SQLUsers group at the SQL Server level, easing administration and permission assignment tasks.

Mapping Windows NT Users and Groups to SQL Server Logins: SQL Server Security Manager

SQL Server relies on the Security Manager application to map Windows NT network IDs to SQL Server login IDs. Security Manager reads the Windows NT security database and creates the logins, permissions, and database groups necessary to take full advantage of integrated security.

The first time you start SQL Security Manager, you are presented with a largely blank window. This first display shows you who has user level access to SQL Server. Clicking on the right button in the paired buttons in the toolbar shows the Admin level users. Figure 27.3 shows a sample server; in this case, all of the users are assigned the login of sa.

FIGURE 27.3.

The SQL Security Manager displays mappings between network users and SQL Server logins.

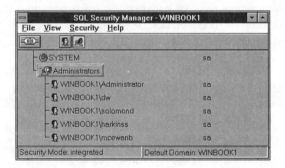

To add new Admin-level users, choose the Security | Grant New… menu sequence. This shows you a dialog box listing all of the groups defined in the Windows NT security database. Select the SQLAdmins group, and the members of that group are automatically added to SQL Server's security domain. (See Figure 27.4.)

Your newly added users appear in the Security Manager window.

Clicking on the left button of the paired buttons shows you user-level groups and their associated logins. Clicking the Security | Grant New… menu sequence enables you to add new user-level IDs to SQL Server. When adding new user-level IDs, SQL Security Manager checks for any Windows NT user IDs that exist in the group and maps them against any Windows NT user IDs that have Admin-level permissions or already exist in syslogins. If a user that Security Manager is attempting to add already exists in one of these categories, SQL Server reports it as an error, using the status dialog box shown in Figure 27.5.

FIGURE 27.4.

The SQL Security Manager showing the newly added SQLAdmins group.

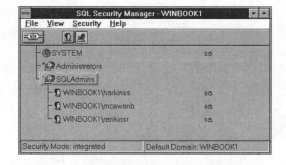

FIGURE 27.5.

This dialog box reports the number of logins, users, and groups added by SQL Security Manager.

In this example, I don't have any errors. Notice that SQL Server has added not only the login IDs, but also distinct user names, as well as a group within the master database for those users (both discussed later in this chapter).

Clicking on Done here displays the main Security Manager window, but with some new information. Notice that it is different from the Admin view. First, the accounts all show the combined machine name (AMS), a backslash separator (common to UNC names), and the individual login name. Also notice that, unlike the Admin permissions, each of these users has been given his or her own SQL Server login. They do not share a login, and they certainly don't share sa!

Testing

Testing integrated security is easy. Start any of the SQL Server client applications (ISQL/w is fastest) and simply enter a servername, but no login ID or password, into the Login dialog box. Choose connect, and you should receive an integrated security connection.

If the connection doesn't work, there are three areas to check before proceeding.

First, check to make sure that the client workstation is using either the Named Pipes or Multi-Protocol Network Library to connect to SQL Server. You can verify this using the SQL Client Configuration Utility, which is used to define the particular network library that a workstation uses.

Second, check that the client workstation actually has access to the network. If a standard login succeeds but an integrated login fails, move on to option three.

Third, make sure that the network ID is properly defined on the Windows NT machine. This means scanning the ID and group definitions in Windows NT User Manager, as well as running SQL Security Manager to detect any conflicts or missing IDs.

SQL Server Logins

To briefly summarize, logins are how users identify themselves to SQL Server. If you are using standard security, you have made a decision to maintain a security architecture for SQL Server that is distinct from the security architecture for the underlying network. Quite often, this option is chosen to maintain application portability across different versions of SQL Server. For integrated security, there are additional issues to consider, but there is a benefit to using Windows NT-based security for SQL Server.

Database Access

After server login security, the next level of security is database access. You manage database access by establishing a link between logins (stored at the server level) and users (stored at the database level). User access to a database is required to use the database (change your current context to the database); it also is required to access any object stored in the database.

> **NOTE**
>
> This information is also added to the memory structure set up for a connection or process, and a review of `sysprocesses` (built dynamically) shows the `uid` and database ID (`dbid`) for a process.
>
> The `uid` is used to identify ownership of objects within a database. Although the ID assigned to an object is used to relate that object with other tables, there is a unique index on the combination of an object name and a `uid` (database user ID). This is why more than one user can have an object with the same name, and avoiding the naming confusion that can result is a very important consideration to remember when determining a development approach.

Adding Users

You grant access to a database by adding a user to the database. Use `sp_adduser` to add users; it adds an entry in the database-level sysusers table. Here is the syntax of `sp_adduser`:

```
sp_adduser login_name [ , name_in_db [ , grpname ] ]
```

To add `rbrown` to the `testdb` database, use the following:

```
use testdb
go
sp_adduser rbrown
go
```

At the completion of the `sp_adduser` procedure, a row is placed in the `sysusers` table in the database where the user was added. The following example shows the contents of the database-level table, `sysusers`, after `rbrown` has been added to the database `testdb`:

```
use testdb
go
select suid, uid, name
from sysusers
go

suid    uid    name
------  -----  ------------------------------
-2      0      public
1       1      dbo
4       3      testuser1
6       4      rbrown
```

The only required parameter is *login_name*, which is checked against the `name` column in the `master..syslogins`. (The login name must already exist in the `syslogins` table.) *login_name* is used to derive the `suid` to be placed into the `sysusers` table.

The *name_in_db* parameter is infrequently used in real life, and its purpose is not to be confused with true aliasing (`sp_addalias`). This parameter is inserted in the `name` column in the `sysusers` table.

TIP

Normally, the default value for this parameter is the string specified for the *login_name*, and (unless you have a very good reason) you should always keep them the same. It makes the matching of database users to server users much simpler. In fact, if a value is not specified or a value of `null` is provided, it defaults to the *login_name*.

The *grpname* parameter defines the group for the user. By default, a user is placed in the group public, which has a group ID (`gid`) of 0, although the word `public` can be specified for this parameter. Groups are discussed later in this section.

Use `sp_helpuser` to get a list of users in a database or to see specific information about a single user, as in this example:

```
Users_name       ID_in_db  Group_name       Login_name        Default_db
---------------  --------  ---------------  ----------------  ---------------
dbo              1         public           sa                master
rbrown           4         public           rbrown            testdb2
testuser1        3         public           testuser1         master
```

Special Users

Two special users can exist in a SQL Server database: dbo and guest.

dbo

The dbo is the database owner. dbo is added to the model database as part of installation (and cannot be dropped); hence the dbo exists in all databases in a server. The dbo can never be dropped from a database and always has a database user ID (uid) of 1.

> **NOTE**
>
> It is unusual for the user ID (uid in sysusers) and the login ID (suid in master..syslogins) to have the same value. The values are predictably the same only for the sa, who is dbo in all databases.

guest

The guest user is provided to grant database access to anyone who logs into the server. The guest user must be explicitly added to a database using sp_adduser (or added to the model database before a subsequent database creation).

The presence of a guest user means that anyone logged into the server can access the database. This is a catch-all to enable access to a database when the login has not been explicitly added as a user of the database (or aliased to another user, as discussed the next section). The guest user always has a uid of 2. Guest permissions default to the permissions granted to the group public.

> **TIP**
>
> Be careful about adding the guest user to the model database, because this means that the guest user will exist in any new database that is created. This could weaken your security strategy.

Adding Aliases (Alternates)

To use a database, a user does not necessarily have to be added explicitly as a separate user of the database. SQL Server provides the capability of relating a login to another login who is already a user of the database.

For example, every database has a user dbo, whose name can be found in the name column in the sysusers table. The sysusers row for dbo includes an suid and a database uid (which is always 1 for dbo). The value specified in the suid column for dbo determines the login ID of the actual database owner—the individual who has all administrative privileges within that database. You can provide database access to additional users *as* dbo by defining aliases within the database for each such user.

> **TIP**
>
> The most common user privilege to be shared with aliases is dbo, which enables several logins to divide the responsibility for database implementation, evolution, and maintenance. This is most common in a development environment, where several users share responsibility for object creation and maintenance.

sp_addalias adds an entry to the sysalternates table, enabling an additional login to access a database as that user:

```
sp_addalias login_name, name_in_db
```

In the next example, mwhite is added as an alias to rbrown in the testdb database. Now mwhite receives all the access and permissions granted to rbrown within this database:

```
sp_addalias mwhite, rbrown
```

Both *login_name* and *name_in_db* are required. *login_name* must be a valid entry in syslogins with no suid entry in sysusers or sysalternates in the current database. *name_in_db* must be a valid user name within the database.

sp_addalias adds a row to the sysalternates table. The login ID of *login_name* is stored in the suid column. The login ID of the actual login mapped to *name_in_db* is stored in the altsuid column.

> **NOTE**
>
> I'd like to meet the comedian who decided that aliases should be added with sp_addalias but stored in the sysalternates table!

Execute sp_helpuser with a user name to get detailed information about a user, including aliases, as in this example:

```
sp_helpuser rbrown
Users_name        ID_in_db Group_name        Login_name        Default_db
----------------  -------- ----------------  ----------------  -------------
rbrown            4        public            rbrown            testdb2

Users aliased to user.
Login_name
------------------------------
mwhite
```

If you examine the contents of the three system tables (syslogins, sysusers, and sysalternates) after adding an alias, you can understand the mapping of logins, users, and aliases.

syslogins and sysusers join on suid. syslogins and sysalternates also join on suid. sysusers and sysalternates join on suid and altsuid, respectively. (See Figure 27.6.)

FIGURE 27.6.

The relationship between the login, user, and alias entities is built on a system user ID (suid) column in the syslogins tables.

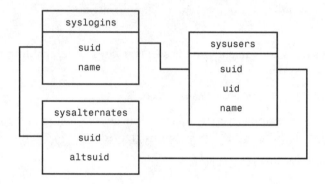

The values from sample versions of sysusers, sysalternates, and master..sysobjects show the correspondence between suid, uid, and altsuid among the tables:

```
select suid, uid, name
from sysusers
where uid > 0
select *
from sysalternates
select suid, name
from master..syslogins
sysusers
suid   uid    name
------ ------ ------------------------------
1      1      dbo
4      3      testuser1
6      4      rbrown
( 10 rows affected)

sysalternates
suid   altsuid
------ -------
7      6
( 1 row affected)
```

```
master..syslogins
suid    name
------  ------------------------------
1       sa
2       probe
3       mon_user
4       testuser1
5       jeff
6       rbrown
7       mwhite
( 7 rows affected)
```

Here are some features to notice about the contents of these tables:

- The dbo of the database is the sa (suid of the dbo in sysusers equals 1).
- Besides dbo, there are two users of the database—rbrown (suid 6 in syslogins corresponds to suid 6 in sysusers) and testuser1.
- mwhite (suid 7) is aliased to rbrown (suid 6) in this database.

How Database Access Works

So what does the server do when trying to determine access to a database? When a person tries to use a database, the server looks for an entry in sysusers and sysalternates to decide whether to grant access. It first looks in the sysusers table to see whether a match can be made on the suid.

A row will be found in sysusers for an suid if the following conditions exist:

- The user has been added through the sp_adduser procedure (normal user addition).
- The user created the database (suid matches with uid of 1, the dbo).
- Ownership of the database has been transferred to the user.

After trying to find a match for the suid in the sysusers table, the server then tries to match the suid column in the sysalternates table.

If a match is found for the suid column in sysalternates, the server then determines the suid that is found in the altsuid column. This value is then matched against the suid column in the sysusers table, as you did previously. Then the uid that corresponds to that suid is used by the user for activities conducted in the database.

If a match is not found in sysalternates, the server then looks at the sysusers table again to see whether the special user guest has been added. If it has, the person assumes the uid of guest within that database.

The database access validation procedure is outlined in Figure 27.7.

674

FIGURE 27.7.

SQL Server database permissions depend on user mappings or the presence of a guest user in the database.

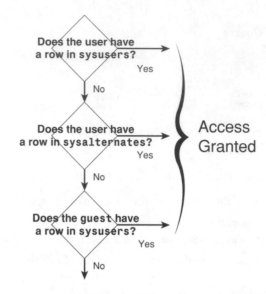

If none of these matches can be made, the person is denied access.

Groups

Groups can be used as part of an effective database security strategy. Object and command permission are granted to users and groups. A user who is a member of a group inherits all the permissions granted to the group.

You can assign a user name to a group with sp_adduser (discussed earlier) or sp_changegroup. Assigning users to groups is a dbo responsibility. There is a detailed discussion of how to implement groups into your permission strategy in the "Permissions" section later in this chapter.

> **NOTE**
>
> SQL Server allows a user to belong to only one group. (This isn't strictly true: A user can belong to one group in addition to public.)
>
> The interesting question is why that limitation exists. It's clear that the structure of the system tables plays a role in that requirement; after all, a user's group membership is recorded in the gid column in sysusers. Permissions are granted to entries in sysusers. Because groups are stored in sysusers alongside users, all permissions checks require that only two tables be read: sysprotects and sysusers.

Public Group

Every user in a database is a member of the `public` group.

> **CAUTION**
>
> Don't forget that if you add a `guest` user to a database, any person that has a valid server login can use that database. The `guest` user will, of course, be able to perform any functions that have been granted to `public`.

It is common for an administrator to grant permissions to the public group rather than to each individual user. For example, if you have 500 users of a database and all users need to select from the customer table, an administrator could execute a `grant` statement once for each user (500 statements) or a single `select` permission to the `public` group.

The `public` group is found in the `sysusers` table in each database with a `uid` of 0, and you cannot delete it.

Adding Groups

Although the public group is a convenient way to grant universal access to database objects, it is inappropriate to use public when you need to grant different permissions to discrete sets of users. You might need to create additional groups to represent different permissions requirements. Add groups with `sp_addgroup`:

```
sp_addgroup groupname
```

For example, to add a `marketing` group to the current database, use the following:

```
sp_addgroup marketing
```

This procedure adds a row to the `sysusers` table with a `uid` of 16384 or larger.

Determining Groups in a Database: *sp_helpgroup*

To determine the groups that exist in a database, or for more information about an individual group within a database, use `sp_helpgroup`:

```
sp_helpgroup [ groupname ]
```

Without any parameters, this procedure reports on all groups in a database. `sp_helpgroup` reports all groups in the database:

```
sp_helpgroup
Group_name                     Group_id
------------------------------ --------
marketing_group                16390
public                         0
```

There will always be an entry for the group `public`. Pass the *groupname* as a parameter to list all users in a group:

```
sp_helpgroup marketing_group
Group_name           Group_id Users_in_group            Userid
-------------------- -------- ------------------------- -------
marketing_group      16390    rbrown                    4
marketing_group      16390    testuser1                 3
```

Drop groups with `sp_dropgroup`, but only if that group does not contain any users:

```
sp_dropgroup groupname
sp_dropgroup marketing_group
```

Use `sp_changegroup` to change a user's group membership. Only the `dbo` can execute `sp_changegroup`:

```
sp_changegroup groupname, name_in_database
sp_changegroup marketing_group, rbrown
```

How Groups Work

`sp_addgroup` adds a row to the `sysusers` table. The `uid` and group ID (`gid`) are assigned the same value (16834 or greater). When you add users to a database without specifying a group name, the group ID of 0 (`public`) is assigned to that person. When you specify a group (either as a parameter in `sp_adduser` or with `sp_changegroup`), the `gid` of that group is placed in the `gid` column for that user.

> **NOTE**
>
> After you assign a user to a group, the user is no longer explicitly assigned to the `public` group. Nevertheless, any permissions assigned to `public` will apply to that user. The `public` group always encompasses all people.

Login Approach

There are several approaches to security in SQL Server systems; the following are the major ones:

- SQL Server login equals the Operating System/Application (OS/App) login.
- SQL Server login is independent of the OS/App login.
- A single login for all users of an application or user type.

SQL Server Login = OS/App Login

This is a fairly maintainable approach to logins. A user is given a login to the operating system. (The operating system could be the client workstation login, network login, or the user login to the server, if the client application runs on the server.) The operating system sets environment variables for the username (and possibly the password) during its login process. Applications read the environment information when logging into SQL Server.

For example, SQL Server facilities such as isql and bcp look for the environment variables USER and PASSWORD when connecting to the server. When the user does not need to specify the "-U" option for isql, the application passes the user name from the environment when connecting to the server.

Administering OS/SQL Server logins is easier because you can develop (administrative or automated) procedures to maintain these user (login) names and passwords in sync.

> **TIP**
>
> Ensure that maintenance procedures such as this will work in your environment. Otherwise, maintaining synchronized names and passwords will drive you nuts.

One drawback of this approach is that users occasionally need to access an application with a different SQL Server login. Applications still must provide a facility for a different login name and password from the one stored at the operating system level.

SQL Server Login Independent of OS/APP Login

To enable separate OS and SQL Server login IDs, applications must include a login function. (Often, when there is some correspondence between SQL Server and OS login IDs, applications automatically populate the login screen with information drawn from the environment.)

This approach is more difficult to administer and maintain than the previous one, but it can provide additional security.

Single SQL Server Login

The single SQL Server login approach is often used by sites that want a single point of control for logins to the SQL Server server. It is simple, but its simplicity has drawbacks.

Only one login exists for an entire application or for each major application piece. When a person invokes the application, the application connects to the server using hard-coded values for the login name and password. This approach has some benefits:

- Users do not need to log into the server explicitly.

- A password changing routine does not have to be written into the application to accommodate password changes. (Applications that use individual logins with the capability of changing passwords often integrate a password changing application to shield users from having to connect to the server by using another interface to change their passwords.)

- The administration activity required to manage logins and passwords is extremely low.

However, drawbacks to this approach include the following:

- A database administrator often executes sp_who to see who is logged into the SQL Server. Part of the output from this command is the login name. If all users log into the SQL Server with same name, the output of sp_who will contain numerous processes with the same login name. If a problem is encountered, determining the actual user associated with a process becomes almost impossible. (To overcome this problem, applications pass the OS login ID as a hostname value when logging in to SQL Server. Hostname values are also included in the sp_who display.)

- Auditing user activity is meaningless. Because every person would be the same application user, you can track only application activities and not individual user activities.

- If an outside source is able to determine the application login and password, that source has free rein of the server. As mentioned previously, auditing cannot be used to target suspects. The application has to change its password, which could require recompilation of the application—not always a desirable thing to do in production.

This approach is not recommended due to these drawbacks. It can be used, however, if it is determined that the reduction in flexibility is worth the reduction in administrative activity.

SEPARATE LOGIN IDS FOR APPLICATION WORK VERSUS AD HOC QUERY

Users often require access to a system through an ad hoc query generator or other front-end tool, in addition to their regular access through an application. If you allow the user to use an application login when running an ad hoc tool, you might find the user updating tables or running stored procedures without the protection or validation normally ensured by the application.

For example, a user who normally uses the application to delete a row from the ten-billion-row sales_history table by retrieving it and pressing a delete button (complete with are you sure? messages!) might be surprised when the delete sales_history statement removes every row from the table.

Unfortunately, you can't restrict most tools from enabling updates to tables or executing stored procedures. Worse, SQL Server never knows whether the user requesting a deletion is running a carefully written application in PowerBuilder or is using `isql` after taking a one-day video course on SQL.

What's the solution?

You could try removing all the neat and interesting front-end products, but you bought SQL Server to enable those products to run.

You could try not to tell anyone how to insert, update, or delete, but that usually doesn't work.

You could require that all updates, inserts, and deletes use a stored procedure (related objects and permissions are discussed later in this chapter), but even that isn't foolproof; if the user can run the procedure from the application, it can be run from a command-line interface such `isql` as well.

One approach is to have two sets of logins: one for users running neat and interesting front-end tools, the other for using applications that are permitted to perform updates. The first set of logins and passwords is known to the users; the second set is based on the user name but known only to the updating applications.

For example, a user `mdoe` with a password `littlelamb` would have an application user name `mdoe_app` and a password `littlelamb_00946`. The login names for the application are visible from `sp_who`, so the passwords need to be difficult to guess. (You might want the password to be derived from the user password and some hashed version of the `uid`. Keeping your password derivation method secret is critical here.)

This approach to logins and passwords is not easy. To make it work, you prevent users from running `sp_password`, so password administration becomes your problem. But with perseverance you can have a system that is safe from the errors of a persistent and uneducated user.

Password Approach

There are several standards that companies use when identifying a password administration plan. These usually fall into one of three categories:

- Password same as login
- General application login and password
- Password independent of login

Whether you use a login approach of "SQL Server Login = Application Login" or not, you still must determine whether the password for that login will be dependent or independent of the login.

Password = Login

At many sites, passwords are identical to logins. Realistically, this is as close to having no password as you can get, because the password for a user is the same as the login name. Therefore, a login for user1 has a password of user1. In this approach, it is very easy for a person to find a way to access the server because only a login name must be determined. Many sites also use a standard for naming logins to a system—for example, market01 through market99, with passwords of market01 through market99, respectively. This is the least secure approach to a user password administration (second only to null). It is also one of the least flexible, because login name and password must remain the same, denying the capability of using password expiration (unless you are using integrated/mixed security).

> **NOTE**
>
> When you talk to hackers about methods they use to guess passwords and break into systems, they invariably tell you that the first password to guess is the login name. (After that comes the literal words, password and secret.)

General Application Login and Password

There are other sites that use a general application login for all users of an application. This means that users access an application, and when the application is connected to the database, it does so as a single general user—regardless of the number of connections it opens. This approach results in a severe reduction in the capability of linking activities to users. When sp_who is executed, for example, all user names are the same. This makes it very difficult to track down who executed a certain command. Fortunately, this approach often enables changing the general user password, depending on whether the application reads its password information from a configuration file or is hard-coded in the application itself.

Password Independent of Login

This approach is the most secure. Each user has a distinct password not related to the login name in any way. The user can change the password periodically, and the use of the "password expiration interval" forces the issue. This approach is normally selected at sites that have regulations (federal) regarding their applications or at sites that are most worried about unauthorized access to the database.

Because each user has a password and the capability of changing it, access to sp_password is required. Unfortunately, many sites want to keep users shielded from database operations because they are not usually accustomed to dealing directly with a database. Because of this fact, a command-line interface (isql) is not an acceptable alternative. This normally results in the creation of a user administration module for users to change passwords. This does increase overall application complexity somewhat, but it is done to continue to shield users from the database.

This is naturally the preferred approach by secure sites and is recommended if your environment is structured to handle the administrative complexities.

Permissions

Permissions are used to control access within a database. This is accomplished through the use of the grant and revoke statements. Any permission that can be granted can also be revoked, so when the word "grant" is used within this section, it can be thought of in the broader sense of controlling access (granting *or* revoking).

The granting of permissions results in the addition of rows to the sysprotects system table. Each database contains the sysprotects table, which means that permissions are database-specific. Because permissions are granted to database users, not server logins, there is no way to grant general access to a login.

Users

Permissions are used to control access by users of a database. In this context, a user is essentially any uid that exists in the sysusers table. The sysusers table initially contains rows for the database owner (dbo) and the public group (public). Additional users of a database are added with sp_adduser, and additional groups in a database are added with sp_addgroup. Therefore, the list of users that permissions can be granted to actually contains both users and groups.

Object Permissions

Granting of permissions on objects is performed using the grant command syntax:

```
grant  {all [ privileges] ¦ permission_list }
  on { table_name [ ( column_list ) ]
  ¦ view_name [ ( column_list ) ]
  ¦ stored_procedure_name }
  to{ group_name ¦ user_name }
[ { , {next_user_or group_} } ...]
  [ with grant option ]
```

Revoking of permissions on objects is performed using the `revoke` command syntax:

```
revoke [ grant option for ]
  {all [ privileges] ¦ permission_list }
  on { table_name [ ( column_list ) ]
  ¦ view_name [ ( column_list ) ]
  ¦ stored_procedure_name }
  to{ group_name ¦ user_name }
[ { , {next_user_or group_} } ...]
  [cascade ]
```

READING sysprotects

When you grant or revoke permissions on a table, SQL Server records that information in a database-level table, sysprotects. Every database includes explicit lines granting permission to system tables to public. (As of this writing, there were 18 rows of default system table permissions in the most recent version.)

Let's add some permissions and see how they affect sysprotects. The following command adds permissions entries:

```
grant all on marketing_table to public
```

Look at the contents of sysprotects after the grant statement:

```
select id, uid, action, grantor
from sysprotects
where id = object_id("marketing_table")
go
```

```
id          uid     action grantor
----------- ------- ------ -------
144003544   0       151    1
144003544   0       193    1
144003544   0       195    1
144003544   0       196    1
144003544   0       197    1
```

The id column identifies the table in the database.

The uid column indicates the user (or group) ID to whom permission is granted.

The action column specifies the type of action affected by the permission. You can decode the action value by referring to the spt_values table in the master database. Permissions actions are identified with the type "T". The output that follows lists all the permission action codes:

```
use master
go
select name, number, type
from spt_values
```

```
where type = "T"
and number > 0
order by 2
go

name                         number      type
-----------------------------  ----------  ----
References                     151         T
Select                         193         T
Insert                         195         T
Delete                         196         T
Update                         197         T
Create Table                   198         T
Create Database                203         T
Grant                          205         T
Revoke                         206         T
Create View                    207         T
Create Procedure               222         T
Execute                        224         T
Dump Database                  228         T
Create Default                 233         T
Dump Transaction               235         T
Create Rule                    236         T
```

grantor records the ID of the user who executed the grant statement.

The object owner grants or revokes permissions on objects to control access to objects within a database. These objects include tables, views, and stored procedures. Permissions default to the object owner, which is why a user who creates an object does not have to grant permissions to himself. However, any other user of the system would have to be granted permission on an object.

NOTE

sa object permissions are not checked. You never need to grant object permissions to the sa.

The types of permissions that can be granted/revoked to these objects include select, update, insert, delete, references, and execute. Select and update can have a column list specified (to control access at the column level), references applies only to tables (and can contain a column list), and execute applies only to procedures. Table 27.1 summarizes how object permissions can be granted.

Table 27.1. Object permissions.

Permission	*Specify Columns?*	*Can Grant On*
Select	Yes	Tables, views
Update	Yes	Tables, views
Insert	No	Tables, views
Delete	No	Tables, views
References	Yes	Tables
Execute	N/A	Stored procedures

Select, insert, update, and delete are pretty straightforward. They indicate whether a user can issue that type of command with a table or view listed in the `from` clause (a normal select or an insert, delete, or update with a `join` clause) or as the object of the action (update table or view, insert table or view, or delete table or view).

> **NOTE**
>
> Text and image columns enable use of the READTEXT and WRITETEXT commands:
> - The capability to use the WRITETEXT command is transferred through update permission.
> - The capability to use the READTEXT command is transferred through select permission.

Execute permission is granted on a stored procedure to enable a user to execute the procedure. This can have very powerful implications because a system can be implemented when access is granted completely to procedures and not the underlying tables or views.

The references permission is part of SQL 6.0 systems, and it applies to the capability of using declarative referential integrity. When implementing declarative referential integrity, the `create table` or `alter table` statement can include a `references` clause to indicate the relationship between tables. This permission needs to be granted only when objects owned by two different users have referential-integrity considerations (a user that owns both objects automatically has references permission). It is not likely that references permission would have to be granted in a production system, because most production systems have all objects owned by the same user name (`dbo`).

A permission list can contain a comma-delimited list of permissions or the word `all` (or `all privileges`). If `all` is specified, only the permissions that apply to the type of object for which the permission is being granted are actually granted.

To revoke permissions on an object to a user, the `revoke` command is used.

```
revoke select on table from user1.
```

The user then can revoke the capability of granting `select` on all columns by revoking the capability of granting on selected columns. This is accomplished by executing this statement:

```
revoke grant option for select on table(column2) from user1
```

Command Permissions

By default, the `dbo` is the only user who can create objects and perform backups. In some environments, users are granted access to these commands. These are called *command permissions*.

> **NOTE**
>
> It's important to differentiate between command and object permissions. *Command permissions* enable users to create objects themselves. This is rarely granted. *Object permissions* enable users to access objects that already exist. This permission must be granted to enable a system to operate.

Command permissions are granted to users by executing the following `grant` syntax:

```
grant  {all [ privileges] ¦ command_list }
  to{ group_name ¦ user_name }
[ { , {next_user_or group } } ...]
```

Here is the syntax for revoking those command permissions:

```
revoke  {all [ privileges] ¦ command_list }
  on { table_name [ ( column_list ) ]
  ¦ view_name [ ( column_list ) ]
  ¦ stored_procedure_name }
  from{ group_name ¦ user_name }
[ { , {next_user_or group_} } ...]
```

Command permissions are granted and revoked to users to control access to certain commands within a database. These commands include the following:

- create database (master database only)
- create default
- create procedure
- create rule
- create table
- create view

These permissions are most often granted in a development environment to enable developers to create objects in the course of developing a system. In a production environment, these permissions are not usually needed.

WARNING

Usually, you should not grant the create database permission to users. create database authority should be reserved for the sa login, or those logins with Admin-level permissions using integrated or mixed security.

If you really need to grant the create database permission, don't give it to the guest user in the master database! Add the login as a new user in the master database, and then grant create database to that new user.

A command list can contain a comma-delimited list of commands or the word all (or all privileges). If all is specified, only those commands that can be executed in that database are granted. This is only an issue with create database; you can grant permission to create databases only within the master database. Note the following about command permissions:

■ The creation of databases usually is performed by the system administrator and normally is not granted.

■ The creation of temporary tables is permitted by any user of the server and does not need to be specifically granted.

Permission Approaches

You should establish the access requirements of tables, views, and stored procedures during the design phase of a system. As each object is identified, the documentation should contain notes on what types of users need what types of access. It is easier to develop an effective permissions plan if you start gathering this information early.

First, define the users of a system. Try to group them logically, based on job description, department, or responsibility (for example, managers, clerks, marketing personnel, billing personnel, and so forth). Often, you will develop systems knowing only the broad user classifications; you will fill in names of users later on. In any case, determine which logical groups will be using a database and define what access is needed to which tables, views, and procedures by each group and the entire database user community as a whole.

> **NOTE**
>
> As you can see, any approach to permissions is deeply associated with a specific login and user approach. Permissions are granted to either users or groups. Most permission plans focus on controlling access to groups, particularly when large numbers of users are involved.

It generally is easiest to grant broad permissions and then limit access to specified users. The easiest way to implement broad permissions is to grant them to groups. Users assigned to a group automatically have the permissions granted to that group. Recall that a group can be any group that is specifically added to a database or the system group `public` (which includes all users of a database).

public

The `public` group is a special group that all belong to even when they are specifically added to a user-defined group. It is important to remember that the `guest` user is, of course, also a member of the `public` group. If you grant permissions to `public`, you are allowing anyone who has access to the database to receive the permissions specified to `public`.

If individual users are added to a database (not `guest`), you have substantial security at the database level. If you are satisfied with database-level security, granting to `public` allows all the users in the database to perform those functions specified. Using `public` is a good approach even when you have several user-defined groups in a database.

Often, several groups exist requiring special access to a select number of tables. Most other tables are available to all users of a database.

Take the example of a database with 100 tables and 10 user-defined groups. If you want to grant select permission on all the tables to all users, granting to each user-defined group requires 10 grant statements for each table. If all groups need select access to all tables, it is easiest to grant select permission to `public` for each table. This requires only one grant statement per table. If one group needs insert, update, and delete access to a table, additional permission can be granted on that table to only that group.

public and guest

As indicated previously, the `public` group contains all users, even the `guest` user. Combining the addition of a `guest` user to a database and using `public` as a means for defining permissions should only be used by those sites that are extremely confident with the security enforced at the server level. When a person gains access to the server, that user then has access to any database that has a `guest` user defined and consequently can perform any activities granted to `public`.

Addition of the guest user invalidates control of access at the database level. However, you can grant permissions to public and revoke permissions from guest to curb the activities the guest user can perform.

> **WARNING**
>
> Make sure you execute permission-related statements in the correct order! SQL Server permissions obey one simple rule:
>
> *Whatever happened last takes effect.*
>
> If you revoke from guest and then grant to public, guest receives the permission because guest is a member of public. There is no hierarchy of permissions. That is, user permissions do not take priority over group permissions, or vice versa.
>
> The safest way to manage permissions is to maintain a script of all the permissions for a particular database. Every time you need to make a change, insert the permission statement into the correct part of the script and re-execute the entire script. In this way, you can avoid unexpected consequences from grant and revoke statements.
>
> Be careful! You probably shouldn't run your big permissions script when users are online. You might end up revoking permissions while users are processing. The only safe way to implement this approach during active hours is to run the script in a transaction or set of transactions, with begin tran and commit tran. However, this can really slow processing dramatically because of locks placed on the system tables.

Granting to User-Defined Groups

Beyond the use of the public group, granting permissions to user-defined groups is the next-easiest way to implement a permission strategy. Of course, this approach is often combined with granting to public or to specific users. The approach is to define logically the access that applies only to a specific group and then grant or revoke permissions to that group.

For example, if only the marketing group needs to be able to perform select, insert, update, and delete on marketing tables, you can add a marketing group and execute this command for each of the marketing tables:

```
grant all on market_table to marketing
```

If you have billing tables that only billing personnel need all permissions to, you add a billing group and execute the following for each of the billing tables:

```
grant all on billing_table to billing
```

What if billing personnel need to select from marketing tables and marketing personnel need to select from billing tables? You can grant select permission on each table to the appropriate group or use the public group by granting select permission on each table in a database to public:

```
grant select on billing_table to public
grant select on marketing_table to public
```

Granting to Specific Users

Granting permissions to specific users requires the most administration but offers the greatest control. Normally, it is not used exclusively in a permission strategy because the addition of each new user requires executing individual grant statements for each object in which access is needed. Granting and revoking to users is most commonly used in combination with granting to public or user-specified groups.

For example, all marketing users can select, insert, and delete on all marketing tables, but only the user super_market_user can update information in the database. In this case, you execute these commands:

```
grant select, insert, delete on market_table to marketing
grant update on market_table to super_market_user
```

(This assumes that the super_market_user is also a member of the marketing group.)

Object Dependencies

Many organizations use dependent objects (views, procedures, and triggers) to implement advanced security structure. Recall from Chapter 1, "Overview of Client/Server," the following points:

- Views can restrict access to specific rows and columns of data.
- Procedures can restrict and validate all data modifications.
- Triggers can perform related updates or update substantive audit records.

In each of these cases, users need access to the dependent object but should not have comparable access to a dependent object.

If object ownership is distributed among several database users, implementing any of these types of advanced security is fruitless. For example, in Figure 27.8, John wants to select from a view owned by Bob, but Mary owns the base table.

FIGURE 27.8.

When the owner of an object and a dependent object are different, permissions must be granted explicitly on both objects.

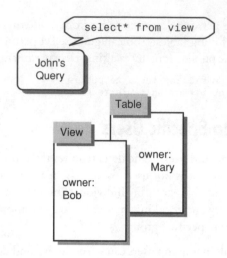

The permissions required for this scheme include the following:

```
[Mary:]grant select on basetable to bob
[Bob:]grant select on viewname to john
[Mary:]grant select on basetable to john
```

The final grant statement, in which Mary permits John to read the table directly, undermines the effect of a view intended to enforce security.

If both the base object and dependent object are owned by a single user, the user needs to grant permission to the user only for the dependent object. Because there is no change in ownership between the dependent and base objects, permissions are not checked.

In Figure 27.9, Mary owns both objects and John wants access to the view.

FIGURE 27.9.

When the owner of an object and a dependent object are the same, permissions on the base object are not checked.

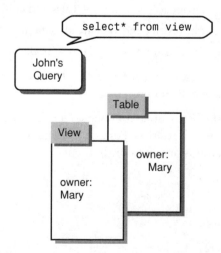

This scheme requires only a single permission statement:

```
[Mary:]grant select on viewname to john
```

Because Mary owns both objects, John's permissions are checked only at the view level and not at the table level. With no change in ownership, permissions are not checked.

Summary

SQL Server security is implemented in four layers: the operating system, the SQL server, the SQL Server database, and the SQL Server object. Each allows greater or lesser control, depending on your requirements.

SQL Server offers a variety of ways to control access to data. Server login and database user approaches affect the way in which a permissions strategy is implemented.

At the object level, most sites grant broad permissions and then limit or grant specific access as needed to minimize the administrative overhead in implementing a permissions plan. This usually involves granting to `public` or a user-defined group, and then revoking or granting specific permissions to a user-defined group or a specific user.

Database Logging and Recovery

28

SQL Server uses a write-ahead log and automatic forward recovery to maintain up-to-the-transaction data integrity, even in the case of erratic or unexpected server shutdowns. This chapter explores how the SQL Server transaction log works and how it manages recovery. You'll understand commits and checkpoints, and how the server manages data integrity through various server events.

SQL Server's use of terms might differ from your prior experience with other database applications or transaction processing systems. For example, you might think of recovery or disaster recovery as the administrative process of getting back to work after a catastrophe, but it means something quite different in the SQL Server world. You need to nail down the meaning of the crucial SQL Server terms first.

- A *transaction* is a unit of work. Transactions can be long or short, and they can involve changes to millions of rows of data or only one. SQL Server promises that every transaction, no matter how long or complex, will run to completion or will be completely reversed if it cannot be completed for any reason. The transaction log is the component of the system responsible for transactional data integrity.

- *Recovery* is the automatic process of reconciling the log and the data. Recovery occurs when the server is started. This chapter examines the recovery process in detail.

- A *backup* is a physical copy of the database or transaction log. The SQL Server term for a backup is a *dump*, and dump is the Transact-SQL command used to initiate backups of either the database or the transaction log.

- *Restoration* is the process of taking a backup of the database from storage and copying it back onto the server.

Backup and restoring are the topic of Chapter 29, "SQL Server Database Backup and Restoration."

What Is a Transaction?

A transaction is a set of operations to be completed at one time, as though they were a single operation. A transaction must be fully completed or not performed at all. Standard examples of transactions include bank transfers (withdraw $500 from checking, add $500 to savings) and order entry systems (write an order for five widgets, remove five widgets from inventory).

All SQL statements are inherently transactions, from grant and create statements to the data modification statements—insert, update, and delete. Consider the following update example:

```
update titles
set price = price * 1.02
```

This statement modifies all rows in the titles table. SQL Server guarantees that, regardless of the size of the titles table, all rows will be processed or no rows will be processed. What if half of the rows are modified and the server fails? When the server comes back up (but before the database is available for use), it rolls back the incomplete transaction, removing all evidence that it ever began. That's part of the recovery process, which is discussed later in this chapter.

SQL Server also includes transaction-control syntax to group sets of SQL statements into single logical work units:

- `begin transaction` starts a unit of work.
- `commit transaction` completes a unit of work.
- `rollback transaction` cancels a unit of work.

The following example enters an order and depletes inventory in a single transaction:

```
begin transaction
   update inventory
      set in_stock = in_stock - 5
      where item_num = "14141"
   insert orders (cust_num, item_num, qty)
      values ("ABC151", "14141", 5)
commit transaction
```

SQL Server guarantees that the inventory will not change unless the order is also entered.

Look at the same example, but with the `rollback transaction` statement instead of `commit`.

```
begin transaction
   update inventory
      set in_stock = in_stock - 5
      where item_num = "14141"
   insert orders (cust_num, item_num, qty)
      values ("ABC151", "14141", 5)
rollback transaction
```

When the server encounters the `rollback` statement, it discards all changes in the transaction and returns the data to the state it was in before work began.

This chapter examines the mechanism used by SQL Server to manage data integrity (both `rollback` and `commit`) in transactions.

What Is the Transaction Log?

The *transaction log* is a database-level system table, called `syslogs`. The `syslogs` table contains a sequential list of all modifications to every object in the database, as well as any information required to maintain data integrity.

The transaction log is

- Shared by all users of a database
- Modified in cache and only flushed to disk at commit time
- Written first (a write-ahead log)

The log is not

■ Usefully manipulated or read with SQL

■ Readable in any useful format

> **NOTE**
>
> There are now third-party utilities that access the log, allowing some direct interaction with the log and providing some measure of "undo" functions. However, nothing in the standard SQL Server suite allows you to interact directly with the log.

A Write-Ahead Log

Write-ahead means that the log is written first, before the data itself, any time that a query modifies data.

> **NOTE**
>
> In addition to standard SQL data modification statements (insert, update, delete), all create statements, permissions statements (grant and revoke), and many system stored procedures (such as sp_adduser and sp_bindrule) change the contents of system tables. The server logs each of these data modifications as well.

When modifying data, the server takes the following steps:

1. Write a begin tran record in the log (in cache).
2. Record the modification in the log (in cache).
3. Perform the modification to the data (in cache).
4. Write a commit tran record to the log (in cache).
5. Flush all "dirty" (modified) log pages to disk.

Commits

A commit flushes all *dirty* (modified) log pages for that database from cache to disk. Figure 28.1 shows the state of the data after the transaction is complete and the commit has taken place.

The server does all of the work in RAM first, before making changes to disk, to improve processing speed. When the process is complete, the only work that is written to disk is any change to the log. However, RAM is volatile. If the server goes down unexpectedly, or if someone pulls the plug out of the wall, the changes to data that are stored only in memory are lost, right? That's where the transaction log earns its keep.

FIGURE 28.1.

The commit process only writes log changes to disk.

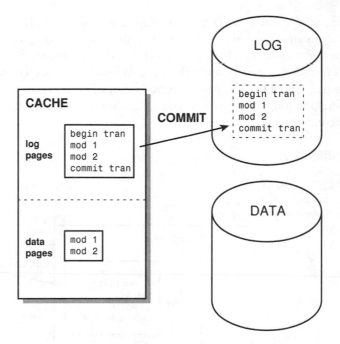

Remember that each modification has been recorded in the log. At recovery time (after the server goes down and is restarted), committed transactions that have not been written to the data area are rolled forward into the data. This is *forward recovery*, or *roll forward*. If the commit tran has been executed and the write to the log has been made to disk, the server guarantees that the data can be recovered when the server goes down.

> **NOTE**
>
> It is interesting to note here that the log is really the part of the database that matters when it comes to recovery and restore. If the disk on which the data is stored catches fire, you can use the information in the log, in combination with your backups, to restore the system up to the last complete transaction. On the other hand, if the log disk gets wet while you are putting out the fire, you will only be able to restore up to the time of the last backup.
>
> If you have to choose between mirroring logs and mirroring data, mirror the logs.

At recovery time, uncommitted transactions (begin tran markers without a commit tran) are rolled back. All data modifications associated with the transaction are undone. This is *rollback*. But how do uncommitted transactions get into the log in the first place?

Frequently, when transactions overlap, the commit tran flushes uncommitted—as well as committed—work to disk. In that way, the "dirty" log pages are copied to disk even though the transactions associated with those log pages are incomplete. This does not commit the transactions, it merely writes the pages to disk. The transaction is still uncommitted at this point. Uncommitted work can be identified by a begin tran entry in the log with no corresponding commit tran. Figure 28.2 illustrates a commit that writes both committed and uncommitted work to the log.

FIGURE 28.2.

The commit process writes all dirty log pages for the database to disk, including those with incomplete transactions.

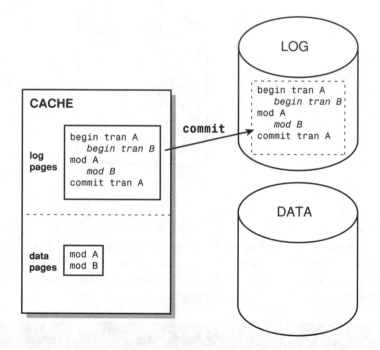

Why write both committed and uncommitted work with every commit? Keep in mind that SQL Server always performs I/O at the page level or higher. Entries in syslogs are ordered by a consecutive timestamp value, so transactions that are processing concurrently are intermingled on a single page.

Remember, also, that the commit process is the crucial bottleneck for an online system. The user is waiting and pages are locked until the commit is complete. By writing out commits at the page level without first weeding out any uncommitted work, the server can streamline commits. If the uncommitted work is subsequently rolled back, the server can record that fact in a later row in syslogs.

Checkpoints

The log is the part of the database that keeps track of data integrity, transaction control, and recoverability. For the server to guarantee data integrity, it only needs to make certain that the log is written to disk. However, if enough transactions pile up in the log without being recorded on the data disk as well, after the server goes down it will take weeks for it to recover all of the committed transactions. When does the data get updated while the server is running? During a checkpoint.

A *checkpoint* writes all dirty pages for the database from cache to disk, starting with the log. (See Figure 28.3.) A checkpoint reduces the amount of work the server needs to do at recovery time.

FIGURE 28.3.

The checkpoint process writes all dirty pages for the database, starting with the log.

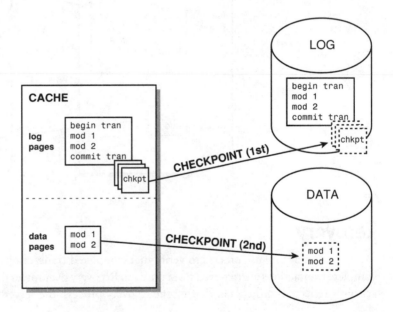

A checkpoint occurs under three different circumstances:

- The dbo issues the checkpoint command.
- The server needs additional cache space.
- The server recovery interval has been exceeded.

Before the checkpoint starts, the server first notes in the log that a checkpoint has been performed in the database. The checkpoint marker enables the server to assume that all committed work recorded in the log prior to the checkpoint marker is reflected in the data.

If there are long-running transactions underway when the checkpoint begins, uncommitted work might be written not only to the log but also to the data. (See Figure 28.4.) The recovery process uses the checkpoint marker in the log to identify work in incomplete transactions that has been written to the data disk by a checkpoint.

FIGURE 28.4.

The checkpoint marker indicates where the last update to the data took place.

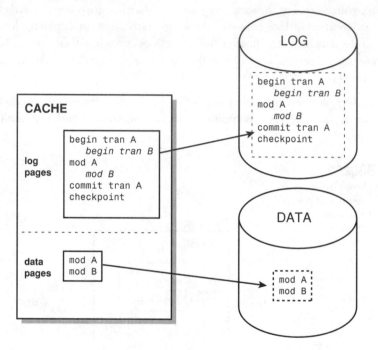

Recovery

Recovery is an automatic process to verify that completed transactions are in the data and incomplete transactions are removed from the data. Recovery guarantees that any completed transaction is reflected in the data. During the recovery process, the server does the following:

- Checks `syslogs` for each database, backing out incomplete transactions and rolling forward completed transactions not in the data.
- Checkpoints the database.
- Drops and re-creates `tempdb`.

Recovery Interval

With the `recovery interval` configuration option, the `sa` can set the approximate amount of time per database that he or she will wait for the SQL Server to start up. For example, to set the server recovery interval to 12 minutes per database, use the following:

```
sp_configure "recovery interval", 12
reconfigure
```

`recovery interval` is a dynamic configuration setting, so the new value will take effect as soon as you issue the `reconfigure` statement. Here's how it works. Once a minute, one of the system processes listed in `sp_who` (which always seems to be stuck on CHECKPOINT SLEEP) wakes up and examines each database in turn. Based on the amount of work recorded in the log for each database, the process determines whether it will take longer than the recovery interval to restore the database. If so, the system process issues an automatic checkpoint. Finally, if the database is set for truncate log on checkpoint, the system process truncates the log.

The length of time it will take your server to recover completely after an unexpected shutdown depends on your recovery interval and the number of databases on the server. The worst-case answer is that it could take the number of minutes attained by multiplying recovery interval times the number of databases. (In other words, 12-minute recovery interval × 20 databases = 4 hours!)

You will seldom encounter the worst case, but even if you do, you can access your own database as soon as recovery is complete. (Databases are recovered in order by `dbid`.)

> **NOTE**
>
> Don't forget that the `shutdown` statement includes an automatic checkpoint on every database. If you issue `shutdown with nowait`, the system skips the checkpoint and shuts down immediately. Server recovery is much faster after a `shutdown` than after a `shutdown with nowait`.

It's tempting to set the recovery interval low to ensure a quick recovery after any shutdown, but the checkpoint process creates overhead when you are running a high volume of transactions through the server. Set the configuration setting to the highest tolerable value.

Recovery Flags

Use the `recovery flags` setting with `sp_configure` to display the names of transactions during recovery. If you use transaction names in SQL code, the names will be displayed in the error log if the transaction is rolled back or brought forward during recovery.

```
sp_configure "recovery flags", 1
reconfigure
```

> **NOTE**
>
> Restart the server after this option to have the recovery flags take effect. During the first restart, transaction names will not be listed. Subsequent restarts will display transaction names as they are processed.

Setting recovery flags enables you to determine exactly which work actually made it into the server before a shutdown. To make good use of the errorlog information, there must be a correlation between SQL Server transaction names and batch or work unit identifiers in the manual process. For example, if the batch number is 17403, the transaction name might be B_17403. Pass the transaction name to the server with the `begin tran` statement, as follows:

```
begin tran B_17403
   ...
commit tran
```

When the Transaction Log Fills Up

If the transaction log fills for any reason, all data modifications to the database will fail immediately. Most standard maintenance measures (dump the log, resize the log) will fail as well. The only reliable way to clear the log is to issue the `dump tran ... with no_log` statement and dump the entire database.

Summary

Transactions ensure consistency of database integrity to manage simultaneous updates and to ensure recovery after a server shutdown. All SQL statements are transactions themselves, and many SQL statements can be combined into a larger transaction.

You need to manage the transaction log, either with thresholds or by regularly monitoring the amount of available space in the log.

SQL Server Database Backup and Restoration

29

Backup is common to any database environment. A *backup* is a copy of a database (or portion of a database) stored on some type of media (tape, disk, and so forth). A *restore* is the process used to return a database to the state it was in at a certain point in time. For SQL Server, a backup is normally referred to as a *dump* and a restore is normally referred to as a *load*, because these are the names of the commands to back up and restore, respectively.

It takes work to define an effective backup-and-recovery plan. This is especially true in *very large database* (VLDB) environments because the complexity of administrative activities is magnified. Timing of activities quickly becomes an issue. For large tables and databases, consistency checks (dbcc), updating index statistics, and index creation can take from several hours to days. When making plans for automating backups, you must consider the impact of these activities as well as application activities.

The backup media you choose also can affect your plan. Dumping to tape devices means that the physical tapes have to be managed. You must consider this in your plan. Additionally, when a tape is full, a subsequent backup will fail, which can affect your entire backup-and-recovery process. When dumping to file devices, you must consider the organization of the directory structure as well as management of the backup files.

Why Back Up?

Backups are a hassle. Why bother? (Why do you have car insurance?) Backups are the easiest and most foolproof way of ensuring that you can recover a database. Without a backup, all data could be lost and would have to be re-created from the source. This is normally an option only for *Decision Support Systems* (DSS), because its data normally originates in some other system. For *On-Line Transaction Processing* (OLTP) or *On-Line Analytical Processing* (OLAP) systems, the majority of data originates on the server. The lost data might not be reproducible.

Backups can guard against table or database corruption, media failure, or user error. They should be performed as frequently as necessary for effective data administration. SQL Server backups can be performed while the database is in use, but generally it is more effective to back up during nonpeak activity periods.

Roles and Responsibilities

The capability of executing the dump and load commands defaults to the dbo of the database. The dbo could be the login who created the database, anyone aliased to the dbo in the database, or the sa login (the sa becomes dbo in any database that the sa uses). Remember that the sa login is the System Administrator, and the dbo is the owner of any particular database. dbo isn't a login; it's a user name, so it resides at SQL Server's database level of security.

You should identify who is responsible for performing backups in your organization. For each of these individuals, create a login and grant the `dump database` and `load database` statement permissions.

As always, the `sa` or `dbo` has the capability of dumping and loading the database.

Types of Backups

There are two types of backups: full and incremental. A *full backup* is a copy of all the allocated pages in your database, including all system tables. (See Figure 29.1.) The system tables include `syslogs`, normally referred to as *transaction logs*. The transaction log is also dumped to ensure that all transactions have been included in the backup.

FIGURE 29.1.

A database backup (`dump database acctg_db`*) copies the entire database, including log and data.*

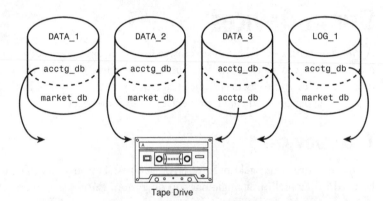

Tape Drive

> **WARNING**
>
> Full backups do not truncate the transaction log, which often is confusing and sometimes disastrous for new database administrators and backup operators. Even if all your backups are complete backups, you must run the incremental backup process periodically to clear the transaction log. Otherwise, you will certainly fill up your log, and processing on that database will halt until you clear the log. (See the section titled "Dumping Database Logs," later in this chapter.)

An *incremental backup* is simply a copy of the transaction log. (See Figure 29.2.) The transaction log contains the transactions that have occurred since the last `dump transaction` command. This is similar to incremental backups of file systems, in which only the files that have changed are backed up. Dumping the transaction log truncates the log, unless the `with no_truncate` option is specified.

FIGURE 29.2.

An incremental backup
(dump transaction
acctg_db) copies only the
transaction log (the
syslogs table).

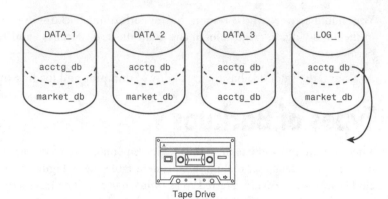

Tape Drive

Dump Devices

A *dump device* is created for the exclusive use of the dump and load commands. When dumping a database or transaction log, you must tell it where to create the backup. Creating a dump device enables you to associate a logical name with the physical backup media. The two most common types of media are tape devices and disk devices.

Tape Devices

A *tape device* records backups to removable tapes. Tape drives can be used alone, or several can be used in parallel for a single backup operation. Purchase as many drives as you can afford, based on the needs of your backup-and-recovery strategy. Tape devices are inherently more secure than disk devices because the media (tape) is removable and portable. Tape capacity has increased dramatically over the last five years. In 1990, standard 1/4-inch cartridges held only 150MB of data. Now, smaller cartridges (4mm and 8mm are common sizes) hold over 50 times more data (8GB). The size and compactness of tapes will almost certainly continue to progress.

Tape devices are used by most production sites. Tape devices provide a removable source of backup media that can easily be moved offsite for additional security. Tape devices adapt to changing database size much more gracefully than do disk devices. Dumping a 50MB database to disk can be easily managed by your file system. As the database grows to 50GB, however, a disk dump will probably prove impossible because most sites do not have that amount of free space in the file system. Additionally, to move the dump offsite, you must back up the dump files to tape.

Disk Devices

A *disk device* is just a file in a directory, usually stored in the file system of your database server. Dumping to a disk device is faster than dumping to a tape device. When you dump to a disk device, you can actually see the file grow if you check the file size at intervals during the dump.

In a break with past behavior, SQL Server 6.0 for Windows NT does not automatically over-write previous backups. In all versions of SQL Server prior to 6.0, backing up a database using a preexisting file resulted in deletion of the original file. Its contents were replaced by the newly created backup. This was called *destructive backup* and was the only behavior SQL Server al-lowed for both disk backups and tape backups. With SQL Server 6.0, that default behavior has changed. By default, SQL Server 6.0 will *append* a backup to an existing file, whether on tape or on disk.

Adding Dump Devices

Use `sp_addumpdevice` to add a new dump device to a SQL Server.

Syntax

```
sp_addumpdevice "tape", logicalname, physical_name, size
sp_addumpdevice "disk", logical_name, physical_name
```

> **TIP**
>
> Prior to SQL Server 6.0, adding dump devices using `sp_addumpdevice` was a require-ment. With the newest version of SQL Server, you don't have to add dump devices with `sp_addumpdevice`; you can provide the physical name as part of the `dump` syntax like this:
>
> ```
> dump tran my_db to disk = "c:\sql60\dumps\my_db_t.dmp"
> ```

Logical Name

After executing this command, you can use the logical name for all dumps and loads; a good practice is to choose the logical name based on the type of device being added. For tape de-vices, use a general name for the tape (`Tape1`, `Tape2`, and so forth). For disk devices, use a logi-cal name indicating the database and dump type (`CustomerDB_dump` or `CustomerDB_tran`, for example).

Physical Name

The physical name is normally predefined for tape devices. Tape devices should be specified using the physical name defined by Windows NT. A common example of the physical name is `\\.\TAPE0`. The following example adds a tape device called `Tape1`. This device recognizes any ANSI tape labels:

```
sp_addumpdevice "tape", "Tape1", "\\.\tape0", 8000
```

For file devices, it is a good idea to organize a directory structure for all your databases. For example, the root directory could be called \dbdump. Each database in your server would be a subdirectory. The CustomerDB subdirectory would be \dbdump\CustomerDB. The filename created is based on the dump type. Therefore, the two dump devices for the CustomerDB database would be created in the following manner:

```
sp_addumpdevice "disk", "CustomerDB_dump",
    "\dbdump\CustomerDB\CustomerDB_dump", 2
sp_addumpdevice "disk", "CustomerDB_tran",
    "\dbdump\CustomerDB\CustomerDB_tran", 2
```

By standardizing your structure, you can now write scripts that accept a database name as a parameter. The entire dump command can be created dynamically. The location of the dump is also known, enabling you to rename the dump file immediately or move it to a different directory to avoid having it overwritten.

Size

The *size* parameter is used to specify the tape capacity in number of megabytes. Use the maximum size allowable for your tape device. The *size* parameter is optional with SQL Server 6.0, because it uses Windows NT to automatically detect the capacity available on the physical dump device. According to Microsoft, this parameter will be removed in future versions of SQL Server, but it is still supported on this release.

Do not be stingy with the number of dump devices added. Using dump devices helps standardize your dump approach, especially for disk devices.

SQL Server 6.0 Backup Functions

Backups in SQL Server 6.0 received significant enhancement and make better use of SQL Server's threading resources. In addition, SQL Server reads and writes 60KB blocks of data for backup, speeding throughput to the backup device. Here are other new features:

- Backups can be *striped* (partitioned), enabling you to specify up to 32 separate devices for dumping or loading a database. The backup manager breaks the database into approximately equal portions and dumps those portions in parallel.

- Backups can be performed remotely, enabling you to dump your database or a portion (stripe) of your database to a device on hardware other than the hardware where your SQL Server resides. This requires a network connection to a remote device, and can support standard Universal Naming Convention network names. (See the Windows NT Server documentation for more information on using UNC names for network resources.)

- SQL Server uses Windows NT backup tape names and resources, so the CONSOLE program is no longer necessary nor included with SQL Server.

- Several backups can be recorded on the same tape. A subsequent reload locates only the file it needs to recover.
- Tape options are expanded.
- Messages can be sent to the session initiating the dump or load, or to an operator console.

Creating Dump Devices with SQL Enterprise Manager

You can also use SQL Server's Enterprise Manager to define tape devices using a GUI interface. In the Server Manager window of SQL-EM, you can add dump devices by right-clicking on the Dump Devices folder and clicking the New menu item on the popup menu that appears to display the dialog box shown in Figure 29.3.

FIGURE 29.3.

Define new dump devices in the Create Dump Device dialog box in SQL Enterprise Manager.

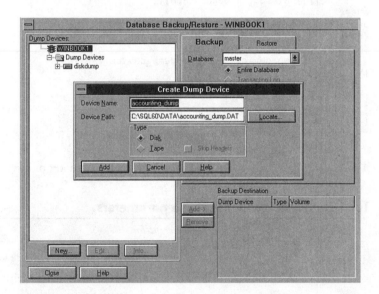

This dialog box enables you to define the logical and physical names, as well as assign the physical location of the device and define whether it is a disk or tape device. In the background, SQL-EM is simply running sp_adddumpdevice, with the parameters containing the values you supply here.

Dumping and Loading

Now that the basics have been defined, you need to take a close look at the dump and load commands. At this point, you should have the backup server up and running and your dump devices identified. Let's look at the dump and load options for both the entire database and the transaction log.

Dumping the Database

Use dump database to make a full copy of your database. The simplified syntax for the dump database command is as follows:

```
dump database databasename to devicename
```

This command is valid for all versions of SQL Server, including those from Sybase. In SQL 6.0, however, the dump command needs to handle several other options, including displaying backup statistics, striped backups, and tape-handling specifications. Here is the full format for the dump database command:

```
DUMP DATABASE {dbname ¦ @dbname_var}
        TO dump_device [, dump_device2 [..., dump_device32]]
    [WITH options
        [[,] STATS [ = percentage]]]
where
dump_device =
{dump_device_name ¦ @dump_device_namevar}
¦ {DISK ¦ TAPE ¦ FLOPPY ¦ PIPE} =
    {'temp_dump_device' ¦ @temp_dump_device_var}}
[VOLUME = {volid ¦ @volid_var}]
options =
[[,] {UNLOAD ¦ NOUNLOAD}]
[[,] {INIT ¦ NOINIT}]
[[,] {SKIP ¦ NOSKIP}]
[[,] {{EXPIREDATE = {date ¦ @date_var}}
    ¦ {RETAINDAYS = {days ¦ @days_var}}]
```

Table 29.1 presents detailed descriptions of each parameter of dump database.

Table 29.1. The dump database parameters.

Parameter	Description
dbname	The name of the database you are attempting to dump.
dump_device	The dump device you defined with sp_adddumpdevice. Optionally, you can directly specify a disk or tape device, even when you are striping them.
retaindays = #_of_days	An option that can be used for any type of dump device. It does not allow the dump to be overwritten until the number of days specified has passed. This is an important option for any production backup strategy.

Several other options focus on how the dump is to be conducted, regardless of the physical device characteristics. You should incorporate several of these options into your backup strategy.

The options in the next six sections apply only to tape devices.

dumpvolume

The option `Specify dumpvolume for production dumps` labels your dump, which then can be specified during a `load`. For example, specify a `dumpvolume` of your database name and the date (`CustomerDB_Jan07`). Then, if you have dumps for January 7–10 on a single tape, you can easily reload the January 7 dump by specifying `dumpvolume` as part of the load.

nounload | unload

The `nounload ¦ unload` option controls the rewinding of the tape. `nounload` should be used unless this is the last dump you want to have on the tape.

noinit | init

The `noinit ¦ init` option determines whether the dump will be appended to the tape or if it reinitializes the entire tape volume. Use `init` when dumping to a tape for the first time or to reuse an old tape. You might use `noinit` to allow for multiple dumps to a single tape.

file = file_name

Use the `file = file_name` option to specify a filename of up to 17 characters in length. This option normally is not specified. By default, the backup server names the file by concatenating the last seven characters from the database name, the two-digit year, the Julian day (1 through 366), and a hex representation of the time.

notify = {client | operator_console}

Volume change messages are sent, by default, to the operator console if available. If not, the messages are sent to the client initiating the request.

The following is an example of striped dumps:

```
— Dump the CustomerDB database across 4 dump devices (Tape1-4).
— Name each volume, initialize the tapes, do not rewind,
— prevent other dumps from overwriting this dump for 2 weeks,
— and send the messages to the client terminal.
dump database CustomerDB to Tape1 dumpvolume = Volume1
    stripe on Tape2 dumpvolume = Volume2
    stripe on Tape3 dumpvolume = Volume3
    stripe on Tape4 dumpvolume = Volume4
    with init, nounload, retaindays=14,
```

Here is an example of multiple dumps to a single tape:

```
— Dump the CustomerDB, ProductDB, and SecurityDB to Tape1
— For the first dump, initialize the tape but do not rewind.
— Dump the second database after the first.
```

```
— After the third database is dumped, rewind the tape.
dump database CustomerDB to Tape1 dumpvolume = CustVol1
    with init
dump database ProductDB to Tape1 dumpvolume = ProdVol1
    with /* no unload is the default */
dump database SecurityDB to Tape1 dumpvolume = SecVol1
    with unload
```

You can dump a database while the server is in use, but doing so causes a substantial performance reduction. Striping dumps across even a small number of devices decreases the total amount of time required to execute the dump, decreasing the duration of the impact. Benchmark user-response times with and without a dump process running to determine the impact on your system.

Dumping Databases Using SQL Enterprise Manager

So why, exactly, are we talking Transact-SQL syntax when Microsoft is shipping this nifty SQL Enterprise Manager utility? Because SQL-EM, behind the scenes, is executing the syntax previously described when you use it to back up databases.

SQL Enterprise Manager displays the Database Backup/Restore dialog box (see Figure 29.4) when you choose Tools | Backup/Restore... from the menu. From this dialog box, you can back up and restore both databases and transaction logs. Enterprise Manager also enables you to create new dump devices, if they are needed.

FIGURE 29.4.

SQL Enterprise Manager supplies the graphical interface that hides many of the complexities of backup command syntax.

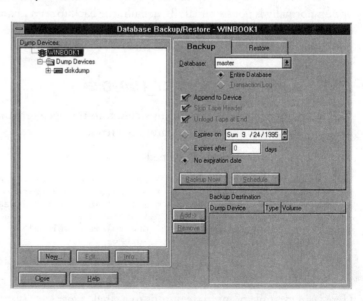

Selecting the database name from the combo box defines which database you are going to back up. The various syntactic options discussed previously are represented as checkboxes and other options.

Striped backups are defined by selecting dump devices from the list on the left and using the Add button in the lower-right corner, adding them to the Backup Destination list of dump devices to be used for the backup. SQL Enterprise Manager, when it builds the DUMP DATABASE statement it will eventually execute, will use the multiple devices listed in the Backup Destination box to construct the multiple-device clause necessary for striped backup.

Whether used as native SQL syntax in a script, or used through SQL Enterprise Manager, the features of SQL Server backup are identical.

Dumping Database Logs

Use dump transaction to make a copy of the transactions that have occurred against your database since the last transaction log dump. This is the simplified syntax for the dump transaction command:

```
dump transaction databasename to devicename
```

dump transaction works similarly to dump database and supports the same options. The only difference between the two lies in the amount of work they do.

```
DUMP TRANSACTION {dbname ¦ @dbname_var}
        [TO dump_device [, dump_device2 [..., dump_device32]]]
    [WITH {TRUNCATE_ONLY ¦ NO_LOG ¦ NO_TRUNCATE}
        {options}]
where
dump_device =
{dump_device_name ¦ @dump_device_namevar}
¦ {DISK ¦ TAPE ¦ FLOPPY ¦ PIPE} =
    {'temp_dump_device' ¦ @temp_dump_device_var}}
[VOLUME = {volid ¦ @volid_var}]
options =
[[,] {UNLOAD ¦ NOUNLOAD}]
[[,] {INIT ¦ NOINIT}]
[[,] {SKIP ¦ NOSKIP}]
[[,] {{EXPIREDATE = {date ¦ @date_var}}
    ¦ {RETAINDAYS = {days ¦ @days_var}}]
```

The special-purpose options are in bold print. These options are truncate_only, no_log, and no_truncate.

truncate_only and no_log

The truncate_only and no_log options are used to prune the transaction log without making a copy of it. As you can see from the format of the command, you either specify one of these options or indicate a device to which to dump the transaction log. Use truncate_only to truncate the log gracefully. It checkpoints the database before truncating the log. Use no_log when your transaction log is completely full. no_log does not checkpoint the database before dumping the log.

Either of these options throws away the log. When the command has been executed, you are exposed. If a disaster occurs before you can dump the database, you will not be able to recover any data that has been added since the last dump. The frequency of dumping transaction logs determines the scope of your exposure.

Any database that does not have its transaction log on a separate device cannot dump the transaction. Every system has a database meeting this characteristic. This usually is discovered when the transaction log for the master database fills up.

Because the master database must fully reside on the master device, the database space is shared between data and log, negating the capability of dumping the transaction log.

To avoid this problem, periodically prune the transaction log with truncate_only (or no_log, if completely full). Make sure you dump the database after logged operations (database creation, user addition, and so forth). For databases that do not require up-to-the-minute recovery, and for databases with no separate log segment, set the trunc log on chkpt option on for the database and dump frequently.

no_truncate

The no_truncate option is exactly the opposite of the previous two options. no_truncate makes a copy of your transaction log but does not prune it. Use this option when you have a media failure of a data device being used by your database. The master database must be available. This option enables the server to dump the transaction log but does not try to touch the database in any way. (In a normal dump tran, a checkpoint is executed. If a database device is unavailable, the checkpoint process cannot write the dirty pages. no_truncate simply backs up the transaction log without checkpointing.)

Dumping the transaction log is disabled after nonlogged operations such as nonlogged writetext, select into, and fast bcp. You can dump a transaction log while the server is in use. The impact on performance should be minimal. It is common to dump transaction logs even during normal business hours.

Transaction Backup Using SQL Enterprise Manager

As with database backup, SQL Enterprise Manager builds a DUMP TRAN statement that reflects the backup options you select using the Database Backup/Restore dialog box. There is one important distinction. Any database can be backed up using DUMP DATABASE. Only those databases that have a separate transaction log can be backed up using DUMP TRAN. As a result, SQL Enterprise Manager detects whether the database is on its own device, and automatically disables the Transaction Log option of the dialog box. In Figure 29.4, the master database is selected for backup, and therefore the Transaction Log option is disabled. For the mktg database in Figure 29.5, the Transaction Log option is enabled because mktg has its transaction log on a distinct device.

FIGURE 29.5.

SQL Enterprise Manager enables the Transaction Log backup option only when a database has its transaction log on a separate device from the data.

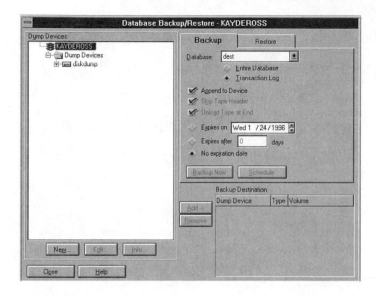

You'll notice that none of the extra transaction log backup options are available from the interface. In order to use the `WITH NO_LOG`, `WITH NO_TRUNCATE`, and `WITH TRUNCATE_ONLY` options of `DUMP TRAN`, you must use the native T-SQL syntax and submit the query from some query-based utility such as ISQL/w or from within the Query Tool window of SQL Enterprise Manager. All other options related to the `DUMP TRAN` statement are available using SQL-EM.

Loading the Database

With SQL Server Enterprise Manager, you can accomplish the same tasks by using a mouse instead of typing SQL code. When you click on the Tools | Backup/Restore... menu sequence, SQL-EM displays the rather enormous dialog box shown in Figure 29.6.

Loading the Database

Use `load database` to load a backup into an existing database. The database can be the database used to create the dump, but this is definitely not a requirement. The simplified syntax for the `load database` command is

```
load database databasename from devicename
```

This command is valid for all versions of SQL Server. Most options available to the `dump` command can be used in the `load`. This is the full format for the `load database` command:

```
Loading a database:
LOAD DATABASE {dbname | @dbname_var}
      FROM dump_device [, dump_device2 [..., dump_device32]]
   [WITH options
      [[,] STATS [ = percentage]]]
```

```
Loading a transaction log:
LOAD TRANSACTION {dbname ¦ @dbname_var}
       FROM dump_device [, dump_device2 [..., dump_device32]]
    [WITH options]
Loading header information:
LOAD HEADERONLY
       FROM dump_device
where
dump_device =
{ dump_device_name ¦ @dump_device_namevar}
¦ {DISK ¦ TAPE ¦ FLOPPY ¦ PIPE} =
    {'temp_dump_device' ¦ @temp_dump_device_var}}
[VOLUME = {volid ¦ @volid_var}]
options =
[[,] {UNLOAD ¦ NOUNLOAD}]
[[,] {SKIP ¦ NOSKIP}]
[[,] {FILE = fileno}]
```

All options listed are identical to the dump command, except for the listonly and headeronly options. If you specify either of these options, information is displayed but no data is loaded. Use these options immediately after a database dump to verify that the load process can read the dump. It can be used for tape or file devices.

listonly

Use listonly to obtain a listing of all dump files on a tape volume. The output contains database name, device name, and date and time of the dump. The = full option provides additional information.

headeronly

Use headeronly to display information about a single dump file. If the device specified is a tape device, information about only the first file on the dump is displayed, unless you specify the file parameter.

> **NOTE**
>
> No one can use the database while load is being executed, including the person executing the load command.

Here are some loading examples. The first shows striped loads:

```
Load database accounting from Tape1, Tape2, Tape3, Tape4
```

The load database command loads all used pages from the dump into the target database and runs recovery of syslogs to ensure consistency. Any unused pages are initialized by the load process. (This is the primary reason that a load can take significantly longer than a dump. The time required to dump a database is proportional to the used pages in the database; the time required to load a database is proportional to the overall number of pages in the database. Therefore, a 50GB database with 20MB of data might take only a few minutes to dump, but the load could take several hours or days.)

Dumps are conducted in order to keep ongoing backups of a database. A `load` is executed to restore a database normally after a corruption or user error occurs. If you are loading for a reason other than a disaster, the current database structure can be used to load the database dump. This does not require any extra work other than ensuring that tapes are loaded (or files are in the correct locations).

Restoring Databases Using SQL Enterprise Manager

From within the same Database Backup/Restore dialog box illustrated in Figures 29.4 and 29.5, you can also restore databases by clicking on the Restore table of the window. The new dialog box, shown in Figure 29.6, provides the same syntactic options that the `LOAD DATABASE` and `LOAD TRAN` statements provide from above.

FIGURE 29.6.

SQL Enterprise Manager supplies the same features and functions that are available in T-SQL for database restoration, but presents them in a more usable format in this dialog box.

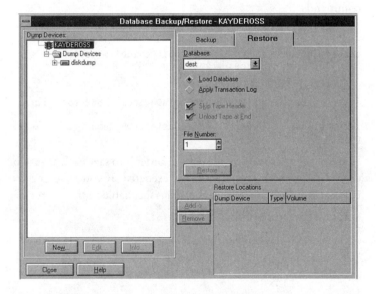

As with the Backup tab, SQL Enterprise Manager automatically detects the database that you want to restore and determines whether you can apply a transaction log backup. If the transaction log is on a separate device, SQL-EM enables the Apply Transaction Log option button. Doing so changes the statement that SQL-EM constructs from `LOAD DATABASE` to `LOAD TRAN`. As with `DUMP`ing databases, `LOAD`ing databases requires a list of source backup devices and a destination database. Having supplied these, and having made sure that the database is not currently in use, SQL Enterprise Manager sends the appropriate `LOAD` command to SQL Server.

Restoring After a Disaster

If the load is a result of a disaster, the database must first be dropped. The drop database might not execute in the case of a corruption. For corrupt databases, use dbcc dbrepair:

```
dbcc dbrepair(database_name, dropdb)
```

A new database structure must now be created. If you are creating a database for the exclusive purpose of loading, use the for load option with the create database command.

Creating for Load

Creating a database for load allocates the structure but does not initialize the pages. Using this option takes significantly less time than a normal create. The database will not be usable except for running a load. The database must be created in the same fashion as the dumped database. For example, if you initially created the CustomerDB database with 1GB for data and 100MB for log and you subsequently altered the database by 500MB for data, execute the following commands:

```
use master
go
create database CustomerDB on DataDevice1 = 1000,
     log on LogDevice1 = 200
     for load
go
alter database CustomerDB on DataDevice2 = 500 for load
go
load database CustomerDB from CustomerDB_dump
go
```

The easiest way to ensure the correct order is to save each create or alter command in a single create script as the commands are executed. If you have not saved your scripts, you can retrieve this information from the sysusages table in the master database:

```
select segmap, "Size in MB"=size/512
from sysusages
where dbid = db_id ("database_name")
segmap     Size in MB
3          1000
4          200
3          500
```

The segmap column refers to the segments defined in your database. Initially, there are three segments in your database: system, default, and logsegment. If you convert the segmap number to binary, you can determine how the segmap relates to segment names:

> 2^0 = system segment
> 2^1 = default segment
> 2^2 = logsegment
> 2^3 = first user-defined segment
> 2^4 = second user-defined segment

The segment mapping for the example database is as follows:

```
             log   data  sys
segmap 2^3   2^2   2^1   2^0    size
3      0     0     1     1      1000
4      0     1     0     0      200
3      0     0     1     1      500
```

Therefore, a `segmap` of 3 indicates a data device (default + system), and a `segmap` of 4 indicates log only.

If you have added user-defined segments (and possibly dropped the default and system segments from a fragment), there are indicators in the `2^3` column and greater. These fragments should be created as data fragments. Because segments are database-specific, the database system tables containing the user-defined segment definitions are loaded in the `load` process, which resolves the segment mapping within the database.

> **NOTE**
>
> If you created your database with the log on a separate device, the log fragments should have a 1 in the log column (`2^2`) only.

Loading into a Different Database

Occasionally, you will want to create an exact copy of a database in your system. First, dump the existing database. Then create a new database to load with this dump. The database does not have to be the same size as the original. The only requirement is that the destination database must be at least as large as the dumped database and have the same beginning fragments as the original database. For example, consider loading the dump from the previous database into a database of 3GB. The command to create this database might be the following:

```
use master
go
create database NewCustomerDB on DataDevice2 = 1000
log on LogDevice2 = 200
     for load
go
alter database NewCustomerDB on DataDevice2 = 500 for load
go
alter database NewCustomerDB on DataDevice3 = 300 for load
go
alter database NewCustomerDB on DataDevice4 = 1000 for load
go
load database NewCustomerDB from CustomerDB_dump
go
```

Loading a Transaction

Use `load transaction` to load a transaction log backup. Transaction logs must be loaded in the order they were dumped. During a `load database`, the data in the dump is copied over the database. After the `load` is complete, the database contains all the data in the database at the time of the dump. The loading of a transaction log is different than loading a database. The transaction log load copies the contents of the dump over the current `syslogs` definition. After the log has been loaded, a recovery takes place. The server marches through the log, applying changes in the log that are not reflected in the database (normally, all records in the log are new transactions). The simplified syntax for the load transaction command is

```
load transaction <databasename> from <devicename>
```

Most options available to the `dump` command can be used in the `load`. This is the full format for the `load transaction` command:

```
load tran[saction] <databasename>
    from <stripe_device> [ at <backup_server_name> ]
        [ density = <density_value>,
          blocksize = <number_of_bytes<,
          dumpvolume = <volume_name> ]
    [ stripe on <stripe_device> ...]
    [ with {
        [ dismount ¦ nodismount ],
        [ nounload ¦ unload ],
        file = <file_name>,
        listonly [ = full ],
        headeronly,
        [ notify = { client ¦ operator_console } ]
        }
    ]
```

Most options listed are explained in the `dump database` section, except the `listonly` and `headeronly` options that are explained in the `load database` section.

The load of a transaction log dump requires significantly less time than a `load database` because the size of the log is normally much smaller than the size of the database itself. No modifications can be made to the database between a `load database` and a `load transaction` (or between transaction log loads).

Additional Considerations

The pieces of the puzzle are starting to fall into place. You have defined the groundwork necessary to begin development of your backup-and-recovery approach. Now you must consider several issues that can affect your plan.

Frequency of Dumps

As mentioned previously, dumps should be executed as frequently as necessary for effective database administration. This is intentionally vague because the frequency of dumps varies based on your requirements. The deciding factor is the duration of time your business can afford for the database to be unavailable after a disaster.

The total time to restore a database is the sum of database load time plus the transaction log load time. The database load is *atomic*: it happens only once during a recovery of a database. The transaction log loads, however, are dynamic. The time to load transaction logs is based on the amount of activity since the database dump.

Consider the difference between a database dumped yearly versus a database dumped weekly, with transaction logs dumped every day between dumps for both. The yearly dump scenario has 364 transaction log dumps between database dumps; the weekly dump scenario has six transaction log dumps. If a disaster occurs on January 4, the time to recover in both cases is identical. Each scenario has a database load (January 1 database dump) and three transaction log loads (January 2, 3, and 4 transaction log dumps). But consider the worst-case scenario. A yearly dump approach could result in having to load a full year's worth of activity, one day at a time. The weekly dump approach would have a maximum of only a week's worth of activity to load.

Therefore, dump your database as often as possible. Ideally, database dumps should occur with no activity on the system. Although this is not a requirement, it assures you that the dump contains the state of your database before and after your dump. If this is not possible, execute your dumps when activity is as light as possible.

Dumps can be executed during normal business hours, but they will have an effect on the performance of your system. Database dumps in SQL Server 6.0 are much less devastating to performance than in earlier versions. This is due to code changes in the implementation of the database dump, increased speed of the process, the capability of striping dumps, and the implementation of backup server as a separate process from SQL Server.

Transaction log dumps are often scheduled during normal business hours, but periods of low (or no) activity are obviously preferred. Dumping a transaction log takes significantly less time than a database dump, and the time required is based solely on the amount of data in the log (which is based on modifications since the last dump transaction). A backup plan for a production system should include transaction log dumps to provide up-to-the-minute recovery. Development environments normally do not dump transaction logs because this type of recovery is not needed. Fairly frequent database dumps usually suffice.

Striping Dumps

Dumps can be striped across as many as 32 parallel devices in SQL Server 6.0. This can significantly reduce the time required to dump or load your database or transaction logs.

In spite of the performance improvement, try to avoid striping. Each stripe can be considered a possible point of failure. If one of the stripes cannot be read, the load will fail. Consider striping when you decide the time required to dump to a single device is too great to fit the activity in your administration window.

Locking

Although SQL Server enables access to a database during a backup (online backup), there is a particular method to its madness. In the backup process, SQL Server locks extents (8 × 2KB pages) for the entire database. As SQL Server copies out used pages (free space is never backed up), those extent locks are released. SQL Server moves sequentially, in extent order, through the database, copying pages and releasing extent locks as it proceeds.

User requests, however, can interrupt this process. If a user connection requests a page that has not been copied out yet, SQL Server suspends its "in order" copy of pages, jumps to the requested page, and backs up the extent on which that page lives. SQL Server then releases the lock on that extent, enabling the user connection to continue. SQL Server picks up from the last sequentially correct position in the database and continues copying out pages until it has finished, or until a user connection requests another locked page.

In this way, a SQL Server 6.0 backup represents a "Polaroid snapshot" of a database. The transactions that the backup process allows do not appear in that particular backup of the database. For that reason, any transactions that are processed after the `dump database` command is executed by the server must be backed up using a subsequent `dump tran` command!

Capturing Statistics

Capture as many statistics as possible about the dump and load processes. It will be invaluable in estimating durations and give you real statistics about the performance of your system. Here are important statistics to gather:

- Total database size (`sp_helpdb`).
- Total number of used pages (for information about `sp_spaceused`, see Chapter 26, "Defining, Altering, and Maintaining Databases and Logs").
- Total execution time (wrap the `dump` or `load` command with `select getdate()`).

For dumps, the time to execute is fairly linear based on used pages. For loads, the time to execute is based on total database size and used pages.

You need to understand and monitor database size and usage when planning backup regimens for databases that have not leveled off in size. During the early stages of a system, data volume can be low. Data is added over time. This increase levels off when your purge and archive criteria kick in.

For example, a 15GB database might be created to support your production system. Initially, it might be loaded with only 2GB of base information (used pages). If your application adds 5GB of data each year and data is purged when it is two years old, the database size levels off at 12GB. Your statistics might show that the 2GB database dumps in one hour. If you have a four-hour dump window, you have to start investigating alternative approaches when your database reaches 8GB. By capturing statistics, you would be able to forecast this problem a full year in advance.

Configuring Tape Expiration

The `retaindays` option to the `dump` command is not the only way to prevent your tapes from being overwritten. Use the `tape retention` configuration option to set a default retention value:

```
/* Configure the default retention to 3 weeks */
use master
go
sp_configure "tape retention", 21
go
reconfigure
go
```

This value is initially set to `0`, which enables tapes to be overwritten by default. Note that the `retaindays` option to the `dump` command overrides the configuration value.

Transaction Logging

It is important to prevent the transaction log from running out of space. When the transaction log fills, no other logged operations can be executed until space is available in the log. This is disastrous in production systems. In version 4.*x*, however, it was a fairly common experience. The DBA was forced to pay close attention to the available space in the log, executing a `dump transaction` before the log ran out of space.

Over time, database activity stabilizes and can be estimated. You should know the amount of time that your system can be active, under normal conditions, before the transaction log completely fills. Based on the amount, schedule transaction log dumps often enough to prevent this situation from occurring. (Dump transaction logs when they are about one-half to three-quarters full.)

Even though you have the `dump transaction` activities scheduled, the system might experience peak activities (end of quarter, fiscal year end, and so forth) that cause the log to fill at a greatly accelerated rate. Version 4.*x* users are still forced to monitor the log using Windows NT's Performance Monitor application to fix this. SQL 6.0 users have the SQL Distributed Management Framework, which allows them to set scheduled tasks to perform transaction log backup and pruning, or define *exceptions* that monitor SQL Server error conditions. That topic is discussed in Chapter 34, "The Microsoft SQL Server Distributed Management Framework."

Monitoring Available Log Space

SQL Server offers the following two stored procedures to monitor space availability. You can use either to get a report on the `syslogs` table.

- `sp_spaceused`
- `dbcc checktable`

`sp_spaceused` checks the reserved column to see how many pages are in use. Relate this to your overall log size to determine availability.

`dbcc checktable` checks each page in a table and provides an accurate reporting of the number of data pages used. As with `sp_spaceused`, relate this value to overall log size to determine availability. If your log is on a separate device, the output is easier to analyze. It reports statistics regarding space used and space free in megabytes as well as percentage:

```
dbcc checktable (syslogs)
```

SQL Server can also use Windows NT's Performance Monitor to monitor log space. PerfMon's Alert subsystem can monitor total space used in megabytes, as well as the percentage of space used. This latter option is only accurate if the log is on its own device. PerfMon enables you to activate ISQL command-line scripts in response to particular events—most notably, setting a percentage threshold over which the log cannot grow. PerfMon relies on a *polling interval* to determine how large the log is, and there is a performance hit caused by this polling action. For 4.2*x*-level servers, it is the only option. For SQL Server 6.0, check out the SQL Distributed Management Framework for how these features have been dramatically improved.

Developing Your Backup-and-Recovery Plan

Consider all your databases when developing the backup-and-recovery plan. System databases have different requirements than user databases.

System Databases

There are four system databases created as part of server installation: `master`, `model`, `tempdb`, and `msdb` (three for version 4.2*x*, which has no `msdb`). `tempdb` is temporary (it is actually rebuilt by SQL Server every time it is started); by definition it is exempt from backups. All other system databases should be backed up, however.

Threats

There are two things to watch out for with system databases:

- Database or table corruption
- Damage to the master device

If a corruption occurs, follow the steps to rebuild that individual database. If the master device is damaged, it has to be reinitialized. This affects the `master`, `model`, `tempdb`, and possibly the `sybsystemprocs` databases (which can exist on the master device or an alternate device).

The *master* Database

The `master` database is not a high-activity database. It is fairly small and is created on the master device with a default allocation of 17MB. This size is adequate for most small installations, but the requirements of larger installations quickly mandate an increase in size. Because it is on a single device, data and log compete for available space and the transaction log cannot be dumped. It cannot grow beyond the confines of the master device.

The following activities result in the insertion or modification of rows in various system tables:

- Creating, altering, or dropping devices
- Creating, altering, or dropping databases
- Adding or dropping logins or users
- Adding or dropping dump devices
- Adding servers

Because `master` controls the server, a database corruption or the loss of the master device can be devastating. The server is unavailable until the `master` database is repaired. Not having a current backup of `master` can be fatal (or at least quite painful). Back up the `master` database whenever commands are executed that insert, update, or delete rows in the system tables. The importance of the backup of this database cannot be stressed enough. Trying to re-create `master` from scratch can be extremely difficult, especially if you have not saved the data from the system tables.

> **NOTE**
>
> I had to attend a SQL Server System Administration course in order to be certified to teach it. Jeff Garbus was the instructor for that course; I came to know him because he certified me to teach that class.

Unfortunately, I didn't pay quite as much attention in class as I should have. Some months later, I was teaching a course at Jeff's corporate offices. The master database became strangely corrupted on the classroom server, (the sa login and password were no longer valid), and it required full restoration of the master device and the master database. I had to call Jeff right in the middle of dinner to have him talk me through the process. Although it took him only a short time to help me fix the problem, I was embarrassed to have to interrupt his family time.

The lesson here is simple: Don't ever underestimate the impact of having to restore the master device and master database. Do yourself a favor, and make it as simple as possible!

NOTE

The master database has no separate log segment, so all backups are full database dumps.

Detecting the Problem

If you lose the master device, the server goes down, alerting you to the problem. Alert messages appear in the errorlog file created by SQL Server, as well as in the Windows NT Event Log application. The normal method of detecting corruption in any database is the suite of dbcc commands. If a corruption does occur in master, the system likely will be affected instantaneously. Often, the server goes down and does not come up, or major errors appear in errorlog (page faults, I/O errors, and so forth).

TIP

If a dbcc detects corruption in master, log a call to Microsoft Product Support Services. Corruption in master or msdb might not be as serious on the surface, but it could be indicative of a problem with the underlying master device. If you are confident that you can solve the problem yourself, start executing the steps in the recovery process.

You must be proactive to avoid a painful recovery. First of all, avoid striping the master database dumps, even if it is a standard for your user databases. Make sure that all of the master dump can fit on a single tape or in an operating-system file. (Based on the normal size of the `master` database, this should not be a problem.) SQL Server must be started in single-user mode to start the recovery process. If the load requires a volume change, you cannot open another connection to tell the backup server that the new tape is in place.

Mitigating the Risk

The `master` database should be dumped regularly, probably on the same schedule as your user databases. If you make a change and you don't want to wait for the backup scripts to run, execute it by hand. As always, you should have scripts saved for every activity that modifies `master`. To be extra safe, bulk-copy the data from the following tables into separate ASCII files:

- `sysdatabases`
- `sysdevices`
- `sysusages`
- `syslogins`

Redefinition of the master device happens within the SQL Server Setup utility. If you have already installed SQL Server, the Setup utility enables you to rebuild the master device. Redefining `master`, and allowing the setup process to complete, gives you a master device identical to when SQL Server was first installed. At this point, `master` has no knowledge of any user databases in your system, nor does the `master` database contain any of the system stored procedures. You have to execute one of the following:

- Loading your current `master` backup (preferred)
- Transferring the data, using `isql` or `bcp`
- Re-creating items from DDL scripts, including `\SQL60\scripts\instmstr`

You should have all the resources to undertake any of these approaches at any time. It is the only way to ensure that the `master` database (and the server) will be available when you need it.

model and *msdb*

The `model` database is copied into any database created with `create database`. It houses those items you want to be available across all databases (rules, defaults, user-defined datatypes, and users). If you have made any modifications to `model`, save all DDL files and back up the database after changes are made.

The `msdb` database holds all of the task-scheduling and error-processing instructions that SQL Executive uses for automated task and alert handling. You should back up this database any time you modify it so that you can restore your scheduled and error-based tasks as quickly as possible.

If you detect corruption in either of these databases, you must re-create the entire master database and master device using the setup utility described earlier.

User Databases

Your business requirements define whether a database should be backed up. Backups are normally a requirement for production systems. Your approach should define the following:

- *Who?* Identify the person or group responsible for backup and recovery.
- *Name?* Outline your naming standards for database names and dump devices.
- *Which databases?* Identify the databases in your system to be backed up.
- *Types of dumps?* Identify whether you will dump the database only, or whether you also will dump the transaction log.
- *How?* Identify whether dumps will use disk or file devices and whether the dump is a single process or striped.
- *Frequency?* Identify the schedule for dumping the database and the transaction logs.
- *Execution?* Determine whether dumps will be initiated by hand or automated. If automated, detail whether it is conducted by an off-the-shelf tool or custom developed. Include all code (dump script and scheduler, if applicable) and make sure that it is commented extremely well.

For database recovery, detail the procedures involved in loading each database. If you are using a tool, outline its use.

Very Large Database Considerations

When developing a backup-and-recovery plan for VLDB environments, several items must be considered. The challenge of a VLDB is its sheer size—everything is larger. Tables are measured in gigabytes, and databases are measured in tens or hundreds of gigabytes. The fact that several SQL Server VLDBs exist in industry today gives credence to the product's capability of handling vast amounts of data. VLDBs are not easy to implement, however, for a variety of reasons. Here are the top 10 VLDB issues:

- Impact of corruption
- Time for recovery
- Time of backups
- Time to perform initial load of data
- Time to update statistics of indexes
- Time to perform database consistency checks
- Time to create indexes

- Impact of incremental batch data loading routines
- Impact of online activity
- Backup media capacity and backup facilities

Based on these items, you need to make several database architecture choices. These choices include the following:

- Physically implementing a single logical database as several smaller physical databases
- Segmenting tables horizontally and/or vertically
- Table or index placement
- Log size and placement
- `tempdb` size and placement

Let's consider the issues list in regard to your choices. The time required to perform database dumps, loads, updates of statistics, and creation of indexes increases linearly with size. Follow these steps:

1. First, consider the amount of time you are willing to be down while performing a recovery (impact of corruption). If you need a database to be recovered within eight hours, determine the size of a database that can be recovered in that amount of time. Note that the load process is much slower than the dump process. Assume that 4GB is the maximum database size that can be reloaded in the defined window.

2. Taking 4GB as a baseline, analyze table estimates for your database. If you have a 40GB logical database, you might need to implement 10 4GB databases. Are any tables greater than 4GB? How many tables can you fit in a database? Are any tables candidates for segmentation based on this determination alone?

3. Develop your utopian administration schedule. For every day during a month, determine what periods of time can be dedicated to administrative activities. Week-ends might be available, but this is not always the case. If you determine that you have five hours per night to perform administrative activities, you then need to determine what activities need to be completed and whether they can be distributed over your available administration time.

4. Determine the rate of the dump process. Take into consideration backup media capacity, speed, and number. Benchmark several scenarios. Create a database and load it with about 2GB of data. Perform several database dumps, a varying number of dump devices (striped dumps), and a number of dump processes that can occur in parallel.

5. Determine periodic activity timings for each of your tables. This should be a matrix with table names down one axis and activities (`dbcc`, update statistics, index creation) across the other axis. After you develop a baseline for these activities, you easily can group tables together to determine the total amount of administration time needed for a certain combination of tables.

6. Determine which activities must take place in a batch window. If you want to perform database consistency checks immediately prior to dumping a database, the time required to perform both activities can be determined from your timings. Assume that a dump takes three hours and a dbcc takes two hours. Although this fits in your five-hour window, it does not consider the fact that you have 10 of these to complete during the course of a week. Perform activities in parallel to determine concurrent processing times. Can you dbcc and dump two databases in a five-hour period?

7. Finalize your schedule and document accordingly.

Summary

Development of a backup-and-recovery approach is not a trivial process. You must consider internal and external forces and determine their impact. In the end, you should document your approach so that it is clear how you plan to handle these activities. Make sure to gather statistics on all activities, and use those statistics to predict future performance.

Although building a good backup-and-recovery plan seems like a tremendous amount of work, it is worth it in the long run. Project plans must allocate time to create the plan, and it should be in place *before* you make your production database available.

Configuring and Tuning SQL Server

SQL Server contains a number of configuration parameters that control the behavior of SQL Server. This chapter examines the available configuration parameters, describing the aspect of SQL Server they control and their defaults and range of values they can be configured for. Chapter 31, "Optimizing SQL Server Configuration Options," looks more in depth at the configuration parameters that have the greatest impact on performance and provide guidelines for tuning them to optimize SQL Server performance.

Configuration Variables

You can change how memory is allocated and examine specific resource allocations that affect memory with the sp_configure stored procedure. sp_configure lists all options for the current SQL Server. Here are the options for SQL Server 6.0:

name	minimum	maximum	config_value	run_value
allow updates	0	1	0	0
backup buffer size	1	10	1	1
backup threads	0	32	5	5
cursor threshold	-1	2147483647	-1	-1
database size	1	10000	2	2
default language	0	9999	0	0
default sortorder id	0	255	40	40
fill factor	0	100	0	0
free buffers	20	524288	204	204
hash buckets	4999	265003	7993	7993
language in cache	3	100	3	3
LE threshold maximum	2	500000	200	200
LE threshold minimum	2	500000	20	20
LE threshold percent	1	100	0	0
locks	5000	2147483647	5000	5000
logwrite sleep (ms)	-1	500	0	0
max async IO	1	255	8	8
max lazywrite IO	1	255	8	8
max worker threads	10	1024	255	255
media retention	0	365	0	0
memory	1000	1048576	4096	4096
nested triggers	0	1	1	1
network packet size	512	32767	4096	4096
open databases	5	32767	20	20
open objects	100	2147483647	500	500
priority boost	0	1	0	0
procedure cache	1	99	30	30
RA cache hit limit	1	255	4	4
RA cache miss limit	1	255	3	3
RA delay	0	500	15	15
RA pre-fetches	1	1000	3	3
RA slots per thread	1	255	5	5
RA worker threads	0	255	3	3
recovery flags	0	1	0	0
recovery interval	1	32767	5	5
remote access	0	1	1	1
remote login timeout	0	2147483647	5	5
remote query timeout	0	2147483647	0	0

```
resource timeout      5          2147483647  10      10
set working set size  0          1           0       0
show advanced option  0          1           1       1
SMP concurrency       -1         64          0       1
sort pages            64         511         64      64
spin counter          1          2147483647  10000   0
tempdb in ram (MB)    0          2044        0       0
user connections      5          15          15      15
```

The descriptions of the five columns in the output are as follows:

- name is the description of the variable.

- minimum and maximum are the valid range of values for the specific variable. Note that these are pulled out of the spt_values table.

- When the server comes up, the values in the permanent table, sysconfigures, are copied into a memory-only table, syscurconfigs. config_value reflects the value in the sysconfigures table, and run_value reflects the value in the syscurconfigs table. Note that not all of the values are necessarily going to be the same.

Configuration values are stored in spt_values, a lookup table in the master database. Rows related to configuration values in spt_values are marked with a type of 'C'.

```
select * from spt_values where type = 'C'
name                   number   type low          high         status
---------------------  -------  ---- -----------  -----------  -----------
CONFIGURATION OPTION   -1       C    (null)       (null)       0
recovery interval      101      C    1            32767        0
allow updates          102      C    0            1            0
user connections       103      C    5            15           0
memory                 104      C    1000         1048576      0
open databases         105      C    5            32767        0
locks                  106      C    5000         2147483647   0
open objects           107      C    100          2147483647   0
procedure cache        108      C    1            99           0
fill factor            109      C    0            100          0
database size          111      C    1            10000        0
media retention        112      C    0            365          0
recovery flags         113      C    0            1            0
nested triggers        115      C    0            1            0
remote access          117      C    0            1            0
default language       124      C    0            9999         0
language in cache      125      C    3            100          0
tempdb in ram (MB)     501      C    0            2044         0
max async IO           502      C    1            255          0
max worker threads     503      C    10           1024         0
network packet size    505      C    512          32767        0
RA worker threads      508      C    0            255          0
show advanced option   518      C    0            1            0
LE threshold percent   521      C    1            100          0
LE threshold maximum   523      C    2            500000       0
backup threads         540      C    0            32           0
backup buffer size     541      C    1            10           0
default sortorder id   1123     C    0            255          0
hash buckets           1504     C    4999         265003       0
sort pages             1505     C    64           511          0
```

```
max lazywrite IO      1506    C    1      255          0
RA slots per thread   1509    C    1      255          0
RA pre-fetches        1510    C    1      1000         0
RA delay              1511    C    0      500          0
RA cache miss limit   1512    C    1      255          0
RA cache hit limit    1513    C    1      255          0
spin counter          1514    C    1      2147483647   0
free buffers          1515    C    20     524288       0
SMP concurrency       1516    C    -1     64           0
priority boost        1517    C    0      1            0
remote login timeout  1519    C    0      2147483647   0
remote query timeout  1520    C    0      2147483647   0
LE threshold minimum  1522    C    2      500000       0
logwrite sleep (ms)   1530    C    -1     500          0
cursor threshold      1531    C    -1     2147483647   0
set working set size  1532    C    0      1            0
resource timeout      1533    C    5      2147483647   0
```

There are two kinds of configurable values, dynamic and nondynamic. *Dynamic values* are those parameters that, when modified, take effect immediately. Some examples are recovery interval, password expiration interval, and default language. Any variables that are not explicitly dynamic will not take effect until the server is *cycled* (shut down and started up again). In the following review of the configuration settings, the dynamic variables are flagged with asterisks (*).

> **NOTE**
>
> Don't forget! You need to *cycle* the server (shut down and restart) for options without asterisks to take effect.

Setting options with `sp_configure` is relatively simple.

Syntax

```
sp_configure "option", value
reconfigure [with override]
```

Example

```
sp_configure "recovery interval", 7
reconfigure
```

In this example, you are setting the recovery interval to 7 minutes. Each configuration option is covered individually next.

> **TIP**
>
> You do not need to enter the entire description—merely enough to make it unique.

The with override option is only necessary if you want to either force the server to configure with options it knows to be invalid or force the server to allow direct updates of system tables. Note also that the values of zero for many variables cause the server to select defaults for those values.

In theory, you do not need to issue the reconfigure command when you issue sp_configure. It is an excellent idea, however, because the reconfigure command double-checks your arithmetic and verifies that there is enough memory to do everything for which you have configured. If for some reason you do not verify these numbers and the server will not come up, start SQL Server with the -f command-line switch described earlier in this chapter to start SQL Server with the default configuration options. Also rebuilding the master database using the SETUP utility resets the configuration parameters to the defaults.

Setting Configuration Options with SQL Enterprise Manager

SQL Server configuration options can be modified using SQL Enterprise Manager in addition to using the sp_configure stored procedure. Highlight the server you want to configure and choose the Server | Configurations... menu sequence to bring up the Server Configuration/ Options dialog box. Click on the Configuration tab to bring up the dialog box displayed in Figure 30.1. The dialog box shows the minimum and maximum values as well as the current running value. The Current column is where you can modify the configuration option values.

FIGURE 30.1.

SQL Enterprise Manager provides a dialog box for changing and viewing SQL Server configuration options.

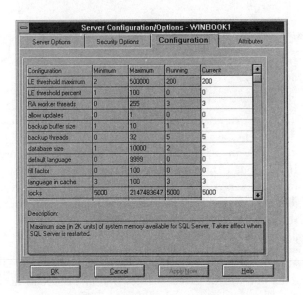

Configurable Values

Here is a detailed list of configuration settings and how they affect server operation and memory configuration. Remember that items marked with an asterisk (*) are dynamic. Standard configuration options and advanced configuration options are marked using "(STD)" and "(ADV)" suffixes. These suffixes *do not* appear as part of the configuration option name. They are included here only for convenience for you, the reader. Don't use these suffixes with the sp_configure command—you will receive an error message. Advanced configuration options are displayed only when the show advanced option configuration option is turned on.

*allow updates** (STD)

Units: 0 or 1 (flag)

Default: 0 (no)

The allow updates option is a flag that directs the server to allow the dbo to modify system tables directly (that is, without using supplied system stored procedures).

> ### WARNING
>
> Turning on allow updates is a bad idea! The first few times I tried this, I permanently crashed the server. Do not do this without the safety net of having Microsoft Product Support Services on the telephone directing you to do so.

Notes:

- In order to turn allow updates on, you have to issue the reconfigure command with override.

  ```
  reconfigure with override
  ```

- The only reasonable time to allow updates is after inadvertent device failure. If a device is not available to the server when the server comes up (the power is down, for example), any databases using that device will be recorded in sysdatabases as suspect. If you update the sysdatabases table (changing the SUSPECT bit), you might be able to bring the server down, power up the offending device, and reconnect to your database. The following shows the update statement you might issue to retry connecting to all suspect databases:

  ```
  update sysdatabases
  set status = status - 256
  where status & 256 = 256
  ```

- After you use the allow updates option, be sure to turn it off. A value of zero says "Do not allow updates"; a value of one says "I'm willing to chance it."

backup buffer size* (STD)

Units: Integer number of backup buffers

Default: 1

Backup buffer size specifies the number of 32-page increments that SQL Server will use for backup I/O. The minimum number of buffers is 1, and the maximum is 10. Therefore, if you specified 10 backup buffers for this option, your next database backup would perform I/O in 320×2KB-page increments, or 640KB per I/O. This option can be very useful for optimizing I/O on Very Large Databases (VLDBs), but setting it is more art than science. Experimentation on your specific platform is the optimal method for using this option.

backup threads (STD)

Units: Integer number of threads

Default: 5

This specifies the maximum number of threads that can be used for a striped database backup operation. Setting this value to 0 disables all striped backup operations. The maximum is 32, although Microsoft's informal testing has shown optimal performance on backup (22 GB/hour) with only six threads. Backup operations can use any number of threads up to this maximum. Backup threads consume very little memory (approximately 18KB), so configuring this for the maximum is not a significant drain on resources.

cursor threshold* (ADV)

Units: Integer number of rows returned by a cursor SELECT statement

Default: −1

SQL Server uses this option to determine how it should populate cursor keysets. If the result set is larger than this option, SQL Server populates the cursor set asynchronously. If the default of −1 is kept, all cursor result sets are generated synchronously. This option can be useful for cursors that use particularly large result sets. If you are going to use asynchronous cursor population, set this value high; small cursor sets are faster to populate synchronously than asynchronously, and setting the option higher reserves asynchronous population for very large cursor sets.

database size (STD)

Units: Integer number of megabytes for default database size

Default: 2

This option is the default size for databases in megabytes. This option should match the current size of the model database at all times. The minimum value for this option is 1, allowing databases to be created on floppy disks. A CREATE DATABASE statement that explicitly defines database size ignores the value for this option.

default language (STD)

Units: Integer value representing a unique language ID

Default: 0 on U.S. English systems

default language tells SQL Server which of the available languages to use for displaying error and print messages back to user workstations. The server always uses the default value (0 for U.S. English), unless the client application login has requested a particular language for that connection. Additional languages receive unique numbers (maximum of 9999) when they are added to SQL Server.

default sortorder id (ADV)

Units: Integer value representing a unique sort order ID

Default: 0 on U.S. English systems

Never change this value using sp_configure! The sort order is actually defined by the BUILDMASTER process in the SQL Server 6.0 SETUP utility. Any changes to the server's sort order should be performed there.

fill factor (STD)

Units: Integer percentage

Default: Zero

The fill factor is the extent to which index pages should be filled (excluding the root) as indexes are created. This includes the data pages of clustered indexes. Note that this is a performance tool.

> **NOTE**
>
> The fill factor required by sp_configure is two words, but the create index statement keyword fillfactor is a single word.

Low fill factors cause index pages to be partially full, which in turn creates more index levels. The performance benefit comes at insert/update time, when row additions are less likely to cause page splits. (Lots of page splits during updates are bad for performance.)

> **NOTE**
>
> A fill factor of zero does not mean that pages will be empty. This is a special case. Clustered index data pages and nonclustered index leaf pages are 100-percent full, and some space is left in the intermediate levels (typically 75-percent full).

High fill factors fill the pages as much as possible. This reduces index levels and increases query performance.

> **NOTE**
>
> Fill factors are not maintained after index creation. To re-create indexes with the fill factors intact, you must drop and re-create the index. Some shops with intensive update applications do this on a nightly basis.
>
> Maintaining fill factors is typically the only reason you might periodically drop and re-create indexes, because SQL Server indexes tend to be self-maintaining and self-balancing.

free buffers* (ADV)

Units: Integer quantity of page buffers

Default: 5 percent of MEMORY configuration option

The LAZYWRITER subsystem, which is responsible for managing background writes as the result of a checkpoint, manages available buffers to ensure that free buffer space does not fall below this level. The minimum number of buffers is 20, and the maximum is one-half the number of buffers available when SQL Server is started.

In effect, this option guarantees that a minimum of 5 percent (based on the MEMORY configuration spec) of SQL Server's buffer space will be freed, so that there are always free buffers available for processing work.

hash buckets (ADV)

Units: Integer prime number of buckets

Default: 7993

This option should not be changed if you have less than 160MB of physical RAM on your machine, unless you are directed to do so by Microsoft Product Support Services.

language in cache (STD)

Units: Integer number of languages

Default: 3

When using a multilingual character set (code page 850, for example), SQL Server is capable of generating error and confirmation messages in multiple languages. This option specifies the maximum number of languages that SQL Server can use simultaneously.

NOTE

The next section discusses *Lock Escalation* (LE) thresholds and management. Prior to SQL Server 6.0, SQL Server would automatically escalate from individual page locks on a table to table locks as soon as the page lock count reached 200. This figure was fixed in the server and did not reflect table size, data usage, table size changes, and so on. In SQL Server 6.0, the point of lock escalation (LE) is configurable using the three options discussed next.

These options are discussed further in Chapter 15, "Locking and Performance," in the Transact-SQL section of this book.

LE threshold maximum* (STD)

Units: Integer number of pages

Default: 200

This option is the maximum number of page locks SQL Server will hold on a table before escalating to a single table lock. If the MAXIMUM value here has been exceeded, a table lock is applied, regardless of whether the PERCENTAGE value (discussed later) has been exceeded.

LE threshold minimum* (ADV)

Units: Integer number of pages

Default: 20

This option is the minimum number of page locks SQL Server must hold on a table before considering escalation to a single table lock. There is a double condition at work: if the minimum value has been exceeded, a table lock will be applied after the MAXIMUM or PERCENT values have also been exceeded.

LE threshold percent* (STD)

Units: Integer percentage of current table pages

Default: 0

The percentage of page locks (above the limit specified by LE MINIMUM) that will trigger escalation from multiple page locks to a single table lock for a query. The default value of 0 specifies that this value should be ignored, and table-lock escalation will then occur at the LE MAXIMUM configured value.

locks (STD)

Units: Integer quantity

Default: 5000

This is the number of concurrent open locks that can be in simultaneous use. If you begin to get error messages saying that locks are unavailable, don't hesitate to bump up the number of available locks by a thousand or two. The memory cost is very low (72 bytes per lock). Note that locks are configured on a server-wide basis, which means that locks are maintained across databases where necessary.

logwrite sleep (ms)* (ADV)

Units: Integer number of milliseconds

Default: –1

This option minimizes disk I/O for log writes on commit statements by delaying the log write for *n* milliseconds. The delay is designed to allow other processes to fill up the write buffer so that more I/O can be accomplished in a single write operation. The default value of –1 specifies that no delay should occur; log writes should occur as commit tran statements are processed. The maximum delay is 500 milliseconds.

max async io (STD)

Units: Integer number of pages

Default: 8

SQL Server uses asynchronous I/O to offload data writes to periods of low disk activity. This option specifies the number of write operations that can be issued asynchronously. There is little benefit with this option if databases are not striped; the disk will be in use constantly, offering little opportunity to delay write operations. Therefore, on systems with databases striped across multiple disks (whether hardware-based RAID or Windows NT stripe sets), this option can optimize I/O to use disk latency periods more efficiently.

This option is used most often by large, bulk I/O operations such as BCP, SELECT INTO, CHECKPOINT, INSERT using SELECT, and so on.

max lazywrite IO* (ADV)

Units: Integer quantity

Default: 5000

Do not change this option unless instructed to do so by Microsoft Product Support Services. This option configures the asynchronous I/O performed only by the LAZYWRITER, not by other general bulk-data operations.

max worker threads* (STD)

Units: Integer quantity

Default: 255

max worker threads defines the number of internal operating system threads that are reserved for handling user connection work. If the user connections value or the current number of user connections is less than the worker threads value, threads are being unused. If worker threads are equal to user connections, optimal thread use will occur. If worker threads are less than the current number of user connections, SQL Server will automatically "round robin" or "pool" user connections across available worker threads.

media retention (STD)

Units: Integer days

Default: Zero

When you attempt to overwrite a database or transaction log dump, the backup server checks to see how long ago this was dumped. The media retention parameter is a safety feature that prevents you from overwriting your dumps prematurely. The operator can override the retention time when he is prompted that there was a violation of the tape retention period. You can also change the tape-retention period for a particular dump by using the retaindays option on the dump commands.

memory (STD)

Units: Integer number of 2KB pages

Default: Varies

This is the most important parameter you will tune. When the server comes up, the first step you need to take is to allocate the amount of memory for the server to allocate. If the allocation fails, the server will not come up, and an error is recorded in the error log. (See the earlier section titled "Memory Utilization.")

The server needs memory to manage devices, users, locks, databases, and objects. All the rest of the memory is used for cache. You can see how memory is used in DBCC MEMUSAGE.

How much memory is enough? As you add memory and the cache grows, SQL Server stores more tables and larger tables in memory, as well as more and larger indexes. If you add more memory, you see substantial performance improvements in repeated queries that require table scans (such as a search for a value in a nonindexed column), and particularly in joins. In general, if the server is too slow, adding memory is a fairly painless first step to improving performance.

In some environments, 32MB to 64MB is plenty of memory. When tables and indexes get very large, substantially more memory (256MB or more) might be required. Remember that on Windows NT, the PAGEFILE.SYS file must grow proportionately to available physical RAM. Check your Windows NT Server documentation for proper page-file management with increased RAM.

nested triggers* (STD)

Units: 0 or 1 (flag)

Default: 1 (yes)

If a trigger modifies a table that has a trigger, the trigger on the second table fires when nested triggers is on (the value equals 1). Otherwise, it does not fire.

network packet size* (STD)

Units: Integer quantity

Default: 4096

This is the default server packet size for all Tabular Data Stream packets. This value should be divisible by 512. Although it is a server default, individual client applications can override this value on a per-application basis. Microsoft's own informal testing has revealed optimal performance to lie between 4096 and 8192 bytes for this parameter. Larger values, up to 8192, should be used for larger data transfer to make them more efficient on the network.

open databases (STD)

Units: Integer number of open databases

Default: 12

This is the total number of databases for which SQL Server builds internal pointers in its kernel and for which it can maintain simultaneous connections. This includes `master`, `model`, `tempdb`, `msdb`, and any user databases that might be used concurrently.

> **TIP**
>
> If the process tries to exceed the configured number, you typically get messages in the errorlog describing the incident. Unfortunately, the message reported to the user is fairly confusing. Avoid this problem by configuring the variable to exceed the number of created databases, and then forget about it. The amount of memory taken up is effectively insignificant.

open objects (STD)

Units: Integer Quantity

Default: 500

This is the number of concurrent open objects that can be in simultaneous use. If you begin getting error messages saying that object connections are unavailable, increase this number. The memory cost is low (40 bytes).

priority boost (ADV)

Units: Integer 1 or 0

Default: 0

This option is used on Windows NT Servers that are dedicated to SQL Server. Using this option boosts SQL Server thread priority on the Windows NT scheduler, increasing the availability of processing resources to SQL Server at the expense of other application on this machine. If you are running SQL Server on a nondedicated machine, this option should not be changed or it will have a negative effect on the performance of other applications.

procedure cache (STD)

Units: Integer percentage

Default: 30

Compiled stored procedure execution plans are stored in an area of memory called procedure cache. The balance of server memory (other than that used by the server for its internal kernel and other variable elements) will be used by the server for data and procedure cache. (See "Memory Utilization," earlier in this chapter.) The procedure cache configuration setting is the percentage of cache set aside for procedures. The larger the procedure cache, the more compiled plans can reside in memory.

At any given time, each user who executes a stored procedure needs his own executable procedure in cache. To establish an initial value for procedure cache, start by leaving enough room in cache to store at least one copy of your largest stored procedure for each concurrent user, plus a fudge factor. Here is an example:

> 100 concurrent users × 60KB (the largest stored procedure) = 6MB × 1.25 (fudge factor) = 8MB

Now you know how large to make the procedure cache, but the procedure cache setting doesn't require the size of the procedure cache; you need to indicate what percentage of cache should be set aside for procedures. If you have 50MB available for cache (run DBCC MEMUSAGE to get available cache and procedure sizes), 8 divided by 50 equals 16 percent. Note that if you use procedures heavily, you might want to increase cache capacity and also the percentage for procedures.

> **NOTE**
>
> Setting procedure cache is more of an art than a science, but it will have a definite performance impact.

The next section discusses Read Ahead (RA) Threading options, which define the operational parameters for Parallel Data Scanning (PDS) operations. You should refer to Chapter 19, "Application Design for Performance," which discusses the PDS architecture and implementation in more detail.

RA cache hit limit* (ADV)

Units: Integer value of pages

Default: 4

Because Read Ahead asynchronously fetches pages from disk to cache, reads from cache by a read-ahead thread provide no benefit. Therefore, this number is the limit of cache reads a read-ahead thread can perform before read-ahead services are suspended. In effect, it is the "off switch" for read-ahead threading, because it turns off read-ahead if the read-ahead thread is finding pages in cache instead of on disk.

RA cache miss limit* (ADV)

Units: Integer value of pages

Default: 3

Because PDS is beneficial when there are substantial quantities of data on disk, this value triggers read-ahead threading. If a single read operating requires <RA Cache Miss Limit> number of reads to disk, SQL Server will allocate an asynchronous read-ahead thread to perform the disk I/O while the user thread is fetching other pages from cache. In that way, it is the "on switch" for *Parallel Data Scanning* (PDS).

RA delay* (ADV)

Units: Integer value in milliseconds

Default: 15

This option should not be changed, particularly for SMP hardware.

RA pre-fetches*

Units: Integer number of extents

Default: 3

This assigns a relative maximum position for the read-ahead scanning position, in terms of extents. Any read-ahead thread uses this configuration option to keep a maximum of <RA Pre-Fetches> extents. The default is three extents, meaning SQL Server will maintain sufficient pages to keep the read-ahead process 3×8 2KB pages ahead of the current page being read by the query itself. When the read-ahead thread has filled cache with the next three extents, the read-ahead thread idles, allowing the user connection thread to catch up.

RA slots per thread (ADV)

Units: Integer value of open buckets per Read Ahead thread

Default: 5

Because read-ahead threads work at the extent level and typical user threads work at the page level, read-ahead threads are more efficient than the worker threads they are supplying. Therefore, a single read-ahead thread is capable of using its otherwise abundant latency to service other read requests. RA Slots Per Thread defines the number of scanning operations that a single read-ahead thread can satisfy at any one time. The number of slots multiplied by the number of read-ahead threads is the total number of simultaneous read-ahead scanning operations SQL Server can support.

This option need not be changed, unless you have an extremely high-performance disk subsystem. Better performance tuning can be achieved by adjusting the number of read-ahead worker threads, rather than adjusting the number of slots per thread.

RA worker threads (STD)

Units: Integer number of total threads from RA pool

Default: 3

This option should be set to the same value as the user connections parameter. This is the number of threads SQL Server will use for Parallel Data Scanning operations. The maximum is 255 threads per server. This number, multiplied by the number of slots per thread, is the total number of simultaneous asynchronous scanning operations SQL Server can support.

recovery flags (STD)

Units: 0 or 1 (flag)

Default: 0 (no)

If this option is turned on, at startup time the server will list in the errorlog detailed information on each transaction that is rolled forward or backward. This detailed information includes transaction names that use BEGIN TRAN and SAVE TRAN statements. If the option is off, only the database name and quantity of transactions rolled forward or backward are listed.

NOTE

This is not a dynamic option, so the server needs to be shut down twice for the change to take effect. During your first restart, transactions will not be named.

recovery interval* (STD)

Units: Integer number of minutes

Default: 5

recovery interval is the maximum number of minutes per database that the server takes during the recovery process. As the server modifies the database, the number of discrepancies between the log and the data increases the amount of time recovery takes to synchronize them and grant control to the users. The server estimates the amount of recovery time necessary and checkpoints individual databases as it perceives an excessive amount of requisite recovery time.

> **NOTE**
>
> It is a common misconception that the recovery interval is the number of minutes between checkpoints. This is not true.

remote access* (STD)

Units: 0 or 1 (flag)

Default: 1 (yes)

The remote access variable determines whether this server can communicate with another one. With SQL Server 6.0 it is imperative that you have this option turned on if you are using replication services. Only the sa login can modify remote access values. This option is only dynamic in SQL Server 6.0 and later versions.

remote login timeout* (ADV)

Units: Integer number of seconds

Default: 5

This option is the amount of time SQL Server waits to make a connection to another server. A value of 0 means that it waits indefinitely.

remote query timeout* (ADV)

Units: Integer value in seconds

Default: 0

This option is the number of seconds SQL Server waits to return results from a remote stored procedure call. The default value of 0 indicates that SQL Server waits until the query is finished.

resource timeout* (ADV)

Units: Integer value of seconds

Default: 10

This option need only be changed if the SQL Server errorlog or the Windows NT Event Log's Application subsystem shows many `logwrite` or `bufwait` timeout warnings.

set working set size (ADV)

Units: Integer 0 or 1

Default: 0 (yes)

Tells SQL Server to request from Windows NT a physical memory range equal to the `memory` configuration option, or equal to `memory` and `tempdb in ram` if that option is activated.

show advanced option* (STD)

Units: 0 or 1 (flag)

Default: 1 (yes)

SQL Server will hide advanced configuration options by default. Advanced options are those noted here using the (ADV) suffix.

smp concurrency (ADV)

Units: Integer number of active threads

Default: 1

This option configures the number of simultaneous Windows NT threads that SQL Server will activate for execution. For single-processor machines, this value should be 1. If SQL Server is running on a dedicated server machine (strongly recommended), this number should be the number of CPUs on the machine.

The special value 0 for this option defines *auto configuration*. Auto configuration uses one less than the total number of processors detected by SQL Server at startup. If your server machine has four processors, setting this option to 0 will have SQL Server use three of those processors by default.

sort pages* (ADV)

Units: Integer number of pages

Default: 64

`sort pages` defines the maximum number of pages that can be used for query sorting operations. Each individual user connection to SQL Server is given this number of pages for sorting space. The maximum value allowed is 511, and increasing sort pages on SQL Server might require increasing the memory configuration option and the size of the tempdb database to reflect greater cache and database space usage.

spin counter* (ADV)

Units: Integer number of resource acquisition attempts

Default: 10 for uniprocessor machines; 10000 for SMP machines

This is the number of attempts SQL Server will make to acquire a resource such as a lock, data page, cache page, or worker thread.

tempdb in RAM (STD)

Units: Integer quantity

Default: 0

If this value is 0, tempdb remains on the master device. This is standard SQL Server behavior. Although it is physically possible to load tempdb into RAM on a machine with less than 64MB of physical memory, it is *strongly* discouraged. tempdb, when in RAM, subtracts memory available for SQL Server caching, so it should only be used when there is sufficient RAM for caching all existing databases.

Although it is not a universally applicable option, if you have systems that use large quantities of temporary tables and stored procedures, it can be a useful performance enhancement—if it is properly tested.

time slice (ADV)

Units: Milliseconds

Default: 100

The time slice is theoretically the number of milliseconds that the server allocates to each user process as the server does its own internal multithreading. In practice, the server uses the time slice as a guideline and might increase or decrease it (transparent to the configuration setting) if processes are taking too long to swap in and out.

> **TIP**
>
> Leave the time slice alone, unless otherwise directed by Microsoft Product Support Services.

user connections (STD)

Units: Integer quantity

Default: 15

The user connections variable determines the number of users who can log in to the server at any given time. Every time a user logs in, it requires a single connection. (A single application could have dozens of connections at one time.)

The user connections variable has the most dramatic effect on configured memory. You need approximately 37KB of memory per user connection. In addition to actual users who are logged into the server, the server consumes user connections for the following:

- One for mirroring SQL Server devices
- One for the checkpoint manager
- One for the checkpoint background I/O manager
- One for the Read-Ahead Threading manager (for parallelizing table scan operations)
- If SQL Executive is started, it will also use two user connections by default (and more if replication is used)
- Additional threads are used by SQL Server for replication processing (which is discussed in Chapter 35, "Introduction to Microsoft SQL Server 6.0 Replication")

The global variable @@max_connections is set to the absolute maximum server connections; the actual number of users who can log in equals @@max_connections minus the system connections in the preceding list. To determine how many connections are currently in use, execute sp_who.

Variables That Use Substantial Memory

Several variables use a substantial amount of memory. They are summarized in Table 30.1.

Table 30.1. Variables that use substantial memory.

Parameter	*Bytes of Memory per Unit*
user connections	37KB
open databases	17KB
open objects	40 bytes
locks	72 bytes
procedure cache	Percentage of remainder of cache
tempdb in ram	Number specified in megabytes of physical RAM, in addition to "memory" configuration option

Summary

Proper memory configuration can help system performance by enabling the server to use the most appropriate amount of memory for cache. Understanding what configuration options SQL Server offers is the first step to understanding how to optimize the configuration of your server, and understanding how those options affect the behavior and performance of your server. You can monitor what the server is doing, and measure the effects of configuration option changes, by using the provided tools or third-party development tools.

Optimizing SQL Server Configuration Options

31

SQL Server 6.0 introduces an array of new configuration options that directly impact the performance of SQL Server. Instead of having only tunable memory options, as in previous versions of Sybase and Microsoft SQL Server, Version 6.0 enables the administrator to manage lock resources and escalation and scanning performance through parallel threading. Used properly, these configuration options can offer worthwhile increases in server performance. Used poorly, they can turn SQL Server into a performance dog just as quickly. Understanding what these configuration options define is just as important as understanding how to change them.

Memory Utilization

Figure 31.1 gives a representation of physical memory on your server box. In this figure, all physical memory is allocated to SQL Server, but the allocation to SQL Server is configurable and is often less than all available memory.

FIGURE 31.1.

Physical memory allocated to the server is configurable, as is the distribution of cache between the procedure cache and data cache.

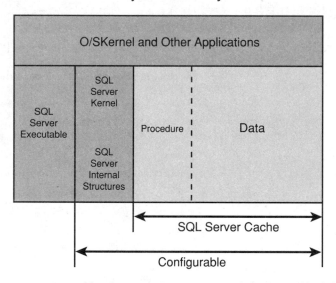

The first chunk of physical memory is used by the operating system, and it is typically defined by the operating system administrator (who is often not the SQL Server system administrator). Under Windows NT Server, the server operating system kernel consumes 16MB, but the server also reserves approximately 50 percent of available physical memory for data caching. This cannot be turned off; it can only be mitigated using techniques discussed later in this chapter.

The next chunk of memory is the server executable. SQL Server is software that is being executed by the operating system. The amount of memory needed for the server executable is approximately 2MB.

When the server comes up, the server refers to a system configuration setting, memory, to determine the number of pages (remember, SQL Server pages are 2KB) of real memory that the SQL server will appropriate when it comes up.

> **WARNING**
>
> If the server does not have enough memory to start properly, it will not start at all. (There is no partial server execution.) If you have misconfigured and the server is unable to get enough memory to start, restart SQL Server using the -f command-line switch. This forces SQL Server to use the default values for all configuration options. Optionally, you can use the SETUP utility and select the Rebuild the MASTER database option, which reconfigures all the memory settings to their default values.

After the server has allocated its total memory pool, it sets aside a portion for its own internal kernel (more on this later), and it uses whatever is left over for cache. For example, if you allocate 5,000 pages for memory and use 2,000 pages for kernel, there will be 3,000 pages for cache.

Cache allows the server to read information repeatedly from memory rather than disk. Because memory is always much faster than disk, sufficient cache size is a critical element in server performance. Cache is effectively divided between data cache, which stores data pages being read or modified, and procedure cache, which stores the optimized executable stored procedures.

> **WARNING**
>
> If you are running SQL Server on Windows NT 3.1 or 3.5, beware of an unusual memory problem that only affects very large-scale systems.
>
> Microsoft wrote SQL Server 4.2x to be capable of physically addressing 2GB of RAM (the maximum value for the memory sp_configure option is 1 million 2KB pages). However, until Windows NT 3.51, Windows NT would only provide a maximum of 256MB of RAM to any Win32 process—even though all versions of Windows NT are capable of physically addressing 4GB of RAM. Attempting to configure SQL Server to use more than 256MB of memory would result in substantial disk access, as Windows NT paged memory access to virtual memory.

> **WARNING**
>
> This "undocumented feature" didn't come out until a year after Windows NT 3.1 had shipped. Its has since been fixed in Windows NT 3.51 and is part of the reason why NT 3.51 is recommended for SQL Server 6.0 installations.

Initial Memory Configurations for SQL Server 6.0

SQL Server relies on Windows NT to provide it with memory. Therefore, configuring memory requires information on how Windows NT itself allocates and consumes physical RAM.

To establish the baseline SQL Server memory configuration, start SQL Server to use 50 percent of available physical memory. Although this might seem wasteful, remember that the remaining memory is consumed by Windows NT Server (16MB), plus Windows NT's own caching mechanism (50 percent of physical RAM/OS Kernel). This 50 percent number, however, isn't as specific or unyielding as it sounds.

Using Windows NT's Performance Monitor application, you can determine the optimal memory configuration for SQL Server with just a little testing. Start Performance Monitor, and choose the Edit | Add to Chart... menu sequence, which displays the window shown in Figure 31.2.

FIGURE 31.2.

Windows NT Performance Monitor allows you to examine finite performance statistics on both Windows NT and SQL Server, making baseline memory configuration easier.

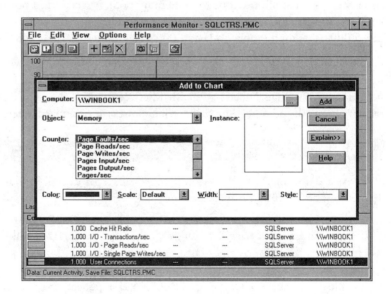

In the Object combo box, select the Memory object. This brings up a fresh list of counters. In the Counter list box add the Page Faults/sec counter. This monitors Windows NT's inability to satisfy memory requests with RAM which results in a *page fault*, forcing it to use PAGEFILE.SYS on disk.

Within SQL Server, use `sp_configure` or SQL Enterprise Manager (see Figure 31.3) to change your memory configuration. Shutdown and restart SQL Server, and watch the PerfMon counters for page faults to see whether SQL Server is using any paged memory. If not, you can gradually increase SQL Server's memory allocation until it starts to rely on the paging file.

FIGURE 31.3.

Setting the memory configuration option using SQL Enterprise Manager.

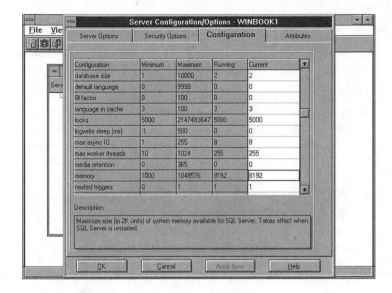

Microsoft has included documentation on recommended settings for initial memory sizes based on available physical RAM sizes. This information begins to deviate from the 50 percent rule after approximately 48MB, but still Windows NT consumes additional RAM as it becomes available. Use the Microsoft guidelines as a starting point, and use the algorithm presented previously to maximize the use of RAM by SQL Server while minimizing performance-crippling pagefile access.

Using the *TempDB in RAM* Option

By default, the `tempdb` database is created on the master disk device by SQL Server. This database can be altered on to other disk devices to increase its size, but it still remains on disk. In the 4.2 release of SQL Server for Windows NT, Microsoft introduced the option of loading the `tempdb` database into RAM to speed page-access operations that involve temp tables, worktables, and sorting operations.

When the `TempDB in RAM` option is set to 0, `tempdb` remains whatever its current size is assigned—that is, the default is 2MB assigned to the master device. Even if the `tempdb` database is extended to other devices, it consumes memory only as its data tables are cached using normal SQL Server caching mechanisms.

When `TempDB in RAM` is changed, the number value used represents the number of megabytes of RAM that SQL Server will use to create `tempdb` in main memory. This memory allocation is *in addition to* the memory allocations already made by Windows NT, the SQL Server executable, and SQL Server's memory allocations for user connections, data cache, and procedure cache. For this reason, Microsoft recommends using this option only if your server hardware has more than 64MB of RAM, and only if an application's queries rely heavily on worktables, sorting operations, and temporary tables. Below 64MB of RAM, SQL Server can use the available memory for cache more efficiently than if it were dedicating a portion of system memory for `tempdb`.

The option of putting `tempdb` into main memory can be an important performance benefit for queries that use sorting operations and temporary tables, particularly when there are large numbers of users using these query constructs. There is a small price to be paid for this option, however. First, SQL Server requires an additional memory block for `tempdb`. But more important, SQL Server still caches `tempdb` tables in data cache as though `tempdb` were still on disk. In other words, SQL Server, for the purposes of cache management and page access, *does not realize that `tempdb` is in RAM*. As such, a given page from a table might be in RAM twice: once in the `tempdb` allocated memory space, and again in the data cache managed by SQL Server. If your temporary tables grow quite large, you can find yourself consuming large quantities of memory very quickly as table pages are duplicated in main memory. For this reason, as well as the others already listed, Microsoft recommends using the `TempDB in RAM` option only in specialized cases, and that thorough testing of application performance follow changing this configuration option.

The safest rule is this: If you want to put `tempdb` in RAM, add enough RAM to contain the entire `tempdb` database. That way, you won't have to sacrifice any of your existing cache space for `tempdb`, and `tempdb` can be accessed in RAM rather than on disk.

Using *DBCC MEMUSAGE* to Validate Memory Configuration

The *Database Consistency Checker* (DBCC) command can detail your memory allocation, which will help you make the best use of memory resources. In order to run DBCC MEMUSAGE, you need to direct the output to your terminal using DBCC trace functions (*trace flags*). Several DBCC trace flags are covered in this book; two very common values are 3604 and 3605.

Here are the important DBCC commands related to memory usage and what they do:

DBCC TRACEON (3604)	Send subsequent DBCC output to the local session
DBCC TRACEON (3605)	Send subsequent DBCC output to the errorlog
DBCC traceoff (3604 ¦ 3605)	Terminate special destinations
DBCC MEMUSAGE	Must be used with DBCC TRACEON (3604) if you want to see the output on your screen

TIP

On some platforms or releases of the server, DBCC TRACEON (3604) must be in its own batch to take effect for the subsequent DBCC MEMUSAGE.

```
DBCC TRACEON (3604)
go
DBCC MEMUSAGE
go
```

Use DBCC MEMUSAGE to determine whether your tuning guesses were correct. It provides extremely useful information about overall memory size, cache size, and the actual objects stored in the cache. This is the memory usage section of DBCC MEMUSAGE:

```
Memory Usage:
                            Meg.        2K Blks          Bytes

Configured Memory:        4.0000          2048          4194304

Code size:                1.7166           879          1800000
Kernel Structures:        0.2440           125           255808
Server Structures:        0.6461           331           677492
Page Cache:               1.0877           557          1140512
Proc Buffers:             0.0156             8            16348
Resource Structure:       0.0008             1              836
Proc Headers:             0.2893           149           303308
```

The first section of the output is the server kernel information. The things you want to look at and consider are

- Configured Memory. This should be the same as what you configured using sp_configure or SQL Enterprise Manager. Here, it is reported in megabytes (4.0000) as well as in 2KB blocks (2048).

- Page Cache. This is the amount of memory configured (by you) for data cache (1.0877M or 557 pages).

- Proc Buffers and Proc Headers. This is the procedure cache (0.0156 + 0.2893 = 0.3049MB).

NOTE

As the system administrator, you can configure the ratio of data cache to procedure cache. If you have the procedure cache configured to 20 (20 percent), you should have 20 percent procedure cache to 80 percent data cache, for a ratio of 1 to 4. These are approximate because SQL Server allocates cache pages on 2KB boundaries.

The second part of DBCC MEMUSAGE is a listing of the top 20 buffered data items (tables and indexes) in cache. The following is a list of the 20 largest contiguous pieces of data in data cache.

```
Buffer Cache, Top 20:
 DB Id   Object Id   Index Id     2K Buffers
 5       240003886   0            118
 5       176003658   0            88
 5       208003772   0            87
 5       176003658   2            57
 5       208003772   2            57
 5       99          0            56
 1       36          0            6
 1       2           0            3
 4       1           0            2
 4       2           0            2
 4       5           0            2
 5       176003658   1            2
 5       240003886   1            2
 1       2           1            1
 1       8           0            1
 1       30          0            1
 1       30          2            1
 1       36          1            1
 2       2           0            1
 2       8           0            1
```

To understand what each item in this list is, perform the following steps. For this example, we will determine what the first and fourth items are on the sample output in the list.

1. Use the appropriate database. You need the name of the database first, so use the db_name() function to convert a database ID to a name:

   ```
   select db_name(5)
   ```

   Now use the database:

   ```
   use perftune
   ```

2. You can use the object_name() to convert the object ID to an object name. (Note that object_name() only works in the relevant database.)

   ```
   select object_name(240003886)
   ```

3. Using the index ID and the following table, you can determine what component of a table is cached.

Index ID	Component of Table
0	Table itself
1	Clustered index
2+	Non-clustered index

   To determine which nonclustered index is cached when the index ID is greater than 1, try the following select statement from sysindexes:

```
select name, keycnt
from sysindexes
where id = 176003658 /* object id from MEMUSAGE */
and indid = 2 /* index id from MEMUSAGE */
```

To retrieve the column names of the index keys for this index, use the `index_col()` function.

```
select index_col(object_name(176003658), 2, 1)
```

The last part of DBCC MEMUSAGE is a list of up to the 20 largest stored procedures in cache, along with the size and number of compiled plans that are in memory for that procedure. An example of the third section is shown in the following output:

```
Procedure Cache, Top 6:

Procedure Name: sp_help
Database Id: 1
Object Id: 1520008446
Version: 1
Uid: 1
Type: stored procedure
Number of trees: 0
Size of trees: 0.000000 Mb, 0.000000 bytes, 0 pages
Number of plans: 1
Size of plans: 0.025528 Mb, 26768.000000 bytes, 14 pages

Procedure Name: sp_monitor
Database Id: 1
Object Id: 1712009130
Version: 1
Uid: 1
Type: stored procedure
Number of trees: 0
Size of trees: 0.000000 Mb, 0.000000 bytes, 0 pages
Number of plans: 1
Size of plans: 0.020489 Mb, 21484.000000 bytes, 11 pages

Procedure Name: sp_lock
Database Id: 1
Object Id: 1584008674
Version: 1
Uid: 1
Type: stored procedure
Number of trees: 0
Size of trees: 0.000000 Mb, 0.000000 bytes, 0 pages
Number of plans: 1
Size of plans: 0.006382 Mb, 6692.000000 bytes, 4 pages

Procedure Name: sp_who
Database Id: 1
Object Id: 1904009814
Version: 1
Uid: 1
Type: stored procedure
Number of trees: 0
Size of trees: 0.000000 Mb, 0.000000 bytes, 0 pages
Number of plans: 1
Size of plans: 0.007292 Mb, 7646.000000 bytes, 4 pages
```

```
Procedure Name: testtemp
Database Id: 6
Object Id: 1436532151
Version: 1
Uid: 1
Type: stored procedure
Number of trees: 0
Size of trees: 0.000000 Mb, 0.000000 bytes, 0 pages
Number of plans: 1
Size of plans: 0.003067 Mb, 3216.000000 bytes, 2 pages

Procedure Name: byroyalty
Database Id: 4
Object Id: 368004342
Version: 1
Uid: 1
Type: stored procedure
Number of trees: 0
Size of trees: 0.000000 Mb, 0.000000 bytes, 0 pages
Number of plans: 1
Size of plans: 0.001348 Mb, 1414.000000 bytes, 1 pages
DBCC execution completed. If DBCC printed error messages, see your System
Administrator.
```

NOTE

Note that SQL Server's stored procedures are recursive and reusable, but not reentrant. If many processes want to run a procedure at one time, the server creates a new query plan for each concurrent execution.

The procedure size statistics reported in DBCC MEMUSAGE refer to the largest, but not necessarily the most frequently used, plans in cache. Unfortunately, profiling Microsoft databases is difficult, because Microsoft has not yet shipped any database profiling tools.

How To Use *DBCC MEMUSAGE* Information

Run DBCC MEMUSAGE regularly to understand how memory is being used in your server. Pay special attention to these issues:

■ Look at the overall memory figures to make certain that you have as much data cache as you expected.

■ Look at data cache to see whether any particular object is monopolizing the cache at the expense of other objects, because it might be appropriate to take other tuning steps on that object.

■ Look at how large stored procedures are, because smaller procedures compile and execute faster.

Configuring Lock Escalation Values

Previous versions of SQL Server implemented locking at two different levels for query processing. A single query could lock individual data pages within a table, or it could lock all of the table pages, depending on the number of pages being read. The "magic number" for lock escalation was always 200 pages. In other words, any query was allowed to allocate 200 page locks on a table. As soon as that query attempted to allocate page lock #201, its locking scheme would be automatically upgraded by SQL Server from 200+ individual page locks to a single table lock. In other words, at the threshold, SQL Server provided access to the entire table.

Although this mechanism introduced substantial efficiency into the algorithms of the locking manager, its impact on query performance, particularly with large numbers of users, is not quite so obvious. The figure of 200 pages is unyielding. If a table as 400 or 4,000,000 pages, a single query acquiring 200 locks forces a table lock. As a result, a single query reading 250 pages (500K of data) from a table containing 5,000,000 pages (a 10MB table), would lock the entire table. This is even more problematic in very large databases where individual table sizes can be gigabytes in size.

Similarly, if a table has only 150 pages, a table lock is never used, even on an unrestricted query. Because the number of page locks on the table never exceeds 200, a table lock can never be used. Obviously, this indicates room for improvement in how flexible SQL Server can be in managing lock escalation.

With SQL Server 6.0, there are configuration options that enable an administrator to adjust not only the ceiling for table lock escalation, but also the floor. Three of the advanced configuration options manage both the availability of lock escalation as well as two points at which SQL Server will upgrade page locks to a table lock.

The LE Threshold Minimum configuration option (remember that this is an advanced configuration option, so you must turn on the Show Advanced option first) sets the minimum number of page locks that SQL Server must acquire before it will consider the option of upgrading to a table lock. In effect, it is the "on switch" for lock escalation. Remember, also, that these are global server configuration options, so the number you specify here will be applied to all queries on all tables.

The LE Threshold Maximum configuration option sets the maximum number of page locks a query can acquire before it is escalated to a table lock. In previous versions of SQL Server, both LE Threshold Minimum and LE Threshold Maximum would be set to 200 if they were configurable. The LE Threshold Maximum value is absolute and does not change based on activity or query size. As a result, this value might mean that smaller tables never receive table locks when needed, whereas very large tables might incur substantial blocking as table locks are applied where they shouldn't be.

The problem of relating lock escalation to table size is solved using LE Threshold Percent. If the LE Threshold Minimum is reached, SQL Server can calculate an approximate threshold, based on current table size, for escalating page locks to table locks. The current table size is determined from information contained in the sysindexes table (see Chapter 10, "Understanding SQL Server Storage Structures."

In order to prevent conflicts between configuration options from confusing SQL Server, there is a strict decision hierarchy that SQL Server uses to define the actual point of lock escalation. First, if the LE Threshold Minimum value is never reached—that is, a table scan operation does not generate *at least* the LE Threshold Minimum number of page locks—SQL Server does not even consider using a table lock. If the minimum threshold is reached, SQL Server upgrades page locks to a table lock based on which of the remaining configuration options is encountered *first*—that is, if the maximum value is encountered before the percentage, locks are escalated. If the percentage is encountered before the maximum, again, page locks are escalated to a table lock.

Remember that using the query-definable locking options overrides any configuration options set by an administrator. These options are considered server-generic, meaning that they apply to all tables. If a query uses the PAGLOCK or TABLOCK keyword, however, the locking scheme defined by the query will override the configuration options discussed here.

Optimizing SQL Server Scanning Operations

SQL Server introduces a whole new way to perform queries that involve scanning operations. Before discussing the configuration of those options, take a look at how this new feature works and examine its impact and usefulness on very large databases.

> **NOTE**
>
> Before reading on, you might want to review Chapter 2, "The Microsoft Client/Server Architecture," for the architectural changes that Microsoft introduced with SQL Server 4.2 for Windows NT. Those changes from the traditional Sybase architecture are responsible for enabling the technological advances discussed in this section.

The capability to use multiple processors vastly increased SQL Server's performance potential, but very large databases exceeding 10 or 20 gigabytes still pose problems for the server. Although SQL Server's transaction performance is excellent by any measure, some new issues arise with very large databases. First, scanning very large tables of many hundreds of megabytes or even gigabytes is very lengthy, even on a multiprocessor system. Why? Because only *one worker thread* is scanning the table for any query. SQL Server 4.2*x* does not have the capability to use multiple scanning threads for a single query, so only one processor is working on a scanning operation at any time. (See Figure 31.4.)

FIGURE 31.4.

With standard table scanning, table scan performance is bound by both the speed of the disk and the capability of a single worker thread to request pages.

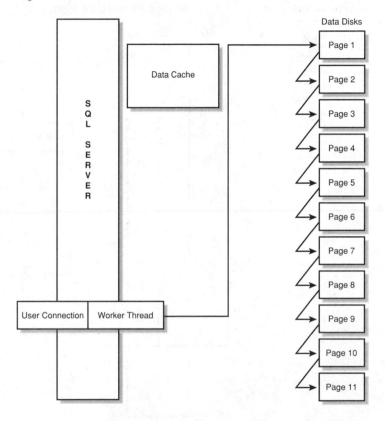

SQL Server 6.0 introduces *Parallel Data Scanning*, which makes use of new *read-ahead threads* to address the limitations of standard table scanning. Read-ahead threads enable SQL Server to use multiple threads for I/O operations even though a single thread has processed a query. (See Figure 31.5.)

For example, in scanning a 2GB table, SQL 4.2*x* uses a single worker thread for the user connection. Because that thread is the smallest unit of work, it can be scheduled to only one processor at any one time. With tables of that size, the likelihood that the entire table will be in cache is obviously low. Therefore, that thread must do substantial disk I/O. Read-ahead threads enable SQL Server to use a background thread to do the disk I/O *in advance* of a worker thread's request for a particular page. In other words, while a worker thread is "surfing" a page chain for data, an additional thread is reading ahead of the current scanning position, loading pages from disk into cache so that the worker thread is always finding data in cache, not on disk. (See Figure 31.5.) On multiprocessor hardware, the statistical probability of these threads being scheduled to different processors is quite high, so a single query operation (worker thread) can now use multiple processors simultaneously to increase query response time. The net effect is that read-ahead threads increase the worker thread cache hit ratio by fetching pages from disk into cache before the worker thread actually requests them.

FIGURE 31.5.

With parallel data scanning, one worker thread can retrieve data pages while another performs the work of a query.

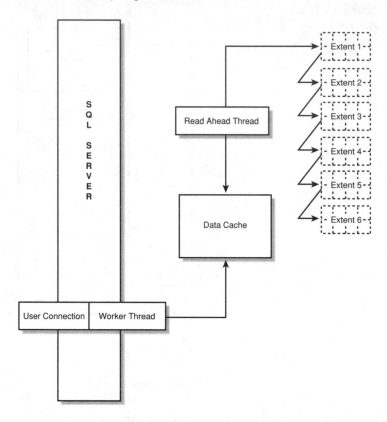

Read-ahead threading is limited to scanning operations, which include both leaf-level index scanning and direct table-page scanning. Therefore, any SELECT statements in which the optimizer chooses a table scan, or any execution of DBCC, UPDATE STATISTICS, CREATE INDEX, and other such operations that scan tables or leaf index levels, will benefit from read-ahead scanning.

Because this operation relies on multiple threads, there is little benefit to spawning threads to do disk I/O when I/O operations are already satisfied by cache. Therefore, a series of new sp_configure options define when read-ahead will be used and how it behaves once activated. Activation and de-activation are controlled by two new advanced configuration options, RA cache miss limit and RA cache hit limit. Because PDS provides benefit only when data is on disk and not in cache, the RA cache miss limit defines the number of sequential read operations that SQL Server will execute on disk before allocating a read-ahead thread to that query. For example, if a query such as `select * from foo` is executed on a 400MB table, SQL Server might find the first 12MB in cache on a large, multiprocessor box. If that query encounters four sequential read operations that go to disk, SQL Server acknowledges the read requests and also allocates a read-ahead thread for that query.

So, how do you turn this off? That's where the `RA cache hit limit` configuration option (the default is three reads) comes in. If the pages that a read-ahead thread is requesting are found in cache, the read-ahead thread contributes little or no meaningful work to the query. Therefore, `RA cache hit limit` enables SQL Server to turn off the read-ahead thread if it is finding data in cache instead of on disk.

How does the read-ahead thread know where to read from? The `RA pre-fetches` configuration option defines the number of extents that a read-ahead thread will keep in cache *ahead of* the current scanning position. With a default value of `3`, a read-ahead will keep three extents, or 24 pages, of data in cache ahead of the worker thread's current read position. Because the worker thread is working with data in 2KB pages, and the read-ahead thread is working with data in extents (eight 2KB pages), a read-ahead thread can quickly fetch extra data before the worker thread is ready to process that part of the page chain. This leaves the unfortunate potential for continuous stopping/starting of read-ahead threads, as well as read-ahead thread idle time. With the `RA slots per thread` option, SQL Server uses that potential idle time by having a single read-ahead thread service multiple worker threads simultaneously.

SQL Server allocates worker threads according to a fixed algorithm. SQL Server is initialized with a specific number of read-ahead threads, configured using `RA worker threads`. The default for this option is 3. The configuration option `RA slots per thread` (default is `5`) says that each read-ahead thread is capable of servicing 5 worker threads, for a total of 15 simultaneous disk-I/O scanning operations. Actual allocation of the threads happens as described in the following example:

1. User 1 logs on and executes an `UPDATE STATISTICS` command on a 2GB table.
2. SQL Server allocates a read-ahead thread and assigns the first slot of that thread to User 1.
3. As more users log in, they also begin various large scanning operations. Each of these new users is assigned first to the open slots on the existing read-ahead thread.
4. When 5 user connections have been serviced, and a sixth needs a read-ahead thread, SQL Server allocates a new read-ahead thread and assigns that sixth worker thread to the first slot of the new read-ahead thread.
5. This continues as read-ahead services are needed.

Multiprocessor hardware is necessary to truly take best advantage of these new configuration options. The overhead of scheduling a multithread scanning operation on a single CPU is, in theory, sufficient to quash the potential benefit of using multiple threads. Specific instances might prove otherwise, but for the most part, multiprocessor systems are needed to make use of this new feature.

In addition to multiple processors, multiple disk channels are also an important "must have" to fully take advantage of Parallel Data Scanning. By parallelizing I/O at the thread, processor, and disk levels, SQL Server can achieve substantial performance gains. During the early beta-testing phases of SQL Server 6.0, internal, and decidedly informal Microsoft tests revealed anywhere from 100 to 400 percent faster reads on a two-processor, four-disk, Intel-based hardware platform. Clearly, the right hardware can be an important aspect in making the most of SQL Server.

The only potential deficiency with Parallel Data Scanning is that the optimizer does not yet account for the performance benefits available for scanning operations using Parallel Data Scanning. In other words, SQL Server now has three different options for processing a query:

- Using a traditional, single-thread-at-a-time table scan
- Using an index
- Using a table scan that triggers read-ahead threading.

The optimizer is not capable of properly calculating the cost of a query using Parallel Data Scanning; therefore the optimizer might choose to use an index to process a query when in fact a table scan that takes advantage of Parallel Data Scanning might be quicker. The math involved in calculating such costs is far too scary to go into in any depth in this book. If you are hosting applications that use multiprocessing hardware and very large tables, however, you should comparison test how existing queries perform using the method SQL Server chooses versus forcing a table scan that uses Parallel Data Scanning to see what the performance differences are. Only through such testing can you determine the true benefit, if any, that Parallel Data Scanning has to offer.

Summary

Although SQL Server 6.0 introduces some new areas in which a system administrator can optimize SQL Server's performance, the real performance-tuning work still belongs with those who write queries. Version 6.0 implements more flexible configuration options and enables an administrator to have a potential impact on performance, but those options have the greatest impact on very large systems that rely on multiprocessing, multidisk-channel hardware platforms.

Measuring SQL Server System Performance

32

IN THIS CHAPTER

Introduction to Measuring Performance

Part of the advantage of using Microsoft SQL Server for Windows NT lies in the integration of the database engine with the operating system. That integration allows SQL Server to rely on operating system services and applications that would otherwise be duplicated in the database engine itself, causing substantial overhead. One area in which this duplication is avoided centers on monitoring performance. By using the Windows NT Performance Monitor, SQL Server administrators can monitor performance characteristics and hunt for potential bottlenecks using a graphic interface that presents immediate, real-time data. Before talking about Performance Monitor itself, take a look at what to monitor, and why.

Why Measure Performance?

Obviously, the ability to measure performance at a systemic level provides administrators with information they need to optimally configure SQL Server for the environment in which it resides, as well as tune particular applications for the specific tasks they execute. Although the activities involved in tuning SQL Server or any application system are more witchcraft than pure physics, the ability to observe changes in a standardized format provides genuine information about the cause and effect of changing configuration options. The problem is getting to the information that you need.

In the Sybase world, that has usually meant profiling databases and queries using a stopwatch and some undocumented DBCC commands. Although useful, the lack of support for such things from the vendor makes performance tuning much harder than it need be. Although Microsoft SQL Server has typically not supported the size or complexity of applications that Sybase SQL Server could, Microsoft SQL Server, through its integration with Windows NT, has been able to provide administrators with more information, such that a given SQL Server can be monitored and tuned more effectively than on any other platform.

What Is Performance Monitor?

Windows NT Performance Monitor is an operating system utility that ships with Windows NT and is used to monitor a variety of performance counters that are provided by the operating system. Performance Monitor is a Win32 application that runs only on Windows NT and relies on Win32 DLLs to interact with the operating system and other applications to provide performance statistics and measurements. Performance Monitor is capable of charting these statistics graphically, as well as take preventative action based on the scope of those statistics. For example, Performance Monitor can execute a command if a particular measurement crosses a specific threshold. In addition, Performance Monitor can be used to log performance statistics to monitor their change over time.

Performance Monitor relies on a defined series of performance *objects*, which are general categories of statistical measures. The performance objects are selected in the upper-left combo box shown in Figure 32.1.

FIGURE 32.1.

Performance Monitor allows you to monitor objects, counters, and instances to provide very precise information about finite elements of SQL Server and other Windows NT applications.

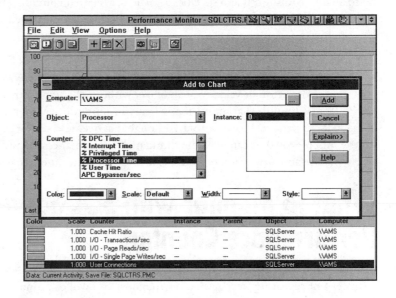

Performance objects include such things as Processor, Physical Disk, Process, and Memory. Each of these has a collection of performance *counters* associated with it, which refers to a particular aspect of that object. For example, the Processor performance object has counters that measure % Processor Time, which measures the total percent of available CPU time being used, as well as Interrupts/sec, which measures the number of interrupts or requests for services being generated by the system. Performance objects and counters are defined by DLLs that integrate with Performance Monitor, telling it what to look for. In some cases, a performance object may also have different instances. *Instances* are unique examples of currently active objects. For example, the Processor object on a single-processor machine will have only one instance: the processor itself. If four processors were present, there would be four items in the Instances list box when the Processor object is selected. Depending on the particular object that you've selected, the Instances list box might contain different items. For example, if you select the Process object, you will see a list of the currently active executables and system DLLs under Windows NT. SQL Server will show up in this list as SQLSRVR, because that is the name of the SQL Server executable file.

If you are uncertain about a particular object or counter, the Explain button can show you more information about that particular counter. A well-documented Win32 application, if it is going to supply PerfMon statistics counters, should have such documentation available for PerfMon to display. All of the SQL Server performance counters have such documentation, even if it is a bit sparse in places.

The default view for Performance Monitor is a standard chart. Depending on how you start Performance Monitor, you will see different counters and objects already displayed. In the SQL Server 6.0 program group, the SQL Server Performance Monitor icon loads Windows NT's Performance Monitor; it also specifies a particular file that contains a predefined list of objects and counters. You can change the statistics that PerfMon uses, as well as save your own custom lists of objects and counters.

The laws of physics are typically unyielding, and both Windows NT and SQL Server are subject to them. Heisenberg's Uncertainty Principle holds true here as elsewhere: You cannot measure the direction or velocity of an object without changing either the direction or the velocity. In real English that means that when you monitor SQL Server's performance you are going to incur performance overhead. Although that overhead can be minimized (or maximized, for the mischievous), it can never be eliminated. Performance Monitor allows you to examine a very precise approximation of SQL Server's performance, not its actual performance.

What to Monitor with SQL Server Performance Counters

Configuring Performance Monitor is discussed in depth in the Windows NT documentation, so instead of repeating step-by-step instructions, you will examine what you need to monitor to see how SQL Server is performing.

Any server application requires four basic sets of services: processor, memory, disk, and network. Consequently, you've just defined the four categories of performance objects and counters that you will want to measure. Although the simplicity of that statement is attractive, you have to remember that not only should you be monitoring the application-level (that is, SQL Server's) performance objects and counters, but you should also be monitoring those same areas at the operating-system level. SQL Server provides many areas to create performance bottlenecks, but so does Windows NT. Sharp SQL Server administrators will learn that not only is SQL Server knowledge required for proper performance monitoring, but also understanding the Windows NT environment as it relates to server applications and networking.

The first object to monitor is `Processor`. For this object, you'll want to monitor either the `% Processor Time` or the `% User Time` counters. The first counter monitors the total SQL Server processor usage by all applications currently executing on the system. For a dedicated SQL Server, the nominal measure for this should be between 60 and 75 percent. This figure, although approximate, indicates that the processor is capable of handling all normal requests for service, but also has available latency for spikes in usage. If your processor usage exceeds 75 percent on a regular basis, consider installing either a faster processor or, if possible, adding a second processor. Windows NT automatically detects new processors and makes them available to SQL Server (see Chapter 30, "Configuring and Tuning SQL Server," particularly the SMP Concurrency option, for more information on this).

The counter `% User Time` is an option because it shows the amount of time being devoted to "non-kernel" functions and applications running on top of the operating system. The counter `% Privileged Time` refers to kernel-level CPU operations, so you'll want the other two counters to measure SQL Server.

For measuring the `Memory` object, you'll want to know SQL Server's memory configuration. That value, combined with the database executable, plus the `TempDB` space (if it is in RAM) has a dramatic effect on this counter. For dedicated servers, you want the `Available Bytes` counter to be as low as possible, without resorting to the use of the paging file. (More on that shortly.)

The disk drive objects and counters require some special attention before they'll work. Because of the substantial overhead (approximately 5 percent of system performance) that the disk counters exact, they are, by default, disabled. To enable the disk counters, you must open a Windows NT command window and type `diskperf -y`. Having done so, the proper registry entry is now set to allow use of the disk counters. Using this option requires shutting down and restarting Windows NT. Leaving this option on permanently is a good way to needlessly drain operating system resources, so remember to reset it after you have completed your performance monitoring work.

For both the `PhysicalDisk` and `LogicalDisk` performance objects, Windows NT will create a distinct *instance* for each *physical volume* that exists in your machine. In other words, if you have a single physical disk partitioned into three logical volumes (hardly wise for a SQL Server installation), Performance Monitor will register a single instance for the `PhysicalDisk` object and three instances of the `LogicalDisk` object. If you have three physical hard disks partitioned as a stripe set, each of those three physical disks will appear as a distinct instance also.

A variety of counters are available, including disk reads and writes. Which you choose is dependent on what type of application your SQL Server is supporting. If it is a decision-support system, then disk reads are going to be more important than disk writes—both in percentage and real terms. For OLTP environments, disk writes are obviously more critical.

For the network, monitoring just SQL Server's performance only gives you part of the story because SQL Server's interface to that network is only part of the equation. The network itself is an entity but is also a component of any client/server architecture. Like the other hardware subsystems, the network is a potential bottleneck and, depending on the cable and topology, could be a bigger one than you expect. If SQL Server is using only one or two of the available protocols, make sure that you monitor the throughput that those protocols are generating. Performance Monitor does allow administrators access to the performance statistics for each protocol stack individually, so comparison testing between protocol stacks for a given application is also possible.

With regard to SQL Server–specific counters, the SQL Server object is the most critical and most often used. Here, SQL Server can display transaction-performance statistics including transactions/sec and writes/sec, as well as displaying reads/sec for OLAP applications. If you are running SQL Server on a multiprocessing, multidisk channel hardware platform, the SQL Server object also includes a collection of very important counters relating to read-ahead performance statistics. Tuning read-ahead caching involves experimenting with different quantities of threads and slots (see Chapter 31, "Optimizing SQL Server Configuration Options," for more information on Parallel Data Scanning) to maximize the RA - Pages Fetched Into Cache/sec and RA - Pages Found in Cache statistics. In addition, having optimized these two, you then want to make sure that the RA - Slots Used counter value and the value of the total number of read-ahead slots (RA Slots × RA Threads) are as close as possible; this indicates maximum efficiency from read-ahead operations for a given workload.

Using *DBCC SQLPERF*

For SQL Server, most of the performance counters are fetched using undocumented DBCC commands. Performance Monitor uses the SQLCTRS.DLL file to list what objects and counters are available. When Performance Monitor polls the SQLCTRS.DLL file for performance statistics, SQLCTRS goes to SQL Server and runs a series of as yet undocumented DBCC commands. The execution of these commands against SQL Server form the majority of the overhead associated with monitoring SQL Server's performance. Certain DBCC options are exposed for general use, however.

The DBCC SQLPERF option exposes three different categories of statistics: IOStats, LRUStats, and NETStats. Consequently, these are the three arguments that must be substituted when executing a DBCC SQLPERF command. IOStats generates information about the I/O statistics since SQL Server was last started or since the last time the options were cleared—whichever is most recent. This is equivalent to using Performance Monitor to report on disk reads/sec and disk writes/sec. Remember, though, that instead of charting these statistics over time, DBCC SQLPERF generates a "snapshot in time" of the statistics. To monitor performance over time, you would have to run this command at regular intervals and record the results. LRUStats reports on the caching efficiency of SQL Server, most notably, the cache hit ration. LRU stands for *least recently used*, which is the caching algorithm used by all versions of SQL Server. The NETStats counter reports on network-related statistics, including bytes sent/sec, bytes received/sec, queue length, and so on.

Why use the DBCC SQLPERF counters? Because the performance drain associated with using them is substantially less than using Performance Monitor. Performance Monitor queries SQL Server at regular intervals and retrieves very large numbers of performance statistics so that they can be charted. DBCC SQLPERF generates text output using PRINT statements and returns them as data to a client application. As a result, the responsibility for recording those results, storing them, and charting them becomes a manual process for an administrator. Most often, that's how this command is used. A regularly scheduled command-line ISQL session pipes in a query that runs DBCC SQLPERF. That query sends the output to an operating-system text file. An administrator moves or copies that text file to an archive directory. As a result, the complete performance history for a server can be stored in a safe location, with minimal (but still present) performance drains being the result.

Summary

If you are troubleshooting a particular performance problem, use Windows NT Performance Monitor. The quantity and variety of information that is available is worth the additional performance hit your server will take during performance tuning and optimization time. If, however, you simply want to track SQL Server's performance as part of monitoring its operational history, use the SQL task scheduling engine (discussed in Chapter 34, "The Microsoft SQL Server Distributed Management Framework") to configure a regularly scheduled, automatically executed batch file that runs SQL, gathers the performance statistics, and redirects the output to a text file. Administrators can then examine, log, and archive these files to maintain operational history information.

Remote Server Management

33

This chapter presents the definition and management of remote servers, privileges, and security.

As your systems grow in size, complexity, or geographic distribution, you might find it necessary to enable your servers to communicate with each other directly. Remote server access in a multiserver environment enables applications to share data (in a limited way) and to access data and functions on other SQL Servers and Open Data Services applications. (See Figure 33.1.)

FIGURE 33.1.

Remote servers include SQL Servers and Open Data Services applications. Open Data Services processes require the same remote server administration as SQL Servers.

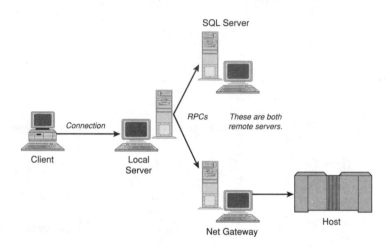

Because the remote server interface can access Open Data Services applications, it also is the mechanism for connecting heterogeneous data sources, including mainframe databases from DB/2 to IMS to VSAM flat files, other non-SQL databases, and nontraditional data sources. The most interesting applications involve the integration of real-time devices (stock tickers, news sources, and data-collection devices).

By definition, a *remote server* is a server that you access as part of a client process without opening a distinct, direct client connection. SQL Server manages communications between servers using *Remote Procedure Calls* (RPC). You call a remote procedure the same way that you call a local procedure; the only difference is that you need to fully qualify the name of the procedure with the name of the server. Here is the syntax:

```
execute remote_server_name.db_name.owner_name.procedure_name
```

You've already used this syntax, with the exception of the `remote_server_name`.

NOTE

With SQL Server and Windows NT, there are actually two different types of Remote Procedure Calls that are available. Windows NT supplies a standards-compliant Remote Procedure Call that enables application-to-application communications both locally and over a network. This RPC is compliant with OSF's DCE (Distributed Computing Environment) RPC specification, so applications that make use of Windows NT RPC services are capable of talking with other DCE-compliant applications, regardless of the hosting platform. For example, a Windows NT application can use RPCs to communicate via TCP/IP to an application running on SunOS or Solaris, and the communication will appear transparent.

SQL Server Remote Procedure Calls are different. Instead of being supplied by the operating system, SQL Server RPCs are supplied by an application and therefore fall outside normal operating-system services. SQL Server RPCs are not DCE compliant, and in fact are a proprietary communication mechanism that works only for Microsoft and Sybase SQL Servers, as well as Microsoft Open Data Services applications and Sybase Open Server applications.

SQL Server RPCs do not interact with the operating system or operating system RPCs. Similarly, Windows NT RPCs neither interact with nor affect SQL Server RPCs. They are mutually exclusive.

No matter what type of external data source you want to access, you need to implement remote servers. Because of the need for remote server features for replication services (discussed in Chapter 35, "Introduction to Microsoft SQL Server 6.0 Replication"), SQL Server 6.0 enabled remote server access by default.

Definitions

For the purposes of this discussion, consider the case in which a client is directly connected to a SQL Server but needs to send and retrieve periodic information to a remote server using an RPC. (See Figure 33.2.)

FIGURE 33.2.

The remote server is accessed through the local server, and the client maintains only a single connection to the local server.

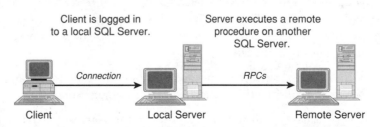

Client is logged in to a local SQL Server.

Server executes a remote procedure on another SQL Server.

Client   *Connection*   Local Server   *RPCs*   Remote Server

First, refresh your memory with a few definitions:

- A *local server* is the server you have logged in to.
- A *remote server* is another server to which you would like to connect from the local server.
- *Remote access* means connecting to a remote server.

To illustrate the configuration of remote servers, here is an example of two servers: a local server (near_server) and a remote server (far_server), as in Figure 33.3.

FIGURE 33.3.

In this example, the name of the local server is near_server. *The remote server is named* far_server.

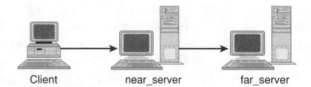

Client   near_server   far_server

Remote Access Cookbook

Ensuring remote access is not difficult, but it is complex. There are several steps to get remote access working properly:

1. Name the local and remote servers on both servers.
2. Configure each server for remote access.
3. On the remote server, define the method for mapping logins and users to the server's own logins and users.
4. Set remote option for password checking.

The following goes through each step in detail. Step 1 names the servers on each server. Until you start working with remote access, server names seem pretty arbitrary. For example, although you specify a named server when logging in, that server name is transformed into an address and port (or an address and named pipe) long before a packet goes out on the network. The server name that you use on your local workstation does not need to correspond to the name in the registry at the server.

With remote servers, the names are relevant to the communication; the names of servers must be defined consistently on each server, or communication will not work properly.

Use sp_addserver to add a server name to the sysservers table in the master database. You need to execute sp_addserver once for the local server name and once for each of the remote servers, as in the following example:

```
sp_addserver local_server_name , local
sp_addserver remote_server_name
```

Note that the local flag distinguishes the name of the local server.

For an example, on the local server (near_server), execute the following:

```
exec sp_addserver near_server, local
exec sp_addserver far_server
```

On the remote server (far_server), execute this:

```
exec sp_addserver far_server, local
exec sp_addserver near_server
```

Step 2 configures each server for remote access. The syntax is as follows:

```
sp_configure 'remote access', 1
reconfigure
```

For an example, on the local server (near_server), execute the following:

```
sp_configure 'remote access', 1
reconfigure
```

On the remote server (far_server), execute this:

```
sp_configure 'remote access', 1
reconfigure
```

Don't forget to shut down and restart each server.

Step 3, on the remote server, maps remote logins and users to the local environment. Here is the syntax:

```
sp_addremotelogin remote_server_name [, local_name [, remote_name]]
```

For an example, on the remote server (far_server), execute this:

```
sp_addremotelogin near_server
```

Step 4 sets remote options as necessary. Here is the syntax:

```
sp_remoteoption remote_server, login_name, remote_name, option, {true ¦ false}
```

For an example, on the remote server (far_server), execute this procedure to set up logins without requiring synchronized passwords between servers:

```
sp_remoteoption near_server, near_server_login, null, trusted, true
```

Adding Servers with *sp_addserver*

Use the sp_addserver procedure to populate the sysservers table. Here is the syntax:

```
sp_addserver server_name [, local]
```

The local keyword identifies the name of the server into which you are signed. (There can be only one local server.) You can verify this by selecting the @@servername global variable. Note that this does not take effect until the server is cycled; until then, RPCs will not work. In this example, you add a local server, near_server, and a remote server, far_server:

```
exec sp_addserver near_server, local
exec sp_addserver far_server
```

To remove a server from the sysservers table, use sp_dropserver. Here is the syntax:

```
exec sp_dropserver server_name [ ,droplogins ]
```

The droplogins keyword also instructs the server to remove all corresponding entries from sysremotelogins (discussed next). The following example removes the entry for server17, created before, and removes all associated logins.

```
sp_dropserver server17, droplogins
```

Adding Remote Logins with *sp_addremotelogin*

Remote logins enable you to map requests to a remote server to that server's local set of privileges and authorizations. *Remote logins are established on the remote server.*

The next three sections explore the three methods for mapping remote logins to local logins on the remote server.

Using the Remote ID as the Local ID

Use this syntax to map the remote ID as the local ID:

```
sp_addremotelogin remote_server_name
```

This is the simplest mapping method. It presumes that the logins are the same on both servers, and maps login to login.

> **TIP**
>
> If users from the remote server need access on your server, don't forget to add them with sp_addlogin.

The following example (executed on far_server) requires each remote login on near_server to have a corresponding entry in syslogins on far_server:

```
sp_addremotelogin near_server
```

Using a Single Local Login for All Remote Logins

If you want a single local login for all remote logins, use this syntax:

```
sp_addremotelogin remote_server_name, local_name
```

This is another straightforward mapping method. Any legitimate user on a server listed in sysservers will be mapped to a single login. In the following example, all logins originating from the server named near_server map to login near_server_user. (You need to run sp_addlogin near_server_user before running sp_addremotelogin.)

```
sp_addremotelogin near_server, near_server_user
```

Using a New Local Name for All Remote Users

Here is the syntax for using a new local name for all remote users:

```
sp_addremotelogin remote_server_name, local_name, remote_name
```

The following is an example:

```
sp_addremotelogin near_server, selected_server_user, mdoe
```

In this example, the login named mdoe on near_server can access far_server using the login selected_server_user. (You still need to run sp_addlogin selected_server_user.)

Removing Logins with *sp_dropremotelogin*

To remove a remote login after adding it, use the sp_dropremotelogin procedure. Here is the syntax:

```
sp_dropremotelogin remote_server [, loginname [, remotename ] ]
```

The following drop statements remove the remote logins added previously:

```
sp_dropremotelogin near_server
sp_dropremotelogin near_server, near_server_user
sp_dropremotelogin near_server, selected_server_user, mdoe
```

Remote Options

A variety of options can be set for specific servers, logins, and remote names. These define the way the server deals with the specific logins. Here is the syntax:

```
sp_remoteoption [remote_server [, login_name [, remote_name]],
    option_name, {true ¦ false}]
```

The only option currently available for sp_remoteoption is trusted which determines whether the local server accepts logins from the remote server without checking passwords. The default is trusted set to false (logins are not trusted), meaning passwords require verification.

In the next example (run on far_server), logins from the near_server that map to the near_server_user login on the local server do not need to verify passwords.

```
sp_remoteoption near_server, near_server_user, null, trusted, true
```

> **NOTE**
>
> If the trusted option is not turned on, you need to establish and maintain synchronized passwords between servers. Very few applications include the capability to transmit a distinct remote password when necessary. For this reason, the trusted option is typically used when mapping remote logins to different login IDs or a single login ID on the local server since it would be unfeasible to try and synchronize passwords in these situations.

Getting Information on Remote Servers

For information on remote servers defined for your server, you can use the sp_helpserver procedure. This procedure reads and decodes information from the sysservers table in the master database. Here is the syntax:

```
sp_helpserver [server_name]
```

Use sp_helpserver without a server name to list all servers defined on your system.

By default, there will be only one server listed in the sysservers table—the name of the local server. Any servers involved with replication will also appear in this list, but only after replication has been configured.

```
sp_helpserver
```

name	network_name	status	id
AMS	AMS	dist	0
KAYDEROSS	KAYDEROSS	rpc,sub	2
NLCWEST1	NLCWEST1	rpc,sub	1

For information on individual logins for a server, use the sp_helpremotelogin command:

```
sp_helpremotelogin [remote_server [, remote_name] ]
```

For a list of remote logins, execute sp_helpremotelogin without a parameter. In the example that follows, there are three different remote logins configured for two different remote servers. The sa logins on both remote servers KAYDEROSS and NLCWEST1 map to the local server login repl_subscriber. All other logins from NLCWEST1 map to the remote_login login ID on the local server. All remote logins are trusted so passwords are not verified.

```
sp_helpremotelogin
```

server	local_user_name	remote_user_name	options
KAYDEROSS	repl_subscriber	sa	trusted
NLCWEST1	remote_login	** mapped locally **	trusted
NLCWEST1	repl_subscriber	sa	trusted

Using Extended Stored Procedures and Open Data Services

SQL Server 4.2 for Windows NT introduced an interesting concept: directly accessing operating system resources from within SQL Server. In implementing its desire to more closely tie SQL Server with Windows NT, an interesting benefit arose: SQL Server could directly call Win32 API functions stored in specially written DLLs. This feature was named Extended Stored Procedures, and represented the first time that any client/server database could directly access and make use of services available to the operating system on which it was hosted.

In order to accomplish this, several requirements must be met. First, in order for SQL Server to call API functions stored in DLLs, those DLLs must be written as Win32 DLLs using the Windows NT API. In addition, the DLLs must also make use of the Open Data Services API, which is an additional, application-level, 32-bit programming interface for developing applications that integrate SQL Server clients and other data sources. Finally, the individual API functions calls must be individually mapped to SQL Server logical names. In effect, creating extended stored procedures is equivalent to writing a header file for a C program or writing an INCLUDE file for a COBOL application.

This level of integration is not possible on any other platform because no other version of SQL Server is so closely tied to its underlying operating system. Remember, Microsoft SQL Server for Windows NT will run only on Windows NT. As such, the only limitations on what resources are available are the features of Windows NT itself.

Depending on the application, extended stored procedures might not be the best way to implement certain functionality using Open Data Services. When using extended stored procedures, the DLL that SQL Server calls is loaded into SQL Server's address space, meaning that any corruptions or protection faults that might occur in the DLL will cause SQL Server to protection fault as well. As a result, extended stored procedures introduce an element of potential failure for SQL Server, depending on the quality and robustness of the DLLs being developed for SQL Server's access.

As an alternative to using extended stored procedures, you can (and depending on the application, possibly should) develop a Windows NT application using the Win32 API that also uses the Open Data Services API. By compiling this application as a separate executable, you gain some important benefits.

First, because it is an Open Data Services application, you can configure the application to appear to SQL Server as a remote server, using the same process described above. In this way, client applications will connect to the Open Data Services application as though it were another SQL Server. Administration is easier for SQL Server administrators because they can treat the ODS application as though it were "just another" SQL Server, making the task of integrating the administration of this application into normal administration routines much easier.

The ODS application isn't considered a special case or exception; it's considered just another SQL Server.

Second, because this application is written as a Win32 executable, you have the option of writing it as a Windows NT *Service*. Services in Windows NT are special applications that make use of, and conform to the rules of, Windows NT's Service Control Manager. Services do not require any desktop interaction; they can run completely in the background. In addition, the Service Control Manager is easily configured using the Services icon in the Windows NT Control Panel. As a result, the AutoStarting properties are easily established, making administration of the application much easier.

Third and most important, because this application is written and compiled to be a separate executable, it runs within its own address space under Windows NT. If this process should generate a protection fault, *only* the ODS application will be trapped out. SQL Server will continue to run unaffected. The prospect of SQL Server failing because of an errant DLL is rather intimidating when you consider that, should you use extended stored procedures, not only will the ODS application be closed down, but SQL Server *and all current user connections* will be closed down as well. If, instead, you rely on remote server access to an Open Data Services application, and if that application fails, only the ODS application will be closed out. SQL Server and all of its current user connections will continue unaffected. The only user connection affected will be the one causing the error in the ODS application. If your application requires high levels of server availability, I recommend that you avoid using extended stored procedures, and use a separate ODS application instead.

Although Microsoft guarantees the integrity of SQL Server in such cases, it cannot guarantee SQL Server's integration with other DLLs. As a result, using separate ODS applications accessed via SQL Server Remote Procedure Calls is typically a more reliable solution.

Summary

Making your server accessible to other servers and able to access other servers requires a number of simple steps. Follow the steps presented in this chapter, and remote access should be working. If you think that you followed the cookbook but remote access is not working, you probably forgot to shut down and subsequently restart the server.

Extended stored procedures represent an interesting and useful technological advance—if it is properly implemented. There are more reliable alternatives, but the business needs of the applications that you support will dictate which is the best choice for your organization.

The Microsoft SQL Server Distributed Management Framework

34

The SQL Server Distributed Management Framework (DMF) is a collection of administrator applications, Windows NT and SQL Server services, and object programmability libraries aimed at enabling the centralized administration of distributed servers. With the SQL Server Enterprise Manager (SQL-EM), administrators can view and manipulate multiple servers from one central console. To achieve this, SQL-EM relies on two other components: the SQL Executive service, and the SQL Distributed Management Objects. This chapter looks at these individual components and their integration into the Distributed Management Framework.

SQL Server Enterprise Manager

With SQL Server 4.2 for Windows NT, Microsoft introduced a suite of very polished administration tools. This was a substantial change for the better. Previous attempts from various vendors—which included such now-historic names as isql, SAF, SA Companion, and Desktop DBA—were good efforts, but they didn't integrate into one desktop all the tasks for which a DBA was responsible. Microsoft's SQL Administrator and SQL Object Manager tools, although possessing a complete feature set, were still a collection of independent applications rather than a central desktop for managing multiple servers. With SQL Server 6.0, Microsoft is introducing such a centralized desktop. The application begins by collecting the various utilities of the SQL Administrator, SQL Object Manager, SQL Transfer Manager, SQL Server Manager, and SQL Setup. From there, it adds administration capabilities for replication, task scheduling, and a detailed viewer of current system and activity.

The desktop interface can be configured to present any server on the network. Servers can also be grouped into nested hierarchies of folders (or server groups), so that the console can logically organize separate collections and groups of servers, and even groups within groups. By relying on a drag-and-drop interface, SQL-EM can easily reorganize the desktop as well. The SQL-EM application does not physically change the underlying server in any way. For example, one administrator creates three server groups named West, Central, and East, and puts servers from cities in those regions into those groups; the servers themselves do not know that any SQL-EM console (my own included) has grouped them or registered them. Another administrator can configure her groups going vertically across the US, such as in North, Central, and South groupings. In both cases, the servers underneath know nothing of the grouping structure on the individual administrator consoles.

In addition, the SQL-EM application does not have an interface into the domain structure of the underlying network. If you are running nested domains of Windows NT networks, SQL Server is only aware of servers that are within the local domain, or servers that might be in trusted domains. SQL-EM does not group servers according to your domain structure, because the server itself does not know how it is registered on a particular administrator's console. Also, SQL-EM only recognizes Version 6.0 SQL Servers.

Architecturally, the SQL-EM application is written to Win32 specifications, and therefore it runs on Windows NT and Windows 95 workstations. The interfaces of the two versions are functionally identical, providing the same drag-and-drop interface for server management, menus, dialogs, and so on, with the Windows 95 version obviously using the new interface components of that operating system. The SQL-EM application has been written to be context-sensitive for right mouse-click operations on both operating systems, so that administrators can choose either desktop, with some important considerations. Because Windows 95 does not use a Service Control Manager like Windows NT does, certain API functions for controlling the SCM are not available in Windows 95. As such, SQL-EM on Windows 95 workstations will not be able to stop, pause, or start the MSSQLSERVER and SQLEXECUTIVE services. For complete control and maximum flexibility of administration for SQL 6.0 servers, Windows NT is the preferred desktop for SQL-EM.

SQL Enterprise Manager relies on two other components—the SQL Executive and the SQL Distributed Management Objects—for many of its administration tasks. With the SQL Executive, the old SQL Monitor becomes more than a simple task scheduler for SQL Server backup services. Instead, SQL Executive becomes an automated administrator of SQL Server, performing according to schedules and responding to system exceptions.

Instead of diving into a grotesque discussion of menu items and dialogs, demonstration of SQL Enterprise Manager's features and interface will come through discussion of configuring automated tasks, exception processing, and configuring alerts and operators.

SQL Executive, Exception Processing, and Task Scheduling

The original SQL Monitor was a useful application for scheduling database backups from within SQL Administrator. With the new SQL Executive service replacing SQL Monitor, the capability to schedule tasks is not limited to simple backup routines. Instead, SQL Executive has been architected to use a collection of subsystems that invoke different types of tasks according to time-based schedules. SQL Executive relies on these subsystems—as well as a new SQL Server system database, msdb—to provide a complete, server-based administrative automation facility to enable timed execution of any SQL Server–related task. These various components are all interdependent, so discussing them becomes a chicken-and-egg problem.

Let's begin by discussing the SQL Executive service and then move into SQL Server's new exception-processing facilities. Then you walk through the msdb database that stores the information necessary for all of these to work. You finish with a discussion of the SQL Distributed Management Objects that are used to create and manage these new tasks and open a new world of administrative programmability previously unavailable to administrators strapped by administrative limitations of Structured Query Language.

SQL Monitor in SQL Server 4.2 allowed administrators to schedule a regular database or transaction log backup. However, what if—before performing that backup—an administrator also wanted to perform a DBCC CHECKALLOC and UPDATE STATISTICS in that database? Previously, that would have required some third party client-based application to manage the schedule for executing a script file containing these various commands. That capability has been provided by applications such as SQL Commander or DesktopDBA for some time, but they are always a separate, *client-based* process. As such, they are subject to all of the points of failure associated with using such an application, and also multi-server administration becomes a configuration nightmare. Instead, SQL Executive relies on scheduling information stored in msdb tables, in conjunction with its own callable subsystems, to put all of the scheduling, activation, and execution history completely within the server itself. The only need for a client process to access this information is for configuration and reporting purposes.

So just what are these subsystems? SQL Server 6.0 initially ships with five different types of tasks that can be executed. The TSQL and CmdExec subsystems are for general use. The other three are reserved for data replication, which is discussed in Chapter 35, "Introduction to Microsoft SQL Server 6.0 Replication." With the T-SQL and CmdExec subsystems, SQL Server can execute Transact-SQL scripts stored within the database or send any command to the Windows NT console command prompt to start off an executable file.

To use the earlier example, an administrator can create a T-SQL script that performs a DBCC CHECKALLOC and an update statistics, and then performs a complete database backup. This script can either be "naked" Transact-SQL stored in msdb, or it can also be a stored procedure call that has the necessary TSQL inside it, allowing you to pass the name of a specific database to process as a parameter, for example. That T-SQL script, whether it is a true script or a stored procedure call, is stored within a table in the msdb database and is read as a character value from those tables.

From there, the command string is passed to the T-SQL subsystem, which executes that command against the appropriate server. CmdExec enables you to specify the command string isql -Usa -P -ic:\backup.sql -o\backup.out, triggering the subsystem to open a background command line task and send that string to the c: prompt, executing ISQL within that window. SQL Executive subsystems then become an access point to the outside world for SQL Server.

SQL Executive has been built to use a layered, modular architecture that relies on a different command processor for each type of subsystem command. As subsystems are added, additional command types are available for processing. The diagram shown in Figure 34.1 illustrates how these pieces fit together.

In conjunction with the msdb database, SQL Executive executes tasks based on scheduling information held in msdb. This scheduling information enables a flexible schedule for task automation, including any combination of time increment or interval measured in months, weeks, days, hours, or minutes. By using the scheduler, administrators can create a backup task that dumps the entire database once each week on Saturday at midnight. A separate task can run only on weekdays at 6 a.m. and perform a transaction log backup instead. Any valid Windows NT command-line syntax or any valid T-SQL command script can be executed in this fashion.

FIGURE 34.1.

SQL Executive relies on five additional components for all task scheduling.

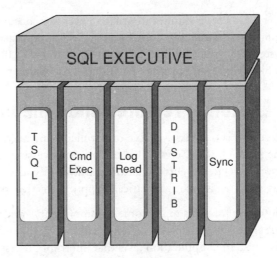

SQL Server Task-Processing Terminology

With all this new technology, Microsoft wouldn't be Microsoft without inventing a slew of new jargon to go along with it. Understanding these terms at least clarifies the units of work that SQL Server and SQL Executive manage, as well as the areas of work that an administrator must manage. Here are some of the most significant terms:

- Task: A task is a series of instructions that are to be processed by one of the SQL Executive's five core subsystems. Tasks that can be scheduled by administrators can be either TSQL statements (including batches of statements and stored procedures, which includes remote stored procedures), or CmdExec statements, which are executables that are run in background Windows NT CONSOLE sessions (from the command line).

- Schedule: A schedule is the combination of date and time interval and increment constructs, which define the execution of a particular task. SQL Executive reads the schedule information associated with each task and executes that task accordingly.

- msdb: A new system database created by SQL Server at installation time that stores all task scheduling, event handling, and alert notification information, as well as a history of all system- and application-generated events.

- Operator: An operator is the designated recipient of a particular alert or series of alerts.

- Event: An event is a system- or application-generated exception that meets three criteria: First, it is posted to the Windows NT Event Log application. Second, it is posted with a source of SQLServer. Third, the SQL Server error message is registered in the master..sysmessages table.

■ Alert: An alert is notification that an event has occurred. Alerts are transmitted using, at present, two media: e-mail (via the MAPI interface and a MAPI-compliant e-mail system), or pager (via the TAPI interface and a TAPI-compliant paging system, such as SkyTel or other message-based paging services provider).

Task-Execution Features and Schedules

Task execution is not just available on a timed, scheduled basis. SQL Executive has also become the heart of SQL Server 6.0's exception processing capability, with which system- and application-generated events can automatically notify scheduled operators and administrators, as well as activate tasks to automatically apply corrective measures.

Before jumping into this topic, some common terms need to be specifically defined. In SQL Server exception processing, three terms are specifically defined. *Events* are exceptions generated at the system or application level that interrupt processing. Although they are more commonly known as *error messages*, there are some additional criteria. Error messages must meet certain criteria before they can be considered events. First, the error must have a severity level of 19 through 25. Second, the error must be logged into the Windows NT Event Log in the application subsystem. Third, that event must have associated with it a source of SQLServer. When these three conditions have been met, a true SQL Server event has occurred.

When an event occurs, SQL Server—in conjunction with the SQL Executive—has two processing options. An *alert*, which is simply notification that an event has occurred, can be sent to an *operator* (or series of operators). An alert can contain alert information, customized messages, and other process-related information. *Operators* are listed and scheduled into the msdb database as well, so that a particular operator on duty at a particular time is notified—a particularly nasty way of delegating beepus interruptus for the newest members in the support organization (depending on your perspective on things). In addition to time-based scheduling of operators, messages of a particular type or severity can be directly assigned to particular operators regardless of their schedule. The actual notification that is sent is delivered using any combination of MAPI and/or TAPI, so that both e-mail and pagers can be contacted for sending out the alert notification.

With alert processing, SQL Server now has the capability to deliver a message of an exception within the system or an application to either the current operator on duty or a particular operator, based on the type of message that is generated. However, simple notification doesn't fix the problem, and automation of those fixes can often be achieved by combining the event detection features of SQL Executive with its capability to execute T-SQL and CmdExec tasks, which is how the final term *actions* is defined.

An action, in SQL Server alert processing, is a T-SQL script or stored procedure or a CmdExec command-line executable or process that is executed in conjunction with an event being detected by the SQL Executive. In this way, not only can tasks be scheduled in terms of time-based execution, but also SQL Server itself can execute tasks based on exception or error conditions that occur at the system or application level. The terms *action* and *task* describe two different ways of invoking a similar command structure. With SQL 6.0, both *notification* and *execution* of corrective measures can be automatically initiated by the server engine itself, without reliance on a separate client application running over the network connected to the specific server.

This feature is available to both the DBMS and any applications running on the DBMS. This is achieved through two important changes to the RAISERROR command. Previously, RAISERROR could only raise custom error strings that had an error number outside the range of 0 to 20,000 because SQL Server reserved these error numbers for its own use. With SQL Server 6.0, RAISERROR can now be used to call both application-level messages (outside the reserved range) and system-level messages that are in the range. Therefore, an application can now return the dreaded error 1205 (Your server command number was deadlocked with another process and has been chosen as the deadlock victim...) or any other standard error message held in sysmessages.

SQL Server 6.0 has a new system stored procedure, sp_addmessage, which enables you to add your own error messages to the sysmessages table, allowing sysmessages to be a central catalog of error messages both for SQL Server and for any applications using that SQL Server. Any message contained within sysmessages—whether created by SQL Server at the time it is installed or added later using sp_addmessage—can be called using RAISERROR. In addition, RAISERROR has a new WITH LOG option that puts the error message into the Windows NT Event Log, with a source of SQL Server. You'll notice that this enables the exception processing capability discussed earlier, by allowing applications to raise both system- and application-level error messages with a severity level greater than 18 (including those added to sysmessages using sp_addmessage), logging them into the Event Log (using the WITH LOG option), and specifying a source of SQL Server (which is handled automatically by RAISERROR). Clearly, this is a powerful exception handling facility that is sure to be a hot topic for database administrators who prefer sleep at 2 a.m. over the shrill cry of a beeper in their left ear.

Within the Win32 API, a subset of that API allows applications to register themselves with the Event Log as *callback processes.* In simplest terms, that registration allows an application to define certain actions that the Event Log itself will take if it receives a particular event, from a specific source, matching particular criteria. When SQL Server 6.0 starts, part of its initialization routine is to register itself as a callback process with the Event Log, and included in that registration are the requirements that make up a SQL Server 6.0 event.

Procedurally, the exception processing architecture of SQL Server 6.0 is quite elegant. (See Figure 34.2.) In step 1, SQL Server generates an error message that is passed to the NT Event log. SQL Server, having already instructed the Event Log to notify SQL Executive in case of any errors, sends notification of a potential error to SQL Executive. In step 3, the Windows NT Event Log contacts SQL Executive, which in turn scans the Event Log for the last-generated message. SQL Executive fetches that message and compares it with configuration information held in the msdb database, in step 5. Based on the contents of msdb, SQL Executive sends e-mail, pages the appropriate operator, or activates the appropriate task, as in step 6.

FIGURE 34.2.

The Exception-Processing Architecture of SQL Server 6.0.

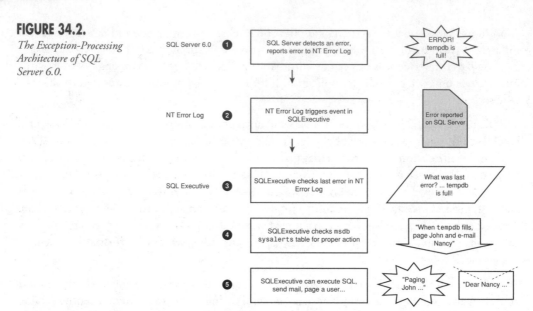

SQL Server Task Execution and Tracking

There are some important implementational considerations to keep in mind when using the exception handling facilities of SQL Server. First, SQL Server records everything it does regarding exception handling. With the `sysnotifications` table, SQL Server records who was notified and based on which particular event. With the `syshistory` table, SQL Server records the execution of all tasks, including those activated by the time-based scheduler or those activated in response to an event. This occurs with each instance of a task being executed, and the log is persistent until it is manually cleared. Therefore, on systems where there are large numbers of scheduled and event-based tasks, pruning that history is an important capacity-management consideration.

Second, each exception is processed within its own context. For example, 12 different users are all executing a stored procedure at the same time. Each of those processes generates an error condition. Each of those 12 error conditions is received, interpreted, and processed independently of the others—which means that, potentially, 12 e-mail messages, 12 pager beeps, and 12 corresponding tasks can be executed. This may or may not be desirable based on the processing of the application. In addition, a task that is called by an exception or event is capable of generating its own events, which starts the process all over again; but, once again, this is within a logical and physical context that is independent of any others currently active on the SQL Server. In this way, a lack of forethought, planning, and most importantly *testing* of the exception handling architecture that you create can lead to a series of closed-loop responses that eventually bring down your server.

The *msdb* database

The msdb database forms the heart of the task scheduling engine. Within msdb, there are five critical tables that hold all of the information necessary for the SQL Executive to function. These five tables cooperate with SQL Executive and store all of the task, operator, event, alter, and execution information for any task on a particular server. They not only tell SQL Executive what commands to execute, but also on what basis that execution should occur. Finally, there is a logging feature within SQL Server that allows for storage of the complete history of SQL Executive's execution.

The systasks table holds all task information. A *task* is an individual unit of work, that can consist of a command-line batch file name, a Transact-SQL script, or a stored procedure call. Any valid command-line syntax (for the CmdExec subsystem) or Transact-SQL statement (for the TSQL subsystem) is considered a valid task, and that call is stored as a text string in the systasks table. The systasks table uniquely identifies each task using a task ID and associates the particular subsystem used to execute that task. In addition, the particular database name and all time-based scheduling information are held in this table. Finally, the last column of the table holds the actual command string that SQL Executive will execute. Therefore, executing select * from systasks will show you any command and all scheduling information for that command on the particular server you are querying.

Similar in function to systasks, the sysoperators table holds information about the operators or administrators who can respond to particular events. With the sysoperators table, SQL Server enables you to specify contacting the operator on duty, contacting a particular operator, or contacting a general *fail-safe* operator for each event. The fail-safe operator is contacted for all events and is a global configuration option for the server. The sysoperators table holds information regarding an operator's schedule, as well as contact information. For example, an individual operator can be contacted using e-mail or pager, so both of those addresses are held in sysoperators, as is the work schedule for that operator. For example, I might be on duty from 6 p.m. to 6 a.m. every weekday, but I might get weekends off. Or, if I happen to exist farther down the corporate food chain, I might be responsible for Thursday, Friday, Saturday, and Sunday nights. In the event that I cannot be contacted when I am on schedule (say, I just happen to jump in my neighbor's Jacuzzi with my beeper still attached to my swim trunks), the fail-safe operator is contacted. All contacts, or contact attempts, are logged and recorded.

The sysalerts table is used to tell SQL Executive which events or exceptions to look for in the Windows NT Event Log and, also, what SQL Executive should do if it ever finds one of those events. The sysalerts table allows an administrator to configure an alert to look for particular characteristics of an event, such as the message ID number, the severity level, or (optionally) text included in the error message itself. In the alert processing architecture for SQL Executive, the sysalerts table is capable of holding a *comparison string* that is used to compare alerts with error messages being generated, so that a single alert could potentially respond to multiple error conditions. For example, there are 13 error messages in the syslogs table that contain the word `syslogs`. However, there is only one `out of space` error for `syslogs`. By using a comparison string of just `syslogs`, I can have a particular alert respond to any of those 13 error messages. However, if I want to trap an `out of space` error, I would use `If you ran out of space in syslogs` as my comparison string, because that uniquely identifies the error I'm attempting to trap. The `sysalerts` table contains the necessary information about operators and tasks to have either or both directly associated with the error. In `sysalerts`, the `task_id` column is associated with the `systasks.task_id` column to tell the alert which task it should execute.

The `sysnotifications` table works with both `sysalerts` and `sysoperators` to join alerts, operators, and also the notification method used to contact the particular operator. These are the only three columns in this table.

The `syshistory` table is an important one. `Syshistory` records the execution history of every task scheduled on a particular SQL Server. With `syshistory`, an individual task's execution data and time are recorded, as is the run duration for the task and its completion status of either success or failure. With this table, SQL Server is capable of maintaining a complete operational history of itself.

There are, however, some important implementational considerations. Although `syshistory` can record every task's execution history, it requires data rows in a table to do so. Therefore, the `syshistory` table can grow to be quite large, particularly in "high task count" servers when much of the exception processing has been automated. Consequently, space and capacity considerations must be addressed early on. Second, the transaction log for this database can become full quickly, because the `syshistory` table will be the destination for many insert statements. Third, the `syshistory` table and the Windows NT Event Log are duplicating many of the same functions. This might not be desirable, depending on how you want to store the information generated by SQL Executive. For example, although the Event Log can hold information, it does run out of space at some point, forcing either a manual save of the file to disk or truncation of the event log itself. As such, it doesn't necessarily represent a permanent storage place for event information. In addition, the Event Log provides no querying interface, which makes searching for repeated occurrences of a single event, or performing trend analysis on the server, very difficult. By keeping that information in `syshistory`, any querying tool can be used to examine the information held there, and administrators can now keep, at the server, valid analytical statistics about the server and start to predict events and trends instead of just respond to them.

SQL Distributed Management Objects

With the creation of System R from IBM in the late 1970s, IBM developers attempted to create a database language that could not only serve as a data retrieval tool for application support but also have standardized administration syntax for operational support. What has resulted from this effort, in spite of ANSI's best efforts, has become a vendor-specific implementation of a variety of commands, procedures, functions, and other inconsistent syntax that have made SQL a kludgy administration facility. For example, creating a space for database storage in SQL

Server requires using the disk init command, which specifies a size parameter for that space in 2KB page units. However, to remove that space allocation, you must use the sp_dropdevice stored procedure. In addition, if you are going to create a database on that device, you must use a number measured in megabytes, not 2KB pages. Such inconsistency has consistently irritated SQL Server administrators. In retrospect, the idea that a data access and retrieval language can also ideally function as a server administration language is ill-conceived.

With the SQL Server Distributed Management Objects, there is consistency in access to administrative commands, procedures, and configuration parameters for SQL Server. With the SQL-DMO, applications that have an OLE Automation interface can manipulate SQL Server through objects, properties, and methods, instead of arcane and inconsistent TSQL syntax. For example, instead of disk init or sp_dropdevice, you can use the CREATE and DROP methods of the DEVICE object (in code, this would be DEVICE.CREATE and DEVICE.DROP), to perform these functions. Any OLE Automation application—in particular, those that have Visual Basic for Applications enabled—can use the SQL-DMO libraries to administer any property or configuration option for SQL Server, or even groups of SQL Servers. With SQL-DMO, the power of collections, or groups of similar object types, can automate many common tasks that must be performed across many objects within a server, or even across many servers. For example, the following sample VBA shows how you can, with a simple FOR...NEXT loop, perform an UPDATE STATISTICS on every table in a database.

```
Sub UpdateStats()
Set MyServer = CreateObject("sqlole.SQLServer")
MyServer.Connect "AMS", "dwoodbeck", "dw"

I = 1
For Each MyTable In MyServer.Databases("pubs").Tables
    I = I + 1
    MyTable.UpdateStatistics
Next
MyServer.Close

End Sub
```

The MyServer.Connect method establishes a standard user connection to SQL Server using AMS as the server name, dwoodbeck as the login, and dw as the password. If you are using integrated security, you can simply specify nulled quotes for these parameters.

Because the SQL-DMO libraries enable you to reference the TABLES collection, which is a dynamic listing of all individual tables within this particular database, I can use the FOR loop to process the command on each table iteratively. This process occurs in serial fashion, so the UPDATE STATISTICS on the first table must complete before the UPDATE STATISTICS on the second table can begin. The TABLES collection referenced earlier is built dynamically by the client application at runtime, meaning that the code does not have to change to take object creation/deletion into account when it is run. Any tables that exist in sysobjects when this code runs will have UPDATE STATISTICS executed on them. Any tables that you create after running this code, or any tables that you drop before running this code, will not be affected.

With one more FOR...NEXT loop, as in the following example, you can expand this operation to perform the UPDATE STATISTICS on each table within each database on your server.

```
Sub UpdateStats()
Set MyServer = CreateObject("sqlole.SQLServer")
MyServer.Connect "AMS", "dwoodbeck", "dw"

For Each MyDatabase in MyServer.Databases
For Each MyTable In MyDatabase.Tables
MyTable.UpdateStatistics
Next
Next
MyServer.Close

End Sub
```

In this example, the code looks at each database as one unique instance within the DATABASES collection and iteratively processes the FOR loop within each database. That nested FOR loop then looks at each table as one unique instance within the TABLES collection and iteratively processes the FOR loop (this one containing the actual UPDATE STATISTICS command) on every table within that collection.

With the release of SQL Server 6.0, the SQL-DMO libraries are a client access method to SQL Server for administrative purposes. There are only limited data access and data retrieval objects for gathering and manipulating data in SQL Server tables. Instead, the SQL-DMO's target audience is administrators who are responsible for managing and maintaining the server's configuration for other applications that use SQL Server for data access. In this way, Microsoft is both providing improved desktop application support for administering servers and also adding the unique capability of programmatic administration of SQL Server. The SQL-DMO libraries encompass all facets of server administration, including replication, task scheduling, security, login management, capacity management for disk devices and databases, and object management. The SQL-DMO libraries are actually called natively by the SQL Enterprise Manager, instead of SQL-EM relying on TSQL commands and stored procedures.

As an implementational note, the SQL-DMO libraries are also Win32-only facilities. Any 32-bit, OLE Automation-enabled program can take advantage of the SQL-DMO libraries, such as the 32-bit edition of Visual Basic 4.0, Excel for Windows NT, Excel for Windows 95, and MS Access for Windows 95.

Summarizing the SQL-DMF Architecture and Features

As this rather lengthy discussion illustrates, Microsoft has spent considerable effort improving the tools available to administrators of SQL Server databases. With a centralized desktop interface for managing multiple servers, as well as building a programmability interface specifically targeted to server administrators and making the upgrade/installation process more complete, the SQL Server administrative facilities finally enable administrators to treat Microsoft SQL Server as a legitimate platform for self-administering, high-availability applications. The final question becomes "How do you make SQL Server do all of these things?"

How to Configure Tasks, Operators, and Alerts

Now that you know what SQL Server can do for you, how do you configure tasks, alerts, and all of the administration-related services? Configuring SQL Server's automated task scheduling begins with the SQL Enterprise Manager application.

In SQL Enterprise Manager, you can display the Task Scheduling dialog box by clicking on the Task Scheduling button on the toolbar (shown in Figure 34.3) or by choosing the Tools | Task Scheduling... menu sequence.

FIGURE 34.3.

SQL Enterprise Manager uses both toolbars and menu sequences to administer servers.

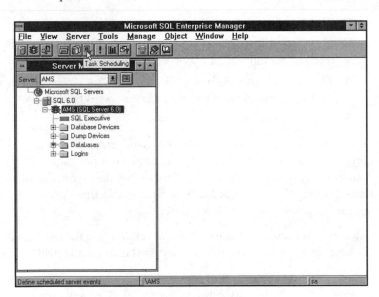

Clicking on the first button in the toolbar (and the only one that is available, if you have no prior tasks configured) brings up the Add Task dialog box illustrated in Figure 34.4. In this dialog box, you will define the identifying properties of this particular task. We'll get to the task schedule in just a moment.

FIGURE 34.4.

SQL Enterprise Manager's New Task dialog box enables you to graphically define task properties, including operator notification and execution schedules.

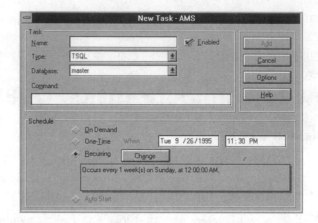

Defining tasks requires defining both the task properties and the task schedule. The properties include the following:

- The task name, which must be unique on the server
- The task type, which for now must be TSQL or CmdExec because the others are reserved for replication
- The database that the task will use (which can be changed in your script, if you choose), particularly if you are calling a stored procedure
- The command string

If you are creating a TSQL task, the command string must be a valid TSQL statement or stored procedure call. Fully qualified naming syntax is support for calling stored procedures that are not in the current database or the database you define for the task. However, the TSQL command string will be compiled and executed within the context of the database that you defined in the "database property" listed above.

Task names must be unique within a server. Because the tasks are stored in the systasks table in msdb, SQL Server has a primary key on the task name field.

There are two other sets of information that you must define for a task. Each task you create has a default schedule (as shown in Figure 34.4), as well as a series of options about the task.

Changing a task's schedule requires you to plan how and when this task should execute. In fact, planning your task scheduling regimen is far more important than learning how to configure such tasks. However, because planning operational support is a shop-specific task, we'll stick to the technical details.

This task will dump the pubs database on a regular schedule. Task names conform to the standards for SQL Server identifiers, meaning 30 contiguous alphanumeric characters with only the underscore (_) character as punctuation. For this task, let's call it DumpPubsTx. Because you are executing a dump database command, the command type must be TSQL. The database is master, because it need not be changed. The command string for this task will be dump database pubs to disk = "c:\pubs.dmp". Notice that TSQL commands cannot return result rows; there is no client application to receive them! However, you can configure a CmdExec task to execute an isql script from the command window, using the -i and -o command-line flags to provide input and output files for the session.

Clicking on the Change button in the lower part of the screen displays the Task Schedule dialog box. (See Figure 34.5.)

FIGURE 34.5.

SQL Server Enterprise Manager enables you to define any combination of increment and interval for both date and time information.

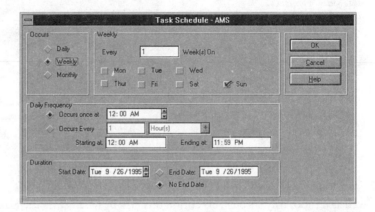

In this dialog box, you first define the increments of days for your task to execute. Execution can be daily, weekly, or monthly, including particular days of the week, days of the month, or particular days during particular weeks during the month.

> **NOTE**
>
> SQL Server 6.0 lets you shoot yourself in the foot with task scheduling however you choose—one toe at a time, or the whole foot! Using this book and the SQL Server documentation, you should have a clear understanding of how to create tasks. Planning those tasks, however, is an important step in creating a truly solid automated administration architecture.

After you have defined the daily/weekly/monthly section of the schedule, the next section defines the "time of day" portion of the schedule. Tasks can be recurring during the day, or they can execute only once on each day at a particular time. The last section of the dialog box enables you to set start dates and stop dates for the schedule as a whole, suspending the task when the "final day" threshold has been reached.

Task options are used to define how SQL Server will track and execute tasks, as well as to define what happens if the task fails. Clicking on the Options button in the Add Task dialog box displays the TSQL Task Option dialog box, shown in Figure 34.6, where you configure task options.

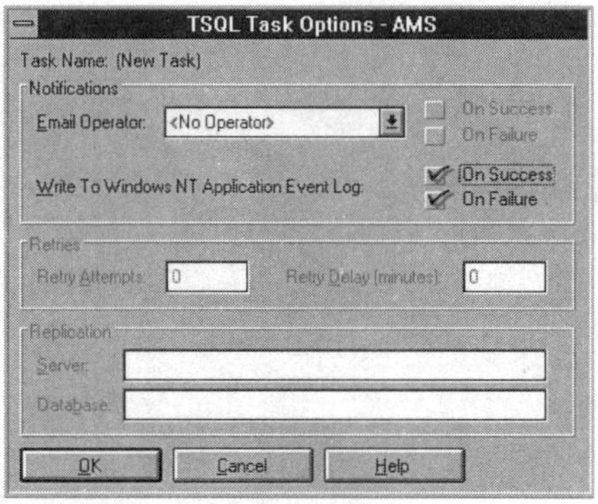

FIGURE 34.6.

SQL Server monitors its own task execution, and it can notify operators if tasks fail or succeed.

Notice that you can e-mail a particular operator (discussed shortly in the section on alerts), as well as temporarily suspend execution of a task by deselecting the Enabled check box. The task remains defined in the msdb tables, but SQL Executive will not execute that task while it is disabled.

Having completed these various options, you can click on OK to go back through the maze of dialog boxes, and your completed task is now available for SQL Executive.

Monitoring Your Server's Task Execution

SQL Server uses the syshistory table to store the execution history of every task, alert, and exception that has occurred on the local server. This information is displayed in the Task History child window. (See Figure 34.7.) All task types, including those used for replication services, are stored here. SQL Server enables you to define a retention period for such log entries, preventing the syshistory table from consuming all of the space in msdb. Clicking on the Task Engine Options button in the toolbar displays a dialog box that enables you to set the maximum number of rows that syshistory can contain. The syshistory table can also be flushed dynamically by using the Clear All button.

FIGURE 34.7.

Enterprise Manager's Task History window displays summary information about individual task executions.

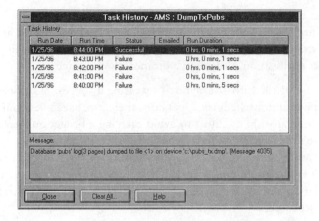

Configuring Operators

Configuring alerts takes place in the SQL Enterprise Manager application. Click on the Alerts button in the toolbar (look for the exclamation mark), or use the Server | Alerts... menu sequence. This presents you with the Manage Alerts child window, which should list the nine demonstration alerts that SQL Server installs by default. Clicking on the Operators tab of the window enables the operators toolbar, which is highlighted by rather cute firefighter's hats. (Can Microsoft design icons or what?) Clicking on the first of the three icons displays the dialog box shown in Figure 34.8, where you can define your operators and their schedules.

FIGURE 34.8.

SQL Server's New Operator dialog box allows you to define who should be notified in the event of a particular exception or error condition.

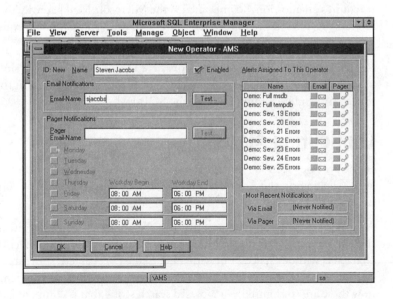

With the Add Operator dialog box, you can define operator names, as well as how they are notified. E-mail notification is provided on demand; that is, any time an alert is generated by an error condition, the designated operator will receive e-mail regardless of day or time. With pager notification, things get a bit more complicated.

Because of the intrusive nature of wearing a beeper, SQL Server allows an administrator to define operator schedules. Operators, therefore, have a vested interest in being very nice to the administrator, in an effort to avoid carrying a beeper on weekends! The schedules allow for active times during weekdays, as well as distinct active times for Saturdays and Sundays. Notice that these schedules are for the whole week, but they can't be varied by week of the month. So, if you're configured as a SQL Server operator, you are on call every week, but only on particular days of the week. The Enabled check box allows you to temporarily suspend an operators schedule.

In the grid at the right, operators can be assigned particular alerts and tasks to which they respond. They can only be notified by tasks that are in this list, or where they are explicitly configured as an operator using the Task Options dialog box.

Microsoft requires the Microsoft Mail 32-bit client (which comes with Windows NT Server and Windows NT Workstation) in order to send both e-mail messages and pager messages. If e-mail is your only wish, only Microsoft Mail is necessary. In fact, setting up a workgroup post office through Windows NT (part of the shipping software) works quite well for small workgroups. Sites that use MS Mail as their primary messaging service are better served with Microsoft Mail Server. In particular, Microsoft Mail Server is required for pager access because it requires an additional component—the Microsoft Mail gateway to TAPI (Telephony API) services. SQL Server requires Mail Server and the TAPI gateway products to send pager alerts to operators.

Remember that configuring operators here means SQL Server is simply adding rows to the `sysalerts` table in the `msdb` database. You can run select queries on this table to verify the information you are adding through the SQL-EM interface.

Configuring Alerts

In the previous section, you opened the Manage Alerts child window in SQL Enterprise Manager. Clicking on the Add Alerts toolbar button displays the New Alert dialog box. (See Figure 34.9.)

Add Alerts defines the error condition in the upper-left corner of the dialog. Alerts use identifiers, so naming alerts forces you to use SQL Server's naming convention of 30 alphanumeric characters without spaces, but with underscore (_) characters. Errors can be defined using one of three criteria: the error number, the error severity (look at the demonstration errors to see how these are configured), or a passed search string that is compared against the error message itself. For example, you could pass the error string `syslogs`, which is contained in 12 different error messages. Any of these 12 messages could trigger this particular alert.

FIGURE 34.9.

SQL Server's New Alert dialog box allows you to define error conditions and how SQL Server will automatically respond to those conditions by error number, by error severity, or by searching for messages that match a particular character string.

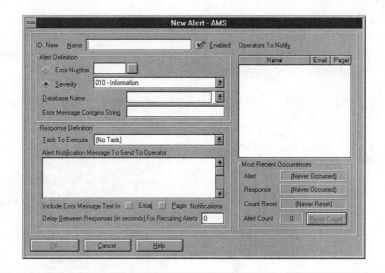

Beneath the alert definition is the *alert response.* This is where SQL Server provides automatic exception processing, by associating a particular task to a particular error condition. You can include notification that the task was fired in the e-mail or pager message that you send to the operator for this alert as well, so that the operator is automatically informed that SQL Server has already taken corrective action in response to the alert. To prevent repeated paging, the Retries interval allows an alert to occur multiple times within a specific period, with no new alert being sent out until that period of time has passed.

As with all SQL Executive features, SQL Server keeps track of both the last date and time a particular operator was notified, as well as the last time an alert was generated for a particular exception.

The Alert Engine Options toolbar button displays the particularly powerful dialog box shown in Figure 34.10. The dialog is important because it allows your server to define a fail-safe operator and pass alerts to another server. The designated server performs the notification operations. The fail-safe operator is notified in the event that no operators are assigned a particular task, or if notification attempts for an operator fail the "retry" number of times.

The Unhandled SQL Server-Event Forwarding Server section of this dialog allows an error condition to be passed to a different server, and that server's SQL Executive and alert configurations trigger operator notification from that server. It is particularly useful if a server does not have access to Microsoft Mail but does have access to the network and another Microsoft SQL Server. Remember, though, that the new server designated as the alert recipient treats that error as a *local* error, so administrators will have to ensure that common error processing routines are specified across all servers.

This feature enables you to centralize all error notification at a single server point. Servers on the network forward their error conditions to the "alert server," which then processes the e-mail and pager notifications. Unfortunately, any task execution must be configured and fired from the local server, so the remote server cannot execute tasks configured to fire automatically in the event of an alert. Alerts can be filtered by severity level, allowing only certain levels to be passed to the forwarding server.

FIGURE 34.10.

The Alert Engine Options dialog box enables you to configure fail-safe operators that are contacted as a last-ditch effort.

Summary

SQL Server's Distributed Management Framework combines a variety of native and foreign technologies to create a new toolkit for SQL Server administrators. Most commonly used will be SQL Server's new exception handling and task automation features, which depend on SQL Executive for their execution. With the delivery of 32-bit development tools for OLE Automation applications, Microsoft now has the additional toolkits necessary to maximize usage of the SQL Distributed Management Objects. By using a standardized object-based API, administrators can circumvent using arcane and inconsistent Transact-SQL statements for server administration.

This chapter represents only the beginning of what you can do with SQL Server's task scheduling features. As is the case with most complex systems, the real difficulties do not lie in the technology or configuring the server. Instead, the real work lies in planning the alert architecture. All of these features require processing power, so careful planning is a must to efficiently use those CPU cycles.

Introduction to Microsoft SQL Server 6.0 Replication

IN THIS CHAPTER

Introduction to Data Distribution Technologies

One of the most powerful features of host-based applications lies not in the size of databases or the number of users that could access centralized data, but in the availability of data and access to it from all points of the globe. The communication technology supporting the traditional host-based computing structure provided the apparatus necessary for multiple, geographically distant application sessions to access the one and only centralized data store. There was no need for a data-distribution interface or facility because there was no data distribution.

With client/server databases, the exact opposite was true. To most MIS professionals, early versions of SQL Server, Oracle, Informix, and so on were merely wanna-be facsimiles of the "real" mainframe-based databases, and worked for small applications that the MIS group would otherwise ignore. In the past 5 to 10 years, both the database engines themselves and the hardware platforms that host those database engines have now grown sufficiently in size and complexity to host large-scale applications that are critical to business operations—and still, there is a need to satisfy the demands of remote access.

The real data-accessibility question isn't the database server or the application; it is connectivity. Remote users on a mainframe system long ago answered questions that network infrastructure planners are only beginning to grapple with on Windows NT– or UNIX-based networks, and at the forefront of those issues is WAN integration. Until the LAN-to-WAN-to-LAN-to-MAN (ad nauseam) issues are resolved, corporations need a means of distributing data that is compatible with existing networks and transports, capable of consuming minimal network resources, and inexpensive. Up to now, the only option has been to choose any two. You could have compatibility, and have it inexpensively, but network consumption was astronomical. You could have compatibility and minimal network drain, but you would have written lots of big zeroes in your checkbook. That is, until now.

> **NOTE**
>
> Asynchronous data distribution has actually been available in SQL Server since version 1.0, as long as you had a number of well-paid people to manage database backup and restoration. For one project I was involved in early on with SQL Server version 1.0 on OS/2 (running on Compaq 386/20s with 16MB of RAM, no less!), we took consolidated financial data from Dun & Bradstreet Millenium VSAM files on our mainframe and moved the data through DCA CommServer (another badge of courage in my war chest) to SQL Server. From SQL Server, stored procedures partitioned the data into the 13 divisions of the company. There were 14 databases involved. The primary server held all of the consolidated data, and then one database for each of the divisions. The data was partitioned into the divisional databases, and then the databases were backed

up to hard disk files. (No, tape wasn't available from Sytos until 4.2, if I recall correctly.) The hard disk files were compressed using a complex data-tokening algorithm (commonly referred to as PKZip by its creator, Phil Katz), and the compressed files were then sent to the administrators of the local divisions, who manually restored the files, loaded them into the local SQL Servers, and—voilà!—data replication.

Considering the bronze-age sophistication of the tools available, the biweekly refresh of data proceeded rather smoothly when all parties involved had been properly trained. The problem was that it took 14 well-trained and, at that point, very expensive SQL Server/LAN manager administrators to keep the whole works up and running, not to mention the support staff and processing time on the mainframe side of the equation.

Clearly, computing structures that provide distributed data and access to a variety of data sources are going to increase in popularity, and have already done so to the point that Sybase, Oracle, and now Microsoft are providing some kind of data replication and distribution technology in their product line. It is important to remember, though, that whether it's through SQL Server's backup/restore facility or through BCP, data distribution is available and cheap if you don't count "people time."

For those solving problems with technology instead of people, SQL Server has also provided a different, programmatic interface to data distribution, using the *2-Phase Commit* (2PC) features of DB-Library. Instead of just distributing data, 2PC actually enables the *physical* distribution of a single *logical* database across multiple servers, or continuously up-to-date copies of the same database on multiple servers. The purpose of such a feature is to provide servers and databases that are perfectly synchronized at all times, at the expense of network resource consumption and multiuser throughput. This, in fact, is the key difference between 2PC and data or transaction replication.

2-Phase Commit gives the capability to apply a single transaction to multiple servers at the same time, and with dependent logging. In the specific case of SQL Server, this last part about "dependent logging" is critical because transaction logs that are on different servers operate independently of one another. With 2PC, a client application is able to modify data on the first server, then modify it on the second server. It validates the change on server 1, and then on server 2. Finally, it commits the transaction on both servers. If the commit on either side fails, *both* sides must have the transaction rolled back. For example, 2PC is an invaluable component to developing applications that rely on fault-tolerant or "hot backup" capable servers. A single client application applies a single transaction across two servers. If the first server is not detected, the client application can notify a central administration desk and then automatically route its transactions over to the backup server. Because both servers have had the same transactions synchronously applied, they are exact replicas of each other during the time they are operational. Although this type of processing is now more commonly implemented with Open Data Services or other gateway applications, 2PC has been a viable alternative for quite some time.

Obviously, the connection, locking, and network overhead of completing transactions using 2PC between even two servers is substantial, and that, combined with the programming fearlessness necessary to write applications that take advantage of this, makes the cost of implementing 2PC applications a very specialized affair. It is also a cost, in terms of overhead and throughput degradation, that is quickly magnified by almost exponential proportions as the number of servers involved increases. Therefore, 2PC is not ideal for simply copying local tables to remote servers to enable easier access. Although replication is a different answer to the question of distributed *data*, it is *not* in any form an answer to the question of distributed *transactions*, for reasons that you'll see soon.

Replication Defined

Replication is the capability to copy one set of data from one source to potentially multiple other sources. Data replication provides a read-only copy of a specific set of data from a data owner to one or many replicate sites. Yes, sports fans, that's right, the copies of data or transactions that you'll be replicating are read-only, and here's why: Replication is an inherently *asynchronous* process, meaning that the *exact timing* of a data change being applied at the source does not affect the exact timing of the change being applied at a replicate site. Therefore, when working in a distributed data environment that uses replication as a model for such data distribution, you must count on the fact that the *only* truly valid copy of the data is the one at the source, because only that one source can be guaranteed to have applied all data changes up through a specific time. For reference, if you were guaranteeing that you were applying a change to data at all sites, and validating that change among all sites before continuing, you would be doing 2-Phase Commit processing—and the overhead of that is just what you're trying to avoid here. Replication trades the overhead and development costs of 2PC for restrictions on how data can be distributed and manipulated.

In any replication model, each record in a given set of data has only one owner. A single set might consist of multiple records, and each of those records might have a *different* owner, but a single record will always have only *one* owner. The reason for this lies in replication's inability to distribute transactions. In an effort to avoid the network and locking overhead of 2PC, a server must be enabled to process transactions. Because SQL Server works at the database level with transaction logs, "versioning" of record changes cannot occur; two servers have no way to figure out which server "owns" the right change. If an application changes record 1 on server 1, and another application changes record 1 on server 2, which change is the "right" change?

The answer to that becomes a *business* question, not a *technological* or *relational* question, because the change itself is tied to the business process, not to any rule or posit of relational theory. The DBMS is responsible only for storing and making available data through means defined by that relational theory. Although deftly written, SQL Server doesn't have the first clue how to resolve the age-old question "Who gets the last donut?" That, unfortunately, is still the domain of the application developer.

Replication provides the capability to distribute read-only copies of a specific set of data to other servers, so that the data is now remotely available to remote users, instead of locally available to remote users. The advantage is data availability that does not depend on weak links between LANs and WANs, and significantly more efficient usage of long-distance network links. Instead of 1,200 users accessing a server from all corners of the globe over a WAN, individual groups of local users can access their own *local copies* of read-only data. Or, as you'll soon see, the local data itself might be the writeable data, and sent back to headquarters as part of a read-only roll-up.

Although this might seem like lots of superfluous talk about relational principles and operating constraints, it will make the discussion of SQL Server 6.0's *particular implementation* of these concepts that much easier to digest. Microsoft has developed an innovative approach to working through some of these constraints, and, in some cases, is still bound by them. Knowing what those constraints are, why they are there, and how to work within them (or choose an alternate technology, such as a transaction processing monitor or 2PC-compliant applications), is critical to properly implement these new features.

SQL Server Replication Terminology

SQL Server 6.0 introduces a whole slew of new terms aimed at befuddling anybody who has ever worked with SQL Server. Actually, Microsoft just needed lots of new words to describe the new features. Some of this terminology focuses on replication and how SQL Server itself functions in a replicated-data environment.

Any single server can function in one of three distinct roles, based on how you configure SQL Server's operation. The first is the "publishing server," which is generically defined as a provider of data. (I'll describe what data it can provide shortly.) *Publishing servers* use *published databases* as the source of the information that they are going to *distribute* to other servers. SQL Server uses a "store and forward" metaphor for actual transaction distribution, and this relies on the second of the server roles: *distributing server*.

A *distributing server* is the server responsible for delivery of the replicated transactions from the publishing server to the subscribing server (more on that shortly) and is the location for the *distribution database*, which is the database that SQL Server uses for its store-and-forward processing. The store-and-forward database has a default name of distribution, but any name is considered valid. For the purpose of consistency, the distribution database will always be the publisher's store-and-forward database for replication. The distributing server role can either be local—that is, a publishing server is also performing its own distribution functions (see Figure 35.1)—or a publishing server can rely on the distribution services of another publishing server, thereby using a *remote distribution server* (see Figure 35.2).

Whether a server is functioning as just a publisher or as both a publisher and a distributor, it is defined by the location of the store-and-forward database. A subscribing server is simply a consumer of data that is provided by one or more publishing servers. The subscribing server functions only as a destination for replicated data.

Microsoft's architecture for SQL Server replication enables a single server to function in any of these three roles. In other words, the subscribing role that a server performs is distinct from any publishing or distributing services it may provide. A single server can publish data, locally distribute that data to other servers, and yet receive replicated data from different servers as well. You'll see this in more detail in the section "Configuring a Simple One-to-Many Replication Model."

In addition to defining server roles, the individual units of work that SQL Server uses for replication have been defined to enable substantially more flexible options for replicating data than previous applications have provided. SQL Server uses both publications and articles to define what is going to be replicated and how. An *article*, which is actually a pointer to a data table, is the smallest unit of work for any SQL 6.0 replication processing. The article is based on a table but is not a table itself. In fact, an article can be an entire table, a subset of columns from a table, a subset of rows from a table, or a combination of the two. As of yet, only table data can be published. A single table theoretically can have an unlimited number of articles that enable publishing of its data. Articles are defined in the sysarticles system table, which is a new addition to the SQL Server database-level dictionary.

By definition, articles must exist within a larger context, which is where publications come in. Any article must be created within a *publication*. The reason for this lies in SQL Server's capability to subscribe either to individual articles within a publication, or to the publication as a whole—giving you a subscription to all the articles in that publication. By doing this, an administrator can create a publication that contains individual whole-table articles. By subscribing to the publication, another SQL Server has just published and subscribed all of the data tables for an entire database!

SQL Server Replication Models

SQL Server 6.0 supports four different "models" of replication. The simplest of these models is the traditional one-to-many data distribution method. (See Figure 35.1.) In this model, a single SQL Server publishes a database and its tables to a variety of remotely located servers, so that clients at those remote sites have local data. In this case, the publishing server is also performing its own distribution.

In cases in which there might be a dial-up or other slow-link connection, however, using a remote distribution server (see Figure 35.2) is actually more efficient. By putting the distribution server on the other end of the remote link, the transactions can be distributed using a local LAN connection instead of an expensive and slow WAN connection.

FIGURE 35.1.

SQL Server supports the typical data-distribution model of a single publisher sending data to multiple subscribers.

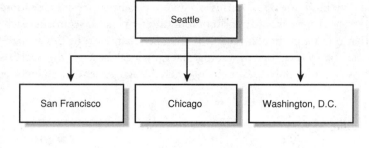

FIGURE 35.2.

SQL Server can also support remote distribution servers, to minimize WAN traffic.

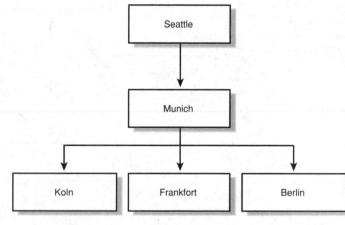

In a complete reversal, SQL Server also supports "corporate roll-ups" of data, although with some additional configuration. Typical examples (see Figure 35.3) include sales roll-ups, where individual point-of-sale units or individual warehouses track their own data changes locally, but feed those changes to a corporate data center for reporting and redistribution purposes.

FIGURE 35.3.

SQL Server also supports multiple publishers sending data to a single subscriber, providing "roll-up" capabilities.

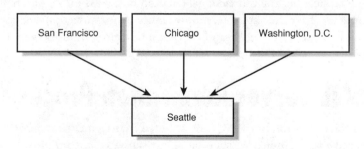

The most complex, in terms of both configuration and management, is the many-to-many model. With this scenario, a single server works as a publisher and subscriber, but to different pieces of information. In effect, it is simply a collection of individual one-to-many models, as shown in Figure 35.4. In this example, a publisher provides location-specific data to the other servers. A table would consist of four different logical segments, each identified by the location that owns a particular record. Remember that, even in this scenario, all changes to a record must be *local* changes, meaning that only local users on the Seattle server can change records from Seattle, only local users on the Chicago server can change records from Chicago, and so on.

FIGURE 35.4.

SQL Server supports multiple-publisher/ multiple-subscriber replication scenarios, but only with locally updated data.

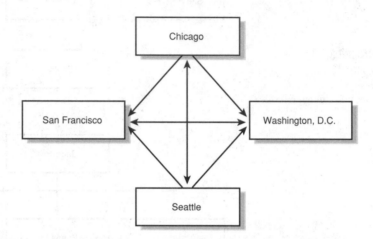

One of the more useful features of SQL Server 6.0 replication is that any SQL Server can perform any of the three functions. The biggest benefits to be gained from replication might actually be for highly transactional systems. One of the biggest problems with large corporate databases has been the often mutually exclusive needs of both *OLTP* (On-Line Transaction Processing) and *OLAP* (On-Line Analytical Processing) users. Anyone trying to process reports on a high-transaction database knows that both processes kill throughput for everybody. Using replication, the transactional data can be loaded into a different, "reporting only" server, or, if you have the hardware, simply replicate the transactional database to a reporting database on the same server. Replication need not be from server to server; it can actually be from database to database on the *same* server!

SQL Server Replication Processing

In the discussion of the SQL Distributed Management Framework in Chapter 34, SQL Executive was supplied with a total of five subsystems. Two of those subsystems are for generic processing (TSQL and CmdExec), whereas the other three are reserved for replication purposes. These other three are LOGREAD, SYNC, and DISTRIB, and they, in concert with SQL Executive, are the "business end" of SQL Server's replication features.

When a database is marked as "published" (using sp_dboption), SQL Server activates the LOGREAD subsystem of SQL Executive. LOGREAD continuously scans the syslogs table of the published database, waiting for committed transactions to be flushed to disk. When those transactions are flushed, LOGREAD scans the newly written pages and, based on their contents, reverse-engineers a SQL statement. That SQL statement, now stored as a text string, is added as a row into a table in the distribution database. How it does this merits further detail. In the distribution database, there are two important tables: MSjobs and MSJob_commands.

The LOGREAD subsystem's function is dependent on not just *what* SQL Server logs for transactions, but *how* those transactions are logged. For example, the query delete authors has 23 rows by default, and generates 23 individual delete statements, each of which corresponds to a unique index value in the primary key of authors (the au_id field). As a result, SQL Server logs 23 individual delete operations in the syslogs table for pubs. When the LOGREAD subsystem sees this, it sees 23 individual operations, but they are still part of a single logical operation: the original delete authors that the application sent to SQL Server. In effect, there is a 1:23 relationship between the original query and the number of individual operations that SQL Server uses to execute that query. MSjobs and MSjob_commands provide a way to resolve that 1:N relationship. MSjobs gives the whole query a distinct job_id, which is used as the common key to MSjob_commands. LOGREAD inserts each of the 23 delete statements as a separate row in MSjob_commands, giving each row a job command ID, and includes the single job_id value as well.

After the rows are added to MSjobs and MSjob_commands, the DISTRIB subsystem is responsible for reading those rows and passing the statements that are held there to the subscribing servers. To do this, DISTRIB uses ODBC and the SQL Server ODBC driver to open the connection. The subscribing SQL Server processes the transaction statement as it would any other. In the event of network failure or other interruptions, SQL Server keeps track of the last successfully executed job_id in the MSlast_job_info table, which SQL Server automatically creates in the subscribing database.

> **NOTE**
>
> In the initial release, Microsoft will be supporting only SQL 6.0–to–SQL 6.0 replication. Expect these features and appropriate documentation with the release of SQL Server 6.5.

Because SQL Server uses transaction statements for replication, rather than simply copying data rows back and forth, replication in SQL 6.0 requires a "baseline" where the publishing table and the subscribing table are synchronized. This is required because each transaction statement represents only a *change* to a value, not a *value itself.* That's where SYNC comes in. Before distribution of transactions can occur, SQL Server uses the SYNC subsystem to take a snapshot of the source data, and copies it to the subscribing database. This involves three important components.

First, SYNC needs to create an object in the destination server, or at least be able to clear an existing object, because SYNC uses BCP to move data. This BCP operation can use either native-format data (if both servers use common code pages and sort orders) or character-format data (if they do not share code-page and sort orders). Obviously, native-format BCP will be faster, so establishing common code-pages and sort-orders is of some benefit for SQL replication. Because BCP only adds new rows (it does not clear existing space), the table must be "clean" for synchronization.

To "clean out" the destination table, SQL Server can auto-generate a *creation script*, which contains the necessary DROP TABLE and CREATE TABLE statements necessary to clear the table. Optionally, SQL Server can use an existing table, and simply TRUNCATE TABLE any existing rows away. After the table has been cleared, SYNC relies on DISTRIB to BCP the source data into the destination table. After the synchronization process has completed, the tables on both the publishing and subscribing servers will be identical—and only then can DISTRIB send transaction statements to the subscribing server.

Configuration Prerequisites for SQL Server Replication

SQL Server relies on its own services, as well as others in Windows NT, to provide replication functionality. The most important of these is SQL Executive. Because SQL Executive will be making a standard ODBC connection into the subscribing database, it must have access to network resources. For this reason, SQL Executive must be able to log on to the network. Although it is the default setup option, the importance of creating a distinct Windows NT domain account for SQL Executive is imperative; this is particularly crucial for data replication with SQL Server.

There are two minimum requirements for SQL Server replication. First, you must have adequate disk space for SQL Server, all of its databases, and both the distribution database and BCP output files. Second, you must be able to configure SQL Server for 16MB of memory. In order to install replication, the memory option for sp_configure must be configured to at least 8,192 pages. Both the stored procedures for replication and the SQL Enterprise Manager (SQL-EM) application check this configuration option, and will not enable you to proceed until it has been properly set. Because SQL Executive makes a standard ODBC connection to the subscribing server, increasing the user connections option on that server is a good idea as well.

Configuring a Simple One-to-Many Replication Model

Although Windows NT and MS SQL Server supply all the necessary operating system utilities and stored procedures necessary to configure SQL Server replication, using the SQL

Enterprise Manager is by far the easiest method to accomplish that goal. What you need to remember is that behind the scenes, SQL-EM is simply executing stored procedures and TSQL commands to configure entries in the `distribution` database, as well as the `syspublications` and `sysarticles` tables of the publishing server.

There are four different configuration steps for using SQL Server replication features:

1. Setting SQL Server's configuration options using `SETUP` and `sp_configure`
2. Configuring a server's roles
3. Creating publications and articles in the published database
4. Creating subscriptions to the publications and articles

Setting SQL Server's Configuration Options

Configuring replication begins with changing the necessary `sp_configure` options in SQL Server. Memory must be set to at least 8,192 pages, and user connections should be increased by 10—but this number is just my own recommendation for testing purposes. The number of publishing and distributing servers, combined with their distribution schedules, will determine how many additional user connections you will need to allocate to avoid running out in normal use.

You must also configure SQL Server for integrated or mixed login security. `SQLExecutive`, through the `SYNC` and `LOGREAD` subsystems, makes an integrated-security connection to SQL Server. Read Chapter 27, "Security and User Administration," for step-by-step instructions on completing this task using the SQL Server Setup utility or using the SQL Enterprise Manager utility. When you have completed these changes, you'll need to shut down SQL Server and restart it. When you do that, you'll be ready to configure SQL Server's publishing features.

Configuring the Server for the Publishing and Distributing Roles

In establishing a replicated-data architecture, SQL Server begins with configuring the data sources that are to be used. In plain English, that means that you need to configure the publishing and distribution servers before you can configure anything else. In the SQL Enterprise Manager application, choose the Server | Replication Configuration | Install Publishing menu items. You will be presented with the dialog box shown in Figure 35.5.

Given that the Install Publishing menu item brought up this dialog box, it might seem odd to define distribution before defining publication. SQL Server needs to know where it is placing what it is publishing, however, before it can know what to publish. This simple example uses a local publishing server, implementing the first of the replication models described earlier. Choosing remote distribution enables the second model. In defining local distribution, SQL Server needs to create the `distribution` database. After having assigned the `distribution` database to a disk device, and optionally a log device, clicking OK activates a series of processes.

FIGURE 35.5.

SQL Enterprise Manager provides the easiest method to configure replication.

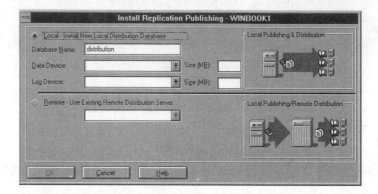

First, SQL-EM edits the Windows NT Registry and sets the name of the store-and-forward database in the `\\HKEY_LOCAL_MACHINE\SOFTWARE\MICROSOFT\MSSQLSERVER\REPLICATION\DistributionDB` key, supplying the value for this key with the name used for the `distribution` database. Second, SQL-EM runs `CREATE DATABASE` using the name supplied for the `distribution` database. In addition to creating the database, Enterprise Manager's third step is to run the `INSTDIST.SQL` script (supplied in the `\SQL60\INSTALL` directory by default) in the `distribution` database, which creates the distribution-role-specific tables that SQL Server needs. (`MSjobs` and `MSjob_commands` are among those created by this script.) Finally, the SQL Server must be able to identify itself as both a publishing and distributing server. This is accomplished by altering entries in the `master..syservers` table. Three new status values for a server have been created: `pub`, `dpub`, and `sub`. Amazing how they correlate, isn't it? SQL-EM runs `sp_addpublisher <server name>, 'dist'` to change the `syservers` entry in the master database to `dpub`. If this were only a publishing server, relying on a remote distribution server, it would be set to `pub`. Because distribution servers must also be publishing servers, `dpub` handles both options.

After you click OK, SQL-EM prompts asks you whether you'd like to define publishing databases and distribution schedules. Accepting this offer brings up the next major dialog in replication configuration, illustrated in Figure 35.6.

A single publishing server works with a fixed distribution schedule. That schedule can be transaction based or it can be time based. A transaction-based schedule keeps a "batch" of transactions, the size of which you specify. Under certain circumstances, particularly horizontal partitioning, you might want to use a transaction batch size of 1, meaning that each transaction is replicated as it occurs (that is, it is sent to each destination server individually). Because of the impact that this can have on network throughput, Microsoft includes recommendations on how to configure this option. Time-based scheduling enables you to send the transactions to replicate every so often—say every three minutes or every hour. Regardless of the number of transactions, the distribution subsystem will send all the transactions for that time block to the subscribing servers.

FIGURE 35.6.

SQL Enterprise Manager enables you to define distribution schedules for server-to-server replication using time-based or transaction-based scheduling.

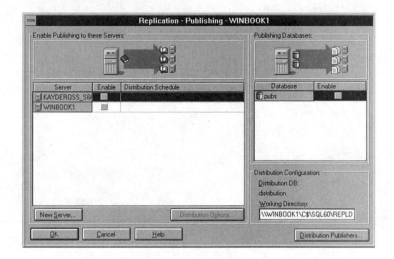

On the right side of this dialog box, you can choose the databases that you want to serve as *publishing* databases. It is in these database that you will create database-specific *publications*, which will be placeholders for your *articles*. I'll talk about article and publication restrictions in a moment. Having marked a database as published (`published` and `subscribed` are new `sp_dboption` parameters), you are now ready to create a publication in your `published` database.

Configuring a Subscribing Server

In order for a SQL Server to receive data, it must be configured as a subscribing server. To do this, you can use SQL Enterprise Manager's Server | Replication Configuration | Subscribing… menu options. Doing so displays the dialog box shown in Figure 35.7.

Enterprise Manager puts the name of the server you are configuring to be a subscriber in the dialog box's title. The left half of the dialog is the list of publishing servers that you want to subscribe to. The right half list is the database that can serve as destination databases for subscriptions.

> **NOTE**
>
> Replication is not dependent on database names. For example, I can publish data from the `pubs` database on AMS to the `dest` database on `NLCWEST1`. In fact, SQL Server can replicate from one database to another on the same server. As a result, any non-system database can serve as a publishing database, subscribing database, or both.

FIGURE 35.7.

Configuring subscribing servers is performed using SQL-EM dialog boxes and screens.

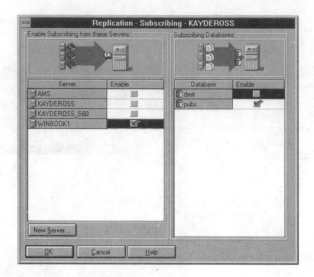

Select the name of the publishing server, and then select the name of the databases that can serve as destinations for subscriptions. You can select a database as a potential destination; it won't actually become a destination database until you have created a subscription, which will happen shortly.

Creating Publications and Articles

Highlight the database you have published, and either choose the Manage | Replication | Publications menu options or click on the Replication - Publishing icon in the toolbar. This brings up the dialog box shown in Figure 35.8.

FIGURE 35.8.

Publications and articles are defined in SQL Enterprise Manager such that articles must exist within a publication.

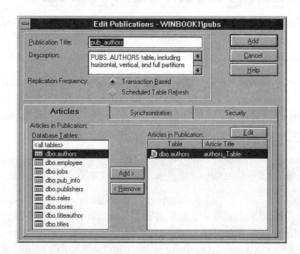

The concept of publication is one of the more difficult to understand, because it is only an abstraction layer: A publication is nothing more than a logical placeholder for articles. In that way, a publication is similar to a directory in DOS. It doesn't really exist physically, but it can still contain files and other directories. In the same way, a publication is nothing more than table entries that enable a one-to-many relationship: A single publication can hold 0/1/N articles, enabling SQL Server to subscribe to individual tables or groups of tables all at once.

Within each publication, theoretically there can be an unlimited number of articles, each of which points to a table. Here, an administrator has created the publication pub_authors, and in it is a single article pointing to the authors table. You might want to review the definition of an article before reading this next point: A single table can be published many times, because each article is merely a *logical pointer* to a table, not a data table itself. In defining the article, SQL Server is defining what data it will *copy from* the table, not the table as an object. Because of this, a single publication could have 12 different articles, all of which are based on the titles table. Each of those 12 tables could be a different view of the data, including combinations of columns, rows, and so on.

You'll notice the Synchronization tab in the lower half of the screen. This tab section defines how SQL Server will process the initial snapshot that's required to establish a synchronous baseline from which all the transactions will be applied. By default, SQL Server uses a native-format BCP file to copy data across. There is a critical assumption in this default value: Both SQL Servers are using a common code-page/sort-order combination. If they do not share this, you must manually set synchronization to use a character-format BCP, or perform the synchronization manually.

If you click on OK here, you're doing just fine. You've just created your first publishing/distributing server, and created a publication and article. You're now set to subscribe to this publication and article.

Defining Subscriptions to Publications and Articles

Defining subscriptions can happen on the subscribing server or on the publishing server. If it's defined on the subscribing server, Microsoft calls that a *pull* subscription. If it's defined on the publishing server, Microsoft calls that a *push* subscription. Regardless of the configuration point, the *work source* is still the same. The LOGREAD subsystem still runs on the publishing server; the DISTRIB subsystem still runs on the distributing server.

Defining Pull Subscriptions

A *pull subscription* in Microsoft terminology is a subscription that is configured from the subscribing server. In simpler terms, an administrator uses SQL Enterprise Manager to configure the subscribing server, and in doing so, identifies publications and articles that the subscribing server wishes to consume. To define a subscription using this method, you can use the

Manage | Replication | Subscriptions menu options or click on the Replication - Manage Subscriptions button in the SQL-EM toolbar. Either option displays the dialog box shown in Figure 35.9.

FIGURE 35.9.

Configuring a PULL subscription in SQL Enterprise Manager requires establishing the subscription from the subscribing server.

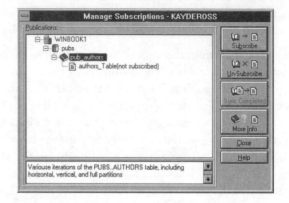

In this dialog box, you can browse the publishing servers to which you have access, as well as the published databases, publications, and articles that are available on those servers. You select the server, database, and publication or article to which you wish to subscribe, and then select the Subscribe button on the dialog. Doing so displays the Subscription Options dialog box shown in Figure 35.10, which enables you to define a number of important subscription properties. Notice that synchronization (the process of making a snapshot-copy of the table so that transactions proceed from a common "baseline" of a table image) can be controlled at the individual subscription level, and the destination database is assigned from the list of available destination databases that you identified when configuring this server as a subscriber. Only those databases that have check marks in the Configuring Subscriptions dialog box will appear in that list.

FIGURE 35.10.

SQL Enterprise Manager will only allow subscriptions to those databases that have the "subscribing" database option enabled.

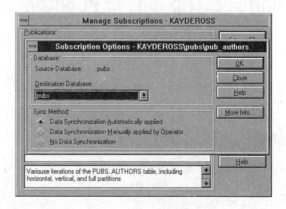

Clicking on OK will put a copy of the authors table from the pubs database on the server AMS into the DEST database on the NLCWEST1 server. You should notice that in the Manage

Subscriptions dialog box, the status for the article has changed from Not Subscribed (refer to Figure 35.9) to Subscribed/Not Sync'ed/Automatic, indicating that automatic synchronization will, but has not yet, occurred.

Defining Push Subscriptions

You can configure a push subscription using the Edit Publications window that you used to define the publication and article. By clicking on the Edit button for the article, you display the dialog box below, which has the all-important Subscribers button on it. In this dialog box, you define who the subscribing server is, and clicking Subscribe enables you to define the destination database for your subscription. After you do this, clicking on OK or Close to close out all the windows runs the necessary stored procedures to configure all of the LOGREAD, DISTRIB, and SYNC tasks necessary to activate the subscription.

Defining Subscriptions Using the Enterprise Manager Topology Map

By selecting the menu options Server | Replication Configuration | Topology, you can display a graphical representation of the servers on your network and configure publications and subscriptions using the same dialogs that you have used through this process. By right-clicking on a server, you can view the publications and subscriptions of a particular server and perform all the operations that you have already completed to create this new publication.

This map gives you a guide to how replication services are enabled between sets of servers. The current server that you are configuring will always appear in a set of light-gray square braces; NLCWEST1 is the current server for the example shown in Figure 35.11.

FIGURE 35.11.

SQL Enterprise Manager enables you to graphically map servers in a replication topology.

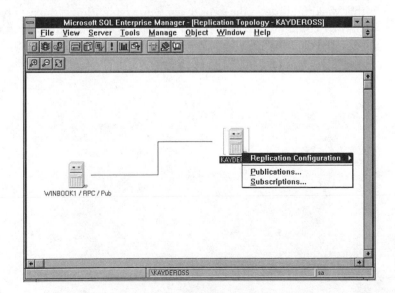

What Happens Next?

The answer to this question is easy: You wait. Fortunately, if you configured the SYNC schedule using the defaults, the next five-minute time increment will cause the SYNC process to fire. This creates the native-format BCP file on the local server, and then SYNC calls DISTRIB to copy that file into the destination table. After the SYNC process has completed successfully, the next batch of transactions will cause DISTRIB to be executed, replicating those transactions to the subscribing server and database. You can monitor all of this in two different areas of the server. First, you can use the Manage Tasks window of SQL-EM to monitor the individual LOGREAD, SYNC, and DISTRIB tasks and make sure that they are running properly. Any error messages they generate will show up here. Also, you can use the Manage Subscriptions window on the subscribing server to monitor the status of the subscription itself. Before any subscription has been created, the status will be "not subscribed." After the subscription has been created, but before the SYNC process has run *successfully*, the status will be "subscribed/not sync'ed." Only after the synchronization process has completed will the status change to "subscribed/sync'ed." That's the magic value, because that's the value that DISTRIB needs in order to receive permission to replicate transactions. You'll see DISTRIB's status in the Manage Tasks window, as well. After all this, watch the task history for all the replication-based tasks, to verify their successful completion.

Summary

SQL Server 6.0 replication is clearly a topic that merits its own book. With all the functionality that Microsoft has encased in one small box, from horizontal and vertical partitioning to ODBC-based heterogeneous replication, SQL Server can now serve as a hub for data distribution through heterogeneous networks. The most important fact to take away from this chapter is that walking through the steps to configure replication is the easy part; knowing how to intelligently configure replication and properly plan an architecture for applications based on distributed data are infinitely more complex.

Defining Systems Administration and Naming Standards

36

As the number of applications that you deploy on SQL Server increases, you will need to develop standards that enable you to administer your servers in a consistent manner. Most companies that successfully implement SQL Server have good standards in place. Standards are created to provide a foundation for administrative tasks, and often result in the establishment of the infrastructure necessary to enable the creation of procedures and scripts to automate activities.

What if you don't have standards in place? The cost of application development without standards is usually very high. The price is paid in effort and delay, as well as credibility. Let's face it: client/server is really no different from any other application environment. Success comes from the right mix of discipline and creativity. Thoughtful standards provide the discipline within which creativity can thrive.

This chapter focuses on those core standards that are needed to enable you to further develop procedures at your environment. It looks at two core activities: first, approaches to organizing databases and servers, especially regarding the development environment; and second, naming standards, from both a SQL Server and an operating-system level. After you decide on names, directory structure, and how you are going to approach development, you can start building those site-specific procedures and scripts to automate activities in your organization.

SQL Server Environment Approach

You must approach development in a SQL Server environment in a consistent fashion, or each development project is destined to waste time performing certain activities. The approach should be focused on providing flexibility for the developer and structure for the database administrator. It also should be built to enable portability of code from the development environment to the potentially many levels of your test environment, and eventually to the production environment.

Defining Environments

Most people who purchase SQL Server are using it to develop new *production* applications. When developing production software, you should assume there will be a development environment, at least one test environment, and a production environment. You must decide how each environment will be supported by SQL Server.

> **NOTE**
>
> Typical environments include development, system test, volume/stress test, user acceptance test, and production. Because there can be several test environments, this book considers them conceptually as a single environment called "test."

For each environment, you must determine the following:

- Is the environment supported by a separate (dedicated) SQL Server or does it share the SQL Server with some other function?

- How are the databases organized on the SQL Server? Is there a database per environment rather than a SQL Server per environment?

The most restrictive environment is a single SQL Server with databases for development, test, and production—the needs of each environment conflict with the other environments. The development environment might require the SQL Server to be rebooted often, but the production environment is likely to have up-time as an important business requirement. The testing environment often is constructed to be able to gather performance statistics. The activity of the development and production environments, however, might skew these performance statistics, and testing might ruin performance for production. It is *strongly recommended* that development, test, and production activities take place on separate SQL Servers.

The Development Environment

The development environment requires the maximum flexibility for developers while enabling the necessary control structures to provide for consistent promotion of code. In designing this environment, several issues should be considered:

- The SQL Server used for development may or may not be dedicated. A dedicated SQL Server is *strongly preferred* because "bouncing" (shutdown and restart) of the SQL Server is a *very* common activity in development. If the SQL Server is shared by several development groups, frequent reboots of the system might have a significant impact on the productivity of developers.

- The SQL Server may or may not be running on dedicated hardware. Dedicated hardware is preferred because occasionally the database hardware must be rebooted. Although dedicated hardware provides developers maximum control, it might not be cost effective. Because this environment is used to unit-test individual modules for *functionality* and not performance, dedicated hardware is not a requirement.

- Although flexibility is at a maximum for the developer, so is developer responsibility. A developer has much more responsibility for administrative activities. Developers often create their own objects (tables, indexes, procedures, triggers, and so forth) in the pursuit of satisfying a business problem. Developers often are responsible for managing their own test data. Organized database administration (the DBA group) still has some responsibilities, however. A DBA may create a base set of objects or manage a core set of data. As always, DBAs still get calls about any problems that a developer cannot handle (killing processes, adding space, and so forth).

- Developers must have a set of tables to use when developing. Define how tables will be organized to meet the needs of all developers. (This is discussed in detail later in this chapter.)

■ Occasionally, a single logical database is physically implemented as several SQL Server databases in production. The distribution of tables to databases should match the production model. (Remember that relating tables from two different databases requires that at least one of the table names be qualified by the database name. If the development environment does not have the same database structure, SQL has to be modified before production implementation, which is likely to introduce new bugs.) Your development environment should look *exactly* like the production environment in the base structure (database, tables, and objects).

If other projects share the development server, create a document to provide information about all groups. It should contain information such as project name, manager, contact name, phone, and specific instructions. Development environments are volatile. You may need to reboot the server to continue development. Because a reboot affects all users on the system, you should contact user representatives to prepare them for this situation.

A Detailed Approach

The development environment is the area in which developers first attempt to create new modules of an application. Development is an iterative process. Multiple revisions of code are normally created in the process of correctly satisfying design requirements. Consequently, the code may have unexpected results on tables. During the refinement of a module, database activities such as DELETE, INSERT, or UPDATE may need several modifications before they are deemed to work correctly. This requires the developer to create test conditions to test individual pieces of functionality. Additionally, new requirements may necessitate the addition or deletion of columns from tables to test the new pieces of code. These changes may become permanent modifications to the existing structures, validated by the iterative testing of an application. The development environment needs to be structured to minimize contention between developers.

Due to the nature of development, it is assumed that the development environment will use a SQL Server separate from the test and production environments. Based on that assumption, you can then determine an approach to development at a database and object level.

There are three main approaches to development in a SQL Server environment. The differences between the approaches are based on whether the developers share a database and whether they have their own copies of objects and data.

The development approach is greatly impacted by the number of *actual* SQL Server databases used to represent the single logical database. An initial approach is to put all tables in a single database. Experience shows, however, that grouping tables into several databases can have significant performance and administrative benefits. The definition of databases in the development environment should be identical to the ultimate production environment to minimize code changes from development to production. If the production environment is organized using several databases, the development environment should also contain several databases.

The following section looks at these three approaches to handling development in a SQL Server environment.

Shared Database and Shared Objects and Data

In the shared database/shared objects and data approach, a single database (or databases) exists for development. All developers use the same objects and data. This approach is sometimes used in very small developments (one or two developers). After the number of developers increases, this approach quickly breaks down.

Advantages

- It simplifies administration. There are fewer objects (tables, indexes, stored procedures, triggers, and so forth) to manage.
- There are reduced storage requirements. There is only one database and one copy of objects and data.
- It is a viable option if your tables are grouped into multiple databases. The development environment is assumed to use a separate SQL server. The names used for databases can be *identical* between development, test, and production environments. Therefore, code that is developed does not have to be modified to be promoted to the next level.

Disadvantages

- There is an almost unavoidable contention for data. Developer 1 might be testing a delete activity on the same row that Developer 2 is using to test an update activity. Development will be impeded as confusion results from "unexpected" changes to data.
- There is a significant decrease in a developer's capability to change the underlying structure to support a hypothesis or test condition. Additionally, Developer 1 might want to add a column that would negatively affect Developer 2's testing.
- Development flexibility is greatly reduced.

Individual Database and Individual Objects and Data

With the individual database/individual objects and data approach, each developer has a dedicated database for development. Because objects are created in the context of a database, the developer therefore has a personal copy of all objects and data. Normally, developers are responsible for all activities with their databases, including data creation and backups.

Advantages

- The developer has the capability to change data or structures without affecting other developers.

- Because object names are created in the context of a single database, all the SQL code can be written to assume the database name and contains only object names, without full database qualification.

Disadvantages

- If tables are grouped into several databases, using this development approach is likely to require code changes to promote code to production. In a single database approach, code is consistent from development to production because there is never a need to *qualify* the name of a table with the database name. In a multiple database scenario, if a query is executed that refers to tables in different databases, at least one of the tables has to be qualified with the database name.

  Consider an example with five developers. The first developer writes code against `customerdb_1` and `purchasedb_1`, the second developer writes code against `customerdb_2` and `purchasedb_2`, and so on. The following is an example of SQL access across databases:

  ```
  select *
  from customerdb_1..customer c, purchasedb_1..purchase p
  where c.cust_id = p.cust_id
  ```

  Migrating this code into the test or production environments requires changes because these environments likely would contain different database names (`customerdb`, `purchasedb`). You have to modify the code to arrive at the following statement:

  ```
  select *
  from customerdb..customer c, purchasedb..purchase p
  where c.cust_id = p.cust_id
  ```

  Changing code from one environment to the next is not recommended. Do not use the private database approach for multiple database implementations.

- The amount of space required to support development increases. Each database will require the space necessary to hold a copy of all objects, procedures, and data. In addition, the minimum size of any SQL Server database is the larger of the default database size (normally configured for 2MB) or the size of the `model` database.

- The number of databases in the server increases. This complicates administrative tasks. It also can affect the recovery process, because SQL Server recovers databases sequentially in database ID order.

> **NOTE**
>
> I was teaching a class once when the SQL Server was rebooted. Our training databases had database IDs of 70 to 80. It took about an hour for our training environment to become usable.

Shared Database and Individual Objects and Data

In the shared database/individual objects and data approach, a single database (or databases) is used for development. Developers do not share objects or data. Each developer is a true user of the database. Objects are created, *and owned*, by the developer. The production objects are created by the user dbo. Code written by the developer does not refer to user name. The normal SQL Server procedure of looking for an object owned by you before looking for an object owned by dbo is leveraged. The SQL that is written acts against the developer's tables when executed in the development environment, and against the dbo's tables when executed in the test and production environments.

Advantages

- Each developer has an individual set of data. A developer has complete freedom to update, delete, and insert data without affecting other developers.

- Migration from development environment to the production environment is eased. All developers work with the same database and object names. This ensures that any SQL created is identical in all environments. No code changes due to different database or object names is necessary.

- Systems spanning multiple databases do not require modifications to promote to production (unlike the Private Database development approach) because the development environment database structure is identical to the production database structure.

Disadvantages

- The number of tables in a single database can be large. A system with 100 tables and 10 developers will have 1,000 tables in the development database.

- Storage requirements are magnified by the number of developers as compared to the shared object approach.

NOTE

Each table and index requires 16KB (one extent) regardless of the amount of data in the table. Therefore, the storage requirements between a private database and a shared database/individual object approach should be equal.

In a private database approach, however, each developer database has its own free space. On average, the total amount of free space required in the private database approach is much greater than the shared free space in the shared database/individual object approach.

Normally, a shared database/individual objects and data approach to development is recommended for multiple and single database installations. The individual database/individual objects and data approach is recommended for single database installations only.

WARNING

Your production requirements may not surface until after development has started. This approach does not work with a multiple database installation. If the decision to implement with multiple databases occurs after development starts, the shared database/individual objects and data approach is able to adapt to the new structure much easier. You may be forced to change your development environment structure completely if you choose the individual database approach. Choose your approach carefully.

Test Environment

There can be several test environments used in the *Software Development Lifecycle* (SDLC). You will test for function or performance. Functional testing is used to confirm that elements of an application or several distinct applications can work together. Performance testing is conducted to verify how the database performs under peak numbers of users, data size, or both.

Functional Testing Environment

Most functional testing can be handled by a single SQL Server. Consider the following when planning this environment:

■ A SQL Server used only for testing is *strongly preferred* because SQL Server should be configured for testing, and the configuration for your application may be different than the configuration needed for the testing of some other application.

- The hardware in which the SQL Server is running may or may not be dedicated. Dedicated hardware is useful in analysis because performance statistics gathered at the hardware level can be related easily to SQL Server, but you are testing functionality and usability across modules here, not performance.

- Objects are created by database administration. Often the files necessary to build the databases structures (DDL scripts) are part of a source code control system.

- There is only one copy of each object necessary to support the system. (A development environment may have several copies of each table.)

- If the tables in the system are physically organized into several databases for performance, recovery, or security reasons, there is only one copy of each database.

- All objects should be owned by the database owner, dbo. This supports the seamless migration of code from the development to the testing environments.

- A core set of data is created that is representative of production data. The amount of data does not need to represent production volumes, because it will be used to support feature, integration, and system testing.

- Logins and users of the test system should be representative of production users. This enforces the testing of the system in the same manner as it would be used by the actual production users. By simulating real users, potential problems such as improper permissions can be identified.

Development logins may be added to enable developers to add specific system test data or to assist in the creation of a core set of data. Developers *should not*, however, have the capability to change the structure of tables or add, drop, or modify any other existing object. Although developers may have access to tables to add or modify data, testing should be conducted using the logins of users representative of production users.

Performance Testing Environment

Performance (or stress) testing should be handled by a different SQL Server than your functional testing environment. This environment will have similar features to the functional test environment, except for the recommendations for servers, hardware, and data:

- The SQL Server used for testing must be configured as it would be in production. Using an identically configured SQL Server is *necessary* because performance data captured is used to estimate production performance.

- The hardware wherein SQL Server is running should be configured identically to the production hardware so that statistics gathered can be considered representative of production performance. This environment is used to validate the system's capability of handling production loads.

■ A core set of data, *representative of production volumes and content*, is created and loaded. The data in this environment is used to test the performance of the system under varying loads. To capture performance and load statistics that are representative of production, production type data must be used.

■ Development logins are normally *not* added to the performance testing server. Logins are representative of production, and all modifications (data or structure) are conducted by database administration.

Production Environment

The production environment is the last and most important environment in the SDLC. The production environment is under maximum control of database administration, and all defined production controls must be implemented and observed. This environment should have the following features:

■ The SQL Server and database hardware used for production should be dedicated. A dedicated SQL Server is *preferred* because it greatly simplifies analysis of performance statistics captured at the SQL Server or hardware level. Most production implementations use dedicated hardware for the production SQL Server.

■ An initial load of data may be required. Database administration normally is responsible for loading the core supporting data (code tables) as well as any other production data needed to support production use of the application.

■ Logins and users are the actual production users. The only other logins added to this server should be for administration reasons. All modifications (data or structure) are conducted by database administration. Security standards and procedures are in place and enforced.

Naming Standards

What's in a name? The answer to this simple question often takes organizations months—or years—to define. Names should be chosen in a consistent manner across all SQL Server systems in your organization; for example, a word should not be abbreviated two different ways in two different places. Consistency with names is one of the building blocks of an infrastructure to which employees and users can become accustomed. Consistent naming enables employees to move from system to system (or software to software) and have basic expectations regarding names. This can help in the transition when learning a new environment.

> **NOTE**
>
> Naming standards are like filing standards. You have to think about the person who is storing the information and the person who will retrieve it. For the person defining the name, the choice should be automatic. For the person retrieving or accessing an object, the name should completely define its content without ambiguity.

Naming standards can be broken into two areas: SQL Server names and operating system names. SQL Server names are the names that you specify in the SQL Server environment (databases, objects, and so forth). Operating system names are the names that you specify for files and directories.

SQL Server Names

In SQL Server, you are responsible for naming the server, each user database, each object in the database (tables and columns, indexes, views), and any integrity constraints (rules, defaults, user datatypes, triggers, declarative constraints). Device names (disk and dump) have different parameters governing their names because they can be somewhat operating-system related.

Capitalization standards must be defined for each type of name. (Should names be in all capital letters, all lowercase letters, or mixed case?) This decision can be different for different groups of names (for example, server names could be in all capital letters and object names could be in mixed case).

Consider also whether to use an indicator of the item being named. For example, does the word database or the abbreviation DB get included in a database name? In the end, your standard should identify whether the customer database will be named Customer, CUSTOMER, CustomerDB, or CUSTOMERDB. For most database objects, the structure of names is the personal preference of the person writing the standard.

> **NOTE**
>
> A naming convention often debated within many shops is whether to use the underscore (_) character between descriptive words and/or indicators (for example, sales_detail) or mixed case (for example, SalesDetail). This author typically prefers using underscores, because that method is, in my opinion, more readable and easier to type. Others tend to prefer the latter because it saves one character per word, which can help to keep names shorter and within size limitations without having to abbreviate as often. It also saves them from having to search for the underscore key on their keyboards. (If only we could convince computer manufacturers to design a standard keyboard with an underscore character that doesn't requiring using the shift key to type, life would be near bliss!)

The method that you choose to use is entirely up to you or your organization's preference. Throughout this chapter, I will attempt to alternate between both alternatives in the examples provided to avoid alienating either camp in this ongoing battle, and provide you the opportunity to see both methods and decide for yourself which you prefer.

Indicators

An indicator is a string of characters embedded in a name to indicate something about the type of object. In SQL Server, these characters are often used to indicate an object type. For example, `CurrDate_Def` could be used as a name for a default setting a column to the current date and time. There are two schools of thought on the use of indicators:

- An indicator is not needed because it can be retrieved from the system tables (the type column in the `sysobjects` table) or is indicated by the table from which you are selecting (`sysdatabases`, `sysservers`). Including it in the name is redundant and a waste of valuable characters. Names are limited by SQL Server to 30 characters long, and naming conventions may often limit them further to be compatible with existing guidelines or other systems (for example, object names within a DB2 environment are limited to 18 characters). An indicator can easily take 4 or 5 characters (`_tbl` or `_view`, for example). This limits the number of available characters in an object name. Indicators can propagate (`Customer_Tbl_CIdx`), further reducing the number of available characters. When users need to use a name frequently, indicators also mean extra typing.

- An indicator is needed because it simplifies reporting—a DBA can tell the type of object from just a listing of object names. Application designers are cognizant of what type of objects they are accessing (for example, the name tells them whether they are selecting from a table or view). Indicators also enable you to use similar, meaningful names for two objects, once with each indicator (for example, `price_rule` and `price_default`).

NOTE

All object names within a database must be unique for the owner. In other words, the `dbo` may own only one object of any name. If you have a rule named `price_check`, you cannot create a constraint named `price_check`. This restriction applies to tables and views as well as rules, defaults, constraints, procedures, and triggers. To avoid being constrained by these names, use indicators, especially for objects that users do not interact with and whose names they will never type (rules, defaults, constraints, and triggers).

Entries in `sysindexes` and `syscolumns` must be unique by table (only one index per table named `name_index`, only one column per table named `price`).

User-defined types are not objects: they are stored in `systypes` instead. Names of types will not clash with objects, but it makes sense to qualify them by type.

If you decide to put an indicator in a name, it is best to make that indicator as short as possible. For object names based on an underlying table (constraints, triggers, indexes), the length of the indicator has an effect on the number of available characters used for the table name. For example, if you decide that insert triggers will be identified by adding the indicator `_InsertTrigger` after the table name, the number of available characters that can be used for the table name can be no greater than 16 (30 characters minus 14 for the indicator). To give as much flexibility to the naming of an object, consider using an abbreviated indicator (such as `_tri`).

Indicators sometimes are placed at the beginning of the name, but you do not usually use this approach. Given an indicator of `tbl_`, a list of all object names groups the tables together. Although it's sometimes useful to list objects by type, you can do that in your SQL:

```
select name, type
   from sysobjects
   order by type
```

Table 36.1 lists the most common indicators used by SQL Server installations throughout the world. Consider that many sites choose no indicators at all.

Table 36.1. Common SQL Server indicators.

Item	Possible Indicators	Preferred
Server	`Server, _Server, _SERV, _serv, SERV, SRV`	None
Database	`_Database, _DATABASE, _DB, DB`	DB
Table	`Table, TABLE, T, TBL, _TBL, _tbl, _t, _T`	None
Column	`_col`	None
Index	Clustered: `ClusIdx, Cidx,_clus,` `_C, _CI, CI`	
	Nonclustered: `_Idx[#],Idx[#],` `NCIdx[#],NCI[#], _I[#]`	`_CI, _Idx[#]`
View	`V_, _V, _View, _VIEW`	None
Rule	`_Rul, _rul, _RUL, _rule, _RULE, R, _R,`	`_Rul`
Default	`_Def, _def, _DEF, _default, _DEFAULT,` `D, _D`	`_Def`

continues

Table 36.1. continued

Item	Possible Indicators	Preferred
User-defined datatype	_TYPE, _Type, TYPE, Type, _TYP, _Typ, TYP, Typ	_TYPE
Stored Procedure	_Proc, _PROC, _Pr, _PR PROC, Proc, PR	_proc
Trigger	InsertTrigger, InsTrig, ITrg, _ITrg	_ITrg
Check constraint	_Check, _constraint, _con, _CkCon, _Chk	_Check
Primary key constraint	_PK, PK, _Pk, Pk	_PK
Unique constraint	_UniqueCons, _Unique, _Uniq, _UN, _UQ	_Uniq
Foreign key constraint	_FK, RI	_FK
Data device	_DISK[#], _Disk[#],_DATA[#], _Data[#], _LOG[#], _Log[#], _IDX[#],_Idx[#]	_Data1, _Log1, _Idx1
Publication	_PUB, _pub	
Article	_ART, _art	
Subscription Table	_SUB, _sub	
Replication Procedure	_RP, _rp, _PFR, _pfr	
Dump device	TAPE[#], _Dump, _Tran,_Log, _Tape[#], _Disk, _DUMP, _TRAN, _LOG, _TAPE[#], _DISK	_Dump, _Tran, TAPE[#]
Scheduled Task	_STSK, _ST, _stsk, _st	
Alert Task	_ATSK, _AT, _atsk, _at	

An Overall Approach

One approach is outlined in Table 36.2. You can use these standards at your site or develop your own. *Make sure that you produce a matrix such as this to distribute to application development projects.*

Table 36.2. Sample SQL Server name standards.

Item	Capitalization	Include Type Name?	Example
Server	ALL CAPS	No	CUST_DEVEL
Database	Mixed case	Yes	CustomerDB
Table	Mixed case	No	CustomerPurchase

Item	Capitalization	Include Type Name?	Example
Column	Mixed case	No	`Age`, `Name`, `Address`, `FaxNumber`, `HomeNumber`
Index	Mixed case `CustomerIdx3` (3rd nonclus) `CustomerCIdx` (clustered)	Yes	(Format of "`TableName[C]Idx[#]`")
View	Mixed case	No	`CaliforniaCustomer`, `PartialCustomer`
Rule	Mixed case	Yes	`ValidSSN_Rul`, `NonNegative_Rul`
Default	Mixed case	Yes	`Zero_Def`, `CurrDate_Def`, `CurrUser_Def`
User-defined datatypes	ALL CAPS	Yes	`SSN_TYPE`, `ADDRESS_TYPE`, `NAME_TYPE`, `PHONE_TYPE`, `COMMENT_TYPE`, `STATE_TYPE`, `ZIP_TYPE`
Stored Procedure	Mixed case	Yes	`Update_Customer_Proc`, `CheckInventory_Proc`
Triggers	Mixed case	Yes	`Customer_ITrg`, `Customer_DTrg`, `Customer_UTrg`
Constraints	Mixed case	Yes	`NonNegative_Check` (check), `Customer_Uniq` (Uniqueness) `Customer_PK` (Primary Key) `CustomerPurchase_RI` (RI)
Publication	Mixed case	Yes	`Pubs2_PUB`, `Sales_pub`
Article	Mixed case	Yes	`authors_art`, `sales_art1`
Subscription	Mixed case	Yes	`authors_sub`, `sales_sub1`
Data devices	Mixed case	???	`Customer_DATA1`, `Customer_LOG1`, `Customer_Data1`, `Customer_Log1`, `DISK1`, `DATADISK1`, `LOGDISK1`

continues

Table 36.2. continued

Item	Capitalization	Include Type Name?	Example
Dump devices	Mixed case	???	`Customer_Dump,` `CustomerDB_Tran, TAPE1`
Sched. Task	Mixed case	Yes	`DumpAllTxSTSK,` `UpdAllStats_stsk`
Alert Task	Mixed case	Yes	`DumpTxNL_ATSK,` `AddMoreDBSpace_at`

The standards outlined in this table are used throughout this chapter.

> **NOTE**
>
> It is probably not a good idea to use indicators in the names of tables or views. Many sites use the table name in the name of other objects. The inclusion of `_tbl` increases the number of redundant characters in the dependent object name (trigger, index, and so forth). In addition, views exist to give users the feeling that their queries are acting against a real table, although they actually are accessing a view. Therefore, the names should be identical in format, and should not contain anything that would distinguish one from the other (`_tbl` or `_view`, for example).

Your standards likely will be different, but the important thing is to be consistent in your implementation of names. Knowing the standards up front can save you days or weeks of costly name conversion changes (with SQL code, administration activities, and so forth).

> **WARNING**
>
> If you haven't already read Chapter 24, "SQL Server Installation and Connectivity," do so now. It contains important information on object names and potential ANSI keyword violations.
>
> In previous versions of SQL Server, Microsoft allowed you to use keywords such as `primary`, `reference`, `user`, and `key` as object identifiers. Because these are now keywords in SQL Server 6.0, they can no longer be used.
>
> In a truth-is-stranger-than-fiction addition to this note, Microsoft itself found this out the hard way. Microsoft's network management application, Systems Management Server, uses an underlying SQL Server as its data storage facility. The SMS team created all of the primary key fields with the name of `key` to make accessing them simpler. Unfortunately, `key` is now a keyword, meaning Version 1.0 of SMS doesn't

run on SQL Server 6.0—it runs only on SQL Server 4.2. Microsoft had to endure a costly migration renaming these offending columns, and ship SMS Version 1.1 for use with SQL Server 6.0. You can avoid such costly mistakes for your applications by reading Chapter 3, "Introduction to Transact-SQL," and avoiding anything resembling an ANSI keyword in naming your objects.

Naming the Server

Name servers according to function. For example, you would much rather have a server named DEVELOPMENT rather than a server named RSR8_AB100. Several companies name their servers according to cartoons or movies. There are Snow White servers (DOPEY, GRUMPY, DOC, and so forth), Batman servers (BATMAN, ROBIN, JOKER, PENGUIN), and Mickey Mouse servers (MICKEY, MINNIE, GOOFY, DONALD). Although these names are fun, they should be used only for development or general server names, because they don't convey any information as to the purpose of the server. Servers intended to support applications should be named in a consistent manner across *all* applications. The following is a good format:

```
systemname_environmentname
```

For the development of a Customer system, you might use CUST_DEVEL, CUST_TEST, and CUST_PROD servers.

> **NOTE**
>
> By default, Microsoft SQL Server for Windows NT takes its name from the NT Server name. This can be changed, but you'd have to edit registry entries to change it, and it really isn't worth the trouble. Therefore, if an NT Server machine is going to be a dedicated SQL Server system, name the NT Server as you would want the SQL Server named.

Naming Databases

Databases should be named according to their contents—for example, the type of data (customer or product) or activity (security or administration). A database containing security tables could be named SecurityDB, and a database that contains customer data could be called CustomerDB. The name selected should be intuitive. (If a document is required to relate a database's name to its contents, it probably is not intuitive.) Some databases are named using a letter followed by three numbers. Would you rather have a database named B123 or ProductDB? *Avoid nondescriptive database names.*

Tables, Views, and Columns

Table and view names should be representative of the underlying data. A customer table should be called Customer; a view of the California customers should be called CaliforniaCustomer. Some organizations like to use nondescriptive table names (TBL0001). *Again, avoid nondescriptive table and view names.* If names are not intuitive, a decode document may be required to relate the table name to its contents. This delays development and makes it harder to write SQL statements. Column names should indicate the data in the column. Name a column containing the age of a customer Age or CustomerAge.

Indexes

A table can have one clustered index and up to 249 nonclustered indexes. Index names should contain the table name and an indicator of the type of index. Some DBAs like to include the column as part of the index name, but compound indexes make this naming scheme difficult to implement. The following are examples of possible index names for the Customer table:

Index Type	Identifier	Index Name
Clustered (max of 1)	_CIdx	Customer_CIdx
Nonclustered (up to 249)	_Idx[#]	Customer_Idx1, Customer_Idx2

> **TIP**
>
> Some application-development tools enable you to perform database administration activities. These tools may already have standard ways to construct names of indexes. Check whether you can modify the format or change your standards to accommodate this new format.

Rules and Defaults

Rules and defaults are implemented at the database level and can be used across tables. Their names should be based on the function that they are providing. A rule that checks for a valid age range could be called ValidAge_Rul, a default placing the current date in a field could be called CurrDate_Def.

User-Defined Datatypes

Here is a good format for user-defined types:

CONTENTS_TYPE

Because user-defined datatypes normally are targeted at certain types of columns, the name should contain the type of column for which it is to be used (SSN, PRICE, ADDRESS) followed by the indicator _TYPE.

Stored Procedures

The name of a stored procedure should be meaningful and descriptive enough to indicate what actions are performed by the SQL statements within the stored procedure. For example, a stored procedure that inserts new entries into the Customer table would be called Insert_Customer_Proc.

SQL Server also allows the definition of customized system stored procedures. These must be created in the master database and begin with sp_. User-defined stored procedures, however, should be named in a way to avoid conflict with existing or future Microsoft-supplied system stored procedures and prevent confusion as to whether a system stored procedure is a standard or user-defined stored procedure. It is recommended that an additional prefix be added to the procedure name after the sp_ to distinguish it from standard system stored procedures. Often, this prefix is an abbreviation of the company name. For example, a custom system stored procedure to display device usage by database for the XYZ Company would be named sp_XYZ_disk_usage. The XYZ indicator identifies this system procedure as one created by the XYZ Company, and prevents it from conflicting with Microsoft-supplied stored procedures.

Triggers

Trigger names should consist of the table name and an indicator of the trigger action (insert, update, delete). A good format is TableName_[IUD]Trg:

Object Type	Object Name
Table name	Customer
Insert trigger	Customer_ITrg
Delete trigger	Customer_DTrg
Update trigger	Customer_UTrg
Update and delete trigger	Customer_UDTrg

NOTE

The indicator consists of seven characters maximum (_IUDTrg, for example). To avoid abbreviation problems, no table name should be greater than 23 characters (30 – 7).

Constraints

Constraint names vary based on the scope of the constraint. Constraints can be used to check for valid values, add unique or primary keys, and establish relationships between tables (foreign keys).

A check constraint checks for valid values in a column or number of columns. Its name should indicate the column(s) and type of check.

Unique and primary key constraints are based on a table and should contain the table name and an indicator (_PK or _Uniq).

A foreign key constraint implements referential integrity between two tables. Its name should contain the tables or columns involved in the relationship and an indicator (_FK or _RI). Table 36.3 shows a sample list of constraint indicators and names for the customer table.

Table 36.3. Sample constraint indicators and names.

Constraint Type	Indicator	Name Based On	Constraint Name
Check constraint	_Check	Column or columns	ValidAge_Check
Primary key constraint	_PK	Table	Customer_PK
Unique key constraint	_Uniq	Table	Customer_Uniq
Foreign key constraint	_FK	Related tables and/or columns	CustomerPurchase_FK

WARNING

Remember that constraints are objects. For an owner, their names must be unique among all objects within the database. You may want to qualify the constraint name by including the table name as well. (In Table 36.3, different tables might contain columns named ValidAge, and their check constraint names would clash.) If you decide to include table names in your constraint names, you face a serious limitation in the length of table and column names.

For example, if you have a table called Institution and a check constraint on the column Date_of_Enrollment, the constraint might be named with the following,

Institution_Date_of_Enrollment_Check

which is much longer than the name length limit. The only realistic solution is to abbreviate the name, but that requires having both the person creating the constraint and the person retrieving information about it know the abbreviation rules. You might want to implement standards for abbreviations as described later in this chapter.

Table-level constraints can evaluate many columns. Include in your naming standard the method of naming table-level constraints. For example, the constraint requiring an invoice amount to be greater than zero whenever the type is "SALE" might look like this:

```
constraint Invoice_AmtType_Check
check ((amt > 0) or (type <> "SALE"))
```

Keep table and column names fairly short, yet descriptive, especially if you plan to use table names in check constraints.

Database Device Naming Standards

A *database device* is physical space that is initialized with the DISK INIT command. After a device is initialized, it is available for use by any database (except for master and model). Selecting the logical name for a device is dependent on what may exist on that device and on a DBA's confidence factor of the eventual use of that device. Devices can be named generically, by database, or by database contents.

Generic Name

Devices can be named generically according to their number or general contents. For example, if you want to name a device according to number, you can (DEVICE1). This approach is flexible, because any part of any database can be placed on the device without confusion. Tracking the databases created on a certain device cannot be easily inferred, however. It often is useful in performance analysis if the device can be easily mapped to a database, type of activity, or type of activity for a database.

Devices can be generically named to represent the *type* of data that will exist on that device (DATA1, LOG1, INDEX1). This provides a DBA with a guideline as to what portion of a database to place on each device. Indicating the type of data expected on the device in the name can cause confusion, however, if space constraints force you to create the data portion of a database on a device named LOG1.

NOTE

After you begin placing database log segments on a device, the SQL Server prevents you from mistakenly placing database data segments on that same device. Go ahead and call a device "log-something" if you are planning to put a log on it immediately.

Database Name

Devices can be named to represent the *database* that will be using the device. The device name can consist of the database name and a device number. For example, the four devices for the customer database might be named `CustomerDB_dev1`, `CustomerDB_dev2`, `CustomerDB_dev3`, and `CustomerDB_dev4`. The name indicates the database intended to be created on the device, but does not indicate the *type* of data. Therefore, log, data, and index data can be created on a device without confusion based on the device name. Indicating the database expected on the device in the name can cause confusion, however, if space constraints force you to create a different database on that device.

Database Contents

Devices can be named to represent the *database* and the expected *contents* to be created on that device. The device name can consist of the database name and the type of contents (data, log, index). For example, the four devices for the customer database could be named `CustomerDB_Data1`, `CustomerDB_Data2`, `CustomerDB_Log1`, and `CustomerDB_Idx1`. The name indicates the database and the type of data expected to exist on the device. This naming scheme requires you to be *very* confident about the placement of databases.

> **NOTE**
>
> Experience has shown that early estimates of index, log, and data requirements are usually way off.

Name devices in the most appropriate manner for your environment, based on the number of databases, whether certain data is placed on separate devices (log, index, data, and so forth), and your confidence that the intended use of the device will not change. (It's probably best if a device named `CustDB_Data1` not be used for expansion of the `ProductDB` database.) VLDB environments are more likely to use the database-contents approach to naming, because databases normally span multiple disks and there is more flexibility for placement.

Dump Device Naming Standards

Recall from Chapter 29, "SQL Server Database Backup and Restoration," that a dump device is created within the Server Manager or by using the `sp_addumpdevice` stored procedure. A *dump device* is used to back up an entire database or transaction log of a database to some type of media. Normally, this media is a local disk or a local tape device. You are required to provide the logical name and physical name of each dump device. This logical name is linked to the physical name. When dumping a database or transaction log, you can dump the database to the logical name (although the physical name can be supplied). The following are examples of three dump commands for the CustomerDB database:

```
dump database CustomerDB to CustomerDB_Dump
dump transaction CustomerDB to CustomerDB_Tran
dump database Customer DB to TAPE1
```

The logical name given to a dump device is normally based on the device type—tape or disk.

Tape Devices

A *tape device* is usually attached or integrated with your database server hardware. These devices normally take 8mm or 4mm tapes, and the tape capacity can be as great as 8GB. Tape devices have simple names. The string TAPE followed by a number is a common approach to a generic tape device name. For example, if you have three tape devices, they could be named TAPE1, TAPE2, and TAPE3.

Disk Devices

Disk device names should be selected with care. Dumping a database or log to disk creates a file on your file system. Each time a dump is executed to a disk device, a file is created whether a file exists or not. If you have not moved the previous dump to a new filename, the file will be overwritten and *lost*. Databases or logs dumped to disk should be copied off to a tape. Disk devices often are used in a development situation, because of the frequency of dumps and the inconvenience of tapes.

It is wise to create two disk dump devices for each database in your system—one for database dumps and one for transaction log dumps. Use the following format for the logical name:

```
DatabaseName_Dump
DatabaseName_Tran
```

Therefore, the CustomerDB database would have two dump devices created: CustomerDB_Dump and CustomerDB_Tran. Here is an example of the possible commands used to create these devices:

```
/* create a disk dump device for database dumping
** of the CustomerDB database*/
sp_addumpdevice "disk", CustomerDB_Dump,
    "c:\dbdump\CustomerDB\Cust_DB.dmp"
/* create a disk dump device for transaction log dumping
** of the customer database*/
sp_addumpdevice "disk", CustomerDB_Tran,
    "c:\dbdump\CustomerDB\Cust_DB.trn"
```

This approach has a number of benefits. Each database will have separate names for each type of dump. This eliminates the possibility of accidentally dumping the CustomerDB dump over the ProductDB dump. Additionally, a consistent naming standard enables you to more easily automate the backup process. Using uniquely named individual dump files for each database prevents a subsequent database dump from overwriting a dump file for another database, should the SQL Executive Task Scheduler fail to move or rename the file for some reason.

Operating System Names

You need to establish a naming standard for operating system files and directories. This standard normally is needed to organize DDL files. You need a DDL file for *every* important action and object that exists in SQL Server. This includes device creation, configuration changes (`sp_configure`), adding users and logins, creating and altering databases, creating objects (tables, views, indexes, and so forth), and granting permissions. Place the files in directories organized to enable you to recreate an entire environment from scratch.

When creating directory and file names, you may have to abbreviate the names of databases or database objects in order to meet file naming restrictions. In order to consistently name your objects and provide for understandable directory/file names, you will need to establish some standard for abbreviating names into filenames. Refer to the section on establishing abbreviation standards elsewhere in this chapter.

Directory Naming Standards

Specifying and organizing directory names should be based on your environment. Here are some important questions to answer:

- How many environments are you supporting (`CUSTOMER_DEVEL`, `CUSTOMER_SYSTEST`, `CUSTOMER_PERF`)?
- How many user databases exist in each server?
- Is there only one database or are multiple databases supported by the server?
- What is the approach to handling Data Definition Language files?
- Are all the creation statements in a single file or is there a file per object?
- Are index creation statements located in the same file as table creation statements?
- How do you intend to grant permissions?

Assume the greatest complexity and level of detail, a directory structure that can handle multiple SQL Servers, and individual creation files for each object.

Base Directory: Server Name

All DDLs for a server/environment should be stored relative to a base directory named according to the server name. For example, if you have three SQL Servers named `CUSTOMER_DEVEL`, `CUSTOMER_TEST`, and `CUSTOMER_PROD`, the base directories would be `\CUST_DEV`, `\CUST_TEST`, and `\CUST_PROD`, respectively.

The base directory should contain every necessary DDL statement to recreate the entire SQL Server. Separating the files from different SQL Server environments by directory enables different environments to contain different versions of the same file. This is helpful in regression testing.

First Subdirectory: Database Name

Under the base directory for the server are subdirectories for each of the databases supported by the server. This includes all user databases *and* the system databases (`master`, `model`).

User Databases

User databases are created to support applications. The name of the subdirectory should be identical to the database name. For the `CustomerDB` database in the `CUST_DEV` server, this is the directory name:

`\CUST_DEV\Cust_DB`

For each user database in the server, there are a number of subdirectories that can be created to hold the various DDL files. Table 36.4 lists possible subdirectories under the user database subdirectory.

Table 36.4. Sample subdirectory names.

Object or Activity	Subdirectory Name
Table	`..\tbl`
Index	`..\idx`
View	`..\view`
Rule	`..\rul`
Default	`..\def`
User-defined datatypes	`..\type`
Triggers	`..\trg`
Constraints	`..\con`
Permissions	`..\grant`
Stored procedure	`..\proc`
Remote procedure	`..\rproc`
Users	`..\user`
User-defined error messages	`..\error`

The directory containing the table creation statements for the CustomerDB database in the CUST_DEVEL server is the following:

```
\CUST_DEV\Cust_DB\tbl
```

The number of subdirectories under the database subdirectory is based on the level of granularity of your DDL files. Some sites like to put all creation statements in a single file. This gives you the least amount of control. To change the creation statement for a particular index, you might have to edit a 70,000-line file. The portion of the file for the index creation is copied into some temporary file or directly into an isql session for execution.

The next level of granularity is to put all creation statements of a particular type into a file—all the table creates in one file, the index creates in another. You still have the same problems with modification and execution, but you have a greater level of control (object type).

The last approach is to have a separate operating system file for each object in your system. This provides you with the maximum amount of control. Sites that use this approach normally save DDL files in a source code control system.

Master Database

The master database subdirectory should contain all files necessary to recreate the base server and all user database structures. After the execution of the scripts in this subdirectory, the server is configured, disk devices are initialized, dump devices are added, logins and users are added, and all user databases are created.

You can use the following subdirectories for the master database:

Object or Activity	Subdirectory Name
Configuration commands	..\config
Device creation (disk and dump)	..\device
Database creation, alter, and setting of options	..\dbcreate
User-defined system stored procedures	..\sysprocs
Addition of logins and users	..\user

The file you want to use to create the dump devices in the CUSTOMER_DEVEL server is \CUST_DEV\Cust_DB\device\Custo_DB.dmp.

Model Database

The model database subdirectory should contain all files necessary to recreate any applicable objects and/or users. The model database normally contains generic users, rules, defaults, user-defined datatypes, and user-defined error messages. These are the types of items that you might want propagated to a new database.

You can use the following subdirectories for the model database:

Object or Activity	Subdirectory Name
Rules	..\rul
Defaults	..\def
User-defined datatypes	..\type
User-defined error messages	..\error
Generic users	..\user

These guidelines should be able to be implemented, in some form, in your own organization. Note that user databases are handled differently than system databases.

File Naming Standards

Name DDL files identically to the object names they are creating, with a concatenated indicator. Of course, the name of the DDL file should be based on its contents. The content of each file is based on the granularity of control needed in your system. A file that contains the create statements for all the objects in a database should not be run to recreate the Order table only. All DDL statements that do not pertain to Order should be deleted before running the script. If you have individual files for each object in your system, however, the Order table can be recreated easily.

For example, a file containing the create statement for the Order table in the CustomerDB database in the development environment has this full path filename:

```
\CUST_DEV\Cust_DB\tbl\Order.tbl
```

File Extensions

It is common in some organizations to name a file with an extension indicating the type of object or activity. The philosophy is similar to indicators in SQL Server names. The extension may be redundant because you know the type of object being created by the name of the subdirectory (..\tbl, ..\rul, and so forth). A file extension, however, is normally provided as a matter of habit. The filename should be the concatenation of the object name and the extension. A rule called `Price_Rul` has a filename of `PriceRul.rul`. Notice the triple redundancy. A rule is created in the `..\rul` subdirectory with a filename of `ValidPrice_Rul` and a file extension of `.rul`. Consider that some sites do not use file extensions to indicate file type. Table 36.5 lists examples of filenames and extensions.

Table 36.5. Sample filenames and extensions.

Object or Activity	Subdirectory Name	Extension
Table	`..\tbl`	`.tbl`
Index	`..\idx`	`.idx`
View	`..\view`	`.vew`
Rule	`..\rul`	`.rul`
Default	`..\def`	`.def`
User-defined datatypes	`..\type`	`.typ`
Triggers	`..\trg`	`.trg`
Constraints	`..\con`	`.con`
Permissions	`..\grant`	`.gnt`
Stored procedure	`..\proc`	`.sp`
Remote procedure	`..\rproc`	`.rpc`
Users	`..\user`	`.usr`
User-defined error messages	`..\error`	`.err`
Threshold	`..\thresh`	`.thr`
Configuration commands	`..\config`	`.cfg`
Device creation (disk and dump)	`..\device`	`.dsk` `.dmp`
Database creation, altering, and setting of options	`..\dbcreate`	`.cre, .alt,` `.opt`
Addition of logins and users	`..\user`	`.lgn` `.usr`

This author typically prefers letting the directory name indicate the type of object or activity with which the script file is associated, and using a generic extension of `.sql` or `.qry`. This is because most query or script management tools out there that run in the Windows environment look for and save files with one of those two extensions by default. It also makes it easier to set up an association between your script files and your query/script management tool of choice within the Windows or Windows NT File Manager.

Source Code Control

Source code control software has been used for a number of years in the development of software to manage changes to application code (COBOL, C, and so forth). Source code control software also can be used to manage changes to DDL. It often acts as a logbook, enabling only one person to check out a file at a time. Checking in a file normally requires text to be provided to indicate why the file was checked out. The version number of the file is incremented each time a file is checked in. Some sites decide to cross-reference the check-in statement with a database change request document.

Capabilities of "cutting a version" of a group of related files should be available. For example, 20 different source code files (each having its own revision number based on the number of times it was changed) can be used to create a C application. Cutting a version relates these 20 files together and logically groups them. Database changes happen for a reason. These changes usually parallel application changes that can be listed as part of the check-in comment.

Source code control gives DBAs a mechanism to manage distinct versions of the database effectively. Through use of this tool, a DBA can identify what versions of DDL files to load to recreate a specific version of a database, object, or stored procedure.

Abbreviation Standards

Because of limitations on the lengths of filenames and database object names, it often is necessary to abbreviate descriptive components of file and object names. It is recommended that abbreviation standards be included in your standards definitions so that all users and developers are using a consistent method of abbreviation to avoid confusion.

Some guidelines for applying abbreviations and keeping names shorter, yet descriptive, are as follows:

- Avoid the use of prepositions in the name (for example, `BIRTH_DT` instead of `Date_of_Birth`).
- When abbreviation is necessary, it is most beneficial to drop the least informative descriptors and abbreviate those that lend themselves most naturally to abbreviation.
- A common method of abbreviation is to remove all vowels from a word, similar to what you see on some vanity license plates.
- Use abbreviations consistently for common identifiers as defined by a master list of common abbreviations, similar to the example provided in Table 36.6.

Table 36.6. Common abbreviations.

Base Word	Abbreviation
NAME	NM
NUMBER	NUM
CODE	CD
COUNT	CNT
AMOUNT	AMT
DATE	DT
TEXT	TXT
ADDRESS	ADDR
FLAG	FL
PERCENT	PCT
TIMESTAMP	TS
IDENTIFIER	ID

Summary

There are a number of SQL Server names to be defined in your environment. Too many SQL Server customers approach development without standards. This is likely to result in costly rework to bring an existing system up to standard after the standards are defined. Sometimes, customers decide not to change the database because of the cost of conversion. This results in a nonstandard SQL Server implementation in your environment.

Application standards are also important but are not the focus of this chapter. You need to develop application standards to be able to build high-performing SQL Server applications consistently. The construction of SQL statements can have striking effects on query performance, and the uniform implementation of triggers, procedures, rules, defaults, and constraints is important in providing a consistent approach to developing SQL Server systems. This enables developers to develop more efficiently because a base structure is provided. It is important that you define standards as early as possible, and monitor the adherence.

It also is important to define naming standards as early as possible and stick with them. Naming standards apply to the operating system as well as to SQL Server. With a consistent approach to naming, you can build upon the underlying structure. Scripts can be written to automate activities on the server, decreasing the overall workload.

Administering Very Large SQL Server Databases

37

When administering a *Very Large Database* (VLDB) environment, a number of items must be considered and reexamined in light of the special issues facing a VLDB. The main challenge of a VLDB is that everything is larger and maintenance tasks take considerably longer. VLDBs provide unique challenges that sometimes require unique solutions to administer them effectively.

What Is a VLDB?

The first question most people ask about VLDBs is what actually is a VLDB? When does a database become a VLDB?

For some people, it depends on how you define "very large":

- A fixed size (for example, 2GB, 20GB, 200GB, 4000GB)?
- When database-restore time exceeds a certain threshold (for example, 4 days)?
- When you're not sure whether to order 25 or 30 more 2GB drives?

In general, there is no easy way to quantify at what point a database becomes a VLDB. Possible definitions may include quantifiable parameters, but these tend to be rather subjective.

Here is the preferable definition:

> *A very large database is any database in which standard administrative procedures or design criteria fail to meet business needs due to the scale of the data.*

In other words, whenever the size of the database causes you to redesign your maintenance procedures or redesign your database to meet maintenance requirements, you are dealing with a VLDB.

VLDB Maintenance Issues

VLDBs present a number of issues for the database administrator, including these important ones:

- Time required to perform dumps and loads
- Time required to perform necessary database consistency checks
- Time and effort required to maintain data (that is, update statistics, reestablish fill factors, increment data loads)
- Purging and archiving data
- Managing partitioned databases

This chapter explores these issues and provides guidelines for implementing solutions.

Managing Database Dumps and Loads

Database dumps are necessary to provide recoverability in case of disaster. Although disk mirroring is a viable method to protect you from loss of data and system downtime due to disk failure, it doesn't protect you from other types of failures that can cause data loss. You still need database dumps in addition to disk mirroring to protect you from the following:

- Physical server failure
- SQL Server failure
- Database failure or corruption
- Table or index corruption
- Controller or disk failure
- User error

The main issue with database dumps and VLDBs is the duration of the database dumps. A SQL Server dump makes a physical copy of all the used pages in a database; therefore, dump time is proportional to the amount of data in the database.

If the time to back up a database is excessive, the time to restore it is even more so. During a database restore, SQL Server will replace all data pages in the existing database with the contents of the dump and initialize or "zero out" those pages not loaded. As a result, the load time is proportional to the size of the database.

The typical ratio between dump and load duration is approximately 1:3. That is, if it takes 1 hour to dump the database, it takes approximately 3 hours to restore it.

When developing a backup and recovery plan for VLDB environments, several issues must be considered:

- What is the impact of corruption and database loss on the application, end users, and company?
- What is the allowable and anticipated duration for database recovery?
- What is the allowable and anticipated duration of database dumps?
- What is the allowable and anticipated time to perform database consistency checks?
- How large are the database dumps going to be, and what are your backup media types and capacities?
- Can database dumps be completed within the defined maintenance window?
- Can the database be restored within an acceptable or required time frame?

The most important of these is the duration of dumps and loads. If you have an available maintenance window of 4 hours per evening to perform your database dumps and a full database dump takes 12 hours, what do you do? Conversely, if you have a requirement that the system, in the event of failure, be up and running within 2 hours, and a full database load takes 24 hours, how do you meet the recoverability requirements?

As stated earlier, because you are dealing with a VLDB, you need to take a more creative approach to database dumps and loads in order to meet your requirements.

The first thing to look at is how to speed up database dumps. One method available in SQL Server 6.0 is striping database dumps to multiple dump devices. If you have four dump devices available and a full database dump to a single device takes 8 hours, dumping to four dump devices concurrently takes just over 2 hours.

Another issue to consider is whether dumps are performed locally or across the network. Dumps across the network are inherently slower than dumps to a locally attached database device. For a VLDB, you want to dump locally.

Another approach often adopted by organizations working with VLDBs is physically to implement a single logical database as several smaller physical databases by partitioning the data. There are two advantages to this approach:

- Database dumps for multiple databases can be performed in parallel minimizing total database dump time.
- Your unit of recovery is the size of one smaller failed database—a single 2GB database loads much faster than a 12GB database.

In order to meet your required dump/load times, you may need to make several database architecture choices. These choices include whether to partition your data horizontally or vertically across databases. This approach essentially breaks a VLDB into a number of "databaselets." There are several advantages to multiple databases:

- If a database failure occurs in one of the databases, database activity may be able to continue in unaffected databases.
- Even if activity cannot continue in the event of a single database failure, the entire system can be up and running faster because the unit of recovery is smaller. Only the smaller single database needs to be restored, because other databases are unaffected.
- Dump load times can be reduced by enabling concurrent dumps of multiple databases.
- Static or archival data that doesn't need to be backed up on a daily basis can be segregated from online.
- It helps to avoid the need to change tapes if database size is less than tape capacity.

The disadvantages to partitioning a VLDB into multiple databases include the following:

- If there are any relationships between tables in different databases, activity may not be able to continue in unaffected databases.

- If there are any referential integrity constraints between tables in separate databases, you may lose referential integrity in the event of a database failure.

- Spreading tables across multiple databases may require application changes to qualify table references fully.

Developing a VLDB Backup/Restore Procedure

There are five steps to designing and implementing a backup/restore procedure for a VLDB:

1. Consider the amount of time you are willing to be "down" while performing a recovery (that is, the allowable impact of corruption or database loss):

   - If you need a database to be recovered within 8 hours, determine the size of a database that can be recovered in that amount of time.

2. Estimate table sizes for your database to determine partitioning sizes and options:

   - If you have a 40GB logical database, you may need to implement 10 4GB databases.

   - Are any single tables greater than 4GB?

   - How many tables can you fit in a database?

   - Are any tables candidates for partitioning based on this determination alone?

3. Develop your utopian administration schedule:

   - For every day during a month, determine what periods of time can be dedicated to administrative activities.

   - Are weekends available? This is not always the case.

   - If you determine that you have five hours per night to perform administrative activities, you then need to determine what activities need to be completed and how they can be distributed over your available administrative time.

4. Determine the rate of the dump process:

   - Take into consideration backup media capacity, speed, and number.

   - Benchmark several scenarios.

   - Perform several database dumps, varying the number of dump devices (striped dumps) and the number of dump processes that can occur in parallel.

5. Finalize your schedule and document accordingly.

Checking Database Consistency

The *database consistency checker* (DBCC) is a systems administration tool that verifies (and, if necessary, repairs) pointers internal to a database and its structures. Remember, DBCC *checks should be run prior to any database dump* to avoid dumping a corrupt database. The worst time to realize you have a bad page pointer is during recovery of a critical database when the load process fails due to inconsistency (this would probably be a good time to update your résumé!).

The DBCC commands typically lock user tables, indexes, system tables, and/or databases when running. In addition, certain DBCC commands, such as DBCC CHECKDB and DBCC CHECKTABLE are very I/O intensive. The more I/O required, the longer DBCC takes. These are the main issues with running DBCC in VLDBs.

If you want to follow the recommendations and run your DBCC commands prior to a database dump, and you have a daily administrative window of 8 hours, but the DBCC commands run for 4 hours and the database dump runs for 6 hours, how do you get everything to run within your administrative window?

In addition, although SQL Server enables a DBCC to run while activity is ongoing in the database, the locking and I/O overhead incurred by DBCC activity may severely impact online performance. If the DBCC commands take several hours to run, this will more likely force you to run them online, negatively impacting system performance.

Developing a Consistency Checking Plan

Your database might contain tables with very different processing requirements. Although it is somewhat mysterious how table corruptions occur, a static table is much less likely to encounter allocation problems than is a highly active table with ongoing allocations and deallocations.

To develop a plan for effectively checking your database consistency in a VLDB, you first need to analyze your tables and rank them in order of importance. For example, where would a corruption have the most serious effects on your system?

Next, analyze each nonclustered index on your table and rank it in order of importance to determine which indexes are most important to check.

Plan to check your high-activity tables as close to your dump as possible, because these tables are more likely to encounter allocation problems. Verify the consistency of these tables as close to the dump as possible. Static tables should need to be checked only after data loads. It is unlikely that corruption will occur once the data has been loaded and indexes created. Therefore, it shouldn't be necessary to check the static tables on a daily basis.

You should always run DBCC CHECKCATALOG immediately prior to the database dump. This DBCC command is relatively inexpensive to run and runs quickly, even on large databases. However, the duration of your CHECKALLOC and CHECKDB commands may not allow them to be run immediately before the dump due to time constraints.

To estimate execution times for your DBCC commands, run DBCC CHECKALLOC and DBCC CHECKDB for each database in your system and note time for completion, running them serially (one after the other) and in parallel (multiple databases at the same time). It is probable that DBCC CHECKALLOC and DBCC CHECKDB, using either of these two methods, cannot be completed in a reasonable time for most VLDBs. Thus, you need to develop a plan that breaks activities into smaller pieces.

Gather data into a table or spreadsheet recording various DBCC times for your tables. This data is needed only for the large tables in your system. All others, such as code tables, can be grouped and considered fairly negligible. The following are commands for which you need to record times:

- DBCC CHECKTABLE for each large table
- DBCC CHECKTABLE for skipping checking of nonclustered indexes
- DBCC TABLEALLOC for each large table
- DBCC INDEXALLOC for each index on the large tables

Next, categorize each table as either static or active. *Static tables* are tables that are not updated (or rarely updated) by the application (for example, tables containing historical data only). *Active tables* are tables where rows are inserted, updated, or deleted by the application on a regular basis. Rank the active tables based on importance to the overall success of the system.

In ranking the importance and criticality of a table, consider whether the data exists only in SQL Server (is created as part of the application) or can be re-created or reloaded from other sources. For example, a purchase table can be updated continuously throughout the day by the application, but a product table can be re-created from a source table on a host machine.

For your static tables, list the frequency that data is added (weekly, monthly, yearly, and so forth). This determines the frequency that you need to run your DBCC commands on the static tables.

If a nonclustered index is corrupted, it can be dropped and re-created as long as the base table is okay. Therefore, consistency of nonclustered indexes are of secondary priority. However, each index is used differently. For example, one index might be used in 80 percent of the queries, but another index might be used in only 3 percent of the queries. The frequently used index is much more important to the system and is a higher priority for checking than the infrequently used index.

Determine the amount of time you have to perform consistency checks in the batch window when you perform database dumps. You will use this period of time to determine which tables to check in that window. To be confident that a table is free of corruption, you need to run DBCC CHECKTABLE and DBCC TABLEALLOC on the table. Determine the time to perform both of these activities, starting with the highest-ranked activity table and working downward to determine which tables can be checked within your batch window.

If you can execute these commands on all activity tables (TABLEALLOC and CHECKTABLE) within the batch window, start adding in the highest-ranked index on each table and continue downward through the indexes until you determine which tables and indexes can be checked in the window before the dump. Consider also the possibility of running CHECKTABLE and TABLEALLOC on different tables concurrently as a way of accomplishing more tasks in a limited time period.

If all active tables cannot be checked within a batch window, during the next maintenance window, start with the point you left off during the last window. This way, over a certain time period (for example, two days or one week), you will have checked all the critical, active tables in the database. Plan to work in checks on your static tables as needed (weekends are a good time to run full checks on all tables).

When putting a consistency checking plan together, it is easy to concentrate on your application tables and forget about the system tables. It is possible for corruption to occur in system tables, and it is essential that you run DBCC commands on the system tables periodically as well.

If you break up your DBCC commands by using DBCC TABLEALLOC and DBCC INDEXALLOC, these commands look only at the allocation pages in use for each table and the index in the database. At some point, you will want to run DBCC CHECKALLOC, which checks all allocation pages in the database, including any allocation pages not currently in use, to check for any allocation page problems.

Data Maintenance

In addition to performing database dumps and checking database consistency on a VLDB, there are other data-maintenance commands that need to be performed on a database. These include updating statistics and purging and archiving data.

Updating Statistics

Index statistics are used by SQL Server to choose the correct access path at query optimization time. SQL Server creates statistics pages for every index in the database at index creation time, but they are not kept up-to-date by SQL Server as data values change or data is updated and deleted.

The DBA should update statistics when the data distribution changes to ensure that valid information is contained on the statistics page.

Update Statistics Scheduling

Typically, you update statistics on your tables by using the UPDATE STATISTICS command on a table:

```
UPDATE STATISTICS customer
```

However, this updates the index statistics serially. UPDATE STATISTICS takes a shared lock on the table for the length of time it takes for completion. This makes the table unavailable for update. On a very large table, this can be a significant period of time.

To speed the UPDATE STATISTICS process, you can update statistics concurrently on multiple indexes by executing UPDATE STATISTICS commands in parallel.

For example, if you have a customer table with a clustered index named `customer_clus` and four nonclustered indexes named `customer_idx1`, `customer_idx2`, `customer_idx3`, and `customer_idx4`, you create five files:

```
/* file 1*/
declare @starttime datetime
select @starttime = getdate()
UPDATE STATISTICS customer(customer_clus)
select "The number of minutes to UPDATE STATISTICS for customer_clus is:",
    datediff(mi, @starttime, getdate())
go
```

Create a similar file for each of the other four indexes and run the five UPDATE STATISTICS processes in parallel. This reduces the overall amount of time necessary to update statistics for all indexes on the table, making the table available to users more quickly.

> **CAUTION**
>
> If you are not using SMP-capable hardware, this can cause considerable strain on the system. Be wary of other activities you are trying to complete in the same time period!

Determine possible periods during the week when the statistics can be updated with little or no impact on online users. For OLTP systems, this likely will be after business hours (during the batch window). For DSS/Data Warehouse systems, the activity is primarily read-only, so update statistics can be scheduled during business hours.

In a VLDB database, you may not be able to update the statistics for all indexes on a table in a single batch window. With that in mind, consider spreading the update of statistics across several days as part of your overall maintenance plan. In addition, you may want to put together an index maintenance plan based on the usefulness and purpose of each index.

The distribution page is used by the query optimizer for estimating rows for nonunique searches or range searches. If you have a unique index on a table and a SARG with an equality operator (=), the optimizer knows one and only one row will match a single value. The distribution page is not used to estimate matching rows. For nonunique or range searches, the distribution page is used to estimate the number of matching rows within the range of values.

Indexes used in range retrievals are your highest priority for updating the statistics. For a unique index used in single row lookups, the statistics don't need to be updated as often, if at all.

Consider a customer table with the following indexes:

- `customer_id`

    Unique, nonclustered. Used for enforcement of uniqueness and single row searches by `customer_id`.

■ state, last_name

Nonunique, clustered. Used to spread contention (activity is by state) and 20 percent of name searches.

■ last_name, first_name

Nonunique, nonclustered. Used for 65 percent of name searches.

■ city, state

Nonunique, nonclustered. Used primarily for management reporting at the end of the month.

■ phone, last_name

Nonunique, nonclustered. Used for 15 percent of online searches.

The maintenance plan for updating the index statistics might be the following:

1. Every Sunday, update index 3, 2, and 5 (or update index 3 on Sunday, index 2 on Tuesday, and index 5 on Friday).

2. On the 25th of each month, update index 4 to support the monthly report.

Update of index 1 is not required.

Purge/Archive Procedures

At some point, the data in a VLDB may grow to a size approaching or exceeding the available database size. At this point, the decision needs to be made either to expand the database, or to purge or archive data to free space.

When purging or archiving data, a number of issues need to be addressed:

■ Locking implications
■ Performance implications
■ Storage and retrieval of archived data

There are typically two ways of dealing with historical data, purging or archiving. *Purging* is the process of removing data from its current location via a delete process. *Archiving* is the process of moving data from its current location to an archival area via a delete and insert process.

To develop a purge/archive strategy, you project database growth over the expected life of your system. Is the database 100GB, growing by 100MB per year, or 500GB, growing by 100GB per year? Over 10 years, the first system grows to only 101GB. The second system, however, grows to 1500GB. Based on physical limitations and the cost of dumps and DBCCs, purging/ archiving data is absolutely critical.

If your growth estimates necessitate removing data from your system periodically, you must decide whether to purge or archive. These are the questions you must answer:

■ Do current business requirements indicate which data is no longer useful to the company?

■ Are there any legal requirements regarding data retention?

■ Is it possible that data requirements may change in the future?

■ Can the data be re-created from another source?

To be able to purge or archive data from your system, you must be able to identify the rows within a table to be purged or archived. Common data characteristics used to purge or archive data include the following:

■ *Time-based.* Data is removed after a certain period of time. Common data elements that can be used are creation date or date of last activity.

■ *Non-time based.* Data is removed based on some element other than time, such as geography (state) or a customer or product list (generated from some source).

Many systems are often designed, developed, and put into production with no regard to purge/archive criteria. If the purge/archive process is not incorporated into the original system design, retrofitting a system to handle purge/archive criteria once it is in production can be extremely difficult and expensive. The time to identify purge/archive criteria is during the requirements analysis of a system, because it is possible that your purge/archive requirements will influence the database design.

To put together your purge/archive requirements and design your purge/archive process, identify the following:

■ How long data should remain in the table

■ The frequency in which data will be purged and archived

■ The element (column) in the table that will be used to identify the rows to purge and archive

Whether you are purging or archiving data, rows must be deleted from the current table. There are four main areas of concern in purge/archive activities that also need to be factored into the design of the purge/archive process:

■ Locking

■ Logging

■ Referential integrity

■ Transactional integrity

Locking and Performance Considerations

When deleting a large amount of data from a table, you must consider the locking implications of the delete and its impact on other online activities. SQL Server will escalate page locks to a table lock when the configured lock escalation point is reached by a single process during a transaction. Extensive archiving also acts as a batch process (which it is, in effect) and grabs an increasing share of a single processor's resources. Additionally, the I/O utilization for the affected disks can create a bottleneck.

One way to avoid locking problems is to perform archival activities when users are not using the system. Here are alternatives to avoid table-level locks:

- Use cursors to restrict rows being modified to one at a time
- Use rowcount to affect a limited number of rows at a time
- Use some other site- or table-specific value to limit pages that are being modified to be under the lock escalation threshold

If the clustered index is on the element used to identify the rows to purge in a table, the necessary rows are organized in clustered index order on the data pages. The number of rows that can be deleted before a table lock is acquired is dependent on the lock escalation threshold settings. The number of pages to be locked should be less than the lock escalation point to avoid a table level lock. Assuming the LE threshold percentage is left at the default of 0, the number of rows that can be deleted without a table lock escalation of the contiguous pages is the following:

```
LE Threshold Maximum × (# of rows per page)
```

If data is not clustered on the element you are using to purge, the pages locked are likely not to be contiguous, possibly a different page for each row. Therefore, you should assume that the number of rows that can be deleted at a time before a table lock is acquired must be less than the LE Threshold Maximum.

Logging Considerations

Rows being deleted from a table are logged in the transaction log. You determine whether your transaction log is large enough to handle the deletion of a large number of rows in a single transaction. To minimize I/O contention, your log should be placed on a separate disk to distribute the I/O.

Although your transaction log might be large enough to handle a single deletion of 500,000 rows from a table, those records remain in the log until they are dumped. Your purge/archive process should be designed to dump the transaction log after the completion of the purge process to clear the log for the next purge or normal system activity.

If your log is not large enough to handle the deletion as a single transaction, break the deletion into multiple transactions, dumping the logs between each transaction.

Referential Integrity Considerations

Data to purge/archive may be spread across multiple related tables. Your purge/archive process must be designed to consider *referential integrity* (RI) implications.

If referential integrity is maintained via triggers, cascading delete triggers may exist on a table where data is to be removed. This can cause the deletion of rows from one table to delete even more rows from a related table. Even though your log may be able to handle the delete from the first table, the cascading effects could fill your log, causing the purge to fail. It could also lead to exclusive table locks throughout your system.

Alternatively, if declarative RI is used to enforce referential integrity or a delete trigger is designed to disallow the delete activity if rows exist in a related table, you are forced to delete from related tables first.

If the purge/archive process is a batch job run during administrative periods, you can drop the triggers or RI constraints before running the purge/archive. If purge/archive is to be conducted during business hours, you probably should leave the triggers on the table.

If there are cascading delete triggers, you perform deletes in small quantities with regard to the number of rows deleted in each table in the relationship, attempting to avoid table locks.

If RI constraints exist or a trigger that disallows deletes while related records exists, you design the purge activity to delete from the tables furthest removed from the base table and work inward to the base table.

Transactional Integrity Considerations

A *transaction* is a logical unit of work. All activities in the transaction must complete successfully or they all should fail. During an archive process, you will likely insert data into a table in a different database and remove the data from its current location. If an error occurs that prevents the process from inserting the data into the new database, your archive process must not delete the data from its current database. Therefore, the insert/delete activity should be conducted in a transaction.

When archiving data with relationships across multiple tables, the design may require you to write transactions that transfer the data from all the related tables before deleting any of the rows. Make sure your design considers multi-table relationships.

Storage/Retrieval of Archived Data

To decide how and where you will archive the data, you need to answer some questions first:

- How available does the archived data need to be?
- Does the system need close to real-time access to the data?

■ What is the maximum amount of time your business can wait before having access to the data?

■ What are any legal requirements for storage and security?

The answers to these questions dictate whether the archived data must be stored online or can be saved into external storage locations, such as BCP files.

Typically, the reason systems are designed with archive mechanisms is to separate infrequently accessed data from the frequently accessed data. With VLDBs, this is often required in order to be able to back up the active data in a reasonable time period or to improve performance for the application that accesses the most frequent data.

"Old" data can often be handled on an exception basis, so a delay in accessing the data may be acceptable to the business and the historical data need not be stored online.

Possible Archive Solutions

If the data is accessed periodically (more than several times per day), the data should be stored online. The data can be stored in a separate table in the same database or in a separate database.

If the data is accessed infrequently (several times per month), the data can be stored externally with a mechanism to make the data available within a certain time period (minutes, hours, or days).

If the data is rarely, if ever, accessed, but must be maintained for legal purposes, some form of external storage is appropriate. The data can be stored in a database dump or in flat files.

Data Archival and Changes to Database Design

In addition to the problems and issues already discussed with purge/archive processes, another very important concern that is commonly overlooked is structural changes to your database over time. Most databases change over a period of time, even after the system is put into production. It is imprudent to ignore this fact when designing the purge/archive process.

Structural changes have much less impact on purge-only applications. If new columns are added to existing tables, it should have no effect on your purge application unless the field added is to become part of the key. If new tables are added to the schema, it should be fairly straightforward to accommodate the new table(s).

Structural changes can have a major effect on archive applications. Data that is archived must be able to be accessed at a later point in time. Your process should be insulated against schema changes as much as possible. If archiving to flat files, also create a file with the table schema in place at the time of the archive. If you use version control software, you may be able to associate the version of the script file used to create the table with the archived table.

If you are using a database approach to archive data, design your application so that it detects a difference between the application schema and the archive schema.

Storage Alternatives for Archived Data

There are a number of options for storage of archival data. Any of the following media types can be used for storing archived data:

- Tape
- Disk
- Optical disk

There are advantages and disadvantages for each type of storage media. A possible solution is a combination of more than one device type, for example, storing recently archived data on disk and older data moved to tape or optical disk.

The advantages of archiving to tape include the "unlimited" capacity of tape storage, the reusability and low cost of tape storage, and the security and reliability of data stored on tape. However, databases archived to tape take the longest to restore to an online state and are more difficult to locate than those on disk or optical disk.

The advantage of archiving to disk is that it provides the fastest access to archived data and makes archived files easy to locate. However, disk storage is the most expensive archiving solution and the files are less secure. You still need to back up the disk to tape or optical disk to protect against data loss due to disk failure.

Archiving to optical disk provides the advantages of high reliability, secure storage, and easier access to archive files than tape. However, unless you use the more expensive rewriteable optical disk, disk platters can be used only once and access times are slower than disk devices.

Data to be archived can be stored on any of the media types in any of the following formats:

- Database dumps
- BCP files
- Database device files

Database dumps are the simplest method of archiving an entire database. However, to restore the data, the destination database must be the same size or larger than the original database dumped, and only the entire database can be restored, not individual tables.

BCP files provide an easier method to restore data to individual tables, and the data can be loaded into non–SQL Server databases if necessary.

One approach sometimes used for archiving data is to archive the device file(s) containing the database to be archived. Here is the typical approach to archiving a database by using file system devices:

1. Freeze update activity on the database, set it to read-only, and checkpoint it.
2. Shut down SQL Server.
3. Copy the device file(s) containing the database to the optical disk or another location on the disk.
4. Restart SQL Server.

To restore a version of the database, use the following steps:

1. Shut down SQL Server.
2. Copy the device file(s) from optical or magnetic disk to the location of the archive database device(s).
3. Restart SQL Server.

You should now be working with an archived version of the database.

Dumping device files becomes a more complex procedure if a database spans multiple devices and it requires a shutdown of SQL Server to copy or replace a device file. This is probably not a viable approach in a production system. The advantage of this approach is that it is typically the fastest way to bring archived data online.

NOTE

Copying device files is not a backup method that is generally supported. It is presented here because it has been successfully implemented by a number of SQL Server customers.

Data-Partitioning Options

When dealing with VLDBs, it might become necessary to partition the database due to SQL Server size limitations or in order to meet your backup and recovery or data maintenance requirements. Partitioning a database does come with some disadvantages—consider these when planning database partitioning.

On the administrative side, you will have more databases to track and back up and more databases to add users to and in which to set up permissions. If any referential integrity exists between tables in different databases, you need some way to maintain the RI between databases during dump/load or if a database is unavailable.

There are two primary ways of partitioning databases: vertical partitioning and horizontal partitioning.

Vertical partitioning of data is the process of drawing imaginary lines through a database schema and placing individual tables in different databases. (See Figure 37.1.) Alternatively, it may also involve partitioning individual tables by columns to separate the frequently accessed columns from infrequently accessed columns and then placing the resulting tables in the same or different databases.

FIGURE 37.1.

Vertically partitioning a large database across multiple databases to minimize the size of each individual recovery unit.

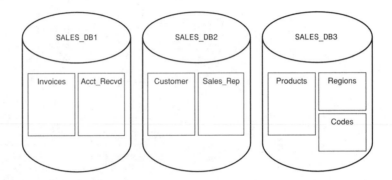

Horizontal partitioning of data involves breaking up tables into logical subsets and placing them into the same or different databases.

Vertical Data Partitioning

The benefits of vertical partitioning over a horizontal partitioning approach is that administration is simplified somewhat because all data for a given table is in a single table in a single database. Additionally, navigation and data access is simplified for end users because they do not need to know which portions of a table are in which database.

Another advantage of vertical partitioning is that the vertical partitioning can be hidden from the end user or application developer through the use of views. If you split a table by columns, a view can be created that joins the two table partitions. (See Figure 37.2.) Users can then select from the view as if it were a single table. This approach also requires the database containing the text table to have the `select into/bulkcopy` option on to enable nonlogged text operations.

No additional work is needed to join databases other than full name qualification (a standard programming practice in many shops anyway). No additional programming needs to be done to handle multi-database transactions because SQL Server automatically synchronizes transaction logs across databases if necessary in a single-server environment.

FIGURE 37.2.

Vertically partitioning a table to separate the infrequently accessed text data from the primary table data.

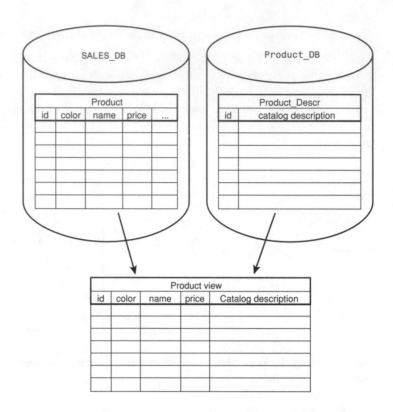

The drawback to vertical partitioning is that if you break up a database by drawing lines through the schema, and relational integrity must be maintained across those lines, recovering an individual unit may be tricky or impossible while maintaining the referential integrity between units. Backups need to be orchestrated and coordinated between databases to maximize RI and minimize recovery time.

Loss of a single database also can cause navigational problems across the entire database or application if necessary tables are not accessible.

When partitioning vertically, you should identify which components of the database get accessed most heavily in order to spread them across databases or devices. This enables you to gain maximum performance by minimizing I/O contention.

TIP

While moving tables around to balance I/O, the shuffling will require the application developers to modify their code to reference the tables.

You might want to consider creating a table containing a list of tables and the databases in which they reside. Application programmers can use this lookup table in their code to qualify the table names dynamically.

Another alternative is to create views in a single database that hide the actual location of the tables from the end users and developers.

Horizontal Data Partitioning

One of the primary reasons for and advantages of horizontal partitioning in a VLDB is the separation of active data from historical or inactive data. This helps to speed access of the active data by keeping it in a smaller table. Users do not need to wade through a lot of historical data to access the current data they need most frequently.

Alternatively, tables may need to be partitioned horizontally to spread activity across databases or devices, minimize locking overhead and contention, or improve performance for table access. Horizontal partitioning also can serve as a security mechanism by enabling access to specific subcomponents of data through database security.

The main drawback to horizontal partitioning is that to retrieve data from more than one table as a single result set requires the use of the UNION statement. For example, if an orders table is partitioned by year into separate databases, pulling data together for a three-year period requires the following command:

```
select name, state, order_num
    from address a, customer c, db1994.orders o
    where a.custid = c.custid
    and c.custid = o.custid
union
select name, state, order_num
    from address a, customer c, db1993.orders o
    where a.custid = c.custid
    and c.custid = o.custid
union
select name, state, order_num
    from address a, customer c, db1992.orders o
    where a.custid = c.custid
    and c.custid = o.custid
    order by state, name, order_num
```

Unlike vertical partitioning, horizontal partitions cannot be hidden from the end user by using views. UNION is not allowed in a view. Queries requiring data from multiple tables have to include the UNION statement explicitly. If you redefine your partitions and move tables around, your users and application developers need to update their queries or application code to reflect the changes.

Horizontal partitioning is usually broken down by using a logical boundary, such as a date-time field, geographical location, department number, or other logical grouping value. (See Figure 37.3.) The advantage to this approach is that is it easy to determine the location of data. However, logical groupings may not provide an even breakup of your tables, or certain logical groupings may be more active than others. If you want to spread your data evenly and randomly spread the access, you might consider using a random hash partitioning scheme.

In Figure 37.3, horizontal partitioning enables the inactive and static data for previous-year activity to be stored in a database separate from the active, current-year data, which needs to be backed up on a nightly basis. At the end of the fiscal year, the current database is renamed and made a historical database, and a new SALES_CURR_DB database is created.

FIGURE 37.3.

Horizontal partitioning of sales data by year across databases.

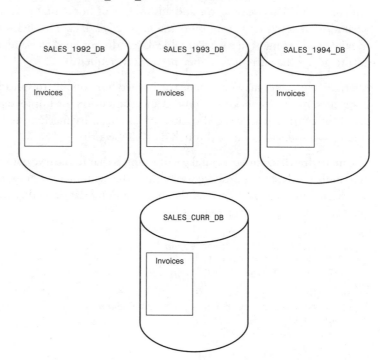

Hash partitioning is a horizontal partitioning based on deriving a hash key, rather than along logical boundaries. The hash key is usually generated by using an algorithm to generate some random value. The benefits of a hashing approach are realized if you experience performance problems with hot spots in your data. Hashing the table is a way of randomly spreading the data across resources, balancing the I/O and data access.

The main drawback to a hashing scheme is that it is harder for end users to determine where the data resides. It is also more difficult to determine the logical recovery unit if a single partition is lost. When using a logical boundary for partitioning your data—for instance, by fiscal year—in the event of loss of a single table, you can rebuild the table by loading the data for that fiscal year. With a hash partition, it is more difficult to determine which rows were lost, and rebuilding the table might require reloading data from multiple source files.

Summary

Although not originally designed as a data-warehousing system, SQL Server is capable of handling large data volumes. The proof is in the fact that a number of people have successfully implemented VLDBs in SQL Server. This is not to say that there aren't a few bumps in the road to making a VLDB work. It requires some advance planning—and at times creative solutions—to deal with the size-related limitations of SQL Server.

PART

V

Introduction to Open Client Programming

DB-Library Programming

38

In the following two chapters, you learn how to create client applications that interact with SQL Server. These chapters are by no means a complete resource; the intention is to introduce you to the basics of DB-Library and ODBC programming.

Examples in this chapter are provided in Visual Basic. Some limited examples are provided in C. The Visual Basic examples are created using Visual Basic version 3, with the Microsoft VBSQL object as the interface to the DB-Library. The C examples have been compiled by using Visual C++ version 1.5 for the 16-bit Windows environment. The development platform is an NT workstation running version 3.51, build 1057.

Essential Pieces of a DB-Library Client

Each DB-Library program has several essential pieces. (See Figure 38.1.) These pieces are entry code, a connection to the server, a message handler to process messages from the server, an error handler to process errors from DB-Library, submission of queries to the server, code to process results returned by the server, and exit code. Examples of all of these pieces are provided as you progress through this chapter.

FIGURE 38.1.

A flowchart of a simplified DB-Library program.

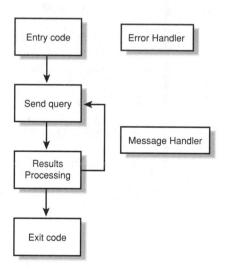

In Figure 38.1, note that the message and error handlers do not connect directly to the main program. These routines are called directly by the DB-Library layer. In C, the functions are registered with DB-Library, and pointers to the functions are passed into the DB-Lib layer. When a message occurs, it is passed from the server to the DB-Lib layer, which, in turn, calls the message handler. When errors occur, DB-Library detects them and fires the error handler. In VB, these functions are registered during initialization, and an event is fired from the VBSQL object. In either case, processing picks up where it left off after the appropriate function exits. A more detailed discussion on these handlers appears later in this chapter under the headings "The Message Handler" and "The Error Handler."

Entry Code

Entry code is very short and simple. The first step is to initialize the library. In VB, this also registers the message and error handlers.

In C, registration occurs separately and is made more complex with the introduction of the two callback functions. Registration of the message and error handlers can occur at any time after calling dbinit(), although, typically, all three functions are grouped together. A good place to call the initialization code is after receiving the WM_CREATE message for your application's main window. (For those of you who are new to Windows programming, this C code appears in the function named in your CreateWindow() call inside WinMain().)

The following code demonstrates entry code for an application program making use of DB-Library:

VB:

```
VersionInfo$ = SqlInit()
```

C:

```
static FARPROC lpdbwinMessageHandler;
static FARPROC lpdbwinErrorHandler;
switch (message){
case WM_CREATE:
(...other window creation code here...)
/* Returning -1 from WM_CREATE indicates Window creation failed */
    if (dbinit() == FAIL) return (-1);
    lpdbwinMessageHandler = MakeProcInstance(
    (FARPROC)dbwinMessageHandler, hInst);
    lpdbwinErrorHandler = MakeProcInstance(
    (FARPROC)dbwinErrorHandler, hInst);
    dberrhandle(lbdbwinErrorHandler);
    dbmsghandle(lpdbwinMessageHandler);
    break;
```

> **WARNING**
>
> If dbinit() returns FAIL or VersionInfo$ = "", initialization of DB-Library has failed. A well-written program must anticipate this and exit gracefully. Calling other DB-Lib functions before successfully initializing the library will be fatal.

Opening a Connection

After initialization has been done, it's time to open a connection to the server. Up to 25 connections are available by default. Microsoft's VBSQL object can manage up to 45 separate connections from a single object by calling SqlSetMaxProcs(). In C, this number can be increased with dbsetmaxprocs().

When opening a connection to the server, a *login record* is first allocated within your local DB-Library. This login record holds several pieces of information relevant to the connection, which must be set inside your application. Two of these parameters are required: the user name and the password. Optionally, a host name and application name can be provided. Finally, after the login structure has been populated, a connection can be opened to the server.

> **NOTE**
>
> A login and password are not required if the following things are true:
>
> ■ The SQL Server is running in mixed or integrated security mode. (See Chapter 27, "Security and User Administration," for more information on security.)
>
> ■ If a login name is provided, it matches the user's network username.
>
> ■ The login is through a trusted connection.

Let's go through each of these steps slowly and show the complete code listing for opening a connection at the end of this section. Here is a code snippet in VB demonstrating allocation of a login structure:

```
ptrLogin% = SqlLogin%()
If ptrLogin% = 0 Then        ' some error encountered
    MsgBox "Error: cannot allocate a pointer to a login"
End If
```

Here it is in C:

```
static LOGINREC *ptrLogin;
/* create a pointer to a login structure */

DBLOCKLIB();
/* Lock the Windows DB-Library */
if((ptrLogin = dblogin()) != (LOGINREC *)NULL){
    /* If ptrLogin is null, allocation has failed. */
(...)
    }
else
    MessageBox(hWnd,
    "Error: Cannot allocate a pointer to a login structure",
    "Example 1",
    MB_ICONSTOP);

DBUNLOCKLIB();
/* Unlock DB-Library */
```

When a login structure has been allocated within DB-Library, you must set some of the parameters within the structure prior to opening a connection to the server. Both the user name and the user's password are required to log in. It's a good idea to set the host name and the application name, too. The host name will show up in the output from sp_who, and is, according to general practice, the network name of the machine running the client application. Both the host name and the application name will appear in the sysprocesses table while this connection remains active. Well-behaved apps identify themselves to the SQL Server so that processes are easily identifiable.

Here, the user name, password, host name, and application name are set. If any of the calls fail, they will return 0, thus setting the whole logical expression to 0. The second example shows a simpler implementation, without extensive error checking.

VB:

```
If SqlSetLUser%(ptrLogin%, "sa") * SqlSetLPwd%(ptrLogin%, "ringding")
➡    * SqlSetLHost%(ptrLogin%, "\\WESTOVER")
➡ * SqlSetLApp%(ptrLogin%, "Example 38.1") = FAIL Then
    MsgBox "Error: cannot update login structure"
    SqlFreeLogin (ptrLogin%)    ' free the login structure
    Exit Sub
End If
```

C:

```
    DBSETLUSER(ptrLogin,(LPSTR)"sa");
        /* set user name to sa*/
    DBSETLPWD(ptrLogin,(LPSTR)"ringding");
        /* set the sa password in the login structure */
    DBSETLHOST(ptrLogin, (LPSTR)"\\WESTOVER");
    /* set host name to the name of your machine, for example */
    DBSETLAPP(ptrLogin, (LPSTR)"Example 38.1");
```

After setting the appropriate values in the login structure, you're ready to ship it off to the server and establish a connection. This is very straightforward.

VB:

```
SqlConn% = SqlOpen%(ptrLogin%, ServerName$)
If SqlConn& = 0 Then MsgBox("Error: Cannot login to the server.",
➡"Example 1", MB_ICONSTOP)
SqlFreeLogin (ptrLogin%)    ' free the login structure
```

C:

```
/* Open a connection to the MSSQLServer server.  NULL indicates failure. */
if((dbproc = dbopen(ptrLogin,(LPSTR)"MSSQLServer")) == (DBPROCESS *)NULL)
    MessageBox(hWnd, "Error: Cannot login to the server.",
    "Example 1", MB_ICONSTOP);
dbfreelogin(ptrLogin);
/* Deallocate login structure in DB-Library */
}
```

After opening a connection to the server, the information in the login structure is no longer needed, and the memory space that was allocated can be returned by calling SqlFreeLogin()/ dbfreelogin(). Note that if several connections need to be opened at one time, the login space can be reused. For example, if dbopen() is called three times in succession, three separate connections are created based on the information in ptrLogin.

> **TIP**
>
> To retrieve a list of server names, call the `SqlServerEnum()` or `dbserverenum()` function. This function can search locally or through the network for available servers. An example is provided later in this chapter, in the section titled "Cool Tricks and Handy Functions."

The following is a complete code listing containing everything in this section.

VB:

```
Dim VersionInfo$, ptrLogin%, SqlConn%

VersionInfo$ = SqlInit()

ptrLogin% = SqlLogin%()
If ptrLogin% = 0 Then          ' some error encountered
    MsgBox "Error: cannot allocate a pointer to a login"
End If

If SqlSetLUser%(ptrLogin%, "sa") *
➥SqlSetLPwd%(ptrLogin%, "ringding") * SqlSetLHost%(ptrLogin%, "\\WESTOVER")
➥ * SqlSetLApp%(ptrLogin%, "Example 38.1") = FAIL Then
    MsgBox "Error: cannot update login structure"
    SqlFreeLogin (ptrLogin%)     ' free the login structure
    Exit Sub
End If

SqlConn% = SqlOpen%(ptrLogin%, ServerName$)
If SqlConn& = 0 Then MsgBox("Error: Cannot login to the server.",
➥"Example 1", MB_ICONSTOP)
SqlFreeLogin (ptrLogin%)     ' free the login structure
```

C:

```
static LOGINREC *ptrLogin;
/* create a pointer to a login structure */
DBLOCKLIB();
/* Lock the Windows DB-Library */
if((ptrLogin = dblogin()) != (LOGINREC *)NULL){
/* If ptrLogin is null, allocation has failed. */
    DBSETLUSER(ptrLogin,(LPSTR)"sa");
/* set user name to sa*/
    DBSETLPWD(ptrLogin,(LPSTR)"ringding");
/* set the sa password in the login structure */
    DBSETLHOST(ptrLogin, (LPSTR)"\\WESTOVER");
/* set host name to the name of your machine, for example */
    DBSETLAPP(ptrLogin, (LPSTR)"SQL Server Unleashed Example");
    /* Open a connection to the WESTOVER server.  NULL indicates failure. */
    if((dbproc = dbopen(ptrLogin,(LPSTR)"SYBASE")) == (DBPROCESS *)NULL)
        MessageBox(hWnd, "Error: Cannot login to the server.",
        "Example 1", MB_ICONSTOP);
    dbfreelogin(ptrLogin);
```

```
/* Deallocate login structure in DB-Library */
    }
else
    MessageBox(hWnd, "Error: Cannot allocate a pointer to a login structure",
        "Example 1", MB_ICONSTOP);
DBUNLOCKLIB();

/* Unlock library */
```

The Message Handler

Defining a message handler is not necessarily required, but it is an essential part of even the simplest DB-Library applications. The *message handler* deals with messages from the server to the client—in this case, from SQL Server to your application. The message handler is fired whenever a print statement is executed by the server, or to report a problem to the client. Using print is common inside stored procedures to pass user-defined messages back to an application.

> **NOTE**
>
> Some common messages are *Login failed* and *Incorrect syntax near...* You can view all system messages by running the query *select * from sysmessages* from the master database. Running on my 6.00.121 (Jun 13 1995 11:32:40) NT SQL Server, I got 1,900 messages.

To better understand the relationship of the client program, DB-Library, and SQL server, consider Figure 38.2.

FIGURE 38.2.

Channels between SQL Server and your client application.

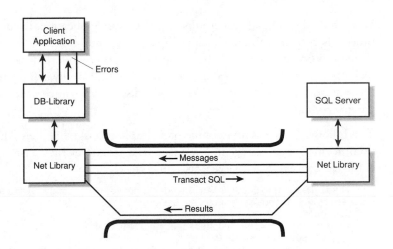

When your message handler is invoked, several parameters are passed in to it: the connection number, the message number, the error state number, the severity level, and the message text.

The connection number corresponds to the value returned by Sql0pen(). It is possible to receive a message that has either an invalid connection number or a connection number equal to 0. In this case, the connection is dead, and steps should be taken to disable it.

The message numbers can be used to trap particular messages. They are also useful for troubleshooting. If users are getting a particular message, they are more likely to report the message number verbatim than a message description. After you receive the message number, you can look it up yourself by issuing a "select * from sysmessages where error=<msgnumber>" query.

> **TIP**
>
> There are some messages that you will want to trap and hide from your users. The first, 4002, is Login failed. This message is followed directly by DB-Lib error number 10003. Only one of these should be displayed. Another message, 5701, is informational only. This message lets you know when your database context has changed. Usually, this message is less informative than annoying.

Messages are also assigned a severity level. The severity level is either 0, or between 10 and 26, inclusive. Severity levels describe the seriousness of the message. Informational messages are assigned a severity level of 0. The most serious ("Lock hash table linkage has been corrupted", for example) have a severity level of 26. Based on this, your program could, for example, pop a message box with an ICON_EXCLAMATION if the severity were over 18, pop an ICON_INFORMATION if between 10 and 18, inclusive, or put the message on a status bar if the severity is 0.

You should be sure to detect deadlocks within your application. If a deadlock occurs, and your process is chosen as the deadlock victim, message number 1207 is passed into your handler. When this occurs, you may either resubmit the previous work or notify your user that a deadlock has occurred and allow the user to take action. Usually, simply resubmitting the work is the best option, because this makes deadlocks, often a source of irritation, completely transparent to your users.

The following code is an example of a simple message handler. This handler displays any noninformational message in a message box. It ignores the Login failed message and the Database context has changed to... message:

```
Sub vbsql_Message (SqlConn As Integer, Message As Long, State As Integer,
➥Severity As Integer, MsgStr As String)
    Dim msg$, Title$, res%
    If Message <> 4002 And Message <> 5701 Then
        If Severity <> 0 Then
            Title$ = "Sql Server Message: Message=" & Message
          Title$ = Title$ & " State=" & State & " Severity=" & Severity
```

```
            res% = MsgBox(MsgStr$, MB_ICONINFORMATION Or MB_OK, Title$)
        End If
    End If
End Sub
```

The Error Handler

The *error handler* receives errors from DB-Library. These errors may report that a SQL server cannot be found, or that the connection has been broken, or that not enough memory is available for a connection to be opened. A list of errors is included in the VBSQL.BI constants file or the sqldb.h include file. This include file is available by purchasing the SQL Server Programmer's Toolkit.

The error handler, like the message handler, is passed a number of parameters. These parameters are the connection number causing the error, the severity of the error, the error number, and the error description.

Sometimes an error occurs from a dead connection. In this case, it is important to take steps within your handler to disable the connection. Attempting to send queries over a dead connection will fail.

> **TIP**
>
> One message that you should always trap and discard is number 10007, "General SQL Server Error". This message is always followed immediately by a message, which can be dealt with inside the message handler. It is often quite bothersome to users to recognize the same error twice within a client application.

Here is a sample error handler, which ignores the general error, checks for dead connections, and attempts a resynch with the SQL server if a nonfatal error has occurred:

```
Sub vbsql_Error (SqlConn As Integer, Severity As Integer,
➥ErrorNum As Integer, ErrorStr As String, RetCode As Integer)
Dim msg$, Title$, ix%, res%

    ' suppress error message for general SQL Server error
    If ErrorNum <> 10007 Then
    ' if the error killed the connection
        If SqlDead(SqlConn%) Or (SqlConn% = 0) Then
            Title$ = "Sql Server Error: Severity=" & Severity & " ErrorNum="
        Title$ = Title$ & ErrorNum & " RetCode=" & RetCode
            MsgBox ErrorStr, MB_ICONEXCLAMATION, Title$
                    ' Change the login icon to logged out
                    frmMain.cbLogin.Value = False
        ' Set connection number to 0 for our array.
        ' Other routines will test SqlConn for zero
                SqlC(0).SqlConn% = 0
        End If
```

```
Else
        ' connection is not dead, so just do
        ' normal message handling here

        ' set up and send a message box
        Title$ = "Sql Server Error: Severity=" & Severity
    Title$ = Title$ & " ErrorNum=" & ErrorNum & " RetCode=" & RetCode
        res% = MsgBox(ErrorStr, MB_ICONEXCLAMATION Or MB_OKCANCEL, Title$)
    End If

        Select Case ErrorNum
        Case SQLEBTOK      ' 10008 BAD TOKEN
        Case SQLETIME      ' 10024 CONNECTION TIMED OUT
        Case SQLEOOB       ' 10027 OUT OF BAND DATA
        Case SQLERPND      ' 10038 RESULTS PENDING
        Case SQLECSYN      ' 10039 SYNTAX ERROR IN SOURCE FIELD
        Case Else          ' ALL OTHER ERRORS
            Exit Sub            ' AVOID attempting a resynch
        End Select

        ' try resynching with SqlOK%
        ' if both succeed then we're A-OK and running.
        If SqlOK%(SqlConn%) Then
          If SqlCancel%(SqlConn%) = FAIL Then
            ' logout
            frmMain.cbLogin.Value = False
          End If
        Else ' Sql not ok.
         frmMain.cbLogin.Value = False
        End If

End Sub
```

Sending Queries

After DB-Library has been initialized and the handlers have been defined, it is time to issue a query to the server. The first step in this task is accomplished with the SqlCmd() function:

```
res% = SqlCmd%(SqlConn%, " select * from sysmessages")
```

SqlCmd places SQL statements into the buffer inside DB-Library. This buffer is maintained until after a query is sent by using SqlExec or SqlSend (see the code sample). The next call to SqlCmd() after either of these function calls clears the command buffer unless the SQLNOAUTOFREE option is on.

Note that in the example, there is a space at the beginning of the query. This is simply defensive programming. Suppose a query has been issued with SqlCmd(). Then suppose that, later in the code, another SqlCmd puts more data into the command buffer. The two queries could end up slapped together, as in select * from sysmessagesselect getdate(). A space never does damage, but could prevent a silly error.

After placing the commands into the command buffer in DB-Library, they must be sent to the server. There are two functions to accomplish this.

Very simple query sending can be accomplished through the use of the `SqlExec()` function. When this function is called, the command buffer is sent, and the function waits until after the server has begun to return results before returning:

```
If SqlExec%(SqlConn%) = SUCCEED Then
(Do results processing here)
```

One of the problems with `SqlExec` is that it ties up your application while waiting for the SQL Server to return its results. During the time `SqlExec` is waiting, no other activity occurs inside your application, and the performance of other programs within Windows is affected. If the results are not ready within the timeout period (by default, 60 seconds), `SqlExec` gives up on SQL Server and returns `FAIL`.

To get over this problem, use `SqlSend`, which sends the command buffer and instantly returns. You have assumed the responsibility for polling the server to determine whether results are ready, but in the meantime, your application (and your system) is free to do other things:

```
res% = SqlSend(SqlConn%)
```

> **TIP**
>
> Use `SqlSend` to do most of the work in your application. `SqlExec` should be used for only the simplest queries.

Retrieving Results

After sending the query, you must poll for results. One way to do this is inside a timer loop: call the timer once a second, or once every half second. Inside, use `SqlDataReady()` to determine whether results are prepared. If they are, call `SqlOK()` to begin retrieving results. A `SqlSend` immediately followed by a `SqlOK()` is the same thing as a `SqlExec()`:

```
If SqlDataReady%(SqlConn%) Then
        If SqlOk%(SqlConn%) Then
```

> **WHY A TIMER IS BETTER THAN A LOOP**
>
> Under Windows, many processes are running together. Whether they're running in a multithreaded environment, such as NT, or in a multitasking environment, such as Windows for Workgroups and the standard Windows 3.1, your process is not alone. If you create a loop such as this one
>
> ```
> While SqlDataReady(SqlConn%) = FAIL
> Loop
> ```

you are fooling Windows into believing that your application has important work to do. This is bad. Using a timer (which, by the way, is a limited resource) enables you to check for results now and then and also enables the rest of the system to get on with whatever else it has to do.

After sending the query, regardless of the method you used, you must call a series of functions to retrieve the results of your query. First, call SqlResults(). This prepares the first result set for processing. Create a loop, such as the one shown here:

```
res% = SqlResults%(SqlConn%)
' Loop through each result set
Do Until res% = NOMORERESULTS or res% = FAIL
    RowType% = SqlNextRow%(SqlConn%)
     ' RowType gets type of row
    Do Until RowType% = NOMOREROWS or RowType% = FAIL
        ' Loop through each row in the result set
        For Col% = 1 To NumCols%
            ColType% = SqlColType%(SqlConn%, Col%)
        ' ColType gets datatype of column
            TheData$ = SqlData$(SqlConn%, Col%)
            ' TheData$ gets Result data
        Next Col%
    Loop
Loop
```

Of course, this code fragment doesn't actually use the data; something has to happen inside the column loop. You've probably noticed that all data returned by using SqlData() is in the form of character data. What about numerical data? Well, for that, you need to use VB conversion functions such as Val(). All the data you receive will be in character format.

In the third line, you make a call to SqlNextRow to retrieve the data in the row. The return value of SqlNextRow indicates whether this is a REGROW (regular row) or a compute row, in which case the value is the (positive) identification number of the compute row. If SqlNextRow returns -2 or NOMOREROWS, the result set is exhausted.

> **NOTE**
>
> Empty result sets will still cause the creation of a result set, and will return SUCCEED from SqlResults(), but will return NOMOREROWS immediately when SqlNextRow() is called.

Exit Code

After using DB-Library, shut it down properly. Before exiting, make sure to call SqlWinExit(). It is also good practice to call SqlExit() prior to calling SqlWinExit(). SqlExit() closes all open connections and frees all allocated login structures. It is identical to calling `SqlClose()` and `SqlFreeLogin()` for each open connection and login structure.

> **TIP**
>
> Closing your connections prevents SQL Server from believing that your application is still running, and is proper etiquette for any application making use of SQL Server. Failing to close all connections before exiting results in `Null DB Process Pointer` errors the next time a DB-Lib application runs. Often, this can lead to W3DBLIB.DLL becoming confused (corrupted in memory) and will force a Windows restart.

When you call `SqlWinExit()`, you inform the VBSQL object that your application is exiting. The library releases the memory it used to track your application. In C, call `dbwinexit()` and `dbexit()`.

Cool Tricks and Handy Functions

During the time that I've been programming DB-Library applications using Visual Basic, I've come across some interesting and challenging problems. This section offers a few of the most interesting functions that you can add to your toolbox to solve these problems. My hope is that you'll find these functions useful, then write me at `102101.164@compuserve.com` to tell me how you improved them.

GetServerList()

One of the first functions I wrote for my VB/SQL toolbox was `GetServerList()`. This function populates a drop-down combobox with a list of all servers detected locally and/or on the network. "Locally" here means in either WIN.INI or SQL.INI, depending on the version of the DB-Library being used. It returns the number of servers found:

```
Function GetServerList (cbx As ComboBox, mode%) As Integer
    ' Retrieves the list of servers from Win.INI
    ' or SQL.INI and/or the network
    ' parameters are ...
    ' cbx  = a combobox to be filled with server names
    ' mode = LOCSEARCH
    '        NETSEARCH (scan the network)
    '        LOCSEARCH + NETSEARCH (both)

    Dim RetVal%, Entries%, ix%, Char0$, Pos%, Length%
    Dim Buffer As String * 255
    Char0$ = Chr$(0)

    ' *** this function sets up the server names in the combo box ***
    ' if you use LOCSEARCH + NETSEARCH, both are searched, but if a
    ' server is available in both lists, it appears twice.
```

```
     ' clear the combo box if enumerating servers
     cbx.Clear

     Do
         RetVal% = SqlServerEnum%(mode%, Buffer$, Entries%)
         If RetVal% > 1 Then Exit Do    ' can't enumerate if > 1: error

         ' scan the buffer looking for Entries%
         Pos% = 1                        ' start in the first position
         For ix% = 1 To Entries%
             ' look for chr$(0) in String, which delimits server names
             Length% = InStr(Pos%, Buffer$, Char0$) - Pos%
             If Length% <= 0 Then Exit For ' this is an error case
             cbx.AddItem Mid$(Buffer$, Pos%, Length%)
             Pos% = Pos% + Length% + 1
         Next ix%
     Loop While RetVal% = MOREDATA%

     ' don't crash if there's no SQL Server entries!!
     If cbx.ListCount > 0 Then
         ' Set the list to the first server and
         ' return the # of servers found
         cbx.ListIndex = 0
         GetServerList = cbx.ListCount
     Else
         GetServerList = 0
     End If
End Function
```

If you install any of the utilities on the disk in the back of the book, you'll see this function every time you log in to a server. All the work occurs inside the `Do...Loop`, where `SqlServerEnum()` is called.

WARNING

Many DB-Libraries will report an out-of-memory condition while calling `SqlServerEnum()`. This fires your error handler with error number 10000.

GetTimeFromServer

Sometimes it's useful to retrieve the time from the SQL Server. Once the time has been retrieved, it is possible to set the time on a client station to match that of the SQL Server. Another good use for this function gives your application a dependable source of date and time for a log file. The SQL Server is a much better source for date and time than a PC client, because the PC is subject to the whims of the user and the state of the PC's battery.

The function accepts a connection number (returned from `SqlOpen()`) and an operation. The operation is just a fancy add-in that isn't critical to the workings of the function; it enables different formats of the `getdate()` string. If the query fails for any reason, it's designed to return the client time. This may not be the best solution to failure; replace the error code with something else if you would like to be aware of failures from calling procedures:

```
Function GetTimeFromSQLServer (SqlConn%, nOp%) As String
Dim Query$, res%
' Accepts connection number and operation.
' The connection number must be established prior to calling
' this function.
' Operation is one of the following:
' SQLTM_ALL = 0       Return complete getdate() string
' SQLTM_DATE = 1      Return date portion only
' SQLTM_TIME = 2      Return time portion only
' SQLTM_ALL2 = 3      Differently formatted ALL;
'                     mm/dd/yy hh:mm (military)

    Select Case nOp%
        Case SQLTM_ALL
            Query$ = "select getdate()"
        Case SQLTM_DATE
            Query$ = "select convert(char(8), getdate(), 1)"
        Case SQLTM_TIME
            Query$ = "select convert(char(8), getdate(), 8)"
        Case SQLTM_ALL2
            Query$ = "select convert(char(8), getdate(), 1)" &
➡ " " & "convert(char(5), getdate(), 8)"
    End Select

    res% = SqlCmd%(SqlConn%, Query$)
    If SqlExec(SqlConn%) = FAIL Then GoTo GOErr:
    ' message handler fires here if there's an error
    res% = SqlResults%(SqlConn%)
    Do While res% <> NOMORERESULTS And res% <> FAIL
        res% = SqlNextRow%(SqlConn%)
        Do While res% <> NOMOREROWS And res% <> FAIL
            GetTimeFromSQLServer = SqlData(SqlConn%, 1)
            res% = SqlNextRow%(SqlConn%)
        Loop
        res% = SqlResults%(SqlConn%)
    Loop
Exit Function

GOErr:
    GetTimeFromSQLServer = Now
    Exit Function
End Function
```

Retrieving Object Information

Another project I wrote required the application to retrieve the names of all databases available on the connected SQL server. From this list, the user selected one database, which caused the application to retrieve a list of tables in the selected database. This was repeated for indexes in the table.

Retrieving information like this can be extremely useful inside your applications. Here is the code that populates a combobox. I placed the query to issue in the box's tag prior to calling

LoadCombo(). (If you ever run a copy of the Aurora Distribution Viewer, you can grin smugly whenever you use it—you now know how we did the interface work!) A picture of the Distribution Viewer at work is in Figure 38.3. A demo version is available on the CD that accompanies this book.

```
Sub LoadCombo (SqlConn%, Box As ComboBox)
On Error GoTo LCHandler
    If SqlCmd(SqlConn%, CStr(Box.Tag)) Then
        If SqlExec(SqlConn%) Then
            If SqlResults(SqlConn%) <> NOMORERESULTS Then
                Box.Clear
                Do Until SqlNextRow%(SqlConn%) = NOMOREROWS
                    Box.AddItem SqlData(SqlConn%, 1)
                Loop
                If Box.ListCount > 0 Then Box.ListIndex = 0
            End If
        End If
    End If
Exit Sub

LCHandler:
If Err = 7 Then
' Out of memory: Some yahoo with over 32,767 tables,
' databases, or indexes.
    Dim t$
    Select Case Box
        Case Box Is frmMain.cbxDatabase
            t$ = "databases"
        Case Box Is frmMain.cbxTable
            t$ = "tables"
        Case Box Is frmMain.cbxIndex
            t$ = "indexes"
    End Select
    MsgBox ("Only the first 32,767 " & t$ & " will appear in the combo box.")
End If
Exit Sub
End Sub
```

FIGURE 38.3.

The Aurora Distribution Viewer, using the code described in LoadCombo().

The queries attached to the comboboxes are listed in the following code. The database selected by the user is used, so that it is the current database for each of the queries. Note that in the last query, the object_id for the table specified in cbxTable is used, which must be passed to SQL Server in quotes. Instead of using a constant QUOTE, defined elsewhere as chr$(34), we also could have used single quote marks.

```
cbxDatabase.Tag = "select name from master..sysdatabases"
cbxTable.Tag = "select name from sysobjects where type = 'U' order by name"
cbxIndex.Tag = "select name from sysindexes where id=object_id("
cbxIndex.Tag = cbxIndex.Tag & QUOTE + CStr(cbxTable) & QUOTE
cbxIndex.Tag = cbxIndex.Tag & ") and indid > 0 order by indid"
```

Programming Potholes

When programming DB-Library, I ran into a few things on the highway of VB code—some of them at 120 mph. Listed here are a few of the specific things about which a beginning DB-Library programmer should be aware.

Versions of SQL Server behave differently. This is a simple, but important, issue to the beginning DB-Library programmer. The version of the SQL Server can be retrieved by issuing a select @@version query and parsing the results.

NULL DBPROCESS pointers can surprise you. If another application has mistreated DB-Library, or if one of your own applications terminates unexpectedly (a General Protection Fault, for example), a NULL DBPROCESS pointer error can occur. This is error number 10001. When your application starts, if a NULL DBPROCESS error occurs, it fires your error handler as soon as it is installed. Anticipate this either by making the 10001 error transparent or by treating it as a special case, or both.

The connection to the SQL Server flows only one way at a time. Figure 38.2 shows a pipe between the client and server, along which flows SQL commands and query results. Keep in mind that if results are flowing through the pipe, no commands can be sent until all results have been processed. Any attempt to do so will cause error number 10038, Attempt to initiate a new SQL Server operation with results pending. Following this error, DB-Library often becomes unstable. You should take pains in every DB-Lib project to avoid sending queries on a connection that is currently waiting for results.

The versions of the DB-Library and the net-library .DLLs are heavily dependent upon one another. Both Sybase and Microsoft have their own versions of the Windows 16-bit DB-library, named W3DBLIB.DLL. There are lots of these around; one is bundled with the Visual Basic VBSQL.VBX, one comes with the Sybase Open Client installation, one comes with the Microsoft Client Installation, etcetera ad infinitum.

Now, take this problem and square it, because the same thing has happened with net libraries. There are net libraries for named pipes, TCP/IP Windows Sockets, Novell SPX, and many others.

This mess is complicated by the fact that, as a third party, your ability to redistribute these libraries is severely restricted. Simply finding a pair of libraries that can live in peace is not enough; afterward, you need to find a way to get your users to install similarly agreeable libraries.

Summary

DB-Library applications are relatively simple to create. Once the basics of the library are clearly understood, creating simple DB-Lib apps is easy. After that, all that is left to do is create an interface.

Using Visual Basic to go against data on a SQL Server is a smart decision. If your applications are performing CPU-intensive operations, externalize them in a DLL written in C for maximum speed. Using VB to program your DB-Lib apps assures a simpler interface for development and maintenance.

Write clever message and error handlers to manage errors generated by SQL Server and the DB-Library itself. The ability to define these handlers enables your application to account for most eventualities.

This concludes our overview of the DB-Library. Whether to use DB-Library or ODBC is a question that you'll explore in the next chapter. Each approach has its benefits.

ODBC Programming

39

Now that you've taken a look at programming using DB-Library, let's look at something Microsoft would much rather have you use: *ODBC*, or the *Open Database Connectivity* interface. This chapter discusses the concept behind ODBC, then provides some sample Visual Basic code using the ODBC API. Many good, exhaustive ODBC books are on the market, and any serious programmer planning to write to the ODBC interface should be armed with them accordingly.

Generally, ODBC enables a single application to talk to a variety of database systems from a single code set, using SQL as a portable method for manipulating data. It accomplishes this through the use of interchangeable ODBC drivers on the client machine. ODBC takes care of some of the things that DB-Lib programmers still need to handle, such as login screens and server lists.

If you are using Visual Basic to create applications, Microsoft has taken steps to make programming to the ODBC layer as easy as possible. In this chapter, you get a close look at how to create simple ODBC applications.

What Is ODBC?

For starters, ODBC enables a single application to make a standard set of calls that are then translated, through the use of an ODBC driver, into statements on the target *Database Management System* (DBMS). It is also possible to use SQL passthrough merely to quote, to the server, SQL statements that are passed without being altered by the driver.

This second method has some merit. Although quoting SQL to the server can, in some ways, limit your application to a specific set of SQL, VB's JET engine gives you, compared to the DB-Lib layer, a blindingly simple way to get at your data. Technical issues concerning the interaction of the JET engine and ODBC should be reviewed by anyone attempting this route. There are other books describing how to approach a project in this manner. This chapter uses the ODBC CLI (Call Level Interface) through Visual Basic.

ODBC Interface

The actual interactions that occur behind the ODBC interface are interesting to explore. There are several layers to the ODBC implementation. (See Figure 39.1 for a model of an ODBC application.)

Sitting on top is an application, which talks to the ODBC driver manager. Of course, the application can be anything. The driver manager decides which individual drivers to call when an application asks for a connection to a data source. Each data source is configured by the user before running the application, and the driver manager handles the interface between the actual driver and the application.

FIGURE 39.1.

Discrete components comprising the ODBC architecture.

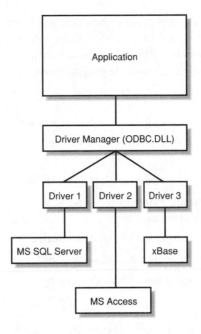

This includes, most importantly, loading the driver. It also includes validation of parameters passed to the driver functions so that the driver need not concern itself with that task. Finally, the driver manager performs some of the ODBC initialization routines. Later on in the sample program in this chapter, you'll see where the driver manager does some actual, observable work.

The drivers do most of the work in the ODBC model. They accept ODBC function calls and translate them into things that the particular data source can understand.

The data sources never know that they are being accessed by ODBC.

API Conformance Levels

When an ODBC driver is written, its creators must adhere to a bare minimum of functionality. Enforcing this conformity is the job of an industry standard such as ODBC—and is a good thing.

Microsoft defines three sets of conformity for ODBC drivers. Each higher level includes the restrictions of the previous level. This is partly due to the inherent differences in data sources; an xBase database has much less functionality than a SQL Server database. An xBase ODBC driver would likely not support Level-2 functionality, because the underlying data source cannot support many of the features mandated by Level-2 conformity.

When product managers start projects that write to the ODBC API, they must make a decision about which level of driver conformance will be required to run their software. To achieve maximum compatibility, PMs might decide to call only core-level API functions. To gain more functionality, PMs can allow their programmers to call Level 1 or Level 2 API functions.

Core-level API functions provide the following:

- Allocating and freeing handles for environment, connections, and statements
- Establishing connections to data sources and using multiple statements on a connection
- Preparing and executing SQL statements over an established connection
- Assigning storage variables for holding parameters in SQL statements and for holding column data in result sets
- Retrieving result set data as well as information about a result set
- Committing or rolling back transactions
- Retrieving error information returned by data source

Programmers can execute the following additional tasks with Level 1 API functions:

- Connecting to data sources with driver-specific dialog boxes
- Sending all or only part of a result column value (useful for long data values)
- Sending all or only part of a parameter value
- Retrieving catalog information about database items (for example, columns, special columns, statistics, and tables)
- Setting options for statements and connections and inquiring about current option settings
- Retrieving information about driver and data source capabilities, such as supported data types, scalar functions, and ODBC functions

Further functionality is provided by the Level 2 API functions:

- Browsing connection information to search for and list available data sources
- Assigning parameter values to arrays and sending them
- Retrieving result column values into arrays
- Retrieving information on parameters, including the number of parameters and parameter descriptions
- Retrieving additional catalog information (for example, privileges, keys, and procedures)
- Defining and using scrollable cursors
- Retrieving native SQL statements generated
- Calling a translation DLL

Using VB to Build a Simple ODBC Application

Functions are called directly from the ODBC.DLL for all the examples in this chapter. Note that you do not use a Visual Basic Data Access Object for these example; although this approach is valid, direct ODBC calls enable you to get closer to the API. This demonstrates its usefulness, while avoiding the overhead of the VB Jet engine.

In Chapter 38, "DB-Library Programming," you used the VBSQL.VBX object to take care of the message handler, error handler, and initialization, then used the CLI to call functions from the VBX. Here, you will do much the same thing by calling all API functions directly from ODBC.DLL.

One difference you'll notice immediately is that return values exist for every function in the DLL. In other words, every function in ODBC.DLL returns a status code. To receive values (for example, a connection number), ODBC changes the value of a passed parameter. This is a much more refined way to do business. In the next example, compare the difference between the DB-Lib `SqlOpen()` and the ODBC `SqlAllocConnect()`. `SqlOpen()` returns the sought-after value (`SqlConn`), and `SQLAlloc()` returns a result code and places the sought-after value (the connection handle `hdbc&`) in the second parameter:

```
SqlConn% = SqlOpen%(ptrLogin%, ServerName$)
res% = SQLAllocConnect(henv&, hdbc&)
```

> **NOTE**
>
> In this chapter, you will be writing to the ODBC 2.0 API; where 2.0 functionality differs from 1.0, it is noted.

Before you start, you need a Visual Basic module that declares all the functions in the ODBC.DLL that you'll be using. If you have ODBC.BAS (included in the ODBC 2.0 SDK), it can be used with some modifications. Here are the declarations you'll be using:

```
Rem Core level API
Declare Function SQLAllocConnect Lib "odbc.dll" (ByVal env As Long, hdbc As
➥Long) As Integer
Declare Function SQLAllocEnv Lib "odbc.dll" (env As Long) As Integer
Declare Function SQLAllocStmt Lib "odbc.dll" (ByVal hdbc As Long, hstmt As
➥Long) As Integer
Declare Function SQLExecDirect Lib "odbc.dll" (ByVal hstmt As Long, ByVal
➥sqlString As String, ByVal sqlstrlen As Long) As Integer
Declare Function SQLFetch Lib "odbc.dll" (ByVal hstmt As Long) As Integer
Declare Function SQLFreeConnect Lib "odbc.dll" (ByVal hdbc As Long) As Integer
Declare Function SQLFreeEnv Lib "odbc.dll" (ByVal env As Long) As Integer
Declare Function SQLFreeStmt Lib "odbc.dll" (ByVal hstmt As Long,
➥ByVal EndOption As Integer) As Integer
Declare Function SQLDisconnect Lib "odbc.dll" (ByVal hdbc As Long) As Integer
```

```
Rem Level 1 API
Declare Function SQLDriverConnect Lib "odbc.dll" (ByVal hdbc As Long,
➥ByVal hwnd As Any, ByVal szCSIn As String, ByVal cbCSIn As Integer,
➥ByVal szCSOut As String, ByVal cbCSMax As Integer, cbCSOut%,
➥ByVal f As Integer) As Integer
Declare Function SQLGetData Lib "odbc.dll" (ByVal hstmt As Long, ByVal
➥col As Integer, ByVal wConvType As Integer, ByVal lpbBuf As String,
➥ByVal dwbuflen As Long, lpcbout As Long) As Integer
```

You also need to have ODBC drivers for your data sources. You should be confident about their proper installation before continuing.

WARNING

Readers familiar with either C or calling Windows API functions already know about this, but if you do not have any experience calling functions directly from DLLs, be aware that a return code of 0 is a customary return value for success. The RETVAL values for SQL_ERROR and SQL_SUCCESS are the opposite of what you might expect: if a function returns -1, it means False, or SQL_ERROR; if it returns 0, it means True, or SQL_SUCCESS.

A Sample Program

The sample program you'll write is a simple one. You will initialize the ODBC library, ask for a list of ODBC data sources to be presented to the user, open a connection to the selected server, ask for a simple, single-column, single-row result set, and output the result to the debug device. Because you'll be writing to the debug device, run this in Development mode inside Visual Basic. The complete example is provided at the end of this section.

To run this program, you need to add the previous defines to a BAS module. You also need to create a dummy form from which your ODBC driver will obtain a parent hWnd handle. In the Form_Load procedure, place a single call to Example391(). Insert the code listed into a subroutine called Example 391.

Initializing ODBC

There are three types of handles defined in the ODBC API. (See Table 39.1.)

Table 39.1. Handle types in an ODBC application.

Handle Type	Definition	Some Functions Referencing
Environment	Memory storage for global information, such as connection handles. There is only one environment handle per application.	SQLDataSources()

Handle Type	Definition	Some Functions Referencing
Connection	Memory storage for individual connection. Each connection is managed by the environment. There may be many connections in a single application, each descended from an environment.	`SQLConnect()`, `SQLConnectOption()`
Statement	Memory storage for a SQL statement. Each statement is managed by its connection. There may be many statements in a single connection. Most of the actual work that occurs in an application references the statement handle.	`SQLGetData()`, `SQLPrepare()`

In order to execute a SQL statement, a statement handle must be allocated. The statement handle requires and references a connection handle, which requires and references an environment handle. First, let's define some variables you'll need in the program, load the form, and paint it. If you try this at home, step through the program with F8 to see how each statement works—merely running this is pretty uninteresting. Figure 39.2 shows the program if it is stepped up through the code listed here:

```
Sub Example391()
' Result code storage, Handle to Database Connection,
' Handle to Environment, Handle to Statement.
Dim res%, hdbc&, henv&, hstmt&

' Fixed length buffer to hold Connection String
Dim ConnectionStr As String * 255

' Work variables
Dim ConnStrlen%, outputlength&
Dim t As String * 255

Form1.Show
Form1.Refresh
```

Now, allocate an environment handle and connection handle:

```
' Allocate environment
res% = SQLAllocEnv(henv&)

' Allocate connection
res% = SQLAllocConnect(henv&, hdbc&)
```

Note that in the `SQLAllocConnect()` call, the environment handle is used to let the ODBC API know which application is requesting a connection handle. The new connection handle is passed back in the `hdbc&` variable.

After you have a connection available, you can open a connection to a server.

FIGURE 39.2.

Code example after painting your sample form, shown here with a background bitmap to avoid programmer boredom.

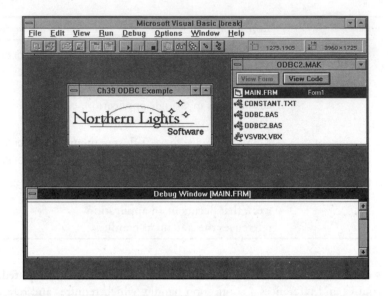

> **NOTE**
>
> Several functions enable you to create a connection. For example, the simplest, SQLConnect(), is a core-level ODBC API function. This means that the function is guaranteed to work in all core-level-compliant (which is to say, all) ODBC drivers. SQLBrowseConnect() is a Level-2 function, the highest. The function featured here is a Level-1 API function.

Open a connection with the following line of code. The result is displayed in Figure 39.3.

```
res% = SQLDriverConnect(hdbc&, CInt(Form1.hWnd), "", 0, ConnectionStr, 255,
➡ ConnStrlen%, SQL_DRIVER_PROMPT)
```

This dialog box is actually launched by the ODBC driver manager. (Refer to Figure 39.1 for a schematic of the call level involved.) Because a data source hasn't yet been selected, a driver can't be chosen; because a driver hasn't been chosen, the driver manager needs to do this work.

After you select a data source, the SQLDriverConnect() function causes the actual driver (SQLSRVR.DLL, for instance) to create a new dialog box to get login information from the user. (See Figure 39.4.) Again, there are lots of ways to get connections to the server; this is only one way to do it. It's certainly possible, and infinitely useful, to create connections based on predefined parameters behind the scenes. (You could update a graph once per minute to reflect changes in a table, for example.)

FIGURE 39.3.

The call to SQLDriverConnect() creates this dialog box. Your dialog box will contain the ODBC sources you have set up in your particular environment.

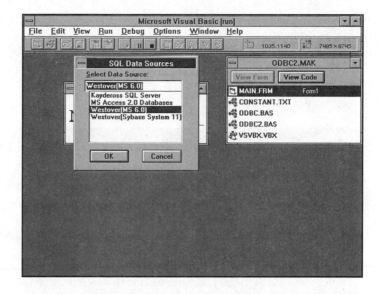

FIGURE 39.4.

After selecting a data source, the ODBC driver manager loads the respective source's driver, which, in turn, presents this dialog box.

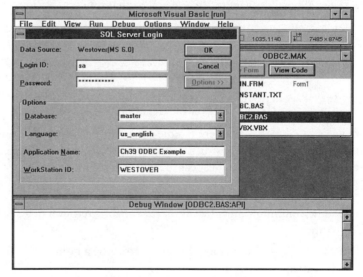

Because you are connecting to a SQL Server, the driver translates your SQLDriverConnect() call into a request for a login, password, and starting database. Once the user has supplied the necessary information, the driver uses it to log you into the server.

After establishing a connection, you are ready to submit a query. To do this, a statement handle is needed:

```
' Allocate a statement handle
res% = SQLAllocStmt(hdbc&, hstmt&)
```

When the statement handle is allocated, prepare one of your work variables, t (for temporary string), with the text of the SQL query. You can change this query to anything that returns a one-column, one-row result set—for example, `select getdate()`. This query is sent to the server using the `SQLExecDirect()` function:

```
t$ = "select count(*) from d1..t1"
res% = SQLExecDirect(hstmt&, t$, Len(t$))
```

> **NOTE**
>
> You might notice some latency after executing this function. On my machine, the ODBC connection has been configured to process results synchronously in order to produce this behavior. This may not be the most desirable behavior, but it is excellent and simple for the purposes of this demonstration.

After results are ready, you need to go out and get them. You accomplish that here with `SQLFetch()` and `SQLGetData()`, although, as with connecting to the server, the ODBC API offers several possible ways to retrieve and format results:

```
' Get a row
res% = SQLFetch(hstmt&)

' Get data from the row's first column
res% = SQLGetData(hstmt&, 1, SQL_C_CHAR, t$, 255, outputlength&)

' Print results to the debug device
Debug.Print Left$(t$, CInt(outputlength&))
```

`SQLFetch()` takes the statement handle and performs a row `fetch` on that handle. After executing a `fetch`, the statement structure contains what can be considered a pointer to a row in the result set. The arguments to `SQLGetData()` include the following:

- The statement handle
- The column number (`SQLGetData()` enables retrieval of a single column of data at a time)
- The type of data (although you're retrieving a numeric result, fetching character data is easier)
- The variable in which the data should be placed
- The allocated length of the output buffer
- The reported length of the data according to `SQLGetData()`

This information is used in the format string passed to the `Print` statement. The remainder of the buffer contains nulls (`chr$(0)`) and looks dreadful in the debug window. Thus, you take only the valid data from the buffer and place it in the debug window. (See Figure 39.5.) Notice that it is necessary to pass a `long` to the API function, but that the `Left$()` call requires an integer.

FIGURE 39.5.

Sample program with results displayed in the Debug window.

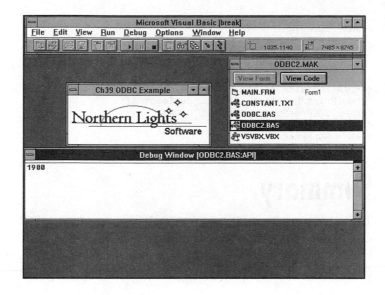

Finally, clean up handles and close connections with a series of simple functions:

```
res% = SQLFreeStmt(hstmt, SQL_DROP)
res% = SQLDisconnect(hdbc)
res% = SQLFreeConnect(hdbc)
res% = SQLFreeEnv(henv)
```

Here is the complete code example discussed in this chapter:

```
Sub Example391()
' Result code storage, Handle to Database Connection,
' Handle to Environment, Handle to Statement.
Dim res%, hdbc&, henv&, hstmt&

' Fixed length buffer to hold Connection String
Dim ConnectionStr As String * 255

' Work variables
Dim ConnStrlen%, outputlength&
Dim t As String * 255

Form1.Show
Form1.Refresh
' Allocate environment
res% = SQLAllocEnv(henv&)

' Allocate connection
res% = SQLAllocConnect(henv&, hdbc&)
res% = SQLDriverConnect(hdbc&, CInt(Form1.hWnd), "", 0, ConnectionStr,
➥255, ConnStrlen%, SQL_DRIVER_PROMPT)
' Allocate a statement handle
res% = SQLAllocStmt(hdbc&, hstmt&)
t$ = "select count(*) from d1..t1"
res% = SQLExecDirect(hstmt&, t$, Len(t$))
```

```
' Get a row
res% = SQLFetch(hstmt&)

' Get data from the row's first column
res% = SQLGetData(hstmt&, 1, SQL_C_CHAR, t$, 255, outputlength&)

' Print results to the debug device
Debug.Print Left$(t$, CInt(outputlength&))
res% = SQLFreeStmt(hstmt, SQL_DROP)
res% = SQLDisconnect(hdbc)
res% = SQLFreeConnect(hdbc)
res% = SQLFreeEnv(henv)
```

Summary

This sample program demonstrates a simple way to connect to a SQL Server by using the ODBC CLI. Using simple API calls and leveraging the resources available to you in the driver and ODBC driver manager, the program presents the user with dialog boxes to find and connect to a server, issue a predefined query, and retrieve and print results.

Legal Agreements Pertaining to the CD-ROM

By opening this package, you are agreeing to be bound by the following agreement:

Some of the software included with this product is copyrighted, in which case all rights are reserved by the respective copyright holder. You are licensed to use software copyrighted by the publisher and its licensors on a single computer. You may copy and/or modify the software as needed to facilitate your use of it on a single computer. Making copies of the software for any other purpose is a violation of the United States copyright laws.

This software is sold as is without warranty of any kind, either expressed or implied, including but not limited to the implied warranties of merchantability and fitness for a particular purpose. Neither the publisher nor its dealers or distributors assumes any liability for any alleged or actual damages arising from the use of this program. (Some states do not allow for the exclusion of implied warranties, so the exclusion may not apply to you.)

By opening this package, you are agreeing to be bound by the following agreement which applies to products supplied by Northern Lights Software:

Aurora is a copyrighted product of Northern Lights Software, Ltd., and is protected by United States copyright laws and international treaty provisions. Copyright 1994, 1995, 1996. All Rights Reserved. Aurora Utilities for Sybase, Aurora Desktop, Aurora Script Manager, Aurora Distribution Viewer, and Aurora Cost Retrieval DLL are service marks of Northern Lights Software. Sybase is a trademark of Sybase, Inc.

Period of evaluation. By installing the software, it is understood that the provided software is for the purposes of evaluation, only, and cannot be used beyond a period of thirty (30) days unless the software is registered. The software can be registered only by Northern Lights Software, Ltd., or its empowered agents.

Limited Warranty. Northern Lights warrants that the SOFTWARE will perform substantially in accordance with the written description delivered with the software, usually in the form of a readme.txt, for a period of ninety (90) days. Any implied warranties are limited to the same period of ninety (90) days.

Remedies. Northern Lights and its suppliers' entire liability and your exclusive remedy shall be, at Northern Lights' option, a refund of the price paid or repair or replacement of the software. This Limited Warranty is void if the failure has resulted from accident, abuse, or misapplication. These warranties are limited to the United States unless you can provide proof of purchase from an authorized non-U.S. source.

No Other Warranties. To the maximum extent permitted by applicable law, Northern Lights disclaims all other warranties, either express or implied, including but not limited to implied warranties of merchantability and fitness for a particular purpose. This limited warranty gives you certain rights. You may have other rights which vary by state and jurisdiction.

No Liability for Consequential Damages. To the maximum extent permitted by applicable law, in no event shall Northern Lights be liable for any damages whatsoever (including without limitation, damages for loss of business profits, business interruption, loss of business information or any other pecuniary loss) arising out of the use of or inability to use this product, even if Northern Lights has been advised of the possibility of such damages. Because some states do not allow the limit or exclusion of liability for consequential or incidental damage, the above limitation may not apply to you.

INDEX

Add to Your Sams Library Today with the Best Books for Programming, Operating Systems, and New Technologies

The easiest way to order is to pick up the phone and call
1-800-428-5331
between 9:00 a.m. and 5:00 p.m. EST.
For faster service please have your credit card available.

ISBN	Quantity	Description of Item	Unit Cost	Total Cost
0-672-30860-6		Windows NT Server Survival Guide (Book/CD-ROM)	$49.99	
0-672-30902-5		Windows NT 3.51 Unleashed, 3E	$49.99	
0-672-30717-0		Tricks of the Doom Programming Gurus (Book/CD-ROM)	$39.99	
0-672-30714-6		The Internet Unleashed, 2E	$35.00	
0-672-30737-5		The World Wide Web Unleashed, 2E	$39.99	
0-672-30706-5		Programming Microsoft Office (Book/CD-ROM)	$49.99	
0-672-30474-0		Windows 95 Unleashed (Book/CD-ROM)	$35.00	
0-672-30602-6		Programming Windows 95 Unleashed (Book/CD-ROM)	$49.99	
0-672-30791-X		Peter Norton's Complete Guide to Windows 95	$29.99	
1-57521-014-2		Teach Yourself Web Publishing with HTML in 14 Days, Premier Edition	$39.99	
1-57521-005-3		Teach Yourself More Web Publishing with HTML in a Week	$29.99	
0-672-30745-6		HTML & CGI Unleashed	$49.99	
❏ 3 ½" Disk		Shipping and Handling: See information below.		
❏ 5 ¼" Disk		TOTAL		

Shipping and Handling: $4.00 for the first book, and $1.75 for each additional book. Floppy disk: add $1.75 for shipping and handling. If you need to have it NOW, we can ship product to you in 24 hours for an additional charge of approximately $18.00, and you will receive your item overnight or in two days. Overseas shipping and handling adds $2.00 per book and $8.00 for up to three disks. Prices subject to change. Call for availability and pricing information on latest editions.

201 W. 103rd Street, Indianapolis, Indiana 46290

1-800-428-5331 — Orders   1-800-835-3202 — FAX   1-800-858-7674 — Customer Service

Book ISBN 0-672-30903-3

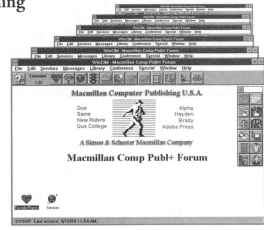